The
STORY
of the
WORLD
in
100 MOMENTS

NEIL OLIVER

PENGUIN BOOKS

TRANSWORLD PUBLISHERS
Penguin Random House, One Embassy Gardens,
8 Viaduct Gardens, London SW11 7BW
www.penguin.co.uk

Transworld is part of the Penguin Random House group of companies
whose addresses can be found at global.penguinrandomhouse.com

Penguin
Random House
UK

First published in Great Britain in 2021 by Bantam Press
an imprint of Transworld Publishers
Penguin paperback edition published 2022

A CIP catalogue record for this book
is available from the British Library.

ISBN 9781804991398

Typeset in Minion Pro by Jouve (UK), Milton Keynes.
Printed and bound in Great Britain by Clays Ltd, Elcograf S.p.A.

The authorized representative in the EEA is Penguin Random House Ireland,
Morrison Chambers, 32 Nassau Street, Dublin D02 YH68.

Penguin Random House is committed to a sustainable
future for our business, our readers and our planet. This book
is made from Forest Stewardship Council® certified paper.

To Trudi, Evie, Archie and Teddy.
All my love, always.

CONTENTS

Introduction 1

1
Enheduanna composes a hymn 9

2
Hammurabi lays down the law 18

3
Rekhmire and the office job 27

4
Cappadocia and the invisible
magic of money 32

5
Grapes and olives and a
Minotaur at Knossos 38

6
Shiva and the oldest cult
religion in the world 43

7
Hyksos, Hebrews and
chariots in Egyypt 48

8
Aryans, the *Rigveda* and the
making of the caste system 53

9
Phoenicians and Solomon's Temple 59

10
Of Homer, *Iliad* and *Odyssey* 63

11
Siddhartha Gautama and the
birth of the Buddha 68

12
Lao Tzu and the *Tao Te Ching* 73

13
Nebuchadnezzar and
the Fall of Babylon 78

14
The expulsion of the
last king of Rome 83

15
Persians, Sparta and the
Battle of Thermopylae 88

16
Socrates, gadflies and
upsetting the status quo 94

17
Thucydides, the Peloponnesian
War and the defeat of Sparta 97

18
Chandragupta, Ashoka and
the Mauryan dynasty 102

19
Mayans sense that time has
no beginning, no end 106

20

Warring States and the coming
together of a place called China 110

21

Julius Caesar crosses the Rubicon 114

22

Primo Levi ponders,
'If This Is a Man' 119

23

The death and life
of Jesus Christ 124

24

Polybius and the cyclical
nature of civilization 129

25

Constantine hailed as emperor
by the Roman army at York 133

26

Ambrose, Bishop of Milan,
brings the emperor to heel 137

27

Alaric the Goth and the
Sack of Rome 140

28

Muhammad hears the
voice of an angel 144

29

A meeting beneath wisteria
and the shaping of Japan 148

30

Charles Martel hammers
a Muslim horde 152

31

Lindisfarne reaps the
whirlwind of the Vikings 156

32

Charlemagne and the birth of
a Holy Roman Empire 160

33

The Treaty of Verdun and drawing the
outlines of France and Germany 164

34

Alfred lays the foundations
for an England 167

35

Charles III of France gives
ground to the Vikings 171

36

In the Church of St Sophia the men
who row make their choice 175

37

Great Zimbabwe and
trade links with China 179

38

Manzikert and the slow-bleeding
of the Byzantine empire 183

39

Emperor Henry IV, Pope Gregory VII
and the Walk to Canossa 187

40

William the Conqueror
and Domesday 189

41

Cathedrals built and spirits raised 192

42
Saladin, Crusading and
the making of an icon of Islam 194

43
Mongols gather to make
Temüjin their paramount leader 198

44
Kupe, the *kuaka* and the land
of the long white cloud 202

45
A divine wind convinces the
Japanese none might beat them 205

46
Dante's *Divine Comedy* 209

47
The Golden Horde and
Black Death in Europe 213

48
The Peasants' Revolt and more
thwarted dreams of utopia 216

49
Johannes Gutenberg asks
Johann Fust for a loan 219

50
The death of Constantine and
the Fall of Constantinople 223

51
Spanish horses arrive
in America 227

52
Martin Luther nails a
placard to a door 230

53
Charles V rules the first empire
where the sun never set 234

54
Magellan and Elcano – around
the world in . . . three years 238

55
Henry VIII goes all out
to impress a woman 241

56
First blast of cannon and a
Mughal empire in India 245

57
Potatoes end famine in Europe
and change the world 249

58
Diego Gualpa finds
a mountain of silver 252

59
Ivan the Terrible, Tsar
of All the Russias 256

60
The Valladolid debate,
slavery and human rights 259

61
Elizabeth I, the Spanish Armada
and the birth of nationality 262

62
Akbar and Elizabeth are dead
and Europe comes to India 265

63
Tycho Brahe dies and Johannes
Kepler accesses his data 268

64

Jamestown and the foundations of
European North America 273

65

The King James Bible and
a language for the world 276

66

Francis Bacon, frozen chicken
and the scientific method 279

67

Isaac Newton, self-isolation
and 'the system of the world' 282

68

Smallpox and the War of
the Spanish Succession 286

69

Thomas Newcomen
and his steam engine 290

70

Clive of India paves the
way for the British Raj 293

71

Pins in milk and
Europe's last witch 296

72

James Madison and the Constitution
of the United States 299

73

Queen Nandi, unsafe sex and
the birth of the Zulu kingdom 302

74

The baker, the mob and
the French Revolution 304

75

Nelson, Trafalgar and the
freedom of the seas 307

76

The world's population
reaches one billion 310

77

The Atlantic slave trade – humanity's
never-ending shame 313

78

Charles Darwin, the platypus
and the *Origin of Species* 316

79

Louis Daguerre and moments
captured for all time 320

80

Marx and Engels unveil
their *Communist Manifesto* 323

81

Sullivan Ballou and
a most uncivil war 327

82

A pub, a book of rules
and the beautiful game 330

83

James Clerk Maxwell
sees light for what it is 335

84

Dostoyevsky sees *The Body of the
Dead Christ in the Tomb* 339

85

The Wright brothers take
to the sky at Kitty Hawk 343

86

Oil in the Middle East and
the poisoned chalice 347

87

7.30 a.m. on the first day of
the Battle of the Somme 350

88

Lenin, the sealed train and
revolution in Russia 353

89

A camp cook and the influenza
pandemic of 1918–20 356

90

Mallory and Irvine and
the quest for Everest 359

91

The German president makes
Adolf Hitler Chancellor 362

92

Pug Ismay, Winston Churchill
and the Battle of Britain 366

93

The liberation of
Auschwitz-Birkenau 369

94

Tomi-San in an
awakening land 371

95

Martin Luther King
and the dream 374

96

A man on the moon
for Mr Gorsky 377

97

Information travels
between two computers 380

98

Aleksandr Solzhenitsyn reveals
the Gulag Archipelago 384

99

A little girl in red 388

100

Harry Patch and the
war to end all wars 391

Today . . . 395

Acknowledgements 397

Illustration credits 399

Index 401

INTRODUCTION

A book called *The Story of the World in 100 Moments* is likely a red rag to a bull. What to leave in? What to leave out? Some or all of everything left out will seem, to some, to have mattered more than some or all of what is here.

So let us confront the obvious trouble and hope thereby to head it off at the pass: this is *my* story of the world and these are *my* 100 moments. Any and every reader will likely question some choices, and that is as it should be. In my imagination I can hear the voices now: 'How could he tell the story of the world and not mention . . .'

I say again: it's my story of the world. The story I choose to tell. If I have an ambition for this book it is that the reading of it might inspire others to think of *their* moments from history – the ones seeming to tell the story that makes most sense to them. Everyone should have some idea, at least, of what's been going on all these years, and also why.

With every day that passes I become more convinced that history is personal, and also a narrative. We tell each other stories about what happened – or rather, what we think happened – and that's all. I love reading and learning about history, always have, but mostly because every story about someone else helps me better to understand the world of me and mine. I have been fascinated by the story of the First World War for the longest time. My doorway into all of that was knowing both my grandfathers were swept up in the storm and lived to tell the tale, wounded though they were. Had either man's story taken a different turn between 1914 and 1918, then I might not be typing these words now. When the subject of the Great War came up at school, it mattered to me because it was family business. More than that, it showed me how close I had come to not existing at all.

I have wondered too if it might be possible to commit to memory a sequence of events that would enable me to feel, just for a little while, that I understand how we all got to where we are now. For a few moments I would like to feel as if I'm holding the whole picture intact inside my head . . . before it all falls apart again like a jigsaw puzzle briefly solved and then held upright.

Like aides-memoire, those events, one after another, might lead me from then to now, like stepping stones through the mire of forgetting, or rungs on a ladder towards the light. I enjoy remembering and I like reciting. I want to hold the shimmering image – mirage though it may be – and see it as one complete picture. The dream would be to stand up and tell it all, the whole story, from start to finish, like a bedtime story. In writing this book I set out to provide myself with the stones, the rungs, so that I might at least lie in bed – on one of those nights when sleep won't come – and work my way through the story of the world, up from the past and towards the present.

In selecting my 100 moments, those that matter most to me, I *had* to leave out everything else. It was painful, made especially hard by my attachment to some events that felt less like steps leading forward or upwards and more like the ways on to roads less travelled but as fascinating as any other. There are moments that only flash bright and disappear, lost for ever. We cannot know what, if anything, was lost with their passing.

I can tell you now that we will be around the halfway mark in this story of the world (chronologically speaking at least, though only fourteen moments into the narrative) before there's more than the barest mention of western Europe, of the dry land that would be Britain and Ireland; of France, Germany, Austria and Italy; of Scandinavia and more. The gigantic continent of Africa will have featured almost from the beginning, but on account of Egypt alone; the expanses to her south and west will have failed to register as the sources of any meaningful moments. By that same halfway mark the Americas, North and South, will have featured not at all.

Noting that those vast tracts are absent from the story for so long is not the same as saying nothing important happened there. What seems unarguable, though, is that the experiments with being human and alive in those parts had not, by 500 BC, offered up any contributions that affected the Middle East, the Near East, the Mediterranean coastline or India and China – the Old World – in any influential or lasting way. In due course the ways of the Old World would affect those of Europe, and of the New World, but the meaningful traffic was one-way for thousands of years, one giving and the other only receiving. Whatever moments sparked into existence elsewhere, whatever potential they might have had for shaping a *narrative* elsewhere, they were lost.

There was (just as a for-instance) a moment in Orkney, the archipelago in the far north of Scotland, that inspired thousands of years of effort but to no avail. The seeming significance of the shape of the circle was noted by Orcadian farmers and the weight of their realization led to a mania for making them. (To say it was noted by farmers *plural* is one thing. Just as likely it appeared for the first time in the mind of just one farmer. Such a moment, lost in time.) By 5,000 years ago the first circles had been chipped and pecked into the bedrock at places like Stenness and Brodgar. Those were later enhanced with circles of stones raised towards the sky. Stenness is older than any other circle in Britain, older than the pyramids of Egypt for that matter, an earlier commitment to grand schemes in search of meaning. Having occurred to someone on Orkney and been enthusiastically adopted there as a means of marking something, tracking something, predicting something, providing the stage-set for something, the idea spread the length of Britain and Ireland – thousands upon thousands of circles like a rash. Whatever notion gave relevance to that thinking and way of being, it lasted for centuries and then millennia, providing inspiration for icons like Stonehenge and Avebury in deepest

England. It lasted as long as Christianity has done, but in the end it had limited reach. By the time the practice petered out and disappeared it had had no impact at all beyond its own hinterland. The reason for their creation is utterly lost. There had been a moment, a brilliant thought, and it had endured for those who chose to care. But in the story of the wider world it had not mattered enough to stay for ever.

The furthest reaches of western Europe were explored from the very beginning. Humans of one sort after another found their way to the Atlantic façade at least a million years ago and their successors kept on coming. Ice ages came and went but always the territory was recolonized by hunters when conditions allowed. After hunters, farmers came west too. There have been grounds for thinking farming began spontaneously in different places across Europe, without the need for its import from the Middle East. Vast swathes of Europe offered fertile soils, and while grains like wheat and barley were imports from the east, indigenous populations may have domesticated their own local plants without having to be taught to do so by immigrants. In time the territory was certainly colonized by outsiders as well, from the east.

The furthest west, by the sounding sea, was a bountiful source of metals and so attracted the attentions of Bronze Age civilizations of the Old World – Phoenicians and others out of the eastern Mediterranean, maybe Joseph of Arimathea, a disciple of Jesus, among them. Rich sources of copper and the richest source of tin were in the British Isles, and from the earliest days of the exploitation of the new magic of metal, prospectors found their way to Cornwall and Wales in search of wealth.

But while the civilizations of the Old World had learned to take advantage of the stuff of which the west was made, they brought home to Mesopotamia, to Egypt, to Byblos and Sidon, to Persia and to Greece nothing but mute cargo. No ideas, no ways of thinking and living made their way from west to east, by ship or overland, during those first millennia after Enheduanna dictated her hymns and Hammurabi laid down the law.

Western noses may be put out of joint by the thought of not mattering for so long. (The west would matter in the end after all, more than any other part of the world before or since.) There are explanations for the slow start. Western Europe is so richly fertile it may have worked against the cultivation of civilization. In Mesopotamia and elsewhere in the Near and Middle East, the environment and climate were less forgiving, more demanding – and especially insistent upon cooperation. While a little European family of mum, dad, grandparents and the ever-growing brood of kids might have been able to make a life for themselves on a patch of green, taking advantage of easy soils and plentiful, gentle rain, folk on the wind-blown terrain between the Tigris and Euphrates rivers, at the mercy of devastating floods and enervating droughts, likely found their lot too much to tame alone. Instead of families working in isolation, thriving well enough but having no pressing need of technological or societal advances, the first cradles of civilization were those that absolutely demanded combined and coordinated effort by hundreds or even thousands of people. As they tamed their unforgiving landscape – irrigating the dusty land, or building levees and baking mud bricks to defy the floods – so they tamed themselves and each other. Having first grown food they next grew cities and kings, and their centralized surplus fed the craftsmen, bureaucrats, merchants, warriors and the rest of the specialists that husbanded civilization itself.

A spark of inspiration is only a spark and will disappear for want of kindling and coaxing. When life-enhancing, life-changing ideas occurred where they could be coddled by hundreds of people working in concert, sparks might become flames ... and flames might grow into illumination that lights up the whole world.

Across the vastness of Africa beyond the Nile and Egypt, beyond the southern Mediterranean coast and its hinterland, circumstances evidently failed to conspire to give rise to civilization for the longest time as well. The Egyptians were in contact with a kingdom to their south they knew as Kush and during the first half of the first millennium BC there were

Kushite pharaohs on the Egyptian throne. So much of the rest of the continent, though, was beyond the reach of written history. Archaeologists have understood climate change to be part of the explanation for the nothingness. Ancient cave art in the interior suggests that before writing was developed anywhere in the world there were grasslands and savannahs where the Sahara Desert is now. People kept horses and cattle, sheep and goats, and it seems at least possible that the seeds of civilization may have been in evidence in southern and western Africa, but that they fell upon desiccating ground and came to nought. Only Egypt, with its life-giving, god-like Nile, survived the great drying that confounded the first farmers elsewhere on the elephant's ear of Africa.

As far as we know, only modern human beings, of the genus *Homo sapiens*, ever found their way into the Americas, via a land bridge across what is now the Bering Strait. Some 25,000 or so years ago there began the penetration of the nearly 9,000 miles of richly varied landscapes, environments and climates that make up North and South. By around 1000 BC there was a civilization of sorts in Mexico by a people called Olmecs. In their wake came full-blown civilizations by Aztecs, Incas and Mayans, but for all their complexity and fascination their reach and influence made no impact on the Old World until the time of contact with Spaniards in the early years of the sixteenth century. When it came, the response their centuries of effort invoked from the technologically superior incomers was outright destruction.

Viewed from high above, as a god might, the darkness of the world was pricked from time to time with single flames that burned and disappeared. For want of numbers, for want of need by enough people working together at the same time, those moments only fizzled and went out. Moments that stayed alight, that were kept alight and made the difference, continued to catch and burn elsewhere.

As time passes, as the modern era dawns, so time speeds up, or seems to. There are so many more of us now (nearly eight billion alive together, for the first time), and in any event the relative crowding filled the more recent centuries with moment – moments – as never before. As W. B. Yeats had it, we are 'turning and turning in the widening gyre'. I do not say that things fall apart – not quite, not yet – but compared to the centuries and millennia of before we seem to be hurtling faster and faster. The future is only a rumour, not to be believed. Right now is all we have, and our understanding and appreciation of it must and shall be helped by remembering, or at least striving to remember, the lives and ways of some that went before. This is my story.

1.

ENHEDUANNA
COMPOSES A HYMN

In so far as a story of the world can have a beginning, let it begin with
Enheduanna, the first named poet. In the moment in question she is in
the temple dedicated to Inanna, goddess of love, beauty and war, and also
to Innana's husband, Nanna, god of wisdom and the moon, in the city of
Ur, in the land of Sumer, Mesopotamia. She is a woman of high status
and the temple is her domain. Either she is a daughter of King Sargon the
Great, founder and ruler of the Akkadian empire that has Ur as its capital, or else someone he values most highly for some other reason. There
is a great deal we cannot know about High Priestess Enheduanna but
what survives is still a sketch of a life.

By the time she walked the earth, 4,300 years ago, humankind had
come a long way, a way so long as to be unimaginable. We are the planet's
youngest apes and that way was walked first by others, the same and not
the same; other apes upright on two legs; other apes that came together
as families, tribes and clans; others that walked into caves tens of thousands of years ahead of Enheduanna's time and by the light of torches
there made art so fine it would never be bettered, not by any ape – not by
Leonardo, or Michelangelo, or Picasso.

By the time of Enheduanna, Ur was a grand city and home to tens
of thousands. Sumer and Mesopotamia, literally 'the land between the

rivers' (Tigris and Euphrates), was where farming was first adopted as a way of life. Tending fields – clearing, irrigating, sowing, weeding, harvesting – demanded collaboration and cooperation by the many. It was a life of repetitive toil but it promised food enough for all. Freed from the dangerous and unpredictable venture of hunting and gathering, the farmers of Mesopotamia worked together to build, of mud bricks baked hard in the sun, villages and towns and also cities like Ur. Strongmen dominated, controlling the stores of food and its distribution. Around them gathered warriors, keen to curry favour. Within the wider population specialists were free to refine and exploit their skills – making tools for work and war, weaving fabric for clothes, shaping gems for adornment – in return for food from the farmers and favour from the strongmen. In time there were more, artists, craftsmen, builders and the like, ready to glorify and aggrandize the growing settlements and their people. This was the birth of civilization, and those that learned its benefits would never look back.

Specialists of another sort told stories. Storytelling was older than farming, as old as hunting . . . maybe as old as speaking. Storytellers composed stories to explain what they had seen and understood of the world and about the gods and goddesses, and told them to the rest so they might know and remember. It was in such a world that Enheduanna lived and died, and her special skill was knowing the invisible, the gods, and acknowledging their power:

> Rising on fearsome wings you rush to destroy our land,
> Raging like thunderstorms, howling like hurricanes,
> Screaming like tempests,
> Thundering, raging, ranting, drumming, whiplashing whirlwinds,
> Men falter at your approaching footsteps,
> Tortured dirges scream at your lyre of despair . . .
>
>   (Enheduanna, 'Lament to the Spirit of War')

Mesopotamia, that land between the rivers, was always subject to the whims and ways of the waters and the weather. Floods destroyed fields and homes; droughts and storms wreaked ruin too. Those elements seemed fickle – sometimes kind and sometimes cruel. Rivers, weather and the sky – night and day – were understood as gods and goddesses and so another specialization was that of appealing to the good side of those forces, those characters that seemed to shape and control lives and deaths.

The roots of Ur are more than 5,000 years deep. Back then the Euphrates was close by the walls and the first city was apparently devastated by a flood. Earlier scholars thought the deluge must have been that described in Genesis, but that idea has been dismissed. The river has changed its course and now lies 10 miles from the site. What was once a thriving city surrounded by lush fields is now ruins in a desert.

In the time of Enheduanna and King Sargon, though, Ur was a place of great wealth and sophistication. Archaeologists working there in the 1920s and 1930s unearthed royal tombs stuffed with riches – gold and silver, gemstones. Kings of Ur had not been in the habit of going alone into the next life. Instead their courtiers and servants were put to death so they might continue to serve. All manner of equipment – weapons, tools, artworks, statues, musical instruments – went into the tombs. In those tombs and elsewhere on the site were found clay tablets bearing writing, including more than a hundred copies of Enheduanna's hymns. There were all manner of remembered stories by then, most so unthinkably old that no one could know who first told them.

Paintings on cave walls had told stories of a sort, had fixed characters and moments in place to last for ever. Some upright apes, apes like us, had used sticks to make marks in the dust – more stories but ephemeral, subject to wind and rain. Writing had been known before Enheduanna's time, centuries before. Someone found that when a reed was cut with a sharp knife the end of the stem had a triangular, wedge shape. This could be pressed into soft clay, and combinations of the shape were soon standardized and recognized as something like an alphabet, or at least a system. This form of writing is called cuneiform, from the Latin *cuneus*, meaning 'wedge'.

Some have doubted Enheduanna was Sargon's daughter. Others have questioned whether she composed the hymns that bear her name – so that the first poet is doubted just as Shakespeare would be forty centuries later. It is true to say the tablets are not originals, made in her presence, but copies created long after her death. Whoever she was – Sargon's daughter or not – the woman called Enheduanna was the only writer of her time who was allowed (or who dared) to write in the first person, appearing alongside the goddess:

Great queen of queens, issue of a holy womb for righteous divine powers,
Greater than your own mother, wise and sage, lady of all the foreign lands,
Life-force of the teeming people, I will recite your holy song.
True goddess fit for divine powers, your splendid utterances are magnificent.
Deep-hearted, good woman with a radiant heart, I will enumerate your divine powers for you.

(Enheduanna, 'The Exaltation of Inanna')

Enheduanna was in the business not just of remembering and retelling stories from before, but also making something new. She was a poet and she wrote – or, rather, dictated to her scribe – in the hope of pleasing the all-powerful, the all-knowing.

Your divinity is resplendent in the land,
My body has experienced your great punishment,
Lament, bitterness, sleeplessness, distress, separation, mercy, compassion, care,
Lenience and homage are yours, and to cause flooding, to open hard ground and to turn,
Darkness into light.

She was surely not the first of us apes that was so moved, moved to assemble words in pleasing rhythms and to make them permanent, not by a long way, but she is the first whose name we know. Many are called, as they say, but few are chosen.

In her moment we could picture her resplendent as the goddess, dressed as befits a high priestess. Men and women of Ur wore clothes of wool first of all and then of flax, long skirts for both and with a shawl to cover all of the upper body but one arm and shoulder. As a priestess, Enheduanna may have shown her piety by favouring wool, the clothing of the elder days. Her dark hair has likely been coiffed by her personal hairdresser, who is called Ilum Palilis. Mesopotamia is a land where winds blow, rising up out of nowhere and driving dust and sand in billowing, choking clouds. Anyone wanting to maintain an elaborate hairstyle, anyone for whom appearance was key to authority, would require the constant attention of a stylist. She wears too her crown of office. Also at her side is a scribe, perhaps her favourite, named Sagadu, stylus in hand and hanging on her words. Whatever her mother called her it was not Enheduanna, for when she was made high priestess of the temple, the most important temple in Sumer, she shed her name and took on a title instead, made of three words: *En* for high priestess, *hedu* meaning 'ornament', and *An*, which is shorthand for the god she serves.

Some of what we know about her comes from an alabaster disc found at Ur in 1927 by British archaeologist Leonard Woolley. Into the front surface of the object, some 10 inches in diameter, are etched four figures; on the reverse are three inscriptions that identify the figures as Enheduanna, her hairdresser Ilum Palilis, her scribe Sagadu and her estate manager Adda.

So in this first moment of the story of the world she is composing, conjuring into being another of the forty-two hymns, the temple hymns that will be remembered ever after. Her companions know to keep quiet while she composes. She has a special interest in praising Inanna. Perhaps she hoped by aligning herself with the feminine and exaggerating her greatness that her own power would be likewise increased, her position improved. For around forty years she served the temple. At some point, after Sargon's death and during the reign of her brother, Rimush, a rebel warlord called Lugal-Ane sought the throne of Ur and Sumer and led a coup. During that time Enheduanna was briefly driven out of her temple, out of Ur and into exile. The experience never left her, and she used it for yet more of her writing:

> Me who once sat triumphant, he has driven out of the sanctuary,
> Like a swallow he made me fly from the window,
> My life is consumed,
> He stripped me of the crown appropriate for the high priesthood.

Lugal-Ane's hopes were dashed soon enough and Enheduanna returned to the temple.

Whether she knows it or not she is, with her writing in this moment twenty-three centuries before the birth of Jesus Christ, making forms, patterns and cadences that will shape the literature of Homer and also the psalms of the Hebrews and the hymns of Christians. In the Song of Songs – the Song of Solomon – are the clearest echoes of the artistry of Enheduanna. Again and again she exalts the goddess Inanna, begging to be destroyed by her and saved by her; to be taken by her and made one with her. By the efforts of Enheduanna, Inanna was made greater than ever before. Such was the power of the goddess, declared her high priestess, she could transform women into men, men into women (both men and women were priests in Ur and there was an apparent androgyny, a blurring in dress and manner in pursuit of getting and being closer to the goddess). When her works are brought together she will offer them up to her father the king and declare to him that such a collection is a first in all the world:

> My king, something has been created that no one has created before.

By this making and keeping of her compositions, Enheduanna is a useful starting point for . . . for something like history. History is from the Greek *historia*, by which they meant 'enquiry'. Now the word describes a record and an analysis of the past.

Perhaps the high priestess of the temple at Ur knew the Epic of Gilgamesh, the oldest story in the world. Gilgamesh was a real person, like Enheduanna. He was a king, ruling from the city of Uruk, not far from Ur, and though he did not compose the epic that bears his name, he is the first named person in history. The most complete form of the epic was not written down until some time after 700 BC but it is older than that by centuries, even by millennia. Like so many heroes who will follow in his train, Gilgamesh goes in search of the meaning of life. Part of the story concerns a terrible flood that wipes the world clean of life, except for a single family that had built an ark. Once the waters subside, this family begins again, and all are descended from them. The Epic of Gilgamesh is older than the Old Testament of the Christian Bible. It is yet another version of a story, a nightmare that occurred to humankind again and again. It makes sense most of all in Sumer, in Mesopotamia, where the farmers came together to carve a world for themselves from the watery morass; where, for all that they had made order out of chaos, the fickle gods and goddesses were in the habit of sending floods to wrest back from man what had been briefly won. The world of the epic is doom-laden, and Gilgamesh must face harsh realities. He goes in search of eternal life but finds, in the end, that the gods have kept it for themselves:

> Oh, Gilgamesh, this was the meaning of your dream. You were given the kingship, such was your destiny; everlasting life was not your destiny.

The Epic of Gilgamesh and other stories were there for Enheduanna to draw upon, to inspire her own creations. Written down, put beyond the ever-rising tide of forgetting that is inevitable for humanity, the epic and other stories were made safe – like gemstones in bedrock – glimpses and traces of the world in which they were created. Enheduanna's hymns did likewise, keeping names and moments, actions and consequences for consideration in the future. From such thin threads is history woven.

Sargon was a diplomat as well as a warlord and understood the long-term gains to be made by pleasing as many of his subjects as possible – the Akkadians who were his own sort, and the Sumerians he had come to rule. His high priestess played her part by making connections between the deities of both worlds, blurring divisions and devotions. Inanna was a local Sumerian goddess when Enheduanna set to work, but through her words she was made one with the grander Akkadian goddess Ishtar, Queen of Heaven. Inanna-Ishtar was greater even than the sum of the parts and would grow to influence the future far beyond Mesopotamia. Even Aphrodite of the Greeks retained some of her DNA, ancient and divine.

The scribes recorded too how Sargon came to be. Pressed into clay, the story became legend and was copied over and over, down through the centuries. Ashurbanipal (685–631 BC), last and greatest of the kings of Assyria, was proudest, most of all, of the library he created at Nineveh. In 1867 an English archaeologist called Henry Rawlinson excavated the ruins and found the copy kept by Ashurbanipal's librarian. Sargon might have been unknown in the modern world, but was returned to the light when the tablet was read:

> In secret my mother conceived me, giving birth to me while hiding,
> Into a basket of rushes she set me and sealed the lid with tar,
> Into the river she cast me but the water did not rise over me . . .

The Legend of Sargon, made safe and kept by writing, had long ago inspired the Hebrew story of the birth of Moses. Like Sargon, Moses was said to have been born into obscurity, set adrift by his mother, but to have risen to greatness among his people.

Here is how stories survived the forgetfulness of fallible apes like us. Enheduanna: daughter of Sargon or not, composer of hymns or not, she is the first named writer. In so far as a story of the world can have a beginning, let it start with Enheduanna.

2.

HAMMURABI LAYS DOWN THE LAW

In the beginning of civilization was the written word. More was needed for a venture so grand – civilization, I mean – but writing was a crucial element. Farmers had won order from chaos, made something out of nothing. Together they had sought to control the waters that gave life and sometimes took it away. Attempts to master the rivers came before writing, before civilization. At Jericho in the Valley of Jordan there was farming, and the irrigation to make it fruitful, perhaps 10,000 years ago. There was a town there of several thousand souls, surrounded by a wall standing 12 feet high and 6 feet thick. There was a tall tower as well, raised by people who knew they had something worth defending.

All across the Near East, in one river valley after another, men and women had come together as farmers. They raised crops and dried bricks in the sun, but with the coming of writing each man and woman would be outlived by the story that made sense of it all. Remembering the nature of civilization, each generation storing it inside their rosy-pink brains like seed grain in a clay pot, was good; having it written down somewhere safe was better. Poets had woven wisdom through the songs they sang, the poems they recited, the stories they remembered and retold; writing, though, thoughts pressed into clay, fixed that wisdom for all time like veins of gold through rock. Now wisdom, once acquired, could be retained and passed on without fear of forgetting. A story of what civilized life was like, how to make it and keep it, was made as durable as the baked clay into which it was pressed, wedge by wedge and word by word.

For century after century, millennium after millennium, more of the tribes of Mesopotamia had laid the foundations of civilization, brick by brick, just as the farmers had made fertile fields out of mud and flood. Sargon's descendants followed him on to the throne at Ur. Enheduanna's hymns were copied and copied again and not forgotten. Other things needful and useful flowed through the kingdom like another river. The first farming tools – sickles, adzes and axes – were edged with blades of flint and obsidian, and since neither existed in Mesopotamia those glassy stones must have come from elsewhere. There was copper in the ground, for metal tools, but the tin for its transformation into the altogether better bronze had had to be sourced and imported too. Already by 2000 BC (at least) there was international trade in the world.

Enheduanna had had her temple but Sargon had his palace close by. In ancient Sumer both Church and state were already on firm footings side by side. The invisible will of the gods permeated all thinking but the king was flesh and blood, and held a power separate from and more obvious than that administered by the priesthood. Sargon's line held Ur until the time of his great-grandson. After the rule of his Akkadians came that of a people from Iran called Gutians, then that of the native Sumerians whom both had dominated, each in their turn. The Sumerian king Ur-Nammu built the Ziggurat of Ur, greatest of many, a looming, tiered wedding cake of a structure made of mud brick and rising into the sky like a Tower of Babel.

That cradle of civilization has had many names – the Fertile Crescent, the Levant, Sumer, Mesopotamia – and whatever it was called by those ancients who knew it, its gravity drew a steady stream of new arrivals. The native Sumerians may always have been where Sargon's Akkadians found them, in what is now the country of Iraq, but everyone else was an incomer: the Gutians (Caucasians out of the north), so too the Elamites and the Amorites. The supremacy of Ur waned and other cities came to matter more. One was Babylon, for some time the greatest city on earth, and famous among its kings was Hammurabi, the lawgiver.

Order from chaos. Once achieved, order must be maintained or it slips away like water through fingers. Left to their own devices, apes like us are a damned mess. Chaos is waiting patiently, ready to flood back and wash away all that has been made. What had been seen to work – fledgling civilization – had to be conserved, repeated and perpetuated. In a place that functioned usefully there had to be assigned roles and jobs for all – some few to set the necessary tasks and many others to carry them out, willingly or not. Each man and woman must know and accept his or her place.

Civilization was like a story with a beginning, middle and end – and also like a ziggurat that rises from a broad and load-bearing base, like the many, to a narrow top made of the few who were gifted the best view of the sky and the cosmos. It was a game in which every player had a part, and a game needs rules or it will not work. Writing made possible not just the keeping of the stories that made sense of the world but also the drafting of rules to maintain the shape of the game. If the rules could be made visible to all, there would be no hope of pleading ignorance as a defence for mistakes and wrongdoing. Writing made possible the rule of law, and King Hammurabi of Babylon set laws into stone so that everyone might see them and know them.

One day in the year 1754 BC (or as close to that year as makes no difference) he stands before a monolith of dolerite, dark and shining like bronze and engraved with the 282 laws that he alone has ordained. It stands more than 7 feet tall, a slim finger of judgement pointing at the sky. It casts its shadow on the ground just as Hammurabi casts his own upon Babylon and all about. In fact he is the first king to bring all of Mesopotamia together. On the reverse of the stele, deeply carved where the fingernail might have been, is a bas-relief Hammurabi must have approved. It shows him standing before a seated representation of the sun god Shamash, son of Nanna, the moon god, and Inanna, beloved of

Enheduanna. If it is meant in part as a likeness of the man, the king, then Hammurabi is strongly made. In the manner of the people of Ur, and of Uruk, who went before, he wears a long skirt on his lower body and a shawl around his torso that reveals his right arm, muscles well defined. His beard is long, elaborately styled, like that of the seated god he stands before, and his head is covered by a helmet. Just as Moses would receive from God the law of the Hebrews, etched into stones, so Hammurabi – likely a contemporary of the biblical Abraham, who may have been from Ur – was handed his laws by another god (though his were shown as a measuring rod and tape).

In Babylonia there was belief in a pantheon of gods. It worked for Hammurabi to promote the notion that not all gods were equal. Above the rest, like the peak of a ziggurat, was Marduk. In the beginning there had been a male deity called Apsu and a female called Tiamat. Their off-spring were uncontrollable, so Tiamat sought their destruction. Alone, Marduk stepped out to face her – great dragon of chaos that she was – and defeated her and cut her into pieces. From her body he made the world and the waters below, and heaven above.

Hammurabi told his people that those other deities had accepted Marduk as their superior then, with the right to rule over them. Understood by all Babylonians was the thought that chaos had always been there, since before time began. Chaos and darkness were not the work of gods – they just . . . were. What Marduk had brought, had achieved by his butchering of Tiamat, was order: light in that darkness, form to replace the nothingness – all that was good. Without Marduk the chaos would rise like floodwater and swallow everything once more. That primacy of Marduk's was hardly Hammurabi's idea, was surely older than him, but it was in his interests to promote it, and so he did.

There was a tradition of seeing the universe as something that had been made, assembled and built like a ziggurat, block upon block. That making had been the work of a paramount god who therefore ruled over all of that creation. The universe was his and so all should be grateful, on account of having been added to that creation, scattered upon it like grounds of pepper sprinkled over a finished dish.

'Let there be light . . .'

Out of that thinking would come, in time, the thought of the One God – of the Hebrews and others. That God was a tamer of chaos, a creator, a builder, a watchmaker capable of work of unimaginable intricacy and perfection. That God had made men and women as well, from dust and spit and the breath of life. In time the Christian faith would continue the thought, with Jesus as the son of a carpenter, another craftsman.

Marduk was a god of thunder and lightning (clearly an idea that had legs). Where men made his likeness he was shown sometimes as a farmer, a sower of fruitful seeds, at other times as a warrior aboard a wheeled vehicle like a chariot. Later his name was changed, to Bel, or Baal, which means 'Lord'.

Found in three pieces by Swiss Egyptologist Gustave Jéquier during the 1901 excavation of the ruins of the city of Susa, 160 miles or so east of the Tigris River in Iran, the so-called Hammurabi stele is on display now in the Louvre. It had been carried away, out of Babylon, in the twelfth century BC as spoils of war by Shutruk-Nakhunte, King of the Elamites, but through all its years and travels it has pointed the way. Hammurabi's 282 laws, known as the Code of Hammurabi, run to almost 4,000 lines of text in cuneiform script. Surely he ran his fingertips over the shining surface of the dolerite and knew that he had done right by his gods and by his people. Men and women, free and bond, might read the law for themselves and thereby be assured of justice:

> Let the oppressed man who has a cause,
> Come into the presence of my statue,
> And read carefully my inscribed stele.

The code specifies two sexes – male and female – and three classes – superior people (free people who owned property), commoners (free people who did not) and slaves – and makes clear the different compensations owing for harm to each. Rights and rules concerning marriage and divorce, and procedures for trade, are graven in stone alongside details of crimes and punishments. Hammurabi's stele has on it the oldest manifestation of *lex talionis*, the law of retaliation, which demands the likes of an eye for an eye:

> If a superior man should blind the eye of another superior man, they shall blind his eye . . . If he should blind the eye of a commoner . . . he shall weigh and deliver 60 shekels of silver. If he should blind the eye of a slave of a superior man . . . he shall weigh and deliver half of the slave's value.

A doctor should charge a superior man 10 silver shekels for treating a severe injury, but only 5 to a commoner and 2 to a slave. If a superior man died under the doctor's care, that doctor should have his hands cut off. If a commoner or slave died, the doctor should only pay a fine.

There had been legal codes before. Archaeologists have found written laws by older Sumerian kings – the Code of Ur-Nammu, builder of the greatest ziggurat, and that of Lipit-Ishtar – but the dolerite stele of Hammurabi towers over all. For a thousand years his laws were copied and taken up by other nations, testament to their authority and worth.

Hammurabi did not – and did not claim – that he himself had invented the wisdom he had ordered carved into his stele. On the contrary he had only collated and displayed, for all to see and to know, the eternal, immutable laws handed down from on high. The right way to be was pre-existing, unquestionable, as old as time. As far back as the time of the kings of Babylon 4,000 and more years ago it was being declared that the law that men and women must obey was a universal constant, pre-ordained. Humanity could not be trusted, could not trust itself, to decide how to behave; only gods had such wisdom. The path to power of those claiming they can talk to a god, intercede on behalf of their fellows, is already well worn by the time of Hammurabi.

If there ever was an age when all men and women considered themselves equal, it was past by the coming of the first civilizations of
Mesopotamia. The Code of Hammurabi, which was not the first list
of laws for men and women to live by, made clear there was a rigid hierarchy. Just like the ziggurat, the many at the base of civilized society
would bear the weight of the superior, property-owning few at the top,
the slaves carrying the heaviest burden of all. Men and women were not
equal either, or not of equal value when it came to crime and punishment:

> If a superior man should break the bone of another superior man, they
>   shall break his bone.
> If he should blind the eye of a commoner, or break the bone of a
>   commoner, he shall weigh and deliver 60 shekels of silver.
> If a man should strike a superior woman so that she lose her unborn child,
>   he shall pay 10 shekels for her loss.
> If that woman should die, they shall kill his daughter.

Wounded men of superior class would see their male assailant suffer the
same injury as that done to themselves. The hurt would demand equal
hurt in return. But where a man killed a woman, even a superior woman,
he was to be left physically unharmed because the crime was deemed less
serious. His daughter, also his property, would be destroyed instead.

Civilization came at a cost. The mass of men and women had accepted
(or had to accept) there would be ceaseless toil in return for the benefits
of permanent homes, streets to walk on, food for themselves and for their
families. The gods had said that it was so, and who could argue with
a god? Property was owned by the few. Those without property were
beholden to landlords and so worked for them in order to pay their way.
Slaves had fewer freedoms still. Each man, each woman was required to
accept his or her place in the scheme, for the collective good. After all, the
rules governing civilization had not been set down by men, but by invisible gods. If the gods had ordained the hierarchy, then so be it.

What was accepted then is accepted now. The civilizations that have functioned over the longest time are those in which the vast majority of individuals play the game by timeless rules they did not set for themselves but accept as 'self-evident'. Western civilization, holding chaos at bay, is fundamentally Judeo-Christian. Even after 2,000 years the foundations are the same. Communism was meant to replace the old ways, establish new values, but lasted only a lifetime and raised the greatest ziggurat of human corpses the world has yet seen. Useful values that work as rules of a game and that improve the lot of as many people as possible are agonizingly hard to come by.

That Judeo-Christian system was founded on the rules of the Old Testament; and rules set by Moses centuries later, that are there too in Deuteronomy and then referenced by Jesus in the Sermon on the Mount centuries later still, suggest those authors knew about and accepted laws set in stone by Hammurabi:

> And thine eye shall not pity; but life shall go for life, eye for eye, tooth for tooth, hand for hand, foot for foot.
>
> (Deuteronomy 19:21)

> Ye have heard that it hath been said, An eye for an eye, and a tooth for a tooth . . .
>
> (Matthew 5:38)

All of this continuity and copying and remembering connects our world of the twenty-first century to a moment in time more than thirty-seven centuries ago, when an ambitious king of Babylon stood in the shadow of a stone he had ordered to be made. No doubt he believed he might benefit personally from having as many people as possible submit to their place in the scheme of things – a scheme that had him atop the highest step of the ziggurat. But even such a man as he knew better, it seems, than to contemplate thinking up his own laws, starting from scratch.

Instead he looked to what had worked in the past, what had worked before and would surely work again. Power, like the law, had not originated from within himself; rather he had acquired and turned to his advantage something that had existed before and that would pass to another after he was gone.

After thirty-seven centuries, in his book *A Story Like the Wind*, the South African writer and philosopher Laurens van der Post would pin down the truth of the eternal nature of the story – how the story was always there and will go on without us: 'The story is like the wind. It comes from a far-off place and we feel it.'

3.

REKHMIRE AND THE OFFICE JOB

This is not a history of the world, it is a *story* of the world. The history of the world interests me less. I want a story I can remember from beginning to end; a set of hand holds on a wall, or rungs on a ladder. I want to lie in bed at night with my eyes closed and imagine snaking my way up this narrative from start to finish. I want a version of events I can memorize and recite like a party trick or one of Enheduanna's poems.

For all the poetry of Enheduanna and all the self-righteousness of Hammurabi and his laws, writing was more likely started by those inclined to be, or coerced into being, bean counters. The first marks pressed into clay were surely counts of crops and cattle, statements of accounts. It was no ancient Justinian, Wordsworth or Austen who first, as it were, put pen to paper. Rather it was someone keeping track of wealth, keeping count of what was owned and owed. We do not know who discovered the trick. Someone in Sumer, in Babylon or elsewhere in Mesopotamia found that marks made in wet clay stayed put when it dried. Rather than remember a number or a deal, it could be created in the world and so made real. A spoken agreement might be challenged or denied later on, but what had been made permanent on a hand-sized slice of clay, for all to see, was proof of the fact, admissible in court. Rather than trust a messenger to remember the details while he travelled, let him carry a note of it instead and hand that over on meeting the client. Once shown to work, writing was perfect for anyone on the make. For every Enheduanna and Hammurabi preserving profound thoughts, there must have been a thousand pen-pushers and desk jockeys keeping the books.

Rekhmire was the governor of Thebes and also vizier to Thutmose III, and then his son Amenhotep II, pharaohs of the Eighteenth Dynasty of the New Kingdom during the second half of the second millennium BC. A vizier was a pharaoh's most senior adviser, trusted, rich and powerful in his own right. The word itself has complicated roots that twist and turn through Turkish *vezir* and Arabic *wazir*, both of which are like *viceroy* and describe one who bears the burden of office. Some etymologists have suggested the word follows in the train of *katib*, which is Arabic for a writer, so that viziers were literate first and foremost.

Katib . . . wazir . . . vezir . . . vizier . . . call him what you will, Rekhmire was employed to keep an eye, likely both eyes, on the money. Here is what truly inspired writing, the invention that changed the world and made history possible. Not a hymn praising a goddess, nor a set of laws to be obeyed, not even an epic for a hero king like Gilgamesh, just the dull necessity of keeping accounts. A pharaoh might have enjoyed reading about how great he was but it mattered more for him to know how rich.

In older days, millennia before Thutmose and Amenhotep, Egypt was two kingdoms, an Upper in the south and a Lower in the north. Around 3200 BC Menes, a great king of Upper Egypt, waged war and achieved dominance over the Lower Kingdom. From then on Egypt was one, a sinuous ribbon of a place strung out along both banks of the Nile that was its artery, and home to a civilization that would last 3,000 years. Menes and his successors were kings. Back then 'pharaoh' was the word to describe the location of the royal court; only in the centuries of the New Kingdom, the time of Thutmose and those who came after, did it mean the king himself. The heart was at Memphis in the north first of all, where the river became an estuary, a single artery harrowed into threads seabound, and only later sited at Thebes, in the south. The fates of all, from highest to lowest, depended on the Nile. Every Egyptian knew their king was responsible for the fertility of the land – that the rising and falling of the river was his gift to give. That belief, in that place, gave life to something that had not existed before. In Ur, in Uruk, in Babylonia and elsewhere leaders, kings, were men. Around and above them, invisible and all powerful, were gods. Gilgamesh had sought something more – eternal life – but his adventures had taught him in the end that such a prize was for gods alone. In Egypt, kings like Menes wedded themselves to the river, to life itself, until two were one. An early depiction of Menes has him digging a ditch through which life-giving water might flow.

In the moment that matters, an entrance is being blocked and concealed. It is the way into Rekhmire's tomb in the city of the dead that is Sheikh Abd el-Qurna on the west bank of the Nile, at Thebes. Egyptologists call it a tomb but Rekhmire's body was not interred inside. His mortal remains were stowed elsewhere, and the space borrowed from the rock at Sheikh Abd el-Qurna kept hidden something else entirely. The tomb is shaped like the letter T, with the entrance opening into the middle of the top stroke, so that a long narrow hall, or chamber, stretches beyond, straight ahead, while two sides of a vestibule are either side, left and right. The moment is the quenching of the light before the scraping of stone on stone and the beginning of the long reign of darkness. As the long, angular shadow grows it falls across and smothers, like blackest lacquer spilled, a host of characters, all the ghosts that will inhabit the space now that men are gone. The walls and ceilings are covered with brightly coloured, skilfully executed scenes and texts describing Rekhmire and his family, but most importantly his duties as vizier, the honours awarded to him and also details about what was owed and paid to the pharaoh by his own people and those of neighbouring states. There is a depiction of the ritual called Opening the Mouth, whereby a statue's mouth was 'opened' to ensure Rekhmire would eat and drink in the afterlife. Nearby are scenes, snapshots, of the Beautiful Feast of the Valley, a ritual celebration of the dead involving lavishly appointed boats on the Nile and conveying hopes for the revival of the departed in the next world. It is all colour and life, in total some 300 square yards of stories in pictures and text, but destined and doomed to an eternity of darkness.

All around are illustrations of what was the pharaoh's due, and what Rekhmire had been responsible for collecting: incense trees from the people of Punt, and also baboons, monkeys and animal skins . . . more baboons, dogs, giraffes, leopards and monkeys from the people of Kush, as well as gold and ivory . . . pots, carts and weapons from Syria, along with horses, a bear and an elephant . . . The demanded wealth seems endless. On other walls are scenes of tribute from Egyptians of the Lower Nile, and on the Mediterranean coast. Elsewhere the vizier oversees the preparation and offering of food for the temple complex at Karnak, or there is the work of the craftsmen who were at his command – carpenters, decorators and goldsmiths, masons and sculptors. Other scenes show fishers, hunters and winemakers.

Collectively the paintings and text are known as the Installation of the Vizier and provide the most detailed description yet discovered of the role of such a man. What was buried in that moment of the closing and sealing of Rekhmire's 'tomb' (or rather fixed in place like a cuneiform mark on clay or hieroglyph etched on stone) was the inevitability of death and taxes. Everyone thinks of the pyramids and the rest of the great public works raised across the kingdom as Egypt's greatest memorial, and so they may be. The most conspicuous, like Karnak and Cheops, were already ancient by the time of Rekhmire, and Thutmose and Amenhotep, and they were the inheritors and beneficiaries of lessons learned by others of their sort and long before. The greatest of the building projects were made possible by the mustering and organization of people and resources on a scale hitherto unprecedented. Thousands of slaves and entire regiments of soldiers were marshalled and deployed, for year after year, for the cutting and hauling of the blocks that made the Great Pyramid. They were fed with mountains of food and lakes of water and wine accounted for and efficiently distributed. It was, all of it, a feat of organization and logistics made possible only by the work of another army – an army of scribes, literate, numerate office workers and bureaucrats trained in a special school at Thebes and employed across the kingdom. Texts survive describing the qualities expected in a good scribe: shrewd and cautious judgement; self-control; conscientious study and respect for those higher in the chain of command. Demanded above all else was demonstrable regard for the absolute sanctity of weights and measures, and respect for private property and legal forms. Only with such skills, carefully applied, were pyramids raised into the sky, whole cities carved from the living rock.

Those bureaucrats, that entire bureaucracy, was what made Egypt . . . Egypt. As well as for the building of public works, the mass of the population had to be organized around the business of growing the food upon which the elites depended. A mostly peasant population bent its collective back throughout the year in fields growing barley, emmer (a kind of wheat) and vegetables. Egypt was made fertile by the Nile but its fields were the work of men and women; so too the canals and irrigation ditches that canalized the water. All such labour was planned and organized by scribes; so too the collection and distribution of the harvest. In the kingdom of the Nile, the king – pharaoh – was life itself. He was not subject to the gods, like kings elsewhere; rather *he was god*. He was raised above all men, and the structure that held him so high was made of bureaucrats.

4.

CAPPADOCIA AND THE
INVISIBLE MAGIC OF MONEY

The end, at least some of the end, is in the beginning. Powerful ideas occurred to our sort early on. Even at the daybreak of civilization, when the foundations of the first cities were still to be laid, synapses crackled in ancestors' brains and conjured into being concepts that would last for ever.

Scattered across the islands of the Yap archipelago in the western Pacific Ocean are thousands of doughnut-shaped stones. They are carved from calcite, a kind of crystallized limestone, and the Yapese call them *rai*. They come in all sizes. Some are small – just an inch or so in diameter – but many are huge: the biggest is more than 12 feet across and weighs as much as several parked cars. They are found all over – by trackways, in clearings, in the middle of villages. For the people of Yap, the stones have functioned as money.

No source of calcite exists on the Yap islands. A millennium and a half ago – and perhaps longer, no one knows for sure – the locals began travelling to the nearest source, on the island of Palau, nearly 300 miles away across the ocean. Maybe some Yapese fishermen were blown there during a storm long ago, and made the discovery by accident – again, no one is certain. Other sources of calcite were identified and exploited on other islands even further away, but most was obtained from Palau. After quarrying and carving, and with a hole drilled through the centre for the purpose of lifting and manoeuvring them, they were loaded on to rafts and canoes and taken back to Yap. Imagine! A stone doughnut weighing tons and suspended between enough canoes to keep it above the waves and transported 300 miles across open ocean. Once set in position, a giant *rai* was never moved again. There was no need.

For the everyday things of life, the Yapese used simple bartering – you give me ten chickens and I will give you this knife. For larger, more expensive transactions, the stones came into play. Let us say a young woman was to be married. If the prospective husband's family owned a *rai*, he might offer it as the bride price. If the deal was acceptable, owner-ship of the *rai* transferred to the family of the father of the bride. The *rai* stayed where it was, where it had always been – by the track, in the clear-ing, wherever – but now everyone knew it had a new owner, and why. If a warrior died in battle and his family wanted to recover his body from whoever had killed him and retained it as a trophy of war, they would have to pay for it. Again, for such a significant transaction, only the exchange of a *rai* would do.

There was value invested in each *rai* in the form of its unique story. For a start there were the details of its making, followed by all the effort and danger involved in bringing it to Yap from Palau, or wherever it had been quarried and carved. Then there would be the endlessly growing story made of its owners – how and why it came to be exchanged each time. The older the stone, the longer and more interesting its story, the greater its value. If a stone had been used to facilitate a marriage that was especially happy or that produced many children, this would add to its desirability. On taking possession of a *rai*, the new owner would learn its story and also become part of it. Unmoving and permanent as a mountain, a giant *rai* was a focus for attention, a fixed point around which much else might revolve.

Archaeologists think the Yapese have been using giant, immovable stones in this way since at least AD 500. The concept involved is not just sophisticated, it is also startlingly similar to some of what gives value to the most modern form of money we have, the so-called 'cryptocurrencies' of the twenty-first century. A currency like bitcoin depends in part upon what is called a distributed ledger. On account of the ledger every interested party can see the valuable item, everyone can see the history of all transactions, but no one has to touch the bitcoin and it never moves in any real sense. It used to be yours, now it is mine, and everyone in the bitcoin community sees this, knows this and accepts this is true.

The investment of value in a *rai* is also inherent in our use of everyday bank accounts. When you are paid at the end of the month, you are not usually handed an envelope full of notes and coins any more. Instead what happens in most cases is that a number, in a computer in your bank, changes to register the fact you have been paid by your employer. When you then pay your mobile phone bill or buy some groceries, that figure changes again and a new figure is also generated in the computer in the bank of your service provider, or of the supermarket. Less for you, more for them. At no point does anyone have to see, far less touch, any real money. No one needs to.

On Yap there is an old story of a *rai* that was being brought to the islands in the usual way. Many miles from land there was a storm and, in order to save their lives, the men in the canoes had to cut loose the stone they were transporting. It sank to the bottom of the ocean, never to be seen again. When they reached land they told everyone what had happened. The story was accepted and the value of the *rai* was neither questioned nor diminished. It was on the seabed but it was still a *rai* and it was exchanged ever after like all the rest. As far as some were concerned, it had the best story of all and so was the most valuable.

When European colonists first encountered the native peoples of North America, in the sixteenth and seventeenth centuries, they found them using strings of polished shells for a variety of purposes. Some told stories from the tribes' histories, some recorded treaties struck between them. Others were used as currency, for exchange. The strings of shells were called wampum, and like *rai*, silver and gold they were, ultimately, proof of work. Usually fashioned by women, the wampum required first of all the collection of whelk and clam shells from the seashore. These were ground down and shaped into uniform cylindrical shapes that were then pierced through with wooden drills tipped with quartz, so they could be strung together to make regular patterns of alternating light and dark beads that were polished with fine sands until they shone. In the early days of the colonies, gold was hard to come by. Either it was squirrelled away or had been sent back to the old country to pay for vital supplies. Left with no other option, the colonists had to use wampum for trade with the locals and among themselves. All worked well enough, for decades, until they imported the means to mass-produce the beads, at which point the value of wampum dropped through the floor. The beads the colonists were making stayed in circulation while the handmade originals, deemed more desirable and more valuable, were stored away. An early version of quantitative easing – like printing cheap banknotes – had prompted a loss of confidence in the currency. The new beads implied no proof of work, and so were worthless.

Our ancestors arrived at this understanding of money – of the essential, invisible value of money – a long time ago. A commodity like silver, a precious metal, was and is hard to come by. Some occurs naturally in pure nuggets, called native silver, but most appears as a constituent element of an ore, bonded with base metals like lead and zinc. Such ore must be ground down to powder and then heated to a temperature close to 1,000°C before the silver will part company with the rest. As long ago as 4000 BC some version of this process was being used in Asia Minor.

By 2000 BC, people in Cappadocia, a part of Asia Minor where silver ore was relatively plentiful, were using bars of silver as currency, as money. At the crucial moment in the story of the world, it occurs to a member of a community there that they do not, each of them, need to carry the heavy metal around on their persons. When it comes to making exchanges, trading for things they need and want, they do not need to pass the silver bars from one person to another. It need never change hands in any physical sense. All that was needed was *knowledge* of how much silver each man owned. Better if everyone left the silver in the same safe place. Since each knew how much silver he owned at any given moment, he did not have to see it any more, far less hold it. He could even carry, if he wanted to, a note of how much he owned on a tablet of dried clay. This realization was also a revelation that would matter, into the future, in many ways.

Silver is valuable not just because it shines and may be used for making pretty things. Silver, like gold, is valuable because it is proof of work. An ingot of silver is the product of hard work – finding the ore, mining the ore, smashing and grinding it into powder, sweating over it while the heat of a furnace coaxes the precious metal away from the base, labouring over it to shape the molten silver into bars of equal size. All of that effort is fixed there in the silver. Gold and silver are also easily stored. A herd of cattle is valuable, but think of the space required for keeping them (compared to the space needed for the quantity of silver or gold of equal value), the food they must eat and the water they must drink. Gold and silver can easily be divided into units – in the case of gold, right down to single grains. Try dividing a cow while still retaining the value of the whole, living animal and see how far you get.

Silver and gold are all of those things – proof of work, beautiful and desirable, easily and cheaply stored, easily divided. What happened in that moment in ancient Cappadocia was even more important to the story of the world: it was the realization that value is an idea shared, shared knowledge that something valuable exists, somewhere; that some have ownership of more than others.

A silver bar, a monolith of calcite, a bag of gold dust, a string of handmade shell beads – each is proof of work, of effort. Coins followed, then promissory notes and cheques, banknotes and all manner of financial instruments. All of these worked either because each was valuable in itself – in the case of gold and silver – or otherwise proved the existence, somewhere, of proof of work. But in truth a man is rich when people know and accept that he is rich, on account of something they do not have to see or hold. Like power, the real value of gold, silver, giant stones and wampum is ultimately invisible and carried in our heads.

5.

GRAPES AND OLIVES
AND A MINOTAUR AT KNOSSOS

Ambitious men wrote that they were kings and gods and other men believed them; inhabitants of those first civilizations learned the law; wealth was accounted for; bureaucrats used writing and counting to organize thousands for building cities and canals, ziggurats and pyramids; surplus food was gathered, centralized and redistributed. All of this was in place 2,000 years and more before the birth of Jesus.

So far this story of the world has been largely about rivers – the Tigris and Euphrates in Mesopotamia and the Nile in Egypt. Civilizations, outline sketches at least, were on those riverbanks 5,000 years ago. By 4,000 years ago the picture was complicated by more rivers – rivers of people on the move within and through the swatch of territory called the Near East. If civilization started there it exerted a magnetic pull. From neighbouring lands came those drawn by its potential. Some would settle quietly in the nest, only becoming what they had beheld. Some would displace the indigenous inhabitants like cuckoos, pushing exiles into new territories where, in turn, their ways proved infectious. At the same time there were those who travelled back and forth, came and went of their own accord and added to the mixing of ideas across an ever-widening area.

Making sense of all the movement is impossible. It is as though restless feet stirred a blinding cloud of dust. As well as by human feet the dust was kicked up by the hooves of horses, an alien species in Mesopotamia until then and ridden or driven in by outsiders, incomers such as Kassites, or the Hyksos whose charioteers would conquer Egypt around the year 1650 BC. Among the wanderers were speakers of the Semitic languages – Akkadian, Arabic, Aramaic, Hebrew, and others besides. There were speakers of the Indo-European languages too, including those who would in time raise the Persian civilization.

By 2000 BC all of the comings and goings had carried civilizing ways into the west, dandelion clock seeds, towards the Mediterranean and Aegean seas. As it would be for thousands of years to come, farming was the mulch from which civilization grew. Surplus food made possible by farming allowed populations to grow. Surplus food made surplus people who might be set to tasks other than farming. Cereal crops had been the mainstay in Mesopotamia and Egypt, but elsewhere other soils and circumstances had farmers seek alternatives. And so the suitability of the olive, the wealth it enabled, provided the conditions necessary for the specialists who wrote, counted, built and crafted; the soldiers who marched, defended and conquered.

The moment that matters next, therefore, is the noticing of the potential of olive trees and grape vines – the crops that changed the Mediterranean world. Like oxygenated blood, the juice of the olive and the grape invigorated people who would grow the civilization that was Ancient Greece. The oldest evidence of the cultivation of olive trees is found in the territory called Israel, specifically the Carmel coast. By 2000 BC they were a mainstay of life on the island of Crete. Cereals were grown there too but the olive and the grape – both of which grow where grain crops do not – flourished in the Aegean islands as they did nowhere else. Crete, the largest, proved best of all.

By at least 2500 BC there were farmers on Crete, doing so well that they had the time for building towns with regular street plans. Those towns were on the coast, to take advantage of the sea. No doubt they had contact with peoples out of the Near East, Egyptian and Mesopotamian prospectors and explorers who carried ideas of civilization among their other belongings. No doubt the Cretans made their own voyages, aboard the deep-hulled ships they included in their murals.

On the walls of that tomb of Vizier Rekhmire at Thebes are depictions of people from Crete bearing, among other things, pottery jugs. A familiar word for them is amphorae, but in the context of Crete at the start of the second millennium BC the better word is *pithoi*, which is Greek and describes a sort of jar as tall as a man and used for storing vast quantities of olive oil and wine, and also grain. The Egyptians of the time had their own word for people from Crete and it was *Keftiu*. Text accompanying the illustration in Rekhmire's tomb reads: 'Coming in peace by the Great of Crete, islands that are in the middle of the sea . . .'

That Egyptian artwork adds colour and detail that might otherwise be absent from the moment. Egyptologists have said those images must represent a later period in the life of Crete but it seems fair to imagine the people and their clothes were little changed from those of before. If so, then just as likely they are the sort that first realized the value, the potential, of the olive trees and grape vines they knew as gifts from the gods. The people are shown with skins dark red. They wear their dark hair long, with curls on the tops of their heads. They wear loincloths and their legs are covered with close-fitting fabric. On their feet are sandals fastened with straps. This may be evidence of trade or it might be what the Egyptians thought it was – namely tribute offered up by grateful neighbours and subjects. Either way such exchanges forged and maintained connections, allowing for the transmission of ideas.

Much of what we know about those Bronze Age folk of Crete around 2000 BC is down to the excavations by Sir Arthur Evans in 1900. His work was centred on Knossos, on the north coast, and what he found there, a great complex of buildings around a huge central court, he called a palace. There were others – in Malia, also on the north coast, and at Phaistos on the south coast – but it seems at least likely that those and all else on Crete were subservient to whoever sat at Knossos. It was Evans who coined the name Minoan to describe the civilization, inspired by later words by Greeks who thought King Minos lived and ruled there with his wife Pasiphaë, daughter of the sun. When Minos offended Poseidon, the sea god cursed Pasiphaë to fall in love with a bull and she gave birth to the monstrous Minotaur. The Minotaur, half man and half bull, they thought, had been kept in a great labyrinth beneath the palace and pacified with young men and women sent to him as sacrifices, until he was slain by Theseus.

With or without a goddess or a Minotaur, there was a palace at Knossos for around 250 years, until perhaps 1600 BC when a volcanic eruption and earthquake on the nearby island of Thera caused devastation. In the aftermath the palace was rebuilt and remained a centre for two more centuries at least.

That Minoan civilization, stubborn in the face of natural forces, was based on farming – of cereals certainly, but also and primarily olives and grapes. That wealth made all else possible. Once identified and realized, the potential of those two crops spread around the Aegean and the Mediterranean. The civilization watered and made fertile by those wonders would, in time, take shape as a place fit for thinking great thoughts – thoughts by Thales, Anaximander, Socrates and all the rest of the first and greatest philosophers.

The olive mattered most of all. It grew deep, into the mind as well as the soil. Much of the terrain – on Crete and elsewhere in what would be the Greek world, the Hellenic world – was arid mountain, and sterile. Impossible for grain, it was a place gripped only by the toughest roots, of the olive and the vine whose thrawn fingers worked and wheedled and held. Better than any other, the olive trees asked little but gave life. In time they would symbolize health and wealth, beauty and wisdom. Perhaps above all the olive meant abundance, plenty. The fruit and the oil were the very stuff of life. The oil could be consumed, and also burned for light and warmth. The bark burned too, and the leaves and twigs were good for stuffing mattresses. The wood provided handles for tools, structure for buildings. Once true trade was established, this for that, olive oil was wealth itself – liquid gold, as Homer had it. Solon the lawmaker of Ancient Greece made harming an olive tree a crime punishable by death. Some olive trees were worthy of worship and called *moria*. The Greek word for giving help, and also for punishment, is *timoria* and has the same root. The medic called Hippocrates would write about scores of treatments won from the olive tree and its fruit. It was used as a contraceptive, applied 'to that part of the womb where the seed falls'. Olive oil was offered up to the gods as a sacrifice. Athletes were anointed with it until they shone, and crowned with the tree's leaves when they triumphed at the Games. The olive branch was a sign of peace after war.

Out of the olive – the fruit that made life for itself and for mankind from the hardest of circumstances – grew wisdom itself.

6.

SHIVA AND THE OLDEST
CULT RELIGION IN THE WORLD

Only five moments gone and already the world has shapes familiar: written words; laws to live by; bureaucrats working late in the office; the sleight of hand of money and wealth. Only five moments gone and a person might think they recognize the place and know it well enough . . . but that which appears simple at first sight has often been altered to look that way, long after the fact.

In the west it has been easy to look at a map of the world – especially the one drawn in 1569 by Gerardus Mercator, a cartographer from the Low Countries – and focus on the strip between the Atlantic Ocean and the Middle East. Mercator's projection made the world simpler and different from how it was. That which exists upon a sphere he rendered into the familiar rectangle that once hung, corners curling, on the peeling wall of every geography classroom. In so doing he laid the basis for a misconception that lasted half a millennium. To help mariners follow trade routes Mercator forced straight lines across the rounded swell of oceans, tight wires across the wet rounding of an eye. As a consequence he implanted a distortion of reality so that North America and Europe were made to appear larger in relation to South America and Africa than they really were, or are. Most conspicuously he made western Europe the centre of the map, and so of the whole world.

The outer skin of a ball has, of course, no centre. In fact, vast terrains belittled by Mercator or pushed to the margins of his map were, for the longest time, untouched and unimpressed by the inhabitants of that ribbon he had aggrandized. Asia felt, for the longest time, little of the existence of Europe. As big as Europe in terms of landmass, India too remained aloof, little noticing or caring about ructions to her north-west, civilizations rising and falling. King Sargon I of Akkad seems to have known about India, at least the part his scribes called Meluhha (thought by historians to mean the Indus Valley – that part of the subcontinent reached first by travellers approaching from the Near East). But while the civilizations of Mesopotamia, and also Egypt, are older than anything of the sort in India, they seemingly had for centuries no meaningful influence there. If they were counted as neighbours at all they were of a distant sort, any noise they might have made while laying their older foundations dulled to murmurs by the insulation of the world's highest mountains and many miles in between.

India was a world unto herself, an inverted triangle made separate not just by mountains towards her north and north-west but also by great swathes of jungle to her north-east. If her landward base was protected, then so too were her other two sides, by the vastness of the Indian Ocean, largely impenetrable until the 1600s. Her climate is tropical, even though much of the landmass does not sit in the tropics. As well as the valley of the Indus in the west there is another great vascular system in the east, the Ganges. Between the rivers is desert, more or less. To the south the land rises to the highlands of the Deccan where forests grew. The mountains in the north hold at bay the cold winds of Asia, saving her from that enervating continental chill. In from the ocean roll clouds that bring the monsoon in the year's hottest months. She is a world entire, and that world gave birth first and foremost not to a nation, or nations, but to a unifying culture of immense power and duration, able to swallow whole and transform all comers. It was altogether different from anything that had grown (or ever would grow) far away to the north and west, in the lands of the Near East, or on the banks of the Nile, or by the waters of the Mediterranean. That ribbon between the Atlantic and Iran would ever be self-obsessed, convinced of its importance to the story of the world, but India mattered to the consciousness of the planet in other ways, different ways.

The moment that matters is the emergence of the god called Shiva, a central figure in the way of life that is Hinduism and regarded by some scholars as the focal point of the world's oldest surviving religious cult. *Shiva* is Sanskrit and was an adjective (meaning 'propitious and gracious') long before it was a name. India kindled the flame of a culture that would survive into the present day, enlightening, shaping and ordering the lives of millions, billions of people. It was a culture imbued always with the power to absorb and assimilate, while remaining unchanged and unchanging. That endurance was founded upon Hinduism.

By the last quarter of the third millennium BC there were cities in the valley of the Indus. Raised of burnt brick – an innovation that made structures proof against the ravages of floodwater – these are attributed to the Harappan culture named after one of them. The city of Harappa was more than 2 miles around, laid out on a rectangular grid plan and home to perhaps 30,000 people. Streets of houses served with internal drainage systems make plain an early obsession with bathing, and so with personal and spiritual hygiene. Mohenjo-daro was another great conurbation in the valley, as meticulously ordered. Both cities had citadels for defence and reached out into their hinterlands with trading networks stretching hundreds of miles. From Mohenjo-daro a canal stretched a mile to a great dockyard on the coast at Lothal.

At a time when circles of sarsen stones were being raised at Stonehenge, and when people were being buried accompanied by metal artefacts and clay beakers all across western Europe, the valley of the Indus was a place of city dwellers. They had mastered writing. Their craftsmen demanded imports of raw materials from a sphere of influence best described as an empire. From as far afield as Mesopotamia they drew what they needed and then redistributed finished goods for the return trips. They had the first cotton fabric in the world and used it for baling goods for export from Lothal. It was at Mohenjo-daro that archaeologists found a piece of steatite stone carved with what may be a representation of Shiva. Called the Pashupati (Lord of Animals) seal and dating to perhaps 2600 BC, it shows a male figure seated in the lotus position and surrounded by all manner of animals: deer, elephant, buffalo and more. It would have been pressed into wet clay to leave its image as an identifying mark.

For long the focus of scholarly attention was on the pendulum of history swinging slowly, back and forth, from one side of the Mediterranean to the other. There, it seemed, was all that mattered. Out of sight of that preoccupation, the Indian subcontinent cradled a flowering of its own. Shiva was there from the beginning, before the beginning. Before there was Harappa or Mohenjo-daro there was faith in a transcendent presence blessed with the power to create and enable life and also to wreak havoc. Lord of destruction, and of reproduction. In time he would be joined by a wife, the goddess Parvati, and their sons Ganesha and Kartikeya. But belief in Shiva may have been old, ancient even, by the time of those Harappan city dwellers. In the Raisen District of Madhya Pradesh at the very heart of India are the rock shelters of Bhimbetka. Archaeologists have established human occupation there from 100,000 years ago. On to the soft sandstone, in shadowed niches, hunters and early farmers painted images of people and animals, the oldest dating from at least 10,000 years ago. One male figure holding aloft a trident and seeming to dance across the stone has been interpreted as an early image of the god who would be Shiva.

In a story of the world it is important to pay attention, from earliest times, to the whole of the place. Archaeologists and palaeontologists are broadly agreed that our species, *Homo sapiens*, had but one source – in Africa. The story of the rise of civilization is different, with flames of that enlightenment sparking in the darkness in many different places, at many different times. In India, as in Asia, civilizations emerged spontaneously, without the need of external inspiration. A focal point in the subcontinent – a centre of gravity holding in place traditions and a culture that would outlive anything in Mesopotamia or Egypt or anywhere else – was and is the religion of Hinduism. It is an encircling net, a web of connections. Spider-like at its centre since a time before the reach of memory, quietly seated in lotus position, is Shiva.

7.

HYKSOS, HEBREWS
AND CHARIOTS IN EGYPT

The great men, legendary patriarchs of the Old Testament, haunt the consciousness of the west. Abraham . . . Isaac . . . Jacob . . . Moses . . . their ghostly presence casts shadows across Judaism, Christianity, Islam and all the way to the modern world. Surely it was real flesh-and-blood individuals who lived and died and inspired the stories, however much those stories may have changed after endless retelling. The first of them, Abraham, was likely one of many refugees or emigrants in the long aftermath of the fall of the Mesopotamian city-state of Ur. Having seen the sense in leaving his homeland, some time around 1800 BC, he evidently came to Canaan, in the Levant, likely with followers. The descendants of Abraham and others like him, with a similar story to tell of dispossession and exile, became the Hebrews first mentioned in Egyptian texts of the fourteenth century BC. Hebrew is a word, a name meaning 'wanderer' that all by itself paints a picture of people restlessly or helplessly on the move for centuries. According to the Bible story, and in a time of famine, there was a movement by some of those Hebrews out of Canaan and into Egypt. One of the named names is that of the patriarch Jacob, remembered as the father of a dozen sons. One of them, Joseph (he of the multi-coloured coat), went ahead of the rest and established himself as a senior official in the service of the pharaoh.

Scholars have imagined this folk movement happening some time during or close to the century of Egyptian history known as the Second Intermediate Period when some of that land was ruled by a mostly mysterious people called the Hyksos. Some sources suggest they rose to dominance in the eighteenth century BC, others say the seventeenth, but there is no consensus. Their name is likely derived from the Egyptian *Hega-khase*, meaning 'foreign kings', and in memory of a time when they were ruled by outsiders. In any event most students of the period are persuaded it was a time when invaders took advantage of unrest within the Lower Kingdom, in the Nile Delta, and asserted their dominance. Only in a period of uncertainty they say, even chaos, could a leader of a foreign people – a Joseph of the Hebrews, for instance – rise to dominate the bureaucracy of a kingdom as formidable as Egypt. After some centuries, perhaps three or four, there was an exodus out of Egypt by at least some of those Hebrews. The leader's name was Moses. After more years on the move they arrived in Canaan – the Promised Land. The Old Testament version of events has both upheavals – the arrival in Egypt, out of Canaan, and then the departure – happening to just one group and their descendants. More recently it has been suggested the story evolved over time to give a sense of shared identity to at least two groups that had made a home in Canaan – one that originated in Egypt, in the west, and a second that came originally out of Mesopotamia, in the east. At least one clue is there in that most famous of names, Moses, which has its roots in the Egyptian language, visible and audible in other famous names like Ahmose and Thutmose.

It would be inconceivable to try and tell a story of the world without considering at least some of the stories fossilized in the Bible. What is more fascinating, as instructive, is to look beyond the shadows cast by names like Abraham, Joseph and Moses and see the people they may have moved among, the people known as the Hyksos. It is especially worth imagining the uprising, the emergence into the light, of those so-called foreign kings.

Perhaps those Hyksos were invaders who had looked on at Egyptian unrest from somewhere beyond its borders and made a move to take advantage when the time was right. Or maybe they were resident foreigners, immigrants, recent arrivals from lands in the east or the north who rose up in a time of crisis, or were pulled into a power vacuum. In any event they were, on account of the technology they had at their disposal, too much for those Egyptians to handle.

There are ancient images of Sumerian soldiers aboard ungainly four-wheeled wagons pulled by asses so that we know the value of vehicles hauled by beasts of burden was identified by others before the Hyksos. As weapons of war those contraptions were limited, perhaps useful only as taxis for transporting armed and armoured men into the thick of fighting on a battlefield.

An Indo-European people called the Kassites, from the Zagros Mountains in Iran, attacked the Mesopotamian civilization of Babylon in the eighteenth century BC. They were beaten off – by a son of Hammurabi the lawgiver, as it happens – but returned in the sixteenth century BC to begin a reign lasting half a millennium. The Kassites were among the first horsemen (they worshipped the beasts) and had learned also to harness those animals to highly manoeuvrable two-wheeled chariots. Wherever the Hyksos came from, by the time they arrived in Egypt they had mastery of chariots too – as well as powerful composite bows and socketed bronze axes. The pharaoh's soldiers then were infantry, foot soldiers, lightly armoured and armed with outmoded weapons like the mace. The world had moved forward elsewhere, leaving old Egypt lacking in the weaponry of the Bronze Age. The wheels of the Hyksos chariots were rimmed with an even younger metal, iron, and thus armed and equipped they ran roughshod over those Egyptians who had never seen nor even dreamed of the like.

Horse-riding was a thousand years old by then, perhaps older, and the folk memory of the first sight of mounted men may explain the Greek legend of the centaur.

So began two centuries of Hyksos rule of Lower Egypt – so that even the pharaohs of Upper Egypt, at Thebes, had to pay them homage. Rule by outsiders is often (always) hard to bear for those who regard themselves as indigenous, who believe a land belongs to them on account of faith in blood and soil. Those native Egyptians nursed the coals of their unhappiness until they could be fanned into wrathful flames. What made the difference in the end, however, was not righteous fury, but technology. Having fallen beneath the iron-shod wheels of the Hyksos, and having been felled by arrows from composite bows and blows from bronze axes, the Egyptians had watched and learned. After a century or so of submission to foreign kings they had mastered the very tools that had been used against them. They adopted the composite bow and, most crucially, took the concept of the two-wheeled chariot and made it all their own. Always fast, driven by one man and used as a moving platform by a second armed with spears, it was elevated by the genius of Egyptian engineers and craftsmen into something truly special, arguably its brightest flower. This is the moment that matters – when the finest chariots in the world were unleashed against those Hyksos.

At Thebes, an Egyptian king called Seqenenre subservient to the Hyksos had his people worship Ra, the old god. The Hyksos king of Lower Egypt, Apopi, sent a force of men to end the old ways. There was an uprising and fighting – Seqenenre himself was killed in battle – but a rebellion had begun and would not be quelled. Seqenenre's son took on the mantle after him, followed by his own son Ahmose I. It was a campaign of years to retake Egypt and in the end the success of it, under Ahmose, depended on the chariot. By the fifteenth century BC the Egyptians had created a vehicle light enough to be carried, if needed and over a short distance, by one man. Instead of solid wood the wheels were spoked, and on an axle positioned not in the centre, as before, but at the rear for maximum manoeuvrability. It was the Egyptians who replaced the spearman with an archer armed with a composite bow. The effect of the coming together of both technologies was revelatory and, in the face of the same, those

Hyksos were expelled not just from Egypt – ushering in the time of the glorious New Kingdom – but pressed all the way to Canaan.

Whatever the truth of the Hyksos, and historians are not agreed, they were defeated, and utterly. Perhaps they were opportunists and rose to dominance only in a time of disruption. Or they may have been invaders right enough, storming across the borders to seize control. There was a time when some suggested some of the Hyksos were enslaved, making them the ancestors of those Hebrews who made their exodus led by Moses. In any event the descriptions of their rule of Egypt are dominated by accounts left by the ultimate victors. Much later, in the first century AD, the Romano-Jewish historian Titus Flavius Josephus would quote the words of an Egyptian historian named Manetho, who kept accounts of the Hyksos occupation of his homeland:

> . . . for what cause I know not, a blast of God smote us; and unexpectedly, from the regions of the East, invaders of obscure race marched in confidence of victory against our land. By main force they easily overpowered the rulers of the land, they then burned our cities ruthlessly, razed to the ground the temples of the gods, and treated all the natives with a cruel hostility, massacring some and leading into slavery the wives and children of others.

Manetho was writing in the third century BC, long after the time of the Hyksos, but the bitterness reads fresh and raw.

Little more than nothing of the Hyksos has been recovered so far by archaeologists, ground into dust by the fast-spinning wheels of the chariots they themselves brought into the land, and which changed everything.

8.

ARYANS, THE *RIGVEDA* AND
THE MAKING OF THE CASTE SYSTEM

By the middle of the first millennium BC the subcontinent of India, that triangle made inadvertently marginal by Mercator, may have been home to a quarter of the world's population. Given the primacy of events elsewhere, the significance often accorded to other pockets of people and their doings, this reckoning is worth noting. Whatever was happening in India in the millennium before Christ was happening to one in every four human beings alive upon the earth.

Whatever the gravity of that space on the map, some consequence of its density, it held in place whatever was there or that wandered in unwittingly. From the far side of some event horizon stretching west to east across the base of the Asian continent, nothing seemed to leave. Somehow the life of the hunter-gatherer, humanity's elders, survived there alongside city life, empires, planes, trains and automobiles down into the twentieth century and longer. Time was warped there too.

As early as 8,000 or so years ago there were farmers in the far northwest, keepers of beasts and growers of crops on soils made fertile by great river systems. More than 4,000 years ago there were burnt-brick cities at Harappa and Mohenjo-daro (and elsewhere in the Indus Valley), where some folk had learned to exercise their minds with the written word and bothered to cleanse their bodies with water fed straight into homes laid out on long, straight streets. By 3,000 years ago other bright minds (but who had, by then, forgotten Mohenjo-daro and Harappa ever existed) were reciting the thousand hymns of praise and knowledge called the *Rigveda*. First committed to the page only in the fourteenth century AD, those compositions known as the Vedas were ancient by then, the stuff of remembering and reciting.

'Aryan' is a word made troubling for many by a nineteenth century complicated by eugenics, and then a twentieth corrupted by Hitler and war. When the *Rigveda* was first being chanted, Aryan meant something like 'high-born', or perhaps 'set apart'. It may also have implied light skin rather than dark, but that much is hard to know, far less to say in a world still in thrall to ideas about ethnicity, race and racism.

Some hundreds of years after the building of the cities and the rise of the civilization called Harappan by archaeologists and Indologists, there was what might be called a disturbance in the force. Some time after 2000 BC a settled way of life with roots dating back several thousand years entered a long period of change. Explanations for this process are the stuff of fevered debate. Since the time of the German historian and Indologist Max Müller, students of Indian history and archaeology have been encouraged to imagine it was an invasive folk movement that altered India for ever. Müller and others proposed that people speaking languages of the Aryan family of tongues (some of the same gave Iran its name) began spreading into India from the north-west, through the mountain range called the Hindu Kush. It was pictured as a flow that lasted hundreds of years. Throughout the nineteenth and then much of the twentieth century, historians wrote about a violent coming together (of oppressor and oppressed) that saw pale-skinned incomers assert their dominance over dark-skinned locals. Superior weaponry was supposed to have been key, along with ideas of what might be called lighter-skinned supremacy. Just as the arrival into Egypt of the Hyksos was assumed to have been blood-soaked, so the Aryans were characterized as aggressors.

They were also pastoralists, herders of sheep and goats, and arrived on horseback and in chariots. In many ways, so the story goes, they were less sophisticated than those among whom they had landed like cuckoos. Interpretation of the archaeological evidence suggested their coming coincided with the collapse of city living and the end of writing for hundreds of years. According to that traditional, Aryan-invasion version of events, the incomers brought with them the seeds of a religion that would, with some modifications, make all the difference. Along with their flocks and chariots they brought a pantheon of gods, and in their heads, alongside the thoughts of deities, they carried the thousand hymns of the *Rigveda*. Their understanding of their place in the cosmos then melded and mixed with that of the Harappan locals to make the foundations of Hinduism.

More recently, in a world less amenable to thoughts of imperialists and colonizers, there have been suggestions of much more at play than violence, more reasons for a harrowing and desiccating of the Harappan civilization, and an assertion that there never was an invasion. It now seems at least possible that climate change played a part, or that there were challenging environmental factors at least. Perhaps rainfall lessened in the headwaters of the rivers. Or did the waterways change their courses, or disappear altogether, so that cities were left high and dry and were therefore abandoned? Since the 1960s and 1970s Indian historian Braj Basi (B. B.) Lal has insisted the agents that brought about the change were all indigenous, homegrown, and that the very idea of a pale invasion becomes an offensive notion with racist overtones.

Much of the debate swirls around the *Rigveda*. On one hand are the traditionalists, descendants of Müller's thinking, who say the memories and stories preserved therein are nothing more than mythology. On the other are those who have carried forward the work of B. B. Lal, and who see in the archaeology, in the *Rigveda* and now in the DNA of the living a story of the continuous evolution of the indigenous population of the subcontinent. No outsiders required.

In common with the oldest stories from elsewhere, some of the verses reach out in search of beginnings:

A time is envisioned when the world was not, only a watery chaos, the dark, indistinguishable sea, and a warm, cosmic breath which could give an impetus to life . . . Who knows truly? Who will declare whence it arose, whence this creation? The gods are subsequent to the creation of this. Who, then, knows whence it has come into being?

(*Rigveda*, Creation Hymn)

Vital, the spark of life, was Agni the god of fire in whose flames sacrifices might be made, winning favour with eternity: 'Oh, Agni, you who gleam in the darkness. To you we come day by day, with devotion and bearing homage . . .'

Mentioned many times in the *Rigveda* is the Sarasvati River – described as 'mother of floods' and 'greatest of rivers'. Archaeological excavation of an ancient settlement in the Punjab, called Bhirrana, showed it was established on the banks of the Sarasvati by 6000 BC, or even earlier. Regarded as a precursor to what became the Harappan way of life, it was home to farmers. Environmental changes saw to it that the river was gone, dried up entirely, by no later than 1500 BC. If the hymns did not arrive in north-west India until the time of the supposed invasion, why do yet more verses refer to a 'glorious' and 'loudly roaring' river . . . a river in its ancient, mighty prime? According to students of B. B. Lal and others, the memory of such a life-giving, natural wonder, fossilized within the *Rigveda*, is evidence the hymns are much older and also homegrown, composed by those farmers who had been in India all along.

The debate goes on, but undenied and undeniable is the rise in India of the unique system of social organization known as caste. The *Rigveda* describes a territory stretching from the Indus in the west to the Ganges in the east, and a population divided, at first, into four: a priestly class of Brahmins, warrior nobles called Kshatriyas, peasant Vaishyas and Shudra

servants. Those born into the first three castes were allowed to hear and
learn by heart the Vedas; those of the Shudra were not. To this day Indians
argue about skin colour. A multi-million-pound cosmetics industry is
based around the promise of turning dark skin light. Always there, full-
square in the foreground or lurking in the background, is the belief that
pale skin is more desirable and visual proof of higher caste. This has
been a painful subject, dismissed by reformers as a misinterpretation
of the Sanskrit of the Vedas. Crucial to the debate is the word *varna*,
which means 'colour' for some and 'temperament' for others. There is no
consensus.

At first there was flexibility in the caste system, with individuals able
to move between the divisions and up through the ranks, as it were.
Intermarriage between groups produced hybrids, and as the generations
passed and intermarriage continued to complicate matters there eventually emerged the system as it survives today, with thousands of castes
called *jati*. Over time the divisions calcified and hardened so that members were restricted to marriages and lives lived within the castes into
which they were born. To this day, caste is a defining characteristic and
fact of life for millions of Indians.

The moment to be imagined, though, is the crystallization of that first
classification, when lines were drawn that would divide and separate
for all time, between the Brahmins who studied and offered advice, the
Kshatriyas who fought and protected, the Vaishyas who provided the
crops and animals, and the Shudra who served all the others. If the journey of a thousand miles starts with a single step, so a decision that would
affect the lives of millions of people had to have occurred first of all to just
a handful, perhaps to a single individual. It was a defining moment for billions of lives yet to be lived, and it is there in the *Rigveda*. Before it could
be written down – before it was woven into verses for remembering – the
thought, the necessity of dividing one individual from another and maintaining that separation for a lifetime, must have occurred for the first
time in just one mind.

Accordingly the story was told and then retold for ever of a creator-being called Purusha, alive at the beginning of it all, who gave up his body to the gods so that by his sacrifice all people might be made: 'The brahman was His mouth, the kshatriya was made of His two arms, then His two thighs became the Vaishyas and from His feet the Shudra was born . . .'

9.

PHOENICIANS AND SOLOMON'S TEMPLE

Attention paid to history, that being the long story of the world, makes the present more heartbreaking than it might be. On 4 August 2020, an explosion in a warehouse by the sea wreaked havoc in the Lebanese capital, Beirut. Thousands of tons of ammonium nitrate, a chemical used for fertilizer, were ignited by fire, causing one of the largest non-nuclear explosions ever recorded. It was between a fifth and a tenth of the fist that flattened Hiroshima and with a mushroom cloud all its own, a ghost come back to haunt the living. Buildings were levelled as though by the hand of a vengeful God. Hundreds of people were killed or injured and hundreds of thousands made homeless. The blast left a crater 500 feet wide, and the sound of it was heard more than 120 miles away in Cyprus.

On account of the civil war that lasted from the 1970s until 1990, and then the unrest and violence of the politics of the Shia Islamists of Hezbollah, Lebanon is synonymous with trouble. I am one of those old enough in the twenty-first century to remember when the country was suffused with glamour in the twentieth. Its mountains are snow-capped so that they called it the Switzerland of the east. Beirut was so chichi it had the nickname the Paris of the Middle East (poor old Paris trades on past glories too now, and so the wheel turns). News reports on television, remembered from my childhood, have Beirut full of dashing men and bonny lassies. It seemed a place where a person might live the highest life imaginable.

How much easier it would be to know less of the past, so that the lesser present had nothing to compare to. Mark Twain is usually credited with the line that goes 'History doesn't repeat, but it rhymes.' There is pain in always knowing what comes next, in sensing the rhythm having heard the chorus at least once before. It hurts to know the song, all that went before the ruin of the latest verse.

Lebanon is a name with roots in the Semitic languages. Stripped of the vowels added later it is l-b-n, which means 'white' and surely refers to those mountains. A better clue or hook to the rest of what follows comes from knowing that the name of the Greek island of Lemnos has similar roots and means the same for the same reasons. For Lemnos is a name with Phoenician origins, and knowing as much makes all the difference.

What is now Lebanon was once home to another of the elder civilizations of the world. The Phoenicians were a Semitic people (Semitic being a reference to the group of languages and so to the people, Arabic people, that share or shared them) who said they established a city they called Tyre on the coast of the Mediterranean Sea around 2700 BC. Archaeologists and historians have decided that that claim, the depth of time at least, stretches credulity, but they will concede there was likely a lively city by that name and on that spot 1,500 years before the time of Jesus. They had Byblos too, and Sidon, and a history long and painful. Their best luck was had on the narrow ribbon by the sea. Inland was arid and sterile, broken by hills that kept the population apart in isolated cells that struggled to cooperate, far less unite. From the coastal cities, summoned by the sea, they embarked on trade in boats and ships and so acted as a conduit linking Africa with Asia.

The pharaohs of Egypt had the Phoenicians fell and bring to them their cedar trees for great building works, and such effort earned them a lasting reputation for engineering skill. At home they were bullied by bigger boys nearby – Egyptians, Hebrews from the Promised Land, Hittites. Home was made for coming from, though, and dreams for going to, and so they set sail across and around the Mediterranean and found their stride. All the while they strove the bullies foundered anyway. Like a game old girl with Alzheimer's, Egypt forgot herself. Mycenae was gone soon enough and others like the Hittites also. In their absence the Phoenicians found the sun and shone in their turn. Some time after 1000 BC (let's say, though no one really knows) they had their moment. The moment that matters to the story of the world is the commission, the job of work, that was the building of King Solomon's Temple. The timing and the event itself are beyond reach, but at least the Old Testament puts it into writing, the supposed words of Solomon himself:

> Now therefore command thou that they hew me cedar trees out of Lebanon; and my servants shall be thy servants: and unto thee will I give hire for thy servants according to all that thou shalt appoint: for thou knowest that there is not among us any that can skill to hew timber like unto the Sidonians.

The Sidonians were the folk of the city of Sidon, Phoenicians whom Solomon knew as the only tradesmen up to the task of the job he had in mind . . . 60 cubits of this, 20 and 30 of that. Elsewhere around the ancient world those entrepreneurs were held in the same regard. As well as builders (and maybe Solomon's temple was their most glamorous effort) they were known as traders and colonizers all around the Mediterranean Sea. They were a people on the make. For all of their attested abilities and prowess they seem always to have had their light hidden under a bushel. Their reach bore all the hallmarks of courage and endeavour – routinely passing through the Straits of Gibraltar and heading north for the archipelago that would be the British Isles so as to trade for tin in Cornwall, the world's richest source of the metal needed for bringing together with copper for the making of bronze. But boastful they were not; they were too busy for that and let no time aside for advertising their worth. As well as the skill of the hand they had other gifts, made manifest by the shaping of an alphabet. Later those letters, scratches in the dust of the world, would be taken up by the Greeks and then the writers of Latin and the rest. The name of their city of Byblos is the root of our English word Bible.

There in the effort of making and doing, building, all gone now, is a moment. Overlooked now, if not forgotten, the Phoenicians exist in that vague space where a word has a familiar sound but no real meaning for most. The temple they built for Solomon was destroyed, utterly, by Nebuchadnezzar II, King of Babylon, in 587 BC. In the aftermath of the siege that made it happen, the elite of the place were taken away, into Babylon, for some kind of exile. Solomon is an immortal name even if most who hear it now have no idea why. For an ever-dwindling number he is the biblical king who composed the eponymous song; for some of a certain age he was the owner of fabled gold mines described by novelist H. Rider Haggard. 'Phoenician' is the same – familiar, but nothing more to add. The temple built on Solomon's orders, in his name, is gone as though it had never been. The Phoenicians who built it, who sailed their ships to Cornwall 3,500 years ago, bear a name that is meaningless to most.

In the moment I think about, picture in my mind's eye, they are on the ground, those architects, engineers and builders, on that high point in the city of Jerusalem. They are the elite of all their kind, called upon to make and build the things others cannot. Elsewhere their ships are at sea, reaching out into the unknown and finding there the makings of an empire – an empire none but a few will even bother to remember. That they are gone now, out of reach or altogether forgotten, cannot eclipse how much they mattered once. Another temple was built on the spot (by others, not Phoenicians) and later destroyed, like the first. Jews still pray or wail at a wall of it, that second effort, in remembrance of all that it had meant. It means something on account of the place where it stands – a place where once another temple stood, built by Phoenicians.

10.

OF HOMER, *ILIAD* AND *ODYSSEY*

Homer may be a figment of the world's imagination, even many figments. Or maybe 'figments' is the wrong word and 'filaments' is better, so that the literary offerings may be spun together to make one thread, like Ariadne's that led Theseus out of the Minotaur's darkness and back to the light. If he existed, that blind bard of Chios, then best guesses have him born around 750 BC. Traditionally regarded as the author of two works, poems – the *Iliad* about the Siege of Troy and the *Odyssey* describing the voyage home of one of its protagonists – next to nothing is known about him. Scholars have speculated that more than one writer shaped the stories and that by the time they were written down at the end of the eighth century BC they were already old. Part of what matters, what makes Homer as immortal as Hector, Achilles, Andromache and the rest of his characters, is the world's seeming need of a Homer, the idea of him at least. In that moment of their setting down into text those stories spun a thread connecting the present and the past – both the present that was Homer's and the present that is ours.

Andromache led the lamentations of the women while she held in her hands the head of Hector, her greatest warrior: 'Husband, you are gone so young from life and leave me in your house a widow. Our son is still but a little fellow, child of ill-fated parents, you and I. How can he grow to manhood? Before that this city shall be overthrown for you are gone, you who kept watch over its wives and their little ones. You leave woe unutterable and mourning to your parents, Hector, but in my heart above all others bitter anguish shall abide. Your arms were not stretched out to me as you lay dying. You spoke to me no living word that I might have pondered as my tears fell night and day.

How can there truly have been any civilization anywhere in the world without words like those having been summoned into being somewhere? Even if they had been thought and uttered and lost in a matter of moments, minutes, then civilization would at least have existed, if only for that little while.

The olive tree had given rich life to Minoans in their palaces on Crete by 2000 BC. Afterwards, after them and during the eighteenth and seventeenth centuries BC, the mainland that would be Greece was home to a civilization remembered as Mycenaean, named after the city of Mycenae. Sometimes its mysterious founders, the Achaeans, are described as yet more chariot-riding invaders – the same picture conjured to explain the arrival of the Hyksos in Egypt, of the Aryans in India – but whether indigenous, immigrant or a mix of both, the Mycenaean civilization that grew to replace the Minoan spread across Greece for the next several centuries. Some time in the middle decades of the thirteenth century BC some Achaeans were likely involved in the destruction of Troy. That city's location in Anatolia (modern Turkey) meant it straddled the geographical point where east meets west, where Asia meets Europe. It squatted across trade routes too, grown rich in taxing traders moving to and fro, and would always have been a target for acquisitive, expansionist foes.

During the centuries after the fall of that city an unexplained darkness fell across the territory of the Greek mainland and the islands of the Peloponnese. The quality of civilization went into decline, withering on the vine. New people arrived from the north. By 1000 BC or so, after a winnowing of the population by some or other horror (plague? natural disaster? who knows?), there are signs of light again. A people called

Dorians arrived, bringing among other things the dialect or language called Doric, a rustic tongue that would be spoken in the Sparta of Leonidas and the 300. There were others too – the Aeolians, and the Ionians who spoke what became Ionic Greek, posh talk. By the time of Homer the people coming together as one from all those arrivals from further north knew themselves not as Greeks (the name that would be given to them hundreds of years later by the Romans) but as Hellenes. They were mostly united by one language by then, the one we call Greek, and Homer could take advantage of its written form. Those Phoenicians who had built Solomon's temple in Jerusalem had spread more than building skills around the ancient world. As traders who roamed as far as Cornwall in search of tin, in their wake they often left their written alphabet. Quite when or how those shapes were acquired by the Hellenes is not known, but when the *Iliad* and the *Odyssey* were finally committed to the page after centuries of mere reciting it was the Phoenician script that was used first of all.

Adam Nicolson, author of *The Mighty Dead: Why Homer Matters*, is among the many who have questioned whether a man called Homer even existed. He has observed that at the very least the author who wrote down those poems was drawing upon centuries of effort already expended to create and to remember characters and events deemed to matter. 'The poems were composed by a man standing at the top of a human pyramid,' he wrote. 'He could not have stood there without the pyramid beneath him, and the pyramid consisted not only of the earlier poets in the tradition but of their audiences too.'

Moments like these, of transformation into the written word of what has previously been passed from mind to mind, are like stubborn pin-pricks of light, light that lasts in the night sky, or synapses firing inside a brain to make a memory. Like Enheduanna, priestess of Ur, and her hymns, like the keepers of the *Rigveda*, the poet or poets remembered as Homer saved some ephemeral sense of an ancient world from the threat of ever being forgotten. In a way that matters they caught and passed those worlds into ours.

It is Nicolson's contention that the stories have their origin in a world before stately kings, when a rough-and-ready warrior class from the flat grasslands of Eurasia, in chariots and on horseback, met and mixed with the polished urbanites of the eastern Mediterranean. In this coupling, consensual or not, Nicolson sees the sparking into being of the origins of Greek culture. In that moment, as long ago as 2000 BC or thereabouts, the double helix of the DNA that would make possible the world of Socrates, Plato and Aristotle was kinked together.

And so Homer, the works in his name at least, are a bridge and a way back into the past. The world described there – of warlords leading and often barely controlling bands of fighting men nominally loyal to them – may, alternatively, have been that which was real in the dark aftermath of the fall of the Minoan and then Mycenaean civilizations. It is all lost in mist now, unlikely properly to be retrieved.

The *Iliad* in particular looks backwards to a time of heroes that may have thrilled its late-eighth-century BC readers while at the same time making them glad such anarchic days were behind them. The *Odyssey* is a different beast – and it is in that difference that scholars sense the hand of at least one other author. It concerns the journey home of Odysseus, King of Ithaca, after the victory over the Trojans. Expecting him after a ten-year absence are his wife Penelope and his son Telemachus, but they must wait. All manner of adventures and distractions lie between Odysseus and his crew and their destination. One of these, the encounter with the Sirens, is of particular interest to Nicolson since for him it forms the thread between the two poems. The Sirens seek to lure Odysseus from his ship and his quest. They tell him stories of heroism, of his past and his youth. For fear of losing him, his crewmen tie their king and captain to the ship's mast. 'They won't be wrecked on the illusion of nostalgia, the longing for that heroized, antique world, because, as the Odyssey knows, to live well in the world, nostalgia must be resisted,' wrote Nicolson.

The moment that is Homer's – Homeric, the moment of utmost

importance – is there in that insistence, in the *Odyssey*, that success in life depends upon remaining tied to the present like Odysseus to the mast.

'Don't be tempted,' Nicolson warned, 'into the lovely simplicities that the heroic past seems to offer.'

It is in this way – standing between an enticing, gilded past and the demands of the present and of the future – that Homer, whoever Homer was, remains as alive and relevant today as he ever was.

11.

SIDDHARTHA GAUTAMA
AND THE BIRTH OF THE BUDDHA

Out of Purusha had come the ancestors of the first castes and so a way of life for millions of human beings. After the *Rigveda* came more words of wisdom in the form of a collection of hymns, aphorisms and thoughts called the *Upanishads*, first written down around 700 BC. From the beginning, Hinduism was a journey undertaken in the hope of understanding the universe and existence within it, and in the *Upanishads* there were hints of a search for a single entity, the singularity from which the universe must have sprung in the first place. It was an old quest already by then, and would only draw more pilgrims on to the path.

Somewhere in the north-east of India, or perhaps the territory we know as the country of Nepal, a prince (and therefore one of the Kshatriya warrior caste) was born to a noble family. Legend had it that at the moment of his conception his mother had dreamed that a great white elephant had entered her side without causing her any pain. It was around 566 BC, and he was Siddhartha Gautama, the man who would be Buddha.

(Now there are Buddha bars for drinking in and Buddha bowls in M&S for eating. Buddha the brand is too tragic to contemplate. Like the co-opting of anything holy, everything holy, at least it might make a person ask who, or indeed what, Buddha ever meant, or means.)

More of the legend has it that his father loved him so much, feared for his wellbeing so greatly, he had him raised in a palace built inside a huge walled garden. Like a Garden of Eden it was meant to protect the lad from all the awful truth and reality of the wider world. In that way of every Eden, however, it could not and did not keep him safe for ever. Unfulfilled by his sheltered existence, Siddhartha climbed the wall one day and fled, never to return. He was in his thirties by then and left behind a wife and child. In short order he saw an old man, a dying man and a corpse and so was confronted, for the first time, by the reality his father had hoped to spare him, that of suffering and death. Then he met a monk and, inspired by the idea of asceticism, spent the next seven years devoted to a life of poverty. Having all but starved himself to death, he was found by a young woman who fed him back to health. From then on he understood what he called the Middle Way, between the two extremes of indulgence and denial. His endless wanderings brought him eventually to a venerable tree, the Bodhi Tree, or tree of enlightenment. Beneath its branches he sat and meditated and finally 'awoke' to complete understanding. *Bodhi* is close to the Sanskrit *bodhati*, meaning 'awake', and also the Proto-Indo-European *beudh*, which means 'aware'. Until his death Siddhartha was described, by his followers, as Buddha, one who is awake – awake to the nature of reality. He said humankind was trapped in an endless cycle of birth, death and rebirth. By accepting as much, a person might reach the state called nirvana and cease the endless suffering, becoming nothing, ceasing to be. More were drawn to him, like motes of dust to an electrical charge. At the end of his life he apparently lay down between two trees and died. Those he left behind believed the Buddha had lived many lives across eternity and died many times. His dying between the trees was different, they said, since at last he had understood enough to end the cycle. He had learned how to be, and how to be gone. In Buddhist terms he had reached nirvana, been blown out like a candle's flame.

So far, so legendary, but from the moment of his awakening under the Bodhi Tree until his death perhaps forty-five years later, the Buddha walked the highways and byways of northern India telling any who would listen about *dharma*. It is a word with no useful single-word translation into English but certainly suggests, among others, concepts like 'truth'.

In a story of the world in moments, it is worth remembering that 'moment' can mean a short span of time and yet also be descriptive of something that lasts for ever – so that we describe an event as being 'of great moment' . . . momentous. The notion, the mere possibility of a human being awakening to reality is surely momentous and worth remembering (whether it happened or not).

Siddhartha Gautama had his moment seated beneath a tree. He awoke to what he regarded as understanding. While this is a foundation story, a founding myth for Buddhists, it surely rings bells for those raised in the shadow of other traditions. A walled garden and the birth of a special son . . . a tree of wisdom . . . an awakening to the truth . . . a wise man teaching a handful of companions and so laying down a path for the following by millions. Familiar elements, moments that jog memories and fire connections in the brain, that make stories memorable. Some 2,200 years after the birth of Siddhartha Gautama, in 1666, Isaac Newton is supposed to have sat beneath another tree in another place. He was resident in the University of Cambridge by then but in that year an outbreak of plague had had him flee to his mother's house, Woolsthorpe Manor by Grantham in Lincolnshire.

A moment beneath a tree in the garden of that house was recorded for posterity by the antiquarian William Stukeley, a younger contemporary and friend of the legendary scientist. In a manuscript held in the collections of the Royal Society, of which both men were Fellows, Stukeley described how Newton had recalled the moment in question. It was the moment when an apple fell from a tree:

After dinner, the weather being warm, we went into the garden & drank tea under the shade of some apple tree; only he & myself. Amid other discourse, he told me, he was just in the same situation, as when formerly the notion of gravitation came into his mind. Why should that apple always descend perpendicularly to the ground, thought he to himself; occasion'd by the fall of an apple, as he sat in contemplative mood. Why should it not go sideways, or upwards? But constantly to the Earth's centre? Assuredly the reason is, that the Earth draws it. There must be a drawing power in matter. And the sum of the drawing power in the matter of the Earth must be in the Earth's centre, not in any side of the Earth.

Therefore does this apple fall perpendicularly or towards the centre? If matter thus draws matter; it must be proportion of its quantity. Therefore the apple draws the Earth, as well as the Earth draws the apple.

In his moment beneath a tree (an apple tree, conveniently enough, like the Tree of Knowledge in that other garden) Newton had understood the truth of gravity, the pull towards the centre, of the apple as well as of the Earth. The apple had not hit him on the head, neither had he had to eat of it (as Eve had done, and then Adam), but he had had his own awakening to understanding just the same.

All those centuries before, beneath another tree, Siddhartha Gautama awoke to an understanding of the apparent oneness of reality, that all things are drawn to a single, central source. Two trees, two men, one realization.

The Buddha was an effective teacher. The way of life he led by his own example was simple and neither knew nor needed any god. Buddhism disregarded the notion of caste and treated women as equal to men. In this way it appealed to the masses, took root and spread far beyond the bounds of India. In time it became the most widespread religion in Asia. Ironically it lost out to Hinduism and then to Islam in the land of its birth, but the influence of Buddhism became part of the great coherence of India, its ability to absorb and digest all comers, to prevail. No god, no easy claim on goodness and no ready blame for badness. The thinking of Buddhism, together with that of Hinduism, gave India and Asia an identity utterly separate from those parts of the world that would follow Christianity or any of the other thinking issuing from the Middle East. In this way the awakening of Siddhartha Gautama, the Buddha, was another moment in the making of the world.

12.

LAO TZU AND THE *TAO TE CHING*

Just as the *Rigveda* was the crystallization of thoughts that would shape Hinduism and so the perception of billions, so another thought occurred in another part of the world and profoundly affected the destinies of billions more.

Between the Middle East and the Atlantic Ocean people learned to see the universe as something made by a creator – an artefact, like a complicated, carefully designed machine. In India the universe was envisioned as an endlessly repeating cycle of births and deaths, summoned into being by Brahma and destroyed by Kali.

English philosopher Alan Watts has pointed out that it was not by accident that Jesus was described as the son of a carpenter, because the Christian God is one who makes, builds, constructs and also dictates what must happen. Watts has, by contrast, likened the Hindu universe to a play – not something made but rather something acted out. 'The Hindu looks upon the universe as a drama,' he said in his 'Essential Lectures'. 'The idea of the universe as the big act. The universe is God playing hide and seek. With himself.'

In thinking about the story of the world it is vital – vital to me, anyway – to know that not just the world but the entire universe has been understood, by other people in other places, quite differently from the western version of events. It is all about perspective, point of view, and other people have seen and see it all differently. Surely a more complete or more interesting picture of the whole is acquired from multiple viewpoints?

Carl Sagan, the noted cosmologist, was apparently aware that more than one path might lead to the same destination, the same understanding. In *Cosmos* he wrote:

> The Hindu religion is the only one of the world's great faiths dedicated to the idea that the Cosmos itself undergoes an immense, indeed an infinite, number of deaths and rebirths. It is the only religion in which the time scales correspond to those of modern scientific cosmology. Its cycles run from our ordinary day and night to a day and night of Brahma (the creator god of Hinduism), 8.64 billion years long. Longer than the age of the Earth or the sun and about half the time since the Big Bang. And there are much longer time scales still.

In the hope of allowing for as many perspectives as possible – a more interesting story of the world – it is necessary to make room for yet another point of view. And so in China, home to other billions, there has been a third way of understanding the universe, indeed the nature of reality itself. In China, for the longest time the universe was understood not as an artefact, or a drama, but as a living thing, one vast organism.

Around 400 BC (and there is no consensus about the date, just endless debate), a book called the *Tao Te Ching* – which means something like 'The Tao Virtue Book', or perhaps 'The Way of Integrity' – was written down for the first time. By 400 BC the idea of 'Tao', which means 'The Way', was already old. One of the most famous names in Chinese history is Confucius, which is the Latinized form of K'ung Fu-Tzu. Confucius lived and died between the sixth and fifth centuries BC and was responsible for framing the thought that, in some ancient, better time, every person had known his or her place and had been happy to perform his or her duty. Confucius had been a bureaucrat or administrator of some kind, but at some point in his life he turned to philosophy and became a teacher instead. So influential were his teachings – called Confucianism – they were to inform and structure Chinese society for the next 2,000 years and more, until the time of the communist revolution, in fact. He espoused the principle that order was the basis for a happy and functional life – a happy and functional world. He believed in a neat and rigid hierarchy, good behaviour, respect for culture and for family. He believed everyone had a position to fill and a duty to perform for the greater good. So enthusiastically were his teachings adopted, and handed down generation after generation, he gave structure to one of the most consistent and stable bureaucracies in the history of the world.

But if Confucius was about man-made order – submission to family, tradition, emperor and empire – there was an older idea that existed before him and that persists to this day. The Way – the *Tao* of *Tao Te Ching* – was understood as an underlying immutable principle of the universe. Confucius knew about The Way but the theory of it was not written down until after his time. The author in question, the first to assemble the thinking into a coherent whole, was Lao Tzu, another character as mysterious and inscrutable as Homer. Almost nothing about him is known for certain, and even that name by which he is known – Lao Tzu, or Laozi – translates only as 'old master'.

Here is the nature of The Way in a 1904 translation of the *Tao Te Ching* by Ch'u Ta-Kao:

> There is a thing inherent and natural,
> That existed before heaven and earth.
> Motionless and fathomless,
> It stands alone and never changes.
> It pervades everywhere and yet never becomes exhausted.
> It may be regarded as the Mother of the Universe.
> I do not know its name.
> If I am forced to give it a name,
> I call it Tao, and name it as supreme.

In the west we exist in a world in which we expect answers to questions, all questions. We are determined that everything, from smallest to greatest, is there to be touched, dissected and thereby understood, if not used and downright exploited. Taoist thinking, understanding, has it that there are unanswerable questions. Accordingly our determination, our compulsion to answer those unanswerable questions is seen by Taoists as the greatest failing of western thinking and the cause of much unnecessary angst.

The moment I think about, wonder about without hope of ever having the details I want, is not the writing down of the eighty-one verses that together make the *Tao Te Ching*; rather it is the first occurrence of the notion of The Way in someone's consciousness. The eighty-one verses came later, shaped most elegantly and concisely by Lao-Tzu, and they have been translated into English hundreds of times, each slightly different from the last. But some fine day in the past, under a Chinese sky, the thought of The Way occurred to someone.

In troubled and troubling times, The Way has a reminder about the nature of leaders and leadership. If the people are not trusted – if human nature itself is not trusted – then there arises the threat of the drift into totalitarianism.

> The best leaders are those the people hardly know exist.
> The next best is a leader who is loved and praised.
> Next comes the one who is feared.
> The worst one is the leader that is despised.
> If you don't trust the people,
> They will become untrustworthy.

In a story of the world it is worth noticing how old the good ideas are – that having been conjured up they lasted ever after on account of being right.

We are struggling in the west, splitting into smaller and smaller groups and fighting among ourselves. In words written down for the first time 2,400 years ago and remembered and recited in some form longer than that are warnings as relevant now as then. More and more we are fretting about the future of our ecosystems, the health of the planet itself. In the *Tao Te Ching* is simple wisdom based on understanding the world as an extension of self. As poem 13 has it:

Surrender yourself humbly; then you can be trusted to care for all things.
Love the world as your own self; then you can truly care for all things.

13.

NEBUCHADNEZZAR AND THE FALL OF BABYLON

King Hammurabi had laid down the law for his Babylonian empire in the eighteenth century BC and the shadow of his hand fell across a strip of territory measuring 700 miles on its long side by 100 miles across, a grand achievement for that time and place. As well as Babylon he had cities at Mari on the Euphrates and at Nimrud and Nineveh on the Tigris. By nearly 200 years after his time the people called Hittites had conquered the world of his descendants but the name Babylon was already unforgettable by then and has survived into the present, not least as a byword for decadence, even for sin and corruption. It was in Babylon that the Epic of Gilgamesh was first made permanent on tablets of clay, and her scientists laid some foundations for mathematics and astronomy.

Hammurabi the lawgiver, master of all he surveyed, may have been one of those figures whose memory, whose shadow eventually gave shape and form in men's imaginations to the image of the One God himself. To this day it is hard in the west, where the Judeo-Christian tradition has held sway, to hear mention of God without imagining a grey-bearded, grandfatherly king of all, his hand stretched out in blessing or in judgement. Also out of Babylon came a story of the summoning of the world from within the swirling waters that came and went in flood. The first men there were made by the gods, out of clay they set into moulds and fired in kilns; strange and yet familiar. From dust thou art.

Further east, in India and China, the nature and texture of the universe and reality would be understood altogether differently, but after Babylon and the other kingdoms of Mesopotamia there took stubborn root the idea of a bearded creator, maker of laws, judge of men, king of kings, seated out of sight perhaps at the peak of a ziggurat. It was an image and a concept that would make all the difference in the world west of Mesopotamia – a world convinced of right and wrong, good and evil, heaven and hell; a world built brick by brick like a ziggurat or engineered into some great, unknowable machine by a master craftsman whose word was law unbreakable.

The Hittites came and went in that same land between waters, and ebbed and flowed until perhaps 1200 BC when their best days were past. There were Indo-European people in the mix as well during the same confused and confusing time, flowing down and through Mesopotamia from the north and further complicating the picture.

After 1200 BC or thereabouts the people called Hebrews – those wanderers – were on the move out of Egypt and heading east, under the leadership of one called Moses. A mix of tradition and history has them as the descendants of Jacob, his son Joseph of the colourful coat and a whole population that had abandoned their homeland, the Canaan of Abraham, during a famine and sought sanctuary under the rule of pharaohs. By the time of their exodus, back to where their ancestors had come from, they obeyed a god, the One God as far as they were concerned, and called him Yahweh. It was Yahweh that was worshipped by the first Hebrew kings, Saul and David, and then by Solomon who had the Phoenicians build him a temple in Jerusalem.

In Mesopotamia after the Hittites there were more new arrivals, or surfacings from the home patch of people whose time had come: Arameans and then Kassites. Another name came and went at the same time, testing the opposition from time to time with jabs and feints, a king here and a king there. These were the Assyrians, and even by the standards of the day they were cruel invaders and cruel masters. In the latter part of the eighth century BC, having hit their stride, they invaded Israel, the northernmost of two kingdoms established by then by Hebrews in the land promised them by Yahweh. Judah was the other, a veritable dot upon the map of the world. The Assyrians remade Nineveh in their own image. In the middle years of the seventh century BC their king was Ashurbanipal who made the library that had the Epic of Gilgamesh among its titles. There were other characters on the stage then too – the Kingdom of Lydia, Scythians out of Central Asia, and Medes from more of the territory we know as Iran. When those latter two joined forces they were able to inflict a final defeat upon the empire of the Assyrians.

There was a last hurrah for Babylon under King Nebuchadnezzar II, whose army sacked Jerusalem in 587 BC. The temple built by the Phoenicians was torn down and the prisoners carried off to Babylon were those of the biblical exile. As slaves they helped build the Hanging Gardens that would be among the Seven Wonders of the Ancient World.

Now comes the moment that matters in the wider scheme of things. Mesopotamia, the land between the rivers, has been the cradle of civilization from the beginning and has mattered for thousands of years. Nebuchadnezzar had made an empire but after him his successors were less able. A whittling and belittling began, with slice after slice of the holdings cut away and falling into the hands of kingdoms rising on the borders. The last of the Babylonian kings was Nabonidus. Perhaps on account of his fate, he is recorded as a man of inconsequential beginnings, a no one from nowhere.

Cyrus II, better known as Cyrus the Great, was the first king of the Achaemenid empire. The Achaemenids had been a minor dynasty out of Iran and ruled a little kingdom there called Elam. Cyrus was made for greatness, however, and during the middle years of the sixth century BC he moved against powerful neighbours like the Lydians and the Medes, absorbing them both. In 539 BC he turned his attention upon Nabonidus and Babylon. Nabonidus fled in the face of his enemy's advance and Cyrus later entered that capital city unopposed. Nabonidus had angered his people anyway. He had favoured worship of the moon god Sin while his subjects remained loyal to Marduk, greatest deity in the Babylonian pantheon. Cyrus had sent messengers ahead of his fighting men to declare he would return Marduk to his rightful place at the centre of things and the Babylonians had rejoiced at the prospect and opened their arms.

In the aftermath of conquest, and having added Mesopotamia to his holdings, Cyrus commissioned the making of a clay cylinder about the size of a rugby ball. Inscribed with Akkadian cuneiform script, it tells of how he saw to it that all those enslaved by Nebuchadnezzar and his heirs, the Hebrews among them, were made free to return to their homelands. More of the script tells how he championed religious tolerance across his empire. Buried in Babylon some time after his coming, it was unearthed in 1879 by archaeologist and diplomat Hormuzd Rassam. (Rassam had, on an earlier expedition, found Ashurbanipal's library and the clay tablets preserving the Epic of Gilgamesh.) Although not found until a century after the American Revolution, the message of the so-called Cyrus Cylinder had by then influenced the contents of that emergent nation's Declaration of Independence. The Greek soldier and philosopher Xenophon, a contemporary of Socrates, had written about Cyrus and his benevolent rule. The book in question, *Cyropaedia*, was read by Thomas Jefferson, principal author and signatory of the Declaration and third president of the United States, and so helped shape the constitution of a nation given to diversity and the tolerance of all faiths.

In the aftermath of Cyrus, the Hebrews had indeed gone home and there rebuilt the temple destroyed in the name of Nebuchadnezzar:

Thus saith Cyrus king of Persia, The Lord God of heaven hath given me all the kingdoms of the earth; and he hath charged me to build him a house at Jerusalem, which is in Judah. Who is there among you of all his people?

His God be with him, and let him go up to Jerusalem, which is in Judah, and build the house of the Lord God of Israel.

(Ezra 1:2–3)

Less well known, less familiar than the end of the Hebrew exile, is that the Fall of Babylon was the end of an era that had lasted since the time of Enheduanna and her hymns. Mesopotamia had, one way or another, endured as an independent presence, a wellspring of civilization, for thousands of years. No more. The ancient world had turned on its axis. Babylonia was gone. Even mighty Egypt was on the wane. Persia, the flowering of Achaemenids and Cyrus and his heirs, was on the rise.

14.

THE EXPULSION OF
THE LAST KING OF ROME

Moments do not last, which is just as well. Like a happy memory, the truth of Classical Greece is probably better reviewed than relived. Like all the rest it was a civilization dependent upon slavery. For all the vaunted benefits of democracy – above all others the word associated with that precocious little entity – women were denied its blessing. There was rule of law but always the accused was presumed guilty. While Greeks were convinced of superiority over all, their world – made of philosophy, literature, art, theatre, architecture and all – was imperfect.

It is important, however, not to go too far in diminishing Greek achievement. On account of available records we know most about Athens, one city-state among hundreds. Even allowing for the possibility that Athenians' achievements were untypical, if theirs was a city that was the apogee of that time and place then it earned its immortality. Athenian democracy was flawed (like every other) but a leap forward for human-kind. There and elsewhere on that little thumb of dry land people saw the value of common sense, the sense of the common man, over blind faith in hereditary rulers. That was a moment in itself.

The philosophers for whom Classical Greece is most famous stepped out of the shadow cast by belief in arbitrary gods and championed rational enquiry instead. It seemed to Socrates, Plato, Aristotle and the rest that existence might be understood by asking questions and looking within, to the soul, for useful answers. Their enquiries fell short of paying attention to the real world, via observation and experiment, and so the scientific method was beyond them. But enough Greeks had seen that existence *might* be understood in a rational manner.

Even in Greece those achievements were only breaks in the clouds. While never quite extinguished, the light of rational enquiry was soon dimmed again by the same old superstitions and by the shrugging of shoulders in the face of what seemed to most like fickle, god-shaped fate. Chaos is a tar pit, all but impossible to avoid, far less escape.

The Buddha had taught Indians that the senses offered only an illusion of reality. People suffered, he had said, on account of enslavement to earthly, sensual wants and desires. By knowing as much, and ceasing to fall for the trick, a person would set himself free to the nothingness (or rather the *no thingness*) of nirvana, which is like a sigh of relief. That search for an end to suffering was all around, and in Greece too. The philosopher Epicurus was born on the island of Samos to Athenian parents and sought to free himself not by denying his senses but by trusting them as the source of truth. Through a modest life of self-sufficiency and simple meals (and much discussion with friends on matters philosophical) a person might know a humble but pain-free existence, and come to accept death as the end of both body and soul, and so of all suffering.

Around the same time Epicurus sought to persuade people of the simple life, a fellow philosopher from Cyprus called Zeno taught that the universe was governed by immutable, universal reason – the *Logos*. If Buddha thought the end of suffering lay in knowing sensory experience was only an illusion, and Epicurus thought senses were key to happiness, then Zeno told his followers to trust the underlying reason inherent in the universe. Perhaps this had hopes in common not just with Buddhism but also with the Tao, as signposted by Lao-Tzu in China. In any event, Zeno said that by following the *reason*able underlying example of the universe a person might live a worthwhile life. For Zeno, all men were alike and good deeds should be performed not in the hope of winning favour from the gods but because such actions were virtuous in their own right, 'For righteousness draweth to itself the souls of men with no lure, no offerings from without, but of its own splendour. Virtue of itself is sufficient for happiness.'

Zeno preached in the roofed colonnades around the city's market square, and since in Greek those are the *stoa*, so his teaching was labelled Stoicism.

Like a dream lost on waking but recalled as somehow memorable, the idea of Classical Greece preoccupied the thinking of those who came after. Philip of Macedon, barbarous neighbour to Greece, was so beguiled, and demanded his homeland be recognized as Greek in nature. His son, Alexander the Great, pupil of Aristotle, made Greece his own – along with Egypt, Persia, Afghanistan and some of northern India. Cities as far apart as Alexandria and Kandahar echoed his name. He said his own mother was descended from Achilles and lived the life of a hero until his death in 323 BC at the age of thirty-three. His erstwhile holdings were shared by his generals then, and though they were torn into parts those disparate territories were marbled through with Greek language and culture. What Alexander left behind was the Hellenistic world.

Egypt was ruled by Ptolemaic pharaohs named after the Alexandrine general Ptolemy who claimed it, until the time of Cleopatra, the last of them. In Asia, vast tracks of Alexander's leavings, from Afghanistan to Syria, became kingdoms for more of his veterans. Seleucus and his sons made the Seleucid dynasty; other soldiers claimed Bactria; General Philetaerus established the Attalid dynasty in Pergamum. When Ptolemy's successors put a stop to the export of papyrus, the *pergamene* animal skins from Pergamum became the *parchment* for the world to write upon next. The thinking of Plato and Aristotle would survive on account of being copied and saved (on parchment, certainly, and on other surfaces besides) by the scholars and scribes of the Hellenistic world – and when the world of Islam took up the torch in the first millennium AD it was a way lit with what had been remembered by those intermediates who had been in thrall to Classical Greece.

The civilization that took most advantage from the achievements of Greece was the product of another moment, being the overthrow of a legendary king in 509 BC. The central part of the peninsula we know as Italy was, by the start of the first millennium BC, the territory of a people called Etruscans. Their origins are obscure but they descended from an Indo-European tribe that had moved west and south some centuries before. They dominated the indigenous Latins (who claimed descent from Latinus, a hero known to Homer's Odysseus) until a time of revolt by the subject peoples. Rome was a Latin city by a bridge on the Tiber and, freed from the Etruscan yoke, her people came into their own.

Those Etruscans had revered, among other beasts, the wolf, and the Romans said they were sons and daughters of the orphan Romulus. Together with his twin, Remus, he had been suckled by a she-wolf after the pair's abandonment by their parents Mars and the vestal virgin Rhea Silvia. After his brother's death, Romulus built a city on the spot where the she-wolf had found them. By her grateful citizens he was made Rome's first king and he established for them the Senate, the gathering of nobles whose responsibility it was to name his, and all, successors.

The moment in question finds us in the presence of Lucius Tarquinius Superbus – the last of seven Roman kings and reviled as a violent oppressor given to gross disrespect for custom and the Senate. News has just broken that his son, Sextus, has raped the noblewoman Lucretia, wife of a powerful husband and daughter of a powerful family. Having reported the crime, Lucretia has taken her own life and now vengeance is at hand. Great men of Rome confront Tarquinius. They are led by Brutus and Collatinus and they tell their king the city will suffer no more of him or his family's excesses. All of them, wives and children, are expelled, cast out beyond the city walls. The time of the monarchy is over, and Rome is a republic. The word is Latin; strictly speaking it is two words, *res publica*, which means 'a public matter'. Rather than the private property of kings and queens, a republic is the form of government that means the population must decide for themselves what must be done. Having emerged there on the banks of the Tiber, it will last for nearly five centuries and change the Old World beyond recognition.

Greece and Rome – two worlds that sit side by side. Of all the frogs croaking around the rim of the Mediterranean, Rome was the most dedicated heir of Greek ways. But while Greek influence had only drifted and adhered, like expensive perfume to fabric, Rome and her Romans would reach out with both hands to grasp and hold.

15.

PERSIANS, SPARTA AND
THE BATTLE OF THERMOPYLAE

Early though it is, so very distant in time, the Fall of Babylon to the people who would be Persians might be regarded as a halfway mark in the story of the world. Civilization was already 3,000 years old by then and had taken root in many places – throughout the Middle East, in Egyptian Africa, in India, in China and elsewhere.

By the middle of the first millennium BC the Mediterranean Sea was another great unifying entity with a pull that held yet more civilized people usefully in orbit. North Africa, forming its southern coastline, was more fertile then, better watered and supportive of more life-giving vegetation, and would continue to be so for a thousand years. Western, northern and eastern coastlines were cradles too, so that an encircling civilization was in evidence, with peoples who spoke one another's languages – Greek and then Latin – and used the surface of the water as a bridge, or perhaps a roundabout, providing access to all and for all. Ships powered by oars and sails took advantage of prevailing winds to roam its length and breadth and so exchange the commodities upon which life depended – metals and fabrics, livestock, grains, olives, grapes and slaves.

The long importance of Egypt was drawing to a close. Nebuchadnezzar of Babylon had captured the old bird in 588 BC, the year before he sacked

Jerusalem. During the second half of the first millennium BC and ever after her throne was occupied always by invaders, outsiders.

The Medes and the Achaemenids were tribes out of Iran. By 549 BC King Cyrus, who took Babylon from Nabonidus and set free the Hebrews, had swallowed the Medes to make a Persian whole. The empire he established rose faster than, and dwarfed, any that had gone before. The secret of his success was similar in spirit to that which would later work for Rome, in that conquered peoples were allowed to go about their business much as before. As long as they paid Persia her due in gold and acknowledged her king as paramount they were left mostly unmolested. Egypt too, old and spent, was made part of the greater agglomeration, and while there was some fragmentation after Cyrus, a subsequent king called Darius would re-establish Persian pre-eminence. Under his rule the empire stretched from Macedonia in the west to the Indus Valley in the east and within it a great mixing of peoples and civilizations was under way that would not be stopped. Stirred into the Persian empire were Babylonians, Hebrews, Indians, Lydians, Medes, Phoenicians and surely others whose very names are forgotten.

Also in the mix were the people who would be remembered as the Greeks. During the centuries after 1000 BC the stomping grounds that had been home first to Minoan and then to Mycenaean civilization were known to those people who called themselves something like Hellenes. On Crete and all across the Peloponnese, on the rest of what we know as the Greek mainland and on the islands of the Aegean, a new identity was in evidence. The olive and the grape, those crops that thrived where others failed, had enabled a growth of population that, over centuries, had driven a spreading colonization far beyond its first cradle. By the middle of the first millennium BC a people united by the Greek language and associated customs had spread the length of the Mediterranean and as far into the east as the Black Sea. Language was a crucial unifying factor, part of what enabled its speakers to understand themselves as one people, and a people apart from others. Those beyond their territories –

who could not speak Greek, whose languages sounded to those who could like the *bar-bar*-ing of lesser souls – were therefore *barbarians* and to be disdained accordingly.

By then those Hellenes had for their edification the poems of Homer – the *Iliad* and the *Odyssey*. He described for them a pantheon of gods and goddesses, confident in the knowledge his readers would recognize and identify with their all-too-human weaknesses as well as their strengths. By the time of the writing down of those works, in the Phoenician alphabet, those Hellenes lived in a world dominated by landowning aristocracies. Like every civilization before them the grunt work was done by slaves, those who had been conquered, or by tolerable resident foreigners called *metics* who handled the work of commerce that for a while at least was infra dig to the Hellenes themselves.

While wealth and power were first based on control and ownership of the limited fertile land upon which might be grown the stuff of life, by the middle of the first millennium BC it was also possible to grow rich through the business of trade that had once been so despised. New men raised up by new wealth and paying their way in silver raised, in turn, armies of professional soldiers. Armed and armoured, these units evolved into the legendary hoplites, literally those who carried the *hopla* – the gear for war. Rather than the single combat of champions, after the fashion of Homeric heroes like Achilles and Hector, warfare moved closer to that which we would recognize: organized bodies of men, all kitted out the same and depending upon one another and on the coordinated, disciplined choreography born only of drill and practice, were set in action against one another in set-piece battles for control of territory.

City-states were established too, wherein citizens came together to make collective decisions about how life should be conducted. Each was a world unto itself, isolated from its neighbours by landscape and by the precise, idiosyncratic details of how best to live. There was a time of tyrants, when new men used new money to take control of the state. The word carries a pejorative meaning now but then it described only strong men who used their wealth and influence to usurp the power of heredi-tary landowners. Homer likely knew tyrants in his time but by 500 BC or so they were gone, replaced by systems of collective people-power that were the foundations for democracy. Athens and Sparta are only the most famous of the city-states; hundreds more operated at the same time, with a greater or lesser degree of success and influence. The people calling themselves Etruscans were in evidence in the Mediterranean by then too, also the Punic people, descendants of the Phoenician traders, with their centre of operations at Carthage, in modern-day Tunisia.

The moment among moments was soon to be at hand. By the advent of the fifth century BC the Hellenic – Greek – city-states were scattered all around the Mediterranean and the Black Sea: it was Plato who described their presence as being like frogs around the rim of a pond, each croak-ing its own song. Those Hellenes and their neighbours were by then well acquainted with the Persian empire and more and more finding its flex-ing of muscles too close for comfort. When Darius was thwarted by the Scythians in an attempt to stretch his northern border into their clan-lands, some of the city-states were emboldened to challenge his forces closer to their own territories. There were jabs and feints, and then in 490 BC an Athenian army triumphed over its Persian foe at the legendary battle called Marathon. The year before, Darius had sent heralds to the other city-states demanding symbolic gifts of earth and water as proof they would submit to his overlordship. At Sparta, ruled uniquely by two kings, the heralds were told to collect the samples themselves and thrown down a well. Executed too were the heralds sent to Athens.

By 480 BC Darius was dead. It was his son Xerxes who invaded Greek territory with an army of a size hard to gauge. While hyperbolic Herodotus reckoned it was five million strong, modern estimates make it between 80,000 and 200,000 men, still a huge host by the standards of the day. Xerxes had had his engineers build a mile-and-a-half-long bridge across the Hellespont – the Dardanelles – and once his army was over it they marched for southern and central Greece where lay the Athens and Sparta that had so insolently defied his father. The only available route took them on a coastal path bounded by precipitous mountains to the north and the sea to the south. At a place defined by three successive pinch points the way was so tight there was barely room for two wagons to pass one another. Nearby were hot springs so that those narrows were called the 'hot gates' – in Greek, *Thermopylae*.

It was there, in terrain that aided a canny, outnumbered defensive force, that the Persians found their path blocked by a relative handful of Spartans led by King Leonidas. Numbering perhaps 4,000 fighting men, the rock-hard core of the force comprised 300 hoplites handpicked by Leonidas himself. In that Spartan way, learned in boyhood and never to be forsaken, those elite warriors would return carrying their shields, or carried dead upon them. Theirs was the way of the warrior. Spartan women knew freedoms unknown to those of city-states elsewhere but understood their purpose on earth was to bear more boys that would be men. Only hoplites killed in battle, or women who died in childbirth, were allowed a gravestone; the only words upon such monuments read *In War*.

For two days the Spartans stood their ground against overwhelming numbers, pausing now and then to comb the blood and gore from their hair worn long. At the end of the second day a local farmer, a traitor, named Ephialtes revealed to the Persians a path through the mountains that would enable a force to get around to the Spartan rear unobserved. At daybreak on the third day, realizing his position was compromised, Leonidas sent away all but his 300. Legend has it that Persian emissaries were sent to goad the defenders then, to let them know they would face innumerable archers whose arrows would block out the sun.

'Good news,' replied the Spartan soldier Dieneces. 'At least we'll be fighting in the shade.'

In the end it was annihilation that they faced right enough, slaughtered to the last man. Their sacrifice, though, the time it bought, enabled the Athenians to ready themselves. At the ensuing naval Battle of Salamis the Persian fleet was scattered. The following year a climactic land battle at Plataea saw Xerxes' men defeated and tossed out of Greece for ever.

There in immortal victory, in the fires of that Persian War, Classical Greece was forged – the Greece of Socrates, Plato and Aristotle, of the world's first great literature, the Greece made of men and women who knew they mattered to the story of the world, the Greece to which other men and women would look back again and again for 2,500 years in the hope of rediscovering a lost idyll. It was hardly the last time west would fight east, when Europe would fight off Asia. It may, however, reasonably be regarded as the first.

16.

SOCRATES, GADFLIES
AND UPSETTING THE STATUS QUO

One day in 399 BC the seventy-year-old Greek philosopher Socrates was handed a cup containing an infusion of deadly hemlock. He had been convicted of corrupting the city's young and of having no regard for the gods. Sentenced to death by poisoning by the city fathers, he calmly took the cup and drained it of its contents. In his work *Phaedo*, Socrates' student Plato described the great man's final moments. He was surrounded by a group of his closest friends. Having swallowed the liquid he was instructed to walk around until his legs felt heavy, or numb, and then to lie down. He did so, and one of his companions pinched his foot, and then his leg, asking him if he could feel anything. Socrates said not, that he felt cold and stiff. He said also that when the loss of feeling reached his heart, it would be over for him. To his friend Crito he said, 'We owe a rooster to Asclepius. Please, don't forget to pay the debt.'

'That shall be done,' Crito replied. 'But see if you have anything else to say.'

Socrates said no more, and a coverlet was laid upon his face. After a little while he seemed to move, but when they removed the cover his friends saw that his eyes were fixed and staring. Crito closed his eyes and mouth. 'Such was the end . . . of our friend; concerning whom I may truly say, that of all the men of his time whom I have known, he was the wisest and justest and best.'

The almost holy trinity of Ancient Greek philosophers comprises Aristotle, Plato and Socrates. Of all the one-named thinkers of that Classical world, it is Socrates who serves as the line in the sand, his existence separating those who went before from those who came after. The way of thinking and analysing that he pioneered – the Socratic method – was about asking fellow thinkers to offer definitions of concepts like courage, justice and piety and then interrogating them until they contradicted themselves and so exposed their ignorance.

By then his friend Chaerephon had asked the oracle at Delphi who, in all of Athens, was wiser than Socrates – and been told that none was. Unable to believe as much, Socrates had set out to prove the answer wrong. He sought all sorts of people famed for their reason and intelligence and tested them with his reasoning, only to learn in the end that none knew anything of note. Since he alone had already known that he was without wisdom, he concluded the oracle had been right after all. It has been suggested that those he bested had been humiliated by the process, and that some of them were determined to lay him low.

He had certainly made of himself a controversial figure. The son of a stonemason and a midwife, he had been a brave soldier – a hoplite – during the Peloponnesian War. In the aftermath of the naval Battle of Arginusae, in 406 BC, many Athenian sailors had been left to drown and there was public outcry back home. The battle had ended in victory for the Athenians but a storm prevented the rescue of many left in the water after the sinking of twenty-five of their ships. Six of the generals responsible were put on trial and Socrates was president of the assembly tasked with establishing their guilt or innocence. Contrary to the mood of the people, he refused to facilitate the generals' conviction and so emerged as what Plato described as a 'gadfly' – one who was prepared to be an irritant and to stand alone, if need be, against the demands of the majority. On a subsequent occasion he defied an order by the oligarchy of the Thirty Tyrants (the pro-Spartan leaders set in place to rule Athens on Sparta's behalf after that city's final victory in the Peloponnesian War).

Socrates left no writing of his own and founded no school, and yet his influence on philosophical thought was greater than that of anyone else. That we know as much about him as we do is down to the details and characterizations recorded in the dialogues of Plato – notably the *Apology*, *Crito* and *Phaedo*, which report his trial, his final days and his execution. By his efforts he transformed philosophy from considerations and intuitions about the natural world and cosmology to the examination of morality and ethics. It was during his trial that he is supposed to have uttered his remark about an unexamined life being 'not worth living'.

Athens was in turmoil following the defeat by Sparta and Socrates seems to have served as a useful scapegoat for those keen to distract the population from many consequences and hardships. Since he had earned a reputation as a seeming critic of democracy, it was easy enough to put him on trial for his lack of cooperation, described then as 'impiety'.

It appears that even though he was convicted on all counts, the Athenian leaders may well have been content had he merely agreed to leave the city and seek sanctuary elsewhere. Socrates, however, was a man who listened, above all, to his own counsel. In fact he told friends he had always had an inner voice – one that seemed inclined to advise him what *not* to do. Despite his own friends' urging that he should flee, Socrates chose to stay and face his fate, calmly and without complaint.

It has been argued that with his dying words Socrates was offering himself as the rooster for Asclepius – the Greek god of healing. A principled man of independent mind, he saw that some sacrifice was needed to cure Athens' ills. By his willing submission to a fate dictated by others, he may have given his life for that greater good. There have always been those ready to face destruction rather than comply with what they know to be wrong, and beneath them.

17.

THUCYDIDES, THE PELOPONNESIAN
WAR AND THE DEFEAT OF SPARTA

'History doesn't repeat, but it rhymes.' Whoever said it first, or wrote it, the truth of the statement resonates. Even this early in the story there are events unfolding, moments instantly recognizable and narratives that match or remind us of what is happening now.

After the long conflict remembered as the Persian War the Athenians were determined to sustain the momentum of victory in the battles at Salamis, Plataea and also at Mycale by creating a league of states (called the Delian League on account of its having been established on the island of Delos). Persia had been cowed and discouraged, driven back behind a line, but the threat of her remained – a dark empire. The league's original objective was to push home the advantage, to use luminous victories as inspiration and so encourage others in Asia, within reach of the influence of Athens and greater Greece, to throw off the Persian yoke. Athens was ever the driving force while Sparta – strange, different, indifferent Sparta, with her own identity, her own way of doing things – withdrew into her space and let Athens and the rest get on with it. Athens demanded support – ships and money – and for as long as there remained alive the generation that had felt Persian aggression, that had known the threat of invasion, most paid their way. As time passed and wounds healed, however, there was forgetting and backsliding, more and more reluctance to keep paying the dues. A great deal of money, far too much in the eyes of some, was spent glorifying Athens herself with great public works including those of the Acropolis – the Propylaea and the Parthenon, original home of the treasures known as the Elgin Marbles. There were divisions within the league as well, with the rich objecting to stumping up while looking on at the poor enjoying the protection of an insurance policy they had not paid for.

The emergence and evolution of the Delian League have been seen as analogous, at least to a degree, to the web of interdependencies that grew in Europe, and between Europe and the USA, after the Second World War. The Greek past had not been repeated, but something about it all seemed to rhyme. Fear and weariness in the aftermath of long and bloody conflict . . . treaties signed to keep allies together . . . always the looming threat posed by a frightening power at bay behind a wall . . . decades of peace leading to complacency in younger generations . . . restlessness by some and a desire to break away . . .

Perhaps the mesmerizing allure of Classical Greece is due in part to its passing away, how it seemed to slip like water or sand through the fingers of those who created it – their descendants' fingers, at least. After twenty years or so, Sparta was sufficiently uncomfortable about Athenian ambition and seeming will to dominate all about her. Her influence served as a fixed point around which Athens' opponents might rally. War, ever ready, reared up once more and would grind and grumble on, years of hostilities broken by periods of desultory peace, until 404 BC. The stretch of bloodshed remembered as the Peloponnesian War began in 431 BC and was recorded by one of its participants, the historian Thucydides, though he never actually named it as such. His book on the subject, called by others *History of the Peloponnesian War*, comes to its last page before the end of the conflict. Not only did he take part in and witness events, he also recorded testimony by protagonists on both sides. Best bets suggest he died unexpectedly or was killed, but his creation is revered by historians as the first work of scientific history.

Time and again his book has been referred to by those seeking to gauge events in their own times, even to predict outcomes. After 1945 and the end of the hot war, the world walked into one that was cold. Different commentators hear different rhymes, or else assonances. Some have decided that since America was a democracy it performed the same role as Athens. The Soviet Union, they say, was a militarized state controlled by a cabal of powerful men, and so reprised the part of Sparta. Others hear the reverse: Athenians bullied their satellites into obedience by the application of fear and violence and so were more like the Soviets, their totalitarian extremes inspiring understandable fear in the minds of those in America, which sought to lead an alliance of free states in need of its protection in the face of overweening threat. It all depends what rhyme a person is tuned for.

Year after year the protagonists played their parts. Sparta had the greatest land army, hoplites drilled until they moved together like a murmuration of starlings, acting and thinking as one and overwhelming any and all. Every year they would descend upon Athens, darkening the farmland needed for life. And every year the Athenians withdrew behind their walls – raised all around the city itself and then sheltering a 200-yard-wide, 5-mile-long corridor to their sea port, Piraeus. Safely shielded within, they could use their fleet – the greatest in Greece – to dominate the seaways and so secure a constant flow of grain and other supplies from elsewhere. While Sparta's hoplites were at war the everyday work back home was performed by *helots*, fellow Greeks the Spartans kept enslaved. Since that unhappy population had to be kept under control, Sparta's army was sent into the field for no more than forty days at a time, sometimes for as little as three weeks, before returning home to ensure control of the subject population. Athens knew as much and so had only to endure siege conditions for that long in any given summer. It was a stalemate, and everyone knew it.

In a bid to break out of the repeating pattern and gain real advantage, Athens looked further afield. Her gaze fell upon the port city of Syracuse, on Sicily. Syracuse belonged to a rival city-state, that of Corinth, and the Athenians reckoned that by taking such a prize they would simultaneously disable a challenger and gain all the wealth required to greatly increase their own navy. So equipped they might dominate not just the Aegean but much of the rest of the Mediterranean as well. Before such reach and power Sparta and her allies would surely quake, so Athens embarked upon the mission remembered as the Sicilian Expedition, of 415–413 BC. The result was a catastrophe – the entire fleet lost, half her army gone and failure complete. Broken economically, militarily and perhaps spiritually, Athens limped on until 404 BC when she sued for peace with Sparta and the rest and accepted the destruction of her ancient walls.

It was a model for events for centuries to come: the old gunslinger riled to violence by an upstart on the make. Sparta had long been recognized as the hard man of Greece that none dared threaten, and sure enough another challenger had bitten the dust. It was not the end of the story, however; the drama had more to deliver. In order to best Athens, Sparta had struck deals with Persia promising the return of those Asian states that had snuck under the protection of the Delian League. She tried welching on the deal but in the meantime lost another war that saw Athens rise again and rebuild her ancient defences. In 387 BC Sparta made peace with Persia and conceded the return of the disputed states. So much intrigue and double-dealing . . . In time Sparta was loathed by all those who had once joined with her to hobble Athens. And at the Battle of Leuctra an alliance of fighting men from two other city-states, Boeotians and Thebans, achieved the unthinkable and defeated a massed force of Spartan hoplites. No one had seen the like, indeed had never dreamed of living to see such a reverse, and the psychological impact was permanent. The tectonic plates had moved in a seismic event and Sparta was humbled. Persia for her own part was back where she had been before so many of her soldiers had fallen at the hot gates.

Sparta's defeat, after so much other strife, was a world-changing moment. After securing victory in the Persian War the Greeks held greatness in their cupped hands. During the century that followed Thermopylae, their arid little peninsula and archipelago of dots on the Aegean Sea had given rise to democracy and to politics (literally the business of the *polis* – the city). Their art and literature would last ever after. Their architecture would command the future dreams of those endeavouring to recreate the perfection that existed in their imaginations if nowhere else. Socrates, Plato and Aristotle began posing their philosophical questions and so taught the world to wonder about the nature and texture of reality itself – nothing less than the quest for the meaning of life.

That so much of that greatness happened against the backdrop of internecine war is a lesson about human nature. Wherever human beings are, a restless fire burns that gives and also takes, and nothing lovely lasts for ever.

Within his *History of the Peloponnesian War* Thucydides records a speech by the great Athenian general and statesman Pericles, who led and inspired his city and his fellows from 460 BC until his death along with uncounted thousands who fell to plague in 429 BC. The speech is remembered as Pericles' Funeral Oration and includes immortal lines about how the perfume of great deeds might linger long after the moment itself:

For heroes have the whole earth for their tomb and in lands far from their own, where the column with its epitaph declares it, there is enshrined in every breast a record unwritten, with no tablet to preserve it except that of the heart.

18.

CHANDRAGUPTA, ASHOKA
AND THE MAURYAN DYNASTY

As the third decade of the twenty-first century gets under way, societies in the west are more and more polarized. Left and Right; Black and White; Good and Bad and Right and Wrong. Identity politics are forcing people to see themselves not as individuals but as members – avatars – of distinct groups determined by race, religion, gender and other character-istics, some they can choose and some they are born with. Differences are declared more defining, more important, than anything that might tran-scend the groups and offer unity, togetherness. The fact that research shows there are more differences *within* groups than *between* groups matters not at all.

Societies have done this to themselves before – individuals clumping like iron filings drawn by magnets – but at other times, in other places, there have been attempts at something altogether different.

Megasthenes was a Greek historian and diplomat sent to India by Seleucus I Nicator (which means 'victor' and is the root of Nike, among other names), one of the generals left squabbling for territory and power after the death of his master, Alexander the Great. His own holding was the bulk of the territory Alexander had claimed in west Asia.

Megasthenes seems to have reached India around 300 BC, just before or just after, beginning a journey that would last years. Alexander's army had refused to travel beyond the Punjab, in the north-west, but Megasthenes made it all the way to Bengal and Orissa in the east, meeting and interviewing all manner of Indians along the way. All that he learned he compiled in a work called *Indika*, now lost but extensively quoted by other writers soon after whose compositions survive.

Megasthenes seems to have been sent into India soon after the signing of a treaty between Seleucus and an Indian king called Chandragupta, founder of the Mauryan dynasty. The moment that matters is one recorded more in the form of folklore than anything that might realistically be considered historical fact, but it counts in its own way – not least because it has been remembered and retold for so long. According to the tradition, Chandragupta had a meeting with Alexander the Great. Chandragupta, so the story goes, had been born in poverty, was abandoned by his own family and later sold into servitude. However or even whether the encounter with the conqueror came about, afterwards Chandragupta is said to have slept and dreamed of a royal destiny for himself. He awoke and found that he was being gently licked all over by a lion. The beast left him unharmed and Chandragupta, his life and sense of self utterly changed, embarked upon a new future. Perhaps the *how* of the change to Chandragupta matters less than the demonstrable fact that a man seemingly born into obscurity drove himself up to the highest place.

From around the sixth century BC there had been a kingdom in the Ganges Valley, near the delta, called Magadha. It was a dominant power, exercising control over a wide area. In 321 BC Chandragupta, having raised an army, deposed the king there and upon the foundations of Magadha raised an empire, the Mauryan, that swallowed the great river valleys of the Ganges and the Indus, and also Afghanistan – which he seized from the Seleucid kings – as well as parts of what is now Pakistan and Iran.

The India of Megasthenes' *Indika* is strange, right enough – to such an extent that many modern historians dismiss him as a fantasist. He certainly told tales of flying snakes and scorpions, of one tribe whose members had eight toes on backwards-pointing feet, and another with snakes for legs. There were men who lived not by eating food but only by inhaling smells. Perhaps he was only reflecting, by the standards of his time, the way isolated groups held outlandish prejudices regarding strangers and outsiders. What is more interesting is the way the India of the Mauryans embarked upon a countrywide experiment in human relations.

The caste system was already long in place, the work of centuries, and society was split largely between the Hinduism presided over by Brahmin priests on the one hand, and Buddhism on the other. Chandragupta was succeeded by his son, Bindusar, about whom less is known. He may have sought to expand his father's empire into the south but there is no consensus among historians. It was under Bindusar's son and heir, Ashoka, that the Mauryan empire and experiment reached its fullest extent, unifying almost the whole of the subcontinent into one entity.

If Megasthenes' history was unreliable, by the time of Ashoka the subcontinent has entered the realm of reliable fact grounded in other sources. By around the middle of the third century BC, Ashoka was in the habit of having his words inscribed in rock surfaces and stone pillars around his vast holdings. During the course of his conquest of Orissa he had inflicted great slaughter, for which he repented. He was, by conversion, a Buddhist, and after the Orissa campaign he experienced some sort of Damascene moment, vowing to eschew violence ever after. The edicts and ideals he had etched in stone have been given the name *dhamma*, or *dharma*, a concept impossible properly to render into English. Within *dhamma* is something of an acceptance of natural law, similar in some respects to the Chinese notion of the Tao, the way of the universe that flows like a river. In both cases the suggestion is that a person might go with the river rather than struggle against it. Rather than convert all of his subjects to Buddhism, Ashoka appears to have sought to encourage tolerance for all. Pragmatism may have been in the mix too – a realization by Ashoka that subjecting everyone to one way of thinking and being was simply beyond the reach of his government and bureaucracy. He was hardly entirely benevolent in any case, since a secret police force of sorts operated throughout society at the same time. His bureaucrats collected taxes to pay for large-scale projects including extending the reach of irrigation and planting endless rows of banyan trees along his roads so as to provide shade for travellers. Ashoka's iteration of the Mauryan dynasty was an attempt to bring order out of chaos by, as far as possible, letting people be. In one of his pronouncements he declared: 'All men are my children.'

For all its success, and for all its potential, Ashoka's grand and unifying idea did not long outlive him. The practical limitations imposed upon his statecraft by the vastness of his country and its disparate population made for an inertia that pulled down his structures like a sandcastle desiccated by the Indian sun. Perhaps in the end the caste system, and the thrall of the Brahmins, was too deeply embedded. After Ashoka and the last of the Mauryans it was a Brahmin dynasty that arose. Unifying ideas based on tolerance and *dhamma*, the way – live and let live – are usually brief bursts of light soon swallowed again by the patient dark.

19.

MAYANS SENSE THAT TIME
HAS NO BEGINNING, NO END

Some time around 25,000 years ago our species reached the Americas via what is now the Bering Strait. Perhaps there was a land bridge all the way across, or else it was a series of boat trips between islands. It appears rising sea levels then severed the link and that no one new reached those continents until the time of the Vikings in the tenth century AD. During the millennia of isolation from the rest of the world, the peoples of the Americas followed their own paths.

The Inuits, those known once as Eskimos, adapted themselves to one of the most unforgiving environments on earth, conjuring into being a culture that enabled them to sustain and to remain in the Arctic territories of what are now Alaska, Canada, Greenland and elsewhere. Further south, on the vast swathe of land between the oceans, traditions of hunting and gathering would evolve and then survive into the modern era. On the eastern seaboard of North America the technologies of farming were developed and settled occupation began that would be maintained until the arrival of Europeans in the sixteenth century. Those ways of life lasted for thousands of years but at no stage did they qualify as civilization.

By around the end of the second millennium BC a culture known to archaeologists as Olmec was flourishing in Central America around a heartland in what is now Veracruz, in Mexico. Here buildings were raised – places of ritual and religion and the product of a level of complexity and sophistication of society deserving of the c-word. The Olmecs practised human sacrifice, a way of living and dying that was to be perpetuated by all the pre-Columbian civilizations of Meso- and South America. There was also a preoccupation with making artworks of clay, stone, jade, obsidian and other materials. The so-called 'colossal heads' carved from blocks of basalt and weighing as much as 50 tons are thought to depict Olmec kings wearing the helmets associated with the 'Mesoamerican ballgame', a sport with profound ritual significance and still played today in some parts; even the word *Olmec* means something like 'people of the rubber', or 'the rubber people', a reference to the hard, solid rubber ball that was central to the game. The Olmecs, and those civilizations that came after them, depended wholly on the cultivation of maize. The gods of the Olmecs, a bloodthirsty lot, became, in one form or another, the gods of their successors.

After the Olmecs came others, Toltecs among them. They or others like them, perhaps the Totona, raised the city of Teotihuacan around 30 miles from Mexico City. In its day, between 100 BC and AD 650, it was home to between 150,000 and 250,000 people and among the six largest cities in the world. As well as domestic dwellings there were scores of pyramids, rivals in scale to those of Egypt. Teotihuacan was overwhelmed some time in the seventh century. Experts debate the cause and the culprits but it seems likely it was symptomatic of the febrile, bellicose atmosphere that evolved in Middle America and lasted until the arrival of the Spanish and Portuguese.

Further to the east, in modern-day Guatemala and Honduras, the Maya had their flowering between AD 100 and 900. The ruins of their civilization – not cities for the mass of the population, but ritual sites for the raising of ziggurats, temples and tombs served by priests – are swallowed now within the rainforests from which they were won in the first place. Like the Olmecs and the rest, the Maya had to clear forest to plant the maize upon which they subsisted. The labour involved was endless and back-breaking and after a few harvests it would have been necessary to abandon the exhausted fields and carve more from virgin forest. In more clearings, vast in scale, they raised their pyramids and the rest of the structures that have beguiled and haunted imaginations ever since.

Also like the Olmec, the Maya were enthusiastic sacrificers of their fellows – men, women and children. It was a cruel and blood-drenched world. Deep in the belief system, running back through time, was an acceptance that life itself was irrigated by the letting of blood. Lesser gods had sacrificed themselves to energize those above them, even powering the heat and light of the sun, and so it was the lot of mortal men to do likewise.

In the valley of the Yucatán the Toltecs, successors to the Olmecs, would be supplanted by the Aztecs in the middle years of the fourteenth century. It was a slow, swirling storm of peoples on the move, warring, rising and falling. Always it was bloody, about taking prisoners of war and offering them up to the gods, cutting out hearts and lopping off heads. Further south was the kingdom of the Incas and more sacrifice and preoccupation with death.

Somewhere in among all the warring and the mania for building, someone started counting days. The coming and going of time likely registered first among the Olmecs, or whoever pre-dated them. Calendars for tracking and predicting the shape of years were in use among several of the peoples of Central America, but among the Maya the making and keeping of a calendar was finessed by individuals acutely sensitive to the passage of time. In 2012 their counting system came to world attention on account of a baseless theory that had it that the Maya calendar predicted the world would end at eleven minutes past eleven on 21 December that year. The Maya calendar is actually three counts running within one another like wheels in a clock. Two of those, the Haab and the Tzolkin, count days of the year. The long count reached back thousands of years and forward for a few thousand more – to 2012. Fantasists imagined the world ending that year, while for the Mayans it meant only the ending of one long cycle and the beginning of another. No civilization before them – save perhaps the Hindus of India – had conceived of deep time in this way. In the moment of the calendar's creation, in the last centuries before the birth of Jesus Christ, some Mayan thinker grasped the concept that time has no beginning, and no end.

20.

WARRING STATES AND THE COMING TOGETHER OF A PLACE CALLED CHINA

Qin Shi Huang, first emperor of China, died on 10 September in 210 BC. Some weeks later, perhaps two months or so, his body was buried in a mausoleum that had been under construction for many years. It lies beneath what is believed to have been a pyramidal structure, in the Shaanxi province of Northwest China, though the passage of years has seen to it that the edifice appears now like a natural hill, covered in vegetation. The tomb has never been excavated but there has been some investigation of the vast surrounding necropolis, an area seemingly stretching for miles in every direction. In 1974 some farmers digging wells in the vicinity discovered the first of the now famous Terracotta Army – thousands of life-size statues of soldiers, acting as a garrison to protect their lord and master. As well as soldiers there were hundreds of chariots and terracotta horses to pull them.

Because the tomb itself has not been touched, in the modern era at least, it is unknown what lies within the man-made hill itself. According to records made afterwards by historians, the tomb is said to have been built as a vast replica of the world the emperor had known in life. Historian Sima Qian, writing a century later and certainly no eyewitness, described an entire landscape, palaces and towers, rivers and seas of liquid mercury, a sky above featuring all manner of 'heavenly bodies'. Supposedly the tomb is yet protected by crossbows loaded and cocked. No one knows for certain.

It is also reported, by some of the same sources, that Qin Shi Huang did not set off into the next world unaccompanied. All manner of slaves and other servants are said to have been buried with him – alive or dead – including those who had helped build the tomb and so knew its secrets. Perhaps thousands died for him that day. Once the emperor's body had been installed, with all due ceremony, the tomb was sealed and buried.

In that moment of its closing, as the darkness fell for ever in the tomb, something of the destiny of China set hard as stone, immobile as the fired clay of the faces of the terracotta warriors. It is important to note that that army of thousands was not composed of identikit figures. While the bodies came from moulds, each face is unique and the work of artists. There are young faces and old, happy and sad, resolute and fearful, just as in life. As Shelley's poem has it about the ruin of Ozymandias, the approximation of life was deliberately rendered on the faces of those warriors: 'its sculptor well those passions read / Which yet survive, stamped on these lifeless things'.

The first syllable of the first emperor's name – Qin – is sometimes spelled Ch'in, or Chin. He was born in 259 BC, and in 247 BC was made king of Qin. He lived in a time of war that involved not just his own swatch of territory but all those around him as well. It was a time of unrest that had rumbled across the land since around 400 BC and which is remembered by historians as the Period of the Warring States.

Another version of civilization had sparked into being in that vast part of the world – altogether a territory bigger than the United States of America – under a tribe called the Shang. Some time in the first half of the second millennium BC they had imposed their will upon thousands of square miles of land on the banks of the Yellow River where it flows through Henan province in the Central China region. After six or seven centuries of Shang dominance came the Zhou tribe (or dynasty) who flexed their muscles over some of the same territory. The Zhou lost control of it all by around 700 BC and it was in the following centuries that that time of endless warring took hold.

It was Qin Shi Huang who established stability at last, in 221 BC, the date recorded as the end of the Period of the Warring States and the establishment for the first time of a unified state that took its name from him, from Qin . . . Chin . . . China.

For all the upheavals, spread across thousands of years, the mass of the people remained what they had always been, which is to say farmers growing millet and other staples. Long before Qin Shi Huang came along there was a wall in the north – or rather many walls, built by many warlords or kings to separate state from state and at the same time keep out barbarians from the far north, outsiders loathed and feared by all. Among many projects, the first emperor of China set about making one of them – one Great Wall as much as 3,000 miles long to mark the northern limit of his empire.

Before and after Qin there was a world there – a world set apart from Europe, and from the Near East, and from the Classical world of the Mediterranean. It was a separateness made mostly of sheer distance and of a natural boundary between east and west made of great mountain ranges. The people – peoples – that established themselves beyond that natural great wall were different from those others to the west, and millennia of separation and different paths followed meant that by the time the west came to meet that east, the difference was permanent and irreconcilable. Never the twain shall meet.

Confucius's lifetime overlaps the period, give or take, when the idea of a republic was crystallizing for the Romans. Rome was on the rise then, becoming what it had beheld of all that civilization among the Greeks. The way of living and doing that Confucius taught set down deep roots in his own part of the world, but it was a part of the world in which civilization was already of an age comparable to that of Ancient Egypt. China, or the land that became China under the first emperor, was utterly different from all the rest and would remain so. Among the emperors and among the people as well there grew a sense that the world beyond the walls – natural and man-made – was merely waiting, and would be grateful for that Chinese version of civilization.

Sealed in Qin Shi Huang's tomb and necropolis, all in an awful moment, were those uncounted thousands of individuals. That fact had hardly been overlooked, since time had been taken to give each terracotta soldier a unique appearance. Here was the world partly shaped by the thinking of Confucius, who taught that peace and harmony depended upon each and every person knowing his or her place. Their unique identities were there, right enough, but best swallowed up like droplets of water in a great ocean. China would be different . . . is different. It is a place where individuals must be sacrificed to the greater collective good directed by the all-seeing, all-knowing one. If not before, then that destiny was certainly made manifest when the light went out for ever inside the tomb of Qin Shi Huang.

21.

JULIUS CAESAR CROSSES THE RUBICON

Totalitarianism begins, said German-born political theorist Hannah Arendt, in contempt for what you have. In an interview for the *New York Review of Books* she said, 'The second step is the notion: "Things must change – no matter how. Anything is better than what we have." Totalitarian rulers organize this kind of mass sentiment, and by organizing it articulate it, and by articulating it make the people somehow love it.'

At the time of writing there is deep uncertainty here in the west, as well as anxiety and anger. Trust in leaders, let alone faith in them, is guttering like a candle flame drowning in its own wax. Calls for change are in the air, even revolution. An end of that which had seemed certain, constant and unassailable is not new in the story of the world. In some important ways it *is* the story of the world.

After the Romans shed their kings and made for themselves a republic in which the people retained sovereignty, there evolved a system that was both effective and enduring. Once established and accepted – by the citizens, the plebs and the proles – the years began to pass, then decades and centuries. The republic was ruled by the Senate and the Senate by two consuls – senior magistrates, men of extensive experience in matters political, judicial and military – elected annually. Below the consuls and the Senate was an intricately complex system of government, of supposed checks and balances and limitations on how long any individual might occupy a position of power and influence. It was altogether pragmatic as well. Roman imperial power expanded, absorbing city-states around it. Soon enough the holdings had grown too huge, and spread over too great a geography, for micro-management to be anything like achievable. Sage Roman heads saw that as long as subject provinces kept paying their dues – in gold, slaves and men of fighting age for the legions – blind eyes might be turned to what the populace actually got up to for much of the time. As long as populations accepted the Roman world view as their own they were left to self-govern. All men owed many years of service to the infantry or to the cavalry and, thus armed, Roman power became ever more muscular, spreading in all directions.

Carthage, in the territory we know as Tunisia, was the principal city of an empire established by the Phoenicians and holding sway over much of the southern Mediterranean. By the middle of the third century BC Carthage and Rome were at loggerheads and so began fighting each other, off and on. Their conflict lasted a hundred years. The Roman rendering of the word Phoenician was *Punic* and so those were the Punic Wars. By 146 BC it was all over for the Carthaginians. Even their own greatest city had been razed, its fields ploughed with salt to make them sterile, and now Rome had Africa for a province. The Greek city-states had been swallowed whole by then too, then France and most of Spain. There was Roman rule in swathes of Asia as well until, by the middle of the first century BC, Rome's shadow fell as far into the east as the Black Sea.

There were any number of memorable figures, men on the make, with unforgettable names like Marius, Sulla and Pompey. The greatest and most memorable of all emerged in 59 BC when a nephew of Marius's wife was given a turn as consul. He was Julius Caesar, and after the consulship came seven years in command of the army of Gaul. He was a commander of genius. Towards himself he attracted the loyalty, the love of the soldiers – loyalty and love they more properly owed to Rome – and so grew powerful, as well as rich from the spoils of victory after victory. He was expected back in Rome but remained in his own world, his own province of Gaul. Intent on more glory, or maybe just playing the game of politics, he made two attempts to conquer the British Isles and was roundly rebuffed both times. When he decided to return to Rome he presented, by his very existence, a potent threat, and other men of ambition watched his approach with mounting alarm.

On he came, towards the eternal city. The physical limit of his authority was the line drawn by the Rubicon River in north-eastern Italy. Roman law dictated that any general crossing that river – re-entering the territory of the republic – must surrender his command. Caesar had other plans, understood another version of reality, and so crossed the Rubicon with his troops held close as ever and awaiting whatever commands he might give. Perhaps *the* moment within *that* moment, of defiance and of ambition, is when he mutters – for himself more than for anyone listening – 'The die has been cast.'

(The intervening centuries have seen to it that no one is quite sure which river was that Rubicon. Benito Mussolini, twentieth-century politician on the make, decided the river flowing through the town of Savignano was likeliest, so that the place was renamed Savignano sul Rubicone.)

Whatever, wherever, for Caesar there unfolded then the events for which he is most famous. Having crossed his Rubicon at the head of his army, he was de facto guilty of treason and faced the ultimate penalty of execution. On the contrary, he said, such action was his duty if the republic were to be rescued from the abuse of others. Pompey was the Senate's choice as the war leader to spare them the advances of a would-be dictator but Caesar out-thought and outfought any sent against him. He pursued Pompey all the way to Egypt and, after his enemy was murdered, amused himself by taking Cleopatra for his lover (or more likely it was she who took Caesar). By 45 BC – just four years beyond the river – he was voted dictator for life. He had defeated all comers and taken control of the Senate to ensure his elevation. He was king of Rome by any other name.

And so totalitarianism, when it comes, is born of contempt for what is there . . . what has been there long enough for it to be taken for granted. Julius Caesar did not finish the republic; it was already dying of wounds not of his making. They murdered him anyway, in the Senate with knives on 15 March, the Ides of March, 44 BC. Those with blood on their hands were soon dead as well.

English art historian Kenneth Clark wrote in *Civilisation* that empires fall not just to barbarians and other enemies from without, but on account of exhaustion and loss of confidence within, 'the feeling of hopelessness which can overtake people even with a high degree of material prosperity'. More than that prosperity, he continued, each needs 'confidence in the society in which one lives, belief in its philosophy, belief in its laws and confidence in one's own mental powers'.

After Caesar the glory that was Rome had centuries still to run. But while the totems and monuments of the republic remained in place, they had been made hollow and impotent. SPQR was the motto that would endure – 'For the Senate and the People of Rome' – but the ultimate sovereignty of the people therein was compromised, an afterthought.

Caesar had crossed the Rubicon, and so had the republic. There was to be no going back. Caesar's adopted great-nephew, Octavian, made complete what had already begun. By 30 BC Cleopatra was dead, of suicide, along with her latest Roman lover, Mark Antony. Together they had challenged Octavian and paid the price. Egypt was Roman thereafter too. Octavian was made consul in 27 BC and honoured with the addition to his name of Augustus (meaning 'venerable'). By 12 BC he was *pontifex maximus* – the greatest priest. What had been a purely religious title for the republic was now politicized and part of the grandeur of a monarch. He would be succeeded by five members of his family. Rome was a monarchy once more, though she always pretended otherwise.

Here is how totalitarianism came to Rome, and how it might come among us now, when a population that has governed itself, for itself, succumbs at last to exhaustion and the forlorn hope that any change is better than the status quo. As Arendt noted 2,000 years later, in the context of the Third Reich, totalitarianism arrives when we regard our present and past with contempt. Caesar and then his great-nephew had sensed exhaustion in the republic (anything is better than what we have). Men of limitless ambition, they saw in that exhaustion mass sentiment they could turn to their advantage. They and their successors organized it, articulated it and, in the years to come, their fellow Romans would learn somehow to love what they were offered next.

22.

PRIMO LEVI PONDERS,
'IF THIS IS A MAN'

In treating, with contempt, that which we have and have had, we court the ending of the world. If not the ending of the world entire then at least the ending of the world we have known and the beginning of another. Having to witness and to live through great change, upheaval, revolution is a constant theme of the story of the world.

Julius Caesar crossed the Rubicon and imposed his will, the will of just one man, upon the Roman republic, changing it for ever before he was finished. It is said that the world is always and only changed by unreasonable people. Reasonable people find ways to accept, to tolerate and to live within the confines of the world as it is (and in spite of the many inconveniences and indignities, great and small); unreasonable people cannot bear such and so seek to change the world until it better suits them. The world also seems split between those people who will, happily or unhappily, do as others tell them, and those who will ultimately refuse to submit. The struggle between order, chaos and new order is older than the beginning of the world's story. The choice between kneeling or standing is as old.

Kings like Hammurabi sought compliance. He may or may not have been an unreasonable man but he had his understanding of the law carved in stone and demanded submission to it. Darius and Xerxes of Persia were surely cut from the same bolt. Cyrus the Great and Nebuchadnezzar were two more kings bent on dominance. Even Lao-Tzu and the Buddha were in their subtle and quiet ways evidently unprepared to accept the conventions of the societies into which they had been born, the version of reality they had been taught, and so sought to bring about change in themselves and others – change that changed the world.

Surely just as interesting in the story of the world, though, are lesser figures than kings and princes, little people all but forgotten now who refused to submit, refused to surrender their understanding of who they were. How much their actions changed the world, if at all, is impossible to gauge. But somehow those efforts affected the whole, like tremors too slight and too deep to be felt on the surface of the earth and yet capable of making infinitesimal alterations that count.

Primo Levi was a Jewish-Italian chemist. During the Second World War he joined partisan fighters engaged in guerrilla warfare with the Nazis in the north of his country. Soon enough he was captured by the enemy and taken to the concentration camp of Auschwitz. He survived, and after the war, while continuing his work as a chemist, he wrote many books about all sorts of things. His testimony concerning his time in Auschwitz was published as *Se questo è un uomo* (If This Is a Man) in 1947. Philip Roth subsequently called it 'one of the [twentieth] century's truly necessary books' and so it surely was, is.

The next moment that matters, a moment partly Levi's and partly another's, is out of time here, and by thousands of years. But some events are so resonant, their ripples so far-travelled, they reach back and forth in time until everything is changed, before and since. Such moments fit everywhere and also nowhere. Those moments, whenever they happen, should make us see all of time differently.

The Nazis' attempt to end every last Jew – man, woman and child – was about more than murder. It was also about dehumanizing the victims, both before and after death. The aim, it seems, was to have them know, before they knew no more, that they were unwanted by the world. As well as being extinguished, excised from the world, they were first to be made to believe that they were lesser creatures, an affront to life itself. Everything about the death camps was designed to break the human spirit, to scour people out until nothing was left but skins easier to throw in the ovens.

After just a week in the camp Levi had given up on any idea of keeping himself clean. Any minutes he had to himself he preferred to spend lost inside his thoughts, or looking up at the sky and wondering if he were seeing it for the last time. He described the communal washroom, into which he and the other inmates were herded every day, as a filthy, draughty building, its brick floor covered by a layer of mud. The water from the taps, when it flowed at all, was foul-smelling and cold. Any attempt at washing in such circumstances seemed to Levi beyond pointless: 'The more I think about it, the more washing one's face in our condition seemed a stupid feat, even frivolous: a mechanical habit, or worse, a dismal recreation of an extinct rite.'

On a morning towards the end of his first week, Levi encountered an old friend, a soldier of the Austro-Hungarian empire named Steinlauf. The ex-sergeant had fought in the First World War and been decorated, receiving the Iron Cross for valour. A man in his fifties, he was a generation older than Levi. The younger watched as the older, stripped to the waist, energetically scrubbed at his neck and torso with the foul, cold water. He finished and reached for his jacket, which he had kept folded between his knees. With this he dried himself before putting the damp garment on again. Having completed his ablutions, he made eye contact with Levi for the first time. The older wanted to know why the younger was not washing. Levi protested that there was no point; Steinlauf insisted otherwise. Here of all places a person must wash, he said, 'precisely because the *Lager* (prison camp) was a great machine to reduce us to beasts – we must not become beasts'. The ex-sergeant, older and wiser, battle-hardened, had learned that even in such a place as Auschwitz it was possible to survive – but that a person must first want to survive, in order 'to tell the story, to bear witness'.

Steinlauf is a small man in the story of the world, a shadow and a ghost, but this is a moment of great significance, perhaps the greatest. For all that he was held against his will in the most dreadful place in the world, facing death and in the grasp of evil shaped and built to make a beast of him before killing him, he would not submit what little remained of his sense of himself. It might be small in the scheme of things, this moment, but it is also everything that matters.

Levi wrote about how he struggled to recall precisely what Steinlauf told him in that moment. Italian was not the ex-sergeant's first language and so Levi had to work hard to recapture the essence of what he had been told. Here is what he understood of the other's lesson:

> . . . to survive we must force ourselves to save at least the skeleton, the scaf-folding, the form of civilization. We are slaves, deprived of every right, exposed to every insult, condemned to certain death, but we still possess one power, and we must defend it with all our strength for it is the last – the power to refuse our consent.

They parted then, Levi and Steinlauf. Even having heard what his friend had to say, even though it stayed with him for ever, still Levi struggled ever after to decide whether or not he was persuaded or convinced of what he had been told. That does not matter. That soldier of the Great War was a man who would not submit, even in the face of overwhelming power. For as long as strength allowed he would wash his face and body without soap in filthy water and dry himself with his own dirty clothes before putting them back on and setting out to greet the rest of his day. Both men are long gone now but Steinlauf was right, is right. From the beginning of the story there have been those determined to win submis-sion from others – Hammurabi, Xerxes, Caesar . . . For as long as there have been kings, or longer, there have been ideas inspired by the desire to wipe away what has been so as to replace it with something else. Right now in the world there are more such ideas, ideologies, some old and some new. There are capitalists and communists, globalists and technocrats. There are those who want the world to remain as it is and others that hold the present in contempt. The world as it has been is under immense pressure and change is in the air, revolution.

There are always men who would be king, unreasonable men who would remake the world in their own image. There are always those who will not submit even when all is lost and they are alone against the towering wave. We are always a hair's breadth from slavery. Our rights are taken from us at a moment's notice. In the end we are all condemned to death, we all owe a death. But we possess one power until the very end. Whatever challenge comes before us, seeks to envelop or even to destroy us – whatever happens, always we may refuse our consent.

Primo Levi made it all the way home. The first of his books was published in 1947. He never really escaped the camp, though. In 1987, at the age of sixty-seven, he was found dead in the ground-floor stairwell of his apartment block in Turin, Italy. His home was on the third floor, and a coroner later recorded suicide as the cause of death. Fellow Holocaust survivor Elie Wiesel commented: 'Primo Levi died at Auschwitz – forty years later.'

23.

THE DEATH AND LIFE OF JESUS CHRIST

The world we live in has the shape it does because a fellowship of Jews watched their leader die on a wooden cross and then said they believed he had come back to life three days later. That such a claim (by a tiny sect among countless other sects) outlived its makers in a world ruled by the Roman empire is impressive. That their claim formed the foundation for a religion that changed the world in every way is nothing short of astonishing. It is hardly more impressive, though, than the survival of the Jewish people and religion that was the cradle and early nursery of Christianity.

The most famous of the kings of Israel – Saul, David and Solomon – might have been in their pomp around the tenth and eleventh centuries BC. No one is sure. King Solomon it was who had had those Phoenicians raise a temple for him, the First Temple, in Jerusalem. Those grand days for Israel, of almost imperial dominance of neighbours (if the stories in the Old Testament are anything to go by), were short-lived. In any event, in 587 BC King Nebuchadnezzar had conquered the place and carried many of the Hebrews into exile in Babylon. By then their glory days were long since over. What they seem to have learned, after Solomon and after exile, was a stubborn determination to endure. Part of their success in that regard had evidently come from choosing to see their history, the unfolding story of their world, as a grand adventure persuading them they were the chosen people of the One God and that by obeying His law, come what may, they would finally be rewarded with His blessing.

Babylon itself, as we have seen, fell to the Persians of Cyrus the Great and in 538 BC those captive Hebrews, some of them at least, seized the opportunity offered them and returned to their Promised Land. They built the Second Temple. They hardly had their troubles to seek, however, and one empire after another had them in its grasp: after the Persians there were the Ptolemies, left behind by the rule of Alexander the Great; after the Ptolemies, Seleucids – more of Alexander's kind. There was a rising, the Maccabaean Revolt of 167–160 BC. Antiochus IV, a king of the Seleucids, had been keen to see his Hebrews live lives more like those of the rest of his Hellenized subjects. Utterly convinced of the rightness of their rituals and ways, they pushed back, and hard. There was a rapprochement of sorts and even some independence for a century or so until the advent of Rome and her soldiers in 63 BC.

However diminished, however put upon, always the Jewish way prevailed, endured, like a candle's flame in cupped hands. By the time Jerusalem and the rest were conquered by Pompey (who later fell before Julius Caesar) and ruled by Rome, Jews were dispersed around the ancient world. They were soldiers, merchants, common citizens of other lands. Their way of life, their beliefs, appealed to many among whom they settled. Above all else their certainty about being God's chosen people was seen by some to make sense of the misery of existence. Jews accepted that their travails were part and parcel of the unfolding drama of the story of the world, their world. They were hard put upon, the tattered outcasts of the earth, but it was all part of the tale and they were the whole point of it, that and the necessary suffering. Like iron ore tortured in the blast furnace they might emerge as tempered steel. They had rules by which to live and believed that adherence to that law would bring them salvation in the end.

King Herod the Great, himself a Jew, was a Roman choice in 37 BC. His preference for foreign, exotic, Hellenistic ways excited the same opposition that had fired the Maccabean Revolt. He came, and slaughtered the innocents, and went, unmourned, and was succeeded by his sons, who were ineffectual. In AD 6 the territory fell under the bailiwick of the

Roman province of Syria, and twenty years later Pontius Pilate was made Procurator of Judaea. Few places proved as troublesome, as incomprehensible to the Romans, as Judaea – and the trouble was rooted in religion. Roman religion was syncretic, which is to say there was belief in an underlying unity and so a willingness to incorporate ideas and practices from other religions they encountered in the world. When the Romans came face to face with Celtic belief at Bath, in Britannia, for instance, and heard the locals say the hot springs were home to a goddess of wellbeing they called Sulis, the Romans intuited a similarity to their own goddess Minerva. Seeing the sense, and the political advantage, of bringing the two together as one and allowing them to co-exist, they named the place Aquae Sulis-Minerva. In Judaea, among the monotheistic sects of Judaism they found people who refused to countenance any mixing of their beliefs with those of the conqueror, or vice versa. For Jews – and then for Christians – there was one way, and one way only, one god, and One God only.

Part of the fascination, and more beguiling than stables, mangers and shepherds, is that it is not even possible to say for certain when Jesus was born. Often you will read the date of 6 BC, so lost is the truth of it. The gospels of Matthew, Mark, Luke and John are commonly (but mistakenly) regarded as eyewitness accounts, written by people who lived alongside Jesus. Biblical scholars, however, accept that the first three – called the synoptic gospels because they share a similar view of the events of Jesus's life – are the work of second-generation Christians, born after his time, and that John, quite different from the rest, may not have been written until the end of the first century AD or even the beginning of the second. As with so much else, there is no consensus.

The apostle Paul – Saul of Tarsus, a Pharisee – is generally accepted as having been born around the same time as Jesus, perhaps 5 BC. He it was who began as an enthusiastic persecutor of early followers of Jesus, indeed a witness to the martyrdom of the apostle Stephen, but to whom Jesus appeared as a bright light and a questioning voice and so made of him a follower as well. Closest in time to Jesus, Paul's writings make no mention of the details of the Nativity, such as feature in Matthew, Mark and Luke. He barely quotes a word of what Jesus had to say. Whatever he knew about Jesus (and surely told others as part of his ministry) he wrote only that he was born, crucified and rose from the dead. Perhaps he was so close to the events in question he was able to allow for a degree of common knowledge in those who heard him preach, and who read his letters.

Whenever, however, Jesus was born into a Jewish world fractured into sects that were often at each other's throats. At Qumran in the late 1940s, in modern Israel's West Bank, around 900 papyrus scrolls were found stored in caves. These are the Dead Sea Scrolls, and among other things they reveal the existence of a sect, with ties to the Sadducees, that believed a final salvation would begin with the coming of a *messiah*, a deliverer.

It seems reasonable to accept that Jesus was born into a family on the downslope from better days. There lingers a suggestion, even an assumption, of connection to a lineage of kings, and the House of David. (When the Romans crucified him – after Pontius Pilate had washed his hands of him in order to appease those Jews angered by the Nazarene's blasphemy – they bothered to put a sign above his head, in Greek, Hebrew and Latin, declaring him King of the Jews.) None of his opponents bothered to deny as much.

He was baptized, in adulthood, by a man named John, who may have been his cousin, and part of the Qumran community, and who thought him the messiah the prophets had promised. The way to salvation he preached afterwards and until his death was simple and rooted in Jewish tradition. Significantly, though, he insisted forgiveness and eternal life were available to Jews and non-Jews alike. In spite of the simplicity of Jesus's message, or perhaps because of it, he aroused the enmity of Pharisees and Sadducees and others besides. If he was not of them – and he chose the company of the poor and broken over men of influence and position – then a loner identified by too many as the messiah was a threat to them. In the Sermon on the Mount he encouraged trust and faith in the One God above all:

> Consider the lilies of the field, how they grow; they toil not, neither do they spin: And yet I say unto you, That even Solomon in all his glory was not arrayed like one of these. Wherefore, if God so clothe the grass of the field, which to day is, and to morrow is cast into the oven, shall he not much more clothe you, O ye of little faith?

In the end it was easier to have him killed by the Romans.

What mattered most of all was a moment following his death – the moment when his followers claimed he had risen from that death. Paul, a contemporary of Jesus, recorded nothing of a tomb, empty or otherwise. What mattered to Paul was that Jesus had accomplished something never known before. In the gospels – which Paul did not mention and which surely came after him – there would be descriptions of a return to a physical body, with wounds that could be touched. For Paul, by contrast, it was about transformation. In 1 Corinthians he wrote:

> It is sown a natural body; it is raised a spiritual body. There is a natural body, and there is a spiritual body. And so it is written, The first man Adam was made a living soul; the last Adam was made a quickening spirit.

There was a belief in resurrection among Jews, but only when God's kingdom was established on earth at the end of time. For Paul, the resurrection of Jesus was a foretaste of the same, a warning that the end of the world was imminent. Here was the message that lasted, down through the centuries: that Jesus would return and usher in the Kingdom of God. That a handful of Jews should have been able to sow the seed of their claim that they had seen a man die and come back to life, that Paul and the rest were able to carry more seeds far and wide, and that those claims would last not centuries but millennia was certainly momentous.

24.

POLYBIUS AND THE CYCLICAL
NATURE OF CIVILIZATION

Maybe Mark Twain was right and history rhymes. Or maybe it has rhythm instead. If so, then when it comes to the affairs of our species that rhythm is languid, ponderous; long wavelengths imperceptible except in hindsight. If the story of the world were a song it would be a long one, drawn out like the world-encircling symphonies of whales.

Julius Caesar's crossing of the Rubicon had been a crescendo, then a clashing of cymbals. His subsequent actions brought change, but although pre-eminent among its kind it was hardly the first or the last time such a moment had occurred. The moments we notice and mark are like the points a mathematician imagines on a curve so that it might be measured and assessed. We need and look for stepping-stones. This is the practice of calculus, or something like it. Time and history might be imagined as a curve, an arc, or perhaps a straight line made of moments like pearls on a string.

All historians have insisted that the soundest education and training for political activity is the study of history, and that the surest and indeed the only way to learn how to bear bravely the vicissitudes of fortune is to recall the disasters of others.

The disasters of others . . . as well as in the past they are all about us now. The death of Europe, the fall of the American empire . . . Before Caesar, there lived a Greek historian who visualized and described elements of human history as having a shape less like a straight line and more like a circle or a rotating wheel. Those are some of his words above. His name was Polybius, and he was born around 200 BC in the Greek city of Megalopolis, in Arcadia. Before Polybius, Plato had looked at how societies sought to govern themselves and noticed a repeating pattern, from good to bad to worse and back around again and again. Others took up the theme and developed a theory of political evolution eventually called anacyclosis, but the writer credited with its best portrayal is Polybius.

If time is a circle, like a clock face, then the hands are surely returning to the start again now, back to midnight. After 2,000 years the west is faltering, failing. Democracy is despised by the demos. We are atomized by the technologies that were supposed to bring us closer together. Those clock hands must be past five minutes to the hour by now, tick-tock, tick-tock. According to the thinking of Polybius, it is all about to end, and also to begin.

Polybius was born into one of the most influential political families in Greece. As a man who would be a historian he was lucky (in some ways) since he was also born into and lived through a time of momentous change. He wrote dozens of books of history and in so doing provided priceless coverage of that period, long before Caesar, during which the Roman republic rose to be the premier superpower of the ancient world, eclipsing and also swallowing the Greek world it had once beheld and so entirely dominating the Mediterranean and far beyond. Polybius lived through much of what he wrote about and was in position to record first-hand accounts of characters such as Hannibal of Carthage and Scipio Africanus. In the case of the latter, Polybius's experience could hardly have been more personal. Once the Romans had crushed all practical Greek opposition (ending with the defeat of King Perseus of Macedon's army at the Battle of Pydna in 168 BC) he was among a thousand hostages, regarded

as leaders and troublemakers of the Achaean region of Greece, taken to
Italy, there to live under house arrest. He entered the family circle of
Scipio, acclaimed general and consul, and grew close to him and them. By
association he gained access to the great and the good, enabling him to
see at close quarters the workings of Roman high society. He saw them
fight and win, against Hannibal and others.

The Greek historian Thucydides had written about the Peloponnesian
War of his own time and is regarded by many, most, as the better writer of
prettier prose. At least one reader of Polybius said no one who started reading his work ever finished it. But he was something other than Thucydides,
maybe something superior in his own way. He was forensic and thorough;
he was painstaking about the importance of detail. Best of all, in the sixth
volume of *The Histories* he neatly explained the way civilizations cycle,
again and again and again, through the same few forms of rule.

First there emerges, from chaos, a wise king who rules fairly and well.
The people love him and so accept the rule of his son after him. All too
soon the subsequent sons and heirs pale in comparison, proving flawed,
spoiled by entitlement. This is the bad form of kingship, its evil twin,
which is tyranny. Powerful men close to the throne lose patience with
some or other tyrant and take command for themselves. This is aristocracy. For a while their rule is good, like that of the wise king but not quite,
and then their descendants and heirs prove as venal as the sons of kings.
What follows is oligarchy, the corrupt rule of rich men. Now the ruled –
the people – take offence at the misrule of the oligarchs and seize control
in the form of democracy. For a while the people govern one another
fairly and then their heirs too lose sight of that which is good. It is all so
enervating. Now comes the time of *mobile vulgus*, Latin for 'the fickle
crowd', which we know as mob rule. In the language of Polybius this
was the ochlocracy, and it was as degenerate as any other failed rule.
This is when the hands on the clock approach midnight. While the ochlocracy devours and debases its own, its members grow desperate for
leadership of another sort, any sort. Now and at last comes a demagogue,

a charismatic figure who will pander to the mob and assure them he has all their interests at heart. Soon there is the return of the chaos that was there at the start, says Polybius, and in time the stage is set for something better, surely something better. Out of the chaos comes a king, a wise king . . . and the cycle starts again.

Perhaps the moment in the story of the world that matters most is when Polybius understood the best hope of civilization was a combination of monarchy, aristocracy and democracy. In the Roman republic he thought he saw the finest flower of that mixing. The royal gloss was there in the presence of the two consuls, the aristocracy was manifest in the Senate, and the people, the *hoi polloi*, were represented democratically, or near enough. His critics have called him a stooge, an apologist for the Romans he lived with. Perhaps he was a compromised historian, but his position enabled him to help his people too. During the 140s BC, when the Greek state of Corinth rebelled against Rome and might have been crushed and sterilized like Carthage, his advocacy on their behalf persuaded the Romans to treat them more lightly than might otherwise have been the case.

Long after his time and into the present day his understanding of anacyclosis has shaped the thinking of those who would build civilizations. Italian Renaissance diplomat and writer Niccolò Machiavelli, author of *The Prince*, was a keen reader of Polybius. The Founding Fathers of the USA saw the wisdom of the mixing of royal, aristocratic and democratic elements to ensure the checks and balances they hoped would save them from tyranny.

In any event, the wheel he saw and understood is still turning. All across the west democracy is under pressure, treated with contempt by the people it has protected. The *mobile vulgus*, the fickle crowd, are loud in their calls for change and demagogues stand ready to do their bidding. In truth one people after another has understood the nature of it. Among the Jews, the eternal outcasts, there is a saying expressed best in Yiddish: 'Laugh, while the wheel turns round.'

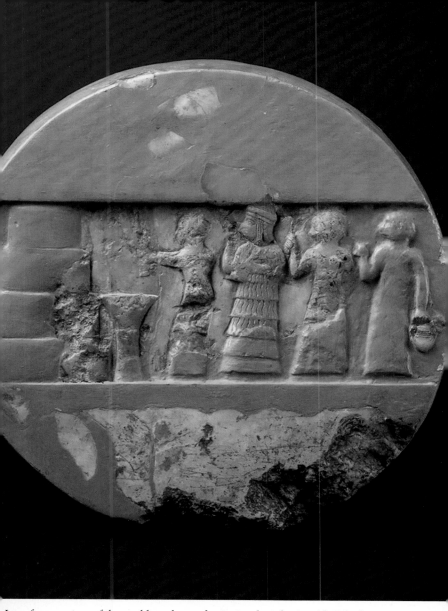

In so far as a story of the world can have a beginning, let it begin with Enheduanna, the first named poet – the central figure with the elaborate hairstyle and carved in relief, on a disc of alabaster excavated at Ur, in Sumer, in Mesopotamia, in 1927, and dated to 2340–2200 BC. Also shown are her hairdresser, Ilum Palilis, her scribe, Sagadu and her estate manager, Adda.

The creator-being Purusha, also called Cosmic Man and central to the foundation of the caste system. In the Hindu tradition Purusha gave up his body to the gods so that by his sacrifice all people might be made.

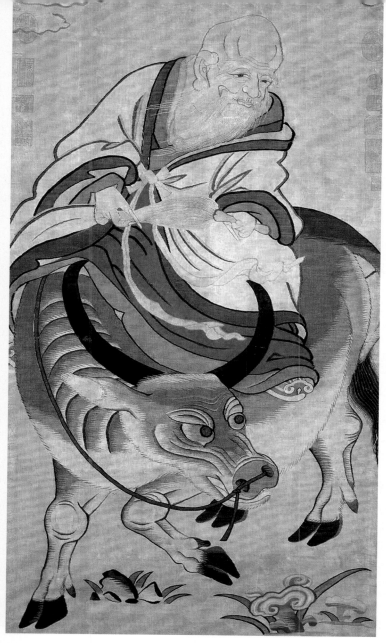

Laozi, or Lao Tzu – the 'old master' – credited as the author of the Tao Te Ching. *First set down in writing around 400 BC, in the form of eighty-one verses, 'The Way of Integrity' seeks to describe the immutable way of the universe.*

The Great Wall, built during the third century BC by order of Qin Shi Huang, first emperor of China – a 3,000-mile-long boundary that ensured east was separated from west; that China was different, and would remain different.

The Great Enclosure, the most famous feature of the massive stone city of Great Zimbabwe. The work of Shona or Gokomere farmers, construction began early in the eleventh century and continued for hundreds of years. The inhabitants of Great Zimbabwe had trade links stretching as far as the Arabian Peninsula, India and China.

Virgil urges Dante to continue on his way towards Beatrice and Paradise. Completed in 1320, Dante's Divine Comedy, *uniting the Classical world with that of Christendom, is regarded by many as the greatest literary work of the Middle Ages.*

The Fall of Constantinople, 1453. After a thousand years and more than thirty sieges, the great Christian city – Rome in the east – falls at last to the Muslim horde of Sultan Mehmet II.

SVR

*The boomtown city of Potosí, in the shadow of Cerro Rico – the 'rich mountain'
of silver discovered by the Spanish, in 1545, in what is now Bolivia. For 300 years
Potosí was Europe's cash cow. By 1650 some 16,000 tons of Potosí silver had flowed
into European coffers.*

25.

CONSTANTINE HAILED AS EMPEROR BY THE ROMAN ARMY AT YORK

Fickle fate and the temporary nature of power are there for all to see on a roughly hewn stone slab on display now in Tullie House Museum in Carlisle. Into a smoothed surface at one end is crudely etched an inscription that reads 'For the Emperor Caesar Marcus Aurelius Mausaeus Carausius Pius Felix Invictus Augustus'. It recalls the reign of Carausius, a usurper who declared himself Roman emperor in Britain in AD 286 and held on to power until his murder in 293. At the opposite end of the same slab, etched the other way up, is a second inscription as rough as the first: 'For Flavius Valerius Constantinus [sic], most noble Caesar'. The latter followed the former as emperor in the west. The skinny slab that had proclaimed Carausius was upended so that his name was buried in the ground out of sight. The other end was smoothed and engraved, and now it was Constantius's name in the sun. How quickly they forget – or rather how quickly they are told to forget.

For half a century before, from 235 to 284, the Roman empire had been struggling under pressure from barbarians outside and usurpers within. At times the whole edifice was close to collapse. In 284 Diocletian became emperor and introduced all manner of reforms. He would rule in the east and his fellow cavalry officer Maximian would rule in the west. In the hope of improving stability each emperor had a junior – a Caesar, an appointed successor. In the east, under Diocletian, it was Galerius, and in the west, under Maximian, it was Constantius. This was the Tetrarchy – the rule of four.

Constantius was vigorous in asserting his authority in his demesne. Carausius – whose name had been in the light, on that slab wherever it once stood – was a naval commander. He had seen his chance and seized it. Under all the pressure of Constantius's efforts to wrest back control, Carausius was murdered by one of his own advisers.

In 303 Diocletian, bloodthirsty devil that he was, launched a final persecution of the Christians, the last of its kind in the whole of the empire. He stood down as emperor in 305 and his successor in the east, Galerius, was as enthusiastic in his pursuit of the same ends. In Asia and Egypt the persecution was cruel and relentless.

Constantius had taken a different path. After the death of Carausius in 293 another usurper, named Allectus, had also had some years swanning around the place as *soi-disant* emperor. Constantius's forces defeated and killed him in 296, along with every last one of the mercenaries Allectus had employed to bolster his position. When it came to persecuting Christians, however, Constantius did no more than pay lip service, little beyond ordering the ruination of some churches and some burning of books. Legends came later that said he was a secret Christian all along and married to Helena (later St Helena) who found the True Cross while on pilgrimage to Jerusalem. There is no proof of any such discovery, any such faith, but legends stick.

Constantine, son of Constantius, might have expected to be made his father's Caesar but was overlooked thanks to the machinations of Galerius, who played Diocletian and others and saw his own favourites elevated. So it was that Constantine, in fear of his life, fled to his father's side in Gaul, in 305, just as the elder was readying himself and his men for an invasion of Britannia. There was campaigning in the north, against the Picts, and then, while resting his forces at York, Constantius fell seriously ill. With death at his shoulder he urged the army to accept his son as emperor after he was gone. And so it was done, and so he was declared, in 306. Throughout the century before, the third century AD, emperors had been made not by the Senate and the people of Rome but by the soldiers of the Roman army, and so it continued in the fourth.

Such a moment: so far from Rome, all that way away in distant Britannia – in the city the Romans knew as Eboracum, the place of the yew trees, York – the elevation of Constantine would change the destiny of Christianity and so the whole world. The same legend that had had Constantius convert to the faith, to please his wife Helena, had the son raised as a Christian at that mother's knee. No one knows the truth of it but after York, Christian or not, he embarked upon a stubborn twenty-year campaign to secure his position. He was no bureaucrat, a soldier rather, and underwrote his power by reorganizing the army and garri-soning men in cities throughout the empire.

Historians have seen in Constantine a man of his time, in that it was fashionable among men of the late Classical period to be swayed by thoughts of one god, if not One God. Most famously, and in what might reason-ably be regarded as another moment of great importance, Constantine claimed to have had a dream on the eve of a vital battle. Outside Rome, on the banks of the Tiber at the Milvian Bridge, he faced the army of Maxentius, who also claimed the imperial throne. Constantine slept and dreamed of the sun, which had been central to his pagan faith, but saw superimposed upon it a cross. Beneath the sun and cross were the words *in hoc signo vinces* – 'in this sign prevail'. Before his troops engaged the enemy the following day he had them paint Christian crosses on their shields. Prevail they did, and Constantine had Rome by 29 October 312.

Thereafter and ever after, Christianity was respected and protected. Like many men and women of that time, Constantine did not seek bap-tism until he was on his deathbed, but after the Battle of Milvian Bridge the religion that had begun as the concern of a rebellious sect became the accepted faith of the Roman empire. Constantine would relocate his cap-ital to Byzantium, in the east, which was renamed Constantinople in his honour. In 325 he summoned the first ecumenical council, the Council of Nicaea. Notionally it was to settle disagreements over the nature of Christ's relationship to God, but the creed that resulted, the Nicene Creed, still describes and declares the faith of the Roman Catholic, Eastern Orthodox, Anglican and Protestant churches:

> I believe in One God, the Father almighty, maker of heaven and earth, of all things visible and invisible. I believe in one Lord Jesus Christ, the Only Begotten Son of God . . .

26.

AMBROSE, BISHOP OF MILAN, BRINGS THE EMPEROR TO HEEL

On Christmas Day in the year 390, the Roman emperor Theodosius – Theodosius the Great – presented himself outside the cathedral in the city of Milan. Rather than any imperial garb he wore only the simple clothes of a penitent. He had been excluded from the Church, from communion and thus from the very presence of God. By some accounts he had been so shunned since the spring of that year. Again and again he had come to the doors of the place, they say, only to have his entrance refused. On each occasion that emperor was denied access by Ambrose, Bishop of Milan. Finally, on 25 December, Ambrose relented and Theodosius was welcomed back into the arms of the Mother Church.

Here was a moment among moments: for the first time a man of the cloth had won submission from a king of kings. By force of will Ambrose had demonstrated that his office, held from God, outweighed that of any other mortal, even an emperor. That Theodosius had been seen to accept the fact, or at least to play along for theatrical effect, showed how far Christianity had come. Just a century before, adherents of the upstart faith had been thrown to the lions in the Colosseum and in the hippodromes of the empire. Now a bishop had shown seniority over the emperor of Rome and that emperor had taken the knee, both knees. There in that moment was born one of the greatest, if not *the* greatest, themes of the story of the world (in western Europe, at least): the endless tug of war between Church and state for the upper hand in the mastery of the people, body and soul.

Ambrose was Roman in every way that mattered, son of a Praetorian prefect and, by the time of his face-off with the emperor, the most famous and celebrated churchman in Christendom. Like an early socialist he insisted the poor be treated not as outsiders but as fully paid-up members of society. In the beginning, said Ambrose, God had intended the resources of the earth to be shared equally by all. That there had evolved a separation of haves and have-nots was on account of nothing more or less than a usurpation by the greedy rich, so that giving to the poor was a rightful and honest redistribution to the many of that which had been unfairly taken by the few.

Theodosius was also devout in his Christianity, a great defender of the Nicene Creed as conjured by Emperor Constantine over the popular and influential Arian heresy of the day. It might reasonably be said that rather than Constantine it was Theodosius who by his edicts and other actions made Christianity the religion of the Roman empire. Ambrose of Milan had been his adviser on Church matters, even if the two had not always agreed on all things.

The matter that made a penitent of the emperor was a massacre in his name in Thessalonika, one of the largest and richest cities in Roman Greece. By 390 the Roman garrison there was made up of Goths. As recently as 378, at the Battle of Adrianople in what is now part of Turkey, Goth rebels had fought and defeated a Roman army. More recently Goths had been welcomed to settle in imperial territory and were living and serving the empire as *foederati* – barbarian peoples made allies of Rome by peace treaties. Tension remained, however, and there were always those citizens who objected to the presence of such outsiders in their midst, especially when they were armed and given authority as in the case of the garrison at Thessalonika.

According to some accounts, trouble started in relation to the sport of chariot racing. Like every large Roman town and city, Thessalonika was home to a hippodrome where charioteers raced and made themselves some of the most feted celebrities of their day. Believe it or believe it not but in the months before the moment in question, one such local legend had been accused of attempting to rape a young male slave. Word of the alleged crime reached the Goth commander of the garrison, named Botheric, and he had had the charioteer arrested and thrown in jail. Racing fans then gathered outside demanding his release, and when they were denied, took matters into their own hands. Botheric and the rest of his men were slaughtered by the mob, the charioteer set free.

Among other characteristics, Theodosius was reputedly a man of quick temper and when he heard what had happened to his garrison in Thessalonika he ordered a nearby Roman force to punish the local population. Apparently he thought better of this rash act and sent word to stand the soldiers down – but by then it was too late. Those men had waited until race day when thousands were gathered in the hippodrome and then indulged themselves in an orgy of violence. Either by sword or the resultant stampede as many as 7,000 Thessalonians are said to have died. A later historian, Theodoret of Cyrus, wrote how the emperor had 'gratified his desire for vengeance by unsheathing the sword most unjustly and tyrannically against all, slaying the innocent and guilty . . . like ears of wheat in the time of harvest, they were alike cut down'.

Theodosius's court was in Milan, and when word of the atrocity reached Ambrose at his cathedral he promptly excommunicated his troublesome parishioner. The extent to which any or all of the aftermath was choreographed by willing participants cannot now be known. Even the details of the massacre – its causes and its scale – are subject to debate. What is certain is that by appearing before his bishop to ask forgiveness for an earthly wrong, Theodosius made plain for all to see that the Church had grounds ever after for declaring it held sway over the rule of mere kings and emperors.

27.

ALARIC THE GOTH AND
THE SACK OF ROME

There is a painting by the late-nineteenth-century French artist Joseph-Noël Sylvestre called *The Sack of Rome*. It marks the invasion of the city by Visigoths led by Alaric in AD 410 and features a pair of near-naked barbarians climbing on the white marble statue of a Roman and placing a noose around its neck so as to pull it down. The statue represents civilization. In the world of today it is a potent image. It brings to mind all sorts, notably the tearing down of Saddam Hussein's statue in Firdos Square in Baghdad in 2003. More recent, and much closer to home, was the pulling down of the statue of Edward Colston – slaver or philanthropist, depending on a person's point of view – in Bristol in 2020. The violent removal of statues, especially by the mob, is a recurrent element of the drama of political protest and regime change.

The Sack of Rome by Alaric and his Goths was a moment and no mistake. Rome was more than a thousand years old by then. It had been eight centuries since the last fall of the city – to the Gauls, led by Brennus, in 390 BC. When those republican, pre-imperial Romans accused Brennus of mistreatment in the aftermath he is supposed to have told them, 'Woe to the Vanquished.' There was more gnashing of teeth when Alaric arrived all those centuries later, but unlike Brennus he was no barbarian, or not what most people might picture on hearing the word. Eight more centuries of Rome had seen Roman ways, *Romanitas*, spread all around the Mediterranean, throughout Europe and the British Isles and into the east. Alaric had been born in the territory that would be modern Romania, north of the Danube in what was once the Roman province of Dacia. Rome had withdrawn by the time of his birth but the place still knew and appreciated Roman ways. In addition to his native tongue he had been schooled in Latin. He was also a baptized Christian – of the Arian heresy, but Christian nonetheless. He led a Gothic army for Rome at the Battle of Frigidus in 394. Emperor Theodosius, he of the massacre at Thessalonika, had faced a rebel force led by a usurper and it had been the sacrifice of the Goths, counting 10,000 slain, that had turned the battle in his favour. In the aftermath Alaric felt slighted, that the letting of the blood of his fellows had been taken for granted and certainly not rewarded. His Roman masters sought to placate him, or just to patronize him, and it was never enough, and Alaric turned on them. In the years to come he would flex his muscles again and again, seeking the respect, position and wealth he regarded as his due, the due of his people. Eventually he brought his forces to the walls of Rome, laying siege to the place again and again. When it came, his and their entrance into the city may have been enabled by a traitor leaving open the Porta Salaria. On they advanced, and for three days the immortal city was looted. Alaric was no barbarian (as previously noted) and while much damage was done and countless gallons of blood spilled, there was restraint by the standards of the day. Since he was Christian too there was more than a nod to leaving holy places intact and respecting the sanctuary of those sheltering within.

But for all that it was less than apocalyptic it was a bloody and cruel sacking just the same. All across Christendom there were cries of woe that sustained ever after, like an endless note reverberating from a plucked string. When Edward Gibbon wrote *The History of the Decline and Fall of the Roman Empire* in the last quarter of the eighteenth century he could still note that this 'awful catastrophe of Rome filled the astonished empire with grief and terror'.

Alaric and his horde withdrew soon enough, their lust and fury spent. They planned an African invasion next, but while they successfully boarded ships, bad weather forced them back to Italy where Alaric died later the same year. According to legend (if nothing else) it was at Cosenza, in Calabria, that he breathed his last. Slaves were put to work to divert a river there and then a grave was cut for Alaric in its bed. There he was interred, with great wealth, before the river was released to its original path so that his resting place was forever drowned. The slaves that knew the truth of it were slaughtered and the site lost for ever.

It was not the end of Rome – not yet – but the decline of which this was a potent symbol would not be halted.

There is a stubborn notion that some creations of humankind grow too big to fail. The story of the world reveals that, on the contrary, empires invariably grow so big they have to fail, and always do. Long before the advent of the fifth century AD Rome was no longer a unified entity in any meaningful sense. Under Emperor Diocletian governance had been split in two so that there was an emperor in the west, in Rome, and another in the east, in Constantinople. For long, too, it had been Roman practice to bring whole populations of erstwhile barbarians inside the tent, in the hope that they might piss out rather than in. As long ago as AD 212 Emperor Caracalla had passed an edict granting Roman citizenship to all free inhabitants of the empire.

By the fifth century it was hard to say who was Roman and who was not, and why. Those like Alaric's Goths, and also Huns and Vandals, who had fought for Rome had understandable claims upon the place they had bled for. By 440 the Huns were led by Attila, who would see them to their high-water mark. His forces were roundly defeated at Troyes in 451 by a nominally Roman army of Visigoths led by their barbarian king Theoderic I. By the time of his death two years later Attila was plotting to become emperor in his own right. Flavius Romulus Augustus, the last Roman emperor in the west, was knocked off his perch by the barbarian warlord Odoacer in 476. There is no consensus as to Odoacer's origins, but he was almost certainly Germanic, possibly a Goth.

For all that the popular notion is of the Roman empire falling beneath barbarian pressure imposed from without, in reality those incomers had as often aspired not to destroy what they beheld, but only to become part of it. Alaric was succeeded as leader of the Goths by Ataulf, his brother-in-law. He it was who is supposed to have declared: 'I hope to go down to posterity as the restorer of Rome, since it is not possible that I should be its supplanter.'

In *Civilisation*, the art historian Kenneth Clark wrote about how the great edifice fails not only on account of existential exhaustion but also fear, 'fear of war, fear of invasion, fear of plague and famine, that make it simply not worthwhile constructing things, or planting next year's crops'. According to Clark, the impact of Romanized barbarians like Alaric's Goths created chaos in the empire, chaos born of that fear and of the exhaustion and loss of confidence it provoked, 'and into that chaos came real barbarians, like the Huns, who were totally illiterate and destructively hostile to what they couldn't understand'.

In that way of history not repeating but rhyming, it is hard to look back at the Sack of Rome and not hear another warning for the modern world. The western Roman empire had burned bright for a thousand years and its light attracted outsiders. Towards its brightness came all manner of moths – immigrants hungry for hope or greedy for whatever might be grabbed. Who belongs and who does not? Who belongs and who must be denied and expelled?

28.

MUHAMMAD HEARS
THE VOICE OF AN ANGEL

Since he founded Islam, a religion that changed and continues to change the world, the birth of Muhammad would be regarded as a moment of note in any story of the world. Muslims generally accept that he was born in Mecca, in what is now Saudi Arabia, around AD 570, and into the Banu Hashim clan of the Quraysh tribe, but the precise date of his birth remains one of many things not known about him. Biographers wrote in later years that Muhammad was orphaned at the age of six and raised afterwards by members of his extended family. Those same writers insisted that even as a youngster he was made conspicuous by his honesty and decency, so that he earned the nickname al-Amin, which means 'trustworthy'. His reputation came to the attention of an older woman, Khadija, who was a merchant in the city. She became his first wife and mother of his eldest children.

More interesting than his birth – and a moment that matters much more in the scheme of things – is the thought of the day in 610 when, he said, the angel Jebreel (Gabriel) appeared and spoke to him: 'Recite, in the name of the Lord, who created; Created man from a clot of blood.'

Reputedly a pious man, he had taken to spending time alone in a cave on Mount Hira, overlooking Mecca. It was there in his darkened solitude that he had his heavenly vision, heard God's truth from the angel's mouth.

It was to Khadija that he reported what had happened to him and she who first offered him support when the significance of it all might have been overwhelming. For the next twenty-two years – until his death, indeed – Muhammad continued to hear the word of God, the God the Arabs knew as Allah. He repeated what he heard – recited the words – and all of it was later collected as the Qur'an, which means 'recitation'. Above all he understood that humankind must bow down to Allah; *Islam* means 'submission'.

Between 619 and 622, and following the death of Khadija, Muhammad felt vulnerable to his opponents in Mecca, those less than welcoming towards his insistence on the worship of One God. It was then that he and his followers moved 250 miles north to Yathrib. This was the migration, or *Hijra*. In time Yathrib would be renamed Medina, the Prophet's City. His status grew, and by 630 he had won the submission of Mecca and the Meccans. There he purged the Kaaba, an ancient stone structure containing idols revered by pre-Islamic Arabs. Muhammad had them cast down – all except a depiction of the Virgin and Child.

By the time of his death in 632 the brotherhood of believers he had created – the *umma* – was far from secure and riven with disputes. Nonetheless, upon the foundations he had laid were built two successive Arab empires. Revolutionary within his teaching was the insistence that the *umma* was a fellowship united not by blood or kinship ties, but by faith alone. All such believers were equal.

As the King James Version of the Bible would do for the English language, so the Qur'an gave a permanent shape to Arabic. For a long time the Jews and the Christians had had their scripture – now the Muslim Arabs did too. Muhammad told his followers that while there had been prophets before him there would be none after. His version of the word of God was therefore the last, and also perfect. Perhaps above all else it was the simplicity of his message that was so potent, a way of living subject to God's will. It was also a portable faith and so perfect for a people on the move.

Into a world of two monotheisms had come a third. Collectively, the followers of all three would be known to Muslims as the People of the Book. The Jews were elder and had ever been wanderers – cast out, exiled and tossed upon a sea of fate, hopeful of a safe harbour. The Christian message had spread like slowly rising water, appearing subtly and without fanfare in places where before it had been absent. Islam was different altogether, more confident and insistent from the beginning, a wave that reared up as if from nowhere and swept across the Old World in a matter of years.

Even without the making of those Muslims, by the seventh century the story of the world was already complicated. The Romans, legatees of the Classical world, had declined and fallen in the west. Into their province of Britannia, furthest north and west of all, their absence had drawn Germanic tribes like Angles and Saxons. Arthur was among the remnants of the *equites* – those Romano-Britons trained to fight on horseback as knights with lances – and would leave behind a legend. Across the Channel, Gaul was claimed by another Germanic tribe, the Franks, who would give their name to France. There were Visigoths in Spain, and Vandals; Lombards in Italy. Justinian had been made emperor in the east in 527 and after him that empire, based at Constantinople, was called Byzantium and Byzantine. From Constantinople he had sought to rebuild all that had been lost, and failed.

In Rome itself the Church had survived, swaddled in imperial purple. The lamb of God had been made to smell right, like an orphan wrapped in another's skin and fleece so that Mother Rome might suckle it. Christianity there could draw, after all, upon power based on the presence of St Peter's bones. From 590 to 604 the Bishop of Rome – the Pope – was Gregory the Great, the same who sent Augustine to England to remind the backsliding locals of faith briefly held and then lost. In a west devoid of Romans, Christianity had ebbed and flowed, finding its way through and among warrior kings emboldened in a world made new by the absence of the old.

The eastern emperors – Justinian and those after him – fought the Sassanids, successors of the empire conquered by Alexander some eight centuries before. There where the sun rose the faith of the risen son confronted Zoroastrianism, an ancient monotheism doomed to setting. So distracted were they with each other, those latter-day Persians and those Romans in the east, they were unprepared for the entrance on stage of a new character. Out of Central Asia came the Avars, latest of the nomads. They had followed in the footsteps of all the Asian hordes that came before. First had been Scythians, known to the Greeks and recorded by Herodotus. After them there were the Hsiung-Nu, ancestors of Attila's Huns. The Avars had been pushed out of Mongolia by Turks and swept down off the Great Eurasian Steppe and into central Europe with enough intent to build an empire of their own. In 558 they had sent an embassy to the court of Justinian. (They also brought to Europe the stirrup, a piece of kit that would change the world in its own way.) It was a whirl of peoples on the move – out of Central Asia and into the sphere of influence of those Persians, and those Byzantines.

So it was into a world filled with uncertainties and possibilities that Islam emerged with an energy and certainty that would affect them all. Muhammad had said he heard the word of God, and enough believed him. That moment in the cave made of a blinding light and a voice had altered the fabric of the world like a seismic event. Everything was different.

29.

A MEETING BENEATH WISTERIA
AND THE SHAPING OF JAPAN

Many are the similarities that have been observed between Japan and Britain, not least by the Japanese themselves. For a start there is the physical: both are made of islands off the coast of a much larger and oft-times threatening and overbearing continental neighbour. In both instances the isolation and necessity of self-reliance have cradled peoples tending to see themselves as special, uniquely blessed.

In Scotland, in 1304, there was a secret meeting between two men on the make. One was Robert Bruce, soon to embark upon years of attritional warfare in pursuit of kingship. The other was William Lamberton, Bishop of St Andrews, in search of a King of Scots who would keep the Scottish Church separate from that of England, and the overweening bishoprics of Canterbury and York. The meeting took place at Cambuskenneth Abbey, by Stirling, and there in the shadows of its towering walls they swore to back each other to the hilt. So it was and so they did, and after much killing and dying they completed their objective.

That meeting was a moment, and no mistake. But it is another covert *tête-à-tête*, in Japan and centuries before, that matters here. In the early seventh century the country was in thrall to a family called Soga. Its patriarch was Soga Umako, who had successfully challenged the powerful Mononobe and Nakatomi families. Those two were closer to the imperial family and Umako needed a tool with which to prise them away to make room for his own ambitions. The Mononobe and Nakatomi clans supported the ancient Japanese religion of Shinto, based on worship of the ancestors and the spirits of nature. Umako had looked to China for a new religion that might be a wedge he could use to break his rivals, and found that Buddhism suited his purposes. Others had sought its introduction but Umako was most determined. Out of the strife that followed, about religion and more, and a climactic battle in 587, the Soga clan emerged victorious. The Mononobe were utterly destroyed and Buddhism was in the ascendant. Umako's choice of emperor was a prince named Sushun but the two fell out before long and Sushun was murdered to make way for Umako's niece, Suiko, as empress. So far so Soga, but as the seventh century progressed that family became over-mighty as well, made too many powerful enemies.

The Mononobe clan had been crushed, but the Nakatomi were still in the game, plotting revenge on the hated Soga. Most powerful among them was Nakatomi Kamatari. The last straw for him, the trigger for his move on the seat of power, was yet another murder. In 643 Soga Iruka, leader of the clan, dispatched the imperial prince Yamashiro Oe and began assuming the trappings of emperor for himself. It was in the aftermath of that killing that the secret meeting took place, between Nakatomi Kamatari and Nakano Oe, son of Empress Kogyoku. They met in the fragrant shade of a wisteria arbour, a flower beloved by Japanese people on account of its strength, and also its ethereal beauty:

> I left the image of wisteria blossoms
> Softly reflected in the pond
> Because it looked so fragile
> It could vanish only with the slightest touch.
> Nevertheless, the waves came and the image was no more.
>
> (Oshikochi no Mitsune, early-tenth-
> century poet of the Japanese court)

There, where the blossoms, tapering clusters of tiny flowers, hung in profusion from twisted tendons of vines to make a haze of colour that shivered in the breeze, they conspired to kill. They sent an assassin to the palace of Empress Kogyoku, where Iruka was in attendance, but at the last moment the would-be killer lost his nerve and the spear dropped from his hand. Nakano Oe was there too, watching, and knowing there was no turning back he took the weapon in his own hand and slew Iruka himself.

In accordance with the plan hatched beneath the wisteria, it was not Prince Nakano Oe who took the throne. There were factions at court, men anxious about their own status, and to allay their fears it was a lesser prince, Karu, who replaced Empress Kogyoku when she abdicated the day after the assassination. He took the name Kotoku and was emperor, but the real power lay always in the hands of the conspirators, Nakano Oe and Nakatomi Kamatari. In 668 Nakano Oe ascended the imperial throne in his own right, as Emperor Tenji, and embarked upon a series of reforms called Taika No Kaishin – the Great Reformation of the Taika Era. Kamatari fell ill and died the following year, but not before Tenji had bestowed upon him the honorific Fujiwara, which means 'the field of wisteria' and which remembered the moment when they had hatched their plans together.

The Fujiwara family – for that was the clan name ever after – retained power by having their daughters marry emperors. The children of those unions were emperors and empresses in their turn, and raised, according to Japanese tradition, by the mother's family. Status flowed downwards to the relatives in the manner of a champagne fountain.

Thus the influence of the Fujiwara clan, the reforms they enacted in the form of Taika No Kaishin, meant the Japanese emperor was more figurehead than real authority. Power lay with the Fujiwara clan, and since the family had always been the bedrock of Japanese society, loyalty to family grew stronger yet throughout the land. After the dominance of Fujiwara there was the Heian era, then the Kamakura. It was during

Kamakura times that there evolved the power of military leaders called *shogun*. Loyalty to family above kings or emperors set Japan on a unique path.

Like Britain, Japan was made a little bit different. Like Britain, she would always be different.

30.

CHARLES MARTEL HAMMERS
A MUSLIM HORDE

Just as a shark needs to keep swimming or drown, so the army of the Muslim Umayyad caliphate that invaded Europe in the early eighth century had to keep conquering or die. A millennium and more before the time when Muhammad's followers would insist theirs was a religion of peace, it was one made only of war and sustained by *ghanima*, the spoils of war. Others of their kind had swept and spread out of their Arabian homeland, pushing west with the Qur'an, the recitation, in their hearts and in their minds, deafening them to any and all. In the years since 632 Islam had been unstoppable: Egypt, Libya, Tunisia, Algeria, Morocco – all conquered. In 711 a Muslim force had crossed the Straits of Gibraltar and, on landing in Al-Andalus – the Iberian Peninsula – they burned their ships. Their leader, Tariq ibn Ziyad, had ordered the conflagration as a symbol of intent. 'We have not come here to return,' he told his followers. 'Either we conquer and establish ourselves here, or we perish.' The great rock would bear his name – Gibraltar is a corruption of Jabal Tariq, being the Mount of Tariq – and it was his intention to put beneath his boot all the lands of the world. The Umayyad caliphate said it was the 'viceroy' of Allah and in order to fulfil that destiny, as described in the Qur'an, all places must be made subject to Him.

Visigothic Spain was skewered first, and then they swept north into the space the Romans had known as Gaul. The devastation they wrought throughout was legendary, remembered ever after even in those gory times. By 725 they were in the shadow of the Vosges Mountains, on the border of the territory that would later be modern Germany. By 731 the Muslim warlord at the head of the conquering horde was Abd al-Rahman. He and they were somewhere north of the Pyrenees by then and that year welcomed the arrival of fresh warriors from North Africa. By the following year, when exactly a century had passed since the death of their prophet, Muhammad, they were in Aquitaine, and the capital, Bordeaux, was put to the torch in June. Odo the Great, the octogenarian Duke of Aquitaine, had history defending his territory from his European neighbours as well as from Muslim Moors, but in the aftermath of his loss before Rahman he and his men made their Hobson's choice and fled north to the kingdom of the Franks, ruled then by Charles Martel, in the hope of aid.

Rahman came on insatiable, thrilled by the thought of riches such as those he had been told bedecked the basilica of St Martin of Tours. He was arrogant, certain none could or would turn him aside. Ready for him was Charles the Hammer, raised to fight from boyhood as a Christian knight. He had come to dominance in Francia in 718 while another army of the Umayyad caliphate was breaking itself against the Wall of Theodosius, the immovable reef of defences surrounding Constantinople – and instead of waiting for Rahman he rode out to meet him on terrain of his choosing outside Tours.

The moment that matters was the clash on fields there of Christianity and Islam – a test to determine which would prevail in the west. Numbers for the opposing forces are hard to come by, misted now by centuries of legend-building. Suffice to say the Muslim army was the greater of the two, probably more than double that raised by Martel's Christians. Rahman's army was built around fast-moving, lightly armoured cavalry, well practised in fighting with lance and sword. Martel's force was dominated by infantry, heavily armoured iron men, and armed with javelins and axes for throwing, swords and knives for slicing.

According to the chroniclers there was a stand-off that lasted a week: two forces eyeing one another across a no-man's land and each unwilling to make the first move. Finally it was Rahman who unleashed his wrath, throwing his cavalry forward in the hope of sweeping his enemy from the field or harvesting them there like tall grass. As one Arab writer later had it, the two armies collided near the River Loire, and while those Muslim horsemen 'dashed fierce and frequent forward' they were galled by the stubborn stand of the Franks.

The *Mozarabic Chronicle* (also known as the *Chronicle of 754*), written in Spain by an unknown Christian (*Mozarab*) author and covering the years 610–754, reconstructed the battle from eyewitness accounts. Containing the first reference to Europeans – *europenses* – in a Latin text, it provides graphic images of the nature of the fighting: 'The men of the north stood as motionless as a wall, they were like a belt of ice frozen together, and not to be dissolved, as they slew the Arab with the sword. The Franks, vast of limb, and iron of hand, hewed on bravely in the thick of the fight.' The chronicle records the death in battle, at the hands of the Franks, of Rahman himself: 'it was they who found and cut down the Saracens' king'.

Unstoppable forces . . . immovable objects . . . time and time again in the centuries to come, one battle after another from one end of the continent to the other would test such opposing forces. At Tours in 732 it was stubborn resolve that counted most – iron-clad men-at-arms standing firm behind a wall made of their shields and bristling with long spears that split the bellies of horses and men alike. They fought until darkness came, and in the morning that followed the Franks awoke to find their foe had fled. Perhaps unmanned by the death of their leader they had abandoned the field. Charles Martel would fight them again and again before finally driving them south of the Pyrenees for ever. In that fire kindled by the striking, flint and steel, of Islam against Christianity, the kingdom of the Franks was made stronger. That year – 732 – had been the high-water mark of the rise of Islam on the European mainland.

In *The Decline and Fall of the Roman Empire*, Edward Gibbon would famously remark that Rahman's Muslims had covered a thousand miles from the Rock of Gibraltar to the banks of the Loire and that the same advance again would have taken them to Poland or to the Scottish Highlands:

> . . . the Rhine is not more impassable than the Nile or Euphrates, and the Arabian fleet might have sailed without a naval combat into the mouth of the Thames. Perhaps the interpretation of the Koran would now be taught in the schools of Oxford and her pulpits might demonstrate to a circumcised people the sanctity and truth of the revelation of Mahomet.

Gibbon did not and could not know that ideas are spread other than by the unsheathed blade or that by the twentieth century the Qur'an would indeed be taught in schools in Oxford, and throughout Britain and Europe besides, to circumcised and uncircumcised alike. To the patient and determined go the spoils.

31.

LINDISFARNE REAPS
THE WHIRLWIND OF THE VIKINGS

At the start of the second week of June in 793, the tide around Lindisfarne was at its highest just after daybreak. On the morning of the 8th, on the horizon towards the east and the rising sun, the square sails of ships were spotted in silhouette. That a little flotilla might be headed to the tidal islet and the Christian community there was hardly noteworthy. By the last decade of the eighth century the Benedictine monastery on Lindisfarne was well established, a light shining bright enough to be seen throughout Christendom. The Gospels named after the island – still regarded as some of the finest artworks of the Anglo-Saxon world – had likely been created in the scriptorium there by artist and scribe Bishop Eadfrith. People and pilgrims came from all over and new arrivals by sea would have been a commonplace.

A holy place then, a holy among holies, but in recent weeks an air of scandal had hung around the priory at Lindisfarne. In April the community had received for burial a nobleman named Sicga. He had taken his own life two months before and it was already scandalous that a known suicide should have been laid to rest in such a place. Add to that the fact Sicga had, five years earlier, murdered his own king, Aelfwald of Northumbria, and it is easy to imagine the gossip. Some had muttered darkly that Sicga's remains ought never to have been brought near Lindisfarne – that there would be hell to pay.

Likely the approach of the ships that June morning saw some of the community make their way down on to the beach, so as to receive the visitors. Once the ships, two or three perhaps, were close enough, those waiting may have noticed prows carved with dragon heads, circular shields hung over the gunwales. The Christian community amounted to perhaps thirty monks, as well as a handful of novices who had not yet taken holy orders. The islet was also home to a lay community of men, women and children. The precise details of what unfolded next cannot be known, because no one survived to tell the tale. The visitors were not pilgrims, neither were they traders. Instead the men that splashed ashore that day were Vikings, from Norway, and rather than a Christian God they worshipped their own – Odin, Thor and the rest of a blood-soaked pantheon. Maybe the butchery began on the beach so that the sand ran red. Those not murdered there or elsewhere were rounded up and carried off as slaves, to lives unimaginable. The church buildings were filled with finery – books bound with gold and jewels, altar pieces as grand, all manner of lovely things conveniently in one place and ready for loading aboard the ships.

In the terrible aftermath, word spread rapidly around the Christian world. That such people had been slaughtered, and in such a place, was bad enough. Worse by far was that the crime had been committed by heathens. All of it had befallen the community just weeks after the funeral of Sicga, regicide and suicide, and for many the murders and mayhem seemed like a punishment wrought by God himself. Alcuin of York, a celebrated churchman working by then in Aachen (in what is now the German territory of North Rhine-Westphalia) as tutor to the children of King Charlemagne of the Franks, was in no doubt as to why Lindisfarne had been made to suffer so much. 'Is this the beginning of greater suffering?' he asked. 'Or the outcome of the sins of those who live there? It has not happened by chance but is the sign of some great guilt.'

Time was slow to heal the wounds so that even by the time English historian Simeon of Durham came to write about the horror in the early twelfth century he was moved to describe it thus:

> They came to the church of Lindisfarne, laid everything waste with griev-ous plundering, trampled the holy places with polluted steps, dug up the altars and seized all the treasures of the holy church. They killed some of the brothers, took some away with them in fetters, many they drove out, naked and loaded with insults, some they drowned in the sea . . .

Christianity had come to Lindisfarne not from Rome, but from servants of the faith's Irish-Celtic variant. Columba had made Iona a holy island of the west, of the setting sun, at the end of the sixth century. Oswald, heir to the throne of Northumbria, had lived in exile there after the death in battle of his uncle King Edwin in 633. He converted to Christianity among the Gaels and when he returned to Northumbria two years later to claim his birthright he brought with him that other, older version of the faith. In time he invited a monk named Aidan to leave Iona behind and begin a new monastery on Lindisfarne in the east, of the rising sun.

After the Synod of Whitby in 664 it was Roman Catholicism that was established as the preferred way of worship and though some churchmen left Lindisfarne then, to lick their spiritual wounds back on Celtic Iona, Roman Christianity was in the ascendant. Lindisfarne's most famous leader was Bishop Cuthbert, and by the time of his death in 687 the place was fully in line with Rome.

Such a moment then – and such an entrance on to the world stage. No doubt those seaborne raiders of 793 did not know themselves as Vikings then, not yet. For the men of the north, the dead time between sowing the fields in the spring and harvesting them in autumn might be spent *a-Viking*, which is to say adventuring over sea in search of gain. *Viking* was not a noun, but a verb – not something one was, but rather something one did.

Having made their presence felt, they would return year after year. It was not just the British Isles that had to adapt to a world altered, but much of western Europe besides. The Muslim civilization of Spain would suffer their attentions too. From three countries they came: Norwegian Vikings would in the main head west, to Orkney and Shetland, to Iceland, Greenland and almost certainly North America; those of Denmark made lives miserable in the British Isles and in northern Europe; while the Swedes headed into the east, across the Baltic to fledgling Russia, the Middle East and perhaps as far as China. Vikings . . . Northmen . . . call them what you will. For the next four centuries at least they would write themselves indelibly into the story of the world.

32.

CHARLEMAGNE AND THE BIRTH
OF A HOLY ROMAN EMPIRE

On the day he was crowned emperor in the Basilica of St Peter by Pope Leo III, Charlemagne (Big Charlie, you might say) looked the part. His court biographer, a comparatively little Germanic chap called Einhard, was careful to record the physical characteristics of the man some historians credit with renewing the Roman empire in the west and thereby laying the foundations for the sort of politically unified Europe that has been pursued as a dream by others ever since. If you were going to call a man 'emperor' you would likely want him 'large and strong, and of lofty stature', as Einhard wrote, and with eyes 'large and animated'. It would be good to see that 'his gait was firm, his whole carriage manly' and to know that 'his health was excellent'. Less welcome perhaps would be the realization that his voice was light and high-pitched and not what might have been expected for a man of his size. That he favoured a bushy moustache is likely neither here nor there, a matter only of personal taste.

As to the moment in question, Einhard (who had joined a glittering firmament of learned men assembled by Charlemagne at his court at Aachen) described how

On the most holy day of the birth of our Lord [800 AD], the king went to mass at St. Peter's and as he knelt in prayer before the altar Pope Leo set a crown upon his head, while all the Roman populace cried aloud, 'Long life and victory to the mighty Charles, the great and pacific Emperor of the Romans, crowned of God!' After he had been thus acclaimed, the pope did homage to him, as had been the custom with the early rulers, and henceforth he dropped the title of Patrician and was called Emperor and Augustus . . .

Lost in time now is the truth as to whether it was all a spontaneous act by the Pope or, as seems altogether more likely, a stage-managed performance following careful preparations by the pair in the weeks and months before. Whatever the truth, it was nonetheless a moment in the story of the world.

If the son of Pepin the Short and grandson of that other Charles, Charles Martel, who had hammered Muhammad's outriders at Tours in 732, looked the part on that day, then the Europe that had borne him did not. West of the River Elbe was a brackish lagoon out of reach of the refreshing tide, a lost world beyond the edge of anything that passed then for civilization. By the time Charlemagne was crowned emperor in 800, a high point and glory for that king among Franks, the civilization of the Romans was a distant memory. The unnamed author of the *Chronicle of 754* had had 'European' as a label for those Christians that defied Islam, but as a breed of folk they were bedraggled. Their leaders might have thought themselves kings but in reality they were warmongers, or no more than warlords, elevated above those who sought their protection only by greater strength of will and greater cruelty when provoked.

Martel's Franks had driven Islam south of the Pyrenees but the infidels had not gone away – far from it. They were in Spain and prowling all about the Mediterranean Sea besides. The civilization that had given them life was orders of magnitude beyond the scope of anything European then. True enough the Umayyad caliphate was gone within a couple of decades of the reverse at Tours, cast out as heresy, but it had been replaced by that of the Abbasid. Under their rule great effort was made to translate into Arabic the wisdom of Ancient Greece, the works of Plato and Aristotle and all of those familiar to twenty-first-century eyes and ears. It was also a time, in the lands of that caliphate, of beautiful architecture and other physical expressions of the appreciation of life's finery. The Abbasid caliphate was a high point – in every way – that would never be, and has never been, repeated in the Islamic world.

If that shabby western Europe was harried in the south by cultured Islam, it was tormented too by Vikings in the north. All around its hindmost coastlines those Scandinavian pirates came raiding, harrowing. Vulnerable, undefended people cowered, disinclined to make plans beyond today. This was the roughened, coarsened world that Charlemagne inherited. He was a Frank, distilled from barbarian stock. His ancestors had settled in the north-east of the land that would be modern Belgium. Like so many other barbarians on the make, those forebears of his had been Roman *foederati*. When some of their sort made a home in Gaul they gave birth to a line of kings called Merovingian, named after Merovech, the first of them. His grandson was Clovis I, who extended the family territory and converted to Christianity around the turn of the sixth century. In the east their neighbours were Avars (those who had learned to better control their horses by the use of stirrups); in the west, Bretons and Gascons; in the south-east, Lombards. The Merovingians were usurped in the end by the father of Charles Martel, who in turn sired Pepin and Charlemagne.

First and always a man of war, Big Charlie spent a lifetime conquering lands and extending his demesne, swallowing Bavaria, Lombardy, Saxony and elsewhere. The cohesion he established could not and would not outlive him, fragmenting with the succession of his sons, but its ghost was remembered and would be summoned again when wanted. He loved swimming and chose Aachen for his court on account of the warm springs that burbled there. He valued education, and therefore men of learning. As well as Einhard, a layman, he gathered to him at his palace school at Aachen no less a figure than Alcuin, the cleric from York – among the most learned men of his own age or any other. Other churchmen of genius or other worth were drawn there too, and Charlemagne, who had learned to read only late in life, was among the most ardent students. According to Einhard he kept wax tablets by his bed upon which he practised his writing. Like the Abbasids out east, Charlemagne ordered the copying of as many ancient manuscripts as he could acquire. In the process of doing his bidding Alcuin and his scribes perfected the form of lettering known as Carolingian minuscule, still revered on account of how it made legible the learning of the past.

By the time of his elevation in Rome, Charlemagne ruled a diverse empire, creeds and colours that stretched from southern Scandinavia in the north to the Adriatic in the south. It was he who reconnected western Europe to the hitherto more cultured worlds to the south and east. He was on friendly terms with the Abbasid caliphate and in 802 received among other gifts from Caliph Haroun al-Rashid an elephant named Abul-Abbas.

Pope Leo had had sound reasons for making Charlemagne emperor, renewed emperor, in the west – political reasons as well as spiritual. Viewed from Rome, the empire in the east had been drifting into heresy then, denying that Jesus was as godly as God, and it mattered to secure the presence of a right-thinking, right-acting man in the west. By placing the crown on Charlemagne's head the Pope had been seen to have the upper hand, the fatherly hand. According to Einhard, his master thought it a mistake ever after. Charlemagne's empire did not outlive him but a Holy Roman Empire had been born, or reborn, and its foundations would be built upon ever after.

33.

THE TREATY OF VERDUN
AND DRAWING THE OUTLINES
OF FRANCE AND GERMANY

Charlemagne was buried in the cathedral at Aachen, close by the hot springs in which he had loved to bathe. His still-warm ghost would haunt Europe for a thousand years and more as men of will sought, when they dared, to recreate the empire he had made. Even the European Union might be regarded as its latest reincarnation. As is often the case, Charlemagne was followed on to his throne – his thrones, indeed – by lesser souls lacking the gravitational pull of personality required to maintain such an entity. The first of them was his youngest son, called Louis the Pious by some. Charlemagne had made plans to divide his holdings between his three legitimate sons (he also had multiple illegitimate offspring by many women who were not his wives), but by the time of his death in 814 only Louis remained alive and so he scooped the jackpot, together with the imperial title.

Louis's reign was fraught, riven with civil wars fomented by his own three avaricious and ambitious sons. His death in 840 was followed by yet more bloodshed between the brothers until the moment in 843 when a peace deal was brokered between them – called the Treaty of Verdun. Louis had named as his successor as emperor his eldest boy, Lothair, and by the terms of the treaty he was granted a rainbow ribbon of lands between the Rhine and Scheldt rivers centred on his grandfather's capital at Aachen and with the comely addition of the kingdom of Italy in the south. This then was the kingdom of Middle Francia, stretching from the Low Countries on the North Sea, over the mountains of the Alps and all the way to Rome in the south. It comprised the old core of Charlemagne's demesne, and by the addition of the Italian lands was supposed to amount to a grand possession. In reality it was a confection crafted only to give Lothair his due. From the outset it lacked any geographical integrity, far less anything much in the way of ethnic or linguistic bonds to unite its population. Without a gravity of its own its disparate elements were pulled in all directions. By its very existence it set in train years, centuries in fact, of covetousness on the part of those in possession of the neighbouring territories to the east and west.

To the east, and into the hands of Louis the German, went the kingdom of East Francia. Here was a population speaking either Germanic or Slavic languages, spread across part of the old Frankish heartland of Austrasia and also taking in the duchies of Alamannia, Bavaria, Saxony and Thuringia. The third tranche carved out by the treaty was the kingdom of West Francia, including Aquitaine, Gascony and Septimania, and granted to Charles the Bald, technically half-brother to the other two.

That Treaty of Verdun, pouring oil on waters troubled by warring brothers, is a moment that matters in the story because it set in train the destiny of much of western Europe until the present day – for West Francia was the land that would be France and East Francia the land that would be Germany. Middle Francia, lacking any natural reason to exist, would hold together only until 855 when it was split between Lothair's own sons and so would give generations of French and Germans reasons to resent one another, to grow bitter and to fight. After Middle Francia it was called Lotharingia for a while, in honour of Lothair's own son. Later still the sound of the name, another contentious ghost, survived in Lorraine, over which much blood would be spilt.

Under Charlemagne they had all of them – West, Middle and

East – been Franks together, united by an identity descending from an emperor worthy of the name. Without his presence they set about the business of forgetting, and so becoming strangers. The inadequacy of Charlemagne's heirs is apparent in the grasping ambition of too many of them. Spoiled by their inheritance and yet unable to live up to it, they fancied the titles and the finery too much. According to those who knew him, while Charlemagne saw the splendour of other men and wished he might echo the greatness that had been Rome, for himself he chose only and wore only the plain blue cloak of a Frankish man.

34.

ALFRED LAYS THE FOUNDATIONS
FOR AN ENGLAND

Together with thirty of his followers, Guthrum the Viking, a leader of men, approached a holy place called Aller, an island of dry ground standing proud of the morass of the Somerset marshes. They were received there by Alfred, King of Wessex, and his retinue, and escorted into a church that had been raised on the site by Saxons. Guthrum and his men were pagans, but that was about to change. The moment among moments saw Guthrum kneel before a circular font and allow himself to be baptized. Having been Guthrum all of his life, he was raised up from the water as Athelstan, Alfred's own adopted son, and a Christian king ever after. For the next twelve days those born-again Christians were hosted by Alfred at his royal estate at nearby Wedmore and afterwards departed Wessex for ever, them and all others like them, as they had promised.

Over 3,000 years into this story of the world and only in a handful of paragraphs have the British Isles merited so much as a mention. Constantine the Great was hailed emperor in York . . . Norwegian Vikings left the first of many bloody fingerprints on Lindisfarne (a light in the dark . . . the windblown seed of Christianity had reached as far). But to all intents and purposes the tale of the rise and fall of civilizations has unfolded with hardly a thought of the place that would, before the end, cast the longest shadow of all.

The Old World and the Classical world had had their effects throughout Europe from the beginning. Hunters who came after the last ice age. Then more ancient folk movements out of the east reached the archipelago as well, either bringing the technologies of farming and then metalworking or else bolstering home-grown efforts. There was a hint of the glory that was Rome, for four centuries or so. Always the flow was one-way, western Europe only taking and not giving, making no impact in the other direction.

Finally Charlemagne, emperor in the west, had felt the absence of greatness, and that glory, and reached out on Europe's behalf to rebuild bridges to the Mediterranean, all the way back to Rome and beyond. Before that, Charles Martel had halted the Muslim advance so that in Charlemagne's empire Christianity was challenged only by the stubborn regrowth of paganism, the hardy annual. For all that, the west had been a cultural backwater or at best an often reluctant sponge fit only for absorbing the ideas of others. With Charlemagne, and the Carolingians who followed him, there was something new at last – not a turning of the tide, not yet, but a whiff of change in the wind.

Having tried their hand at smash-and-grab raids for half a century and more, the Vikings laid plans for wholesale conquest and colonization – from Orkney in the north to the furthest south of Angle-land. In 865 the Mycel Hæþen Here arrived – the Great Heathen Army. Thousands of them, a coordinated effort out of Scandinavia, set about toppling the Anglo-Saxon kingdoms that had grown in fields left fallow by the departure of the Romans in the fifth century. By the time of the Great Heathen Army, these may have numbered four – Mercia, Northumbria, East Anglia and Wessex.

One by one they fell, but in Wessex there was an obstacle immovable at last in the face of what had been an unstoppable force. Aethelred was king there until his death in battle with the Vikings in 871. He was replaced on the throne by his younger brother Alfred, and at last that Angle-land, that England, had a hero unforgettable.

His biographer was Asser, a Welshman welcomed into Alfred's court. His *Life of King Alfred* describes a thoughtful man, persuaded of the value of education and devoted to improving the lives of his people through a mix of reading, writing and religion. 'But yet among the impediments of this present life, from infancy up to the present time, and, as I believe, even until his death,' wrote Asser, 'he continued to feel the same insatiable desire of knowledge, and still aspires after it.'

As a boy of four he was sent by his father to Rome, to be blessed by the Pope. As the youngest of five sons he might have been expected to take holy orders and live a life of religious devotion, but one by one his elder brothers died before him. A Viking army commanded by that Guthrum came close to knocking Alfred over as well. His nadir was in January 878 when a surprise attack sprung upon his fortress at Chippenham saw him chased into hiding in the marshes of Somerset, around Athelney, with just a few of his followers. He raised a new defence there in the wastes and sallied forth from time to time to wage guerrilla warfare. It was during those weeks and months that, according to the legend at least, he took shelter with a poor family. One day he sat by the fire and so the wife asked him to watch the bread cakes she had placed there to bake. Alfred grew distracted by his troubles and let them burn. That wife, not knowing him for her king, cuffed him around the head and had him help her make some more.

By May he was ready and rode out of Athelney to tackle Guthrum in pitched battle at a site recorded by Asser as Ethandun, now thought to be Edington, in Wiltshire. His foot soldiers formed a shield wall and advanced until they, in Asser's words, 'overthrew the pagans with great slaughter'.

Edington could not and did not remove the Viking threat but in hindsight it was the beginning of the end for Guthrum's ambitions. Alfred was a wily tactician and played the long game. He it was who established the *burhs* – a network of fortified towns dotted across the kingdom, each of them home to a body of fighting men that could quickly be summoned to face down any threat. He set about raising a navy so that the enemy, famous for its longships, might be tackled at sea as well if need be.

By such endeavour was Guthrum ultimately thwarted. After Edington, Guthrum had fled with his battered army, back to the fortress at Chippenham from which they had ousted Alfred months before. Alfred laid siege to them and after three weeks the Vikings were broken. Alfred had Guthrum promise he would convert to Christianity and then sign up to a treaty – the Treaty of Wedmore. By its terms the foreigners would remove themselves from Wessex. Alfred would have the southern and western half of the land while Guthrum would rule in the north and east – the so-called Danelaw, where Scandinavian law prevailed.

It would be during the reigns of Alfred's sons and heirs that the Vikings were finally brought to heel, but even by the time of his death in 899 the squatters had accepted they were under his thrall in all but name. Thanks to his diligence, the foundations of England – and so of Britain – were laid during his lifetime. By his commitment to learning, for himself and his subjects both, he elevated the character of the people. Christianity was secure, and the structure he applied to his kingdom – division into shires, hundreds and hides – was to last for a thousand years.

35.

CHARLES III OF FRANCE GIVES GROUND TO THE VIKINGS

By the first decade of the tenth century AD the kingdom of West Francia had been exhausted, both physically and financially, by the depredations of Scandinavians living then at the mouth of the River Seine. On the momentous day of 1 September 911 the leader of those Northmen – named Rollo, and so huge no horse could carry him (so that he was called 'the walker') – came to Saint-Clair-sur-Epte in north-central France, close by Paris itself. Waiting to receive him and his retinue was Charles the Simple, king of that West Francia. (In his day, the epithet 'simple' referred not to any lack of wit on his part but to his straight-forward ways of talking and behaving.) Rollo – which is the Latinized form of the Scandinavian *Hrolfr* – had come to make peace with Charles, to sign a document remembered as the Treaty of Saint-Clair-sur-Epte. Just as Guthrum had done for Alfred of Wessex, so Rollo had also agreed to be baptized a Christian. In return he would receive a huge tranche of West Francia stretching inland from the English Channel to the banks of the Seine. Charles had previously tried to fob off his tormen-tor by offering the gift of Flanders, but Rollo had declined on the (quite accurate) grounds that the land there was uncultivable. The territory he gained instead would become, in time, the Duchy of Normandy – literally 'the land of the Northmen' – some of the most fertile soil in all of France. He would also receive the king's own daughter, Gisela, as his bride.

The moment came, the moment within the moment, when the giant Rollo the Walker was expected to kneel and kiss the foot of his feudal master – after all, he would be holding territory as a generous grant from a king and visible gestures mattered. In return for receiving such largesse he would vow not just to stop raiding West Francia on his own account, but also to hold at bay any other Vikings who might arrive from the north and seek to do what he and his fellows had been in the habit of doing. Rollo looked down upon the lesser figure of Charles and, instead of kowtowing as required, glanced at one of his lieutenants and signalled he should do the honours instead. That lieutenant was a giant too (though not quite as big as Rollo, apparently) and accordingly he stepped towards the little king, bent and grabbed the monarch by the ankle and raised the royal foot to his lips. Charles the Simple, straight-talking, straightforward man or not, fell flat on his back.

The Viking raids on West Francia had not begun in Charles's reign but more than a lifetime earlier. Just as the Norwegians had made their presence felt in England at the end of the eighth century, so others of their kind had soon turned their attentions to mainland Europe. West Francia was easy prey, with rivers like the Seine and the Loire allowing their longships to penetrate many miles inland. Their raiding was relentless and everywhere. Paris itself was within easy reach. In 845 the Viking Reginherus – whose life may have inspired the legend of Ragnar Lothbrok – laid siege to the city and only withdrew when Charles the Bald, another Carolingian after Charlemagne, gave him 7,000 lb in gold and silver. By the 860s a monk called Ermentarius could write, from his monastery on the Atlantic-facing island of Noirmoutier:

The number of ships grows: the endless stream of Vikings never ceases to increase. Everywhere the Christians are victims of massacres, burnings, plunderings: the Vikings conquer all in their path, and no one resists them:

they seize Bordeaux, Perigeux, Limoges, Angouleme and Toulouse. Angers, Tours and Orleans are annihilated and an innumerable fleet sails up the Seine and the evil grows in the whole region. Rouen is laid waste, plundered and burnt: Paris, Beauvais and Meaux taken, Melun's strong fortress levelled to the ground, Chartres occupied, Evreux and Bayeux plundered, and every town besieged.

For ten years, until 898, Odo, Count of Paris, was king of the West Franks. Charles the Simple had been crowned king in 893 but his rule amounted to little until Odo, the choice of the nobility, died. Charles inherited a land tormented by Vikings. Another siege of Paris had ended in 886 and afterwards their leader, the aforementioned Rollo, had kept his men in the area so they could raid at will, capturing slaves and anything else of value. The protection money paid by Charles the Bald in 845 had been the first of many payments. Straight-thinking Charles the Simple knew such a tactic could only lead to ruin and when his nobles suggested buying off the pagans with land, he saw the sense. The condition that they convert made more sense yet, and Charles saw that by making them fellow Christians their raiding ways would have to be set aside – Christian, after all, must not harm Christian. For ever after those Vikings would be inside the tent and so pissing out.

Rollo was as good as his word, as were his descendants. As Charles and his nobles had foreseen, having given him a seat at the table they had also given him cause to protect what was now his. In so doing his territory of Normandy became a buffer zone, holding other Vikings at bay. After the Treaty of Saint-Clair-sur-Epte there are no more accounts of Viking violence via the Seine. More importantly in the long run – and here is why this moment matters, the moment of the upending of Charles while a Viking kissed his foot – those Northmen of Normandy became, in time, proper Franks and so proper Frenchmen. Rollo accepted the Carolingians as his superiors (because it suited him to do so) and as more Northmen arrived in his territory they duly adopted local ways, learned the local language.

A century after Rollo's death, the Duchy of Normandy was held by one of his descendants. Called William the Bastard by some, on account of his mother having not been married to his father, Robert I of Normandy, he came into his inheritance in 1035 and had to fight for a quarter of a century to secure his throne. William had his eyes on a bigger prize, and when, six years later, in 1066, he set about taking it for his own, his triumph would be the last laugh on behalf of every Viking before him that had contemplated the throne of England.

36.

IN THE CHURCH OF ST SOPHIA
THE MEN WHO ROW MAKE
THEIR CHOICE

They were Rus' from Kiev. They had been sent by Vladimir, leader of their kind – Vikings, we would say. Emperor Basil II, Basil the Bulgar Slayer, had entertained them first, in the Sacred Palace. The following day they were taken, those barbarians out of the wilderness, into the sacred, beating heart of Constantinople which was itself the beating heart of Byzantium. They were rough souls raised in hard places and now they walked beneath the dome of the Church of St Sophia, raised on the orders of the Roman emperor Justinian four and a half centuries before their time. There is no record kept of what they said there and then as they looked about them, poor souls. The central dome was so high above their heads it may have appeared to float in heaven. While they watched, the Patriarch, leader of the Christian Church in the east, led the congregation in worship, a full pontifical service. The air was heavy and heady with incense; choirs sang all around them and in the galleries above. There was gold everywhere, and jewels and holy vestments of finest silk. Perhaps those Rus' felt like ants crawling beneath the sky. Months later they stood before Vladimir, back in Kiev, and he saw that they were changed and asked them why.

'When a man has tasted something sweet,' their spokesman said, 'he does not want anything bitter.'

Intrigued, Vladimir asked him about the Church of St Sophia, what had gone on there.

'We knew not whether we were in heaven or earth,' came the reply. 'For on earth there is no such vision nor beauty, and we do not know how to describe it; we know only that there God dwells among men.'

Or so the oft-told story goes, at least. That first experience of the splendour of the Church of St Sophia by the Rus' (which was a name not of their own choosing but one applied to them by those who saw them come out of the Baltic in their longships, and meaning 'the men who row') is legend now. Their ancestors were Swedish Vikings who had rowed and sailed into the rivers that penetrate the Baltic's southern coastline, like the Volga and the Volkhov. The first capital they made then (around 860, while others of their sort were tormenting the west of the European continent and the British Isles) is Novgorod now. An account called the *Russian Primary Chronicle*, made by a monk named Nestor, has it that the locals had cried out for leadership, for strangers to come and set them on the right path. 'There was no law among them, but tribe against tribe,' he wrote. 'Discord then ensued among them, and they began to war one against another. They said to themselves, "Let us seek a prince who may rule over us and judge us according to the Law."' Emissaries made it as far as the homeland of the Rus' and according to Nestor said, 'Our land is great and rich but there is no order in it. Come to rule and reign over us.'

So far, so convenient, and apparently three Rus' brothers duly obliged and crossed the sea to the land of the Slavs to do for them what they could not do for themselves. They were Rurik, the eldest, who made a home for himself in Novgorod; Sineus, who founded Beloozero; and Truvor, who established Izborsk. Sineus and Truvor were soon dead and after them Rurik ruled alone, eventually moving his base of operations to the place that would be Kiev, on the Dnieper River. Whatever the truth of Nestor's account, by the end of the ninth century a population of Swedish Vikings held sway in the land of the Slavs to such an extent that the place was later named Russia in their honour. From their homeland they imported exotics like amber, swords of steel, walrus ivory, birds of prey, honey, beeswax and fur. They brought and bought and sold slaves too, but above all else they coveted and sought the silver of the Abbasid caliphate, which had overthrown that of the Umayyads, who had once pushed into Europe as far as Tours. While the Umayyads had had Damascus, in Syria, for their capital, the Abbasids preferred Baghdad, on the banks of the Tigris River in Iraq, in what had been Mesopotamia where civilization began (many moments ago now). The Abbasids were in the business of silver mining, in Afghanistan and elsewhere, and the Rus' would go to the ends of the earth in pursuit of it.

With longships suited to rivers as well as to the sea they pushed further and further south and east on voyages that brought them not only to Baghdad but Constantinople and God knows where else besides. The city founded as the capital of the Roman empire in the east was nearly five centuries old by the time the Rus' trembled amid its magnificence. Muslim warriors of the Umayyads had broken themselves upon its defences (the Wall of Theodosius) around the same time their brothers of the *umma* were being chased out of Frankish territory by Charles Martel.

In the latter years of the tenth century the Rus' were ruled by Vladimir and he had grown bored of the pagan ways of his ancestors. Accordingly he dispatched emissaries to find followers of the supposedly great faiths of the world. They would learn about their ways and, by a process of elimination, find a new religious path the Rus' might follow. The Jews duly told how they had been driven out of their homeland by their God and the Rus' were not impressed by their tale of never-ending woe. If God did not smile upon their ways, why should the Rus'? They were forbidden, after all, to eat pork (which was bad enough), but utterly abhorrent to those virile men was their talk of circumcision for their boy children. The Muslims subsequently told how they did likewise – no pigs and no foreskins – but worse by far, and the principal reason for the rejection by the Rus' of Islam, was the revelation that they took no alcohol.

And then they walked through the doors of the Church of St Sophia and found where God walked among men.

Legend is woven through all of it, of course. More modern research has suggested Vladimir may even have been raised a Christian before assuming the pagan ways of a Viking to please his fighting men. Christianity was all around the Slavic peoples like rising water by the tenth century, but it was the western Christianity of Rome. When Vladimir led his people on to the eastern path, the path of what we know as *Orthodox* Christianity, he set a destiny for the Russian people that prevails to this day. If the Viking ancestors had turned to Rome or to Judaism or to Islam, the story of the world would have been altogether different.

37.

GREAT ZIMBABWE AND
TRADE LINKS WITH CHINA

Some time around 1830, people speaking one of the many dialects of the Bantu family of languages established themselves on territory in the Central Plateau of southern Africa. They were the amaNdebele, similar in many ways to the people of the Zulu kingdom, to whom they were related. Like the Zulu, the amaNdebele were a fledgling nation – independent of spirit, proud of the fighting skills of their warriors and fiercely loyal to their king.

The territory into which they had pushed and settled was another heaven on earth (in the Bantu language *amaZulu* means 'the place where heaven is', so that the Zulus had already called themselves the people of heaven). Soil deep and rich, well watered and well drained; plentiful game; there was gold in the rivers, and copper as well. All in all it was a fine place to be and yet the amaNdebele encountered there, in such prime real estate, a resident population they found it easy to despise. They called them Mashona and found them lacking in all but the merest vestiges of an organized society. Surely such as they hardly deserved to live in such desirable territory? Unified by a language and little else, and with nothing of the kind of sophisticated social hierarchy the amaNdebele lived by, the Mashona quickly became near vassals of the incomers, or little more than prey to be pushed around and abused at will. That those Mashona were so reduced by the early decades of the nineteenth century meant that no one, neither the amaNdebele nor anyone else, gave any thought at all then to what their ancestors may have been like, what they might have accomplished long ago.

From around AD 200 there was established in the same territory a culture known to archaeologists as the Gokomere. It was the creation of people speaking an earlier variant of the Bantu tongue and they were farmers and pastoralists. The Gokomere were the ancestors of the Mashona and by around 500 they had established trading links with other groups all the way to the coast of the Indian Ocean. In time the contacts in the east were Muslim but there was Swahili (a word of Arabic origin and meaning 'of the coasts') as a common language. Via the coastal ports the Gokomere and their immediate descendants, the Shona, were plugged into a trade network that reached the Horn of Africa, the Arabian Peninsula and the Bay of Bengal in India. By 800 the Shona had gold to trade, and also copper and elephant ivory.

The moment of note in the story of the world came (for the sake of argument) around 1000. Some or other of the farmers – of the Gokomere, or the Shona – had paid attention, over the years, to the nature of the local granite outcrops. Under the extreme heat of the African sun and then the intense cold of night, the bedrock had split along fault lines, creating deep fissures. The altitude of the Central Plateau – well above 5,000 feet in places – had exacerbated the effect, and those observant farmers began adding heat of their own into the mix, in the form of fire, to accelerate the cracking. By experimentation they had learned how to split whole sheets of granite away from the bedrock. Armed with iron tools they could then work and shape the rock into regular blocks ideal for building. Some day at the dawn of the eleventh century work began (the laying of some cornerstone, as it were) on the construction of what would grow, during the four and a half centuries to come, into the greatest complex of stone buildings south of the Sahara Desert – the city of Great Zimbabwe.

The scale of the place suggests it may have been home to between 10,000 and 20,000 people. There were three distinct complexes spread across some 1,800 acres. Earliest of all was what is known to archaeologists now as the Hill Complex – stone walls around and upon the summit of the steepest hill in the area. Most famous of the three – what most people mean by 'Great Zimbabwe' – is the feature called the Great Enclosure. Work may have begun there around 1200, not long before Magna Carta, and continued for hundreds of years. The roughly circular wall, enclosing an interior more than 800 feet across, is many feet thick and more than 30 feet high. Inside is a second circular wall, and between the two a 33-foot-tall tapering circular tower thought to represent a giant grain store. Close by the Great Enclosure is the Valley Complex, the remains of many mud-brick buildings that may have been homes for the mass of the population. Aside from the houses, the construction technique at Great Zimbabwe is dry stone throughout and demonstrates great skill on the part of the masons. Excavation revealed a number of sculpted stone birds, each around a foot tall and interpreted as representations of eagles. These may once have sat atop pedestals within the Hill Complex.

Also found throughout Great Zimbabwe is evidence of a trade network across thousands of miles – pottery from China and Persia, silver coins from Arabia. Whichever Shona elite made its home in the city, between the thirteenth and fifteenth centuries, was evidently in control of trade up and down Africa's east coast. For reasons not yet properly understood, the place was abandoned during the fifteenth or early sixteenth century – perhaps prompted by population pressure, climate change that caused drought, or some other pressure on available resources.

Often described in older western literature as a lost city, the truth is that people living nearby were always aware of the place. There is some debate as to the origin of the name but a general consensus has it that 'Zimbabwe' is a reference, in some variant of the Bantu language, to stone houses.

A Portuguese explorer, Captain Vicente Pegado, described the ruins in 1531, the first European to do so:

> Among the gold mines of the inland plains between the Limpopo and Zambezi rivers there is a fortress built of stones of marvellous size, and there appears to be no mortar joining them . . . This edifice is almost surrounded by hills, upon which are others resembling it in the fashioning of stone and the absence of mortar, and one of them is a tower of more than 12 fathoms high. The natives of the country call these edifices Symbaoe, which according to their language signifies 'court'.

After Pegado, the next European to stumble upon the remains was a German-American hunter called Adam Render. Word of it all reached Englishman Cecil Rhodes at the very moment when he was plotting to assemble the territory he would eventually name Rhodesia, after himself. Rhodes dispatched to the site English archaeologist James Theodore Bent, who could not bring himself to accept that the city had been the work of black African people. Instead he focused his (and his employer's) attention upon a single wooden lintel he claimed had been crafted by Phoenicians (the same who built the First Temple for King Solomon). All too soon Bent and Rhodes and the rest of those with a stake in claiming southern Africa for their own were telling the world the city was a copy of the palace of the biblical Queen of Sheba. Far from being the work of the black man, Great Zimbabwe had been raised, they said, by wandering Jews, or Phoenicians, or Arabs. Any suggestion in public, far less acknowledgement, of the true genesis of Great Zimbabwe was outlawed on pain of personal ruin.

It was all a great falsehood, spun and perpetuated by white men determined to keep black men away from any claim on a land rich in gold and ripe for colonizing. Not content with denying them wealth, they denied them the achievements of their ancestors as well.

38.

MANZIKERT AND THE SLOW-BLEEDING OF THE BYZANTINE EMPIRE

The fighting was over. It had ended in a rout. For the first time the Byzantine army had been bested by a force deployed by heathens. An army of Seljuk Turks led by Sultan Muhammad bin Dawud Chaghri, known to his followers as Alp Arslan, the heroic lion, had driven the Byzantines from a field slick with Christian blood. As if defeat were not humiliation enough, the Byzantine emperor, Romanus IV Diogenes, had been captured and brought before the Turk.

'What would you do if I was brought before you as a prisoner?' asked Alp Arslan of his captive.

'Perhaps I would kill you, or else exhibit you in the streets of Constantinople,' replied Romanus.

'My punishment is far heavier,' said Alp Arslan. 'I forgive you, and set you free.'

Alp Arslan was right, and Romanus would surely have fared better had he remained among the Turks. Instead he returned to his own forces. Back in Constantinople he was deposed by a coup, blinded and exiled to die.

In slow motion, spread across decades and then centuries, Byzantium reeled in the aftermath of the defeat. By the standards of the day – 26 August 1071 – the losses on the field at Manzikert had been light. The senior commanders had lived to fight other days, indeed to intrigue against the emperor. What had been upended, though, like Charles the Simple by the Viking who kissed his foot at Saint-Clair-sur-Epte, was the long-held belief that the Byzantine soldiers would never be bested by those of Islam, that east could never beat west. The illusion of invincibility, once extinguished, would not be rekindled. Emperor Romanus had taken with him as his second-in-command Andronicus Ducas. In the confusion of the rout, Ducas declared the emperor had been killed and fled the field with men who might have made a difference. In the months of aftermath it was that same Ducas who conspired against his emperor. Some say he spoke out against the blinding but . . . *meh*.

Underlined above all else was the irresistible nature of the rise of the Seljuk Turks . . .

After millennia of irrelevance, by the start of the second millennium AD ideas and people out of western Europe were making their presence felt in the older, wider world. During the high days of Rome, Christianity had landed there like a windblown seed and taken root. When it might have withered away in the absence of imperial dominance, it survived in the nooks and crannies furthest west of all, on the Atlantic façade of the British archipelago, before creeping back. It was a stubborn plant, and its flourishing would affect the European world like no other, and so the wider world.

Charlemagne had remade the connection to the civilized worlds of the Mediterranean and the Near East, and people in the west began to care once more about what was happening in the lands of the rising sun. There, in the second millennium, four civilizations co-existed – Byzantium, China, India and Persia.

In China, the Ch'in of Qin Shi Huang had prevailed for just twenty years before they were succeeded first by the Han dynasty – from 206 BC to AD 9 – and then, after some years of uncertainty, by the Later Han for two more centuries. After the Later Han, and four centuries of disunity and the rule once more of independent kingdoms, a sense of cohesion had been re-established by the Sui dynasty between 581 and 618. Under them some of the great work of creating China's Grand Canal was set in train – by the end around 1,100 miles of waterways linking the Yangtze River valley with that of the Yellow River valley in the north. The Sui, short-lived by Chinese standards, were succeeded by the Tang. Their capital was at Chang'an, in the Shaanxi province in the centre of the country where the Silk Road ends, or begins. Chang'an means 'perpetual peace' and such sentiment was made manifest in the cosmopolitan nature of the place. Given its location the city drew travellers and merchants, vagrants and vagabonds, from Arabia, Central Asia and Persia. Tolerant of religions, the city made a home for Muslims, Nestorian Christians and Zoroastrians. The Tang dynasty was a cultural high-water mark, one of many to come, but by 907 they were gone, eventually replaced by the Later Liang dynasty.

The death throes of the Tang, the momentary loss of cohesion, provided opportunities for others, though, in other places. The Turks were a Central Asian people and during the sixth and seventh centuries they established and maintained what might reasonably be described as an empire spanning a great swathe of territory. Expansion and invasion by Arabs out of Arabia in the second half of the seventh century brought about the break-up of that empire, until the advent of the tenth century and the collapse of the Tang when all bets were off once more. Central Asia shrugged, like a bull pestered by flies, and the Oghuz Turks were among those jostled and displaced by movements elsewhere. The Turks had been pagans but among them were the Seljuk clan whose folk had run across and mingled with Arabs in Transoxiana. Impressed with and persuaded by Islamic ways some Oghuz, the Seljuks among them, went so far as to translate Persian and Arabic books into their own language. It was Muslim Seljuks, then, who crossed the Oxus River (roughly from present-day Uzbekistan and Tajikistan) towards and into lands that had been Byzantine and Christian. Then it was into Palestine and Syria, Asia Minor, and on to the battlefield of Manzikert.

Atlas had shrugged and people had moved, or toppled like dominoes so that one pushed against another. The Seljuk Turks had moved and had begun the conquest of Asia Minor, turning its people towards Islam. It was those Seljuks who called their leaders 'sultan', and the sultanate they built with Manzikert at its heart they called Rum, which was their version of Rome because they saw themselves as heirs apparent. Christ had been set aside and it was as a pistol shot that echoed around the world. The consequence of Manzikert, the loss there, was the call to set Christ back upon his throne. That call would roll and echo, and in time summon the Crusades.

39.

EMPEROR HENRY IV, POPE GREGORY VII AND THE WALK TO CANOSSA

On 28 January 1077, the gates of the Castle of Canossa were opened and Henry IV, Holy Roman Emperor, stepped inside. He had been waiting for three days and nights, barefoot and fasting, while all around him a blizzard blew. For the duration of his wait he had been wearing only a hair shirt, the traditional garb of the suffering penitent. Once inside he was brought before Pope Gregory VII and went down on his knees to beg forgiveness and ask that his excommunication be ended. When he was done, Gregory absolved him and welcomed him back into the Church. That night the two of them – and also Countess Matilda of Tuscany, whose castle it was – took communion together. There was a dinner then and, according to one chronicler, Henry took no food and spent the whole meal digging his fingernails into the table.

The ending of the so-called Walk to Canossa is regarded as one of the most memorable moments in the whole of the Middle Ages. Like other kings and emperors before him, Henry had assumed the right to choose bishops for his cities. The technical term was investiture, and by the time of Henry and Gregory, the right was hotly contested. Apart from anything else, it was a tradition and a practice that had underlined the dominance of Crown over Church.

Pope Gregory, whose given name was Hildebrand, was a zealous reformer determined that his office, received from God, should have and be seen to have the upper hand in the relationship between earthly and sacred power. The stage was set for drama, and one thing having led to another in a power struggle between two ruthlessly stubborn men, on 22 February 1076 Gregory excommunicated the Holy Roman Emperor, theoretically depriving him of his right to rule. Henry's friends abandoned him and his opponents sharpened their knives. A council of German princes decreed that if Henry did not win absolution from the Pope within the year, he would be deposed as emperor and a new candidate sought.

Europe was agog, and for a time it seemed likely Germany and Italy would go to war to settle the matter.

In December 1076, together with his wife and infant son and an entourage of fifty, Henry set out for Italy. The Pope was known to be at Canossa – and staying with Matilda of Tuscany, who had her own territorial troubles with Henry – and on 25 January the following year the emperor arrived outside the gates. By Gregory's own account, written soon after, the emperor appeared suitably chastened and in no mood for trouble:

> Once arrived, he presented himself at the gate of the castle, barefoot and clad only in wretched woollen garments, beseeching up with tears to grant him absolution and forgiveness. This he continued to do for three days until all those about us were moved to compassion at his plight . . . indeed, they marvelled at our hardness of heart . . .

As to what really happened inside the castle, historians have debated the possibilities ever since. Also discussed is whether Henry was ever as submissive as he had seemed. Some have argued that by so perfectly and wholeheartedly playing the part of the penitent, he left the Pope with no option but to absolve him. In any event, within three years the two were again at each other's throats. The fight over who should invest bishops would rumble on for centuries to come.

40.

WILLIAM THE CONQUEROR
AND DOMESDAY

In 1085 King William I of England did not have his troubles to seek. No change there, then. The man who had been known (still was known, by some) as William the Bastard had fought all his life for that to which he felt entitled. He was descended from Rollo, the Viking who had won Normandy from the French king Charles the Simple. He had been Duke of Normandy since 1035 and fought until 1060 to make himself secure there. In 1066 he had invaded England and defeated the Anglo-Saxon king Harold Godwinson. For most of his life he had had to fight to retain his throne there too. Around 1051 he had married Matilda of Flanders. She would be the love of his life and a source of his strength and determination as well as mother of his children.

Their eldest was Robert, nicknamed Curthose, which means 'short stockings'. He had been at his father's throat for years, seeking to replace him on the throne, and in 1085 he was at it again, egged on this time by King Philip of France. William's half-brother, Odo, Bishop of Bayeux, was urging the king's English and Norman subjects to rebel against him, and King Malcolm III of Scotland was prowling on the English border, ready to make trouble of his own for the English king. Worst of all, most dangerous of all, King Cnut of Denmark was on his way to England, together with Robert the Frisian, Count of Flanders, and a great army. All in all, quite a moment.

To add to his woes, William was old and ailing by then. His beloved wife and queen, Matilda, had died just two years before and his heart was adrift. Rollo had been a big man, and in his later years William was, not to put too fine a point on it, fat. Old, fat and broken-hearted . . . but he was still a fighter, and he ordered great swathes of the English coast laid waste so there would be no scavenging for food by any invaders from the Continent. He was in Normandy when he heard reports about Cnut being on the move, and he crossed to England to command from the front. With him he brought a vast army of his own, mercenaries in numbers so great the chroniclers were amazed: 'a larger force of mounted men and foot-soldiers than had ever come into this country'. William had always been and still was a skilful organizer and planner. So that he could ensure they were fed and watered, he had them quartered on various of his nobles' estates.

A moment of note then occurred, around Christmas that year, when William was holding court at Gloucester. According to the *Anglo-Saxon Chronicle* it was there that he 'had much thought and very deep discussion with his council about this country – how it was occupied, and with what sort of people'. In fact he was looking ahead with a view to paying for the war he thought must soon come. With that in mind, and finally to establish to the nearest penny how much the kingdom was worth, he

> sent his men all over England into every shire and had them find out how many hundred hides there were in the shire, or what land and cattle the king himself had in the country, or what dues he ought to have annually from the shire . . . Also how much land his Archbishops had, and his bishops and his abbots and his earls . . . there was no single hide nor yard of land . . . nor one ox or one cow or one pig left out . . .

The result of that moment in Gloucester was the Domesday Book – after Magna Carta, the most famous document in English history. Within just a hundred days the first draft, covering England south of the River

Tees, was completed. By August 1086, at Old Sarum in Wiltshire, William was poring over the survey's findings and planning ways to use the data as the basis for new taxes. William's commissioners and scribes called it a *descriptio* – a Survey of All England – but the common people knew it as Domesday. In *Domesday England*, Welsh historical geographer Sir Henry Clifford Darby described it as 'probably the most remarkable statistical document in the history of Europe. The continent has no document to compare with this detailed description covering so great a stretch of territory'.

Long before Darby's day, writing in the 1170s, Richard FitzNigel, treasurer to Henry II, commented that its attention to detail put them in mind of the Day of Judgement in the Book of Revelations:

> The natives call this book Domesdei, that is, the day of judgment . . . for just as no judgment of that final, severe and terrible trial can be evaded by any subterfuge, so when any controversy arises in the kingdom . . . its word cannot be denied . . .

41.

CATHEDRALS BUILT
AND SPIRITS RAISED

Mountains of stone were raised to exalt the Christian God from the fourth century onwards. Ground was broken for Etchmiadzin Cathedral in Armenia in 301; the Church of Divine Wisdom (the Hagia Sophia) was built in Constantinople between 532 and 537, and for a thousand years and more was the largest cathedral in the world; Charlemagne ordered the building of a cathedral at Aachen, where he liked to bathe in hot springs, in 796.

Such effort has been part of being human and alive for thousands of years and all over the world. The Carnac Stones in Brittany; Silbury Hill and stone circles throughout Britain; the ziggurats of Mesopotamia; pyramids in Egypt and Central and South America – all expressions of awe in the face of the invisible.

During the late eleventh and twelfth centuries in Europe, a continuation, an evolution, of that urge to raise stone towards the sky saw a veritable explosion of cathedral building. Just as it is foolish to try and think like a Neolithic builder, so there is little point in imagining precisely what moved the people who designed and then built the great structures that soon punctuated the story of the European landscape, spires rising behind hill after hill, beyond forest after forest.

A moment of note was the laying of the foundation stone of Durham

Cathedral in 1093. Frenchman William of St Calais had been made Bishop of Durham by William the Conqueror in 1080. Historian Simeon of Durham described him as 'very conscientious in matters divine and worldly business', and he also took on a major supervisory role in the Domesday survey. It seems likely it was his practical skills as an administrator that drew him to the king's attention. In any event, it was as bishop that he oversaw the design and the early years of the build at Durham, including the laying down of the first stones – cut, like the rest of the necessary blocks, from the cliffs alongside the River Wear and raised to the building site with winches.

Work continued at Durham for generations. All over Europe it was the same as populations sought to glorify their God in stone. It was in the fabric of the great cathedrals of those centuries that Gothic architecture achieved its finest flowering. As well as providing grand spaces, backdrops for ceremony and ritual, the artists and sculptors of the age were able to use the cathedrals as canvases upon which to tell the stories of the Bible in stone and coloured glass for the mostly illiterate general public.

But as English art historian Kenneth Clark observed, what mattered most in the story of the world was the impact such places surely had upon the hearts and minds of those living in their elegant shadows. 'Much of the year was spent in darkness, in very cramped conditions. What must have been the emotional impact of the inconceivable splendour, which overwhelmed them when they entered the great monasteries or cathedrals.' From modest, humble homes of timber and turf, wattle and daub, they came to stand before and walk inside structures that are edifying and awe-inspiring even now, in the secular twenty-first century. Not until manned flight and rockets to the moon would spirits be invited to soar as high.

42.

SALADIN, CRUSADING AND
THE MAKING OF AN ICON OF ISLAM

After the defeat of the Byzantines at Manzikert in 1071, the world was a different place. There for the first time east had beaten west, and the shockwaves rippled across time. The Seljuk Turks who inflicted the blow were late converts to Islam and so had the zeal of those making up for lost time. Where before Christians had generally enjoyed peaceful access to the Holy Land, in the years after Manzikert those Turks increasingly blocked the way. In the hope of reclaiming the territories there was a First Crusade between 1095 and 1099, ending in the bloody sacking of the Holy City of Jerusalem as well as the creation of the Principality of Antioch, the County of Edessa, the County of Tripoli and the Kingdom of Jerusalem – known as the Crusader states. A Second Crusade between 1147 and 1150 ended in defeat for the soldiers of the cross outside the walls of Damascus. Jerusalem remained the capital of a Christian kingdom but the Muslim tide was ever on the rise.

On 4 July 1187, at the Battle of Hattin, a Muslim force led by Salah ad-Din – Saladin, Sultan of Egypt and Syria – secured a spectacular victory over the armies of the Crusader states. Riding high on the wave of his success, he entered Jerusalem as conqueror just three months later, on 2 October, ending nearly ninety years of Christian dominance. The shock of those two triumphs for Islam triggered the Third Crusade. Three kings sallied forth unwisely from Europe – Philip II of France, the Holy Roman Emperor Frederick I 'Barbarossa' of Germany, and Richard I of England. By June 1191, Philip and Richard had joined the siege of the vital port of Acre that had been under way since 1189. Frederick was dead by then, drowned en route while crossing the Saleph River in Turkey, and relations between Philip and Richard had soured. The Siege of Acre lasted two years and was a misery of suffering and dying for all concerned.

Richard was among the thousands who fell ill, possibly from malaria, during his months outside the walls, and, according to the best of the accompanying stories, word of his plight reached the ear of Saladin himself. Apparently moved by the thought of the suffering of a fellow ruler, he dispatched one of his own physicians in the hope of bringing comfort. Islamic medicine was the finest in the world in the twelfth century, and as well as a doctor Saladin also saw to it that a box of snow was delivered to the English king, so that his fever might be soothed. Snow, in the Holy Land, in high summer . . . no mean feat in itself.

In *The Talisman*, one of Scottish author Sir Walter Scott's most popular novels, it is Saladin himself who travels in disguise to the English encampment so that he might minister to the king with his own hands. Introduced to the Christians as one Adonbec el Hakim, he is challenged on arrival at Richard's bedside by the Grand Master of the Knights Templar.

'Infidel, hast thou the courage to practise thine art upon the person of an anointed sovereign of the Christian host?' he asks.

Undaunted, el Hakim replies, 'The sun of Allah shines on the Nazarene as well as on the true believer, and His servant dare make no distinction betwixt them when called on to exercise the art of healing.'

El Hakim brews a potion, with the help of the eponymous talisman, and Richard is made well.

In the story of the world there are moments that ought to have happened, even if they didn't. The chivalric icon of the Islamic world risking his life to come to the aid of his foe is surely one.

Like the rest, the Third Crusade gave birth to much shameful horror. Having finally gained access to Acre, Richard eventually ordered the execution of 2,700 Muslim men, women and children who had been trapped inside. Inexcusable obscenity that it was, that butchery came four years after Saladin's slaughter of 200 Templar and Hospitaller knights taken as prisoners after Hattin. On 6 July 1187 he had had them beheaded by Sufis – holy men unused to wielding weapons of war. Swords in clumsy hands rose and fell as many as six or seven times on some necks, adding much unnecessary suffering. Militarily speaking it might have made sense to dispatch those foes rather than keep them as potentially dangerous prisoners, but the sickening brutality of their ending was unforgivable even by the blood-soaked standards of the day.

Despite the ugliness – or perhaps because of it – later Christian writers sought to make legends of Saladin and Richard both. In his *Divine Comedy*, Dante would install Saladin in Limbo, the softer, outer edge of Hell reserved for those who had not known the benefits of the teachings of Jesus and so were, like unbaptized infants, to be spared the real suffering of the damned. Saladin is there with worthy figures such as Homer and Horace, Socrates, Plato and Aristotle. (Muhammad himself is in the Eighth Circle of Hell, the worst but one, as punishment for having led souls away from Christ.)

The lionizing of the Lionheart is understandable, but the elevation of the infidel Saladin might be surprising. As the years passed so memory of and reference to his many undoubted cruelties were allowed to fall away, replaced by tales of kindness and honour. It was reported that during the Battle of Jaffa, in 1192, Richard had his horse shot out from under him. Since it was unseemly for a king to walk, Saladin is said to have had not one but two replacement mounts sent to his rival. In the centuries to come, Saladin was made an icon of chivalry, always and only just and good. In time it was a commonplace to believe he had been secretly knighted by a soldier of the cross, even that he sought and received baptism on his deathbed in 1193.

Perhaps the reinvention of Saladin was born out of the determination of writers in the Christian west to come to terms with the inexorable rise and success of Islam. How could it be that God had granted the victories of the First Crusade and yet overseen their undoing in subsequent adventures? After the Third came a Fourth – as ugly, or ugliest of all.

For many the explanation for the failure – the failures – seemed to be that Saladin must have been God's instrument, a scourge sent to punish Christians for their sins, for falling short of the ideal. Since Christian kings like Richard of England and Philip of France had fallen out with one another during the Third Crusade, Saladin's steadfastness at that time was aggrandized so as to turn a brighter light on their shortcomings.

Islam was here to stay and so there had to be a coming to terms. Saladin was made as a pearl, formed around otherwise irksome grit inside the oyster.

43.

MONGOLS GATHER TO MAKE TEMÜJIN THEIR PARAMOUNT LEADER

The Onon River rises on the eastern slopes of the Khentii Mountains in north-eastern Mongolia. From there the water flows more than 640 miles to the Pacific Ocean. The Onon is one of the ten longest rivers in the world and its reach is great.

On a day in 1206 all the nobles of the Mongol tribes gathered by the river there, at its source, for a great *quriltai* – a general assembly. Attendance at a *quriltai* was mandatory but the need to be by the Onon that day in 1206 was especially pressing. In a clearing a large white tent had been erected, so large its roof was held aloft by wooden pillars bedecked with gold. As well as Mongol oligarchs there were emissaries of foreign states, including a future emperor of China. The first business of that day provided the moment that matters – being the request by those nobles that one among them, the one they had gathered to honour, accept a title created specifically for him. He was Temüjin, son of a powerful family, and he said he would do as they wished on condition that every Mongol give him unquestioning obedience, do his every bidding and slaughter any and all if commanded by him to do so. Every one of those present agreed, and prostrated themselves before him. So be it then, said Temüjin, henceforth he would be their Genghis Khan, a title meaning 'hardest ruler', or perhaps 'the blacksmith who makes the strongest iron'.

Genghis Khan spent a decade bringing the disparate clans together as a nation. The speed of his achievements was breathtaking and by the time of his death in 1227 he ruled an empire four times larger than that of Alexander the Great and twice that of any Caesar. The shadow of his hand was over a territory that stretched from the Pacific Ocean, where the Onon had its estuary, to the shores of the Caspian Sea. All of it was an act of will, backed by simple military tactics carried out by disciplined, well-trained warriors led by generals of ability. Their cavalry were supreme; they had mastered siege warfare so that city defences were overcome when necessary. Soon it was by reputation that he conquered, having demonstrated a taste for brutality that terrified most populations into submission before an arrow was shot. When a city surrendered to him without resistance he let the inhabitants be, often doing no more than impose upon them a ruler of his own. Resist, and he was as likely to slaughter every soul. In 1218 he turned west, sending his generals along the silk roads, into Transoxiana and northern Iran. He built pyramids of the skulls of Persians before making his way 5,000 miles into Russian territory.

Over such a vast demesne, communication was vital, and Genghis Khan exploited a vast network of post-houses, positioned at careful intervals along the roads and trails, so that messages could be moved by men on horseback at a rate of 200 miles a day.

Mongol culture had been riven by loyalties to family and clan, and so too the blood feuds that accompany such systems. Genghis Khan eroded that ancient, traditional structure by moving and mixing people by the thousands and tens of thousands until he had spun a web in which all were caught, and made loyal only to his own family.

Even the death of Genghis Khan was the stuff of legend (the truth of it long since lost, along with the location of his grave). According to the *Secret History of the Mongols* – a text likely completed just a year after his death, its accuracy hotly debated – he sought out the daughter of a foreign king and took her for a concubine. As they lay down together the girl took a knife from within the folds of her clothing and castrated him.

His bodyguards heard his cry of pain but when they reached him he asked only that they take the girl away and let him sleep. The *Secret History* tells us he sleeps yet, like King Arthur, ready to return to his people when their need is greatest.

If he failed to take the king's daughter, she was one of very few who avoided his attentions. The most famous quote attributed to him has it that 'A man's greatest work is to break his enemies, to drive them before him, to take from them all the things that have been theirs, to hear the weeping of those who cherished them, to take their horses between his knees and to press in his arms the most desirable of their women'. He was an abuser of women and girls on a monstrous scale, of that there can be no doubt. Analysis of DNA collected from 2,000 men across Eurasia and published in 2003 suggested his genetic inheritance was scattered across the entire continent. He may have 16 million male descendants – one in every 200 men alive today.

However he died, wherever he died, he was succeeded by his third legitimate son, Ögedei. As his father would have wished, Ögedei completed the conquest of northern China before turning his attentions to the west once more, and to Europe. Albanians, Austrians, Croatians, Hungarians and Poles, all of them felt the wrath of and fell before Ögedei's Mongols. At the Battle of Legnica, on 9 April 1241, even the knights of the Teutonic Order, who had affected the outcome of war in eastern Europe for a century and more, were utterly routed. Those knights were among a combined army of Europeans thousands strong, with Poles and Moravians to the fore, and yet the tactics of the enemy were superior. By some accounts the victorious Mongols filled nine sacks with the right ears they cut from the fallen so they might properly count the dead.

China, India, the Near East, Europe – all felt the impact of the Mongols. Such was their influence across nine million square miles of territory, historians write about a veritable Pax Mongolica that facilitated (relatively) safe trade from Europe in the west to China in the east. By the time the Venetian Marco Polo was in the court of Kublai Khan – grandson of

Genghis Khan – China had demonstrated its power to absorb and change all comers. Kublai was the last with the gravity to hold the centre. With his death in 1294 the old Mongol empire was essentially no more. Unlike his nomadic predecessors he was a man of settled luxury. Like Chinese emperors before and after, he and all the khans considered themselves kings of all humanity. They worshipped Tengri, the sky god, who reigned over all and had the Mongols and their khans as his representatives on earth. When emissaries came from other states they were therefore received not as equals but as subjects bringing tribute.

The Mongol empire had risen like a sudden storm, without warning. Genghis was the heart of it. His mother was Hoelun, wife of Chiledu, a great warrior. According to the *Secret History*, rivals came to take her and, fearing for her husband's life if she resisted, she surrendered to them. Before leaving him she told Chiledu, 'If you but live, there will be maidens for you on every front. You can find another woman to be your bride, and you can call her Hoelun in place of me.' Finally she took off her blouse and threw it to him, saying, 'Take this with you so that you might hold it to your face and have my fragrance as you go.' Hoelun was given as wife to Yesugei, father of Temüjin.

The time of the Mongols was brief in the scheme of things, in the story of the world, but their scent has lingered, clinging everywhere it touched.

44.

KUPE, THE *KUAKA* AND THE LAND
OF THE LONG WHITE CLOUD

Humankind has been inspired by the birds for the longest time, and no wonder: flight is the dream and always has been. At Vedbaek, by Copenhagen in Denmark, archaeologists found a 7,000-year-old grave containing the remains of a woman and a baby. It has been assumed they died together, in childbirth. The infant had been set down on the wing of a swan. It seems at least reasonable to imagine those left behind and grieving, hunters all, were aware of the annual flights of migratory birds, that leave and then return. Maybe they hoped that like the swans, their lost loved ones would come back when the time was right.

Surely, like the rest of humanity, those ancient hunters also envied the gift of flight and wished that they too could soar in the blue. From then, before then and until now, people have craned their necks and watched the birds. All in good time the species *Homo sapiens* would find their way into the sky, and into space, with the help of magnificent flying machines. Long before that happened they were moved to follow in the wake of birds, over land and sea.

Some time around the middle of the thirteenth century there came a moment when the watching of birds sparked a voyage of discovery. Just as the north Atlantic was explored in the middle part of the Middle Ages by brave men in boats – those Vikings – so the investigation of the southern vastness of the Pacific Ocean was pioneered by inhabitants of the Polynesian islands. In the main, the Pacific was colonized by people expert in the use of double-hulled canoes and sailing south-west, out of Polynesia. By paying acute attention to wave forms and currents, by noting and navigating by the position of lights in the sky, by imagining the Earth was fixed and that the sky moved above them, those mariners sewed together the infinitesimal dots of islands scattered like fallen leaves across the thousands of square miles of blue. The most notable exception was the voyage embarked upon by a man remembered as Kupe. The truth of him is lost to storytelling and legend. So important is he to so many different groups, a dizzying range of versions of his story have been fixed in the memory and handed down to the present.

His moment was one of realization, a pinpoint of light sparking in darkness. For the sake of argument the moment of illumination came on a day in the year 1250. Even the name of the island that was home to him has been blurred by myth-making, so that it is remembered as Hawaiki – as unknown now and legendary as any Avalon. It seems certain it was in north-east Polynesia. On that day, in that moment, Kupe's attention was caught by the flight of birds – a flock of hundreds, thousands of godwits, a species his people knew as *kuaka*. They came every year, always from the north-east and always heading south-west.

To Kupe and his people the *kuaka* were a mystery, for they were never seen to land.

'Kua kite te koanga kuaka?' they asked one another – Who has seen the nest of the kuaka?

'Ko wai ka kite I te hua o te kuaka?' – Who has ever held the egg of the kuaka?

Those they saw every year were hardly strays, lost in the emptiness; rather they were so numerous they reminded Kupe of the chips of wood that flew in profusion from the adzes wielded by those hollowing the hulls of the dug-out canoes.

In the moment of note, it occurred to Kupe that birds so determined, so focused and so many must be making for land – land as yet unknown to him and his folk. In the vastness of the Pacific, land was a priceless resource. They grew kumara (sweet potato), yams and taro and were ever on the look-out for new soil for cultivating. Kupe's moment of revelation inspired him to undertake the voyage that would put a human foot on the last landmass to be colonized by the species. Together with his wife Kuramarotini and others faithful to him, Kupe set sail aboard his great double-hulled canoe *Matahorua*. The voyage would have required sailing south-west, leaving behind the familiar tropical easterly trade winds and finding their way across an area of unpredictable and un-familiar currents and winds. Soon enough they might have encountered strong headwinds out of the west and tempestuous, cold seas. Towards the end of spring, however – the time of the *kuaka* – those same latitudes are often sat upon by a zone of high pressure that brings warm winds out of the east. Such conditions – to which Kupe had been alerted by the annual migration of the *kuaka*, from their breeding grounds in Siberia to warmer climes in the south – would have made a journey into the south-west relatively peaceful.

By such means did Kupe and his fellows find their way across Te Moana Nui a Kiwa – the Pacific Ocean – to the islands that, according to the legend, Kuramarotini named Aotearoa – the land of the long white cloud . . . New Zealand. It seems most likely they struck North Island first, and knew it as Te Ika-a-Māui – the great fish of Maui.

That the exploratory journey that carried humankind to the last land-mass they would settle was led by birds seems perfectly reasonable. Kupe, or someone like him, was of ancient stock. They lived by looking, by see-ing what mattered, by hunting the things they needed. By watching birds, reading their flight and drawing the right conclusions, he completed the settlement of the world.

45.

A DIVINE WIND CONVINCES
THE JAPANESE NONE MIGHT BEAT THEM

Once Kublai Khan had bettered the soldiers of the Song dynasty and become the first emperor of the Yuan – Mongol – dynasty, much of China and Korea were beneath the shadow of his hand, along with Mongolia. More of his kind, other Mongol leaders to whom he was related by blood or marriage, held sway across an empire stretching from modern-day Hungary to Siberia's Pacific coast. (Timur the Lame, who came after him and them, was cut from the same cloth. The last of the great Mongol khans, he would bring an Ottoman sultan to battle and destroy him after hearing the other boast that he was the greatest in the world. Mongol khans were, above all, arrogant and proud, driven to dominate any and all.)

In 1281 Kublai dispatched 140,000 soldiers aboard a fleet of more than 4,000 warships to invade and conquer the islands of Japan. Since the time of the Fujiwara, Japan had evolved as a place of rival families, rival clans. There was a shogun, the strongest military leader to whom they notionally deferred, but always the other clans circled and fought among themselves, sharks around a bigger shark. There was an emperor in a palace but his was a hollow crown. Either he agreed with the shogun and was left in peace, or he disagreed and was overruled. It was a fractious state, a managed anarchy, and in the face of a determined threat from without, on the scale of that unleashed by Kublai Khan, distinctly vulnerable.

The shogun and the clans had known what was coming, and why. Long before sending his armada, Kublai had dispatched emissaries to demand the Japanese emperor travel to his capital at Dadu (now Beijing) and there kowtow to him. To kowtow was to *k'o t'ou* – to kneel and literally 'bump the head' on the floor in obeisance. The Japanese emperor might have been little more than a sock puppet, but he was the shogun's sock puppet and no one else's. The khan's men were beheaded and the shogun, the clans and their samurai – their knights in armour – hunkered down and prepared for war. Kyushu Island was closest to Korea, the likely point of departure for Chinese warships, and so the Japanese built a great wall across Hakata Bay, facing the Tsushima Strait and the threat.

It was in the spring of that year that word reached the shogun of the imminent arrival of the Chinese fleet. First to arrive were ships full of conscripts from Korea – recently conquered by Kublai and harbouring little affection for him. Unable to breach the defensive wall, they anchored off the coast and so were sitting ducks for night-time raids by samurai who rowed out under cover of dark and set the ships ablaze. It was nearly two months of stalemate before the main body of the armada arrived. Now the defenders were hopelessly outnumbered and facing almost certain defeat – when there came the moment worth noting. It was 15 August, and while the samurai waited, swords in hands, and while the khan's warriors edged closer to land, the sky darkened. All eyes looked west as the sea reared up beneath the massed ships, and a terrible wind began to blow.

Three centuries before a great storm would break a Spanish armada and save England from invasion, a typhoon had come to save Japan. All but a handful of Kublai's warships were sent to the bottom of the Tsushima Strait. Some hundreds of sailors and soldiers, at most a few thousand, made it ashore and were hunted down by the samurai and slaughtered to a man.

If all of that was not miracle enough, what broke Kublai's heart was the fact it was happening to him for the second time. In 1266, while he was still about the business of breaking the Song dynasty, Kublai had first turned his attention to the islands of Japan. Emissaries were dispatched then as well, to tell the emperor there that he was required to submit to his neighbour and send tribute. They returned empty-handed. During the following five years he sent five more parties of messengers but each time the shogun had their boats turned back before they could make landfall. By 1271 his conquest of China was complete and so Japan would have his full attention. For three years he had his shipwrights at work building a great fleet of hundreds of warships.

In 1274 an armada of perhaps 900 ships dropped anchor in Hakata Bay. There was no wall then and the fighting men made it ashore in their thousands. The Japanese warrior code of *bushido* commanded every samurai to face his foe in single combat. But as each stepped out in turn, the Mongol warriors paid no heed to etiquette and fell on the lone warriors en masse, as wolves around a stag. The invaders were well trained and disciplined, moving as coordinated units in practised set-pieces. The samurai, for all their bravado and undoubted bravery, were no match. But as night fell on the fighting, a wind rose and rain began to fall. Back aboard the fleet, the seamen looked about them and knew. In the hope of safety, they headed out to sea and deeper waters but there was no sanctuary to be had. All through the night and the day that followed a typhoon punished them like a vengeful god. When it was over, as much as a third of the fleet was on the seabed and thousands of men were lost. Their hearts broken, the rest limped home to tell their khan what had befallen them.

When it happened again seven years later, the Japanese said they had been saved by *kamikaze* – divine winds. Kublai Khan apparently agreed, for he sent no more warships. For Japan it was a defining moment, of the sort that only seeming miracles can make happen. If their prideful self-belief had had them think they were invincible before, the coming to their aid in time of need of not one but two *kamikaze* was as a hook that pierced the national psyche and held fast. Even as the might of the United States of America and the rest of the Allied forces was brought to bear upon them in the Second World War, still the Japanese believed a divine wind would save them.

46.

DANTE'S *DIVINE COMEDY*

In Europe, and for hundreds of years, the work of educating men (and it was mostly men who were educated) was done by the Church. Universities were established throughout the continent from the end of the eleventh century – Bologna in Italy and Oxford in England being the first of them – and then appeared in city after city – in Salamanca, in Spain; in Cambridge, in England; in Padua, in Italy; in Coimbra, in Portugal – during the four centuries to come. The Christian religion remained central, ghosting in the background of every subject, a guiding force, so that the faith directed learning while being canalized and disciplined in return. (In seeking to ensure and maintain the primacy of God they inadvertently began the work of honing men's minds and so made of them axes sharp enough, in the end, to cut down the old-growth forest blocking the sunlight of reason – and at such cost! But those days were yet to come.)

Ancient learning from the Classical world came to Europe via Islam, countless works having been translated for use by the scholars of that other faith. The University of Bologna was founded in 1088 but centres of learning in the Islamic world were already old by then. Al-Quaraouiyine, in Morocco, was founded in 859; Al-Azhar, in Cairo, in 970. There were others besides. That the works of Aristotle, Euclid and the rest (Chinese and Indian thinkers included) reached Europe in the Middle Ages was down to the efforts of Islamic scholars who revered them first. On arrival in the west that ancient learning was absorbed by Christian universities ('appropriated' might be the more apposite word) until it could be passed off as their ancestor: the Greek thinkers were the fathers, the scholars of Christian Europe their true sons.

If they thought highly of the likes of Aristotle, it was an educated man of the Roman world those Christians came to worship almost as one of their own. That was the first-century BC poet Virgil. His *Eclogues* (also called the *Bucolics*, since they were principally concerned with the lives and times of shepherds), *Georgics* and *Aeneid* are still among the most famous in all of Latin literature.

Virgil's Eclogue 4 is different, and significantly so. It tells the story of a boy child whose coming signals the start of a golden age on earth, a world from which fear itself is banished:

> . . . and the majestic roll
> Of circling centuries begins anew:
> Justice returns . . .
> With a new breed of men sent down from heaven.
> Only do thou, at the boy's birth in whom
> The iron shall cease, the golden age arise,
> Befriend him . . .
> Under thy guidance, what tracks remain
> Of our old wickedness, once done away,
> Shall free the earth from never-ceasing fear.
> He shall receive the life of gods, and see
> Heroes with gods commingling, and himself
> Be seen of them, and with his father's worth
> Reign over a world at peace.

For this work if no other, Virgil was seen by European Christians as nothing less than a prophet. He lived and died before the time of Jesus Christ and yet he was (is?) regarded as having prophesied His coming. A boy . . . a golden age and an end to fear . . . a boy who will receive the life of gods and reign over a world of peace . . . Those scholars seeking to close the gap between the Classical world and their own saw in Virgil the perfect bridge. He lived and died as a pagan but like an Old Testament Isaiah he had apparently felt the warmth of a sun not yet risen but burning beyond the horizon.

The moment that matters in this context came in 1320 when Italian poet, writer and philosopher Dante Alighieri completed his *Divina Commedia*. A Florentine by birth (in 1265), he had been exiled from the city in 1301 after finding himself on the wrong side of a tortured dispute between political factions – namely Guelphs and Ghibellines – supporting either the Pope or the Holy Roman Emperor. It was during his resultant exile that he wrote, among other poems, the *Divine Comedy*. Initially highly regarded, it eventually fell from grace until the time of the Romantics, beginning around 1800. Rehabilitated, it might be regarded as the great-est literary masterpiece of the Middle Ages. It is certainly a cornerstone of Italian literature. Dante was aware of the need to create a unified Italian language from among the dialects spoken in his time and by com-posing his *Comedy* in *his* Italian, being the spoken tongue he himself preferred and understood best, he achieved that aim at least.

The moment of completion, in 1320, was a long time coming. He had begun the work in 1308, creating the first of what would be more than 14,000 lines of verse, divided into a hundred cantos (a division of a long poem). Written in the first person, it opens with Dante lost in a wood. It is the night before Good Friday and he is thirty-five years old (half the biblical allocation of three score and ten). The whole adventure will last until the Wednesday after Easter, in the year 1300, and those days will see a journey through Hell, Purgatory and Paradise. Since the real-life Dante was in exile, his feelings of being lost and far from home are only fitting. He begins:

> His glory, by whose might all things are moved,
> Pierces the universe, and in one part
> Sheds more resplendence, elsewhere less . . .

Dante is not alone on his odyssey. Beatrice, an embodiment of perfect love, the ideal woman, will see him through Paradise – but his guide through Hell and Purgatory is Virgil. By the end of the way, by the completion of the last lines –

> Power, here, failed the deep imagining,
> But already my desire and will were rolled, like a wheel, that is turned equally
> By the love that moves the Sun and the other stars.

– he has created something without equal.

W. B. Yeats called Dante 'the chief imagination of Christendom'. By his genius, he wedded the Classical world to that of Christendom. It was a marriage that would last.

47.

THE GOLDEN HORDE
AND BLACK DEATH IN EUROPE

In the autumn of 1346 the army of the Mongol khanate, the Golden Horde, led by Jani Beg, was besieging a Genoese port called Kaffa, in the Crimea, on the Black Sea. They were Muslims, and since the traders beyond the walls were Christian there was no end of bad feeling. Those Mongols were recent converts to Islam but it was those Christians that monopolized trade in the region. There was an important slave market and business was good for all, regardless of faith. Religious strife was a running sore, though, and the most recent round of trouble had first flared two years before. Jani Beg's men had laid siege then too, but Kaffa was well defended and, being a port, easily supplied by sea. The Mongols backed off, but a couple of years later they were back, armed with siege engines.

Sieges are hard to maintain at the best of times, soldiers tending to boredom and thoughts of home and likely to slip away, like grains of sand through a commander's cupped hands. During that autumn of 1346, however, there was an outbreak of plague among the besieging force. Men fell like cropped grass, with painful lumps – buboes – in groin, armpit or on either side of the neck. Black marks appeared on their faces and bodies. They had terrible fevers and vomited, or coughed up blood. Within three to five days, most victims were dead. The Mongols had seen the symptoms before, but beyond the walls the Genoese were less familiar with its signs. Determined that those Christians should share the horror, the attackers loaded the corpses of their dead into their siege catapults and flung them over the walls into the city. It may have been one of the earliest uses of biological warfare in the story of the world. In any event it must have been quite a moment when the first of the human missiles landed, splitting on impact. For hours the bloated and rotting bodies of the dead rained down. The inhabitants of Kaffa did what they could, gathering the dread windfalls and dumping them into the sea. But by then it was too late, and the Black Death had come to Kaffa.

The siege was lifted the following year but the die was cast. Ships had already sailed, and months ago . . . to Constantinople, to the west coast of Anatolia, to the Mediterranean Sea and to Europe.

The Black Death – also remembered as the Great Mortality, or the Bubonic Plague, or just the Plague – came to humans via fleas on black rats. Unlike brown rats, their black brethren like living close to people. They are also happy aboard ship. The fleas of the black rat carry the bacterium *Yersinia pestis* and it is this that makes people so very ill. Archaeologists have found *Yersinia pestis* in the DNA of skeletons of eastern European people who died in the early centuries of the third millennium BC. When those nomads moved into the west, following their herds of cattle, they likely brought with them a form of the Black Death. Great changes to populations then – an ancient winnowing that reached as far as the British Isles at that time – may indicate how long our species has been under threat, from time to time, from blood in fleas on black rats.

Between 1346 and 1353 around a third of the entire population of Europe died of the Black Death – tens of millions of people. Britain may have lost as much as 40 per cent of its inhabitants during those years alone. Some experts, including Norwegian historian Ole Jørgen Benedictow, have suggested the death toll across Europe might have been as high as 60 per cent.

The Plague would come again and again for centuries, but the pandemic of 1346–53 was an event that altered the course of the story of the world like nothing before or since. War and trade alike were put on hold, whole swathes of farmland left unsown. Most people accepted it had all been a divine judgement, punishment of sins, but for those who survived there were beneficial changes too. The power of landowners was diminished for want of people to work the land. Wages rose, for those working the land and for craftspeople in the towns. Some historians have traced the kindling of the Renaissance to the aftermath of all the dying. As it turns out, nothing – not even blood-red war – has as much power as a pandemic to change the face of the world.

48.

THE PEASANTS' REVOLT AND MORE
THWARTED DREAMS OF UTOPIA

Dotted like diamonds through the stuff and story of the first and largest popular uprising in English history are all manner of memorable moments. So mythologized has it all been, so important has it seemed for those in search of the roots of socialism and Marxism and a dozen other *isms* besides, it is also hard to know where the facts of the matter end and the ideological fantasies take over.

Often recounted, just as a for-instance, is the dance around a bonfire in Cambridge by an old woman called Margery Starr. As the rising flames consumed charters, letters patent and privileges, as well as the archive of the university – all possible records of who had ever owned what and whom – old Margery whirled and twirled among the flying ashes and scintillating sparks shouting, 'Away with all the learning of clerks! Away with it!'

It is a potent image, and one of many recalling, or seeming to recall, days when thousands upon thousands of poor people saw a chance to throw off the shackles of their poverty, their serfdom, and to stand proud, as men and women, the equals of lords and ladies (at least in their own eyes but also, surely, in the eyes of God).

For the purposes of this story of the world, however, the moment that lingers is when John Ball (a radical priest excommunicated in 1366, or thereabouts, for sermonizing about the need for a classless society) appeared before a gathering of thousands at Blackheath, outside London, on 7 June 1381. He was not just an excommunicant but also, most recently at that time, a prisoner languishing at His Majesty's convenience. Since 1376, at least, he had been in and out of the clink on account of his persistent troublemaking and rabble-rousing. Some Kentishmen had freed him from Maidstone prison and he had accompanied them thereafter to the aforementioned Blackheath and his moment in the sun. He was known to many of those gathered, and when they saw him they cheered. He began to speak, and told them many things. It was reported, or at least alleged, that he incited those listening to set about the killing of lords and ladies and other nobs. In the moment that seems to have about it all the stuff of historical significance, he asked his audience, 'When Adam delved and Eve span, who was, then, the gentleman?'

Well versed in scripture (more so than we), those listening knew what he meant. In the Garden of Eden, God had created a man and then a woman. He had not created lords and peasants. The notion that some should have while some had not was the creation of men alone and, according to Ball's way of thinking, utterly and damnably wrong.

It was also the time of the Hundred Years' War, started by King Edward III in pursuance of his claims in France and by 1381 still burning in the reign of his son and successor Richard II, a lad of fourteen years. Wars cost absurd amounts of money and the people of England were being made to foot the bill via a newly created poll tax. It was charged at a standard rate of a few pennies, then a shilling – chump change to a rich man but a last straw to break a poor man's back. There were all sorts of other grievances besides. It was just thirty-odd years since the worst of the Black Death. Almost half the population had died and those left alive, the poor at least, had had the temerity to think their relative scarcity might make them more valuable. They had hoped for better wages, and those hopes had been met for a while. But by 1381 the landowners and other employers had fought back, and laws passed to force pay back down again had led to furious anger. By the time the likes of John Ball were shouting the odds, England was a tinderbox of unexploded hurt and rage.

During some of that summer, that unforgettable summer, uncountable thousands of men and women marched on London. Modern historians have sought to make it a revolt not just by peasants but by the middling class as well (as though there were *Guardian* readers in the fourteenth century), sensitive to the needs of the poor, but who really knows, now?

Kentishman Wat Tyler emerged as leader and spokesman. Officers of state were butchered. Important buildings were burned to smoking rubble so as to destroy records of servitude. The boy king met the rebels at Mile End on the 14th of the month and made promises about free trade and ending serfdom and forced labour – promises he had no intention of keeping.

The Tower of London surrendered to the rebels and England's chancellor and treasurer, figureheads of the hated poll tax, were parted from their heads. On the 15th little Richard met the rebels again, at Smithfield. There was fighting, and Tyler was cut down and killed by the king's men. That was the end of it in London but outside the bubble there was more trouble. It was all over within a month of starting, however, and in the end it had achieved next to nothing. There would be no more poll tax (not until the time of Prime Minister Margaret Thatcher, at least), but any dreams of a socialist utopia had been scotched in the egg. It was ever thus.

49.

JOHANNES GUTENBERG
ASKS JOHANN FUST FOR A LOAN

The intellectual achievements of the Classical world had been recovered and returned to the west by Islamic scholars. Euclid's geometry, revealed in his *Elements*, was the foundation for maths teaching until the start of the twentieth century and came to Latin via Arabic. The work of Ptolemy came west via Arab scholars too; the Greek astrolabe that enabled navigation was rediscovered first by Arabs; familiar numbers and the decimal point, Indian in origin, came via the Islamic world, along with the medicine of the Greeks Aristotle, Galen and Hippocrates. Historians would call the reconnection to the Classical world a 'renaissance' but it might also be described as a revivifying, as of dry soil by irrigation.

Whether in Arabic or in Latin, all of the impact of the knowledge depended upon the circulation of information to as many fertile minds as possible, and in the middle of the fifteenth century an innovation by a sometime goldsmith in Mainz, in Germany, made all the difference.

Little is known of the early life and career of Johannes Gensfleisch Gutenberg. He was born around 1400, the son of a patrician of Mainz, and between 1430 and 1444 he was likely working as a goldsmith, or in some other part of the jewellery trade, in Strasbourg. Sometimes he is described as 'the diamond polisher of Mainz'. Historians have assumed, or at least suspected, that Gutenberg was developing a sideline in printing in Strasbourg by at least the late 1430s. In any event, he was by no means the only craftsman dabbling in the fledgling industry in those years and even earlier. What he seems to have offered, however – his immortal contribution – was the realization that the existing method of carving words and images into wood, and using those for printing, was wholly inadequate. Instead he incised letters into the ends of wooden rods and pressed those into sand to create moulds into which a molten alloy might be poured. Once set, those pieces of 'moveable type' might be assembled into pages of text. A further innovation of Gutenberg's was to come up with a way of mixing ink and oil to create a liquid more inclined to stick to the type and so produce a better print. For the press itself he copied the essential technology of those ancient machines used for extracting juice from grapes to make wine.

By 1448 he was back in Mainz and working out of his Hof zum Humbrecht workshop, just off the town square. One day in May 1450 he approached wealthy local businessman and moneylender Johann Fust in the hope of making him an offer he could not refuse. Having shown Fust a few pages of printed text, and having explained how his technique would produce in a couple of weeks a quantity of books that would take years of effort by scribes copying by hand, he secured a loan of 800 guilders – a considerable sum. That moment – of their coming together in partnership – set in train a revolution. It was a moment as important to the world as the invention of writing almost 5,000 years before, and its product – a means of swiftly disseminating information to as many people as possible – would have no challenger until the advent of the Internet in the second half of the twentieth century.

Businessman Fust wanted to get the product – finished books – to market as soon as possible. Gutenberg strove for perfection. He had had to agree that his prototype press and the rest of his equipment would serve as collateral and the pressure was on. After two years he had to ask for a further 800 guilders and this time Fust agreed in return for being made Gutenberg's partner. When none of the loans had been repaid by

1455, Fust successfully sued Gutenberg and gained ownership of the whole enterprise. To add insult to injury, the day-to-day running was taken over by his son-in-law, Peter Schöffer, who had been Gutenberg's apprentice and best employee.

By then, however, Gutenberg had completed his masterpiece – the edition of the Bible that bears his name. Since the first completed copy went into the library of one Cardinal Mazarin it is also known as the Mazarin Bible or, on account of it having forty-two lines of text on each page, the 42-line Bible. Some collectors regard it still as one of the most beautiful books ever printed. The court settlement also gave Fust ownership of the type for the Bible, and for a second Gutenberg masterpiece, a psalter.

It might be no exaggeration to say the advent of printing in this way enabled information to 'go viral' for the first time. Where before books, the work of monks labouring endlessly in their scriptoria, had been rare and inaccessible to all but a handful of the elite, now they could infect the many. The first books, printed between 1455 and 1500, are known to specialists as incunabula, a Latin word meaning 'cradle' or 'swaddling clothes' and suggestive of the newly born. The *Index to the Early Printed Books in the British Museum: From the Invention of Printing to the year MD; with Notes of those in the Bodleian Library* by English bibliographer Robert Proctor was published in 1898 and is still the foundation work that shows the spread of the emergent technology through Europe during that first half-century. Something like 35,000 separate editions – some running to many hundreds or even thousands of copies – were produced by fifteenth-century presses. Germany and Italy were most productive, and in Venice alone the printers turned out more than a million copies of 4,500 separate editions.

For all the times when the world has been altered by the action or thinking of a single individual, there are others when it has taken the partnership of two. Had Steves Jobs and Wozniak not met in 1971 (brought together by mutual friend and soon-to-be employee Bill Fernandez), the world would have technology but perhaps no Apple and no iPhones. Had either Larry Page or Sergey Brin failed to sign up to Stanford University's computer science graduate programme in 1995, there would be search engines on the Internet but no Google.

Somewhere in Mesopotamia, 5,000 years ago, a series of marks pressed into wet clay with the cut end of a reed enabled writing for the first time. It was the skill that empowered Enheduanna, high priestess of Ur, and all the writers who followed in her train. Writing was the first information revolution. The creation, in 1974, of TCP/IP – Transmission Control Protocol/Internet Protocol – would give order and structure to the movement of information on the Internet and so enable the third information revolution. Between those two, sandwiched in the middle of the trinity and at least as important as those others, is the printing press built by Gutenberg and paid for by Fust.

50.

THE DEATH OF CONSTANTINE
AND THE FALL OF CONSTANTINOPLE

In the early hours of 29 May 1453 a gate in ancient walls was breached at last. Through the portal of the Christian city of Constantinople poured Muslim warriors thrilled by the thought of fulfilling a prophecy of conquest made many centuries before by their prophet, Muhammad. Word of their insolent presence spread as fire within dry tinder. The spirits of the citizens within, tormented and terrified by weeks of siege, broke at last, and the sounds of wailing and disbelief filled the air.

'The city is fallen!' they cried. 'The city is fallen!'

Constantine Palaiologos, in Christ True Emperor and Autocrat of the Romans, was with a remnant of his army when the dread sounds of disaster reached his ears. Looking towards the Gate of St Romanus he saw the banners of the Ottoman Sultan Mehmet II appearing on one high point after another, like licking flames driven by the wind. He called out to the defenders around him, urging them to stand and fight once more. Every other time, day after day, they had obeyed, and willingly; now they turned and ran, joining a flood of civilians seeking escape even when there was no hope.

According to the legend that outlived him, Constantine was last seen alone on the battlements of the city, perhaps near the Gate of St Sophia and overlooking the tens of thousands of enemy soldiers crowded below and awaiting their chance to come in. He had cast off any vestige of his imperial garb and was dressed as a simple soldier. Taking a sword from the dead hand of a defender, he leapt from the walls – out and down like a drop of rain into an ocean. Later in the day Mehmet would parade a severed head, telling one and all it was that of the emperor. In truth no one could tell if his claim was true or false, and in any event no other trace of Constantine, last of the Romans, was ever seen again.

Prophecy had always stalked the streets of Constantinople. It had been named after Constantine I (the same that was hailed emperor in York, by the army of his father, Constantius) and rumour had always had it that the life of the city would begin and end with emperors of the same name.

Theodosius II had had a great double wall raised to protect the landward side of the city, so great it was named after him. Constantinople occupies the tip of a peninsula, where the Bosphorus holds Europe and Asia at arm's length. Two bodies of water to the south – the Sea of Marmara and the Golden Horn – form the apex of a triangle that points roughly east. From above, through eyes half shut, the landform has the look of a hippo's head, blunt snout sniffing towards the Bosphorus. It is across the neck of the peninsula, forming the base of the triangle as it were, that the Wall of Theodosius lies. Constantinople then is Istanbul now, the cultural capital of Turkey, and the history of east and west is marbled through the place like fat through beef.

From beginning to end, the citizens of Constantinople called themselves Romans. It was a New Rome Constantine had built and until its falling, dying day it was assumed by all in the Christian west that it would, somehow, always be there. Emperor Justinian had dedicated the Church of St Sophia – greatest of all churches, the same that won the hearts of those Russian Vikings – in 537. It was the Orthodox faith that was cradled there – literally the *true* and *correct* form of Christianity.

Before 1453 and Sultan Mehmet, Constantinople had withstood more than thirty sieges. Like a mountain range or some other natural feature on a geological scale, the Wall of Theodosius was regarded as permanent, immovable, for ever. The centuries came and went and Constantinople and the Byzantine empire changed, right enough, their fortunes ebbing and flowing, but always they seemed certain to survive. Always too, until the end, it remembered it was Roman. In 800 the Pope made an emperor of Charlemagne, in the west, but the Autocrat of the Romans was always and only in the east.

The Battle of Manzikert in 1071 had shown that soldiers of Islam could defeat those of Christ. In 1204 the climax of the Fourth Crusade – that awful scourge unleashed by the shock of Manzikert – saw the sacking of the city by brother Christians. Those crusaders shared the imperial territories between them and yet still Constantinople prevailed, stubborn as the Wall. In little over half a century, by 1261, the Byzantine empire was restored – a relative shadow of its former self, but restored nonetheless.

Far away and long ago, in China at the beginning of the tenth century, the Tang dynasty had stumbled and fallen. The power vacuum left by the Tang had set dominoes toppling, entire peoples moving. Out of Central Asia then had come the Oghuz Turks, and from among them the Muslim Seljuk clan. Also from the Oghuz, in all likelihood, came Osman, a prince among his people – a *ghazi* in their tongue. Those he led came to be called Osmanlis and then Ottomans. Among his successors was Bayezid I who besieged Constantinople, styled himself Sultan-i-Rum – Sultan of Rome – and was a significant threat to the empire until 1402 when he boasted of being the greatest ruler in the world. Word reached the ear of Timur the Lame, the last great Mongol khan, who brought Bayezid to battle at Ankara and utterly destroyed him. Bayezid tried to flee in the aftermath but was captured and brought to Timur. Long afterwards there persisted, in Europe at least, the legend that Timur had kept his captive in an iron cage that was pulled behind his dogs.

The intervention of Timur was a last reprieve for those Romans of Constantinople. Christians in the west disapproved of the Orthodox ways of those Christians in the east and so had long turned a blind eye and a deaf ear to the diminution of the empire, its surrounding and erosion by the heresy of Islam. Mehmet II was Bayezid's great-grandson and just twenty-one years old when he arrived before the Wall of Theodosius with a host uncountable. He brought heavy guns in his train and for the best part of two months used them to pound the ancient defences and the city within. In the end it was a door left open (by mistake or by treachery) in the Gate of St Romanus that made all the difference.

After more than a thousand years, the city had fallen. After 2,000 years a direct line of descent from the Classical world of Athens and Rome had been cut through with an Ottoman scimitar. Into slavery went 50,000 Christian souls, and the Church of St Sophia, the greatest church in Christendom, was turned into a mosque. East was east and west was west and nothing could ever be the same again.

51.

SPANISH HORSES ARRIVE IN AMERICA

When Christopher Columbus returned to the Americas in 1493, so did horses. The Genoese navigator and explorer landed that time on the Caribbean island of Hispaniola, and the horses he unloaded there were Spanish, like his patrons. Later the Spanish conquistador Hernán Cortés would bring more – to the mainland – and by the middle years of the sixteenth century there were horses in Argentina, Brazil, Florida, Mexico, Panama and Peru. British, French and other colonists brought even more, and soon enough the beasts were back in North America too.

Columbus's second voyage was just a year after his first ('when he'd sailed across the ocean blue in fourteen hundred and ninety-two', as we used to learn in primary school). For the first time since the Vikings in the tenth century he had shown that seamen might head into the west in search of land, as well as into the east. Columbus would remain convinced he had found an alternative route to Asia, the *West Indies*, and it was others after him who understood the Americas as new continents entirely.

For the species *Equus ferus caballus*, however, it was a return to those continents after thousands of years. Palaeontologists believe the wild horse was wiped out there by the first bands of human hunters in the millennia after their crossing of what is now the Bering Strait around 25,000 years ago.

American cartoonist Gary Larson imagined the return. In one of his cartoons a ship lies at anchor on the horizon while a rowing boat containing two dopey-looking conquistadors ferries a horse, sitting upright and stony-faced, towards land. Already onshore is a third Spaniard, accompanied by two more horses, up on their hind legs like humans. There are two comic-book Indians, feathers in their hair, and one is politely shaking the hoof of one of the horses. The second horse is pointing inland with one raised foreleg, an excited expression on its face as it contemplates the potential of the place. The caption of the cartoon reads: 'Circa 1500 AD: Horses are introduced to America'.

All the comedy of an 'introduction' set aside, the return of horses was a moment of note. If indigenous peoples saw trouble ahead from the two-legged incomers, they were quick to see the positive potential of those on four. Along with iron tools and, later, firearms, the horse enabled the development of a way of life that was hitherto impossible. Between 1539 and 1542 Spanish conquistador Francisco Vásquez de Coronado led an expedition from Mexico into the Texas panhandle and the south-west of North America. He was looking for a city of gold he called Quivira and while he found no such place, he was the first European to describe the lifestyle of the Plains Indians. In *The Journey of Coronado, 1540–1542, from the City of Mexico to the Grand Canyon of the Colorado and the Buffalo Plains of Texas*, published in 1896, George Parker Winship described the lifestyle the Spaniards encountered among a tribe they knew as the Querecho. They lived, he wrote,

in tents made of the tanned skins of the cows. They travel around near the cows killing them for food . . . They travel like the Arabs, with their tents and troops of dogs loaded with poles . . . these people eat raw flesh and drink blood. They do not eat human flesh. They are a kind people and not cruel. They are faithful friends. They are able to make themselves very well understood by means of signs. They dry the flesh in the sun, cutting it thin like a leaf, and when dry they grind it like meal to keep it and make a sort of sea soup of it to eat . . . They season it with fat, which they always try to secure when they kill a cow. They empty a large gut and fill it with blood, and carry this around the neck to drink when they are thirsty.

The Querecho were likely those known later as the Apache, and the cows they depended upon, the buffalo. Like the first hunters everywhere, those in North America had always moved on foot. In the case of the Querecho, domesticated dogs were beasts of burden, pulling travois loaded with belongings. Coronado had horses with him, but not enough to trade with the locals. Gradually in the decades and centuries to come the indigenous peoples obtained horse herds of their own. Elsewhere on the plains of North America, as was true of the indigenous peoples of Central and South America, there were settled farmers subsisting on maize. But it was the horse culture that shone like a well-buffed bridle. Once they had enough to equip every member of the tribe, the archetypal Plains Indian culture blossomed in its fullest form. With horses, the hunting of the buffalo was made infinitely easier, and a first icon of the American West was born.

The large print gave, however, while the small print would take away. The life made possible for the first Americans by the introduction (or rather, reintroduction) of the horse was their finest flower. In the scheme of things it was as brief as any blossom, flourishing through the eighteenth and nineteenth centuries and crushed under foot by the advent of the twentieth. It was a grim portent. From South to North the coming of Europeans to the Americas was a death knell for the indigenous peoples. Beware of Europeans bearing gifts.

52.

MARTIN LUTHER NAILS
A PLACARD TO A DOOR

By his perfection of the art of printing, Gutenberg of Mainz had forged the tools of an information revolution. Where before the communication of new ideas had depended upon copying words by hand, a process that made the creation of a single book the work of weeks, or months, and therefore ruinously expensive for all but the elite, now it was possible to churn them out in minutes and hours at a price that increased the viable audience by orders of magnitude.

In this twenty-first century there is routine talk of a statement 'going viral' – as in spreading at exponential speed via the Internet. By the turn of the sixteenth century there was the first hint of the power latent within an idea when it might be printed and circulated by the hundred . . . and then by the thousand . . .

On 31 October 1517 an Augustinian monk named Martin Luther approached the castle church in the town of Wittenberg on the River Elbe, in Saxony in the north-east of Germany. In his hand he held a document he had written himself, in Latin, listing ninety-five ways in which he thought the Catholic Church had strayed from the path of righteousness. In 1515 Pope Leo X had authorized and encouraged the sale of indulgences to help finance the building of the new St Peter's Basilica in Rome. Indulgences were get-out-of-jail-free cards that promised sinners they would spend less time in purgatory and so proceed more quickly to heaven – and Luther was appalled by their very existence. The first of his 'theses' read: 'When our Lord and Master Jesus Christ said, "Repent," he willed the entire life of believers to be one of repentance.'

Luther's own parishioners had told him how a Dominican friar named Johann Tezel was in the area of Wittenberg selling indulgences to any and all, promising forgiveness of everything from adultery to theft. For Luther it was a dread sign of how far the Church had fallen from any sort of Christian ideal. While he had never before been moved to court controversy, he was devout and well read and certain of the necessity of every man and woman to earn forgiveness by making of themselves better people.

The rest of his document was more of the same, developing the notion that forgiveness was earned and not bought. He had sent a copy of the *Ninety-five Theses* to the archbishop of Mainz, who sent it to the Pope in Rome. Now he took a hammer and nailed a second copy to the church door for all to see.

At first the archbishop was intent only on having Luther stop talking about indulgences. Matters escalated beyond everyone's expectations or wants, however (including Luther's, at least at first), on account of the printing presses that began mass-producing copies, in German, of the *Ninety-five Theses* and then Luther's subsequent offerings.

Perhaps Luther was flattered by the realization that he was rather a good writer, and reaching a large and growing audience of enthusiastic readers. In any event he was emboldened and began circulating, via pamphlets, other ideas more challenging, threatening indeed, to the Church. Soon he was broadcasting his belief – this one revolutionary in ways that objection to the sale of indulgences had not been – that there was more required for entrance to heaven than just going to church and performing the rituals. . . going through the motions, as it were. That well-trodden route to St Peter's gate, made of communion, confession, mass and the rest, was called 'works', but now Luther was telling his audience that faith was the key. For longer than anyone could remember the Church had persuaded everyone that access to salvation was through them, a gift that was theirs to give or to withhold. Now Luther was kindling in the minds of many that a man, a woman, might establish a direct line to God, that salvation was secured via grace, and that grace was a gift from God alone. It was the responsibility, the obligation, of every individual to find the way to salvation within his or her own heart.

Pope Leo refused to take his employee seriously. 'Luther is a drunken German,' he said. 'He will feel differently about it when he sobers up.'

Defiant in the extreme, Luther replied that the Pope was no better than 'any other stinking sinner'.

Luther's words and ideas spread, finding fertile ground in Germany and beyond. He opposed the quick fix of confession and absolution; he condemned the traditional celibacy of the clergy. The Church moved to cancel him. He was excommunicated in 1520 and promptly stood before wondering onlookers and burned the bill. Defiant again in front of an imperial Diet, he was driven into hiding, perhaps even kidnapped by those determined to keep him out of harm's way.

Whenever challenged, Luther said his thinking was based purely on his reading of the Bible. In order that others could have better access to scripture he translated the New Testament into German. Once again it was the printing presses and type perfected by Gutenberg that put copies into the hands of the many.

Luther had been a trenchant champion of the Catholic Church. That he should go down in the story of the world as the midwife of the rebellion that split the faith in two and gave birth to what was soon called 'Protestantism' surely surprised no one more than the man himself. By the 1530s Lutheranism and Protestantism – in many forms – were spreading throughout Europe. Luther opposed many of those forms himself. One especially virulent strand of rebellion against the Catholic Church took the form of Anabaptism, whose followers objected to infant baptism and insisted that such an act of commitment to God could and should be undertaken by adults only. In 1534 the city of Munster came under the control of Anabaptists and the proto-society its leaders sought to establish has been regarded by some commentators as a foretaste of communism. There was polygamy in Munster and rumours of other amoral behaviour before a violent put-down. So revolutionary was Anabaptism it had raised the ire of Catholics and Protestants alike.

What had begun as one devout churchman's opposition to the sale of forgiveness had, within less than a decade, upended the Catholic Church as effectively as a Viking warrior had once upended Charles the Simple of France. Reformation was a wave that washed back and forth across Europe in the decades to come. In Switzerland, French-born John Calvin was inspired, by Lutheranism, to conjure the austere brand of reformed faith that bears his name and would spread as far as North America in time. Whatever Luther had intended when he hammered that nail into the church door in his hometown, a spider web of fractures, cracks and fissures spread from the blows all across the world.

53.

CHARLES V RULES THE FIRST EMPIRE WHERE THE SUN NEVER SET

Since the time of Charlemagne in AD 800 there had been an emperor in the west, a Roman emperor made holy if and when he was crowned by the Pope. On 23 October 1520, Charles I, King of Spain, was crowned in the cathedral at Aachen. He had been challenged for the throne by Francis I of France and England's Henry VIII. Henry had dropped out of the race early doors, but the imperial crown, like the presidency of the United States, was essentially for sale to the highest bidder. Since Charles had the deepest pockets, the seven electors, whose gift the crown was, found him their preferred candidate, surprise, surprise.

Three bishops (not a Pope, not yet) presided over the proceedings in Aachen. Charles was the fifth emperor of his name and he sat upon Charlemagne's throne beneath the octagonal dome of the Palatine Chapel, near the sarcophagus containing that first emperor's remains. Charlemagne had ordered the building of the chapel in 796 and two years later Alcuin of York, the same holy man who had written about the horror of the Viking desecration of Lindisfarne, recorded that the work was close to finished. It was less than a lifetime since Constantine, the last emperor in the east, had fallen beneath the scimitars of the Muslim Turk at the Gate of St Sophia in Constantinople.

Quite a moment. Nearly a decade later Charles would be crowned by

Pope Clement VII and made holy, right enough. That would be in the San Petronio Basilica, in Bologna, on 24 February 1530, amid all possible pomp. Before receiving the imperial crown he would, for some other moments, don the Iron Crown of Lombardy that had at its heart a thin encircling thread, silver in colour and said to have been beaten from a nail recovered from the True Cross, one of those that had pierced the flesh of Jesus.

That Pope Clement had agreed to the coronation was quite something in itself. By allowing it, and officiating there, he was declaring to all that what was needed was a peace accord to bring together as one the Christian west – and that Charles was the man for the job. Only the year before, Suleiman the Magnificent, Sultan of the Ottomans (the same Ottomans that had, under Mehmet II, taken Constantinople in 1453 and made a trophy of the head of the last emperor), had brought a Muslim horde numbering in the hundreds of thousands up to the very gates of Vienna before being driven off.

Before his high day in Rome, Emperor Charles would face the wave of religious unrest inadvertently summoned by Martin Luther. Four years after the posting of his ninety-five theses on the church door, Charles summoned Luther to explain himself at the Diet of Worms. He promised the turbulent priest safe conduct (and was as good as his word) but failed to change the other's mind. By the Edict of Worms he outlawed Luther, saying:

> You know that I am a descendant of the most Christian emperors of the great German people, of the Catholic kings of Spain, of the Archdukes of Austria, and of the Dukes of Burgundy. All of these, their whole life long, were faithful sons of the Roman Church . . . After their deaths they left, by natural law and heritage, these holy Catholic rites, for us to live and die by, following their example. And so until now I have lived as a true follower of these our ancestors. I am therefore resolved to maintain everything which these my forebears have established to the present.

By those words Charles made plain an otherwise implicit truth – that it was religious unity that held his empire together. And what an empire it was, so vast in its reach that for the first time in the story of the world one man held sway over holdings where the sun never set from one day's end to the next. No one before – no Persian, no Roman of the Classical world, no Genghis Khan – had stretched his arms around the globe. His mother was Joanna, daughter of Ferdinand of Aragon and Isabella of Castile. From her he had inherited both Spanish kingdoms, the Kingdom of Sicily and the Spanish holdings in the Americas. His father was Philip the Handsome, eldest son of Maximilian I who had been Holy Roman Emperor before him. From Philip, Charles inherited the Low Countries, and from his grandfather a swathe of territory taking in Germany, Austria and northern Italy.

Charles was a son of the Habsburg line – one of the two great houses of Europe from the fifteenth century onwards. The Habsburgs were German-Austrian and their rivals were those of the French house of Valois. By the sixteenth century, the Habsburgs were dominant. Charles's brother was Ferdinand, King of Bohemia, Croatia and Hungary, his eventual successor as Holy Roman Emperor. Charles V was King of the Romans; emperor-elect; semper Augustus; King of Spain, Sicily, Jerusalem, the Balearic Islands, the Canary Islands, the Indies and the mainland on the far side of the Atlantic; Archduke of Austria; Duke of Burgundy, Brabant, Styria, Carinthia, Carniola, Luxembourg, Limburg, Athens and Patras; Count of Habsburg, Flanders and Tyrol; Count Palatine of Burgundy, Hainault, Pfirt, Roussillon; Landgrave of Alsace; Count of Swabia; Lord of Asia and Africa.

Detractors would say that he had not the linguistic skills required to speak from the heart to so diverse an empire. For his own part, Charles is supposed to have said: 'I speak Latin to God, Italian to women, French to men and German to my horse.'

He had the ambition and the sense of himself as a man sent by God to lead the Christian world. Much though he aspired to encompass the world, to rule from one side of the globe to the other, the means did not yet exist to make it possible to be seen and accepted as ruler in the hemispheres of west and east at the same time. 'Too big to fail' is a claim made again and again. Maybe anything too big, any attempt to place everyone under one rule, one ideology, must fail, in the sixteenth century or in the twenty-first.

54.

MAGELLAN AND ELCANO — AROUND
THE WORLD IN . . . THREE YEARS

There is still fun to be had pretending everyone thought the world was flat until Columbus crossed the Atlantic, that ocean blue, in 1492, but pretence it is. In the sixth century BC Pythagoras knew the world was shaped like a globe. Aristotle said the same a couple of centuries later, pointing out that constellations in the southern sky grew higher for a person travelling south. Goodness knows how long ago the ancients first looked at an eclipse of the moon and saw that Earth's shadow upon it was curved instead of straight. Eratosthenes in the third century BC . . . then Ptolemy . . . then the Venerable Bede in the 700s AD . . . on and on it goes, one observer after another recording that the Earth was and is a ball and not a plate.

Almost harder is to envisage the world as Europeans really did up until around the turn of the fifteenth century. Even the learned counted only three continents – Africa, Asia and Europe – grouped tight around the Mediterranean Sea. Jerusalem was, for most, the geographical centre of that world, like the maker's decal on the ball. (Vikings had crossed the Atlantic half a millennium before, but that fact had evidently slipped from everyone's memory.)

It may be that the knowledge hiding in plain sight – that a ship might sail west and end up in the east – was simply overlooked until it was needed. That need came when those on Europe's Atlantic façade, with their backs against the blue wall of the sea, had to come to terms with how the overland routes into the east were coming up against the buffers – of Muslims in the Balkans and the eastern Mediterranean, of confident Russia further north. Europe was full of people, and the roads east were increasingly blocked with them.

Ship design had come on apace – with proper rudders, multiple masts, sails jib and lateen (from 'Latin') – so that sailors could tack against the wind instead of only waiting for wind at their backs. By the fifteenth century the ship's compass had been at play in Europe for 200 years or more and there were tables recording the position, at noon each day, of the sun and the Pole Star over the horizon in northern latitudes.

Matters political were complicated by the Treaty of Tordesillas, in 1494, by which the Pope had given Portugal the trading rights to everything in the east, while Spain had all in the west.

For the fun of it this time, the moment that matters is made of the money troubles faced in the second decade of the sixteenth century by Castilian ship's captain Juan Sebastián Elcano. As a younger man he had been a soldier helping to press Spanish claims in the Italian Wars, and also in Algeria in North Africa. Seeking a more peaceful life he later settled in Seville and became captain of a merchant ship. A soldier he was, a sailor he was, a businessman he was not, and all too soon he had borrowed too much money from a variety of aggressive companies and sponsors. Pressed to settle his debts, he gave up his ship. The ship, however, was not his to sell, and by its surrender he had broken the laws of Spain. The moment came when he threw himself upon the mercy of Charles I, who agreed to pardon him on condition he join an expedition just then being put together on his behalf by the Portuguese mariner Ferdinand Magellan.

Having run out of options, Elcano agreed and signed on as a master aboard one of a fleet of five ships destined to depart into the west in search of the Spice Islands . . . which lay, as everyone knew, in the east. They set sail from Seville on 10 August 1519 – the flagship *Trinidad*, the *San Antonio*, the *Concepción*, the *Santiago* and the *Victoria*.

Magellan – fiery, bellicose and committed to the sort of brutal discipline required to keep hundreds of men in line for years at sea – is the man named by most as first to circumnavigate the globe. He took them on an odyssey and no mistake: via Tenerife, Cape Verde and Sierra Leone, across the Atlantic to Brazil, to the Plata estuary and then to Patagonia where the *Santiago* was lost. Then the *San Antonio* fled for home, making it back to Spain and claiming the rest had foundered. Magellan found and then led the remaining three through the 350-mile-long strait that bears his name. They took a hundred days then to cross the vastness – 64 million square miles of ocean they called Pacific. By 15 March 1521 they were in the Philippines – and there Magellan's nature had him pick a fight that cost him his life, on 27 April, and those of several of his crew. The little flotilla limped onwards without him and them. By the time they left Borneo on 8 July they had insufficient men for three ships and so burned the *Concepción*.

Elcano (he that was among them only on account of bad debts) was, by desperate men, made captain of the *Victoria* on 16 September. On 8 November, two years and three months after leaving Seville, the two surviving vessels arrived in Maluku, in the Spice Islands. Suitably loaded with their prized cargo of spices, they took their leave of the islands and of the severely leaking *Trinidad*, later lost as well. Elcano was in charge of the whole exploit by then and plotted a course west, to Spain. After a month and a half they rounded the Cape of Good Hope (on 19 May 1522), and, after yet more hardship and death, returned to Seville on 8 September. They had been gone for three years and Elcano, rather than Magellan, was the captain at the end of it all. A debtor he had been but now a hero (even if no one remembers his name now). There were eighteen other Europeans left alive to tell their tales, and four from Maluku.

For what it is worth, King Charles was impressed enough to let Elcano augment his own coat of arms with the legend 'You Went Around Me First'.

And so he had.

55.

HENRY VIII GOES
ALL OUT TO IMPRESS A WOMAN

Martin Luther had been moved by faith to question the selling of indulgences to lessen the time spent in purgatory by sinners. By so doing he had inadvertently triggered the religious revolution that was the Reformation. Luther was a pious and educated man, well read in matters theological, and his motives seem to have been (at first, at least) altogether virtuous. Having troubled his own house, he had inherited the wind; having sown the storm, he had unleashed a whirlwind that would kill uncounted thousands in the name of his God.

Within a few years of the nailing of his ninety-five theses to the church door in Wittenberg, it was the earthly desire for a pretty woman that had the king of England launch a reformation of his own that would, inadvertently or not, set more Protestants and Catholics in deadly hate the one against the other.

On 29 December 1524, a company of knights prepared to defend a castle on behalf of some maidens. The castle was a stage set, assembled in the tiltyard of the royal palace at Greenwich, the whole event a carefully planned drama choreographed to let some well-heeled young men about court show off their combat skills in front of royalty and pretty ladies. Just as the first half a dozen likely lads prepared to go into action against some similarly suited-and-booted attackers, a pair of oldsters, bearded and bewigged, rode between the young guns and Queen Catherine of Aragon where she sat with her ladies-in-waiting. With theatrically shaking hands one of the silver-haired veterans produced a petition for reading aloud. Among much purple prose it was declared that 'Although youth had left them and age was come, and would prevent them to do feats of arms; yet courage, desire and good will remained with them, and bade them to take upon them to break spears, which gladly they would do . . .'

Queen Catherine acceded to their request and, with the flourish of the finest amateur dramatics production, the pair removed their wigs and false beards to reveal no less a duo of knights than King Henry VIII and Charles Brandon, the Duke of Suffolk and Henry's brother-in-law and closest friend. One by one they took on and bested the young knights. Henry and Charles were thirty-three and thirty-nine years old respectively and soon age and guile were giving youth and innocence a dangerously hard time. In *Six Wives: The Queens of Henry VIII*, English historian David Starkey suggested that alongside Queen Catherine that day was twenty-three-year-old Anne Boleyn, lady-in-waiting and already the holder of the king's heart. The daughter of a good family, she had been at court for a couple of years by the time of the jousting at the so-called White Castle. Her elder sister, Mary, had been Henry's mistress before her. Mary was a married woman, wife of William Carey, a Gentleman of the Privy Chamber, but such details were of no concern for that king or any king.

The moment worth noting may be when, before the White Castle, Henry pressed his attack so hard upon one Anthony Browne – a contemporary of Anne's who had spent time with her at the French court – that he came close to parting the youngster's head from his body. 'Was King Henry also fighting in Anne's presence? And for her?' wrote Starkey. 'To show that he alone was fit . . . ?'

It is a fascinating thought and, if he is right, the making of a moment of importance. It was then or soon thereafter that Henry fell completely under Anne's spell. She was young and pretty and, more importantly, a lady-in-waiting to his wife and so in his line of sight.

'How do we begin to covet?' asked Hannibal Lecter in *The Silence of the Lambs*. 'We covet what we see every day.'

Henry's marriage to Catherine had, for him, already run its course. She had been wedded first, for five months, to Arthur, Henry's elder brother. Arthur's death at fifteen years, from the mysterious malady remembered as the sweating sickness, turned an unexpected spotlight on the then ten-year-old Henry. Along with the throne, he inherited his brother's widow.

The prime objective of a king then was the making of a son, to ensure the continuation of his line, but Henry and Catherine were barely blessed. There was a stillborn girl in 1510 and then a boy, right enough, on the first day of 1511. Little Henry, Duke of Cornwall, lived for less than two months. There were two stillborn sons – in 1513 and 1515 – and then a daughter, Mary, who lived and reigned in time, and unhappily.

Who knows how that man and that woman, Henry and Catherine, coped with all the loss, but as the teens of the sixteenth century gave way to the twenties, Henry's want of a son had him look elsewhere for a source.

'Heaven has no rage like love to hatred turned,' wrote English Restoration poet William Congreve. 'Nor hell a fury like a woman scorned.'

It would be imprudent to guess at either emotion in the case of that king and queen, but by 1527 Henry was earnestly seeking to divorce his first wife and marry his second. His case rested on the so-called Leviticus curse, from Leviticus 20:21: 'And if a man shall take his brother's wife, it is an unclean thing. He hath uncovered his brother's nakedness: they shall be childless.' Determined to find just cause and have the Pope annul his union with Catherine, Henry grasped at the notion his marriage to his brother's widow had been, and was, unclean. They had had their daughter, Mary, but on account of the wrongness of their coupling they (or rather he) had been denied the son he so desperately craved.

Henry's line, that of the Tudors, was young. His father, also Henry, had been the first of them and the pressure, then, to make a male heir and so perpetuate that line is hard to comprehend now. Obtaining papal approval of his separation from Catherine – what he called his 'great matter' – became an obsession. Pope Clement VII refused to oblige him and so in 1532, having secured the support of his Parliament, Henry embarked upon the process of having himself declared Supreme Head on Earth of the Church of England, completed with the 1534 Act of Supremacy. He was undoubtedly torn. In 1521 he had condemned Martin Luther and been rewarded, by Clement's predecessor Adrian VI, with the title of Defender of the Faith. Until the end of his days he would consider that he and the English Church he led were Catholic in all but name.

Anne would bear him a daughter, Elizabeth, but no son. He would have Anne's head cut off once the shine had gone off her, as it had gone off Catherine. There would be four more wives. Jane Seymour bore him Edward – Edward VI – and died in the infected aftermath. He divorced Anne of Cleves and had Catherine Howard beheaded like Anne Boleyn. Catherine Parr survived him. Wanted or not, intended or not, the Reformation and all its attendant horrors had come to England.

56.

FIRST BLAST OF CANNON
AND A MUGHAL EMPIRE IN INDIA

The subcontinent consumed all comers, changing them and making them her own version of whatever they had been before. In Book IX of Homer's *Odyssey* the ship is blown off course by a storm and comes to rest on the island of the Lotus-eaters. There some of the crew begin eating of the lotus flowers and are changed, forgetting themselves and losing any desire to leave. The natives of the place freely offer the newcomers their intoxicating food, 'which was so delicious that those who ate of it left off caring about home, and did not even want to go back and say what had happened to them'. The north-western frontier offered a doorway into India, and once through it, any invaders seemed to find it hard to leave, and more importantly harder to change the place they had found. Instead, they were as often changed by India.

After the time of Chandragupta and Ashoka and the Mauryan empire came a people called the Kushanas, from the borderlands of China. They made art of the Buddha and so helped make a god of him. Persian kings came and went. Always they remained towards the north, never properly penetrating beyond the Deccan plateau. There was trade between India and Egypt . . . between India and the Hellenistic world . . . with Greeks and then with Romans. In the early fourth century AD there rose in India the Gupta civilization, first of all under another Chandragupta, in 320.

The language of Sanskrit was a unifying presence in the subcontinent, common to north as to south. The great works of storytelling, the *Mahabharata* and the *Ramayana*, took on a final polish on account of its rhythms and cadences. The Gupta civilization saw a flowering of Hindu ways and thinking, and also those of the Buddha. The years and centuries passed and always India retained a gravitational pull, holding in place a culture with Hinduism and Buddhism at its heart. There was animal sacrifice and worship of idols; women were increasingly oppressed, controlled within an already rigid caste system. There was the custom of *suttee* by which widows were expected to throw themselves on to the funeral fires of their dead husbands. At the same time there was profound philosophical thought about the very nature of reality, about the endless round of birth and death – the hamster wheel of *Samsara* – and the hope of stepping away from it all and into the blissful nothing of nirvana, as the Buddha had outlined. It was all as intoxicating as anything the Lotuseaters had had to offer.

By the eighth century there was Islam in India too, first of all on the west coast out of Arabia, then on the Deccan. Having found the subcontinent, as raiders and then as traders, they kept coming. By the eleventh century there were Turkic people in the Punjab, settling and colonizing. Hinduism and Buddhism survived all the while in the presence of an Islamic empire centred on the valley of the Ganges, along with the Christianity that had arrived via the western seaboard in the first century AD. At the end of the fourteenth century the Mongol Timur the Lame (the same who would buy a little time for the Christians of Constantinople by breaking their arch tormentor Bayezid on the field at Ankara) was triumphant in Delhi after a bloody invasion that left piles of corpses in his wake. Islam held sway in Delhi in the aftermath but in a less than unified form under a succession of sultans.

In 1483 a descendant of both Timur and Genghis Khan was born in the territory known now as Uzbekistan. He was Zahir ud-din Muhammad but would earn for himself the nickname of Babur, which means 'the tiger'. He succeeded his father as emir in 1494 and just three years later, aged fourteen, led an army to conquer the oasis city of Samarkand. He lost control of the place – and much else – soon after, but his reputation was made. His fortunes rose and fell, sometimes in exile and sometimes not, as he sought to emulate his ancestors, until 1521 when he was invited to oust Ibrahim Lodi, Sultan of Delhi. Lodi had enemies around his throne and some of them, nobles of Afghan descent, looked to their countryman Babur, resident in Kabul by then, as an alternative. The resultant effort took five years to accomplish.

The moment of note in the story of the world was the sound of cannon fire on the level plain outside the city of Panipat in Haryana, some 60 miles north of Delhi. Babur's army of perhaps 25,000 – primarily cavalry – was greatly outnumbered by that of Lodi. Estimates vary but it may have amounted to as many as 100,000 fighting men and 1,000 war elephants, armoured and magnificent as any image from a child's storybook.

Aware of the disparity in numbers, Babur had prepared the ground. With his right flank secured against the city and his left protected by a great trench camouflaged with branches, he deployed his secret weapon in the centre of his lines. Unknown to Lodi's men, Babur had obtained and brought heavy artillery. Behind long lines of wagons lashed together with ropes and protected by heavy shields he positioned his ranks of cannon. Lodi's force advanced towards Babur's narrow front and when the artillery opened fire it must have seemed as though the gates of hell had opened wide. That First Battle of Panipat, on 21 April 1526, was perhaps the first fought in India using heavy guns. The effect was dramatic, and cataclysmic. Never having heard or seen the like, Lodi's elephants panicked and stampeded, trampling hundreds of his men. Sultan Lodi was among those who tried to flee the rout, but he was cut down and beheaded, dying alongside as many as 20,000 of his own warriors.

Panipat did not secure Babur's throne but he had thereby laid a cornerstone of what became the Islamic Mughal (a corruption of 'Mongol') empire in India. His life was always testing, always challenging. He had his capital at Agra but was challenged by rivals again and again, notably by the Hindu Rajput princes. Even after a great victory over them at the Battle of Khanwa in 1527, still the Rajputs threatened his rule. When Babur died in 1530, aged forty-seven, he was succeeded by his twenty-two-year-old son, Humayun. He too would have to fight for years to consolidate his control, but the Mughal empire would reach its high point under his son, Akbar – Akbar the Great.

All of it had sprung from Babur. He had been a tiger, and also a lover of books and poetry and gardens. He was buried, as he had commanded, in a garden, in a tomb without a roof and open to infinite sky.

57.

POTATOES END FAMINE IN EUROPE
AND CHANGE THE WORLD

Columbus sought the Americas to silence the doubters and prove that a ship might sail west to find the east. In his wake came those conquistadors like Cortés and Francisco Pizarro seeking gold and other riches. Along the way, and more by accident than by design, Pizarro's men found a treasure more valuable than all the rest, and with much more power to change the world.

In Peru, while some of their number went about the business of capturing, ransoming and then executing the Incan emperor Atahualpa, other Spaniards took a moment, a crucial moment, to notice some of the locals eating a foodstuff they called *chuno*. It was a stew, and at its heart was a variant of the plant known around the world now as the potato. The Incas had found that by leaving the tubers to freeze during the night, and then thawing them during the day and repeating the cycle over and over, they were transformed into soft lumps. These were squeezed to remove moisture and then stored for anything up to ten years and more. Once cooked, the preserved *chuno* took on the texture of gnocchi and was so nutritious and sustaining it was the staple food of the Inca army. Having appreciated the potential, the Spaniards began taking *chuno* – and the potatoes themselves – aboard their ships as dependable rations that helped them avoid the predations of scurvy.

Spanish monks in the Canary Islands were the first Europeans to cultivate potatoes, beginning in the 1560s, and by the following decade the plant was on mainland Spain. During the 1580s it spread to Britain, Belgium, Germany, the Netherlands, Ireland and France. Uptake was slow at first and many populations greeted the incomer with suspicion, claiming that eating, even touching, the plant would lead to all manner of ailments including leprosy, syphilis and sterility. For long the crop was fed only to animals. In France, King Louis XVI was persuaded of the value of the potato and, *pour encourager les autres*, took to wearing its flower in his buttonhole. His wife, Marie Antoinette, wove the blooms into her hair. The public-relations exercise worked and soon French farmers were growing potatoes and French people were eating them.

Historians including the American Alfred W. Crosby have made the case that the arrival of the potato in Europe changed the world. In his 1972 book *The Columbian Exchange*, Crosby suggested that the voyages of Columbus began the work of stitching back together a world torn apart by geological processes. Once upon a time the dry land of the world was a single continent, known to geologists as Pangaea. Eons of upheaval and drift caused by the movement of tectonic plates had seen to a separation, and then the evolution of unique ecosystems on the disparate landmasses. In the Americas, the nightshade plant (genus *Solanum*) gave birth to tobacco, sweet peppers, chilli peppers, eggplant (aubergine), tomatoes, potatoes and all manner of variants besides. The wild potato was toxic to humans but by a process of experimentation lasting centuries the Incas produced domesticated plants that were among the most nutritious on earth. Something in the region of 5,000 potato varieties are stored in the International Potato Center in Peru.

Before the potato, Europe was a continent of famines. Historian Fernand Braudel has calculated that French peasants endured more than one national famine every decade between 1500 and 1800. As if that were not bad enough, he also noted in *Civilization and Capitalism* that it was a woeful underestimation of reality since it 'omits the hundreds and hundreds of *local* famines'. All over the continent it was the same, and always had been. Famine was a fact of life, and death.

After the potato, Europe was changed for ever. For centuries the staples had been wheat and barley but the easy-to-grow import provided more nutritious food faster on less land than any other food crop, in any terrain. During the eighteenth and nineteenth centuries Ireland was so dependent upon the potato that half the population ate no other solid food. In other northern European countries the same was true for as many as a third of people. Dependency on a single crop was a double-edged sword, and when the potato blight arose in the middle years of the nineteenth century (the mould *Phytophthora infestans* likely came to Europe from Peru, aboard ships loaded with the seabird guano used to fertilize the soil) the consequences were brutal. In 1845 an estimated three quarters of a million acres of potatoes were lost to the disease in Ireland alone. The next two years were even worse, and the resultant starvation killed more than a million Irish people. Perhaps as many as two million fled the country, emigrating to the New World whence the plague had come.

The potato had both given and taken away. Its positive impact on the continent was the one that endured, however, and the population growth so boosted the energy of the countries of northern Europe that they were able to reach out and place the shadows of their hands over the Old World and the New. The story of the world has been shaped by the earnest endeavours of men and women, by the forces of nature, and in no small part by the humble spud.

58.

DIEGO GUALPA FINDS
A MOUNTAIN OF SILVER

By the Treaty of Tordesillas in 1494, the world (the world of international trade, at least) was divided between Spain and Portugal. By its terms, and with the connivance of the Pope, Spain gained rights to everything worth having, outside of European waters, west of a line of latitude running 370 leagues west of Cape Verde, off the west coast of Africa; Portugal got its hands on everything east of the same line. It was just two years since Columbus had found the Americas between his flotilla of ships and his intended destination of Asia, and already there was a need to settle matters between the two great Atlantic trading nations. The Pope was on board (since when did the Church turn up its nose at the chance of a fast buck?), but after Luther and the Reformation, Protestant states respected Tordesillas not at all.

Spanish conquistador Hernán Cortés proceeded to eviscerate the empire of the Aztecs in Mexico, much as those locals had split open the chests of uncounted victims of human sacrifice. The home team was utterly overwhelmed – partly on account of the superior tactics and technology of the invaders but in no small part because their own creation myth had predicted the return of the pale-skinned, bearded god who had been the making of Aztec civilization in the first place. When Cortés turned up fitting the bill, the chest-splitters were existentially rattled, all the way to their undoing.

In 1531 Francisco Pizarro invaded and conquered the Peru of the Incas. The following year he captured their last emperor, Atahualpa, and demanded a room full of gold for his safe return. Despite the payment of the ransom (amounting to a million pesos once it was melted down and cast as coins), Pizarro had the Inca executed by means of the garrotte. Out of the Americas and into Spain flowed a fortune in gold and silver beyond the dreams of avarice. Atahualpa's price was dizzying on its own. The same value again was taken out of Cuzco, and when the loot arrived back in Spain it was enough to destabilize the money markets of Europe. And that was before the finding of silver at Potosí.

Into the New World the Spaniards brought the diseases of the Old – chicken pox, diphtheria, influenza, malaria, measles, typhus and yellow fever. Estimates for death tolls – from violence certainly, but mostly from disease – run as high as 90 per cent of the indigenous population, and beyond, during the first 130 years of contact.

It was in 1545 that there came another moment worthy of remembrance: an indigenous man named Diego Gualpa, employed by the Spanish, discovered an entire mountain of silver the locals called Potosí, in what is now Bolivia. It was soon a boomtown, home at first to tens of thousands of workers, and then hundreds of thousands. The Spanish called it Cerro Rico – the rich mountain – and during the second half of the sixteenth century its output accounted for two-thirds of all the silver mined anywhere in the world. By 1650 some 16,000 tons of Potosi silver had flowed into European coffers. Potosi silver was the cash cow for Europe for 300 years. Even today there is a Spanish term – *valer un potosí*, to be 'worth a potosí' – that describes an unimaginable fortune. Miguel de Cervantes used the same in his novel *Don Quixote*.

That which enriched the lives of Spaniards and others was the making of a hell on earth for those indigenous people forced to extract the ore and process it into silver. Long before the Spanish arrived, the Inca aristocracy had demanded labour from their population via a system called *mit'a*, by which each person owed his masters the sweat of his brow and the strength of his back. That tradition was exploited by the Spanish mine owners, and uncounted thousands of people were swept into the deadly misery, to be consumed like oxygen by a fire. One Spanish observer, Domingo de Santo Tomás, wrote, 'to the complete perdition of this land, there was discovered a mouth of hell, into which a great mass of people enter every year and are sacrificed by the greed of the Spaniards ...' Another, Rodrigo de Loaisa, described the mining work in detail: 'The Indians enter these infernal pits by some leather ropes like staircases ... Once inside, they spend the whole week in there without emerging, working with tallow candles. They are in great danger inside there ... If 20 healthy Indians enter on Monday, half may emerge crippled on Saturday.' If the mines did not kill them, then the heavy use of mercury in the extraction of the silver, topside, from the crushed ore was lethally toxic too.

The Spanish had found great wealth in their holdings in South America. In the main they restricted their operations to New Spain (which was what they called Mexico), Peru and some of the Caribbean islands, but their shadow was from sea to shining sea. While King Charles, back in Spain, liked to imagine he was ruling the Americas directly, in practice the tyranny of distance made that impossible. In truth his colonies were independent kingdoms where Crown-appointed governors ruled as they saw fit. As long as the bullion kept flowing back to Spain, along with the tobacco and sugar grown on the plantations, all was well.

Spain also exported to the Americas a form of feudalism that enabled the near slavery of the indigenous population in those mines and elsewhere. A landowner would be granted, by the Crown's representatives, an *encomienda* – a number of villages populated by locals who were under his notional protection in return for a share of their labour. It was a system that had been applied first in Spain, over Moorish territories reclaimed during the Reconquista. In both cases it was a means of dominating non-Christians and was part of what created the long-term difference between the societies that evolved in Catholic South America under Spain and, later, Portugal, and those that took shape in North America under offshoots of English and other Protestant and non-conformist societies. In the North, the rights of the individual to property and protection by law, underscored by religious tolerance – or, at least, enough space to allow different faiths to keep out of each other's way – produced in time the United States of America. In the South, absolutism and the feudalism of *encomienda*, strengthened and legitimized by inflexible Catholicism, produced populations that saw better futures for themselves north of the border.

If only the Spanish had called it quits at horses.

59.

IVAN THE TERRIBLE,
TSAR OF ALL THE RUSSIAS

Russia seems more than a country, even more than a continent. It is certainly the biggest country in the world – twice the size of China or the USA. A journey from the city of St Petersburg in the west to the Pacific Ocean in the east takes in eleven time zones. For all that geographical heft, it is home to just around 145 million people – a population dwarfed by the 450 million of the EU. Much of its mass is made up of the wastes of Siberia, rich in mineral wealth but an exceptionally hard place in which to survive, far less thrive. Russia's vastness is, anyway, about more than numbers. Like the ice and taiga of Siberia, the very idea of Russia feels impenetrable. In some ways Russia . . . *Russian* . . . seems more like a state of mind.

When more people were familiar with the many words of Winston Churchill, before and during the Second World War, his line about Russia was among the best known, and often quoted thereafter. During a radio broadcast on 1 October 1939, he said, 'I cannot forecast to you the action of Russia. It is a riddle wrapped in a mystery inside an enigma . . .' Those words are less well known now, but even when they were routinely quoted by this commentator or that, the second half of the line was usually left out: '. . . but perhaps there is a key. That key is Russian national interest.'

Keeping something the size of Russia together is like herding cats. If you had a mind to, you might round up a territorial vastness stretching for thousands of miles in every direction and populated by all manner of peoples, European and Asian and every creed and colour. You could give that vastness a unifying name. But holding all those souls and entities in place when what they often seem to want to do is spin off into space requires a massive centre of gravity.

The roots of the Russia of now go all the way down to those Rus' of Kiev, 'the men who row', a relatively tiny clump of cells held in place first of all by Rurik, the Swedish Viking. In the Church of St Sophia in Constantinople they had found the Christian God most beguiling of all. Those newly Christian Rus' made Russia but it was a small thing still, and vulnerable to invasion. That sense of vulnerability was always there – that threat from beyond the horizon – and has never left them. By the thirteenth century, tormented by Mongols, the Russians made a new capital for themselves at Moscow. Now they were the Grand Principality of Muscovy, but the vulnerability remained.

Ivan Vasilyevich was born on 22 January 1440 – Grand Prince of Moscow and Grand Prince of All Rus' – and ascended his father's throne in 1462. In 1472 he married Sophia Palaiologina, younger sister of Constantine XI, last emperor of Constantinople. From their union came the double-headed eagle of the Russian coat of arms. That Ivan was Ivan the Great, and under his rule the country tripled in size. He saw his demesne as successor to the Roman empire, and said Moscow was the new Rome. He was the first of his kind to style himself *tsar* – a corruption of 'Caesar' – and Sophia was his tsarina.

The moment of note in the story of Russia, and therefore of the story of the world, was the naming of his grandson, also Ivan, as the first Tsar of All Rus' in 1547 at the age of sixteen. He would come to be known as Ivan the Terrible – a translation of the Russian *grozny*, which has more to do with being powerful than evil, so to speak. He could be evil too, though, and no mistake. In 1570 he would sense treason in the city of

Novgorod and sent soldiers of his bodyguard, the *oprichnina*, to torture and slaughter tens of thousands of citizens – men, women and children. The Massacre of Novgorod is only the most notorious product of the paranoia and cruelty that characterized much of his behaviour in the later years of his reign.

Under that Ivan, Russia began its great spread – east into the Ural Mountains, south to the Caspian Sea and the Black Sea and north into the Arctic. The spread would be inexorable, and within a hundred years Russia had swallowed Siberia all the way to the Pacific. He paved the way for other legendary figures – Peter the Great, Catherine the Great. By the end of the Second World War Russia stretched west to east from Berlin to the Pacific, and north to south from the Arctic to Afghanistan.

Always the successful control of Russia, of the USSR, has been about ruthless strength at the centre – the gravitational pull of a black hole from which nothing, not even light, should escape. The end of the Cold War and the fall of the Iron Curtain after 1989 would see a lessening, but the Russian state of mind – which is the state of mind of the strong man, and a tendency to submit to such – prevails. There are always those who prefer order, even cruel order, to the possible chaos of dissolution lying in wait.

In his speech of 1939 Churchill also quoted British Liberal John Bright, speaking at the end of the American Civil War: 'At last after the smoke of the battlefield had cleared away, the horrid shape which had cast its shadow over the whole continent had vanished and was gone for ever.' Since the time of Ivan the Terrible the shadow cast by the strong men of Russia has never gone away.

60.

THE VALLADOLID DEBATE, SLAVERY AND HUMAN RIGHTS

In August 1550, fourteen theologians gathered inside the grand hall of the Colegio de San Gregorio in the Spanish city of Valladolid. They had been summoned by their king, Charles I (who was also Holy Roman Emperor Charles V, made holy by the Pope), to hear a debate about the human rights (or not) of the Native Americans in the Spanish colonies. Before the *junta*, or jury, were two more men – humanist scholar Juan de Sepúlveda and Dominican friar Bartolomé de las Casas. Each would take a side in the debate and any decision resulting from their efforts would affect the lives of men and women living then and millions yet to be born.

Ever since the discovery of the New World by Columbus at the end of the fifteenth century there had been pain in the hearts of some – and not just those conquered and colonized. While it is easiest to think of cruel and murderous conquistadors, bent on pillage and extortion as many of them were, there were also souls among those Europeans who were prompted to ask questions about what it meant, after all was said and done, to be human.

In 1511 another Dominican friar, Antonio de Montesinos, had watched the rapaciousness of the conquerors on the island of Hispaniola and declared: 'I am the voice crying in the wilderness . . . the voice of Christ in the desert of this island . . . you are all in mortal sin . . . on account of the cruelty and tyranny with which you use these innocent people.'

'Are these not men?' he asked. 'Have they not rational souls? Must you not love them as you love yourselves?'

From the beginning of the colonization there had been that system of *encomienda*, whereby Spanish nobles were granted, by the king, little kingdoms of their own and rights to the labour of the native people living there. They had wanted slaves, and while *encomienda* dealt the cards slightly differently for the sake of some or other propriety, the hand amounted to the same for those under the yoke.

Back in Spain, back in the grand hall in Valladolid, Sepúlveda made arguments about a place and people he had never seen. He was all theory and book learning. He reached back in time to the thinking of Ancient Greece, and Aristotle of Athens, who had decided some men were meant to rule while others were lesser and meant to be slaves. Those 'savages' in the New World were cannibals, said Sepúlveda. They made sacrifices of each other and tore out living hearts, which was true. Such behaviours made it plain those creatures were of the lesser sort Aristotle had had in mind when he defined 'natural slaves'. As well as being enslaved, Sepúlveda continued, they should be forcibly converted to Christianity. Those savages were idolators and sodomites, he stated, the lowest of the low. Indeed, he added, Spain was justified in making war upon them, 'in order to uproot crimes that offend nature'.

While Sepúlveda had no personal experience of America or Americans, Bartolomé de las Casas was different. His father had been a friend of Columbus. Las Casas himself had been on Hispaniola at the beginning of it all and, as a young man, had taken part in slave raids. He had owned slaves of his own. When that Dominican friar Montesinos had asked 'Are these not men?' Las Casas had answered that no, they were not. Later, and in the manner of St Paul on the road to Damascus, the scales fell from his eyes. In time he became a Dominican friar himself and for the rest of his life he campaigned for the rights of the natives as fellow human beings.

In 1537 he was instrumental in persuading Pope Paul III to pass the bull Sublimis Deus that declared the native people rational beings. In 1542 he was part of the drafting of the so-called New Laws, intended to end the *encomienda* system altogether. By 1550 King Charles was minded to go so far as to summon the *junta* at Valladolid, to hear yet more about the great philosophical question of the age: how was European man to conceive of those he had found on the other side of the ocean?

It was the duty of every man, said Las Casas, to protect the vulnerable. He had read as much in Ecclesiasticus: 'Deliver him that suffereth wrong from the hand of the oppressor . . .' More wisdom he quoted, from Church Fathers St Augustine, greatest Christian thinker after St Paul, and also St John Chrysostom, who had hated the abuse of power and the neglect of any needy or suffering: 'Do you pay such honour to your excrements as to receive them into a silver chamber pot, when another man made in the image of God is perishing in the cold . . . ?'

The *junta* sat in 1550, and then again the following year. In the end, their judgement was . . . that there was no judgement. They favoured neither argument strongly enough and so each side claimed a victory of sorts. The *encomienda* system had been stalled a little while, but soon regained its old momentum. What was certain was that Bartolomé de las Casas emerged, and was regarded ever after, as that most staunch of all the defenders of the native peoples of the Americas. All of this happened long before the British emerged as the kings of the Atlantic slave trade. What mattered, what is momentous, is that the doubt was there at the beginning of European contact with the New World – doubt about such treatment of fellow man. It would not be until the nineteenth century and William Wilberforce and the Abolition Movement he represented that slavery would be undone. But even as enslavement began, and all the while the horror unfolded, there were plenty who knew that it was wrong.

61.

ELIZABETH I, THE SPANISH ARMADA
AND THE BIRTH OF NATIONALITY

The British Isles have done well out of being just that – isles. Separation from the main has, down through the millennia and then the centuries, been more advantage than disadvantage. William Shakespeare made a great deal of it of course in, among countless instances, the words he put into the mouth of John of Gaunt, in *Richard II* – all that 'royal throne of kings, this sceptred isle' stuff, and: 'This fortress built by Nature for herself / Against infection and the hand of war . . . / This precious stone set in the silver sea / Which serves it in the office of a wall / Or as a moat defensive to a house . . .'

It was patriotism he was weaving, in support of a royal house still anxious then about legitimacy and keen to make a unity out of dynasty and nation. All of that was deliberate on the part of the Bard because he was ever in the business of sucking up to royalty – Tudor royalty. By his time they were more than an upstart house, the usurpers they had been when the first of them, Henry VII, had seized the crown on Bosworth Field. Elizabeth I (Good Queen Bess, as the faithful were encouraged to call her) had been on the throne for nearly four decades by the time Shakespeare wrote *Richard II*, and by then England had woken up to nationhood.

Some of it, perhaps a great deal of it, was the work of Elizabeth herself. She was fifty-four years old when she arrived at her fort at Tilbury, on the Thames, on 9 August 1588. It was a year and a half since she had sanctioned the execution of the Catholic Mary, Queen of Scots. Protestant Elizabeth had held her cousin prisoner for nineteen years by then and her beheading, in Fotheringay Castle in Northamptonshire, had been by way of a final solution to a problem. If Elizabeth was loved by many of her English subjects there were plenty, both in her realm and on mainland Europe, who felt otherwise. Catholic King Philip II of Spain had come to regard her as an affront to any throne. She was his former sister-in-law, on account of his having been married to Mary Tudor, Elizabeth's half-sister and predecessor as queen. Philip eventually joined those in whose interests it was to view Elizabeth as illegitimate. She had been born to Anne Boleyn, second wife of Henry VIII, after his scandalous divorce from the Spanish Catherine of Aragon. Many – Philip and the Pope included – considered the second marriage unlawful, unholy, so that Elizabeth was no more than a bastard, and unfit to rule.

On the abdication of his father, Charles V, Holy Roman Emperor, Philip became ruler of Spain, the American colonies and the Spanish Netherlands. Mary had died in 1558, replaced by Elizabeth, and at first Philip sought her hand in marriage as well. When he asked her first to renounce her Protestant faith she refused. He was the first of many suitors she would rebuff, and surely the most powerful.

For Philip, the beheading of the Queen of Scots was a convenient last straw. He had seen in her the chance of returning a Catholic to the English throne and when word of the regicide reached him he was moved to make war – to knock Queen Bess from her throne and sit upon it himself. In May 1588 his 'great and joyous Armada' set sail from Lisbon. Towards the end of July the Spanish leviathans clashed, inconclusively, with the smaller, more manoeuvrable vessels of the English fleet, commanded by Francis Drake. In early August the Armada was anchored off the French coast, at Calais. Just 25 miles away, at Dunkirk, were the transports ready to carry a Spanish army – commanded by Alexander Farnese, Duke of Parma, and tens of thousands strong – across the Channel, to the Thames and London. The Armada was to escort them, but instead those ships came under attack from English fireships, loaded with pitch and sulphur and set ablaze. Having slipped their anchors to escape, the Spanish fell foul of a change in the weather – 'a Protestant Wind' that blew them north. Unable to turn for home they had to circumnavigate the archipelago. Only half the ships and half the men would ever see Spain again.

While the wind blew, England waited. The Armada had been galled, but what of the army waiting at Dunkirk? Would they come now? It was in that atmosphere of waiting, tension unbearable, that Elizabeth came to Tilbury. It was the moment that more than any other made her memory immortal – made England, England. Eyewitness accounts have her appear like a goddess of war. She was all in white, plumes in her hair, a breastplate over her gown and astride a white horse. Unafraid, she moved among her troops, 20,000 of them, with a bodyguard of just half a dozen. Here was her moment and she began to speak, addressing her soldiers as 'My loving people': 'We have been persuaded by some that are careful of our safety, to take heed how we commit our selves to armed multitudes, for fear of treachery; but I assure you I do not desire to live to distrust my faithful and loving people. Let tyrants fear.' She had come there, she said, 'to live and die among you all; to lay down for my God and for my kingdom, and my people, my honour and my blood, even in the dust'.

Historians are happy to conclude the words were hers, and spoken there and then rather than being imagined later by some other. Here was the queen who would never marry any man, who was married instead to England and the English. She was, in that moment, the embodiment of all of it.

I know I have the body of a weak, feeble woman; but I have the heart and stomach of a king, and of a king of England too . . .

England was a nation.

62.

AKBAR AND ELIZABETH ARE DEAD
AND EUROPE COMES TO INDIA

Good Queen Bess – she with the heart and stomach of a king – died on 24 March 1603. She was sixty-nine years old and had reigned for forty-four years. Akbar the Great – third Mughal emperor and grandson of Babur, the first of them – died on 27 October 1605. He was sixty-three and had ruled his empire for forty-six years. Their lives had run on parallel tracks. As their long reigns drew to a close, the fates of England and India were about to converge with consequences that would have been unimaginable for either monarch.

The coming together got under way while both were still alive, on a memorably cold New Year's Eve in 1600, and it was quite a moment. Both grand performances were well into their third acts when Elizabeth granted a Royal Charter to the Honourable Company of Merchants of London Trading into the East Indies. Thus was created what became known as the British East India Company – a straightforward money-making venture to begin with, but ruling the subcontinent in all but name before the end.

According to English poet Edward FitzGerald's translation of Stanza XLVIX of the *Rubaiyat of Omar Khayyam*:

> 'Tis all a Chequer-board of Nights and Days
> Where Destiny with Men for Pieces plays:

Hither and thither moves, and mates and slays,
And one by one back in the Closet lays.

If so, then at that moment when she was granting 218 merchants a monopoly of trade with all lands lying east of the Cape of Good Hope, no one would have thought much of Elizabeth's position on the board. Her kingdom barely counted as a great power, even in the context of Europe. Those watching her make her mark on the necessary paperwork that day might well have been trembling – not with cold, with excitement rather, at the potential of all that lay ahead. But their queen was in a corner, overlooked, hemmed in by crippling debt. Akbar the Great was the king, presiding over one of the most powerful empires in the world. The population of his city of Calcutta was greater than that of the whole of England.

Chess had come out of Persia around AD 600. In its early form, the queen was a relatively minor piece – in fact it was not called the queen, but the adviser. The king was always most important, and to be protected at all costs. To lose the king was to lose all. Along the Silk Road the game travelled, all the way to Europe eventually. And then something happened in the west that had not happened before. Between 1362 and 1654, eighteen women reigned as queens in thirteen different European kingdoms: Isabella of Castile . . . Catherine of Aragon . . . Mary Tudor . . . Elizabeth I . . . The world was changing, and the game of chess changed to reflect it, though hardly a soul noticed at the time. As a result of all those powerful women the piece that had been only the adviser was given the combined powers of a rook and a bishop, and renamed the queen. With the advent of Gutenberg's printing press, the rules of chess were formalized and circulated as never before and the power of the queen on the chessboard spread around the world.

The Persian cry of '*shah mat!*', which means 'the king is helpless', is rendered into English as 'checkmate!' Unbeknown to Akbar, as his reign drew to an end a new destiny was taking shape for his successors. He was not helpless – not yet, and never would be – but the move made by Queen Elizabeth as one year rolled into another would change the world.

After Akbar came his son, Jahangir, and then his grandson, Shah Jahan, who had the masterpiece of the Taj Mahal raised as a tomb for his favourite wife. Shah Jahan was imprisoned by his third son, Aurangzeb, who sidestepped his elder brothers as well in his determination to seize control.

For a century, since Babur, the Muslim Mughal empire had been tolerant of India's other faiths, but Aurangzeb was a zealot. Zoroastrians, Christians, Buddhists, Jains and especially Hindus suffered his intolerance. Temples and other sacred places were destroyed; the poll tax on non-Muslims – the *jizyah* – that had been done away with by Akbar was reinstated. Akbar had gone so far as to try and bring Hinduism, Islam and Zoroastrianism together as a hybrid faith – a failure in the end, but a sign of good intentions. Aurangzeb wanted only Islam. There were rebellions, and in the Deccan a heartland of Hindu resistance gave birth to the Mahrata empire, under the visionary leadership of Shivaji Bhonsale, and committed to Hindu self-rule. During the second half of the eighteenth century, the empire controlled 250,000 acres of territory – one third of the subcontinent. Aurangzeb died in 1707 but the hornets' nest he had stirred among the hillmen of the Deccan, those Mahratas, was in large part the undoing of the Mughals. India always prevailed, swallowing its own children as well as outsiders.

And all the while Mughals fought with Mahratas, and Muslim with Hindu, elsewhere on the chequerboard of nights and days other pieces had been moving. Madras Fort George was settled by the English in 1639, their first toehold. By the turn of the eighteenth century there would be posts in Bombay and Calcutta too. There were Portuguese prospectors as well, and later French. In the same year Aurangzeb died, the parliaments of England and Scotland came together as one and Britain was born. Above all it was British pieces, rooks and castles, bishops and pawns, working together, that were poised to check the Indian kings and queens with mate in mind.

63.

TYCHO BRAHE DIES AND JOHANNES
KEPLER ACCESSES HIS DATA

That Earth was the centre of the universe, around which the sun and all else revolved, had been accepted fact since the time of Ptolemy of Alexandria in the second century AD. Such thinking was in agreement, after all, with the Bible. God had created the Earth and then set the sun and moon in the sky above. Always the assumption had been that Earth was a fixed point, the immovable centre of creation. As Psalm 104 expressed it, God had 'laid the foundations of the earth, that it should not be removed for ever'.

Aristotle had said the same in the fourth century BC. It was altogether a stubborn notion. Having accepted Earth was stationary, Ptolemy set about explaining the nature of the observable movements of the sun, moon, planets and stars. Greek thinkers, Aristotle among them, had been determined that all heavenly bodies followed perfect – which is to say circular – orbits of the Earth. Simple observation, however, made it hard to see how that *could be* the case, even when it was assumed that it *was* the case.

Ptolemy was not the first genius to try and make the evidence fit the conviction after the fact, but his system was the most complete and persuasive. The so-called Ptolemaic system was a triumph of determination to make what was *seen* comply with what was *believed*. He envisioned

Earth sitting at the heart of a nest of invisible spheres (like hamster balls, one inside the other in the manner of a Russian doll) within which the heavenly bodies were fixed. Those spheres rotated and the sun, moon, planets and stars had their own circular orbits in the gaps between the spheres. It was a system of Byzantine complexity . . . and yet it worked. Founded on a profoundly flawed premise though the Ptolemaic system was, the predictions it enabled about the movements of the lights in the sky worked well enough for navigators up until the time of Christopher Columbus.

Francis Bacon, Attorney General and Lord Chancellor of England, is usually the name mentioned in relation to the advent of the modern scientific method that would upend those ancient assumptions. He was certainly a bright light among others of similar mind, men beginning to emphasize the need to observe the natural world and to test ideas by means of experimentation.

Before effort of that sort there was *On the Revolutions of the Celestial Orbs* by Nicolaus Copernicus, a Polish churchman, published in 1543. He was not a scientist and instead wrote up a hunch born of his own imaginative genius, that it must be the sun at the centre of all, with Earth, moon and planets in orbit about it. Here was a *heliocentric* system, sun-centred, and as striking for Christendom and Christians as a slap across the face. What was required – and what was coming – was scientific proof of what Copernicus had merely intuited.

Among those busily observing, and recording data, in the middle years of the sixteenth century was the Danish nobleman and astronomer Tycho Brahe. Originally destined for a career in theology and law, Brahe's destiny was changed by his witnessing of a solar eclipse in 1560, when he was thirteen. Then and there began his fascination with astronomy and, from the beginning, an understanding of the need for accurate observation. In 1572 he observed the appearance of a supernova, a new star in the constellation Cassiopeia, and his reports of his findings made him famous. By comparing his own measurements of the phenomenon, made in

Denmark, with those recorded in England by astronomer Thomas Digges, he was able to show an apparent absence of parallax. The implication was that the new star was a vast distance from Earth, and in his book on the event – *De Nova Stella*, published in 1573 – he declared that the understanding of the universe as laid out by Aristotle (and so, by association, Ptolemy) must be wrong.

With the financial support of King Frederick II of Denmark and Norway he built two observatories on the Danish island of Hven, as well as equipment needed for tracking and measuring the movements of heavenly bodies. This was in a time without the telescope (not generally available until the middle of the seventeenth century), and much of Brahe's contribution was made possible by skilful use of a mural quadrant, a huge angle-measuring device built into a wall erected upon a meridian. For twenty years he watched and measured the movements of planets against the fixed stars, creating a database of planetary positions of unprecedented value. He also catalogued the positions of 777 stars that were, by an order of magnitude, more accurate than anything previously achieved.

Brahe proposed a system to replace not just that of Ptolemy (whose vision of the cosmos was wrong) but also that of Copernicus, whose vision was quite right. The Tychonic system envisioned all the planets, except Earth, orbiting the sun, while the sun orbited the Earth. Had the story ended there, it would be one of well-researched failure. Fortunately for the store of human wisdom, Brahe's orbit was intersected by that of Johannes Kepler.

It was a coming together of opposites. Brahe was born rich and maintained an extravagant lifestyle. He was flamboyant in style and wore a metal nose (some said gold, others silver or brass) to cover wounds sustained in a sword fight. He was also secretive and guarded his data jealously. Kepler was from poverty, the son of a mercurial mercenary father and a profoundly eccentric mother. While Brahe was proud and grand, Kepler was self-effacing and self-deprecating.

Kepler had won fame in 1596 with the publication of *Mysterium Cosmographicum*, in which he laid out a fantastical and yet elegant and imaginative theory of the movement of the celestial bodies. Impressed by the leaps of thought revealed in its pages, Brahe went against his own secretive nature and invited Kepler, twenty-five years his junior, to join him. His patron, King Frederick, had died and he had fallen out with his successor, Christian IV. Forced to abandon Denmark he had curried favour with Rudolf II, the Holy Roman Emperor, and set up a new observatory at Benatky near Prague. It was there that Brahe and Kepler attempted to collaborate, and within months they were at each other's throats. Kepler took his leave but Brahe persuaded him to return.

The moment of greatest significance was the unexpected and premature death of Tycho Brahe, on 24 October 1601. The official cause of death was bizarre enough, being a burst bladder caused by him attending a royal gala and, so the story goes, being too embarrassed to excuse himself to use the facilities. Conspiracy theorists used to insist he was the victim of murder by mercury poisoning – with the finger of guilt pointing either at King Christian, in revenge for Brahe's alleged affair with his mother, or at Kepler himself. Brahe's remains were exhumed in 2010, however, and tests ruled out any significant trace of the element.

Whatever the cause of his death, his absence gave Kepler unobstructed access to all of the data Brahe had so meticulously collected and carefully withheld. So armed, and having taken up the prestigious post of Imperial Mathematician, Kepler produced the three laws of planetary motion that bear his name. In a break from Aristotle and Ptolemy more profound, and more meaningful by far, than that of Brahe, he painted a picture of planets moving in elliptical orbits of irregular speeds.

Without Brahe's data, Kepler would have been without foundations upon which to build. The achievement born of their bad-tempered union was followed in due course by that of the Italian Galileo Galilei, more famous and infamous by far. Unlike his predecessors he was equipped with a telescope and used it finally to wipe away any surviving faith in ideas like those of Aristotle and Ptolemy and to underline the truth of Copernicus. He observed that Venus, like the moon, had crescent phases. To his amazement he discerned two little 'handles' on Saturn and what he interpreted as another, lesser solar system orbiting Jupiter. The Milky Way, which seemed an ethereal ribbon of smoke to the naked eye, was, through the telescope, awash with stars.

Brahe's dying words had been: 'Don't let my life have been in vain.' On account of an unlikely sequence of events – of the sort that fill the story of the world – it had not been.

64.

JAMESTOWN AND THE FOUNDATIONS
OF EUROPEAN NORTH AMERICA

That the fates of North and South America have been so utterly different is due in no small part to the manner in which each was colonized by Europeans.

Spain was furthest ahead in the game, having begun settlement in Central and South America in the fifteenth century. Those colonies were little kingdoms, little Spains, where King Philip liked to imagine his personal rule extended across the Atlantic Ocean, and they were run on the *encomienda* system. It was slavery by any other name, and those locals that did not die of European diseases soon succumbed to hardship and cruelty in mines and elsewhere. The Spanish imposed their religion too, enforcing conversion to their Catholicism. At every meaningful level, the Spanish presence in the Americas was backed by Church and state.

Spain claimed North America too, by right, but its ability to press that claim fell short of the realistic or the practical. The English explored the coastline and in 1585 established a first colony on Roanoke Island in what is now the state of North Carolina. It withered and failed, and its replacement, set in place two years later, fared no better. When relief ships returned to the place in 1590, not a soul was found and rumour

persisted ever after that all had either been massacred by the locals or
else assimilated by them and spirited away.

The moment that counted in the long run came on 4 May 1607 when a
flag was raised above a fortification soon known as Jamestown, in honour
of King James VI and I of England. Elizabethan prospectors dispatched
by Sir Walter Raleigh had explored the eastern seaboard and a vast swathe
north of 30 degrees of latitude was soon claimed and named Virginia
after Her Majesty. In contrast to the Spanish model to the south, the
British Crown was more inclined to privatize its efforts to colonize its
share of the New World. The Virginia Company of London was a joint-
stock company established by James in 1606. Adventurers would shoulder
the risks – both personal and financial – and the Crown would take its
cut of any proceeds.

Among the risk-takers was sometime mercenary John Smith, son of a
tenant farmer in Lincolnshire. Having earned his battle scars fighting the
Spanish and the Ottoman Turks he returned to England long enough to
insert himself into Raleigh's schemes for wealth in virgin territory on the
other side of the Atlantic. He was a handful from the get-go, and shackled
for mutiny on the way out. The feckless aristocrats around him were
lucky he was there, however, and by deciding against executing him on
arrival they helped assure their survival in the face of desperate conditions in a malarial hellhole.

Before they were to be regarded as settlers and Americans, they were
more like ship-wrecked mariners on a hostile shore. Incompetent governance all but saw to their undoing, but the emergent leadership of men
like Smith secured their survival, although only just. Though much
embellished by Smith himself – notably in his accounts of twice being
saved from death by the intervention of Pocahontas of the local Powhatan
tribe – it is generally accepted that he helped establish amicable relations
with the indigenous neighbours. Jamestown struggled through early
years and a 'starving time' but was well established by the end of the
second decade of the century. Its presence, its name, lured the first of

thousands of British colonists. Among the traditions exported were individual rights to property, rights to legal protection – and thereby the foundations of what became the United States of America. Those outlines of freedom, flawed though they were and are, help explain why immigration in the Americas in the modern era has been predominantly from South to North.

THE KING JAMES BIBLE AND A
LANGUAGE FOR THE WORLD

Johannes Gutenberg had launched a new age of information when he perfected the printing press. That he might never have got the job done without the financial backing of his sometime partner Johann Fust is indicative of the entrepreneurial dynamism that characterized the later Middle Ages. The feudal system was on the wane and an emergent middle class made of aspirant merchants and inventors, on the make and in pursuit of new money, was on the rise. Those new men had risen from among the world of the poor and the ways and means of their recent ancestors hung about them like a lingering scent, of the soil, of the sea and of the mine. Among themselves the poor – and so the new middle class to whom they had so recently given birth – spoke English to each other; the nobles above them, and the academic churchmen, spoke Latin and French. For hundreds of years the Bible had existed only in Greek, and then Latin, and so was in effect an audio book for most – strictly for listening to. Any poor man – or woman, or child – wanting the word of God had no alternative but to sit in church and hear it recited by another.

Gutenberg had begun to change all that in 1455 with the printing of his Bible. It was in Latin, right enough, but it had shown how copies of a printed text might be for the many instead of the few. Up came the middle class, and among other things they wanted to read the word of

Imperial mathematician Johannes Kepler, author of the three laws of planetary motion that bear his name. Although of unquestionable genius, Kepler's achievements would not have been possible without access to the data gathered by his less famous collaborator Tycho Brahe.

The birth of the British Raj: triumphant after his victory at the Battle of Plassey in 1757, Lieutenant Colonel Robert Clive, employee of the British East India Company, greets Mir Jafar, newly installed Nawab of Bengal and puppet of the British.

Shaka, son of Nandi, warrior king of the Zulus. By the time of his death in 1828 he ruled a population of 250,000 and had laid the foundations of a Zulu kingdom that would defy and defeat the British army in Africa.

The Wright Brothers take to the sky: after earning their wings piloting gliders, in 1903 Wilbur and Orville built the first ever powered-flight aircraft. That same year Orville completed the first flight – a distance of 120 feet – at Kitty Hawk.

Within eight weeks of the outbreak of war in 1914, three-quarters of a million British men had volunteered for service. For many of those their first action would be 1 July 1916, the first day of the Battle of the Somme.

The radioactive plume from Fat Man, the atomic bomb dropped on the city of Nagasaki on 9 August 1945, seen from Koyagi-jima, nearly 10 kilometres away. In a single lifetime Japan had been transformed from a medieval kingdom, cut off from the outside world, into a twentieth-century superpower. A flash of man-made light would change it all again.

'I have a dream . . .' The Civil Rights Act outlawing discrimination based on race, colour, religion, sex or national origin was passed by Congress the year after Dr Martin Luther King Jr's speech in Washington in August 1963. It was intended to mark the advent of a new American Republic and yet the US – together with much of the rest of the world besides – is presently as mired in race hatred and division as it has been at any time since the life and death of Dr King.

Through a glass darkly . . . Neil Armstrong is reflected in the visor of Buzz Aldrin's helmet as he takes this photograph of his fellow astronaut joining him on the surface of the moon.

God for themselves, so that as the sixteenth century progressed there was more and more demand for translations of the Bible into the languages they actually spoke in their homes, being the vernacular. Gutenberg had had a hand in it, and so too had Martin Luther, that turbulent priest of Wittenberg. He had nailed his ninety-five theses to a door and then someone took them down and printed them for general circulation. The rest of his ideas were printed as well, and so the Reformation had been born. A central plank of that movement – that revolution – had been about encouraging every person to read the Bible for himself, for herself. Taken together, the printing press and the Reformation taught Protestants to read, that each might save his own soul by making a direct and personal connection with the Almighty.

English theologian John Wycliffe had overseen a translation of the Bible into English that was completed by 1384. Luther translated the Bible into German in 1522, and then four years later William Tyndale offered a version of the New Testament, based heavily on Luther's, in English. The first full Bible in English was the work of ecclesiastical reformer Myles Coverdale, in 1535. Among the most beloved translations into English was the Geneva Bible, and Coverdale had a leading hand in that one as well. It would be the favourite of figures including Shakespeare, John Donne and John Bunyan, author of *The Pilgrim's Progress* in 1678.

Among all those lights, a greater illumination yet was made by the Bible commissioned by King James VI and I in 1604 and completed in 1611. He was no sooner on the throne, in 1603 after the death of Elizabeth I, than he was being harangued by Catholic and Protestant alike and all creeds in between. All wanted reassurance, if not dominance, at court and in the land. Among other ambitions he had for his Bible, James hoped it would be as oil on troubled water. Furthermore the Geneva Bible had all manner of marginal notes, some of which might be interpreted as undermining royal authority, and he planned to excise those too.

The resultant King James Version is also, and most importantly, a foundation for the English language spoken today. It is littered throughout with turns of phrase coined for that Bible that are with us still: out of the mouths of babes . . . fought the good fight . . . do we see eye to eye? . . . signs of the times . . . the powers that be . . . rise and shine . . . a fly in the ointment . . . a thorn in the side . . . a man after his own heart . . . the apple of his eye . . .

The moment worth imagining in a story of the world was in Stationers' Hall, close by St Paul's Cathedral in the City of London, and the premises then (1610) of the Worshipful Company of Stationers. There and then began the reading aloud of the finished work. The KJV would be read in every church and so it was necessary, vital, to ensure it sounded right, that its rhythms and cadences would lift hearts and souls. There in that hall its verses rose and rang. Its language sounds archaic now but resonates as it did then. It is a translation of great simplicity based throughout around a structure of ten syllables and the de-dum-de-dum iambic rhythm familiar to Shakespeare. That reading in Stationers' Hall, after the moment of its beginning, would take most of a year.

English is the language of the world, of the Internet, and its most important founds are in and of the KJV. Its idioms are there in popular songs, its stories were the inspiration for more novels than might be counted, from *Moby Dick* to *The Old Man and the Sea*. Beyond the England of its birth its influence travelled aboard the ships of empire to India and Africa. Like no other, it was the book that changed the world.

66.

FRANCIS BACON, FROZEN CHICKEN AND THE SCIENTIFIC METHOD

They say Pond Square, in London's Highgate, is haunted by the ghost of a half-plucked chicken. Reported sightings are few and far between now but there were documented encounters during the Second World War and in the 1960s. As recently as the 1970s a courting couple claimed their passionate embrace among the stately London plane trees of the square was interrupted when the avian apparition dropped from the sky and landed beside them. After running in circles for a few moments, squawking all the while, it apparently vanished into the thin air from which it had come.

The legend of the spirit chicken is a footnote to a story, a moment, almost as strange, involving Sir Francis Bacon, sometime Lord Chancellor of England and eulogized by some as a father, if not *the* father, of the scientific method.

Born in 1561, in London, he was a man with an eye on a future made better for humankind by the philosophy of science. Central to his thinking was that it was not enough merely to think one's way to explanations for the workings of the world, as the Greek philosophers had done. He wrote of those ancients that they 'assuredly have that which is characteristic of boys; they are prompt to prattle but cannot generate; for their wisdom abounds in words but is barren of works . . .' Rather, he said, it was necessary – vital – to devise and perform *experiments* to test ideas, and then to analyse any results. This was the scientific method, in essence the same that underpins scientific investigation to this day.

Bacon was a man of many parts, imagined by some as the real author of Shakespeare's plays. In his time he was also a jurist, statesman and author, a favourite of Elizabeth I and also close to her successor James VI and I. Appointed Lord Chancellor in 1618 he fell into debt – and from grace. Leaving behind the world of politics then, he focused on science. And so it was that in the spring of 1626 the moment came that fixed him for ever in the firmament of scientific stars . . .

On a fearful, cold April day he was travelling in a carriage with a Dr Winterbourne. By way of conversation, Bacon suggested it ought to be possible to preserve meat by freezing it, but his companion was unconvinced. They were passing through the village of Highgate at the time and, determined to prove his theory, Bacon had the carriage driver pull to a halt outside a house. He climbed out and knocked on the door. A woman answered, and after a few minutes Bacon had purchased a chicken from her. He had her partially pluck and gut the carcass before taking it to snow-covered ground nearby, in what is now Pond Square. There he packed the bird's cavity with snow and then, having placed it inside a bag, he packed more snow around it, dug a hole and buried the bundle. Back in the carriage, Bacon was severely chilled – to such an extent that Dr Winterbourne had the carriage divert to the nearby home of the Earl of Arundel, where Bacon was put to bed. The cot had been heated with a hot pan but no one had slept in it for a year or more and the sheets were damp. His condition worsened rapidly, and within a few days he was dead – although not before finding the strength to write a note for his absentee host, Arundel: 'I was . . . desirous to try an experiment or two touching the conservation and induration of bodies . . . it succeeded excellently well . . .'

What more can a man do to demonstrate the value of experiment than to make himself a martyr to the process?

In an unfinished novel called *New Atlantis* – published in 1627, the year after his death – Bacon had imagined a utopian island where the search to expand human knowledge was paramount. The very heart of the place was a college 'dedicated to the works and creatures of God . . . The End of our Foundation is the knowledge of Causes; and the secret motion of things; and the enlarging of the bounds of Human Empire, to the effecting of all things possible'.

Bacon has been made a milestone, or a touchstone – an icon of sorts – but he was not alone in coming to the conclusion that observation and experiment were keys to understanding the natural world and the wider cosmos. Kepler was there at the beginning too, and Brahe and Galileo. English physician William Harvey observed and described the circulation of blood from the heart to the brain and the rest of the body. They were few, but they were on the right path. With the advent of the seventeenth century, and the coming of tools like the telescope and the microscope, humankind was taking its first steps towards the modern world.

67

ISAAC NEWTON, SELF-ISOLATION
AND 'THE SYSTEM OF THE WORLD'

At the time of writing, Britain and much of the world is in a time of quarantine the government has called 'lockdown'. A pandemic has been abroad in the land and whole populations are mostly confined to their homes. For some it has been unbearable; for others the captivity has been a time of productivity. Time will tell, but it is hard to imagine anyone equalling, far less improving upon, Isaac Newton's record of achievement while hiding from another plague, in another time.

Deaths from an outbreak of bubonic plague (now there's a disease to worry about) were first reported in the winter of 1664. By the summer of the following year cases were in the thousands. The Great Plague of London was in full infectious flood and households were sealed behind doors painted with the prayer 'Lord have mercy'. It was not just London. There was dying all over. Newton was a student at the University of Cambridge then, and when it closed in fear of the outbreak he returned to his childhood home, at Woolsthorpe Manor in Lincolnshire. For the next eighteen months he happily stayed put, thinking and writing. He would subsequently describe that time as the most productive of his life.

Armed with a prism, he pondered why light passing through glass was split into rainbow colours. His deductions from his observations enabled him to comprehend, for the first time, that refraction was the cause and that invisible 'white' light passing through a prism was made to give up its secret. Spun within the white were threads of colour, different rays refracted at different angles. Each ray appeared differently to the human eye – red, orange, yellow . . . Understanding of the science of optics was changed for ever.

Such an advance might have been enough for a lesser mortal, but Newton was constitutionally incapable of avoiding the act of noticing, and of making sense of what he noticed. What others failed to notice – walked by, as it were – made Newton stop and gawp. Just as light through a prism was split into rays of colour, so phenomena passed through Newton only to be frayed into threads of understanding.

Also during his isolation he gave thought to the movement of objects in flight. Why did a shot arrow draw an arc in the sky – rising, slowing and falling? Why did a fired cannonball do likewise? In time he shaped his understanding into three laws of motion: that an object will remain at rest, just as an object in motion will remain in motion, unless acted upon by an external force; that the force acting on an object is equal to the mass of that object multiplied by its acceleration; that for every action there is an equal and opposite reaction.

So it was that while walking in the orchard of Woolsthorpe Manor, with an always questioning mind and helplessly noticing, he observed the moment of a single apple parting company with its stalk and falling to the ground. Why had it done so? Why not sideways, or upwards? And if an apple fell always towards the centre of the Earth, why not the moon? Why did it stay in place above, and the sun likewise? Natural philosophers understood that a ball on a chain might be swung around and around. Were that chain to break, then the ball would fly off . . . so why did the moon and other objects stay in place in the sky rather than float away like boats untethered?

While the mass of people would shrug and get on with their lives, Newton did the mathematics; in fact he invented the mathematics, to which he gave the borrowed name of *calculus*. He conceived of the force of gravity holding everything in position in relation to everything else, from largest to smallest.

More than twenty years later, on 5 July 1687, the fruits of Newton's thinking were published as *Philosophiae Naturalis Principia Mathematica* ('Mathematical Principles of Natural Philosophy'), perhaps the greatest work of science ever written. Of gravity he noted: 'all matter attracts all other matter with a force proportional to the product of their masses and inversely proportional to the square of the distance between them'. If the truth of that sentence is hard to grasp, then get in line.

As well as a genius, Newton was a man of idiosyncrasies. He was also competitive and keen to protect his scientific advances from copying by others. For those reasons he made his work inscrutable and so deliberately spun his *Principia* so as to make it hard to understand. The line above is as simple as Newton gets. Elsewhere his truth is cloaked by references to the Bible, to historical figures, to everything he could think of. Nineteenth-century English scientist William Whewell was among the many made to wonder at the depth of Newton's understanding. He wrote:

> The ponderous instrument of synthesis, so effective in Newton's hands, has never since been grasped by one who could use it for such purposes; and we gaze at it with admiring curiosity, as some gigantic implement of war, which stands idle among the memorials of ancient days, and makes us wonder what manner of man he was who could wield a weapon we can hardly lift as a burden.

Newton's understanding changed the world of science and would direct the study of it for the next two centuries. He said himself that understanding gravity let him 'explain the system of the world'. In so doing he told another story of the world, one utterly beyond me. Some of it remains inscrutable even now, and that is how the genius wanted it to be. Mere mortal that I am, I think of the fictional physicist Sheldon

Cooper in the TV comedy show *The Big Bang Theory*. In one scene he has taken delivery of a new laptop and considers its inbuilt operating system. 'My new computer came with Windows 7,' he says, more to himself than to anyone listening. 'Windows 7 is much more user-friendly than Windows Vista. I don't like that.'

That, right there, is Newtonian too.

68.

SMALLPOX AND THE WAR
OF THE SPANISH SUCCESSION

On 6 February 1699 a six-year-old boy died in a grand home in Brussels, in what was then the territory known as the Spanish Netherlands, where his father, Maximilian II Emanuel, Elector of Bavaria, was governor-general. He was Joseph Ferdinand Leopold, of the house of Wittelsbach, and his passing was unexpected. According to some accounts he died of smallpox; others reported he was seized by fits and ceaseless vomiting and there were claims the boy had been deliberately poisoned. Some fingers were pointed at the Holy Roman Emperor, Leopold I of Austria, who had stood to gain a great deal once little Joseph Ferdinand was gone. However it occurred, it was a moment, and quite terrible – as is the death of every child.

It is hard to imagine now the extent to which Europe was once made not of nation states but of vast landed estates. These were the territories ruled, for centuries, by monarchs and nobles, and the fates of millions of ordinary people depended upon the deals they struck with one another without so much as a by-your-leave from the individuals actually living there. By war, by marriage and by treaties of one sort or another a relative handful of families agreed and disagreed about precisely who owned what. It was not national but *notional* lines that separated the jealously guarded holdings, and the patchwork created by those demarcations shimmered and flickered like a mirage, or like the lights of the borealis, never seeming to stay long in one place before changing again.

After Elizabeth I, England had a sense of herself as a nation state, but that had been made by geography and the English Channel as much as by anything else. The French and the Spanish were on the road to modern national identity as well, but overweening dynastic ambitions continued to blur their outlines when it suited this king or that.

On 9 June 1660, the young King of France, Louis XIV, had been wedded to the Spanish Infanta Maria Theresa, eldest daughter of King Philip IV of Spain. As part of the deal she agreed that neither she nor any children she might bear would ever inherit the Spanish throne. Philip was supposed to pay his daughter a vast dowry, in compensation, but never did. Within a year Louis was mooching around, eyeing the Spanish Netherlands and hinting that perhaps the legal barrier keeping her and hers from the Spanish throne might be null and void as a result.

It was not the beginning of the dynastic trouble to come – that was made of wars, marriages and treaties stretching back over decades and centuries – but the marriage of Louis and Maria Theresa was a serving of yet more strong spice to an already dyspeptic stomach.

As the second half of the seventeenth century drew to a close, the temperature all over began to rise. Along the way Philip IV had sired a male heir. He was Charles (Carlos) II and he was less than ideal. Tales of his physical and mental failings abound, so that by some estimates he was little more than a functioning idiot, barely able to walk. A penchant for inbreeding in the royal house of Habsburg had, apparently, gifted him among other handicaps an outsize head and a facial deformity called prognathism – being a severely protruding lower jaw and an underbite so severe it was hard for him to eat and speak. Any and all of the above may have been exaggerated, but while the kindest commentators note that he was popular with his subjects there seems little doubt he was weak of mind and physically poorly, to such an extent that he was never expected to live long. From the day and hour of his birth, his imminent death was being predicted by someone, somewhere.

Unfit or not, the vast scale of the empire he had inherited from those wars, marriages and treaties that preceded him meant many heads were pondering what must happen if and when he eventually did die. As well as the Spain of the Iberian Peninsula, Charles held the previously mentioned Spanish Netherlands, rich colonies in the Americas, and territories around the Mediterranean, in Italy, in North Africa and in the Philippines.

Among his collection of ailments, real or imagined, was an inability to father any children from either of his two wives. He had no surviving siblings and so the prime candidates for inheriting his fabulous demesne, on account of that dizzying back catalogue of inter-family marriages and alliances, were the Habsburg emperor Leopold I of Austria and Louis XIV of the House of Bourbon.

European countries great and small held their collective breaths. Not since Emperor Charles V had so much been held by one ruler. As the clock counted down on the always-ailing Charles, all manner of so-called partition treaties were assembled and signed in a paper storm of diplomacy.

While France, Austria, England and the Netherlands plotted and manoeuvred, seeking to settle on the candidate least likely to do any of them any harm, Charles made little Joseph Ferdinand his heir. His unilateral decision ruffled feathers – especially those of Louis and Leopold – but it was logical and legal. Neither France nor Austria would gain Spain and so the European balance of power need not be destabilized. All might have been well . . . until the little boy died fitting in his bed.

With all to play for once more, the rival powers got back to seeking carve-ups to suit their own ends. As the last months of the seventeenth century slipped by, and with ink drying on paperwork that seemed to have averted the detonation of dynastic dynamite, Charles signed a version of his will that handed the whole kit and caboodle to Louis's grandson, Philip, Duke of Anjou. In spite of earlier partition treaties he had signed – designed to prevent just such an undivided inheritance going to any one soul – Louis agreed that Philip should succeed Charles.

Horrified and/or infuriated by the turn of events, Emperor Leopold, England and the Dutch Republic came together as the Grand Alliance to challenge French audacity. Thus began the War of the Spanish Succession and a dozen years of fighting before Louis signed the Peace of Utrecht, of 1713–14. By its terms, never again would the thrones of Spain and France come together as one. Philip was confirmed as King of Spain but with the loss of the Netherlands, most of the Italian territories and also Gibraltar and Menorca. The Battle of Blenheim, fought in Germany in 1704 and won by the combined genius of John Churchill, 1st Duke of Marlborough, and Prince Eugene of Savoy, has been described as one of the most significant in history, preventing Louis establishing the sort of dominance enjoyed by Alexander the Great, or the Romans. Of the victors, Britain gained most, emerging as a naval power and with control of Gibraltar and Menorca in the Mediterranean and the trading rights in Spanish America. Louis gained nothing but debt, and on his deathbed, a year after Utrecht, muttered, 'I have loved war too well.'

69.

THOMAS NEWCOMEN
AND HIS STEAM ENGINE

Figures as diverse as Isaac Newton and Lao Tzu intuited and understood the interconnectedness of all things. In *My First Summer in the Sierra*, published in 1911, the Scottish-American naturalist John Muir demonstrated awareness of the same reality when he wrote: 'When we try to pick out anything by itself, we find it hitched to everything else in the Universe.'

So it is with history, and in truth every moment (like every thing) is connected to every other, by invisible chains that pull and rods that push. As much is neatly revealed by the story of the Industrial Revolution. Most historians have it start in England, in the early eighteenth century, with Thomas Newcomen's steam engine. From there the fire of invention and change spread around the world. Newcomen's achievement, dated 1712, was a moment of note and worthy of attention. He had begun with the well-established fact that heat from a fire transformed water into steam. It followed that that steam might be directed into a cylinder via an opened valve. The cylinder was not sealed; rather it contained a close-fitting piston that might rise and fall inside. First the steam raised the piston; then cold water, sprayed into the cylinder from outside, caused the steam to condense, creating a partial vacuum that pulled the piston back again. The expansion and contraction, first pushing and then

pulling the piston, operated a pump that could move water – notably out
of the way of miners in a coalmine.

Newcomen's steam engine was an embodiment of interconnectedness:
a pump ... operated by a cylinder and piston ... inside which H_2O
appeared first as steam, making a large space, before being transformed
into water occupying a small space. By exploiting the connections, big
followed by small, Newcomen could move water from where it was not
wanted to some place where it was welcome.

But the truth is that Newcomen's achievement did not exist in
isolation – hardly. By his endeavour he had made a contribution to a long
story of observation, experiment and invention stretching back millennia. He was, by trade, a blacksmith from Devon, and since 1698 had been
in partnership with fellow Devonian Thomas Savery, a military engineer
and inventor who in 1696 had patented a means of moving a boat via
paddle wheels. By 1698 Savery had come up with a pump powered by
steam and also intended for removing water from coalmines. It was then
that his path crossed that of Newcomen's and by 1712 their connection
had duly advanced mankind's understanding of the potential of har-
nessed steam applied to the concept of a pump.

Savery was hardly the first to sense, far less to exploit, the potential of
steam. Egyptian-born Greek engineer Hero of Alexandria has been credited with the invention of a device called an aeolipile – a spinning globe
powered by steam exiting two pipes (or jets) attached to its north and
south poles – in the first century AD. The story of steam power may not
even start with Hero, since others have credited Roman engineer and
architect Vitruvius with having invented an aeolipile of his own in the
first century BC.

Newcomen did not start the Industrial Revolution, but he was certainly
handicapped by its not having started *yet*. There were no mass-produced
parts and each of his components had to be made, instead, in the traditional way – by hand and by individual craftsmen. There were no railways
to move either those parts or the coal (which was his fuel) so that he had

to station his enterprise close by a mine. Letters delivered by horse- and manpower were the only means of communication, so that the sharing of clever but incomplete ideas was slow and limited. The Industrial Revolution was made of stages on a long and winding road, countless contributions by countless people in all manner of places.

The story of steam, like the story of everything else, is about connections all the way back to some time before remembering. Always the heat that matters most comes from human observation and invention.

70.

CLIVE OF INDIA PAVES
THE WAY FOR THE BRITISH RAJ

Aurangzeb had set aside his father, Shah Jahan – he of the Taj Mahal – to take the throne of the Mughal empire in India. By the time he died in 1707 his zealotry had seen to its fatal weakening. The Hindu Mahratas had flowered in the Deccan and then spread throughout a vast swathe of the subcontinent. After Aurangzeb the time of the Mughals was over (even if they did not know it then) and the cohesion they had provided at the height of their power was lost. Like a castle made of sand on the beach, the structure dried out and lost all shape; winds of change saw to its erosion and collapse. India became once more a place of independent, rival kingdoms – a patchwork made of Islam, Hinduism and also Sikhism. Persians saw their opportunity and were soon flowing across the border, securing territory of their own.

While those internecine struggles rolled and rumbled – the fighting of dinosaurs – fast-moving little mammals had moved and spread unseen, exploiting niches and thriving in ecosystems of their own making. These were the Europeans – Dutch, French and British. Each had its version of an East India Company. The British, with their base at Calcutta, in the basin of the Ganges, were in the shadow of the Dutch at first. For the Europeans it was all about trade, not religion, and this focus mattered. The French allied themselves with the Mughals in the hope it would make the difference. It did not, and as one diminished so did the other.

By the seventeenth and eighteenth centuries it was not just matters Indian that made the difference. The story of the world was a tapestry of interwoven threads, of Byzantine complexity. In the middle years of the eighteenth century Britain endeavoured to push into French territory in North America. They came to blows in 1756 and each side sought support from those other Indians, the Native Americans, so that tribe was set against tribe. The tribes of Europe were at it on that continent too – Austrians, Prussians, French and the British all in a stew.

On the subcontinent the same predatory and/or defensive behaviour around territory led to fighting between French and British there too; even before the outbreak of the European–American Seven Years' War, France and Britain were wrestling for control. France allied herself with the nawabs – the nobles of the fractured and fracturing Mughal empire – and challenged the British in Bengal. Much like the Romans of 2,000 years before, the British had no real interest in imposing a new faith or a new ideology on the peoples of India. They wanted access to Indian things, the wealth of India, and as long as that trade was allowed to prosper the Brits had made it clear that Indian people should continue to live and worship as before. But in 1756 the Nawab of Bengal, Siraj ud-Daulah, entered the fray and seized Calcutta, occupying the British Fort William in the process. Notorious is the treatment meted out to a few dozen prisoners – British and Indian soldiers and also some civilians – in the aftermath. Between sixty and seventy were crammed into a small cell and kept there overnight on 20 June. This was the 'Black Hole', and in the morning the majority of them, more than forty, had died of heat and suffocation. It seems unlikely that the nawab was aware of the incident until it was over, but for the British East India Company it was a useful ugliness.

Lieutenant Colonel Robert Clive, an employee of the company and prominent in its private army, led an armed force to retake Calcutta. He had succeeded by 2 January 1757 and then, in the June of that year, came the moment of note. A few miles outside the city of Murshidabad, the Mughal capital of Bengal, at Plassey, Clive brought the nawab to battle. Significantly outnumbered though he was – with a force of around 3,000 compared to the nawab's 50,000 – still the British adventurer was able to secure victory. By the standards of the day the Battle of Plassey, on 23 June 1757, was a relatively bloodless encounter but its long-term significance was enormous. Siraj ud-Daulah himself was captured trying to flee the field on the back of a camel. He was later murdered by an assassin, but long before then he was replaced as Nawab of Bengal by a puppet of the British.

No one, least of all the British government, understood the significance of the moment as it happened. In the aftermath, a small number of British troops was sent out to support those of the company, but as a show of intent it was meagre. Unexpected or not, Clive's success at Plassey (with the loss of just twenty-two British soldiers) was a decisive moment like no other on the way to British domination of India. The Mughals were finished in every way that mattered. The Dutch too were a spent force by then. The French lost their nerve or their resolve (or both) in the months and years ahead until Britain had almost inadvertently been left alone on the chequerboard of nights and days. The Battle of Plassey had been one of the most significant in world history. The British Raj was born.

71.

PINS IN MILK
AND EUROPE'S LAST WITCH

Anna Göldi was forty-seven years old when she was put to death in the little town of Glarus, in Switzerland, on 13 June 1782. She was taken to the town square and there, in front of the townspeople, her head was cut off with a sword. Before her head was parted from her body, she was broken in every way that mattered. She is remembered as Europe's last witch and is the last person known to have been executed there for the crime of witchcraft. Glarus was small, among other small towns in a narrow valley. Steep slopes of mountains cast shadows, making darkness that conceals.

Göldi was born in the town of Sennwald, in the St Gallen canton of Switzerland, in 1734. Details of her life are blurred by storytelling but she had a child out of wedlock and the baby died soon after birth. Göldi was blamed in some way, no doubt and not least for the sin of having a baby at all while unmarried, and put in a pillory for pelting with rotten food. She was then placed under house arrest, but escaped. There was another child, by another man, before she found work in Glarus, around the year 1780, with a well-to-do family called Tschudi.

Göldi was a good-looking woman – that much seems obvious. She was a tall and voluptuous brunette, long-haired and dark-eyed. She had a healthy complexion. Jakob Tschudi was a local magistrate, a man of influence and power, locally at least. He was married with children when, into his home, came Göldi, to take on some of the childcare and so, in a way that is subtle but that mattered, acquired some influence of her own. In any event there bēgan an affair of sorts, between the husband and the nanny – an old story. If there ever was any love, any kindness, it did not last. The old story ran its course and Göldi was sacked, put out of the house.

There were other stories then. The Tschudis said there had come a day when one of the children found a steel pin in her cup of milk. There had been pins in the bread as well, and the finger of guilt was pointed at the help.

All of this happened in 1782. While the people of Switzerland and the rest of Europe were in the thick of the Enlightenment and having their eyes opened to science and reason, Anna Göldi was arrested and accused of witchcraft. She was tortured, of course. How else is a witch to be made to confess? They hung her up by cords around her thumbs and put weights on her feet to dislocate her joints. The confessions she made in her misery sound laughably scripted, except the horror of it all meant no one was laughing. She said Satan himself had come to her in the form of a black dog. It was he who had given her the needles. Cut down from the ropes, she immediately said none of it was true, that she was innocent. So they hung her up once more and hurt her more severely until she said it all again, about Satan and his needles. Göldi could neither read nor write but with one ruined hand she made her mark on a paper detailing her crimes. Soon after that she was taken to the square and the swordsman.

Göldi would speak no more, and that was the point after all. Jakob Tschudi had the power and, he no doubt thought, more to lose than she. Maybe she came back to him after her sacking and threatened to tell all unless . . . unless . . . Maybe that was all the provocation he needed to raise a storm to destroy a woman scorned.

1782. In the November of that year Britain would recognize the independence of the United States of America, and the *Philosophical Transactions of the Royal Society* would devote much space to the study of a Great Meteor that passed through the night sky . . . and an unmarried woman and her severed head lay cold in an unmarked grave, denounced as a witch. The ultimate cancelling.

It was all wrong. The people of Glarus, great and small, knew it was wrong, that there was no such thing as witchcraft. A powerful man feeling threatened, backed by others who knew better and cared nothing for scientific fact, far less the truth, if it did not fit the narrative, had made claims that flew in the face of all reason. The powerless people around them kept their heads down and were silent for fear of drawing the same deadly heat upon themselves. No doubt in their homes they spoke the truth together – that they were being duped, frightened into accepting as right what they knew to be wrong. It was not the first time scientific fact and reason were set aside by powerful men for the sake of expediency, and it would not be the last.

72.

JAMES MADISON
AND THE CONSTITUTION
OF THE UNITED STATES

Ever since High Priestess Enheduanna and her hymns, the story of the world had been written down – not in full but in part. Over millennia of writing, more and more pieces of the picture were assembled, pieces of a puzzle never to be completed. Magna Carta, the great charter to which King John had put his seal in 1215, was deemed so important – enshrining as it did some rights inalienable – it was copied and preserved. Its creation was a moment in its own right. Down the centuries it influenced more thoughts and those subsequent evolutions were remembered in writing too.

The American War of Independence (also remembered as the American Revolutionary War) began in April 1775 when, with trouble brewing, British soldiers sought to seize weapons stored at Lexington, Massachusetts, and shots were fired. The Declaration of Independence was signed in 1776, more unforgettable words: 'When, in the course of human events, it becomes necessary for one people to dissolve the political bands which have connected them with another . . .'

The fighting continued until 1781. After the British surrender at Yorktown both sides entered into the negotiations that culminated, in 1783, in the Peace of Paris, by which Britain formally recognized the independence of the fledgling nation named the United States of America. More years of talking and writing followed.

As early as 1781 there had been the Articles of Confederation that gave the states a basis for union. Strong feelings within individual states – hunger for independence within independence – had rendered the resultant central, federal government too weak and ineffectual. In the hope of rectifying the problems, and finding terms for closer union and stronger government, there was a constitutional convention in Philadelphia in 1787. After four months of talking, there was a written constitution, ready for ratification by the summer of the following year. *E pluribus unum* – out of many, one.

Just as the Romans had thrown off the yoke of a king, their last king, in 509 BC, so those Americans of 1788 had turned their backs on Britain's George III in favour of a republic – *res publica* – by which government was understood to be a public matter, for the people to decide.

The significant moment this time was in the framing of the first line of that constitution. Credit for its writing is usually given to James Madison, Founding Father and later fourth president of the US. In his short biography of Madison, Pulitzer Prize-winning American historian Garry Wills described his subject as 'this unimpressive little man with libraries in his brain'. Impressive or not, Madison was the lead architect of a document that borrowed some thinking from Magna Carta but also struck out on its own to create a basis for government that would change the world just as fundamentally as that ancient English charter. The USA is still the best idea for a country any has had so far. Its constitution begins:

> We the People of the United States, in Order to form a more perfect Union, establish Justice, insure domestic Tranquility, provide for the common defense, promote the general Welfare, and secure the Blessings of Liberty to ourselves and our Posterity, do ordain and establish this Constitution for the United States of America.

If the thinking of Magna Carta haunted the document, so too did the organization of government in Britain. By making room for a president as head of state, the authors of the constitution mirrored the presence of a king in Parliament. They had done away with one monarch only to replace him with another. A person might say the Americans' is elected, but by now there are proto-dynasties – Kennedys, Bushes, Clintons – and the presidency is nudging as close to hereditary as that person might want to get. If there are Obamas and Trumps the Younger to come, it will hardly surprise.

They wanted an independent nation of their own, but modelled it in so many ways upon that which they had been at such apparent pains to fight off. Those Founding Fathers were, all of them, sons of the colonies, of empire, after all and, as is usually the case, that which is bred in the bone 'will not out of the flesh'.

The power of the people was the bass note that resonates still. Time and again presidents would claim it as their true north. Abraham Lincoln would invoke his fellow citizens three times in just the single line that ended his immortal Gettysburg Address of 19 November 1863, when he said he hoped 'that government of the people, by the people, for the people shall not perish from the earth'.

But that amorphous entity – *the people*, whoever they are – would also be the rock upon which American hopes would founder and almost perish. A nation based on the power of the people must decide whether that *democracy* is best exercised in pressing home the decision of the majority, or by protecting at all costs the rights deemed inalienable (even if, and perhaps especially if, those rights are held by a minority). Within a lifetime, that constitution and that nation would be tested by a civil war that would come within a hair's breadth of tearing the Union to shreds. The battle between majority decisions and the protection of inalienable rights is still being fought today.

73

QUEEN NANDI, UNSAFE SEX AND
THE BIRTH OF THE ZULU KINGDOM

Nandi is a name from the Bantu family of languages and means 'the sweet one'. She was born around 1760, daughter of Inkosi (Chief) Mdingi of the Mhlongo clan, and on a day in 1786, or maybe 1787, she caught the eye of Senzangakhona kaJama, a chief among the neighbouring Zulu clan. They were a small people then, the Zulus – perhaps 1,500-strong – but Senzangakhona was haughty and proud enough for a thousand times that number. Custom banned full sex between unmarried couples but a practice called *ukuhlobonga* was allowed – foreplay short of penetration, also known as *amahlaya endlela*, 'the fun of the roads'. In the moment that mattered, however, Nandi and Senzangakhona went that significant bit further down the road and a child was conceived.

Once her bump began to show, Nandi's father took her before Senzangakhona and asked him what he intended to do about his daughter's predicament. With great disdain Senzangakhona replied that he did not believe Nandi was pregnant. Instead, he said, she was suffering from infection by a parasitic beetle called *iShaka*, which was known to cause swelling of the intestines and disruption of a woman's menstrual cycle.

The Zulus laughed to hear it and, humiliated, Nandi and her father returned home. When the child was born she named him Shaka, so that Senzangakhona's insult would not be forgotten. Privately Nandi adored her son and would fight for him like a lioness. Wherever no one was listening she called him *umlilwana*, her 'little blazing fire'.

Under her guidance, and showered in her love, Shaka rose to dominance. By 1816 he was king of the Zulu people, and by the time of his death, twelve years later, his iron rule was rigidly in place over a population of 250,000 people. He changed the way his warriors fought, favouring hand-to-hand combat with short stabbing spears called *iklwa* (the Zulu language is onomatopoeic and *iklwa* mimicked the sucking sound of the spear point when it was pulled back out of a body). He devised the 'horns of the buffalo' formation by which his men spread out to encircle their foe while the units comprising the head and chest pushed in behind to crush them. In battle, any man who so much as hesitated before engaging an enemy would return home to find Shaka had ordered the beating to death of his family. Having been shown their bodies, the inadequate warrior would then be killed too.

Always Shaka was mindful of the power of women, taking counsel not just from Nandi but also from her sisters Mkabayi, Mmama and Nomawa. When Nandi died in 1827 he ordered years of mourning – no children to be born, no milk to be used, no crops planted. Thousands of men and women were executed for seeming insufficiently grief-stricken and countless cows were slaughtered so that their calves might share his pain.

The madness he displayed, the cruelty that was excessive even by his own murderous standards, likely provoked his assassination in 1828. By then, however, he had laid the foundations for greatness. Under his descendant Cetshwayo kaMpande, the Zulu kingdom would have its finest flowering – defying, taking on and defeating, with spears and shields, a British army wielding modern rifles and artillery at the Battle of Isandlwana in 1879. The Zulu spirit born of Shaka would bloody the nose of the British empire and have her red-coated soldiers honour them as among their bravest foes of all time. The Zulu kingdom had been a lone, independent obstacle in the way of British plans to force southern Africa into a British-ruled confederation. That unity would be achieved, but the independent identity of the Zulus was for ever.

74.

THE BAKER, THE MOB
AND THE FRENCH REVOLUTION

On 21 October 1789, a baker named Denis François was in his shop on the Rue de la Juiverie, in Paris, when a mob appeared outside. Accounts vary, but he was either accused of selling mouldy bread or of swindling his customers by some other nefarious means. His principal accuser was a hungry woman, one of the legion of the poor. Those were the so-called 'October Days', in the immediate aftermath of the sparking of the French Revolution, and feelings were running as hot as the inside of any baker's oven. It was just three months since the Storming of the Bastille, on 14 July, and three years, give or take, before the guillotine would make its first appearance in the Place de Grève, in Paris, for the execution of a highwayman on 25 April 1792. The tumbrils of the Terror were yet to roll but the baker's moments were numbered nonetheless.

Some of François's accusers shouted that he had been stockpiling and hiding loaves to bump up the price or otherwise deprive the people of bread. It was two weeks since thousands of women armed with weapons looted from the city armoury had marched on the Palace of Versailles, on 5 October, to make their protests within the hearing of Louis XVI. The very next day, the king and his family had returned to Paris and the mob was emboldened.

Outside his shop, François protested his innocence but he was dragged to the Place de Grève – by the mayoral palace known as the Hôtel de Ville and for hundreds of years a place of protest as well as of public torture and execution. There, in front of the baying crowd, he was first hanged by the neck from a lamppost and then decapitated. His pregnant wife, who had been dragged alongside him, was forced to kiss the bloodied lips of her husband's severed head. Soon after the lynching, the recently created National Assembly declared martial law that allowed for the execution, on sight, of any protesters refusing to disperse when ordered to do so.

All of it was indicative of the extent to which it was supposedly hunger – specifically shortage of bread, or else anger at the continually rising price of that staple foodstuff of the French poor – that sparked the French Revolution. Those thousands that stormed the Bastille (and the hundred or so who gave their lives in the effort) had apparently had it in mind there might be grain stored there, as well as arms for insurrection. When the king and his family had returned to Paris after the march by the women on 5 October, the crowds in the city had celebrated by chanting: 'We have the baker, the baker's wife and the baker's son. We shall have bread!'

Anne Robert Jacques Turgot, who had been one of the king's advisers before the trouble really started, had advised his master, above all else, 'Ne vous mêlez pas du pain' – 'Do not meddle with bread.'

The bread upon which the poor subsisted was not the familiar white baguette of wheat flour associated with France today; rather the mass of the population subsisted upon coarse loaves made of barley or millet. For several years before the Revolution there were poor harvests. Coupled with an accelerating growth in population, the food shortages were more than poor people could take. What made the tinder dry enough to catch and hold the flames of revolution were the added pains of inflation, rising taxes and landlords opportunistically raising rents. In the resultant febrile atmosphere Louis had, with a view to airing complaints and finding solutions, summoned the Estates General – representatives of the clergy, the nobility and the commoners – for the first time since 1614. They

assembled on 5 May 1789 and by the summer they had morphed into the
National Assembly, which described itself as representing all Frenchmen
equally rather than differentiating between classes as France had always
done before.

In time it would define the French constitution, and along the way the
Assembly did away with feudalism, created a representative government
with separation of the powers of the executive, the legislature and the
judiciary, made all men equal before the law and took control of land
previously held by the Church. Those who were in favour of the Revolution
sat on the left of the king, those opposed on the right, establishing a
political tradition that has prevailed in speech and print, if nowhere else,
ever since.

Some changes to society were good. Travelling alongside the determination to effect kindly reform, however, was brute cruelty and the exercise
of petty vengeance. Such was the so-called Terror, in which some 30,000
were murdered, across a year and a half, in all manner of score settling.
It might have been supposed that the Revolution was about fairness –
equality, and all that. It may have been, in some cool heads, and the French
effort defined the politics of revolution for the wider world. But in the
heart of the mob, as always, it was an excuse to take revenge on any that
seemed to have had it better. Vengeance was served not only to the rich,
to the powerful, to those who had lived by the oppression of others; it
was also meted out against any within reach whose lives seemed a little
more comfortable, who had earned for themselves a little bit extra. As the
Russian mobs would do to the kulaks, so the French did to those, like
Denis François, who had had the temerity to get a little bit ahead of their
neighbours. His lynching was only a moment – ugly and cruel, and only
a moment – but it told truths about the human animal: that revenge is
too tempting for too many, that revolutions devour their children, and
that the mob is hungry not just for nobles, but for neighbours too. It's
never about bread.

75.

NELSON, TRAFALGAR
AND THE FREEDOM OF THE SEAS

The French Revolutionary government called the Directory (another iteration of command and control in the aftermath of 1789 and the National Assembly) held power from November 1795 to November 1799. Under its thrall the French economy regained ground lost during the bloodshed of the Terror and the army rediscovered winning ways. It was also a profoundly corrupt institution, and when it fell to a coup d'état and cleared the way for Napoleon Bonaparte there were few tears shed other than by those politicians whose noses had been knocked out of the public trough.

Since 1792 the Revolution had been under threat, variously and collectively from Austria, Britain, the Netherlands, Prussia, Sardinia and Spain. These travails would continue after Napoleon came to power, but under his leadership – as a general, then as First Consul, and finally as emperor – France would exert great influence over much of the European continent.

Napoleon was a demagogue (of the sort that would have been recognized by the Greek Polybius as he drew his circle of anacyclosis). Whenever it suited him he ran roughshod over the rights and freedoms the Revolution had supposedly been all about. Opponents and malcontents were thrown in jail without trials. Freedom of speech and of the press was stamped upon unless they spoke and wrote well of the despot he became.

The French Revolution had been greatly inspired and shaped by that of North America, and in both the truth of 'the power of the people' was as hard to pin down and know as the position of the lights of the borealis. In Napoleon's hands it was his own to do with as he saw fit – as long as he kept giving the proles bread and victories.

The loss that counted most came not on land but on sea, at Cape Trafalgar. The moment that lingers from it all is a grim one. The British fleet was commanded that day, 21 October 1805, by Admiral Horatio Nelson, from the deck of his flagship *Victory*. In the thick of the fighting, he was spotted by a French sniper high in the rigging of the warship *Redoutable*. A well-aimed musket ball struck the admiral in the chest, below his collarbone, passed through his body and lodged in his spine. He was carried below, to the cockpit. There he lingered for hours, and in much pain, while the battle raged above and around him. Slowly the ebb and flow of war turned in Britain's favour. Those men not required on deck gathered around their commander. He was propped on bedding packed against the massive oak timbers of *Victory*'s hull. There was little that could be done to ease his suffering but he bore it with some dignity. 'I am a dead man,' he whispered to his friend Thomas Hardy, the ship's captain. 'I am going fast. It will all be over with me soon.'

Some time between 4.30 and 5 that afternoon, he succumbed to his hurt – but not before Hardy had been able to assure him the day was theirs . . . his.

'Thank God, I have done my duty,' he said.

If Nelson was the master at sea, Napoleon dominated the land. That Frenchman was a soldier of audacity and genius in equal measures. He was charismatic – reckless and yet successful. As a gambler he always seemed to know how far to push his luck and the French people loved him for it. In battle after battle he played his hand magnificently until 1812 and his invasion of Russia, when that freezing vastness damned near swallowed him whole. He had invaded with a Grand Armée half a million strong. Mikhail Kutuzov was the Russian commander who awaited them on the approaches to Moscow. At the Battle of Borodino on 7 September the combined death toll was perhaps 75,000 men – the equivalent of a packed jumbo jet crashing every three minutes from dawn till dusk. Kutuzov and his survivors melted away afterwards, back into Moscow and out the other side. Napoleon entered the empty city and waited, but Kutuzov was gone, waiting for winter to do his work for him. Only 120,000 of the French force made it out of Russia.

After Russia, and whether he knew it or not, Napoleon's ambitions of world domination were bleeding from mortal wounds. There were many more steps of the dance of death but in 1815, at Waterloo, he would be finally and utterly undone. He offered his surrender aboard the British warship *Bellerophon*. 'I have come to throw myself on the protection of your prince and laws,' he said.

Over dinner with Captain Frederick Maitland that evening he told him, 'If it had not been for you English, I would have been Emperor of the East. But wherever there is water to float a ship, we are sure to find you in our way.'

For all that Napoleon had held sway in continental Europe until 1815 and Waterloo, he had been forever hobbled by then. At Trafalgar, Nelson and his Royal British Navy had seen to that. What he and they achieved was more than one victory. What was secured in that moment, as victory was seized just as Nelson died, was the freedom of the ocean sea. For the next century the ships of the Royal Navy would maintain that freedom for all.

76.

THE WORLD'S POPULATION
REACHES ONE BILLION

Some moments are impossible to pin down – even if we know they must have happened.

On an unknown and unknowable day some time in the first decade of the nineteenth century (for that is as close as anyone has figured it), a child was born whose arrival took the world's population to one billion for the very first time. By that point, by that special moment, there had been human beings on earth, of one sort or another – *Homo erectus* . . . *Homo neanderthalensis* . . . *Homo sapiens* – for two million years and more. All that living and dying, the survival against the odds of those individuals that lived long enough to make more people who, eventually, made the people who made us. English author and artist Mervyn Peake wrote a poem called 'To Live is Miracle Enough', and so it is: 'The doom of nations is another thing / Here in my hammering blood-pulse is my proof . . .'

It took a further one and a quarter centuries before that number doubled, and then only thirty more years to reach three billion. At the time of writing there are nearly eight billion of us alive together on the blue marble, drawing upon all her resources, breathing the air and exhaling carbon dioxide. We seem to be adding an extra billion every fifteen years or so now. There are projections about further rises – to a peak and then a fall – but any predictions about the future are unwise. It has been calculated that all of us, nearly eight billion, would fit, neatly stacked like logs for winter fires, into the hollow presently filled by Lake Windermere in Cumbria, England.

We are small, but we are formidable. We are also many, and no mistake, and vulnerable. As flies upon a great bull's back we might be swatted at any moment. More than from anything else, and throughout the story of the world, we have been at risk from each other.

Peake was sent by a British newspaper to record, in drawings and paintings, the liberation of Belsen concentration camp in north-west Germany. He already knew it was miracle enough to be alive. In 'The Rhyme of the Flying Bomb' he imagined a sailor with a baby in his arms, running through London's streets during a raid while tons of explosive rain down: 'A ton came down on a coloured road / And a ton came down on a gaol / And a ton came down on a freckled girl . . .' Behind the barbed wire of Belsen he saw how easily we might be dispatched by those with a mind to look us in the eye while so doing. As well as drawing, he was moved to write. In 'The Consumptive' he described the ending of a little girl:

> If seeing her an hour before her last
> Weak cough into all blackness I could yet
> Be held by chalk-white arms, and by the great
> Ash coloured bed,
> And the pillows hardly creased
> By the tapping of her little cough-jerked head –
> If such can be a painter's ecstasy
> (Her limbs like pipes, her head a china skull)
> Then where is mercy?

Where is mercy?

That moment in the early 1800s, that rounding of the first billion of us, is a moment at which to pause and take note. As the numbers grow un-imaginably large, larger, we are in danger of losing sight of the individual . . . the little girl, sick and dying. As the numbers grow larger still each one of us, any one of us, might vanish, like tears in rain. Each one of us, every one of us matters – or else none of us do.

77

THE ATLANTIC SLAVE TRADE —
HUMANITY'S NEVER-ENDING SHAME

During the eighteenth century the British were the world's most enthusi-astic enslavers of fellow human beings. The determination to treat others as property is an ugliness in humanity's soul. For millennia it has been pursued by people of every sort, but for 200 recent years it was British hands that were mostly deeply steeped and stained. That it happened far from the homeland, out of sight and out of mind in the plantations of the West Indies, cannot shield us from the fact that millions of African men, women and children were swallowed whole by a singular trade in the hands of its ultimate practitioner.

On 25 March 1807 the Abolition of the Slave Trade Act, outlawing the purchase or sale of those already enslaved, was passed in the House of Commons by a vote of 283 to 16. At that time there were perhaps 700,000 enslaved people in the colonies, and for them, nothing changed. Slaves they had been and slaves they continued to be. Britain later acquired territories in South America where slavery was still the norm anyway. So much wealth was based on slave labour, and blind eyes and deaf ears were turned to the plight of those still owned.

A moment that matters concerns a man named Samuel Sharpe, born into slavery in the parish of St James, on the island of Jamaica, in 1801. He learned to read and write and joined the local Baptist church, becoming a deacon. He was eloquent and passionate and those who heard him preach remembered his words. By 1831, literate slaves like Sharpe were reading newspaper reports about efforts by abolitionists in Britain. Rumours grew around the facts, like weeds, until there was a spreading belief that emancipation was close – even that it had come to pass. It was in that febrile, excited atmosphere that Sharpe became involved in plans for a strike. The sugar cane was harvested around Christmas and so Sharpe suggested to his followers that they should lay down their tools then, in protest at the very notion of slavery. Word of the planned sit-down drifted like smoke throughout St James and then to the parishes of Trelawney and Westmoreland. Sharpe had planned a peaceful protest, but others made preparations to fight any opposition. Slave owners heard the rumours too and soldiers were sent to stand ready in St James. There were warships in Montego Bay.

Perhaps the moment came on 28 December, when a house belonging to a slave owner was set alight. Any hopes Sharpe might have had for a peaceful protest were dashed then, and matters turned bloody. After eight days of rebellion by as many as 60,000 slaves around 200 of them lay dead, along with a dozen or more whites. The revolt was over. Hundreds of slaves were convicted of rebellion and hanged, their heads cut off and displayed on pikes placed around the plantations. Samuel Sharpe was the last to die.

On the night before he was hanged he gestured through the bars of his prison cell and said, 'I would rather die upon yonder gallows than to live in slavery.'

Sharpe's erstwhile owners were paid £16 in compensation.

The so-called Christmas Rebellion lit a fire under the British Parliament as well. The crude and cruel violence in its aftermath was an affront to many. There were enquiries and anxious questions asked. By then, those in favour of abolition were in the ascendant in Parliament. The necessary Act was passed in 1833 and came into force the following year. Even then, enslaved people were not set free, and for years lived instead as unpaid 'apprentices'. To compensate the slave owners for loss of property the British Treasury, in 1837, took out the biggest loan in history. In today's money it would amount to hundreds of billions of pounds and was not paid off by taxpayers until 2015.

In 1808, in the aftermath of the ending of the trade, the Royal Navy's West Africa Squadron had been established to apprehend anyone flouting the law. By the time it was disbanded in 1860, 150,000 slaves had been freed from 1,600 illegal slave ships. Some 2,000 Royal Navy sailors had given their lives to the effort.

And yet for all that, slavery is with us still. Still out of sight and out of mind they make cheap clothes in English factories, clean their owners' homes; others, children included, are passed around for sex. Back in Africa, where dubious regimes reign, more slaves, more children among them, mine the cobalt used in the batteries for computers, smartphones and electric cars. Slavery of one sort or another will always be with us.

78.

CHARLES DARWIN, THE PLATYPUS
AND THE *ORIGIN OF SPECIES*

Since ancient times it had been speculated and assumed, given the weight of all the landmass in the northern hemisphere, that there must be a great counterbalancing land in the south – a Terra Australis. When Europeans found and began mapping the place, from the seventeenth century onwards, they brought the Latin name with them. Dutchman Willem Janszoon was in the Gulf of Carpentaria by 1606. The English naval captain James Cook was in Botany Bay by 1770, and the first European settlement was founded in Sydney in 1788. Australian historian Geoffrey Blainey coined the term 'the tyranny of distance' and used it as the title for his classic 1966 text about his homeland, and that southern continent does, and likely always will, feel far from the rest of the world. The impact of Europeans upon the first Australians has been discussed and rightly lamented for lifetimes now. Less often considered are the influences that have flowed in the other direction, one in particular.

The continent of Australia began its long, languid journey towards its present location on the little blue ball we call Earth more than 200 million years ago. Until then it had been part of Gondwana, a supercontinent covering much of the southern hemisphere, for many more hundreds of millions of years. Then Atlas shrugged and a parting of the ways began – a parting made at the speed at which fingernails grow. As the great raft that would be Australia began sliding north, so the rest of Gondwana cracked and fractured; the Indian Ocean, the south Atlantic and the Southern Ocean would fill the spaces made. Australia has not stopped moving and every year slips around 70 millimetres towards the north and west, closer to the equator and the continent of Asia.

All the while proto-Australia had been part of Gondwana, the plants and animals growing or roaming upon her swatch of vast territory had been much like those on the rest of the supercontinent. Notable among them was the presence of marsupials, those mammals that bear unready young that must complete their development inside maternal pouches. Once upon a time there were marsupials all over the continent of South America as well but when that raft's northward drift had it bump into North America the resultant influx of the rest of the mammal family – those more fleet of foot, more fecund, more aggressive – duly sounded the death knell for the pouch-bearers there. Adrift and alone, the marsupials of Terra Australis would be safe and sound in a world all their own for millions of years to come, until much more recent proximity to the Asian mainland would make possible colonization by other species, including *Homo sapiens*. Suffice it to say that by the time the twenty-six-year-old Charles Darwin stepped ashore in New South Wales, in January 1836, Australia had been on a voyage altogether more epic than his.

By then he had been the naturalist aboard HMS *Beagle* for four years. Seasick throughout, he had suffered for his science but his weeks ashore would change his life and also humankind's understanding of the story of the world. He had been an enthusiastic (if untrained) naturalist when he joined the voyage of discovery. He was lucky too, born into that class of British men blessed with the kind of family money that precluded the necessity to earn a living. He was a direct descendant of the English naturalist Erasmus Darwin and also the potter, industrialist and abolitionist Josiah Wedgwood. Originally destined for a career as a clergyman, he had defied his father's wishes and followed his heart into a career in science.

The moment of note came some time in that month of January, near a little township in the Central Tablelands, just west of the Blue Mountains, called Wallerawang – the name a corruption of that applied to the place by the local Wiradjuri people and meaning something like 'plenty of water'. It was on or around the 19th, near sunset, while walking beside a little creek, that Darwin caught his first glimpse of the living curiosity that is the duck-billed platypus. So downright odd that British biologists examining the first specimens believed they were dealing with a hoax – a composite creature stitched together from parts of multiple species in the manner of a little Frankenstein's monster – the platypus is from a class of mammals called monotremes. There are only two examples of monotremes, the other being the equally peculiar echidna, a spiny hedgehog of a thing. Monotreme means 'one hole' and refers to the fact that both the platypus and the echidna have a single orifice for reproduction and excretion. They also lay eggs, and then the hatched young suckle on their mothers' milk.

Accompanied by the Wallerawang property's overseer, a Scotsman named Andrew Brown, Darwin watched several platypuses playing in the water: 'very little of their bodies were visible, so they only appeared like so many water Rats. Mr Brown shot one; certainly it is a most extraordinary animal.' Later he spent hours examining the little corpse and considered how the platypus fitted into the ecological niche that was, back home, occupied by the water rat (the creature that inspired Ratty in *The Wind in the Willows*). Elsewhere he would watch kangaroo rats and see how they filled the role of English rabbits.

While everyone else might only have watched, wondered at the strangeness of the platypus and then moved on, the encounter haunted Darwin's imagination. Born and raised in a world in which most people, even educated, thinking people, were still in thrall to the creation story of the Old Testament, he could not help but notice a conundrum: why would an omnipotent, omniscient God solve the same problem in different ways in different places? If there was a watery niche to fill, why create a water rat for Europe and North America and a duck-billed platypus for Australia? In his diary he wrote: 'A Disbeliever in everything beyond his own reason might exclaim, "Surely two distinct creators must have been at work; their object however has been the same and certainly in each case the end is complete." ' He thought of both creatures and struggled to make sense of the extraordinary differences between them. 'What would the Disbeliever say to this? Would any two workmen ever hit on so beautiful, so simple and yet so artificial a contrivance? It cannot be thought so the one Hand has surely worked over the whole world?'

Darwin and the *Beagle* are mostly associated with the Galapagos Islands, with the finches and the giant tortoises and the rest. His time in Australia is overlooked by most, if not entirely forgotten, and yet it was there and only there that he recorded the sparking of that momentous thought. It was more than twenty years after his return to England that he published *On the Origin of Species*, in 1859. In time he would be labelled, among other things, 'the most dangerous man in Britain'.

We take for granted that Earth's life forms produce more young than could ever survive – that it is only those best adapted to their environments, on account of individual differences, that prevail in each case. That idea, so seemingly obvious and which changed for ever our understanding of life on this planet, depended upon Charles Darwin and a visit to Australia. All those years before, in the presence of the platypus, Darwin had set out on the greater journey of his life. By the end of it he had shaped the best and most complete scientific idea anyone has had so far.

79.

LOUIS DAGUERRE AND
MOMENTS CAPTURED FOR ALL TIME

There is no way of knowing when our species first noticed, far less exploited, the phenomenon of the *camera obscura* – the 'dark chamber'. In the fifteenth century Leonardo da Vinci wrote about how a smaller image of a brightly illuminated subject – like the sunlit frontage of a building, for instance – would appear upside down on the wall of a room directly opposite, if its light was allowed to pass through a small hole in a wall facing that subject. The effect was particularly useful for an artist like Leonardo, because a piece of paper could be placed in the way of the beam of light to enable the tracing of the inverted image. He was hardly the first. Ancient Greeks like Aristotle wrote about the same trick, as did tenth-century Arab physicist Ibn al-Haytham, known in the west as Alhazen (and whose writings were known to Leonardo). Some audacious scholars have suggested the cave artists of the Palaeolithic may have exploited a variation of the same technique tens of thousands of years ago.

The camera obscura effect is the same in every way as that exploited for, and by, the pinhole camera. Even the human eye works the same way, with the pupil as the pinhole and the retina as the surface receiving the reflected image.

Although both camera obscuras and pinhole cameras have been in operation for millennia, modern photography was an invention only of the nineteenth century. The oldest surviving photograph – the image made permanent – was taken in 1826 or 1827 by French inventor Joseph Nicéphore Niépce. It shows the view – gloomy and indistinct as a half-remembered dream on account of the primitive nature of his technique, using naturally light-sensitive Bitumen of Judea – from an upstairs window of a house on his estate in Burgundy. Niépce subsequently collaborated with fellow Frenchman Louis Daguerre, another innovator. Niépce died in 1833 but Daguerre persevered alone and developed what became known as the daguerreotype photography process.

His moment of note came in 1839 when he removed the cap covering the lens of his camera and allowed light to flood the surface of a sheet of copper inside coated with light-sensitive silver iodide. He and his camera were in the Place de la République, in Paris, facing south towards the Boulevard du Temple. The buildings and rooftops are unmistakably Parisian but the shot is made heartbreakingly poignant by the presence, down in the left-hand corner, of two people. They are a shoeshine boy and his customer, the first souls to have their images made permanent in that way. Even more haunting is the knowledge that countless other people passed through the frame and escaped capture, vanished like thieves in the night. On account of the relative insensitivity of silver iodide on a copper sheet, Daguerre had needed a ten-minute exposure. Only the shoeshiner and his client had stayed still long enough to leave their marks. All the rest had slipped by, elusive as the photons they had helplessly and unknowingly reflected.

The invention of photography (the term itself first coined only in the nineteenth century) is a moment of the utmost importance in the story of the world. After the advent of a way to keep moments, to trap them for ever like bugs in amber, we would be confronted by our nature and its consequences as never before. Mistreatment of our fellow human beings has been part of that nature from the beginning. We are born neither good nor bad but with the capability to do either, or both. Before photography our crimes against fellow humanity were remembered first as spoken stories and then described in written documents. There was art too – paintings of scenes – but these were only ever subjective and hardly as affecting as the images only photography may seize. A photograph reflects back at us the reality of our impact on others.

There have been slaves for ever – black, white and brown and owned by black, white and brown. There have been subject peoples, captured and misused. Down through unsnapped millennia there have been victims of torture, murder and every other abuse under the sun. There have been billions of invisible lives and deaths, inflicted on all, crimes by all. Only we of latter days have been caught out. The music stopped and ours, of all the generations, have been the ones left standing to answer for the record of our actions made of photons' traces, fixed on paper or on the screen. People of every colour and creed have been dreadful, each in their turn and in every way imaginable, to every other. The camera has only been catching a few of us at it for less than two centuries.

The photograph leaves us no alternative but to look wronged people in the eye. African slaves on American plantations were the first enslaved people whose reality we could not deny, not even to ourselves. The faces of Native Americans, driven off their ancestral lands and made to pose in costume, were the first such people to look down the lens with hearts broken. Maoris in New Zealand . . . Australian Aborigines . . . indigenous peoples all around the world have had their images recorded, made marks indelible. Now and for ever, on account of Bitumen of Judea, silver iodide and the rest, we cannot forget who they were, what we are, what all of us have always been.

80.

MARX AND ENGELS UNVEIL THEIR *COMMUNIST MANIFESTO*

According to Karl Marx, at the moment of the publication of the work known around the world as *The Communist Manifesto*, 'a spectre' was haunting Europe. That spectre, he wrote in his famous, infamous opening line, was communism itself and the haunting or possession to which he referred had hardly gone unnoticed by others: 'All the powers of old Europe have entered into a holy alliance to exorcise this spectre.'

Published anonymously at the end of February 1848 by the Workers' Educational Association and originally called *Manifesto of the Communist Party* in its first iteration, it was composed in German, ran to twenty-three pages and appeared bound in a dark-green cover. Just to be precise, with regard to such a portentous document, the moment of that printing happened inside premises at 46 Liverpool Street, in Bishopsgate, London. Together with his friend and fellow German Friedrich Engels (a twenty-eight-year-old heir to a Manchester-based milling family), twenty-nine-year-old philosopher and thwarted bon viveur Karl Marx had sought to have the spectre do their bidding and inspire worldwide revolution. They collaborated on the form and content, but Marx alone, skilful wordsmith, authored the final draft. He was a master of the art of the polemic. *The Communist Manifesto* is a work of some genius. It would be tweaked and republished many times and do no end of harm.

In 1848 a spectre haunted Europe right enough, there was no denying it. The aftershocks of the French Revolution of 1789 had rumbled and rippled. From around 1815 to 1870, those convulsions would affect (or afflict) states and populations beyond the borders of France. Like a hernia protruding in a place of strain, a painful, pain-filled tendency towards revolution bulged in one place after another, displacing old ways of being, of ruling, of being governed – or else erased them altogether. Directly or indirectly, the febrile atmosphere of which communism was a part meant that it was during the nineteenth century that the state assumed more power over the lives of citizens than ever before.

The Congress, or Treaty, of Vienna of 1814–15 had aimed to create a permanent peace for Europe – a settlement of all the grudges and unrest left over from the French Revolution and the wars waged by Napoleon. For four decades its central tenets held firm, providing a scaffold to hold up that peace of 1815 and the means by which smouldering fires of change might be snuffed out before they caught fully light. That it held as long as it did was down to the fear of revolution that stalked the lands even while the spectre of communism was still taking shape. Revolution is often a dirty word so that it is worth remembering that during the first decades of the nineteenth century the unquiet ghosts of the French Revolution were made, at least in part, of calls for representative government, personal freedom, freedom of the press and the like – honest and familiar wants. There was hunger too for nationalism felt by some, and for liberalism by others.

By 1848 the continent of Europe seemed on the verge of a conflagration nonetheless, one that might consume the old peace poorly wrought. By the summer of that year every major city bar London and St Petersburg could be seen only through a haze of rising political heat. Radicals of the working class, or liberals of the middle class, found voices of varying volume in Paris, Milan, Venice, Vienna, Prague, Budapest, Krakow, Munich and Berlin and called for the end of old conservative regimes. By then, of course, the manifesto penned by Marx and Engels was already in the hands of militants. In 1847 Marx had given the name 'Communist League' to those of like mind in France, Germany and Switzerland. Workers throughout the world were, he said and wrote, to unite. In their manifesto, he and Engels laid out a potent theory that concluded socialism was not just desirable but the inevitable consequence of industrialization. Marx likely first ran across the term *proletariat* (to describe the wage earners, the working class that toiled under the oppression of the capitalist system) in the writings of the Swiss economist Jean Charles Léonard de Sismondi. And so it was that he took the term for his own and prophesied that inevitable revolution would see that proletariat rise up triumphant and overthrow the oppressive class – those he termed the *bourgeoisie*, who owned the property, the factories and the rest of the means by which capital was made and squirrelled away.

If Marx, let alone Engels, were possessed of genius (and let us give the devil his due), then it was the genius of some version of prophecy. *The Communist Manifesto*, as it has come to be known, was, among other things, ahead of its time. In the Europe of 1848, the industrialization of society necessary to dehumanize and so propel the proletariat into open revolt had not yet come to pass in France, or in Germany, or elsewhere on the continent. What yet prevailed was the pride of artisans and craftsmen still fighting to retain their independence and to avoid the crushing cogs and wheels, powered then by steam engines, that could make mince meat out of the pride of working people. For want of the necessary numbers of suitably oppressed factory workers and the like (and those hordes would be tortured or suborned into being soon enough) there was inadequate kindling for the fires Marx imagined would forge them into steel for cutting.

He and Engels might instead have been predicting the anxieties haunting the workforces of the twenty-first-century west. Now we fret not about steam engines but about the influence of Big Tech and artificial intelligence, how their reach into our lives seems infinite and unrestricted. 'The bourgeoisie has stripped of its halo every occupation hitherto honoured and looked up to with reverent awe,' Marx wrote. 'It has converted the physician, the lawyer, the priest, the poet, the man of science into its paid wage labourers.'

In some of what was enshrined in the manifesto are notions too that are open to misinterpretation or abuse even now (especially among those still bent upon the upending of society, just as that Viking once upended King Charles the Simple of France). Hard it is to know if Marx and Engels ever lamented the bloody, broken-hearted changes they foresaw, or if they rather fancied them as the necessary birth pains of a new world order more to their liking, slippery with the blood resulting from the clumsy sewing up of gaping wounds between those that make and work the machines and those that own them and reap the profits of their power.

> The bourgeoisie cannot exist without constantly revolutionising the instruments of production, and thereby the relations of production, and with them the whole relations of society . . . Constant revolutionising of production, uninterrupted disturbance of all social conditions, everlasting uncertainty and agitation . . . All that is solid melts into air, all that is holy is profaned, and man is at last compelled to face with sober senses his real conditions of life, and his relations with his kind.

Engels was a rich man's son and Marx a dyspeptic malcontent who liked fine food, a good drink and more than the odd cigar, but who lacked the wit or the will to pay for any of it by the sweat of his own back. He leeched from family – his own and his wife's – and from Engels too, and repaid not a jot. Before listening to those who would change the world it is worth noting how they run their own lives and treat those closest to them. Jenny von Westphalen, Marx's wife, lamented how their life together might have been better if he had spent 'more time earning capital than just writing about it'. He fathered a child by their maid, Hélène Demuth, and then disowned the lad, called Frederick, leaving it to Engels to raise him as his own. Talk about exploitation of the workers.

81.

SULLIVAN BALLOU
AND A MOST UNCIVIL WAR

Civil war is among the worst wounds a society might inflict upon itself. It may be the worst of all. America's was fought between 1861 and 1865 and cost the lives of around 620,000 men – 2 per cent of the population. The same hurt inflicted today would mean six million dead. By some estimates the Battle of Antietam on 17 September 1862 is the bloodiest day in American history, with a casualty count of 22,654 men.

Like the First World War lying over the horizon then – less than a lifetime away – the American Civil War can seem too much to take in, too many numbers. It is made more comprehensible, the hurt more immediate, by taking time to consider what happened to just one family among the thousands.

In his documentary about the war, director Ken Burns gave prominence to a letter by Sullivan Ballou, a major in the 2nd Rhode Island Infantry Regiment that fought for the Union at the First Battle of Bull Run, the first major clash of the war. It was addressed to his wife, Sarah, mother of their two young sons. In the opening paragraph of the letter, dated 14 July 1861, he tells her it seems likely they will go into action in just a few days: 'Lest I should not be able to write you again, I feel impelled to write a few lines that may fall under your eye when I shall be no more.'

The formal tone is unfamiliar to a modern world – especially one in which letter writing between spouses has, anyway, all but fallen away. The moment in question is when Sarah opens the envelope and begins to read. The content of the whole of the text is close to unbearable. Woven through the staid and formal paragraphs are lines of intimacy:

> The memories of the blissful moments I have spent with you come creeping over me, and I feel most gratified to God and to you that I have enjoyed them for so long. And hard it is for me to give them up and burn to ashes the hopes of future years, when, God willing, we might still have lived and loved together, and seen our sons grow up to honourable manhood around us.

As he wrote, and as she read, it was just eighty-five years since the signing of the Declaration of Independence that had made their land a nation. In two and a half years their president, Abraham Lincoln, would stand in the aftermath of Gettysburg, another charnel house, and confess his inability – the inability of any and all still living then – to hallow the graveyard there:

> It is rather for us to be here dedicated to the great task remaining before us – that from these honoured dead we take increased devotion to that cause for which they gave the last full measure of devotion – that we here highly resolve that these dead shall not have died in vain – that this nation, under God, shall have a new birth of freedom . . .

Lincoln's words . . . Ballou's words . . . hard to read, both, on account of the sound of men's hearts breaking over the wedge of loss remembered, loss to come. Lincoln had a premonition of his own death, in a dream that found him walking into a room in the White House and seeing his own covered corpse laid out. Perhaps Ballou was no more than a realist, perhaps a fatalist, but he wrote as one who feared the worst, but loved his wife.

Never forget how much I love you, and when my last breath escapes me on
the battle field, it will whisper your name . . . But, O Sarah! If the dead can
come back to this earth and flit unseen around those they loved, I shall
always be near you; in the brightest day and the darkest night . . . always,
always, and if there be a soft breeze upon your cheek, it shall be my breath,
or as the cool air fans your throbbing temple, it shall be my spirit passing
by. Sarah, do not mourn me dead . . . for we shall meet again . . .

First Bull Run was a victory for the Confederates, who remembered it
as First Manassas. Major Ballou was shot in the leg, and a week after its
amputation he died in hospital. He was thirty-two years old. Like bad
weather, civil war is never far away – and dangerously close whenever a
population thinks such bad days are only behind them. It is always ready
to come again to break more families and more hearts.

82.

A PUB, A BOOK OF RULES
AND THE BEAUTIFUL GAME

Football's origins are hard to discern. Archaeologists have found evidence of an ancient pitch marked out with lines in Kyoto, Japan. In the third century BC the Han Chinese had a game that involved kicking a ball into a net, and the Ancient Greeks played something similar too.

What we do know is that the game has been a worry to the powers that be for the longest time. Some of its earliest iterations reek of violence and disorder. As a person might expect, the bloodiest forms of the game were to be found among the British. There are those audacious scholars who say the Celts would celebrate any battlefield victory over the Roman squatters by taking some laurelled head and making a plaything of it. Others have it instead that the game surfaced in these islands only after the Romans departed – 500 years later, perhaps – among Anglo-Saxons celebrating victories over Vikings by using for a ball the head of some or other luckless Dane. Certainly from the Middle Ages, the length and breadth of Britain, in one town after another, there are records of rambunctious ball games played by sprawling, brawling mobs of men and boys. Rules were in short supply (if they existed at all) and treated only as a hindrance to the pursuit of messy mayhem. Teams might number hundreds of players. On Orkney there is still the Kirkwall Ba Game, a centuries-old confection kicked off on New Year's Day close by the doors of the town's St Magnus Cathedral. 'Ba Games' are common throughout Scotland in particular – at Duns, Jedburgh and Roxburgh in the Borders, at Scone in Perthshire, and elsewhere.

Scotland's King James I was especially irked and alarmed by what he saw as the baleful influence of the game upon the hearts and minds of men and boys who should have been practising the skills of war. In 1424 he banned it outright with a suitably blunt proclamation, in parliament, that read: 'Nae man shall play at fute-ball.'

It had been much the same story south of the border. Chaos around the game, played in the streets and squares, provoked some London merchants to seek a ban of their own. In April 1314 King Edward II obliged them: 'there is a great noise in the city caused by hustling over large balls from which many evils may arise which God forbid; we command and forbid, on pain of imprisonment, such game to be used in the city in the future.'

On and on it goes, down through the centuries – a litany of complaints about boys playing with their balls. Edward III issued his own ban in 1349, and in 1477 Edward IV did likewise. Again and again it was framed by the notion that boys distracted by ball games would neglect their archery practice. Ned IV had it that 'No person shall practice . . . football . . . but every strong and able bodied person shall practice with the bow for the reason that the national defence depends upon such bowmen'.

By the eighteenth and nineteenth centuries the irresistible progress of first an agricultural and then an industrial revolution came close to achieving what kings and other spoilsports had thus far failed to do. Enclosure of land and then the density of building in towns and cities – factories, and the houses for the poor souls who would work in them – smothered the open spaces that had been used for rough play by hundreds if not thousands of players. Industrialized lives – regimented hours in factories and mines – denied working people the time for play. Only in the middle years of the nineteenth century did employers make room for a half-day on a Saturday, enabling men to gather for games in the afternoon. In some industrial towns – notably Sheffield – the half-day was midweek, on Wednesday, creating the same precious air bubble of free time.

Into the latter part of the 1700s the then endangered sport of football found refuge (if that is the word) in the English public schools – in those days barely recognizable, to modern eyes, as places of top-flight education. Those establishments then were veritable bear pits where the sons of rich families exercised their *Lord of the Flies* tendencies and only the fittest survived. On the playing fields of Eton, Charterhouse, Harrow, Rugby, Winchester and the like, football was an escape valve for pent-up aggression and general rowdiness. Every school, it seemed, played its own version and followed its own rules. In some the ball was only kicked with the feet; at others it was for catching and running with as well. The game played at Rugby stayed true to its earliest traditions and so took a specific path into the present day. Whatever the idiosyncrasies, everyone in every case called the game football.

Over time the masters of such schools came to realize that the rigours and demands of the game, the physicality, the threat of injury, might help turn unruly boys into fearless and uncomplaining men – leaders of governments, perhaps, and of the burgeoning empire. Practical problems arose, however, when teams from different schools came together in the hope of exercising their muscular Christianity and settling rivalries. Since each played its own variation on the theme, confusion was inevitable.

And then on the evening of Monday, 26 October 1863, in the Freemasons' Tavern on Great Queen Street in the West End of central London, close to where Holborn tube station is now, some former public schoolboys met to formalize the rules of the game of football. According to the official record they came together 'for the purpose of forming an Association with the object of establishing a definite code of rules for the regulation of the game'. Taking part in what was apparently a heated debate were representatives of Barnes FC, Blackheath Proprietary

School, the Civil Service, Charterhouse School, Crystal Palace (no relation to the modern team of the same name), Crusaders, Forest (Leytonstone), Kensington School, No Names (Kilburn), Perceval House (Blackheath) and Surbiton. Together they formed the original Football Association, and on that day, and on several days thereafter, the details were thrashed out. Approval was given first of all to a list of thirteen rules, and while there were later revisions, the groundwork had been completed for the modern game. The Rule Book of Association Football – or The Football Association Laws – was first published later that same year.

While sport in all its forms has been a defining force, shaping countless lives down through the centuries, even millennia, football has been something more and different. Take it or leave it, love it or loathe it, none but the hardest heart and emptiest head could or would seek to deny that football (or 'soccer', the short form of 'association football') has brought meaning to billions of lives in a way that only religions might challenge. Once the rules were set down, the game spread like a virus, the length and breadth of Britain and then around the world. The first international match, between England and Scotland and ending in a goalless draw, was played in 1872. France caught the bug the same year. Canada was next in 1876. By now the game is everywhere, known to everyone.

Football – that game that needs only a ball, a handful of players, castoff jumpers for goalposts and familiarity with those rules of 1863 – matters. Even those who have no love for the game (and I place myself in that camp) must accept its power to win and hold hearts. For its devoted followers, football provides the certainty of belonging to something grander than the self. The triumphs and disasters of The Club provide alternative heartbeats by which to measure a life. And then . . . and then on the field of play a lone figure might transcend all that had seemed possible on earth and briefly shine, like a flash of sunlight, for some few seconds of individual, unforgettable glory.

Scotsman Bill Shankly, player and legendary manager of Liverpool FC, is usually credited with the line that bears noting in this context: 'Some people believe football is a matter of life and death. I am very disappointed with that attitude. I can assure you it is much, much more important than that.'

83.

JAMES CLERK MAXWELL
SEES LIGHT FOR WHAT IT IS

Ancients like the Buddha and Lao Tzu had had intimations of the connectedness of all things. The Hindu view of the world is older, oldest, and goes further, seeing everything as part of the immortal creator Brahman. In the *Upanishads*, the revered Hindu texts, Brahman, neither male nor female but both, is all things at once:

> It is made of consciousness and mind: It is made of life and vision. It is made of the earth and the waters: It is made of air and space. It is made of light and darkness: It is made of desire and peace. It is made of anger and love: It is made of virtue and vice. It is made of all that is near: It is made of all that is afar. It is made of all.

That thought comes and goes, like crests and troughs on the ocean of time. It is accepted, and then not. With the arrival of the scientific method, elements of the same idea were rediscovered like fragments that might be put together to reveal a whole. Albert Einstein tried – and failed – to unite disparate phenomena, to find a theory that would explain everything in a few lines of mathematics. Before him, Isaac Newton had demonstrated that the force that pulled an apple to the ground was the same that held planets in their orbits. German philosopher Immanuel

Kant, a central figure of the Enlightenment of the eighteenth century, reached towards some of the same thinking when he proposed that all knowledge is relative – that we know nothing about things other than by appreciating their relationship to other things.

Modern physicists accept a trinity of sorts – giants of science deserving of a reverence close to worship – with Newton on one side and Einstein on the other. In the middle of the line-up, for those in the know, is Scotsman James Clerk Maxwell.

Author Basil Mahon opens *The Man Who Changed Everything: The Life of James Clerk Maxwell* with the line: 'In 1861, James Clerk Maxwell had a scientific idea that was as profound as any work of philosophy, as beautiful as any painting, and more powerful than any act of politics or war. Nothing would be the same again.' Appropriately enough, in the face of such grandeur, it is hard to pin down the moment. But it was in 1865 that Maxwell produced a paper entitled 'A Dynamical Theory of the Electromagnetic Field', revealing to his mostly uncomprehending scientist contemporaries a light that was too bright for them (as was he, come to that). What he had realized – and there is no way to be sure when that moment of realization occurred – was that electricity, light and magnetism were all manifestations of the same phenomenon.

Maths is the language that the universe speaks, and beyond the reading of all but a few. Some hint of what Maxwell had intuited might be appreciated by thinking about how ice, water and steam are just three physical manifestations of the same thing. According to Mahon, also a scientist and a lifelong admirer of Maxwell: 'The theory predicted that every time a magnet jiggled, or an electric current changed, a wave of energy would spread out into space like a ripple on a pond. Maxwell calculated the speed of the waves and it turned out to be the very speed at which light had been measured.'

Scientists had long suspected a link between the electricity they could generate and the magnetism they could feel. The nature of that connection, however, was beyond them – until Maxwell. 'At a stroke,' wrote

Mahon, 'he had united electricity, magnetism and light. Moreover, visible light was only a small band in a vast range of possible waves, which all travelled at the same speed but vibrated at different frequencies.'

The elegant equations with which Maxwell expressed his understanding are regarded, by the cognoscenti, as among the most beautiful maths ever written. That which he had comprehended was so far in advance of most of his contemporaries it was as though a time traveller had come back to the nineteenth century to demonstrate a portable nuclear power station to a steam-powered world.

If the necessary maths is too much for most, it is at least worth knowing that it is the application of his equations that has enabled radio, television, radar, mobile telephony and the interconnectedness of the Internet. He truly was a man who changed *everything*.

Towards the end of his life, Einstein was offered an honour by the University of Edinburgh. By then the great man was festooned in such baubles and so initially declined to attend the inevitable ceremony. Soon afterwards, however, he got back in touch to say he would come after all. He had realized Maxwell had once lectured in the hall in which the award was to be made and so his one condition was that any carpet or other flooring be lifted from the surface of the stage so that he might briefly tread the same boards as his predecessor. Einstein freely acknowledged that without having been able to stand on the Scotsman's intellectual shoulders, he would not have seen the way ahead to his theories regarding relativity.

'One scientific epoch ended and another began with James Clerk Maxwell,' he said.

American theoretical physicist Richard Feynman, a recipient of the Nobel Prize in Physics, would later say: 'From the long view of the history of mankind – seen from, say, 10,000 years from now – there can be little doubt that the most significant event of the nineteenth century will be judged as Maxwell's discovery of the laws of electromagnetism.'

Geniuses are often difficult men, or at least challenging to be around in private life. Feynman certainly ruffled feathers; Newton was so awkward in his dealings with his fellow human beings it has been supposed, by modern medics, that he may have been autistic. By all accounts, Maxwell was charming in every way. He was close to his family and a devoted husband and father. He made and maintained friendships that lasted from boyhood until the end of his days. He was described always as good-natured, a man who bore no grudges and never took himself too seriously. He happily acknowledged his own mistakes while being gentle around the shortfalls of others. It seems no one who knew him ever had a bad word to say about him.

As soon as he could speak, as a child of one or two years, he began asking questions about the world around him. Anything and everything caught his eye and inspired in him a spirit of investigation. As a toddler he would point to whatever he had noticed and ask, 'What's the go o' that?' If the answer failed to satisfy him, his inevitable follow-up question was: 'But what's the particular go o' that?' Perhaps he came as close as anyone ever has – as close as the Buddha, or Lao-Tzu, or Jesus, or any seer – to understanding the connectedness of all things.

Even now the fullest extent of the revelation of Maxwell's equations has not been realized. Above all it is their beauty that prevails. British physicist Paul Dirac said in *Scientific American*, 'It is more important to have beauty in one's equations than to have them fit experiment.' Maxwell's contribution to the story of the world, the significance of his moment and moments of revelation, may be that he turned a light on the beauty of it all.

84.

DOSTOYEVSKY SEES *THE BODY*
OF THE DEAD CHRIST IN THE TOMB

In 1867 Russian novelist and philosopher Fyodor Dostoyevsky found himself standing before a painting in the Kunstmuseum in Basel, Switzerland. He was with his wife, Anna, and the artwork in question was *The Body of the Dead Christ in the Tomb*, by German artist Hans Holbein the Younger and painted between 1520 and 1522. It is a life-size depiction of the dead Jesus, in oil and tempera on limewood, and measures 200 cm by 30.5 cm. It offers a letterbox view of the tomb, or a cross-section giving sight of what lies within. In a style known to art critics as 'grotesque' it portrays an emaciated body laid out on a cloth-covered slab. Jesus is unmistakably dead. Three wounds are visible – a puncture of the right hand, of the right foot, and a gash in the right side of the ribcage. The hand and the foot are tinged green, suggesting putre-faction. Most troubling is the depiction of his face. More than a profile, the head is turned, or rather slumped, slightly towards the right, and so to the viewer. The lifeless eye is open, the mouth sagging. Like the hand and foot, the face has a greenish hue. Long hair is unkempt, swept back from the forehead and falling down over the edge of the slab. It is altogether unsparing.

Anna Dostoyevsky wrote in her diary that she had to pull her husband away from the painting, so transfixed did he appear to be. Dostoyevsky suffered epilepsy throughout his life and she feared he was so affected by the image he might experience a seizure.

It was in the aftermath of the viewing that he began work on his novel *The Idiot*, which was published the following year. The couple were living in poverty, moving from address to address between Switzerland and Italy. Dostoyevsky was a chronic gambler and his habit only made their circumstances worse. By his own estimate, *The Idiot* was an attempt to 'depict a completely beautiful human being'. His central character is Prince Lev Nikolayevich Myshkin, a good and open-hearted young man, an epileptic, and a target for those older and less wholesome figures who seek to manipulate him.

Epilepsy was a constant presence for the author, his condition almost certainly exacerbated by hardship and sometimes terrible stress. In 1849 he had been convicted of circulating banned literature and sentenced to death by firing squad. He and others were in position before the rifles when their sentences were commuted to jail terms in exile in Siberia. Those moments of imminent death haunted Dostoyevsky ever after.

While in exile he told a friend about his experiences during the advent of one particularly memorable seizure:

The air was filled with a big noise and I tried to move. I felt that heaven was going down upon the earth, and that it had engulfed me. I have really touched God. He came into me myself; yes, God exists, I cried, You, all healthy people, have no idea what joy that joy is which we epileptics experience the second before a seizure. Mahomet, in his Koran, said he had seen Paradise and had gone into it. All these stupid, clever men are quite sure that he was a liar and a charlatan. But no, he did not lie, he really had been in Paradise during an attack of epilepsy; he was a victim of this disease as I am. I do not know whether this joy lasts for seconds or hours or months, but believe me, I would not exchange it for all the delights of this world.

How strange would it be if so many moments that changed the story of the world were born out of epilepsy? Was it joy, ecstasy like that described by Dostoyevsky, that inspired Muhammad's recitation? Was it something similar for the Buddha? For Jesus Christ? Historians have speculated that when Emperor Constantine envisioned the cross in the sky before the Battle of Milvian Bridge, and heard the promise of victory under that sign, he too was in the grip of the ecstasy before an epileptic seizure. What of St Paul on the road to Damascus – the blinding light and the questioning voice he heard as that of Jesus?

Before Anna could pull her husband away from the painting of the dead Christ he had told her: 'A painting like that can make you lose your faith.' In *The Idiot*, Myshkin is visiting the home of Parfyon Rogozhin – whose character is sly and selfish, the opposite of his own well-meaning ways – when he sees a copy of the painting of the dead Christ upon a wall. 'That picture!' he says. 'A man could lose his faith looking at that picture!'

Jesus is dead in Holbein's painting. As was his mission on earth, having been made flesh, he has experienced everything that it is to be a mortal man. His incarnation has been complete. The Greek term *kenosis* translates as 'self-emptying' and refers to the way in which Jesus surrendered and lost every scintilla of his divinity so that he could know life and therefore death. When he died on the cross, his dying was real in every way in order that his sacrifice would indeed spare the rest of humanity from the need ever to do likewise.

Friedrich Nietzsche's *The Gay Science* was published in 1882 and included the fateful pronouncement, by the Madman, that 'God is Dead'. Nietzsche described Dostoyevsky as 'the only psychologist ... from whom I have something to learn', and, by some means likely never properly to be understood, both writers outlined the same fate for humankind in a world without belief in God. Almost in parallel with each other the novelist and the philosopher thought themselves into the twentieth century and foreshadowed the horrors there. The Madman asks:

Where has God gone? I shall tell you. We have killed him – you and I. We are his murderers . . . What did we do when we unchained the earth from its sun? Whither is it moving now? Whither are we moving now? Away from all suns? Are we not perpetually falling? Backward, sideward, forward, in all directions? Is there any up or down left? Are we not straying as through an infinite nothing? Do we not feel the breath of empty space? Has it not become colder? Is it not more and more night coming on all the time? Must not lanterns be lit in the morning? Do we not hear anything yet of the noise of the gravediggers who are burying God? Do we not smell anything yet of God's decomposition? Gods too decompose. God is dead. God remains dead. And we have killed him. How shall we, murderers of all murderers, console ourselves? That which was the holiest and mightiest of all that the world has yet possessed has bled to death under our knives. Who will wipe this blood off us? With what water could we purify ourselves? What festivals of atonement, what sacred games shall we need to invent? Is not the greatness of this deed too great for us? Must we not ourselves become gods simply to be worthy of it? There has never been a greater deed; and whosoever shall be born after us – for the sake of this deed he shall be part of a higher history than all history hitherto.

Perhaps Dostoyevsky saw it first, in Holbein's *Dead Christ*. It was, in any event, a moment worth noting.

Around and around the names keep coming, out of the past and into the present. English physicist Oliver Heaviside wrote about James Clerk Maxwell, another visionary of another sort, and said the intellectual giants among us 'live the best part of their lives after they are dead'. 'His soul will live and grow for long to come,' he wrote, 'and hundreds of years hence will shine as one of the bright stars of the past, whose light takes years to reach us.' Something of the same sentiment is there in the words of Nietzsche's Madman when he tells his audience that 'deeds require time even after they are done, before they can be seen and heard. This deed is still more distant from them than the distant stars – and yet they have done it themselves.'

85.

THE WRIGHT BROTHERS TAKE
TO THE SKY AT KITTY HAWK

On 9 February 1969, the first Boeing 747 'jumbo jet' took to the skies over western Washington state, USA. When chief test pilot Jack Waddell opened the throttles on its four jet engines they delivered a combined 174,000 lb of thrust. A few weeks later, on 2 March, French Air Force pilot André Turcat was at the controls of a prototype Concorde for her maiden flight over Toulouse, France. On 1 October that same year she would go supersonic – breaking the sound barrier – for a whole nine minutes. The world of which this is the story had been made smaller.

All three moments in the same year, and just over sixty-five years, not even a lifetime, after Orville Wright had piloted the first powered flight in the history of the world on 17 December 1903. From take-off to landing, at Kitty Hawk on the Outer Banks of North Carolina, he and the *Wright Flyer* managed a distance of just 120 feet – considerably shorter than the 195-foot-8-inch wingspan of Jack Waddell's jumbo jet.

Orville was a shy and gentle soul. Wilbur, that other Wright brother of legend, was older and the more seriously studious of the two. They had two elder brothers, Reuchlin and Lorin, and a younger sister, Katharine, and the family lived in Dayton, Ohio, where their father, an ordained minister, was the editor of a newspaper. Their mother, Susan, had died of tuberculosis in 1889.

The moment, of such importance that it changed the world, came after years of study, experimentation and effort by many thinkers and innovators. By the 1890s the bicycle was the next big thing in the US and the younger Wright brothers, together with their sister, smartly got on board. They opened a workshop and, with the help of a talented mechanic and machinist called Charlie Taylor, from Illinois, set about selling and repairing the newfangled contraptions. Taylor was an innovator in his own right and he it was who built the engine used for that first powered flight. He wanted to be a pilot too, but it never happened.

It was altogether an inventive and exciting time, when once distant technological horizons were pulled closer by the determined efforts of those committed to expanding the boundaries of the possible. Much of it was driven too by the understanding that there was money to be made in making the results of innovation accessible to the general public. By the end of the nineteenth century George Eastman had come up with the Kodak camera, the first to put photography into the hands of the amateur, and Isaac Singer had offered up the sewing machine that bears his name.

For the Wright brothers it was the observation of the flight of birds that made the difference. At Kitty Hawk it was seabirds they watched and somehow they intuited that it was the curved shape of their wings that, when offered up to a headwind, provided the necessary magic of lift. There were experiments with a makeshift wind tunnel too, and practice with gliders. In this they were following in the footsteps of many innovators including French-American engineer Octave Chanute, German Otto Lilienthal – known as 'the flying man' on account of his well-publicized flights aboard gliders of his own design – English inventor and aviation pioneer Sir George Cayley, and even Leonardo da Vinci, whose drawings had made plain the necessity of mimicking the ways of birds.

What the Wright brothers understood, perhaps more than anyone else, was the necessity of giving control to the pilot. Others had made useful progress with the design of wings and engines, but it was the Wrights who set themselves properly to giving the pilot the means to make the moment-by-moment adjustments required to ride and take advantage of the ever-changing currents of air. The death of Lilienthal in 1896, when one of his gliders stalled and crashed, gave them the impetus to perfect their approach.

It was Orville at the controls of the *Wright Flyer*, with its 40-foot muslin-covered wingspan and 12-horsepower petrol engine, for that immortal first powered flight by a heavier-than-air craft. For the moment and moments in question they had built a runway of 2×4s, which they nick-named 'Junction Railroad', down the bank of a sand dune called Kill Devil Hill. It was a biplane – two wings, one above the other – and Orville lay on his front on the delicate surface of the lower. His hips were in a cradle connected to cables that gave him, via body movements, the ability to simultaneously alter the shape and curvature of the wings and control the rudder. A stiff 27 mph wind was blowing and it was cold, but with a view to keeping his weight down Orville chose not to wear his coat. The wind blew, the engine roared into life and, with Wilbur gently holding one wingtip to keep it steady until the last moment, the take-off got under way, down Kill Devil Hill and then . . . and then up and away. In the end the flight lasted just a dozen seconds but for that thread of moments a man had been in control of an engine-powered flying machine in the air.

Their clergyman father had repeatedly told his boys, 'It's given only to God and angels to fly.' But he was wrong.

Some moments of import are noted at the time of their happening, but the Wright brothers' first flight, its significance, was stubbornly ignored at first. Soon enough, and with the help of a more powerful engine, they were able to make flights of 25 miles, or even more, and yet the US government twice rejected their offer to let them in on the technology. Even that first rise and flight and landing had gone largely unobserved. The world of newspapers had let the event brush past them like a stranger in a crowd. In his elegant, intimate telling of the adventure in *The Wright Brothers*, Pulitzer Prize-winning American author David McCullough described how the scene was witnessed only by 'three men from a nearby Life-Saving Station, one local dairy farmer and a curious 18-year-old boy'.

The nature of their achievement registered first in Europe and then, once the momentum began to build, the rest of the world began to wake up to what it meant. Within a decade the Wrights were in the aircraft-building business. By 1912 Britain had added a Royal Flying Corps to its military, and by the end of the First World War that fledgling had evolved into the Royal Air Force. The motto of the service, coined by classically educated pilots, was, and is, *per ardua ad astra* – 'through endeavour to the stars'.

To the stars it would be, and on 20 July 1969 – the same year as those flights by the jumbo jet and Concorde – two representatives of a species that had barely believed in the possibility (let alone the utility) of powered flight just over sixty-five years before, walked on the surface of the moon. A splinter of wood from the *Wright Flyer* was aboard Apollo 11, along with some muslin from a wing, and so flew to the moon and back. On 19 April 2021, another piece of her fabric, the size of a postage stamp, fluttered aboard a little helicopter called *Ingenuity* that stayed aloft for some moments in the thin air of Mars. The world has been made to seem smaller in an infinite universe, and the possibilities are as limitless.

86.

OIL IN THE MIDDLE EAST
AND THE POISONED CHALICE

On a day in mid-June 1908 English engineer George B. Reynolds was at work in the Zagros Basin in Persia. He had been there several years by then, looking for oil. He had just been handed a telegram from his employer, the Scottish Burmah Oil Company. It was ordering him to 'cease work, dismiss the staff, dismantle anything worth the cost of transporting to the coast for re-shipment, and come home'.

Instead of doing as he had been told, there and then, Reynolds merely smiled and kept working.

He had originally been hired for the job by fellow Englishman William Knox D'Arcy, an adventurer who had made himself rich from a gold mine in Australia. In London, and bored of living the high life, D'Arcy had been approached by Armenian Kitabchi Khan, on the look-out for investors for a new venture in Persia, modern-day Iran. On 28 May 1901 D'Arcy and his partners struck a £20,000 (£2.2 million in today's money) deal with the Persian ruler Mozaffar ad-Din Shah Qajar. This would become known as the D'Arcy Concession and it granted him, for sixty years, exclusive rights to prospect and drill for oil in a swathe of Persia covering almost half a million square miles.

The First Exploration Company was set up by May 1903 and D'Arcy appointed self-taught geologist and engineer Reynolds as his head of field operations. That there was likely to be oil in the Zagros Basin was no secret. By the middle of the nineteenth century archaeologists and geologists alike had reported numerous areas of natural 'seepage' of both oil and bitumen, and anyway, the locals had always been aware of such.

Early signs were encouraging, but by 1905 D'Arcy's pockets were close to empty. Conditions in the field were severe – heat, remote locations and the presence of aggressive local tribesmen. It was a testing environment, and costly, and D'Arcy agreed to a deal that gave control of his rights to the newly formed Glasgow-based Concessions Syndicate Ltd, in turn financed by the Burmah Oil Company. By then the Royal Navy was planning a change of fuel for their warships, from coal to oil, and it had been deemed prudent, at the highest levels of government, to keep the D'Arcy Concession in British hands.

Reynolds kept working regardless. It is easy to imagine that in those far-off days when international communications were still quite a lot less than instantaneous there was often a lag, messages passing one another like ships in the night. On 26 May 1908, Reynolds' team struck oil, discovering the world's largest oil field in the process. It was what became the Masjed Soleyman field, which means 'the Mosque of Solomon'. Word of the find reached the British government in the form of a coded message that directed the reader to lines from two psalms. Once assembled it read: 'That he may bring out of the earth oil to make him a cheerful countenance . . . the flint stone into the springing well.'

It was not until the middle of the following month that Reynolds received the telegram, dated 14 June, advising him to shut up shop and come home. By then the story of the world had changed yet again. In years to come oil would be found all over the Middle East – throughout the Arabian Peninsula, in Iraq, Kuwait, the United Arab Emirates, beneath the Caspian Sea and elsewhere besides. In 1944 geologist Everette DeGolyer estimated that 300 billion barrels of oil were saturating the rock of the Middle East, with as much as a third of that 'greatest single prize in all history' in Saudi Arabia.

In the years following the First World War, Reynolds relocated to Venezuela and there found the giant La Rosa field – so that a self-taught prospector, barely remembered today, was responsible for finding two of the world's richest sources of oil.

Unimaginable, obscene wealth lay in store for some. Oil and its by-products would reshape the world. But for many of those living on top of it, the presence of oil has, as often as not, been a cause of great suffering. Economists and others talk about 'resource curse' and note that countries rich in non-renewable resources have had a tendency towards less economic growth and, perhaps more importantly in the long run, less in the way of democracy and human rights than those in countries not so blessed.

87.

7.30 A.M. ON THE FIRST DAY
OF THE BATTLE OF THE SOMME

Within eight weeks of the outbreak of war in August 1914 three-quarters of a million British men had volunteered for service. Unlike the rest of the great powers, Britain had had no mass-conscripted army when the fighting started. Well aware that the small professional army she did have would quickly be overwhelmed, Horatio Herbert Kitchener, Secretary of State for War, had put out the call for volunteers – *Your Country Needs You*, and all that. A wave of patriotism and the excitability of young men saw thousands, and then hundreds of thousands, step forward in all their eagerness. Among them were those men and boys who formed what became known as the Pals Battalions as men in workplaces, or from the same streets, or as members of clubs joined up to serve together, shoulder to shoulder. All over Britain it was the same. In London, in Birmingham and Bristol, in Cambridge and Cardiff, in Hull, Leeds, Manchester and Newcastle, in Edinburgh and Glasgow and elsewhere besides there was nothing less than a desperation to be together with friends, colleagues, neighbours and teammates for what was being billed as the adventure of a lifetime.

Hastily trained, the first of them were in northern France and on the Western Front by the middle of 1915. For many of them, thousands upon thousands of them, their first action would be the first day of the Battle of the Somme. That butcher's yard would remain in business until November 1916, but it is the first day, 1 July, that has for generations since come to symbolize the futility and loss of the whole war. For many people, the first day of the Somme *is* the First World War.

In the *Times* and *Telegraph* newspapers, in the In Memoriam sections, there has been a traditional entry, year after year:

> 9th and 10th BNS., K.O.Y.L.I. – To the undying memory of the Officers and Men of the above Battalions who fell in the attack on Fricourt (Somme) on July 1, 1916.
>
> 'Gentlemen, when the barrage lifts.'

For the week before that day of days, Allied troops had bombarded the German lines with heavy artillery – the barrage in question. The thinking was that a million and a half shells would obliterate the barbed wire and the rest of the defences, so that British infantrymen could walk in formation and unopposed across no-man's land to occupy the enemy positions. In fact the barrage had only made the wire an even more jumbled and impenetrable obstacle, and the moment the barrage lifted – as in stopped – the German soldiers emerged unscathed from reinforced bunkers deep underground and set up their machine guns.

Thousands of soldiers, those of the Pals Battalions among them, stepped out on to no-man's land and into oblivion. Here was the deadliest day in British military history with 57,470 casualties, 19,240 of whom had been killed.

Prior to the Somme a British soldier wore a single dog tag. In the event of his death it was removed to ensure his pay was stopped (the British army did not pay dead soldiers). Such was the shameful heap of slain, however, the burial parties could not keep up, not nearly, and while the army bureaucrats knew who was dead, right enough, they could no longer tell which corpse was which. In any event, many bodies had been mangled beyond recognition or else turned into pink mist that blew away on the wind. Here was the reason for the myth-making of 'The Missing of the Somme' – the notion that thousands of men had disappeared that day, and on many days that followed. Here was why so many gravestones read only 'A Soldier of the Great War', for want of a name long since lost. Serried ranks of Portland stone, set in place later on top of mass graves of mangled dead, created an illusion of order. After the carnage of the Somme every British soldier received two tags to wear around his neck – one for removal to ensure the stopping of his pay while the other remained with his corpse that he might go into the ground beneath a stone bearing his name.

There would be no more Pals Battalions. None had foreseen a day like the first day of the Somme . . . a day that wiped away so many men from one street, from one factory, from one family. After the Somme some care was taken to ensure men who knew each other were spread between battalions, so as to prevent such heartbreaking clusters of loss.

In *The Great War and Modern Memory*, American war veteran and writer Paul Fussell explained the genesis of the 'In Memoriam' quoted above. In the last moments before the attack began a group of officers and their commander waited in their mess, behind the lines in a Picardy farmhouse. On being asked to propose a toast to the CO, the senior company commander raised his glass amid the din of the ongoing bombardment.

'Gentlemen,' he said, 'when the barrage lifts.'

The First World War is a litany of numbers troublingly large – of volunteers and conscripts, of casualties and deaths, of bullets and shells fired – until the scale of it is numbing, incomprehensible. By November 1914 France was a million casualties down with four years of fighting still to go. It is hard to imagine that anything remotely similar would be allowed to happen now, but not impossible.

88.

LENIN, THE SEALED TRAIN
AND REVOLUTION IN RUSSIA

Time and again it has been single individuals who have altered the story of the world. The Buddha, Confucius, Jesus Christ, Muhammad – a long list of people who by their actions, or communicated thoughts, changed the narrative for millions or even billions of people.

At around 11 p.m. on the evening of 16 April 1917, Vladimir Ilyich Ulyanov stepped down from a train just arrived at the Finland Station in the city of Petrograd in Russia. Some fifteen or so years earlier he had adopted the pseudonym Lenin and it was as Lenin that he would change the world.

It was quite a moment, that arrival. In *To the Finland Station*, his 1940 history of socialism, American writer and critic Edmund Wilson described the destination as 'a shabby, stucco station, rubber grey and tarnished pink'. It was altogether dreary and unprepossessing, and hardly suitable for a capital city, and yet there it was that Lenin set foot back in his homeland after years in exile as a would-be revolutionary. Years later Winston Churchill would look back on the moment and describe Lenin as nothing less than a 'plague bacillus' injected into the body of a Russia terribly weakened by the First World War and lacking the immune system necessary to fight him off. Like a syringe, that train plunged Lenin into the already feverish country, and the disease of communism he carried would quickly spread. As he emerged on to the platform and approached a triumphal arch raised for the occasion, a band played revolutionary tunes like 'La Marseillaise' and a large crowd of well-wishers cheered their welcome.

Lenin had dreamed of revolution since 1887 when his brother was executed for his part in a plot to murder Tsar Alexander III. He trained and worked as a lawyer and by 1895 was helping to organize Marxist groups in St Petersburg. In the December of that year he was arrested along with other leaders of the 'Union for the Struggle for the Liberation of the Working Class', jailed for one year and exiled to Siberia for a further three. After his release and during the early years of the twentieth century he was abroad in western Europe, in London among other places. In 1903 he was part of the founding of the Russian Social Democratic Workers' Party (RSDWP) and from the outset championed the Bolshevik majority in favour of military action to achieve their desired ends. The Menshevik minority endured their final humiliation, at the All-Russian Congress of Soviets in Petrograd in November 1917, when Leon Trotsky loudly dismissed them 'into the dustbin of history'.

There was a revolution in Russia in 1905, for which Lenin returned, but Tsar Nicholas II brought the trouble to an end by offering reforms, before welching on the deal. By 1907 Lenin was in exile again. During the First World War no other country was hurt as badly as Russia – more men dead, the economy shattered. By March 1917 there were riots in Petrograd, by starving people demanding food. Soldiers joined the protests, and on the 15th Tsar Nicholas abdicated. A provisional government – led by Minister of War Alexander Kerensky, and seeking to mollify the *soviets* or councils of soldiers and workers – replaced centuries of tsarist rule.

Lenin had been living quietly in Zurich, in Switzerland, with his wife Nadezhda Konstantinovna Krupskaya. He was in his late forties by then and had been coming to the conclusion that he was too old for revolution, that his time had passed, when Germany saw an opportunity to knock their enemy Russia out of the war. Kerensky and his colleagues had maintained the war effort in the face of mounting opposition, but his administration had been weak and ineffectual from the beginning. One hefty push (or one more infection injected into its bloodstream) would likely see it fall. Lenin and his lieutenants were therefore put aboard a train departing Zurich at 3.10 p.m. on 9 April. This was the fabled 'sealed train' that would pass through Germany, Sweden and Finland without customs checks as though it had never been there. That would be the way Lenin described events anyway, adding polish to his own legend, though in truth he and his colleagues disembarked in Frankfurt where they enjoyed a one-night break from the train.

Conditions aboard were simple. Lenin issued tickets for use of the toilet – first class for those in need of the actual facilities, and second class for anyone just wanting a quiet place in which to smoke. German soldiers occupied part of the train, supervising the Russians' every move, and a chalk line drawn on the floor marked the international border between the warring states. The train was loaded on to a ferry for the crossing of the Baltic Sea, and in Stockholm Lenin disembarked a second time for a brief stretching of the legs. They passed through the Grand Duchy of Finland and then turned south again for arrival in Petrograd. When Soviet artist Mikhail Sokolov reimagined the scene many years later, he made space directly behind his depiction of Lenin for the grinning face of one Joseph Stalin, who was not even there on the day but wished with all of his self-obsessed heart that he had been.

Lenin set to work at once, writing and preaching his Marxist gospel of revolution and calling first of all for the overthrow of the provisional government. Things did not go his way at first and, having been labelled by the authorities as a German agent, he was forced to flee back to Finland in July. His infection had taken hold, however, and for a nation on its knees with war wounds and starvation his echoing calls for 'Peace, land and bread' – all that the people wanted if they were to start new lives – would not be silenced. By October he was back in Petrograd, and the following month the Red Guards of his Bolsheviks succeeded in replacing the provisional government with rule by soviets. Russia and the world would never be the same.

89.

A CAMP COOK AND THE INFLUENZA PANDEMIC OF 1918–20

Face coverings to be worn in public . . . funerals limited to fifteen minutes' duration . . . no entry to towns or permission to travel on public transport without official certificates . . . hefty fines for those breaking the rules . . . the influence of scientists in the ascendant as governments rely on them for advice . . . hopes for vaccines . . .

All of the above sound like tactics for coping with Covid-19 in the third decade of the twenty-first century; in fact they were in place in 1918 as the world coped with a fourth year of war and a flu pandemic that would kill more people than the most lethal outbreak of the Black Death in the middle years of the fourteenth century. Just before breakfast time on 11 March 1918, Sergeant Albert Gitchell, a cook at Camp Funston in Kansas, reported to the hospital block with what he described as 'a bad cold'. He had a headache, sore throat, pain in his muscles and a high fever. No sooner was he admitted than Corporal Lee Drake was at the front desk describing the same symptoms. Moments after that, Sergeant Adolph Hurley would join them on a ward set aside for those with contagious conditions. In *The Great Epidemic*, American author A. A. Hoehling described how one Surgeon Colonel Schreiner found himself all at once dealing with a flood of ailing servicemen: 'By breakfast time, the telltale medical manifestations were as obvious to Colonel Schreiner as the inscriptions in a family Bible.' By lunchtime that day he had 107 men struggling with near identical symptoms: 'Fever 104 degrees. Low pulse, drowsiness and photophobia. Conjunctivae reddened and mucous membranes of nose, throat and bronchi, evidence of inflammation.'

Although widely circulated and quoted, historians now challenge the validity of naming Gitchell (or indeed anyone else) as Patient Zero of the deadliest pandemic of all time. There were reports of the same illness in other camps in Kansas and in New York City around the same time. Spain was a neutral country and since her journalists were not hidebound by wartime censorship, excited reporting of the pandemic led simultaneously to exaggeration of its impact in that country and to the disease being labelled 'Spanish Flu'.

With millions of men on the move on account of the war, it is impossible now to say where the first cases originated. It hardly matters. As 1918 wore on there were outbreaks throughout Africa and Asia, in North and South America, in Europe and in the islands of the south Pacific. In India its effects were especially severe, with as many as fifty deaths per thousand people. As with the Covid-19 outbreak that began in 2019, there were many who pointed at China as a likely source. Wherever it originated, it was a virus mutation that sidestepped almost everyone. Herd immunity was undone. There are innumerable stories of people taking ill in the morning and dying the same day. For many there was the complication of cyanosis – a depletion of oxygen in the blood so that they slowly suffocated, bloody froth trailing from mouths and noses.

By the time the storm of the pandemic had blown itself out, in 1920, as much as a third of the world's population had been infected. Estimates of the overall death toll range from 20 to 100 million – as much as 5 per cent of the 1.9 billion people alive at the time.

In 1918 Europe especially, and the world in general, was exhausted by war. Populations weakened by food shortages and other privations, and also by the enervating toll taken by awful, endless stress, were in no state to face a new variant of an already dangerous disease like influenza. In

The Great War and Modern Memory Paul Fussell wrote about how irony, or the appreciation of irony, was a consequence of the war for the European populations worst hurt by the attritional nature of the fighting. There had been no all-encompassing war for the best part of a century and most people were incapable of imagining what lay ahead – how terrible it would be. 'Irony is the attendant of hope,' he wrote, 'and the fuel of hope is innocence.'

The irony for those still alive in the early spring of 1918 was that a killer more efficient than the war was on its way. By the time the guns fell silent, bullets and shells, barbed wire and poison gas – as well as all manner of other illnesses – had claimed 20 million lives. The pandemic that followed on another horse of the apocalypse would claim twice that number and more.

90.

MALLORY AND IRVINE
AND THE QUEST FOR EVEREST

At the climax of the 1924 Everest expedition English mountaineers George Mallory and Andrew Irvine made an attempt on the summit. They set out together on 4 June from Advanced Base Camp, at 21,330 feet. On the 8th, from a position far below, at Camp V, fellow expedition member Noel Odell watched a legend sketched on to a canvas made of snow and ice and rock by two tiny dots of black. In his diary he wrote: 'At 12.50 saw M and I on ridge nearing base of final pyramid.' Some days later he added more:

There was a sudden clearing of the atmosphere, and the entire summit ridge and final peak of Everest were unveiled. My eyes became fixed on one tiny black spot silhouetted on a small snow crest beneath a rock step in the ridge; the black spot moved. Another black spot became apparent and moved up the snow to join the other on the crest. The first then approached the great rock step and shortly emerged on top; the second did likewise. Then the whole fascinating vision vanished, enveloped in cloud once more.

There was but one explanation. It was Mallory and his companion moving, as I could see even at that great distance, with considerable alacrity, realizing doubtless that they had none too many hours of daylight to reach the summit from their present position . . .

With that, they were gone from sight. No trace of either was found until 1999 and the Mallory and Irvine Research Expedition timed to mark the seventy-fifth anniversary of their disappearance. Mallory's body was found and identified by a piece of clothing tagged with a label bearing his name.

It has long been speculated that perhaps . . . perhaps the pair had had time to make it to the summit and that they died on the descent, having had their moment on the roof of the world.

There in the tragedy of their loss is the unblemished heart of adventure, the very meaning of endeavour . . . *per ardua ad astra*. Defeated in the end or not, still Mallory and Irvine reached an altitude, in 1924, that would not be bested for thirty years. More important, they reached even higher than that summit in the story of the world for they had pushed beyond their own limits and so into the invisible. Two black dots and then . . . and then . . .

Everest was successfully climbed for the first time in 1953 by New Zealander Edmund Hillary and Nepali-Indian Sherpa Tenzing Norgay. Theirs was an extraordinary achievement, right enough, the summiting of the world itself.

Something of Mallory and Irvine would surely appeal to Homer. Something in their striving seems to reach higher, much higher than the 29,031 feet of Everest, the highest point on earth. The death of Captain Robert Falcon Scott – Scott of the Antarctic – has more romance than the life of Roald Amundsen, who beat him and his party to the South Pole in 1911. Scott and his companions reached the pole some weeks after their Norwegian rivals and died on the way home, overtaken by the elements and also by time. In the same way and for some of the same reasons Mallory and Irvine, two dots, remain suspended in the space between earth and for ever. Their fall, their loss, adds an immortal grandeur to the question of what it is to be human and alive. Theirs was the grandest adventure.

'A man's reach should escape his grasp,' wrote Robert Browning, 'or what's a heaven for?' The American poet Emily Dickinson put it best of all in a poem she composed in 1859:

> Success is counted sweetest
> By those who ne'er succeed.
> To comprehend a nectar
> Requires sorest need.
>
> Not one of all the purple Host
> Who took the Flag today
> Can tell the definition
> So clear of victory.
>
> As he defeated – dying –
> On whose forbidden ear
> The distant strains of triumph
> Burst agonized and clear!

91.

THE GERMAN PRESIDENT
MAKES ADOLF HITLER CHANCELLOR

Adolf Hitler was summoned to the office of the elderly and ailing German president Paul Ludwig Hans Anton von Beneckendorff und von Hindenburg at noon on 30 January 1933. So reluctant was the old man to hand the reins of government to one he regarded as an uppity pleb, a veritable chancer, it is said he barely looked the other in the eye for the duration of the formalities. As recently as 26 January he had privately told a group of his closest friends: 'Gentlemen, I hope you do not think I can call this Austrian corporal Chancellor.'

Be that as it may, by the time the two men parted company on that day of days the corporal was Chancellor and the most significant moment of the twentieth century had taken place.

They could hardly have been more different men. His country's most decorated marshal of the First World War, Hindenburg was regarded by the old-fashioned faithful as the embodiment of German decency and honour. Aged eighty-five and in failing health, he was also on the way out. Hitler was a civilian, a politician, but one on the make and on the rise, and in spite of any outward demonstrations of deference it was known that he regarded his uniformed superior as a reactionary 'old ruin'.

Since the rise of Hitler heralded such world-changing upheaval, and inflicted such shaming horror on the species *Homo sapiens*, it feels vital to understand how and why it happened, why *he* happened. There is no easy answer, and it may be enough to accept that he simply gave voice to all the bitter regret and resentment that had curdled in the gut of Germany and many Germans since the war to end all wars. By the Treaty of Versailles she had been made to accept sole blame for the outbreak of hostilities in 1914. The democratic republic that had been set in place, named Weimar after the town where its assembly first met, was an affront to the national pride of many mourning an imperial past. Those two conditions were enervating enough, but any hopes of long-term success for a self-consciously progressive young democratic republic were most likely to be dashed by economic reality. Europe had been shattered by four years of cannibalistic, attritional fighting and economic depression was inevitable. The victorious Allies had indulged themselves with the illusion that Germany had been hobbled, gelded, and so would not rise or trouble her neighbours ever again. Pretending she was no longer there, that they could not see her, was as meaningless as a child covering his eyes rather than acknowledge the presence in the room of that which scares him. By dint of her history, her innate potential as an industrial powerhouse – even just her place on the map – Germany was always going to matter in Europe, and hugely so; maybe not today, maybe not tomorrow, but soon, and for the rest of our lives . . .

When in 1882 the German philosopher Friedrich Nietzsche declared the death of God at the hands of humankind in *The Gay Science*, far from celebrating the fact he mourned it, and predicted it would lead to no end of suffering in the century to come. In the absence of God, men would believe not in nothing but in anything. Sure enough, into the void were pulled new ideologies as people, denied sight of the old compass, sought other bearings, false coordinates. Just as it did everywhere else, revolutionary Marxist communism was soon abroad in Germany, upsetting the natives. Fascism was there too, and good old-fashioned nationalism, raised up from a shallow grave.

Hitler was pulled inexorably into the mix, a willing thorn in the side of all who wanted a peace founded upon a quiescent Germany. Austrian by birth, he had indeed been the chancer Hindenburg recognized. Having failed to get into Vienna Academy to further his dreams of life as an artist, between 1904 and 1913 he lived on his wits in the city, selling sketches as postcards and doing odd jobs including beating carpets. When the First World War broke out he volunteered for service in a Bavarian regiment, rising to the rank of corporal and being recommended for the Iron Cross. After the war he continued to serve the army by spying on fringe political parties. In 1920 he joined one of them, renaming it the National Socialist German Workers' Party.

A walking, talking malcontent, his undoubted gift for oratory enabled him to spin his various hatreds and resentments into speeches that burrowed, like ear worms, into the thoughts of those who listened to them. By 1923 he was confident enough to attempt the overthrow of the Bavarian government but the effort was crushed by the authorities and sixteen of his 'storm troopers' were killed by machine-gun fire. Hitler was wounded, along with his accomplice Hermann Göring, and during his time in prison he dictated his autobiography *Mein Kampf* (My Struggle) to Rudolf Hess. Freed after less than a year he was unabashed and back on the campaign trail with his party's mix of radicalism and bitter criticism of all those who had shamed the nation by signing the Treaty of Versailles. In 1932 he challenged Hindenburg for the presidency. He lost, but in the elections of July that year his party emerged as the largest in the Reichstag, the German parliament. The following year the old man was persuaded to offer the post of Chancellor to the Austrian corporal by a previous incumbent, conservative Franz von Papen, who reasoned, as many in positions of authority had done before him, that it would be better to have the rabble-rouser inside the tent, pissing out.

In February 1933, Hitler made his first address as Chancellor, making plain his contempt for Marxists in the process:

The warning signs of this approaching disintegration are all about us. In a single gigantic offensive of willpower and violence, the communist method of madness is attempting to poison and disrupt the volk, which is shaken and uprooted to its innermost core . . .

Peasants, workers and bourgeoisie must all join together to provide the building blocks for a new Reich. The government will therefore regard it as its first and foremost duty to re-establish Volksgemeinschaft – the unity of spirit and will of our volk.

It will preserve and defend the foundations upon which the power of our nation rests. It will extend its strong, protecting hand over Christianity as the basis of our entire morality, and the family as the germ cell of the body of our volk and State.

It will reawaken in our volk, beyond the borders of rank and class, its sense of national and political unity, and its resultant duties.

It will establish reverence for our great past and pride in our old traditions as the basis for the education of our German youth.

It will declare a merciless war against spiritual, political and cultural nihilism. Germany must not and will not drown in anarchistic communism . . .

Like a lightning rod he had channelled all those grievances he could exploit. Germany's predicament, her loss of pride, her economic misery were variously and collectively the fault of the signatories of Versailles . . . capitalists the world over . . . communists. During the Weimar years Jewish people had risen to more influential positions than had been the case before, and so Hitler blamed them as well.

He controlled and then exploited the mass media. He declared the February 1933 burning of the Reichstag building a communist plot and, in the general election he insisted upon, empowered Göring to break up any meetings of opposition parties. The Nazi majority that resulted, slim though it was, made way for the 'Law to Remedy the Distress of People and Reich'. Also known as the Enabling Acts, they were the means by which Hitler secured the power to enact laws without the say-so either of the Reichstag or the president.

Hitler purged his own party of opposition in 1934 on the Night of the Long Knives, and when Hindenburg died in August that year, he was absolute ruler of Germany.

92.

PUG ISMAY, WINSTON CHURCHILL AND THE BATTLE OF BRITAIN

It is a day in August 1940 – that summer revered by those in thrall to the legend made of Spitfires and Hurricanes, the fighter pilots of the Royal Air Force and the immortal days remembered as the Battle of Britain.

Still stunned by the horrors of the First World War, Britain had been slow to accept the reality of the danger posed by Adolf Hitler and his Third Reich. Having trusted diplomacy (and its handmaiden, appeasement) for too long, the nation's defences were in no state to fight a war in 1939. For his own part, Hitler was in no mood for anything protracted either. Germany's resources were limited and stretched and all depended on lightning success, instant knockdowns of all foes. Events at Dunkirk had frightened the living daylights out of the British government, bringing the realization that only the English Channel stood between Britain and the enemy.

For a time the spotlight was turned on to the Royal Air Force, as a vital line of defence while other efforts were prepared. Hitler had plans for a seaborne invasion, codenamed Unternehmen Seelöwe (Operation Sea Lion) and scheduled for September 1940. Before that, by the end of August, he wanted the RAF swept from the sky, just to be sure.

Under Air Chief Marshal Hugh Dowding, Fighter Command had been split into groups, each responsible for fending off the Luftwaffe from their own patch of sky. Number 10 Group defended the south-west of England, Number 12 Group the Midlands and the north. London and the south-east were under the care of Number 11 Group, and the necessary moment happened inside their operations room at Uxbridge.

General Hastings Lionel 'Pug' Ismay is there with Prime Minister Winston Churchill. They are meeting with Air Vice Marshal Keith Park, to see for themselves how fraught and dangerous is the reality in the sky over their heads. The fighting is as intense as can be, Spitfires and Hurricanes duelling with Messerschmitt 109s and 110s in a desperate struggle for control as German bombers lumber close by like whales.

Churchill takes a moment to ask Park how many aircraft and pilots he has in reserve. Park tells him, quietly and calmly, that there is no reserve, that every man and plane is in the sky.

The fight goes on, wave after wave, minute after minute, spreading into hours. Churchill will not leave the room until he knows the outcome. Pug, his chief military assistant and staff officer, waits too. Finally word reaches Uxbridge that the German aircraft are pulling back, short of fuel and with no option but to return home to bases on the European mainland. The RAF has held the line, and Churchill and Pug take their leave.

Inside their staff car as they begin the journey back to Chequers, Pug begins to say something. Churchill holds up one hand.

'Don't speak to me yet,' he says quietly to his friend. 'I have never been so moved.'

Both men are silent for a while. The car's tyres hum and hiss on the tarmac and the miles pass.

At last Churchill looks Pug in the eye and speaks: 'Never in the field of human conflict has so much been owed by so many to so few.'

Pug remained silent but as soon as he got home he repeated his boss's words to his wife. That night he wrote them down in his diary, that he might never forget them. There was no need. Churchill would speak the same words a second time, in Parliament on 20 August, and a legend would be born.

There is no saying now what difference the Battle of Britain made to the outcome of the Second World War. Long and hard have been the debates on the subject, whether or not it was the effort of 'the few' that stopped Hitler launching the invasion of these islands. Historians have argued instead that Operation Sea Lion was called off not because of the Battle of Britain (a name and an endeavour some claim was Churchill's own invention, part of a self-aggrandizing scheme to make those efforts seem to have mattered more than they did) but on account of Hitler's realization of the need to leave Britain alone while he tackled the USSR. The truth of it all is hard to discern.

What did matter, though, was the effect that doughty defence, in the skies over the south-east of England, had on a generation's sense of itself. The stubborn perseverance and survival of the RAF in the face of the Luftwaffe (and Churchill's coining of the legend of 'the few') became embedded in the nation's concept of what it was to be, to have been, British. The identity that was internalized by the fighting generation of 1940 was passed then, like DNA, into their children and grandchildren. The technical, tactical truth of the significance of the events of that summer was neither here nor there. Generations of British men and women were invited to grow up believing all things were possible for those brave enough to try. It was potent stuff, and for good or ill it mattered.

93.

THE LIBERATION OF
AUSCHWITZ-BIRKENAU

On 27 January 1945, soldiers of the Red Army of the USSR arrived at the gates of Birkenau, the largest of the three camps making up the Auschwitz complex in southern Poland. The site had been selected by the Nazis because it was the spot on the map where several railway lines intersected, making it easy to transport captives there. Some of the world inside Birkenau would be filmed, in the days ahead, by a Russian cameraman named Alexander Vorontsov. It was around six in the evening when he stepped inside the camp for the first time, and into the first of many barracks. It was dark, and since he had no lights he did not film anything that day.

'A ghastly sight arose before our eyes,' he reported later. 'A vast number of barracks . . . People lay in bunks inside many of them. They were skeletons clad in skin, with vacant gazes . . .'

It has been estimated that of 1.3 million people sent to Auschwitz, 1.1 million were murdered. Around a million of those were Jews. By January 1945 there were perhaps 60,000 prisoners still behind the wire. On the 18th, around 56,000 of those able to move had been marched out of the camp, towards death camps in Germany. A quarter would die on the way, murdered or otherwise succumbing. The 4,000 or so left behind were too sick, too old or too young even to attempt the march. Starvation, diarrhoea, typhus – all manner of disease stalked those still clinging to life.

Among them was that Italian chemist Primo Levi. With a friend he ventured into the abandoned SS quarters. They found food, vodka, medicines and eiderdowns and took them back to share with other inmates.

Elsewhere, soldiers found warehouses full of personal belongings – hundreds of thousands of items of clothing, hundreds of thousands of pairs of shoes, tons and tons of human hair, teeth and gold fillings.

Here, in this moment called liberation, is the Second World War, or rather the reason the Second World War had to be fought. Beyond politics, beyond ideologies, beyond battles were men, women and children murdered – executed – for the crime of being alive in the world.

Cameraman Vorontsov said the memory of those moments stayed with him 'my whole life long. All of this was the most moving and most terrible thing that I saw and filmed during the war. Time has no sway over these recollections. It has not squeezed all the horrible things I saw and filmed out of my mind.'

Here is war – any war, every war. Every war ends in a pile of corpses too large to count.

In 1979, UNESCO added Auschwitz to their list of World Heritage Sites, and in 2005 the date of 27 January was made International Holocaust Remembrance Day.

94.

TOMI-SAN IN AN AWAKENING LAND

Early on the morning of 9 August 1945, in the city of Nagasaki, on Kyushu Island in Japan, sirens howled their warning once again. The inhabitants were less alarmed than they might have been. Nagasaki had been spared the worst of the carpet-bombing experienced by other locations in Japan, and when the all-clear was sounded, around 8.30 a.m., no one was surprised that no planes had come, no bombs had fallen. Just after 11 a.m., and without any warning at all, the sky was filled entirely by the brightest flash of light. Moments later came the thunder of a monstrous explosion, and soon after that a great blast like the sweeping hand of a wrathful god. For anyone left with eyes to see, let alone looking in the right direction, there might have been a glimpse of an American B-29 bomber named *Bock's Car* departing towards the south. Its payload had been a single atomic bomb nicknamed Fat Man by its makers. Three days before, on 6 August, another B-29, *Enola Gay*, had dropped another atomic bomb, called Little Boy, on to the city of Hiroshima, on Honshu Island.

The flash of brightest light and the blast of god was the ending, all in an instant, of around 40,000 people in Nagasaki. Within five years, radiation sickness being what it is, the death toll from that one bomb was more like 100,000. No one knows for sure, or ever will, how many were undone by that brightness and that thunder.

The flash was a moment, and no mistake; but the moment in question in this story of the world came just over two weeks later, on 26

August. Kuraba Tomisaburo – Tomi-San to his friends – was seventy-five years old, and a widow for two years, when he hanged himself with a length of clothesline in a room in his house at number 19 Minamiyamate, some 3 miles from the epicentre of Fat Man's devastation. When his body was found his feet were still on the floor and his body was tipped forward so that he was curled like an unborn baby. His eyes were open. Before taking care of himself he had strangled his beloved pet dogs.

Tomi-San was the only son of Scots-born merchant and adventurer Thomas Blake Glover, who had arrived in Japan in 1859. Aged just twenty-one he had been in China, working for British company Jardine Matheson, when new business opportunities lured him from Shanghai to Nagasaki. Initially in the green tea trade, buying and selling, he soon opened his own company and broadened his business horizons. He was ambitious, and in time would establish the business that is today Mitsubishi; he was also part of setting up the brewery that still makes the famous Japanese beer Kirin. Not content with the life of a merchant, Glover immersed himself in politics. He sided with rebellious factions plotting to overthrow the then military government of the Tokugawa Shogunate. Against laws both British and Japanese he supplied his new friends with modern weapons and when they achieved their aims and established the Meiji Restoration government, complete with emperor, he found himself on the winning side. He brought to Japan the technology of the steam train and was no small part of the transformation of his adoptive homeland from a medieval feudal kingdom of sword-bearing knights in armour into a twentieth-century superpower capable of taking on and beating Russia and China. He died in 1911, at the age of seventy-three.

Along the way he had fathered Tomi-San by his Japanese common-law wife Maki. She was left behind when he met and later married Awajiya Tsuru, by whom he had a daughter, Hana. Once settled with Tsuru he went back to Maki and persuaded her to give up Tomi-San, six years old by then. Money is said to have changed hands, and there are those who say Italian composer Giacomo Puccini knew their story when he wrote *Madama Butterfly*.

Tomi-San fell always between two worlds. He spent time with his father's family in Aberdeenshire, Scotland, but felt an outsider there as he did in Japan. He was scholarly, and hard-working like his father. In 1899 he married Nakano Waka, like him a child of a British merchant and a Japanese woman. They had no children.

When war broke out they were often harassed by members of the Kempeitai, the Japanese military police: since both had western heritage they were automatically under suspicion. Waka died in 1943 and after nearly half a century with a soulmate Tomi-San was alone with their dogs. Then the bomb dropped and much of the city was laid to waste. Death and dying were everywhere. Soon the dazed survivors were talking about the imminent arrival of Allied soldiers and Tomi-San reasoned – no doubt rightly – that having spent the war under the suspicion of the Japanese, he now faced spending the rest of his life under the suspicion of the Americans and the British.

Tomi-San's life was a moment of sorts, in the grander scheme of things. He fell between two worlds in more ways than one. He had been born, in 1870, into the past. For more than 200 years, from 1633 until 1853, Japan had been closed, under the *sakoku* ('closed country') policies of the Tokugawa Shogunate. Only in 1853 had US Navy commodore Matthew Perry led the Black Ships expedition that forced the country to open up to formal trade with the west. Tomi-San had been born while Japan was just waking up from that slumber of isolation. He lived to see her rise to greatness and then fall into utter humiliation. Spanning such an abyss can be too much, and it was too much for Tomi-San.

95.

MARTIN LUTHER KING AND THE DREAM

When American Baptist minister and civil rights activist Martin Luther King Jr stepped up to the podium late in the day on 28 August 1963, he was sixteenth on the official programme of events. It had been 87°F at noon and most speakers before him had overrun their allotted time. Between a quarter and half a million people had filled the Washington Mall but given the heat and the long day a drift had begun towards the shade of trees, or to the reflecting pool and its promise of respite for sore feet.

There had been many opportunities for people-watching and star-spotting. Scattered through the crowd (four-fifths black and one-fifth white) were all manner of celebrities: movie stars like Sammy Davis Jr, Sidney Poitier, Charlton Heston and Marlon Brando; singers like Josephine Baker, Harry Belafonte, Marian Anderson, Odetta Holmes, Mahalia Jackson, Lena Horne, Joan Baez and Bob Dylan; famous activists including Rosa Parks and the Little Rock Nine. The regular people, the rank and file, had travelled through the night to be there and the buses and trains had been arriving in the nation's capital since daybreak. Hour after hour they had stood within sight of the memorial to Abraham Lincoln, the president who had made the Emancipation Proclamation a century before, promising freedom to the enslaved. All in all, it would take some effort and charisma to inject fresh energy into proceedings already on the wane. What was needed was another Gettysburg Address.

Into that languid, somnolent atmosphere stepped King, in white shirt, black suit and black tie. He had been up much of the night tweaking his speech and now he began to read it from a page almost tattered and all but illegible on account of late additions and crossings-out. What he said in those first moments and minutes was good but it was safe and, for the most part, some way short of unforgettable. There were no big screens in 1963 and for the majority of the crowd he was just a dot. For those gathered to hear someone crystallize the hopes of millions in the face of decades, centuries of inhumanity, he was minuscule – as minuscule as Mallory and Irvine had been to their witness when they stepped towards legend and immortality on the face of the highest mountain on earth. How might he stand out and make the difference now?

From nearby came the voice of Mahalia Jackson, a gospel singer whose voice had moved King's heart just before. 'Tell them about the dream, Martin,' she said. For some moments he kept to his prepared text. And then Jackson said it again, shouted out the words: 'Tell them about the dream!'

So far he had told them about the unfulfilled promises of the Founding Fathers . . . about the fierce urgency of now . . . All at once, and in the afterburn of Jackson's exhortation, he set his prepared speech aside and grasped the podium with both hands while he spoke from his heart.

'So even though we face the difficulties of today and tomorrow,' he said, 'I still have a dream.'

Those were words he had used before, in other speeches, and his aides had advised against using them again. It was a 'trite' sentiment, they said. If that were so, it was too late now.

I have a dream that my four little children will one day live in a nation where they will not be judged by the colour of their skin but by the content of their character. I have a dream today. I have a dream that one day, down in Alabama, with its vicious racists . . . one day right down in Alabama, little black boys and black girls will be able to join hands with little white boys and white girls, as sisters and brothers. I have a dream today . . .

Ever since the moment when King stopped speaking that day, historians and others have debated how much his words mattered. Right away there were activists who lamented the thought of 'dreamers' at the front of their movement when what was needed were leaders. More recently it has been accepted as one of the greatest speeches of the twentieth century. The March on Washington had been organized in support of civil rights legislation proposed by President John F. Kennedy's government. The Civil Rights Act outlawing discrimination based on race, colour, religion, sex or national origin was passed by Congress the following year. It was intended to mark the advent of a new American Republic.

At the time of writing, the United States of America – and much of the rest of the world besides – is as mired in race hatred and division as it has been at any time since the life and death of Martin Luther King. Racial harmony – when men and women are judged by character and not colour – remains, at most, a dream.

96.

A MAN ON THE MOON FOR MR GORSKY

It is well known that Commander Neil Armstrong set foot on the moon on 21 July 1969. The time was 2.56 in the morning (Coordinated Universal Time), and by then the Apollo lunar module *Eagle* had been on the surface of Earth's satellite for six hours and thirty-nine minutes. Less familiar is the knowledge that, before the moon walk and while still inside *Eagle*, lunar module pilot Buzz Aldrin took communion, with bread and wine prepared for him by the pastor of Webster Presbyterian Church in Texas, where he was an elder.

> For the bread of God is he which cometh down from heaven, and giveth life unto the world.
>
> (John 6:33)

His name was Edwin Eugene Aldrin Jr, but in childhood his younger sister had struggled with the word 'brother'. 'That's my buzzer,' she would say, and a short form of the word was soon his nickname.

High above, still in orbit, was Apollo 11's command module, *Columbia*, piloted by the third astronaut, Michael Collins.

In the shadowy black-and-white footage of the landing, recorded by a camera fixed to the outside of *Eagle*, Armstrong lingers on the bottom rung of the ladder. He talks about how easy or not he thinks it will be to climb back up, and about how the landing module's big round feet have sunk just an inch or two into the fine 'powder' of the surface. It is prosaic stuff, strangely calm and surreal in the context of a man about to step down on to a new world.

Perhaps the most famous element of the story of that first moon landing is the line he uttered during the first moments after he finally set foot on the surface. His words were slightly muffled and the American commentators narrating the live broadcast took a few moments to work out what, precisely, he had just said. 'That's one small step for [a] man,' they decided, 'one giant leap for mankind.'

It was just over sixty-five years since the Wright brothers' first flight at Kitty Hawk, and a moment like no other had been, nor could ever be. For the first time, a human being had left the home planet behind and stood and walked elsewhere in the universe. It may be the greatest single moment in the story of the world.

Aldrin joined Armstrong on the surface soon after. Among other tasks – collecting samples and such – they planted a US flag together and spoke to President Richard Nixon. He told them, 'For one priceless moment in the whole history of man, all the people on this earth are truly one.'

Since 1955, the USA had been locked into the 'space race' with the USSR. The Soviets had got off the ground first and stayed well ahead until the early part of the following decade. Their satellite *Sputnik 1*, first of its kind, was launched on 4 October 1957. Yuri Gagarin became the first human in space on 12 April 1961, and was followed by the first woman, Valentina Tereshkova, on 16 June 1963.

President John F. Kennedy had declared, in 1961, that the USA would put a man on the moon and bring him safely home 'before this decade is out'. Between 1960 and 1973 he and they would spend $28 billion on the dream ($283 billion in today's money). By 1969 and the success of Apollo 11, the Americans had won the space race, well and truly.

Least well known of all, but an anecdote so perfect it almost qualifies as a moment of the story of the world all on its own, is the rumour regarding what Armstrong really said while he briefly occupied the inches between the bottom rung of the ladder and the surface of the moon. 'Good luck, Mr Gorsky,' he (is supposed to have) said. According to aficionados on the Internet, Armstrong had told friends about a child-hood memory of overhearing the married couple who lived next door to him, the Gorskys, having an argument. They were in their garden, and in response to something the husband said, the wife told him he would receive oral sex from her 'the day that boy next door walks on the moon'.

97.

INFORMATION TRAVELS
BETWEEN TWO COMPUTERS

Since the time of Enheduanna there had been writing and so a means to share information without speaking face to face. Before her time, and after, there were those who desired to control information and have it make them powerful. Hammurabi had been one, with his laws graven in stone. Chandragupta was another, with his edicts on rocks (but he seems to have had hopes that the ideas he was sharing might bring people together). After thousands of years, Johannes Gutenberg introduced printing to the masses and books became a commonplace. After millennia of information being easily controlled by the powerful – by kings, by the Church – the printing press set it free to circulate as never before.

At 10.30 p.m. on 29 October 1969 (twenty-eight days after Concorde went supersonic for the first time) the message 'lo' arrived on a computer screen at Stanford Research Institute in Menlo Park, California. It was shorthand for 'login' and had been sent from the University of California Los Angeles (UCLA) 350 miles away, by a programmer called Charley Kline. Brief and to the point, it was the first message sent and received via what became the Internet.

Some moments were the effect of two minds connecting. Gutenberg might not have reached his goal without his sometime partner and financier Johann Fust; Johannes Kepler had needed the obsession of Tycho Brahe; Marx had needed Engels, for ideas certainly, but most importantly for money; Orville Wright may never have got into the air without the steadying hand of his brother, Wilbur. The Internet would not have happened without the coming together and collaborating of the unlikeliest of bedfellows – being the US military and a bunch of Californian academics in the habit of dropping acid and dreaming of a tech utopia. The former were rattled by the Cold War and, in the event of an attack by the enemy using nuclear weapons, wanted a means to have remote command and control of their computers. The latter were tired of having to book slots on the few-and-far-between computers that existed in the world, and then travelling to wherever the machines were in order to use them, and so desired remote access of their own. Many of those first computer geeks were also devotees of the 1960s counter culture and dreamed of a time when worldwide sharing of ideas across an egalitarian, open-access network would enrich all of humankind. The irony of it all was that in order to make their dream a reality the academics needed the kind of investment that was only available (then, at least) from the government, specifically in their case the US Defense Department's Advanced Research Projects Agency Network. Charley Kline's message had therefore been sent via the ARPANET. Only later would the term 'Internet' be coined, as a shortened form of 'Internetworking', referring to the practice of interconnecting multiple computer networks.

The list of those whose intention it was to create something that would enrich rather than negate human potential is a long one. English computer scientist Tim Berners-Lee was working at the Conseil Européen pour la Recherche Nucléaire (CERN) in the late 1980s when he first developed the use of hypertext (an extant idea) as a means by which documents stored on computers might be linked to one another. The result was the blue-highlighted words on screen that can be 'clicked' upon to open related documents. By his efforts – and he gifted his technology to the world for free – Berners-Lee gave birth to the World Wide Web that makes some sliver of the near-limitless store of data that is the Internet more easily accessible to users.

As it turned out it was neither the military nor the hippies who inherited the new world of the Internet. Instead it was to be a relative handful of business owners imbued with the libertarian, free-market economic theory of the likes of Milton Friedman and the ethical egoism of novelist and philosopher Ayn Rand.

In *Move Fast and Break Things*, American author Jonathan Taplin described the rise to dominance of tech billionaires like Peter Thiel of PayPal, Bill Gates of Microsoft, Sergey Brin and Larry Page of Google and Mark Zuckerberg of Facebook. He contrasts their ruthless pursuit of market dominance and profit with the ethos of Internet pioneers like Doug Engelbart. At what went down in history as the Mother of All Demos at the Association for Computing Machinery/Institute of Electrical and Electronics Engineers (ACM/IEEE) in San Francisco in December 1968, Engelbart demonstrated the potential of what he had in mind. Into an unsuspecting world in which a computer was a machine for arithmetical and mathematical calculations, he introduced a prototype device – an array of technology available then and assembled by him and his team into a functioning whole – for navigating the Internet, before the Internet existed. Taplin described how Engelbart had it in mind to 'provide a tool for individual empowerment: the user could access the world's knowledge, create inspiring content, and share it with anyone'.

Berners-Lee was an inheritor of the Engelbart ethos, so that at least as recently as the 1990s there survived an intention that the Internet should remain egalitarian, providing equal access to any and all comers. But the potential to wield power is seductive, and attractive. Social media platforms like Zuckerberg's Facebook and more recently Twitter, founded by Jack Dorsey, have tapped into an apparently insatiable human appetite to be seen and to be liked even – if not especially – by people we do not know. The platforms are free, but in order to take advantage of the 'freedom' users must sacrifice more private information about themselves than has ever previously been collected by any government in history. Two old adages are relevant: 'Vanity trumps privacy' and 'If you're not paying for it, you're the product'.

Content at the moment for sites like YouTube and Facebook is harvested from the great stores of music, literature, films and the rest of the arts assembled by creative types during the past several thousand years. As the wise man said, 'We are living inside the corpse of a whale. There's plenty to eat right now – but only because there was a whale.' If and when those assembled riches are consumed, it will not matter overmuch. Users are already cheerfully providing the next generations of content themselves, while the platform owners profit by selling yet more personal data to advertisers.

Against all expectations of those in their respective rooms at UCLA and the SRI that October evening in 1969, the Internet is now the personal fiefdom of a number of mega-rich tech wizards, unelected and uncontrolled by none but their shareholders, who might be counted on the fingers of both hands.

98.

ALEKSANDR SOLZHENITSYN REVEALS
THE GULAG ARCHIPELAGO

Over and over, the story of the world has turned on the words of one person. In the case of at least one book, the change of direction was the effect of one author and also of tens of millions of unquiet ghosts given a voice and a monument by his testimony. In his author's note at the front of a 1986 abridgement of his masterwork, Solzhenitsyn noted that 'material for this book was given me in reports, memoirs and letters by 227 witnesses, whose names were to have been listed here'. Already then, before so much as a word of the text itself has been read, the number of world-changing individuals has grown from one to many. In the next paragraph, he wrote: 'What I express here to them is not personal gratitude, because this is our common, collective monument to all those who were tortured and murdered.'

By the time the reader embarks upon the text proper, he or she is minded to think not of the one, nor of the 227, but of the 60 million known to have died in the Gulag Archipelago. Of course that is only the number that actually died – who were tortured and murdered or otherwise succumbed to the conditions – and the reader's imagination must be haunted too by the thought of the uncounted millions more who passed through that same system and survived.

The moment that matters is that of the original publication, when those words, names and ghosts were first brought into the light. The first of the three volumes of *The Gulag Archipelago* was published in Paris on 28 December 1973. *Gulag* is, or was, the Russian-language acronym for the network of prison and labour camps that existed like islands.

And this Archipelago crisscrossed and patterned that other country within which it was located, like a gigantic patchwork, cutting into its cities, hovering over its streets. Yet there were many who did not even guess at its presence and many, many others who had heard something vague. And only those who had been there knew the whole truth.

Aleksandr Solzhenitsyn was born in Kislovodsk in 1918. He graduated from university in Rostov in 1941 with a degree in maths and physics. He was a good soldier of the Red Army, with a distinguished service record in the Second World War, but after making disparaging comments about Stalin's prosecution of the war (in letters to a friend) he was sent into the Gulag system from 1945 to 1953, followed by what might have been a sentence of lifelong internal exile in Kazakhstan. With Stalin dead and gone, however, and under the rule of Nikita Khrushchev, Solzhenitsyn was rehabilitated and began writing fiction, winning the Nobel Prize in Literature in 1970. It was his great work of non-fiction, however, more than 1,800 unsparing pages recounting the lives and deaths of those made victims of Stalin's reign of terror, that should be read by everyone and for ever.

It is, in every way, devastating – a forensic account of horror after horror, cruelty after cruelty, inflicted by a communist regime that had realized (as such regimes always do) that their desired ends might only be reached by force and fear. In the aftermath of publication, in 1974, Solzhenitsyn was arrested in Russia and deported to West Germany, stripped of his Russian citizenship. He later settled in the US but in 1994, his citizenship restored, he returned to his homeland. He died of heart disease in 2008.

Republished many times, *The Gulag Archipelago* has sold millions of copies. Given the sheer heft of the three-volume edition, however, many fewer people are likely to have read it than bought it. In spite of the subject matter it is by no means only depressing. It is about the journey of a human spirit – perhaps *the* human spirit – out of darkness and into the light. In the third volume, in the chapter titled 'The Ascent', Solzhenitsyn explains how he came to understand his own reality, the truth of himself. With all the time that his imprisonment afforded, he had looked back over his life and seen that while his sentence had not been justified at all by his criticisms of Stalin, he had hardly led a blameless life. He considered his own actions as a soldier and saw that he had been guilty in those years of unjust acts of his own:

> Slavery nurtures in you the shoots of contradictory feelings. Once upon a time you were sharply intolerant . . . Formerly you never forgave anyone. You judged people without mercy. And you praised people with equal lack of moderation . . . You have come to realize your own weakness – and you can therefore understand the weakness of others.

In March 1946, in a speech he gave at Westminster College in Fulton, Missouri, in the presence of US president Harry S. Truman, former British prime minister Winston Churchill made his famous remarks condemning Soviet Union policies in Europe: 'From Stettin in the Baltic to Trieste in the Adriatic, an iron curtain has descended across the continent.' That iron curtain, set in place by the Russians at the end of the Second World War and forcibly separating Europe into the free west and the Soviet-controlled east, remained in place until 1991. Its removal was the work of many people, known and unknown, and including figures such as Mikhail Gorbachev, Ronald Reagan, Margaret Thatcher and Pope John Paul II. By then, however, the world had long since been invited to look behind that curtain and see the reality of the Soviet system. That revelation was the work of one man more than anyone else, one writer speaking for himself, for hundreds and for millions – Aleksandr Solzhenitsyn. He said himself it was the Gulag that taught him what he needed to know, what everyone needs to know:

> It was granted to me to carry away from my prison years on my bent back, which nearly broke beneath its load, this essential experience: how a human being becomes evil and how good. In the intoxication of youthful successes I had felt myself to be infallible, and I was therefore cruel . . . It was only when I lay there on rotting prison straw that I sensed within myself the first stirrings of good. Gradually it was disclosed to me that the line separating good and evil passes not through states, nor between classes, nor between political parties either – but right through every human heart – and through all human hearts.

99

A LITTLE GIRL IN RED

Little girl in red – it has been a recurrent image: *Don't Look Now* . . . *Schindler's List* . . .

In the nineteenth century, at a place called Birka, on the island of Björkö on Lake Mälaren in Sweden, archaeologists found the grave of a little Viking girl. She had been laid down with some riches, including a gilded brooch they imagined had been fixed to her dress. Since red was the most expensive colour to achieve in the tenth century, it has been suggested the dress, long turned to dust, was red. Another little girl in red – that one remembered as Birka Girl, and as haunting as the rest. It is a vision that lingers, like the ghost of a bright light that drifts upon the darkness behind closed eyelids, before fading to yellow and blue and is gone.

On 21 December 1988, Pan Am Flight 103 from London's Heathrow to New York's John F. Kennedy airport was blown into pieces at an altitude of 31,000 feet above the Scottish town of Lockerbie. A bomb in a suitcase, stowed in a forward luggage hold of the Boeing 747-121, had been detonated by a timing device. All 259 passengers and crew were killed, along with eleven people on the ground in Lockerbie. The wreckage was scattered over 850 square miles.

The moment that must be remembered, an encounter between a little girl in red and a passenger called Chas, happened earlier in the day and aboard another flight. Their paths crossed inside a Boeing 727 flying from

Frankfurt to Heathrow. The little girl was Suruchi Rattan, aged three, one of a family of five making a trip from New Delhi to Detroit. She was wearing bright red clothes for the journey. She and they should have been on an earlier flight that would have made a different connection in London, but one of the children had been taken ill while the plane was taxiing towards the runway, and the pilot made the unusual step of returning to the gate to let them all off. The child, a little boy, recovered soon enough and seats were found for them aboard a flight timed to connect with Pan Am 103 instead. The 727 landed and just over half of the passengers – Suruchi and the rest of the Dixit-Rattan family among them – joined Pan Am 103, a 747 called *Clipper Maid of the Seas*, for the onward leg of their journey. Suruchi, in her red *kurta* and *salwar*, smiling and playful, had been an eye-catching addition to the flight to London. She had toddled up and down the aisle, played peek-a-boo through the headrests on her seat row. In that way of little children she had captivated several of those around her. The passenger called Chas parted company with the Dixit-Rattan family there and then, his own plans taking him elsewhere.

In the aftermath of the tragedy at Lockerbie, one of countless bouquets of flowers delivered to the town hall from countless broken-hearted people was accompanied by a card that had on it: 'To the little girl in the red dress who made my flight from Frankfurt such fun. You didn't deserve this. God bless, Chas.'

The downing of Pan Am 103, the murder of 270 people, triggered the largest and most complicated criminal investigation in Scottish legal history. In 1992, after years of western sanctions against his country, Libyan leader Muammar Gaddafi handed over two suspects – Abdelbaset al-Megrahi and Lamin Khalifah Fhimah, two Libyan intelligence officers. After the trial that followed, Fhima was acquitted of all charges but al-Megrahi was found guilty and sentenced to life imprisonment. He was released in 2009, on humanitarian grounds, after being diagnosed with prostate cancer. He died back home in Tripoli in 2012, pleading his innocence to the end.

All of thirteen years before two planes were flown into New York's Twin Towers, the terrorist atrocity of Pan Am 103 changed the world, opened another door leading from the world of before to the world of after. Teeth have been on edge ever since.

Since our species were hunters for 200,000 years, and we are descended from those hunters, our attentions are caught by eye-catching things – small and bright. The little girl in red – small and bright and irreplaceably precious – is one of those.

100.

HARRY PATCH AND THE WAR TO END ALL WARS

Some moments are beginnings; others mark the end.

On Saturday, 25 July 2009, Englishman Harry Patch died peacefully in his residential home in Wells, Somerset, aged 111. He had been Britain's last surviving fighting veteran of the First World War. Max Arthur, author of *Last Post*, a 2005 book that documented the recollections of twenty-one old soldiers, said Harry described the battlefield of Passchendaele as the single most depressing place on earth – 'hell with a lid on'.

Seven days before Harry Patch died, Henry Allingham died at the age of 113. He had been Britain's oldest man and a fellow veteran of the battlefields of the Western Front. They were, Harry and Henry, the last leaves to fall from an old British tree.

Harry's dying was a moment like no other in the story of the world. The First World War . . . the Great War . . . the War to End All Wars . . . the conflict has been described as a set of iron railings separating two worlds. The world that was – the world of before, an innocent Edwardian horse-drawn world where women still wore crinoline dresses – was still visible from the bloodied, mutilated world of after, but it could never be visited again, never touched again. Everything on this side of the railings, our side, is different, and for ever.

Harry was born in 1898, in Combe Down, near Bath in Somerset. His

eighteenth birthday came just in time for the advent of conscription. He
was a machine gunner at Ypres – Passchendaele – from June until a day
in September when a shell detonated close by him and three friends. He
alone survived, but with shrapnel wounds to his stomach.

When it was all over he took up the trade he had trained for before the
war – plumbing – until he retired in 1963. He outlived three wives and
both of his sons.

'We each owe a death, there are no exceptions,' wrote Stephen King in
The Green Mile, '. . . but sometimes, oh God, the Green Mile is so long.'

Every year on the anniversary of his wounding, and of the deaths of
his comrades, Harry would lock himself away to remember and to grieve.
Not until he turned a hundred did he breathe a word of any of it to
another living soul. When he did start talking it was to say that war was
not worth it. He said he and the team of machine gunners did their
best to wound and not to kill, aiming for legs and feet. He called the
whole of it organized murder and not worth a single life, 'let alone all the
millions'.

The Unknown Warrior was entombed in Westminster Abbey on 11
November 1920. 'They buried him among kings because he had done
good toward God and toward his house.' Maybe so. Harry Patch's funeral
was in Wells Cathedral, eighty-nine years later. Between them those two
soldiers – one known and one not – hold the war suspended, defying
Newton's gravity, alpha and omega. The Great War, four years made of
moments unthinkable, drew a line between two soldiers and across the
story of the world. What came after, everything that came after, was different from what had gone before.

Chief of the General Staff, General Sir Richard Dannatt, spoke for
many when he said of Harry Patch: 'He was the last of a generation that
in youth was steadfast in its duty in the face of cruel sacrifice and we give
thanks for his life – as well as those of his comrades – for upholding the
same values and freedoms that we continue to cherish and fight for
today.'

This is my story of the world, and I say we are still in the aftermath of that great war, and the greater war that followed twenty-one years later, an awful and corrupted coming of age. Some historians have called the years' from the start of the one to the end of the other a second Thirty Years War. Maybe yes and maybe no, but we are bleeding still from septic wounds. Heat simmers out of sight, underground, as it were, like a fire in a coal seam ready to break out at any time and in any place. We are the children and grandchildren of damaged generations. To think we are beyond those years, those consequences, is a mistake most egregious. Those years from 1914 to 1945 were the most transformational of all the years since Enheduanna and her hymns. In all the story of human-kind, they were the worst by far, because we inflicted that worst upon ourselves.

Ur and Babylon; Egypt, Persia, Greece and Rome; rise and fall; mil-lions of souls on the move from east to west; kingdoms and empires, holy and not; war and war and war again; New Worlds; there and back again. And then came the twentieth century after the birth of Jesus Christ and all hell broke loose once and for all. Never before such butchery. Never before such violation of all that it had been to be human and alive. Industrialized slaughter of innocent and guilty alike. The Somme and Passchendaele; Stalingrad and Berlin; Auschwitz and the Holocaust and the Gulag Archipelago – on and on and on, an obscene litany of shaming and shameful names.

For as long as Harry Patch and his ilk were alive there was a living link to all that was done wrong. For as long as he and they were among us, those who had been and seen, we had witnesses and therefore their testament from their own mouths. 'Testament' has its roots in the Proto-Indo-European language – specifically *tri-st-i*, which means 'third person standing by'. It evokes the notion of a witness, someone seeing and remembering. Now that Harry is gone, he and my own grandfathers and the rest, the connection to the reality of it all is broken. The eleventh of November is Remembrance Day, but we will not remember properly now because none of us were there. Now and for ever the Somme and Passchendaele are myths like Thermopylae, or Carthage. We have crossed the Rubicon. The witnesses to the second war are endangered now and will soon be gone too. Harry and others like him around the world, grey sentinels all, were the links to the worst of times. Without them we are blind and dumb to the reality of those most awful moments of the past. Now we must just talk about things none of us have seen. We must be careful.

Harry Patch was outlived by others who gave service, including Canadian John Babcock, who died in 2010, and American Frank Buckles and English-Australian Claude Choules, who both died in 2011. Englishwoman Florence Green, of the Women's Royal Air Force, was the last known veteran of the war from any country when she died on 4 February 2012, aged 110. But Harry Patch was the last of the fighting soldiers, those who pulled triggers in the charnel houses and heard the bullets flying. He was at Passchendaele, which was hell on earth and made by men. His death cut the cord connecting us to all of that.

'He was the last,' said General Dannatt. Harry Patch was the last, and so we must remember.

TODOT . . .

. . . is my last day writing this book. This is another moment in the story of *my* world, if not *the* world. Today is all there is. The past is gone, and the future does not exist. This moment, right now – this is it. I read somewhere that *Time* is a magazine, which is true. At least you can hold a magazine, even keep a magazine. You can't do that with time with a small 't'.

In this moment I am thinking about my middle child – my eldest boy. He is fifteen years old now but in the moment I am thinking about he is a little more than one, a lot less than two. In that moment we are in a café near our home and he has been let down – and disastrously – by his nappy. We hurry home. I stand him in the bath and give him a shower, clean him up with warm water and soap. I carry him into a bedroom, and while I wrap him in a towel and stoop to dry him, skin pale as milk, he has his arms around my neck.

All out of the blue he says, into my ear, 'I love you.'

I am taken aback. I free his arms from around me and lean back so I can look him in his eyes.

'Why?' I ask. It is a stupid question, but it's out and away before I can think of a better one.

'Because you're lovely,' he says.

I replay that scene over and over, year after year. I think about everyone who has lived and died before me and us, about how everyone's life has mattered to those who loved them and washed them in warm water and wrapped them in warm clothes. I think about thousands and thousands of years of love.

I think about my eldest child, my daughter, who is eighteen now. She was born in London, in Guy's and St Thomas' Hospital. Like the other two would be in time, she was an emergency C-section and she was handed to me to hold while the surgeon and nurses took care of my wife. I stood with her in my awkward arms, inside a little space made of four blue nylon curtains. As I swayed, leaning my weight on one leg and then the other, the light came and went across us. I looked into her eyes, so fixed upon my own, and knew that everything was different and for ever.

I think about my youngest boy. He is thirteen. A few days ago he was in hospital for a routine procedure. I was with him while the anaesthetic took effect. I looked into his eyes while the gas did its thing. I watched him being switched off. I was with him again in the recovery room, while he came back on, dreamy and lost. I knew then, as I have always known, that he and his brother and sister and their mother are my whole world.

At the time of writing we are in a second year of lockdown, on account of a pandemic that is not at all like the one in 1918. Their mother and I spend many moments – hours and days – wondering what our children's futures will be.

I look back over the words I have written for this book, from page one to this one, and know that while all of its stories are interesting to me, these last moments recounted here, these moments with my children, are the story of my world.

ACKNOWLEDGEMENTS

The Story of the World in 100 Moments – what on earth was I thinking? I was about two and a half 'moments' into the writing of it when the scale of the task began to dawn on me. Soon enough I was struggling to keep my footing, so to speak, in danger of being swept away by the torrent of necessary names, places and dates. By the time I emerged at the end of it all, my mind was spinning.

Never in my life, therefore, have I been more grateful for being in the careful, attentive hands of the exemplary team at Transworld. Throughout the often dizzying complexities I was kept on solid ground by the editorial gifts of Susanna Wadeson, Daniel Balado, Helena Gonda, Katrina Whone and Sharika Teelwah. I really cannot sufficiently stress the importance and value of their contributions. In ways impossible to list or count, they ensured a cohesion and sense of order that might otherwise have been beyond me. To each and all, my grateful thanks.

Likewise the care shown by proofeaders Tom Atkins and Lorraine McCann, and indexer Gary Kirby, whose attention to detail always leaves me in humbled awe. Picture research, that crucial task of finding just the right image from among so many, was undertaken, and wonderfully, by Jo Carlill. The elegant page design is by Dan Prescott and production was skilfully overseen by Catriona Hillerton. Again, to each a thousand thanks. Further gratitude to Ella Horne, in charge of marketing, and to Tom Hill for looking after the publicity, upon which so much depends.

As one who has, contrary to all advice, always judged books by their covers, I have to say how delighted I am with the jacket design and illustration by Andrew Davidson and Beci Kelly. Yet more thanks, of course, to the excellent sales team of Tom Chicken, Laura Garrod and Emily Harvey, and also to the marvellous field sales teams.

Once again I am also grateful beyond words to my literary agent, Eugenie Furniss at 42 Management & Production, who has been holding my hand on the matter of books for more years than I can remember.

Lastly I owe more than I can ever say to my wife Trudi, for her endless support and encouragement, with a particular emphasis on those days, not infrequent, when I am seen to be feeling especially sorry for myself. I would be lost without you, Trudi, and you know it. Thanks finally to our children, Evie, Archie and Teddy, for being, as I have noted before and elsewhere, the point of it all.

Any and all mistakes in the text are mine and mine alone.

ILLUSTRATION CREDITS

First plate section

Calcite disc of Enheduanna, daughter of Sargon of Kish. Courtesy of the Penn Museum, object no. B16665

Purusha, the thousand-headed Cosmic Man, stands on Vishnu © akg-images/Science Source

Laozi (Lao Tzu) riding a blue ox. Anonymous scroll painting on silk, Song Dynasty (960–1279) © Bridgeman Images/Pictures from History

The Great Wall of China at Jinshanling © Darrell Gulin/Getty Images

The Great Enclosure at Great Zimbabwe © DeAgostini/Getty Images

Virgil urges Dante to continue the way towards Beatrice and Paradise © Mary Evans/Iberfoto

The Turks seize Constantinople in 1453 (Siège de Constantinople par les Turcs en 1453). Tirée du manuscrit 'Le Voyage d'Outre-Mer', folio 207v. Bibliothèque Nationale de France, Paris. Miniature © 2021. Photo Josse/Scala Florence

Detail from *Cerro Rico and the Imperial Municipality of Potosí* (1758) by Gaspar Miguel de Berrío. Museo de Charcas, Sucre, Bolivia © akg-images/Gilles Mermet.

Second plate section

Painting of Johannes Kepler, c. 1620 © akg-images

Robert Clive and Mir Jafar after the Battle of Plassey © Prisma Archivo/Alamy

Shaka Zulu © Topfoto

Wilbur Wright piloting a test glider at Kitty Hawk, October 1902 © Getty Images; the Wright Brothers' first powered flight, 17 December 1903 © Getty Images

British Army recruitment poster from the First World War © Library of Congress, Prints & Photographs Division (reproduction no. LC-US2C4-10896)

Fat Man's radioactive plume seen from Koyagi-jima, 9.6 km from Nagasaki © Getty Images

Dr Martin Luther King Jr after delivering his 'I Have a Dream' speech in Washington DC, 28 August 1963 © Getty Images

Buzz Aldrin walks on the surface of the moon during the Apollo 11 mission © NASA.

INDEX

Aachen 157, 160, 162, 164, 234
Abbasid caliphate 161–2, 163, 177
Abd al-Rahman 153, 154, 155
Abolition Movement 261
Abolition of the Slave Trade Act (1807) 313
Abraham 48
academics, Californian 381
accounts 27–8
Achaeans 64
Achaemenid empire 80, 89
Acre 196
 Siege of 195
Act of Supremacy (1534) 244
Adrianople, Battle of 138
Advanced Research Projects Agency Network
 (US) 381
Aelfwald of Northumbria 156
Aeolians 65
aeolipile 291
Agni 56
Ahmose I 51
Akbar the Great 248, 265, 266–7
Akkadians 16, 19
Alaric 140–2, 143
Alcuin of York 157, 162–3, 234
Aldrin, Buzz 377, 378
Alexander III, Tsar 354
Alexander the Great 85, 102–3, 125
Alfred, King of Wessex 167, 168–70
Allectus 134
Aller 167
Allingham, Henry 391
Alp Arslan, Sultan 183
alphabet 61–2, 65
amaNdebele 179–80
Ambrose, Bishop of Milan 137, 138, 139
Amenhotep II 28
American Civil War 327–9
American War of Independence 299–300

Americas 106, 227
 European conquerors 229, 249–51, 252–5
Amundsen, Roald 360
Anabaptism 232–3
anacyclosis 130, 132
Ancient Greece 39, 42
 Dorians 65
 Mycenaeans 64
 origins of culture 66
 see also Classical Greece
Andromache 63
Anglo-Saxon Chronicle 190
Anne of Cleves 244
Antietam, Battle of 327
Antiochus IV 125
Apaches 229
apes 9, 11
Aphrodite 16
Apollo 11 346, 377
Apopi 51
Apsu 21
Aquae Sulis-Minerva 126
Arameans 79
Arendt, Hannah 114, 118
Arginusae, Battle of 95
Arian heresy 136, 138, 141
aristocracy 90, 131, 132
Aristotle 85, 95, 101, 162, 238, 260, 268,
 270, 320
armies 90
Armstrong, Commander Neil 377–8,
 378–9
Arthur, King 146, 200
Arthur, Max 391
Aryans 54–5
Asclepius 96
Ashoka 104–5
Ashurbanipal 16, 80
Asser 169

Association for Computing Machinery/ Institute of Electrical and Electronics Engineers (ACM/IEEE) 382
Assyrians 80
Atahualpa 249, 251
Ataulf 143
Athelney 169
Athens 83–4, 91, 97–8
  expenditure on public works 98
  Peloponnesian War 98–100
atomic bombs 371
Attila the Hun 142
Augustus, Flavius Romulus 142
Aurangzeb 267, 293
Auschwitz 120–2, 369–70, 370
Australia 316–17, 319
Avars 147, 162
Aztecs 6, 108, 252

B-29s 371
Ba Games 330–1
Babcock, John 394
Babur 246–8
Babylon 20, 21, 62, 78, 80, 125
  Cyrus II 80–1, 81–2
  fall of 82, 88
Bacon, Sir Francis 269, 279–81
Baghdad 177
Ball, John 216–17, 218
Ballou, Sarah 327–8
Ballou, Sullivan 327–8, 329
bank accounts 34
Bantu language 179, 180
barbarians 90
bartering 33
Basil II, Emperor 175
Bastille 304, 305
Battle of Britain 366–8
Bayezid I 225
Beautiful Feast of the Valley 29
Beirut 59
Bellerophon 309
Belsen 311
Benedictow, Ole Jørgen 214
Bent, James Theodore 182
Bering Strait 6, 106
Berners-Lee, Sir Tim 381, 382
Bhimbetka 46
Bhirrana 56

Bible 49
  English version 277
  Geneva Bible 277
  King James Version 277–8
  printing of 276–7
bicycles 344
Bindusar 104
birds 202, 203–4
Birka Girl 388
Birkenau 369
bitcoins 34
Bitumen of Judea 321, 322
Black Death 214–15, 356
Black Hole incident 294
black rats 214
Black Ships expedition 373
Blainey, Geoffrey 316
Blenheim, Battle of 289
Bock's Car 371
Bodhi Tree 69–70
The Body of the Dead Christ in the Tomb (Holbein) 339, 340
Boeotians 100
Boleyn, Anne 242–3, 244, 263
Boleyn, Mary 242
Bolsheviks 354
Bonaparte, Napoleon *see* Napoleon Bonaparte
bookkeeping 27–8
books 221, 380
Borodino, Battle of 309
Botheric 139
bourgeoisie 325, 325–6
Brahe, Tycho 269–72, 281, 381
Brahma 73, 74
Brahman 335
Brahmins 56–7
Brandon, Charles, Duke of Suffolk 242
Braudel, Fernand 250–1
bread 304–5
Brennus 140
Bright, John 258
Brin, Sergey 222, 382
Britain
  American independence and 299–300
  colonialism of 273–5
  conscription for First World War 350
  football 330
  slavery 313–15
  trade in India 294

Britain, Battle of 366–8
British East India Company 265–6, 293, 294
British Isles 262–4
Bronze Age civilizations 4
Brown, Andrew 318
Browne, Anthony 242
Browning, Robert 360–1
Bruce, Robert 148
Brutus 86
bubonic plague 282
Buckles, Frank 394
Buddha *see* Siddhartha Gautama
Buddhism 69, 70, 71–2, 104, 149, 246
Bull Run, First Battle of 327, 329
Burmah Oil Company 347, 348
Burns, Ken 327
Byblos 62
Byzantium (Constantinople) 135–6, 183–4, 225

Caesar, Julius *see* Julius Caesar
calcite 32–4
calculus 283–4
calendars 108
Calvin, John 233
Cambuskenneth Abbey 148
camera obscura 320–1
Canaan 48, 49
cannons 247
Canossa, Castle of 187, 188
Cappadocia 35–6
Caracalla, Emperor 142
Carausius 133, 134
Carey, William 242
Carlos II, King of Spain 287–8, 288–9
Carolingian minuscule 163, 168, 173
Carthage 115
Casas, Bartolomé de las 259, 260–1
caste system 56–7, 104, 105
    Mauryans 103–4
cathedrals 192–3
Catherine of Aragon, Queen 242, 243, 244, 263
cave artists 320
Cayley, Sir George 344
cedar trees 60–1
Celts 330
Cerro Rico 253
Cervantes, Miguel de 253
Cetshwayo kaMpande 303
Chaerephon 95
Chandragupta 103, 380

Chang'an 185
Chanute, Octave 344
chaos 20, 21, 22, 84, 131, 132
    Roman Empire 143
chariots 50
    Egyptian 51
    racing 139
    see also two-wheeled chariots
Charlemagne (Big Charlie) 160–3, 164, 166, 168, 184, 192, 234
Charles I, King of Spain 234–7, 239, 240, 254, 259, 261
Charles Martel (Charles the Hammer) 153–4, 161, 168
Charles the Bald 165, 172, 173
Charles the Simple (Charles III) 171, 172, 173, 189
Charles V, Holy Roman Emperor 236, 263
chemical explosion 59
Cheops 30
chess 266
China
    Confucius 74–5, 112, 113
    differences from other countries 112–13
    dynasties 184–5
    Qin Shi Huang 111, 112, 113
    Taoism 75–6
chivalry 196
Choules, Claude 394
Christ, Jesus *see* Jesus Christ
Christian IV, King 271
Christianity 124, 135, 184
    in education 209
    Lindisfarne 158
    progress of 137–8
    war against Muslims 153–4
Christians 146
Christmas Rebellion 314
Ch'u Ta-Kao 75
chuno 249
Church and state 19, 137–8
    power struggle 188
Church of Divine Wisdom (Hagia Sophia) 192
Church of St Sophia 175, 176, 178, 226, 257
Churchill, Winston 256, 258, 353, 367, 386
circles of stones 3–4
city-states 90, 91
    under Roman rule 115
Civil Rights Act (1964) 376
civil war 327–9
Civilisation (Clark) 117, 143

civilization(s) 4, 5–6, 18
  birth of 10
  cost of 24–5
  establishment of 88
  Gupta 245, 246
  Harappan 54, 55, 56
  Mesopotamian 19, 24, 80
  Mycenaean 64
  order and chaos 20
  rules 20, 24–5
  Western 25
  see also Ancient Greece; Classical Greece;
    Egypt
Clark, Kenneth 117, 143, 193
Classical Greece 83–4, 85
  achievements 83, 84
  allure of 98
  forging of 93
  war against the Persians 91–3
  see also Ancient Greece
Classical world 219
Clement VII, Pope 235, 244
Cleopatra 85, 116, 117
climate change 55
Clipper Maid of the Seas 389
Clive, Lieutenant Colonel Robert 294–5
Clovis I 162
Cnut of Denmark, King 189, 190
Code of Hammurabi 22–3, 24–5
Cold War 99, 381
Colegio de San Gregorio 259
Collatinus 86
Collins, Michael 377
colonists 34–5
colonization 260, 273–5
colossal heads 107
Colston, Edward 140
Columba 158
Columbia 377
The Columbian Exchange (Crosby) 250
Columbus, Christopher 227, 238, 249, 252, 259
communism 25, 323–6, 353, 363
Communist League 325
The Communist Manifesto (Marx and Engels)
    323–6
composite bows 51
computers 380–1
  remote access 381
Concepción 239, 240
Concessions Syndicate Ltd 348

Concorde 343
Confucius 74–5, 112, 113
Congreve, William 243
conquistadors 227–8, 259–60
conscription 350
consent 122
Constantine I (Constantine the Great) 134–6,
    224, 341
Constantine XI Palaiologos 223–4
Constantinople
  fall of 223–6
  sieges 223–4, 224–5
Constantius 133, 134, 135
continents 238
Cook, James 316
Cooper, Sheldon (TV character) 284–5
Copernicus, Nicolaus 269, 270, 272
Corinth 132
Coronado, Francisco Vásquez de 228, 229
Cortés, Hernán 227, 252
Cosmos (Sagan) 74
Council of Nicaea 136
Coverdale, Myles 277
COVID-19 pandemic 356–8
creationism 318
Crete 39–40
Crito 94
Crosby, Alfred W. 250
Crusader states 194
Crusades 194–7
crypto-currencies 34
cuneiform 11–12
Curthose, Robert 189
Cuthbert, Bishop 158
Cyropaedia (Xenophon) 81
Cyrus Cylinder 81
Cyrus II 80–1, 81–2, 89, 120

da Vinci, Leonardo 320, 344
Daguerre, Louis 321
Danelaw 170
Dannatt, General Sir Richard 392, 394
Dante 196, 211–12
Darby, Sir Henry Clifford 191
D'Arcy Concession 347, 348
D'Arcy, William Knox 347–8
Darius 89, 91, 119–20
Darwin, Charles 317–19
Darwin, Erasmus 317
De Nova Stella (Brahe) 270

Dead Sea Scrolls 127
Declaration of Independence (US, 1776) 81,
    299, 328
The Decline and Fall of the Roman Empire
    (Gibbon) 155
DeGolyer, Everette 348
Delian League 97–8, 100
demagogues 131–2, 132
democracy 83, 131, 132
Demuth, Hélène 326
dhamma/dharma 70, 104
Dickinson, Emily 361
Dieneces 92
Diet of Worms 235
Diocletian, Emperor 133, 134, 142
Dirac, Paul 338
Directory 307
disease 253
distributed ledgers 34
Divine Comedy (Dante) 196, 211–12
Domesday Book 190–1
Dorians 65
Dorsey, Jack 382
Dostoyevsky, Anna 339, 340
Dostoyevsky, Fyodor 339–42
doughnut-shaped stones 32–4
Dowding, Air Chief Marshal Hugh
    366–7
Drake, Corporal Lee 356
Drake, Francis 263
Ducas, Andronicus 184
Dunkirk 366
Durham, Bishop of (William of St
    Calais) 193
Durham Cathedral 192–3
Dutch East India Company 293, 295
'A Dynamical Theory of the Electromagnetic
    Field' (Maxwell) 336

Eadfrith, Bishop 156
Eagle 377
Earth
    as centre of the universe 268
    circumnavigation of 240
    shape of 238
    stationary 268
East Francia 165
East India Company *see* British East India
    Company; Dutch East India Company;
    French East India Company

Eastman, George 344
Eclogue 4 (Virgil) 210
Edict of Worms 235
Edington, Battle of 169–70
education
    ancient learning 209–10
    by the Church 209–10
Edward II, King 331
Edward III, King 217, 331
Edward IV, King 331
Edward VI, King 244
Egypt/Egyptians 5–6, 28–9, 31,
    44, 49
    defeat of the Hyksos 51–2
    foreign rulers 51
    two-wheeled chariots 51
    waning importance of 88–9
Einhard 160–1, 163
Einstein, Albert 335, 336, 337
Elam 80
Elcano, Juan Sebastián 239, 240
electricity 336–7
electromagnetism 336–7
elements (weather) 11
Elgin Marbles 98
Elizabeth I, Queen 262–4, 265–7
empires, fall of 117, 142
Enabling Acts (1933) 365
encomienda 254–5, 260, 261, 273
Engelbart, Doug 382
Engels, Friedrich 323, 325, 326, 381
English language 278
Enheduanna 9–17, 222, 299
    appearance 13
    hymns 4, 11, 12, 13, 16, 19
    writings 10, 12, 14
Enola Gay 371
Ephialtes 92
Epic of Gilgamesh 15, 78
Epicurus 84
epilepsy 340–1
equites 146
Eratosthenes 238
Ermentarius 172
Estates General 305–6
Etchmiadzin Cathedral 192
Etruscans 86, 91
Euclid 219
eugenics 54
Euphrates 5, 10, 11, 38

European–American Seven Years'
    War 294
Evans, Sir Arthur 40–1
Everest, Mount 359–60
experiments 280–1

Facebook 382, 383
famines 250–1
farming 4, 18, 39
    origins of 10
    tools 19
Farnese, Alexander, Duke of Parma 263
fascism 363
Ferdinand II, Holy Roman Emperor 236
feudalism 254–5, 276
Feynman, Richard 337, 338
Fhimah, Lamin Khalifah 389
fickle mob 131, 132
To the Finland Station (Wilson) 353
First Crusade 194, 197
First Exploration Company 347
First World War 1–2, 350–2, 354, 391, 392
Fitzgerald, Edward 265–6
FitzNigel, Richard 191
floods 11
foederati 138, 162
football 330–4
Football Association 333
four-wheeled wagons 50
Fourth Crusade 225
Francis I, King of France 234
François, Denis 304–5, 306
Franks 146, 154, 161
    see also Charlemagne (Big Charlie)
Frederick I 'Barbarossa', Emperor 195
Frederick II of Denmark, King 270, 271
Freemasons' Tavern 332
French East India Company 293–4, 295
French Revolution 304–7, 308, 324
Friedman, Milton 382
Frigidus, Battle of 141
Fujiwara family 150
Fussell, Paul 352, 358
Fust, Johann 220–1, 276, 381

Gaddafi, Muammar 389
gadflies 95
Gagarin, Yuri 378
Galapagos Islands 319
Galerius 134

Galileo Galilei 271–2, 281
Ganges 44
Gates, Bill 382
Gaul 115–16
The Gay Science (Nietzsche) 340–1, 363
Geneva Bible 277
Genghis Khan 198–200
George III, King 300
Germany 363
    Weimar 363, 365
    see also Hitler, Adolf; Nazism
Gibbon, Edward 141, 155
Gilgamesh 15, 29
Gitchell, Sergeant Albert 356, 357
Glarus 296, 298
Glover, Thomas Blake 372–3
gods 10, 12
    pantheon of 21–2, 90
Godwinson, Harold 189
Gokomere 180
gold 35, 36
Golden Horde 213–15
Göldi, Anna 296–8
Gondwana 316–17
Gorbachev, Mikhail 386
Göring, Hermann 364, 365
Gorsky family 379
Gospels 126, 128
Gothic architecture 193
Goths 138, 139, 140, 141, 142
Grand Alliance 289
Grand Canal 185
Grand Principality of Muscovy 257
granite 180
grapes 39–42
gravestones 92
gravity 71, 284
Great Enclosure 181
The Great Epidemic (Hoehling) 356–7
Great Heathen Army (Mycel Hæþen) 168,
    169–70
Great Plague of London 282
Great Pyramid 30
Great Wall of China 112
Great War see First World War
The Great War and Modern Memory (Fussell)
    352, 358
Great Zimbabwe 180–2
Greece see Ancient Greece; Classical Greece
Green, Florence 394

Gregory the Great 146
Gregory VII, Pope 187, 188
'grotesque' art style 339
Gualpa, Diego 253
Gulag Archipelago 384–7
The Gulag Archipelago (Solzhenitsyn)
   384–5, 386
Gupta civilization 245, 246
Gutenberg, Johannes Gensfleisch 219–22,
   230, 276, 277, 380
Guthrum the Viking 167, 169–70
Gutians 19

Habsburg empire 236
   Carlos II 287–8
Haggard, H. Rider 62
Hammurabi, King 4, 20–6, 78, 119, 380
   stele 20, 22–3
Han dynasty 184
Hanging Gardens 80
Hannibal of Carthage 130, 131
Harappa 45, 46
   Harappan civilization 54, 55, 56
Hardy, Thomas 308
Harvey, William 281
Hattin, Battle of 194, 196
heavenly bodies 268, 269, 270
Heaviside, Oliver 342
Hebrews 48, 79, 80, 81–2, 125
Hector 63–4
Hega-khase 49
Helena 134, 135
Hellenes 65, 89–91
Hellespont 91
helots 99
Henry IV, Holy Roman Emperor
   187, 188
Henry VII, King 243–4, 262
Henry VIII, King 234, 242–3, 244
Hero of Alexandria 291
Herod the Great, King 125
Herodotus 91
Hill Complex 181
Hillary, Edmund 360
Hindenburg, Paul von 362, 364, 365
Hindu Kush 54
Hinduism 45, 55, 68, 71, 74, 104, 246,
   293, 335
Hippocrates 42
Hiroshima 371

The Histories (Polybius) 131
history 1
   Enheduanna 15
   recording disasters of others 129–30
   rhythm of 129, 143
History of the Peloponnesian War (Thucydides)
   98–9, 101
Hitler, Adolf 362–5, 366, 368
Hittites 60, 61, 78, 79
HMS *Beagle* 317, 319
Hoehling, A.A. 356–7
Hoelun 201
Holbein the Younger, Hans 339
Holy Roman Emperors 187, 188, 234–7, 263,
   271, 286
Homer 63, 65–7, 90, 91
Homo Sapiens 46
hoplites 90, 92, 95
horse-riding 50
horses 39, 227–8, 229
hot gates (*Thermopylae*) 92
Howard, Catherine 244
Hsiung-Nu 147
Humayun 248
Hundred Years' War 217
Huns 142
hunting and gathering 10, 106
Hurley, Sergeant Adolph 356
Hyksos 39, 49–51, 52
   defeat of 51–2
hymns
   Enheduanna 4, 11, 12, 13, 16, 19
   Rigveda 55, 56
hypertext 381

Ibn al-Haytham 320
identity politics 102
The Idiot (Dostoyevsky) 340
iklwa 303
Iliad (Homer) 63, 65, 66, 90
Inanna 9, 13, 14, 16
Incas 6, 108, 249, 250, 253–4
incunabula 221
India 44–5, 46–7, 245–6
   ancient life in 53–4
   Aryans 54–5
   Battle of Plassey 295
   Black Hole 294
   British/French conflict 294
   caste system 56–7, 104, 105

India (*cont.*)
  culture 246
  encroachment of the Europeans
      293–4
  independent, rival kingdoms 293
  indigenous change 55
  internecine struggles 293
  Islam 246, 267
  jizyah 267
  Mauryans 105
  Mughal empire 247–8, 267
  population of 53
  skin colour 54, 55, 57
Indians 294, 322
indigenous peoples 322
Indika 103
Indo-European languages 39
indulgences 230–1, 241
Indus 44, 45–6
Industrial Revolution 290,
    291–2
industrialization 325
  spare time for workers 331–2
information 380
  books 221, 380
  worldwide sharing of 381
  see also printing
Ingenuity 346
In Memoriam (First World War) 352
Installation of the Vizier 30
International Holocaust Remembrance
    Day 370
Internet 381–2, 383
Inuits 106
investiture 187, 188
Iona 158
Ionians 65
Iran 19, 54, 80
Ireland 251
Iron Curtain 386
irony 358
Iruka, Soga 149, 150
Irvine, Andrew 359–60
Isandlwana, Battle of 303
iShaka 302
Ishtar 16
Islam 71, 85, 144, 146, 147, 197, 293
  education 209–10
  growth of 152
  in India 246, 267

Ismay, General Hastings Lionel 'Pug' 367
Israel 80, 81–2
  imperial dominance 124
Ivan the Great 257
Ivan the Terrible 257–8

Jackson, Mahalia 375
Jacob 48, 79
Jaffa, Battle of 196
Jahangir 267
James I and VI, King 274, 277, 331
Jamestown 274–5
Jani Beg 213
Janszoon, Willem 316
Japan 148–50, 205–8, 371–2
jatis 57
Jefferson, Thomas 81
Jéquier, Gustave 22
Jericho 18
Jerusalem 125, 194, 238
Jesus Christ 22, 25, 73, 124, 126–8, 339, 340
Jewish people 62, 120–1, 124, 146
  belief in One God 22, 79, 124, 126, 128
  dispersal of 125, 177
  as God's chosen people 124, 125
  murder of 369–70
  unfolding of history 124
Joanna of Castile 236
Jobs, Steve 221
John Chrysostom, St 261
John Paul II, Pope 386
Joseph of Arimathea 4
Joseph (Old Testament) 48, 79
Josephus, Titus Flavius 52
Judaea 126
Judah 80
Judeo-Christian system 25
Julius Caesar 115–18, 119
junta 261
Jupiter 272
Justinian 146, 147, 175

Kaaba 145
Kaffa 213, 214
Kamakura era 150–1
Kamatari, Nakatomi 149–50
kamikaze 207–8
Kant, Immanuel 335–6
Karnak 30
Kassites 39, 50, 79

Keftiu 40
Kennedy, President John F. 376, 378
kenosis 340
Kepler, Johannes 270–1, 281, 380
Kerensky, Alexander 354–5
Khadija 144, 145
Khan, Kitabchi 347
Khrushchev, Nikita 385
Kill Devil Hill 345
King Jr, Martin Luther 374–6
Kirkwall Ba Game 330–1
Kitchener, Horatio Herbert 350
Kitty Hawk 343, 344, 378
Kline, Charley 380, 381
Knossos 40–2
knowledge 336
Kogyoku, Empress 149, 150
Kotoku 150
Krupskaya, Nadezhda Konstantinovna 354
Kshatriyas 56–7
kuaka 203, 204
Kublai Khan 200–1, 205–8
Kupe 203–4
Kuramarotini 204
Kush 5–6
Kushanas 245
Kutuzov, Mikhail 309

Lal, Braj Basi (B.B.) 55, 56
Lamberton, William, Bishop of St
    Andrews 148
landed estates 286–7
Lao Tzu 75–6, 120, 290, 335
La Rosa field 349
Larson, Gary 227–8
Last Post (Arthur) 391
Later Han dynasty 184
Later Liang dynasty 185
Latins 86
law of retaliation (*lex talionis*) 23
leaders/leadership 76
league of states 97–8
Lebanon 59, 60
    see also Beirut
Lecter, Hannibal 243
Legnica, Battle of 200
Lemnos 60
Lenin, Vladimir Ilyich 353–5
Leo III, Pope 160–1, 163
Leo X, Pope 230–1, 232

Leonardo da Vinci *see* da Vinci, Leonardo
Leonidas, King 92
Leopold I of Austria, Holy Roman Emperor 286
Leopold, Joseph Ferdinand 286, 288
Leuctra, Battle of 100
Levi, Primo 120–3, 370
Leviticus curse 243
light 336–7
Lilienthal, Otto 344, 345
Lincoln, Abraham 301, 328, 374
Lindisfarne 156–9
Loaisa, Rodrigo de 254
lockdown 282
Lockerbie 388
Lodi, Ibrahim, Sultan of Delhi 247
Logos 84
Lombards 146, 162
Lothair 164–5
Louis the German 165
Louis the Pious 164
Louis XIV, King of France 287, 289
Louis XVI, King of France 250, 304, 305
Lucretia 86
Luftwaffe 366–7, 368
Lugal-Ane 14
Luther, Martin 230–3, 235, 241, 244, 277
Lutheranism 232
Lydians 80

Maccabaean Revolt 125
Machiavelli, Niccolò 132
Madison, James 300
Magadha 103
Magellan, Ferdinand 239–40
Magna Carta 299, 300, 301
magnetism 336–7
Mahon, Basil 336
Mahrata empire 267, 293
Maitland, Captain Frederick 309
maize 107–8
Malcolm III of Scotland, King 189
Mallory and Irvine Research Expedition 360
Mallory, George 359–60
Manetho 52
Manzikert, Battle of 183–4, 185, 186, 194, 225
Marathon (battle) 91
Marduk (Bel, Baal) 21, 22, 81
Maria Theresa of Spain 287
Marie Antoinette 250
Mark Antony 117

marsupials 317
Marx, Karl 323–6, 381
Marxists 364–5
Mary, Queen of Scots 263
Mashona 179–80
Masjed Soleyman field 348
Matahorua 204
Mathematical Principles of Natural Philosophy
    (Newton) 284
maths 336–7
Matilda of Flanders 189, 190
Matilda of Tuscany 187, 188
Mauryan empire 103–4, 105
Maxentius 135
Maximian 133
Maximilian II Emanuel, Elector of
    Bavaria 286
Maxwell, James Clerk 336–8, 342
Maya 107–8
Maya calendar 108–9
Mayans 6
Mazarin Bible 221
McCullough, David 345–6
Mecca 144, 145
Medes 80, 89
Mediterranean Sea 88
Megasthenes 102–4
al-Megrahi, Abdelbaset 389
Mehmet II 223, 224, 226
Meiji Restoration government 372
Mein Kampf (Hitler) 364
Meluhha 44
Menes 28, 29
Mensheviks 354
Mercator, Gerardus 43–4
Merovingian dynasty 162
Mesoamerican ballgame 107
Mesopotamia 5, 10, 11, 15, 44
    civilization 19, 80
    see also Babylon
messiah 127
middle class, emergence of 276
Middle Francia 165
Middle Way 69
Milky Way 272
Milvian Bridge, Battle of 135
Minerva 126
mining 253–4
Minoans 41
Minos, King 41

Minotaur 41–2
mit'a 253–4
mobile vulgus 131, 132
Mohenjo-daro 45, 46
monarchy 132
money 32–7
Mongol empire 198–201, 205–7, 213–15, 257
Mongol khans 205
Mononobe family 148–9
monotremes 318
Montesinos, Antonio de 259–60, 260
moon landing 377–9
moria 42
Moses 16–17, 21, 25, 49, 79
Mother of All Demos 382
motion, laws of 283
Move Fast and Break Things (Taplin) 382
Mozarabic Chronicle 154
Mughal empire 247–8, 267, 293
Muhammad 144–5, 147, 196
Muir, John 290
Müller, Max 54, 55
Munster 233
mural quadrants 270
Muslims 144, 146, 177–8
    war against Christianity 153–4
Mussolini, Benito 116
Mozaffar ad-Din Shah Qajar 347
My First Summer in the Sierra (Muir) 290
Mycenae 61
    Mycenaean civilization 64
Mysterium Cosmographicum (Kepler) 271

Nabonidus 80, 80–1
Nagasaki 371
Nakatomi family 148–9
Nandi 302, 303
Nanna 9
Napoleon Bonaparte 307–8, 308–9
National Assembly 305, 306
National Socialist German Workers'
    Party 364
Native Americans 294, 322
nawabs 294, 295
Nazism 120–1, 365, 369–70
Near East 38
Nebuchadnezzar II, King 62, 80, 88–9,
    120, 124
Nelson, Admiral Horatio 308, 309
Nepal 68

Nestor 176–7
New Atlantis (Bacon) 281
New Laws 261
New World 251, 253, 259
  colonization of 274
  savages in 260
New Zealand 204
Newcomen, Thomas 290–2
Newton, Isaac 70–1, 282–4, 285, 290, 335,
  336, 338
Nicene Creed 136, 138
Nicolas II, Tsar 354
Nicolson, Adam 65–7
Niépce, Joseph Nicéphore 321
Nietzsche, Friedrich 340–1, 363
Night of the Long Knives 365
nightshade plants (*Solanum*) 250
Nile 28, 29, 30, 31, 38
Ninety-five Theses (Luther) 230, 231,
  241, 277
Nineveh library 16
nirvana 69, 84
Nixon, President Richard 378
Norgay, Tenzing 360
North America 273–4
  British/French conflict 294
  colonization of 273–5
Novgorod, Massacre of 258

ochlocracy 131
Octavian 117
October Days 304
Odell, Noel 359
Odo, Bishop of Bayeux 189
Odo, Count of Paris 173
Odo the Great 153
Odoacer 143
Odyssey (Homer) 63, 65, 66–7, 90, 245
Oe, Nakano (Emperor Tenji) 149–50
Ögedei 200
Oghuz Turks 185, 225
oil 347–9
Old World 3, 4, 6, 87, 146, 168, 251
oligarchy 131
olive oil 40, 42
olives 39–42
Olmecs 6
  culture 106–7
Onon River 198
Opening the Mouth 29

Operation Sea Lion (Unternehmen Seelöwe)
  366, 368
oracle at Delphi 95
order 74–5
On the Origin of Species (Darwin) 319
Orissa 104
Orkney 3
Orthodox Christianity 178
Osman 225
Oswald 158

Pacific Ocean 203–4
Page, Larry 222, 382
Palaiologina, Sophia 257
Palatine Chapel 234
Palilis, Ilum 13
Pals Battalions 350–2, 351, 352
pandemics 282, 356–7
Pangaea 250
Panipat, First Battle of 247
Papen, Franz von 364
Park, Air Vice Marshal Keith 367
Parr, Catherine 244
Parvati 46
Pashupati (Lord of Animals) seal 46
Pasiphaë 41
Passchendaele 391, 392, 394
Patch, Harry 391–2, 393, 394
Paul III, Pope 261
Paul the Apostle 126–7, 128
Peace of Paris (1783) 299–300
Peake, Mervyn 310, 311–12
Peasant's Revolt (1381) 217–18
Pegado, Captain Vicente 182
Peloponnesian War 98–100, 131
People of the Book 146
pergamene animal skins 85
Pericles 101
Period of the Warring States 111, 112
Perry, Matthew 373
Persia/Persians 88, 89, 347
Persian war 91–3, 97
Peru 249, 251, 253
pharaohs 28–9, 30
Philip, Duke of Anjou 289
Philip II, King of France 189, 195, 197
Philip II, King of Spain 263, 273
Philip IV, King of Spain 287
Philip of Macedon 85
Philip the Handsome 236

Philosophiae Naturalis Principia Mathematica
    (Newton) 284
philosophy 96
Phoenicians 60–2, 65, 115, 182
photography 320–2
Pilate, Pontius 126, 127
pinhole cameras 320–1
pithoi 40
Pizarro, Francisco 249, 253
Place de Grève 304, 305
plague 213–15
Plains Indians 228, 229
planetary motion, laws of 271
Plassey, Battle of 295
Plato 85, 91, 94, 95, 96, 101, 130, 162
platypus 318, 319
poets 18
    Enheduanna 9–17
poll tax 217, 218
Polybius 129, 130–2
Pompey 116, 125
Pond Square 279, 280
poor, the 138
population 310–11
Portugal 252
potatoes 249–51
Potosí 253
powered flights 343–4, 345–6
printing 219–22, 230, 232, 380
    Bible 276–7
Proctor, Robert 221
proletariat 325
Promised Land *see* Canaan 125
proof of work 35, 36–7
property 24
Protestantism 232
Proto-Indo-European language
    69, 393
Psalm 104 268
Ptolemaic system 268–9
Ptolemies 125
Ptolemy 85, 219, 238, 268, 270
public schools 332
Puccini, Giacomo 373
pumps 291
Punic people 91, 115
Punic Wars 115
Purusha 58
pyramids 30, 31, 107, 108
Pythagoras 238

Qin Shi Huang 110–11, 112, 113, 184
Queen of Sheba 182
queens, influence of 266
Querecho 228–9
questions 76
Qumran community 127
Qur'an 145, 155
quriltai 198

Ra 51
radiation sickness 371
rai 32–3, 34
Rajputs 248
Raleigh, Sir Walter 274
Rand, Ayn 382
Rassam, Hormuzd 81
Rattan, Suruchi 389
Rawlinson, Henry 16
Reagan, Ronald 386
reasonable/unreasonable people
    119, 123
Red Army 369
Red Guards 355
Redoutable 308
Reformation 232–3, 241, 244, 277
Reginherus 172
Rekhmire 28–31, 40
Remembrance Day 393
Remus 86
Render, Adam 182
republic (Roman) 114–15
republics 86–7
resource curse 349
resurrection 128
revenge 304, 306
On the Revolutions of the Celestial Orbs
    (Copernicus) 269
Reynolds, George B. 347–8, 349
Rhodes, Cecil 182
Richard I (Lionheart), King 195,
    196, 197
Richard II, King 217, 218
Richard II (Shakespeare) 262
Rigveda 54, 55, 56, 56–8
Rimush 14
Rurik 176, 257
Robert the Frisian, Count of Flanders 189
Rollo ('the walker') 171–2, 173, 174,
    189, 190
Roman Catholicism 158

Roman religion 126
Romans 114–15, 146, 330
  emperors 135
  see also Constantinople
Romanus IV Diogenes 183, 184
Rome 86–7, 112, 115
  decline of 142
  sacking of 140, 141
  SPQR motto 117
  subject provinces 115, 142
  totalitarianism 117–18
Romulus 86
Roth, Philip 120
Royal Air Force (RAF) 346, 366–7, 368
Royal Navy 315, 348
Rubaiyat of Omar Khayyam (Fitzgerald)
  265–6
Rubicon River 116
Rudolf II, Holy Roman Emperor 271
Rugby 332
Rule Book of Association Football 333
rules 20, 24–5
Rus' of Kiev 175–8, 257
Russia 177, 256–8
  First World War 354
  revolution 354, 355
  sealed train 355
Russian Primary Chronicle 176
Russian Social Democratic Workers' Party
  (RSDWP) 354

The Sack of Rome 140
sacrificial offerings 58, 107, 108
Sagadu 13
Sagan, Carl 74
Sahara Desert 6
Saint-Clair-sur-Epte, Treaty of 171, 173
Saladin 194–5, 195, 196–7
Salamis, Battle of 92–3
samurai 207
San Antonio 239, 240
Sanskrit 246
Santiago 239, 240
Sarasvati River 56
Sargon the Great, King 9, 12, 14, 16, 19, 44
Sassanids 147
Saturn 272
Savery, Thomas 291
Schöffer, Peter 221
Schreiner, Colonel 356–7

scientific method 279–80
Scipio Africanus 130, 131
Scott, Captain Robert Falcon 360
Scott, Sir Walter 195
scribes 13, 31
Scythians 80, 91, 147
Se questo è un uomo ('If This Is a Man',
  Levi) 120
Second Crusade 194
Second Intermediate period 49
Second World War 366–8, 370
Secret History of the Mongols 199–200, 201
Seleucid dynasty 85, 125
Seleucus I Nicator 102, 103
Seljuk Turks 183, 184, 185, 186, 194, 225
Semitic languages 39
senses 84
Senzangakhona kaJama 302
Sepúlveda, Juan de 259, 260
Seqenenre 51
Sermon on the Mount 128
Sextus 86
Seymour, Jane 244
Shah Jahan 267, 293
Shaka Zulu 302–3
Shakespeare, William 262
Shang 111
Shankly, Bill 334
Sharpe, Samuel 313–14
shell beads 34–5, 36
Shelley, Percy Bysshe 111
Shinto 149
ship design 239
Shiva 45, 46
Shivaji Bhonsale 267
shoguns 151, 205–6
Shona 180, 181
Shudra 56–7
Shutruk-Nakhunte 22
Sicga 156, 157
Sicilian Expedition 100
Siddhartha Gautama 68–70, 71, 72, 84, 120, 335
Sidonians 61
Sikhism 293
silver 35–6
Sima Qian 110–11
Simeon of Durham 158, 193
Sineus 176
Singer, Isaac 344
Siraj ud-Daulah 294, 295

Sismondi, Jean Charles Léonard de 325
Six Wives: The Queens of Henry VIII
    (Starkey) 242
skin colour 54, 55, 57
slavery/slaves 23, 24, 30, 80, 90, 261, 273, 322
    British 313–15
    in Classical Greece 83, 90
    of Qin Shi Huang 111
smallpox 286
Smith, John 274
Socrates 94–6, 101
Socratic method 95
Soga family 148, 149
Sokolov, Mikhail 355
Solomon, King 61, 62, 79, 124
Solomon's Temple 61, 62
Solon 42
Solzhenitsyn, Aleksandr 384–7
Somme, Battle of the 350–2
Somme, Missing of the 352
Song dynasty 205, 207
South America 273
South Pole 360
Soviet Union *see* USSR (Union of Soviet
    States Republics)
Spain 252, 253, 254
    colonialism of 273
Spanish Armada 263–4
Spanish Flu 356–8
Sparta 91, 92, 97, 98
    deal with Persia 100
    as "hard man" of Greece 100
    military defeat 100
    Peloponnesian War 98–100
specialists 10
Spice Islands 239, 240
Sputnik 1 378
St James Parish 313, 314
Stalin, Joseph 355, 385
Stanford Research Institute 380
Starkey, David 242
Starr, Margery 216
stars 269–70
Stationers' Hall 278
statues 140
steam 291–2
steam engines 290–1
Steinlauf 121–2
Stenness 3
Stoicism 85

Stonehenge 3, 45
storytelling 10, 11
strongmen 10
Stukeley, William 70–1
Sublimis Deus 261
submission 121–2
Sufis 196
Sui dynasty 185
Suleiman the Magnificent 235
Sulis 126
Sumerians 19
surplus food 38, 39
survival 121–2
Sushun 149
Swahili 180
Swedish Vikings 176, 177
Sylvestre, Joseph-Noël 140
Syracuse 99–100

Taika No Kaishin (Great Reformation of the
    Taika Era) 150
Tang dynasty 185, 225
Tao Te Ching 74, 75, 76, 77
Taoism 75–6
Taplin, Jonathan 382
Tariq ibn Ziyad 152–3
Tarquinius Superbus, Lucius 86
Taylor, Charlie 344
TCP/IP (Transmission Control Protocol/
    Internet Protocol) 222
Temüjin *see* Genghis Khan
Teotihuacan 107
Tereshkova, Valentina 378
Terracotta Army 110, 111, 113
Terror 304, 306, 307
Teutonic Knights 200
Tezel, Johann 231
Thatcher, Margaret 386
The Way (Tao) 75–6
Thebans 100
Theodoret of Cyrus 139
Theodosius II 224
Theodosius the Great 137, 138, 139, 141
Thermopylae 101
Thessalonica 138, 139
Thiel, Peter 382
Third Crusade 194–5, 196
Thirty Tyrants 95
Thirty Years' War 393
Thucydides 98–9, 101, 131

Thutmose III 28
Tiamat 21
Tigris 5, 10, 22, 38
time, concept of 109
Timur the Lame 205, 225, 246
tin 61
Tokugawa Shogunate 372, 373
Toltecs 107, 108
Tomás, Domingo de Santo 254
tombs 11
  Kings of Ur 11
  Qin Shi Huang 110–11, 113
  Rekhmire 29, 30, 40
Tomisaburo, Kuraba 'Tomi-San' 372–3
Tordesillas, Treaty of 239, 252
totalitarianism 76, 114, 117
  in Rome 117–18
trade 90
Trafalgar, Battle of 308, 309
Trinidad 239, 240
Trotsky, Leon 354
Troy 64
True Cross 235
Truman, President Harry S. 386
Truvor 176
Tschudi family 296–7
Tschudi, Jakob 296–7
Tshushima Strait 206
Tsuru, Awajiya 372
Tudor, Arthur 243
Tudor, Mary 243, 263
Tudors 262
Tullie House Museum 133
Turcat, André 343
Turgot, Anne Robert Jacques 305
Turks 185
Twain, Mark 60, 129
Twitter 382
two-wheeled chariots 50, 51
Tychonic system 270
Tyler, Wat 218
Tyndale, William 277
tyrants 90–1, 131
Tyre 60

ukuhlobonga 302
Ulyanov, Vladimir Ilyich see Lenin, Vladimir Ilyich
Umako, Soga 148–9
Umayyad caliphate 152–3, 161, 177

umma 145
United States of America (USA) 99
  Articles of Confederation 300
  civil war 327–9
  constitution 300, 301
  Founding Fathers 132, 300, 301
  independence 297, 299–300, 328
  majority decisions/protecting inalienable rights 301
  presidency 301
  racial hate 376
  space race 378
universe 21–2, 68
  Chinese understanding of 74–5
  cycle of births and deaths 73, 74
  Hindu 73
  perspectives on 73–4
universities 209–10
University of California Los Angeles (UCLA) 380
Upanishads 68, 335
Ur 9–10, 11
  clothing of people 13
  wealth and sophistication 11
Ur-Nammu 19, 23
US military 381
USSR (Union of Soviet States Republics) 99, 378, 384–7
  see also Russia
Utrecht, Peace of 289

Vaishyas 56–7
Valley Complex 181
value 33–6
van der Post, Laurens 26
Vandals 142, 146
varna 57
Vasilyevich, Ivan see Ivan the Terrible
Vedas 57
Venerable Bede 238
Verdun, Treaty of 164–5
Versailles, Treaty of 363, 364, 365
Victoria 239, 240
Victory 308
Vienna, Treaty of 324
Vikings 106, 157, 158–9, 162, 168, 172–3
  Great Heathen Army 168, 169–70
Virgil 210–11
Virginia Company of London 274
Visigoths 140, 142, 146

Vitruvius 291
viziers 28, 30
Vladimir 175–6, 177, 178
Vorontsov, Alexander 369, 370

Waddell, Jack 343
Waka, Nakano 373
Walk to Canossa 187
Wall of Theodosius 153, 226
wampum 35
War of the Spanish Succession 289
warfare 90
warriors 10, 92
Waterloo, Battle of 309
Watts, Alan 73
Webster Presbyterian Church 377
Wedgwood, Josiah 317
Wedmore, Treaty of 170
Weimar 363, 365
West Francia 165, 171–2
Western Europe 4–5
Westphalen, Jenny von 326
Whewell, William 284
White Castle 242
Wiesel, Elie 111
Wilberforce, William 261
William the Conqueror (William I, William
    the Bastard) 174, 189–91
Wills, Garry 300
Wilson, Edmund 353
Winship, George Parker 228
Winterbourne, Dr 280
wisdom 18, 23–4
witchcraft 296, 297, 298
Woolley, Leonard 13
World Wide Web 381

Worshipful Company of Stationers 278
Wozniak, Steve 221
The Wright Brothers (McCullough)
    345–6
Wright family 343
Wright Flyer 343, 345, 346
Wright, Orville 343–6, 378, 381
Wright, Wilbur 343–6, 378, 381
writing 18, 380
    cuneiform 11–12
    origins of 222
    rules 20
Wycliffe, John 277

Xenophon 81
Xerxes 91–2, 93, 119–20

Yahweh 79, 80
Yapese 32–4
Yathrib (Medina) 145
Yeats, W.B. 7, 212
Yersinia pestis 214
York (Eboracum) 135
YouTube 383

Zagros Basin 348
Zahir ud-din Muhammad *see* Babur
Zeno 84–5
Zhou 111–12
Ziggurat of Ur 19
ziggurats 20, 38
Zoroastrianism 147
Zuckerberg, Mark 382
Zulus 179, 302, 303

ABOUT THE AUTHOR

Neil Oliver was born in Renfrew in Scotland. He studied archaeology at the University of Glasgow and worked as an archaeologist before training as a journalist. Since 2002 he has presented various TV series including *Coast* (in the UK and in the Antipodes), *A History of Ancient Britain*, *Vikings* and *Sacred Wonders of Britain*. He is the author of several non-fiction books and one novel. He lives in Stirling with his wife, three children and two Irish wolfhounds.

The Story of the British Isles in 100 Places

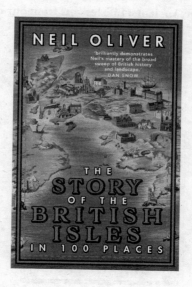

The Story of the British Isles in 100 Places is Neil Oliver's very personal account of what makes these islands so special, told through the places that have witnessed the unfolding of our history. Beginning with the footprints made in the mud by humankind's earliest ancestors, he takes us via Romans and Vikings, the flowering of Christianity, through civil war, industrial revolution and two world wars. From windswept headlands to battlefields, ancient trees to magnificent cathedrals, in each of his destinations is a place where, somehow, the spirit of the past still lingers. Beautifully written, his book is majestic, awe-inspiring, a kaleidoscopic history of a place with a story like no other.

'Everyone should have two copies – one for the car and one for the house to plan journeys . . . a reminder to think more about the places you pass and less about your route, because every British journey is through rich history.'
Edward Stourton

Wisdom of the Ancients: Life lessons from our distant past

In a time that is increasingly fraught with complexity and conflict, we are told that our wellbeing relies on remaining as present as possible. But what if the key to being present lies in the past?

In *Wisdom of the Ancients*, Neil Oliver takes us back in time, to grab hold of the ideas buried in forgotten cultures and early civilizations. From Laetoli footprints in Tanzania to Keralan rituals, stone circles and cave paintings, Oliver takes us on a global journey through antiquity and distils the wisdom of the distant past into twelve messages that have endured the test of time.

'Neil Oliver writes beautifully – bringing the past to life and letting us see ourselves in a new light.'
Professor Alice Roberts

HOW TO BE A

SUPER READER

- READ FASTER
- UNDERSTAND MORE
- REMEMBER FOR LONGER

RON COLE

piatkus

PIATKUS

First published in Great Britain in 2009 by Piatkus

Copyright © 2009 by Ron Cole

The moral right of the author has been asserted

Every effort has been made to identify and acknowledge the copyright
holders. Any errors or omissions will be rectified in future editions provided
that written notification is made to the publisher.

A CIP catalogue record for this book
is available from the British Library

ISBN 978-0-7499-4230-4

Edited by Carol Franklin
Text design and diagrams by Emma Ashby

Typeset in Giovanni by
Action Publishing Technology Ltd, Gloucester
Printed and bound in Great Britain by
MPG Books, Bodmin, Cornwall

Papers used by Piatkus are natural, renewable and recyclable
products sourced from well-managed forests and certified
in accordance with the rules of the Forest Stewardship Council.

Mixed Sources
Product group from well-managed
forests and other controlled sources
www.fsc.org   Cert no. SGS-COC-004081
© 1996 Forest Stewardship Council

Piatkus
An imprint of
Little, Brown Book Group
100 Victoria Embankment
London EC4Y 0DY

n Hachette UK Company
www.hachette.co.uk
www.piatkus.co.uk

Contents

Acknowledgements   vii

PART 1 Starting Out   1

1   The lowdown on SuperReading™   2
2   Overcoming your reading challenges   19
3   Before you begin   34
4   Reserving judgement and setting goals   44
5   Testing your reading effectiveness   54

PART 2 Your New Basic Reading Technique   71

6   Introducing hand pacing   72
7   Previewing   92
8   Eye-Hop™   115
9   Parroting   134
10   Reviewing and embodying   142

PART 3 Building on the Basics   161

11   Pattern reading   162
12   Visualisation and affirmation techniques   192

PART 4 Further Techniques and Strategies   209

13   Learning and memory   210

14   Focusing your mind   244

15   Look to your future   268

APPENDICES   273

Appendix A   It's About Time   274

Appendix B   Reading Tests and Answers   281

Appendix C   Calculating Your Reading Speed   305

Appendix D   Reading Effectiveness (R.E.)

                Scores and Progress Graph   309

Index   323

About the author   333

Acknowledgements

In mostly chronological order, I wish to thank:

The Roman scholars who came up with the concept of 'the room'.

Evelyn Wood for getting the ball rolling with speed reading.

Shanna McBain for putting in a good word for me at Hewlett-Packard.

Mariam Ghazvini for giving the course a chance at Hewlett-Packard, and championing it through the lean years.

Judy Peterson, whose continued enthusiasm at Xilinx was brilliant.

Bonita Steers for suggesting that the testing could be improved.

Reto Stamm for making Eye-Hop™ accessible to everyone.

Jackson Chow for continuing to support SuperReading™ for students.

Claire de Than for her steadfast belief in the project and her desire to help her law students.

Dr Ross Cooper for his support and professionalism in evaluating the SuperReading™ course for dyslexics, and spurring great ideas for improving the testing procedure.

Don Schloss for promoting SuperReading™ among the dyslexic population.

Doreen Montgomery for finding a super publisher.

Anne Lawrance for believing in SuperReading™ and fully supporting this project.

Carol Franklin for brilliant editing and determining the best order of topics.

All the educators and decision makers who approved SuperReading™ to be taught.

All my students for taking a chance, giving it a go, and proving time and again that the techniques work.

PART ONE:

Starting Out

1.

The lowdown on SuperReading™

There are probably several reasons why you want to be a 'super' reader. You may have stacks of reports you need to get through, you may be drowning in emails, you may be revising for exams or you may have problems keeping focused. Whatever your reasons are for buying this book, my goal is to help you become a highly effective, confident reader. If you work your way through the advice in this book you will learn how to understand what you read and remember what you need.

In simple terms, you will be able to handle any reading 'assignment' that comes your way intelligently, enthusiastically and efficiently. In the days and weeks ahead you will change your attitude towards reading. Whether you love reading or you dread it, your improved skills will make reading something you will always look forward to. Also, you will learn how to use memory tools that will help you retain any information for as long as you wish.

If reading is a chore for you, take heart. Just a couple

of days after picking up this book you will already be reading better. It has been written in a conversational and humorous tone, as if I'm talking to you. If you can simply invest a little time each day, I promise you that your abilities will quickly improve.

What's the SuperReading™ story?

This book is based on the highly successful SuperReading™ course that I have been teaching for over 14 years. So, how did it all come about? Back in the mid-1990s I was a life coach coaching clients to have more success in their work. Some of my clients were concerned about where their time was going. They told me they would get to work, start work on a couple of projects and suddenly it was lunchtime. Before they knew it the day was over. Where had all their time gone and why had they accomplished so little? To find out, I asked them to track their time on paper every 30 minutes of the working day. We discovered that time, apart from the unavoidable amount spent travelling, was disappearing into two main areas: meetings and reading. For the first area, I gathered information on running a tidy meeting, with tools like deciding in advance how long to give each topic, assigning a time keeper and ending the meeting at the time that was agreed upon, no matter what.

Then there was reading. What could be done? One option we considered was to hire someone else to read material and provide an executive brief highlighting the main points. The problem was that important items could be missed or misinterpreted. Another option was to transcribe written work to audiotape, but focusing on what is being said can be difficult, going back over bits you've missed is cumbersome and it can take even longer than reading. Or, of course, they could just ignore the material. Unfortunately, that could have serious consequences. As one client, a manager at Sun Microsystems, said: 'Fifteen years ago I could just go to trade shows and keep up to date on the industry. Ten years ago I could read quarterly synopses of what was happening and not fall behind. Five years ago I could just about get away with monthly newsletters. Now that the industry has become so competitive and fast-paced, and I'm a high-level manager making multi-million-dollar decisions, I need information almost daily because things can change so quickly. I must be totally up to date or we could lose millions. And I can't trust anyone else to know what I need. That's why I took this course.'

I looked into 'speed reading' to see if that would help. It was sort of OK for novels, but for business or legal reading it just didn't help people to get everything they needed and not miss important points. So I experimented. I got people together and tried various techniques. The techniques that were successful went on to form the backbone of the SuperReading™ course. While SuperReading™ is related to speed reading, this book focuses on comprehension first. I feel that going fast is meaningless if you do not understand what you've read and cannot recall it. Traditional 'speed reading' courses get you to skip words and sometimes whole sections of what you are reading. With SuperReading™ you do not have to do that. You will read every word and understand it while going faster and faster over time.

The most important development I devised was the Eye-Hop™ exercises (see chapter 8). I had heard that it was important to read in groups of words, instead of just one word at a time. So I worked at a series of exercises with words separated into groups and found that regular practice reading these allowed people to surpass their present speeds greatly, while maintaining or even improving their comprehension. The Eye-Hop™ exercises are the hallmark of SuperReading™ and you will find examples on pages 126–131.

Who could this book help?

This book could benefit anyone who is reading at the level of a nine-year-old or better. Since 1996 the Super-Reading™ course has been taken by engineers, doctors, lawyers, dentists, managers, university students, students at all levels, salespeople, administrative assistants, teachers, professors, researchers, mums, dads and grandparents. It has been taken by fast readers, slow readers, pleasure readers, business readers, dyslexics, children and adults with attention deficit hyperactivity disorder (ADHD), avid readers and people who (previously) hated reading. The basics of SuperReading™ are appropriate for people of any age, but some of the high-level Eye-Hop™ exercises (see chapter 8 for all you need to know about this) may be too sophisticated for most primary school children, depending on their mental development.

What will you gain from this book?

Once you have worked your way through this book you will have learned some simple skills and techniques which will improve your ability to focus, read, retain and recall information. You will know when you are taking in what you have read and when you are not. You will be able to regain and maintain your concentration when it slips. You will become confident that whatever the reading challenge you are presented with, you have the best tools for doing a great job with it. You will feel assured that even when your reading stack is high you will be able to get through it in record time. You will also find you can get past dry, poorly written material and glean just what you need from it. Your self-esteem will rise as you realise you can perform brilliantly.

Remember: whenever students, of any age, apply these simple techniques, they tend to rise to the top of their class. Here is a comment from a professional in Silicon Valley, California:

CASE STUDY

'Hi Ron,

I took your SuperReading™ class earlier this year, along with my co-worker, Tim. As you know, we are both taking an MBA programme that involves night classes. For the last year, we have been going each week, and seeing our standing in the course among our 100+ peers.

'Our professor posts the grades outside the door each week. We see our student number, our grade, and our ranking in the class. In the past, before your class, our ranking was all over the grid. One week I could be number 7, the next week 101 and the following week number 75. Since the third week of SuperReading™, Tim and I have occupied the number 1 and 2 positions, and nobody can surpass us! Each week we jockey between ourselves and the rest of the class has to fight for number 3.

'To us, this demonstrates the power of the skills we learned from you. In a way, we're no smarter than we were before SuperReading™. What we have is the ability to understand and recall what we read. Perhaps we are smarter. It depends on how one defines intelligence. Either way, our reading skills have set us above about 120 other professionals struggling to enhance their careers.

'So we both send you a big "thank you". We're spending half the time studying and getting far better results. It's just how you said it would be.'

FRANK T., ENGINEER, ADVANCED MICRO DEVICES (AMD)

Frank's comment neatly sums up the benefits of SuperReading™. Frank and Tim cut out half the time they spent studying and were the best in their class. All it took was about three weeks' study with good tools. The 'full effect' of SuperReading™ means *all* the tools coming together, making them as brilliant a reader as they will become while they are on the course. With Frank, as with most people, he did not require the 'full effect' to rise to the top of the class, and achieved high levels within three weeks. Because many people's reading and recalling skills are so poor, they do not require the full effect of SuperReading™ to overtake others. Frank and Tim completed the course in about the year 2000. This book in your hands now has even better tools than Frank and Tim had available to them. Apply them and you too will be the best reader in your group. However, if everyone in your group has bought this book, then all bets are off! What's really important is that you become the best reader you can be.

'Your biggest competitor is your own view of your future.'

WATTS WACKER AND JIM TAYLOR

(lecturers and business people, authors of *The 500-Year Delta*)

How long will it take before I see some results?

SuperReading™ is not a pill you take or a jab in the arm to make you a better reader. It's a series of simple concepts combined together to make a powerful set of tools. Most people who take the course will see significant improvement in their comprehension within a few days. They notice that they drift off less and retain information better. Some see a qualitative difference in the first hour or two. For the full effect of all the tools to come together takes most people five to seven weeks. Some people have accomplished this in as little as three weeks, but that is quite rare.

As the memory tools come into play retention is increased. After the first two months you can experience a slow and steady gain from that point. For example, you may begin the course with a Reading Effectiveness (R.E.) score of 100 (for a full explanation of R.E. scores, see page 309). Three weeks later it may be in the 300 range. After six or seven weeks it may be in the 500 to 800 range. After ten weeks you could reach 1,000 to 1,500. After that, if you keep practising the advanced techniques and the growth techniques, it is possible to surpass 2,000 within another three months, around 20 weeks in total. While few people achieve this, it is only because of other commitments and the fact that they are very happy with R.E. scores of around 600 to 800, which already makes reading much more fun, efficient and worthwhile.

SuperReading™ skills will save you around 20,000 hours in a typical career. Some people will save more time than that. Whether you are reading for pleasure, study, work, self-development or any other reason, these skills will bring both efficiency and pleasure to your efforts.

The key to success

The key to success in SuperReading™ is to follow the steps like you would a recipe for a cake. Reading the lessons doesn't take very long at all. Even with your present reading skills you could read all the lessons in an hour or two. It's not so much a question of knowing what's in this book; it's more about practising it. Most of the tools in the book you can simply read about and begin using straight away. However, the Eye-Hop™ exercises (you will find out about these in chapter 8) require 40 minutes of investment per day and will take between four to eight weeks to master. Once you've mastered them, the benefits will last you the rest of your life.

'Striving for success without hard work is like trying to harvest where you haven't planted.'

DAVID BLY

(politician and writer)

What if I don't like reading?

Some people on my courses hated reading. It seemed like hard work to them. They were looking to change that because their job required them to read volumes. Like them, probably the reason you don't like reading is that it has been difficult for you. It feels like work because, for you, it is work! I have observed people go from hating reading to loving it after doing the Super-Reading™ course. This is especially true for young people, though age is only a consideration if you allow it to be. The bottom line is that when you can do something really well with relatively little effort, you don't mind it so much. If you need to read, or at least understand how vital it can be to your success, your new skills can motivate you to do more and improve.

Now it all comes down to attitude. If you are open and willing to give it an honest go, you will see that reading can be fairly effortless and quite rewarding. Just hang in there and keep at it for a while. If you have a positive attitude it will open you up to more possibilities. Your brain will respond and give you a more positive experience.

'Your Attitude determines your Aptitude which determines your Altitude!'

BOB MOAWAD

(motivational speaker)

How will I know I'm progressing?

You may be wondering about what benchmarks or signs will be good indicators of your progress. You already know the timeframes of what to expect in terms of days, weeks and months. I realise we're living in a society that often expects instant gratification and results. Many of the skills in this book can work 'straight out of the box'. However, it depends on how you are doing at any particular moment. A tool that might get great results for you on Thursday may not have had the same effect on Tuesday. That is why it's so important to reserve judgement (I talk more about this in chapter 4). ALL of the tools in this book CAN work; the real questions will be which ones work best for you or which way they will work best for you.

CASE STUDY

The early groups I taught, back in the mid-1990s, were only tested on their reading speed on the first day of the course. Four weeks after her reading test one woman commented that she felt her speed hadn't increased much at all. Her reading speed felt the same to her, although she thought her comprehension was definitely greater. I gave her group another speed test at four weeks. Her speed had risen from 175 w.p.m. to 660 w.p.m. She was astounded. This happens because each day we 'normalise' to our new speed. She ended up reading novels from a speed of 800 w.p.m. to well over 1,000 w.p.m.

When we grow gradually we often cannot see the changes happening. If you've ever had the experience of not seeing a child for a year or two, and then you see them again, they look far bigger to you. To their parents the changes are less noticeable because they are with them every day. You may find the same experience with your reading. During classes I get reports from my students. They sometimes say how a colleague has commented on how quickly they are reading. Sometimes this takes them by surprise, as they have not noticed the change in their reading themselves.

This book comes with a set of tests that will help you to gauge your own progress in both speed and recall. The tests are quite rigorous and in different subjects, and will represent a fairly accurate estimate of your abilities. There is also another method, personal testing, which will test you on areas you already have an interest in (see page 68). You may find these results will be more rewarding and accurate. Mostly your scores will go up from week to week. Occasionally they go down, but don't worry; this is normal and may be due to a number of factors from sleep to stress to your interest in the subject, and whether you have recently begun a new reading skill. With all that in mind, you will be amazed how your scores do generally go up over time, despite all the factors that can affect reading.

The testing section will help you determine your present reading abilities. These tests are important; they will help you measure your progress. While skipping them would get you into the lessons more quickly, the lessons are only an hour away! I strongly recommend doing the testing.

What else is in this book?

This book will not only cover powerful reading skills, but also the power of attitude, affirmation, learning and memory. Let's start with attitude!

'Whether you think you can do a thing, or whether you think you can't, you're probably right!'

HENRY FORD

(founder of Ford Motor Company)

Your brain believes what you tell it. If you are convinced that you can do something, you are virtually unstoppable. If you are convinced that you will fail at something, your brain will find many creative ways *not to* succeed (in other words, fail). Think of this book as being like a recipe. Follow the instructions and the 'cake' will taste great. Leave out any of the ingredients, and it will not come out as you hoped. Here's my most important thought on that: given enough time and effort, you can become a super reader, absorbing information quickly, accurately and recalling it when you need to. The ONLY question is how long it will take you, not IF you can.

The other components of the book revolve around useful skills and tools such as developing your vocabulary, spellings, Info-Mapping™, note taking, visualising and setting goals. The more of these you employ, the sooner your reading and recall skills will grow to full potential. You may or may not see all the relationships between and among these various skill sets. Each one can help build others. For example, taking notes after you read will demonstrate to you how much more you are recalling. That feedback can enhance your attitude, which may help you accept some of the more esoteric concepts, such as visualisation and affirmation (see Chapter 12). Success with those may spur you to try developing another area you may not have otherwise considered. The more positive steps you take the better the results.

Why are SuperReading™ skills so important today?

In order to cope with today's reading demands you can't be using 19th-century skills. Email alone threatens to overwhelm many people. Unless you are immortal, you must budget your time. Why spend three hours reading a document when you could do a better job of it in one hour? Most of us have so much to do. We have projects on hold and more waiting in the wings after those. By investing a few hours following the techniques explained in this book you can save hundreds of hours per year. The average UK and US employee now spends an average of 15½ hours per week reading. That's up from 7½ hours per week in 1996. You can reclaim those lost hours with the skills you learn from this book. The next six weeks of your life will go by in a flash whether you do this or not. Imagine – had you started this a mere six weeks ago, today you would have read this far in less than half the time and actually remembered most of it!

'The illiterate of the 21st century will not be those who cannot read and write, but those who cannot learn, unlearn and relearn.'

ALVIN TOFFLER

(writer and futurist)

A part of you may well be wondering if you can really double your reading abilities. That may not seem possible. In fact, it's not only possible, it's inevitable. Once you understand how you will measure your progress it becomes clearer. Let's start with reading speed. Most people read around 150 to 200 words per minute (w.p.m.). Easy novels could be read from 200 to 300 w.p.m. or a bit faster (though with lower comprehension). Difficult textbooks could be 100 w.p.m. or slower. Taking 200 w.p.m. as an average, if you ended up reading similar material at 400 w.p.m., you would have doubled your speed. If you look at the speed charts in Appendix D, this will become clear.

Moving on to consider average comprehension/ recall, this is between 30 and 60 per cent at comfortable speeds (200 w.p.m.). Average comprehension/ recall above 320 w.p.m. will probably be quite low, around 20 to 40 per cent. When you boost that to 80 per cent comprehension after following the advice in this book, you've more than doubled your effectiveness again. Combining both figures means you've quadrupled it.

In short, this book will teach you the skills you need to absorb information in today's ever changing world of learning. Information content will change over time, but our brains and the basic way they function will not. Prepare to learn how to take better advantage of that wonderful brain of yours. No matter what you may have thought of it in the past, it has only performed to the level at which it was taught and programmed. You are about to take it to the next level with the right tools and a little encouragement. So listen well: YOU CAN DO THIS! You have been duly encouraged!

'There comes a moment when you realise that virtually anything is possible – that nothing is too good to be true.'

KOBI YAMADA

(CEO of Compendium Inc., a leading strategic communications company)

SUMMARY

- Anyone can greatly increase their reading abilities in just a few weeks, by following the advice in this book.

- You will have to put in some effort to achieving these improvements, but probably less than you think.

- If you have the right attitude you will do even better.

- Improved reading skills will allow you to read and understand more in less time, reducing stress and allowing you to recall more information.

- As Benjamin Franklin said, 'Time is money.'

2.

Overcoming your reading challenges

I want you to become a confident, excellent reader. This means that you are able to approach a reading 'assignment' intelligently and enthusiastically, getting all you need from it in a relatively short amount of time. Also, you will have the tools and ability to retain whatever you wish, for as long as you wish. And I want you to continue to use your improved skills so they will continue to improve. I want you to read anything and get the most you can from it in the least amount of time, and enjoy the process.

I do realise that you may have specific concerns or worries about your ability to benefit from this book. Before I go on to address some of these worries, I can honestly say that in 14 years of teaching people Super-Reading™ only one person on one of my courses has not been helped; a woman whose eye muscles had been badly damaged in a car crash and was unable to move her eyes without moving her head. So, unless you have similar serious eyesight issues, you will be able to benefit from this course. Indeed, you will be able to do brilliantly.

I can't anticipate all your concerns in this chapter, but here are some questions I am often asked by students before they take the course.

What if my eyesight is not all it should be?

 Reading is a visual art. If you can't see, you can't read. If you need corrective eyewear you should take care of this before starting the course. If your eyesight is a problem, you may not reap all the benefits you are otherwise capable of achieving. If you have any doubts at all about your eyesight, you should consider visiting a 'behavioural optometrist'. These are vision specialists who look for problems that may not be picked up by high street optometrists. They offer training classes that can solve problems such as:

- eyes tracking too far inwards or outwards
- eyes not focusing where you're looking
- sensitivity to certain wavelengths of light
- severe eye dominance (where the brain accepts only limited amounts of information from one eye in favour of the dominant eye).

Each of these problems can be 'fixed' with relative ease. There are other problems they can help with, which are more technical. These thorough eye exams can be especially important for children. In the UK, you can find specialists at the following website: www.babo.co.uk.

What *if* I read really slowly?

You may be wondering if this course can help you even if you're a really slow reader. The answer is yes it can and yes it will, as the following example shows:

CASE STUDY

A mother called me to ask about her daughter who was the slowest reader in her school. When all the other children had finished a reading assignment she was barely halfway through. To make it worse she had poor recall of the text. A friend whose son had been through the course was doing really well. The mother, a doctor, was about to have her daughter tested to check for learning disabilities and other possible problems. Before putting her through that the friend convinced her to give SuperReading™ a try. Luckily I was running a course that very weekend. Two weeks later this young girl was the fastest and best reader in her class, and three weeks later was the best in her school. After the course there was no question that she was the best and also no question that there was anything wrong with her. All she needed were some good tools, which did wonders for her self-image and she later improved in all subjects.

Being a slow reader is usually just a sign of poor reading tools. In the following chapters you will be learning simple tools that will have a profound impact on your reading. By adopting these tools and techniques you will speed up and get more out of your reading.

What if I'm a bit of a perfectionist?

Are you afraid you'll miss something if you go fast? While that is a legitimate concern, you need not worry. You will always be in control of your speed. You will NOT be like a car with the accelerator pedal stuck down. While there is virtue in being careful in order to get it right, soon your brain will be working faster by natural means. What will feel slow to you will be quite a bit faster than you read today. The difference is the skills you will develop between now and then. Remember the lady in chapter 1 who thought she wasn't reading any faster? She may have been just as careful as before. The fact is that you will be reading in a more focused and concentrated way. As your competence increases, you will be able to handle more material in less time while paying attention to detail. The difference is that you won't have to get stressed over it.

It's a good idea to let go of the concept of perfection. It is not attainable. It is a myth; a dangerous, frustrating and sometimes debilitating myth. Replace it with the concept of excellence, which can actually be achieved.

The key is in knowing when to stop. Once you've achieved excellence, walk away; you're finished. Besides, you know that all that extra effort you put into things isn't always appreciated by most people anyway. Only you know the difference.

> **ASSIGNMENT**
>
> For the next 21 days, be aware of when you have achieved excellence with projects you undertake. Once you get there, say to yourself, 'I have achieved enough with this. I'm going to let it go now and watch the consequences.' Track your projects and see what happens.

What if I tend to drift off when reading?

Do you drift off a lot while you are reading? Do you keep losing the plot and sometimes have to reread entire sections? Help is on the way. There are two tools that you will get in the first couple of lessons in the book – pointing and previewing (see pages 75 and 92) – that will virtually eliminate that phenomenon, which I call 'distracted reader syndrome'. One of the causes of this syndrome is reading too slowly. Your brain believes it can multitask and think about other things. It has learned how to fool you into thinking you are reading by pronouncing the words in your head but not processing them deeply. This book will help you become more aware and keep your focus.

What if I am already a fast reader?

What if you believe you are already a fast reader? What can this book do for you? In fact, fast readers are often poor recallers. I've had loads of people join a course because the company needed more delegates to justify the cost. Some people came in believing they were already superior readers. What they found was that they had high speed, but low comprehension and recall. They would argue that for their job all they needed to do was scan material for a few important points and they had become very good at that. Others felt they were 'very fast readers' and didn't really need to learn anything more, but they felt it might be handy to pick up a pointer or two.

What they realised was that they had probably missed some important points over the years by skimming instead of reading. They were able to achieve even higher speeds while increasing their comprehension and recall. They were previously unaware that their recall had been so low.

What if I have dyslexia or other learning challenges?

I've had many people in my classes with dyslexia, dyspraxia and other barriers to reading/learning. I have seen them all make significant progress in their reading and recalling abilities. While some of them have not achieved as highly as non-dyslexic delegates overall, two things were fairly consistent. One was that their 'ratio of improvement' was on par with non-challenged learners. That is to say, if most people saw a five-fold increase in their overall abilities from their starting point, so did people with learning challenges. The other interesting factor is that most of the dyslexic learners ended up with higher numerical scores than non-challenged readers without SuperReading™ skills.

In a 2008 study of adult dyslexic students at London South Bank University, they all saw significant improvement as a result of taking the SuperReading™ course. One of the surprising findings was that those coming in with the poorest abilities saw some of the largest gains.

Here is an interesting quote from Dr Ross Cooper, principal lecturer LLU+, London Southbank University: 'When we piloted SuperReading™ with a group of dyslexic students at London Southbank University, their reading effectiveness more than doubled in ten weeks. I have known nothing like it. I have always advocated individual support for dyslexic students, but this impact was achieved in a group of 15. Just imagine how much better their university learning experience would have been had they completed the course before starting their studies.'

How SuperReading™ overcomes the problems of 'standard reading'

The way we were taught to read at school (known as 'standard reading') is adequate, but it is not effective enough for today's informational demands. Whether people are taught 'phonics' or 'real reading', the methods of reading that are taught in most schools as a standard have inherent problems concerning concentration, comprehension and retention. The so-called information superhighway implies high speed and high volume; but we are limited by our ability to absorb the information we need in the time we have available. The following pitfalls hold us back. My feeling is that knowing and understanding these pitfalls will aid you in overcoming them.

'He who has a why can endure any how.'

FRIEDRICH NIETZSCHE

1. Unconscious and conscious regression
Regression means 'to go back'. Both conscious and unconscious regression cause problems for readers but the techniques of SuperReading™ can deal with both effectively.

Unconscious regression

We may believe that our eyes track straight across the page when we read, but special sensors reveal that the eyes can wander as much as 18 times per minute. This is known as unconscious regression and is a source of poor concentration, since we are 'reading' in one place while our eyes look in another place. You will learn two tools (pointing and previewing in chapters 6 and 7) that will help you overcome this regression.

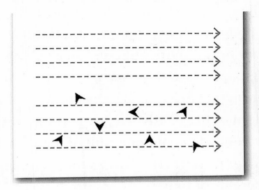

Unconscious regression

Conscious regression

Another form of regression occurs when we stop, back up and read something we have just read (or tried to read). While this makes some sense for a standard reader, it really holds us back from having higher comprehension. The same two tools of pointing and previewing referred to above will help with this form of regression as well.

The quick brown fox jumps over the lazy dog.

2. Reading word by word

While reading one word at a time was necessary in our earliest days at school, nobody ever told us how to progress on to reading multiple words at a time. One problem with reading word by word is that our eyes get tired! The eye muscles are among the weakest in the human body and when they must refocus with every word, they begin to tire. SuperReading™ teaches you to read in groups of words at a single glance – and get all the meaning! (See chapter 8.) Over time, you will learn to read four or five words at a glance (or more), so your eyes need only do about one-fifth of the work required for standard reading. This means that you can read for longer periods of time.

3. Sub-vocalisation

Pronouncing the words we are reading in our head is known as sub-vocalisation. This is a limitation because we cannot read and comprehend well much faster than we can speak, and top speech speed for most humans is about 300 w.p.m. By reading four or five words at a glance using SuperReading™ techniques, the brain gives up on trying to 'say' the words, and simply understands the meaning without pronouncing them all. When you are able to read several words at once, you will notice that as your speed goes up, so too does your comprehension. This would seem to defy logic, but only with your present reading tools. When you can see and understand a group of words at a time, you are able to engage more of your 'right brain', which is capable of tremendous understanding.

In the 1960s experiments showed that the two sides of the human brain were responsible for different functions. It was discovered that information from your left eye goes to your right brain, and information from your right eye goes to your left brain, with the optic nerves crossing one another behind your forehead. It seems that your left brain is mostly verbal, logical, numerical and serial, while your right brain is pictorial, spatial, holistic, creative, non-linear, musical, arty, intuitive and emotional. Most people tend towards one or the other. The ideal is to have balance or synergy between the two. People who combine right-brain inspiration with left-brain logic often transcend ordinary accomplishments. Celebrated examples would be Leonardo da Vinci, Einstein and Michelangelo. By using their whole brain, they were able to think in ways other people found difficult or impossible. When you read using more of your right brain you have a fuller experience of the text. Stories come alive when you are able to see and experience a book. Business reading can improve as well. Indeed, any experience where you can involve both sides of the brain will be positively enhanced.

4. Poor vocabulary

> **ARE YOU FAMILIAR WITH THE WORDS IN BOLD?**
>
> **Sargute** – shrewd
>
> **Ascesis** – self-discipline
>
> **Cromulent** – acceptable
>
> **Freck** – to move quickly
>
> **Halcyon** – calm
>
> **Redolent** – fragrant

If you don't understand enough of the words you read, your comprehension will suffer. SuperReading™ has a system to help you record, understand and recall new words. (See pages 241–2.) Vocabulary is an important area of life. People judge us by the words we use. Your ability to think is either helped or hampered by your vocabulary. If you don't know a word you cannot think of that concept in order to solve a problem or express a point. Building up a resource of useful words will help you become a better reader (and writer as well).

5. Poor organisation

Most people simply pick up a book and start reading. When they reach the end they put it down and move on to something else. They employ no effective strategies for extracting the information they need and remembering anything that is vital. SuperReading™ teaches

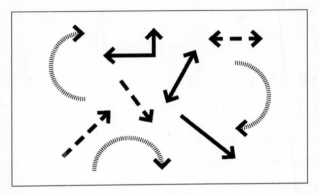

Poor organisation

you strategies to improve your organisation, including a few minutes of eye exercises each day.

6. Poor attitude

Many people believe themselves to be poor readers and worry that there's little that can be done to fix their situation. They may even tell themselves and others what a slow reader they are. Some people become cynical, and do not believe that new tools can help them. These people can be their own worst enemy. They may have tried some things before and found them to less helpful than expected. Usually, they have not reserved judgement (see pages 44–7) and thereby not given those tools adequate practice.

Please note: I've taught thousands of people, and can confirm those who doubt either themselves or the tools end up performing the most poorly. Negative attitudes yield negative results. People who expect to do well (and persist) tend to accomplish more, and in less time.

'The only disability in life is a bad attitude.'

SCOTT HAMILTON
(Olympic ice skater)

Another important point is that for many people, their greatest progress comes towards the end of the course. Once again, please reserve judgement on your skills and on your progress until the end of the book.

'The key to everything is patience. You get the chicken by hatching the egg, not by smashing it.'

ARNOLD H. GLASOW
(frequently quoted humour writer)

SUMMARY

- You will have a few challenges to overcome before you can become a super reader, potentially ranging from problems with your eyesight to a poor attitude, but follow the advice in this book and you will succeed.

- The only thing you don't know exactly is how many weeks it will take you (but note, I am not saying months or years).

- Using the tools in this book will help you overcome just about any challenge you will face in your quest to be a super reader. Just stay with it, be patient and you will succeed.

3.

Before you begin

believe it's important to understand how you learn things. With that knowledge you can look out for learning opportunities that play to your strengths. You can also put some effort into bolstering the areas in which you are weak. This is useful because often it's not possible to control how information is presented to us. We must take it as it comes.

There are many different types of learners, and there are two main ways to determine the type of learner you are: the psychological and the physical. Let's look at the psychological first.

The psychology of learning

There is a spectrum of attitudes among learners, ranging from people who are not interested in learning at all to people who are very eager to learn, understand the benefits and put in every effort to master a new skill regardless of any obstacles. They jump in with both feet and are certain that they will conquer this new thing. Most people fall somewhere in between the two extremes. Near the top are people who understand and appreciate the benefits of SuperReading™ and are looking forward to giving it a go. Near the bottom are people who are very sceptical and are tempted to abandon ship at the first setback or when they realise it might take a lot of time or effort. In between are those who are sceptical but rather hopeful. It goes without saying that the people at the lower end of the spectrum make life much harder for themselves. Their cynical views hamper their ability to learn (see the brain scan experiment on page 221).

Where do you fit on the psychology of learning scale?

1 Not interested in learning (prisoner to your past experience/beliefs)
2 Very sceptical, but will take a small chance
3 Sceptical, but hopeful
4 Fairly confident, need to experience it
5 Fairly committed, only vague doubts
6 Appreciate benefits, will give it a go
7 Very eager, will master new skills no matter what (take no prisoners).

It is really important to work out where you are on the psychology of learning scale. If your attitude isn't right, the rest hardly matters. As you will soon learn, your brain will work to the capability in which you believe in yourself. The skills in this book are not rocket science. While innovative, they are really quite simple. As simple as they are, a cleverly cynical brain can usually find a way to sabotage just about anything. Only your attitude that this can work (by putting in enough good effort) can save you from the fate of the truly cynical. Their fate is to miss out on the best skills and abilities because they did not give themselves a fair chance to embody them.

Visual, audio and kinaesthetic (VAK) learning

When it comes to the physical aspects of learning people are divided into visual, audio and kinaesthetic learners. Visual people learn mainly through their eyes. The world makes sense to them when they can **see** the meaning or how something works. Audio (or aural) people **hear** how things work. There are two kinds of audio learners: analogue and digital. Analogue audio people learn by hearing sounds from outside their body. Digital audio people learn by repeating what they hear outside internally using their 'inner voice'. Kinaesthetic people must **touch or experience** something in order to learn it well. They learn best by doing. They can also experience the emotional aspects of what they are learning.

The representational system preference test

This brief quiz (also known as the Rep Test) will give you an indication of how your brain likes to process information from your environment. There will be more explanation after you answer the five questions. Please read the instructions very carefully.

For each of the following statements, please place a number next to every phrase. Use the following system to indicate your preferences:

  4 ....Closest to describing you

  3 ....Next best description

  2 ....Next best

  1 ....Least descriptive of you

Use all four numbers in each of the five sections – there are NO ties in a section.

1. **I make important decisions based on:**

   ....gut-level feelings

   ....which way sounds best

   ....what looks best to me

   ....precise review and study of the issues

2. **During an argument, I am most likely to be influenced by:**

   ....the other person's tone of voice

   ....whether or not I can see the other person's argument

.............the logic of the other person's argument

.............whether or not I feel I am in touch with the other person's true feelings

3.   I most easily communicate what is going on with me by:

.............the way I dress and look

.............the feelings I share

.............the words I choose

.............the tone of my voice

4.   It is easier for me to:

.............find the ideal volume and tuning on a stereo system

.............select the most intellectually relevant point concerning an interesting subject

.............select the most comfortable furniture

.............select rich, attractive colour combinations

5..............I am very attuned to the sounds of my environment

.............I am very adept at making sense of new facts and data

.............I am very sensitive to the way articles of clothing feel on my body

.............I have a strong response to colours and to the way a room looks

Now bring down your values and write them in for each question:

1: _____	2: _____	3: _____	4: _____	5: _____
K _____	A _____	V _____	A _____	A _____
A _____	V _____	K _____	D _____	D _____
V _____	D _____	D _____	K _____	K _____
D _____	K _____	A _____	V _____	V _____

Now add up the values for each letter (add all the 'Vs' together, then all the 'Ks', etc.)

V.................... Visual   K....................Kinaesthetic
A.................... Analogue Audio   D....................Digital Audio

Interpreting the Rep Test

The questions in the Rep Test were designed to discover what kinds of information your brain prefers to use to understand the world. For example, how do you get your news each day? You have choices of newspapers, TV, radio, friends, the internet, cable and satellite broadcasts. Which do you prefer? If that was not available, what would your second choice be? And your third choice? Any of those choices will tell you what's happening, but you will prefer one choice over another. The Rep Test will tell you which sensory modality you tend to prefer. Now, read on to see what your scores tell you about how you like to learn. The first three answers tell you about your intuitive nature and the last two tell you about your physical relationship to the environment.

V stands for Visual. This is information that comes in through your eyes.

K stands for Kinaesthetic. This involves a combination of emotional feelings and body awareness.

A stands for Analogue Audio. Take your fingers and make a tapping sound on your table or desk. That tapping caused the molecules in the table to vibrate. They in turn caused the air molecules to vibrate. That reached your inner ear and caused your eardrum to vibrate. Those vibrations became nerve impulses and reached your brain. At that moment you experienced the sound. 'A' stands for the sounds that are outside of you in the environment.

D stands for Digital Audio. Right now, sing to yourself the words to 'Happy Birthday'. Did you hear it in your head? Yes? That is Digital Audio. You experienced hearing, but the 'sound' did not originate in the outside environment (with vibrating air molecules). It started and ended inside your head. That is very different from Analogue Audio, which is a more passive experience.

What the scores indicate:
Anything **12 and above** is significant.
Anything **16 and above** is highly significant.
Anything **19 and above** is rare. With these scores you

are so dominated by that mode that special allowances should be made. You have so much dependence in that area of input that it can be seen as both a real advantage when available and a possible handicap when denied. For example, a person who has a very high Visual score and a very low Audio score will have a difficult time learning in a classroom where lecture is the only delivery method.

A score of 7 or below is relatively rare. It would almost seem that the brain is avoiding that mode for some reason. Remember, there is a default of 5 even if a mode scores last in all 5 categories!

Over time your scores can change. You can train yourself in any area and your brain will respond by giving that mode a chance. This is especially true of Visual and Kinaesthetic learning. You can train your Visual mode by using the picture visualisation technique (see page 192).

Most importantly, remember that this test indicates your preference. Even a score of 10 or less does not necessarily mean you are not good at that skill. It simply means that skill or modality is not your brain's first choice when it goes about interpreting the world. It's only a rule of thumb. Do NOT get carried away with this test. Always see your outcomes as advantages.

ASSIGNMENT

Taking into consideration what you have learned about how you learn, make one change per day about how you take in information, either in reading, listening or observing. For example, if you are a kinaesthetic learner, a hands-on course would be better for you than a lecture only. You learn primarily by doing, touching and trying. If you are primarily an audio person, a lecture is fine, as you can easily interpret words and do not need to experience a concept to understand it.

SUMMARY

- Knowing what kind of learner you are is an advantage to a super reader; you can learn to play to your strengths.

- If you are a visual learner, sit at the front of the class or lecture theatre. Whatever the teacher puts on the board will be inspiring and stimulating to you.

- If you are more of an analogue audio learner, you can sit further back, as long as you can hear what the teacher is saying.

- If you are a kinaesthetic learner, try to find courses that supply hands-on experience. You will learn better by touching, doing and manipulating objects.

- If you are digital audio, you need to be able to repeat things to yourself verbally. You could also verbally explain the material to someone else. You work best when you can hear your voice in your head.

4.

Reserving judgement and setting goals

The purpose of this chapter is to instil in you an open mind and a willingness to stretch beyond your present understandings and limitations. That is what the concept of reserving judgement is all about and why it is so important to SuperReading™ success. Once you have got to grips with reserving judgement it's time to set yourself some goals and really put your new-found commitment into practice. The concept of ideation or brainstorming is also useful for generating ideas and stretching yourself.

Reserving judgement

 Imagine you are going on a voyage across the sea. You leave port and set sail for a distant land. You're out there on the vast, open waters. You're making good time, but it's a big ocean! There are days and days of nothing but sea and sky. Finally, you spot land and make port soon after. Dry land at last! Thinking back, you realise that

for 99 per cent of your voyage you could not see your destination! You had charts and a compass, but until you actually saw the land, and the desired port, there was no other real proof that things were going well.

Achieving something can be much the same as that sea voyage. Very often we can't see any perceptible change or progress until we're near the end, and then suddenly it's there. We realise that we have achieved what we set out to do. Faith and persistence have helped many people achieve seemingly impossible tasks.

Learning a new skill can also be compared to a sea voyage. Or consider a ten-month-old child learning to walk. They have bumbled around for weeks or months barely able to stand. They wobble and fall many times. Then, one day, suddenly, they're walking! Before they know it they're running! A child learning to walk is the perfect example of faith and persistence in action, and it will be helpful to remember this mindset as you go through the book.

New skills take time and even when you master a skill it may be that you do not see its apparent benefit right away. You have to keep on going long enough to give it a fair chance to work for you. This is where the concept of reserving judgement really comes into play. If you're feeling that a new skill is not paying off, you're being prematurely judgemental and not giving it adequate time to work for you.

There is no substitute for experience. Intellectually understanding something is not the same as doing the thing. You will receive the most benefit from this book if you reserve your judgement and keep practising the skills. Although you can be taking tests each week, the time for measuring your full progress is after you have absorbed and mastered all the skills. Arguing with the ideas presented here will not help you. Indeed, some of these ideas may defy your traditional sense of logic. However, if you learn these ideas and push ahead with them, they will benefit you for the rest of your life. Only by practice, persistence and finally mastery will these skills have a lasting, positive impact on your life. So relax and enjoy the voyage.

Contract with yourself

Before you go any further, take a look at the following contract, which defines what is meant by reserving judgement, and if you want to go further, sign it now!

I understand the significance of practising a specific new skill for at least 21 days (or 21 times) before I decide whether it is valuable to me.

I declare my willingness and determination to fully apply each new skill that I learn.

I declare that I will practise each new skill with enthusiasm and diligence for at least 21 days in a row, and then and only then consider its effectiveness.

SIGNATURE ....

DATE ....

ASSIGNMENT

After you have signed your contract with yourself, for the next 21 days carry a card with you that says, 'I am reserving judgement.' Look at it at least five times per day and jot down notes about the times you have found it helpful. After the 21 days are up, write down your thoughts about the assignment you have just carried out. In what areas of your life did reserving judgement make a difference? You may be surprised how effective it is and how often it can come into play.

Setting goals

 It is very important to have goals, both in life and, more specifically for the purposes of this book, in your reading. Those people who regularly set clear goals and keep after them tend to achieve them. In my work as a personal coach, the first thing I do is get people to write down what it is that they want to achieve. I suggest you do the same.

The categories listed below are suggestions for the kinds of things you can look forward to reading. Simply write down a list of all the things you would like to either become an expert in or would just like to know more about. Whenever you hear about a book or subject that intrigues you set it down as a goal to preview (for more on this see page 99) or read.

You can put a time frame to it if you like. You may

want to put down those things you would like to read in the next six months, in the next two years and the next five years. If you like, you can also prioritise your reading, not just by dates but by letters. Give a rating of 'A' to the books that are of most importance in your life now. Give a 'B' to those that are significant but not critical. Give a 'C' to those that you'll get to some day. You can put both a deadline for completing a book and one for starting the book. Sometimes the start dates hold more power than the end dates! Keep referring back to your list at least once a week. Every day is even better if you can manage it.

When you have read them, take notes on these materials using the note-taking method explained on page 147–151. You can keep a separate notebook for all the things you have learned. It feels good when you can check off a book you had written down for reading. As the months go by you will be surprised at how many books you will have read using these methods. And with SuperReading™, you will have really read them!

When goal setting, the rule is:

Be brave,
Be bold,
Believe.

Then be relentless.

Reading goals

Write down goals for what you would like to read in the months and years ahead. Draw up a list of books, magazines, journals and authors you are particularly interested in. You could make an Info-Map™ (see chapter 10) of your ideas and add to it as you come across more reading materials that you would like to read. With each, write down a start date and a completion date. Check them off as you complete them!

Here are some headings to get you started:

- Autobiographies
- Biographies
- How-to
- Inspirational
- Self-development
- Spiritual

And don't forget to include subjects relating to your own particular hobbies and interests.

> 'You must have long-range goals to keep you from being frustrated by short-range failures.'

CHARLES C. NOBLE

(former Dean of Syracuse University, 1946)

ASSIGNMENT

Review your goals in the first 30 minutes of your day and in the last 30 minutes of your day. That's all you need to do. Actions will follow automatically.

Ideation

Ideation (formerly known as brainstorming) has been around for a long time, and is a useful tool to help you generate ideas. Start with a blank sheet of paper. Visualise it full of great ideas, and then begin to write. Extend two lines out from every idea (whether you use the idea or not). Do not judge whether a thought is good or not. Just write it down. To get to buried treasure, you must dig through loads of dirt. Most of what you come up with will be fairly useless, but that's OK and is expected. As two-time Nobel Prize winner Linus Pauling said, 'To have a great idea you must have many ideas.'

You can fill several pages this way. If you feel you've run out of ideas, visualise more, then put pen to paper and start it moving again. More ideas will come to you. When your first piece of ideation is finally complete, circle the best ideas. You can take those and repeat the process on another page! The more you do this the better you get.

Here are the six simple steps to successful ideation:

1 Be clear about your purpose, like how to increase your profits, or perhaps planning a themed party.
2 Visualise a page (or pages) full of ideas.
3 Start writing.
4 Go fast – put down whatever comes to mind.
5 Do not judge any of it.
6 When you are finished, visualise; put pen to paper and start writing more. The 'starting writing' will encourage more ideas to come forth.

ASSIGNMENT

Do at least one ideation session per week on various topics that either interest you or are part of your projects.

What if I'm still a bit sceptical?

Not to worry. I'm going to share a concept with you, which when you master it could change your life. First I'm going to ask you a possibly painful question. How many skills or ideas have you heard or experienced in your life that you felt would be of great benefit to you? How many of those are you not using on a consistent basis? Most people roll their eyes and let out a sigh. The fact is that we try things and then somehow lose track of them and forget them. Months or years can go by until we are reminded about them. We wonder what happened. We started out excited and eager to use them. Somewhere along the way they were lost. How did that happen?

One reason it happened is because we never really took these ideas to our hearts. They never became 'second nature'. Why? There are a couple of reasons. One possibility is that our 'comfort zone' never expanded to embrace it. This is the part of the mind that accepts something as a normal part of who we are, that is consistent with who we believe we are at an unconscious level. Comfort zones cover many different areas of life: wealth, relationships, fashion, cars, praise, tidiness, noise, violence, humour, physical contact and many more.

Another reason we lose track of skills is that we tried them but they didn't work fast enough for us. Some things take time to master before we get the kinds of results we were promised. This is especially true if the skill in question is far outside our comfort zone! In fact, there is often a direct relationship between how far outside the zone it is and how good it would be for us.

It turns out that we must practise such new skills consistently over a long enough period of time for them to feel natural to us. Interestingly, the minimum number of days (the magical 21) it takes for something new in our life to feel normal is fairly cross-cultural. This concept was first put forward by Dr Maxwell Maltz in his book *Psycho-cybernetics*, written in 1960.

SUMMARY

- Give yourself a fair chance to master each skill.

- Set goals for the subjects and authors you want to read.

- Practise ideation on topics that interest you.

- Be patient and keep at it. Remember you need to practise your new skills over a long enough period of time that they feel like 'second nature'.

5.

Testing your reading effectiveness

Testing your abilities is one of the keystones to success in SuperReading™. This is done by checking your reading effectiveness (R.E.) level before starting the course and at intervals as you work your way through the book. That is what this chapter is about. Whenever you take a test you learn something about yourself that goes beyond the scores.

At one time the only reading comprehension tests available used multiple-choice questions to determine comprehension and recall. The 'fill in the blank' tests I have devised are a far more accurate assessment of memory and comprehension skills. These tests are tough!

How to test yourself

The first thing you need to do is find out what your present reading effectiveness (R.E.) level is. You will be measuring both your speed and your comprehension/recall. You will do this by reading a 400-word essay and answering ten questions about it. Afterwards, you will repeat the same steps again. At that point you will correct the tests, and look up your speed and R.E. on the tables in Appendix D. You will find one test in this chapter and there are others in Appendix B.

When reading the test essay, please read it for comprehension. Do not try to go fast. Read at your normal speed, knowing there will be fill-in-the-blank questions to answer when you've finished. Do not look at the questions on the essay until you come to answer them. You will have to time yourself on the reading in minutes and seconds.

Read every word of the essay. Read through it once. When you are done, check your time. Immediately record your time. For example, if you take 2 minutes and 14 seconds; write down 2:14. Now move on to the questions. If you cannot recall an answer after about 20 seconds, let it go. How long would you keep trying to remember a fact in a conversation before moving on to the next point? When you have answered the ten questions, turn the page and read the essay a second time (time yourself again). When you are finished, record your time and then answer all the questions again.

When you read the essay for the second time, try to learn enough to get 100 per cent on the re-test. (Remember that you only time your reading of the essay. You do NOT time yourself answering the questions.)

Remember:

- Do not look back at the essay when answering the questions
- Spelling doesn't matter in this instance
- Read through the essay once for the first test. Do not go back over it before answering the questions.

SUMMARY

- Read for comprehension.

- Time your reading for both test and re-test in minutes and seconds.

- It's not an 'open book test' – you must recall your answers from memory.

- Questions are not timed.

Testing phobia

Do you tend to freeze up or get anxious when you take tests? Does the very word 'test' fill you with dread? Do you feel wary when it comes to testing? If any of the above applies to you, relax! It's OK – really. Whatever happens on the tests is fine. Your scores will probably increase over time. As you realise that your reading ability is getting better, you will not mind testing so much. You may even find that you look forward to it. Whatever happens with the tests, it's all irrelevant compared to your daily reading abilities. Those will certainly improve whether the tests reflect that or not. Consider this: if you had a choice between having great reading skills and doing well on these tests, which would you choose? Of course, most people would choose having great reading skills. Having the tests confirm that is just icing on the cake. Relax and see what happens. Never let your test scores deter you from using the techniques. Also, do not become over-confident if your test scores skyrocket. That can be almost as dangerous as getting discouraged if they fall.

What about erratic scores?
Most of the time, you will find that your scores go up. However, that may not always be the case as there are many factors that can affect them adversely.

Why would they go up and down? There are a variety of reasons, including:

- your interest in the material
- how much sleep you've had
- whether or not you are eating a balanced diet
- your present stress levels
- the time of day
- the day of the week
- environmental distractions
- how many deadlines you have
- whether you are ill or becoming ill
- relationship challenges.

Or perhaps your scores dip because you are using a new skill or technique. Skills take time to develop and sometimes you may be using a relatively new skill that has not come to full power for you. If you have your eye on the big picture, a dip in your scores now and then is nothing to be concerned about.

If you do find your R.E. score has dropped, you can take more than one action. You can check to see that you are on track in learning and adopting new skills. You can go over the list of items that can interfere with reading. Or, you can simply think of it as a blip and look forward to an increase in your score in following tests.

I know that SuperReading™ is a rock-solid, logical reading improvement method. You *will* get better and better in your abilities. Always remember the big picture and don't worry about any temporary setbacks. You will rise above them and be brilliant.

Testing and English as a second language

If your first language is not English, your vocabulary may hold back your scores for a while. Be aware of this possibility as you take tests and perhaps see your scores go down once or twice. If your scores have been good and then suddenly dip, it may well be due to not understanding all the words in a particular essay. Stopping to work out the meaning of a word will count against you, as the clock is running and your reading time is half the formula for determining your reading effectiveness score. This is worth remembering because all the tests are on different subjects and you cannot tell in advance which ones may give you more of a vocabulary challenge.

If English is not your first language you should not get discouraged and remember that you need to keep your eye on the big picture even more than native English speakers.

Scoring yourself

Now that you know all about the theory behind testing, the next topic to look at before you embark upon the tests themselves is scoring. Remember that you do not score your tests until you have completed both the test and the re-test.

Here's how to score your tests:

1 When you get an answer totally correct, either in the test or the re-test, give yourself a score of 10.
2 Give yourself a zero when you get an answer wrong or leave it blank. Numerical answers must be totally correct or you score zero.
3 Score 5 for a partially correct answer. For example, if the correct answer is 'Alexander Fleming', you get 5 points for 'Fleming' and 10 points for 'Alexander Fleming'.
4 Add up your numbers – this gives you your comprehension score. For example, 70 points represents 70 per cent comprehension.

5 Turn to Appendix D. In the left column of the
   table, look up the time you noted down for your
   reading, both for the test and then for the re-test.
   The number immediately to the right of your
   reading time is your words per minute (w.p.m.)
   score. Make a note of this.

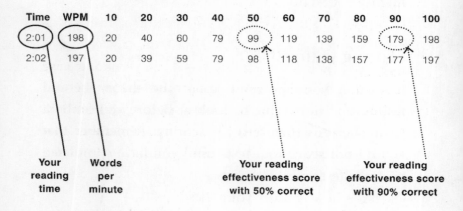

Time	WPM	10	20	30	40	50	60	70	80	90	100
2:01	198	20	40	60	79	99	119	139	159	179	198
2:02	197	20	39	59	79	98	118	138	157	177	197

Your   Words   Your reading   Your reading
reading   per   effectiveness score   effectiveness score
time   minute   with 50% correct   with 90% correct

How to find your reading effectiveness (R.E.) score

6 The numbers across the top of the chart refer to
   your comprehension score, or number of correct
   answers. If, for example, you got five answers
   correct (5 x a score of 10), follow down the 50
   column until it meets the row your time is on.
   The number where the column and row meet is
   your reading effectiveness (R.E.) score. If your
   score on a test is an odd number, such as 75, then
   your R.E. score would be the figure between 70
   and 80. You will need to calculate that for your-

self. For example, if your reading time was 2 minutes and 4 seconds and you scored 75 points, your R.E. score would be halfway between 135 and 155, i.e. 145.

You can test yourself either once a week or fortnightly. After you have worked through all the techniques in the book (this should take from six to eight weeks) you can test yourself monthly or even quarterly. Once a test has been read you should not use it again. Although, after you have followed the steps in this book, you would be surprised at how little you recall from your first tests, because your skills were low at the beginning.

Reading test 1

The first test follows. Further tests are in Appendix B and you can take them in any order. You will need a stopwatch (to count minutes and seconds) and a pen or pencil. Start your stopwatch; then begin to read. No note taking!

Test 1: Biography of George Stephenson

George Stephenson was a British engineer who designed a famous and historically important steam-powered locomotive named Rocket. He is known as the father of British steam railways.

George Stephenson was born in Wylam, England,

west of Newcastle upon Tyne. Stephenson grew up near the Wylam coal mine, and in 1802 began working there as an engine-man. For ten years his knowledge of steam engines increased, until in 1812 he stopped operating them for a living, and started building them.

Stephenson designed his first locomotive in 1814, a travelling engine designed for hauling coal. Named Blucher, it could haul 30 tons of coal in a load, and was the first successful flanged-wheel locomotive. That means it was the first locomotive to use flanged wheels to rest on the track. Over the next five years, he built sixteen more engines.

As his success grew, Stephenson was hired to build an 8-mile railway from Hetton to Sunderland. The finished line used a combination of gravity pulling the load down inclines and locomotives for level and uphill stretches. It was the first ever railway to use no animal power at all.

In 1821, a project began to build the Stockton and Darlington Railway. Originally the plan was to use horses to draw coal carts over metal rails. Stephenson convinced company director Edward Pease to change the plans. Three years later Stephenson completed the first locomotive for the new railroad. It was at first named Active, but later renamed Locomotion. Driven by Stephenson himself, Locomotion hauled an 80-ton load of coal and flour for nine miles, reaching a top speed of 24 miles per hour. The first purpose-built passenger carriage, dubbed Experiment, was also attached, and held a load of dignitaries for the opening journey. It was the first time passenger traffic had ever been run on a steam-driven locomotive railway.

While building the S&D line, Stephenson had noticed that even small inclines significantly reduced the speed of the locomotives. Even slight declines made the primitive brakes almost useless. He concluded that railways should be kept as level as possible. On future railways he executed a series of difficult cuts, embankments and stone viaducts to smooth the route.

As the Liverpool and Manchester line approached completion in 1829, a competition was held to decide who would build the locomotives. Stephenson's entry was Rocket, and its impressive victory made it the most famous machine in the world.

Note down your reading time; then answer the questions on the next page:

TIME ....

QUESTIONS

Biography of George Stephenson

1. In what city was Stephenson born?
2. How long did Stephenson work at the coal mine?
3. What was the name of Stephenson's first locomotive?
4. What kind of wheels did his first locomotive have?
5. On the Hetton to Sunderland line, what did Stephenson use for pulling loads down declines?
6. Who was director of the Stockton and Darlington Railway?
7. Stephenson named an engine Active. Later, the name was changed to what?
8. What was the name of the first passenger carriage run on a steam railway?
9. Name one feature Stephenson used after building the Stockton and Darlington line to keep the railways level.
10. What was the name of the most famous machine in the world (at that time)?

Now go to the next page and read the article again.

Time yourself!

Test 1: Biography of George Stephenson

George Stephenson was a British engineer who designed a famous and historically important steam-powered locomotive named Rocket. He is known as the father of British steam railways.

George Stephenson was born in Wylam, England, west of Newcastle upon Tyne. Stephenson grew up near the Wylam coal mine, and in 1802 began working there as an engine-man. For ten years his knowledge of steam engines increased, until in 1812 he stopped operating them for a living, and started building them.

Stephenson designed his first locomotive in 1814, a travelling engine designed for hauling coal. Named Blucher, it could haul 30 tons of coal in a load, and was the first successful flanged-wheel locomotive. That means it was the first locomotive to use flanged wheels to rest on the track. Over the next five years, he built sixteen more engines.

As his success grew, Stephenson was hired to build an 8-mile railway from Hetton to Sunderland. The finished line used a combination of gravity pulling the load down inclines and locomotives for level and uphill stretches. It was the first ever railway to use no animal power at all.

In 1821, a project began to build the Stockton and Darlington Railway. Originally the plan was to use horses to draw coal carts over metal rails. Stephenson convinced company director Edward Pease to change the plans. Three years later Stephenson completed the first locomotive for the new railroad. It was at first named Active, but later renamed Locomotion. Driven by Stephenson himself, Locomotion hauled an 80-ton load of coal and flour for nine miles, reaching a top speed of 24 miles per hour. The first purpose-built passenger carriage, dubbed Experiment, was also attached, and held a load of dignitaries for the opening journey. It was the first time passenger traffic had ever been run on a steam-driven locomotive railway.

While building the S&D line, Stephenson had noticed that even small inclines significantly reduced the speed of the locomotives. Even slight declines made the primitive brakes almost useless. He concluded that railways should be kept as level as possible. On future railways he executed a series of difficult cuts, embankments and stone viaducts to smooth the route.

As the Liverpool and Manchester line approached completion in 1829, a competition was held to decide who would build the locomotives. Stephenson's entry was Rocket, and its impressive victory made it the most famous machine in the world.

Note down your reading time; then answer the questions on the next page:

TIME ....

QUESTIONS

Biography of George Stephenson

1. In what city was Stephenson born?
2. How long did Stephenson work at the coal mine?
3. What was the name of Stephenson's first locomotive?
4. What kind of wheels did his first locomotive have?
5. On the Hetton to Sunderland line, what did Stephenson use for pulling loads down declines?
6. Who was director of the Stockton and Darlington Railway?
7. Stephenson named an engine Active. Later, the name was changed to what?
8. What was the name of the first passenger carriage run on a steam railway?
9. Name one feature Stephenson used after building the Stockton and Darlington line to keep the railways level.
10. What was the name of the most famous machine in the world (at that time)?

Now go to page 301 in Appendix B and get the answers.

Grade yourself! On page 322 there is a graph on which you can record your scores so you can chart your improvement over time at a glance.

If your score was low, don't despair. *How to Be a Super Reader* will help you improve.

The personal testing method

I also recommend testing yourself in a less formal manner. Using reading material that you read often, like a journal, book or other source, time yourself reading for a specific number of minutes (from three to eight). Then put the reading material aside and write down everything you remember from the text. Then count the number of lines you read and write that on your answer sheet. Revisit similar material six weeks later and read for the same amount of time. Just make sure there is more material there than today, because you will get further than you did today. You could do this every two weeks, or however often you wish. I'm certain you will be pleased with the results, assuming you followed the recipe for reading success.

ASSIGNMENT

Test yourself using the personal testing method every six weeks.

SUMMARY

- Testing is not absolutely necessary but it is highly recommended because it can show that you are making progress.

- If you test yourself, you will begin to 'normalise' your top speed, comprehension and recall, meaning that it will get better and you will 'forget' how bad it was before.

- Do remember that scores can drop for all sorts of reasons, from stress to lack of interest in the subject. Do not get disheartened!

- If you feel you did very badly, remember the big picture. Soon you will be a super reader. It's only a matter of time.

PART TWO:

Your New Basic Reading Technique

6.

Introducing hand pacing

Now begins your journey through the skills that will turn you into a super reader. The following chapters outline and detail the techniques you will need to learn and use, and are really the 'How to' part of the book. You will be covering hand pacing (in this chapter), previewing (chapter 7) and learning to read multiple words at a glance (chapter 8). From this point on, you will be altering your behaviour, and this will improve your results. This is where your positive 'can-do' attitude and belief will harness the power of your brain and improve your ability to read, retain and remember written information.

After each new tool is introduced, I suggest a reading assignment to give you the opportunity to practise your new skill. Remember that sometimes new skills may cause a temporary drop in performance. This is because you are not only performing the new technique, you are also thinking about how you are doing it. That splits your attention for a little while. Don't worry. Your ability will pick back up again and surpass what it was before.

Are you ready to leave old habits behind and move forward with simple, powerful techniques? If your answer is yes, then let's proceed.

First things first. Before you start reading, you need to think about how you are sitting.

Are you sitting comfortably?

You may not realise this, but the way you sit affects your reading ability. If you are like most people, you probably just pull your chair up to a table and start reading. Before you do that, I would like you to turn your chair 45 degrees, allowing your elbow to rest on the table. If you are right-handed, please rotate your chair to the left, or anti-clockwise and rest your right elbow on the table. If you are left-handed, swivel your chair to the right, or clockwise and rest your left elbow. (See the illustrations overleaf.)

Now, hold your book with your free hand, either flat on the desk or propped up to about 30 or 40 degrees to bring the text to a friendlier angle for your eyes. You can prop it up with some books or anything that brings up the far edge about 2 or 3 inches (5 to 8 cm). Be relaxed, and swivelling left and right from your elbow, you will use your finger to follow the lines as you read the paragraph that follows. When you read, go as fast as you can **with** comprehension.

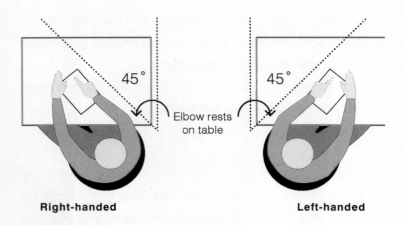

Right-handed   **Left-handed**

For most people, sitting like this is very natural and easy. And if it does not feel natural, it will very soon. Sometimes it takes a few minutes because you are doing several new things at once. Do not judge yourself or these techniques harshly. Be patient. Even people with the most negative attitudes only take a day or two to get used to it. For most people, within a week they can't imagine going back to reading 'the old way'. At first, you will not only be reading, you will also be thinking about pointing and pacing (you will learn all about this in the rest of this chapter). This may even distract you from the meaning of the words. This newness will wear off and soon you will ignore your finger and how you're seated and focus on the words. Do you understand this paragraph? If so, you are doing just fine. If you are totally lost, just keep reserving judgement (see chapter 4), until you get it.

Hand pacing

When I'm teaching the SuperReading™ course, I get everyone's attention and then throw a soft object the length of the room. I then ask who watched the object. Everyone raises their hand. Then I ask whether they made a conscious decision to watch it or if it was more a reflex. Virtually everyone agrees it's a reflex, as there's little time to make a considered decision. Why is this important? Because I want you to understand that the tool you are about to learn is well thought out. It makes sense and works very, very well. It is one of the foundations of this programme.

So why did I ask about watching the object? I asked because it is natural for humans to pay attention to a moving object. All animals do. It's natural because that moving object might be a predator come to eat us. Our ancestors had to watch out for all sorts of nasty beasts like lions and tigers and snakes and scorpions and who knows what. Those who paid attention to movement lived. There is a technical term for those people who did not pay attention to moving objects: lunch! We can use this natural reflex to our advantage.

If you are right-handed, raise your right hand. Left-handers raise your left. Now point to the sky.

 That forefinger doing the pointing is your new reading tool! Use it to pace yourself as you read. Do this by moving it under the words you are reading in a smooth, fluid motion. Most children in societies with written languages often use their fingers to keep their place as they read. Most educators have been told to 'correct' this tendency. Funny, but it turns out that using the hand is a natural, intuitive technique that works very well with the right tools. You're now getting those tools.

Hand pacing is quite wonderful. When I ask graduates even years after they have finished the Super-Reading™ course, hand pacing is always one of their top three tools. Without hand pacing, they say, their minds wander off and they waste untold hours of their precious time. It also stops them reading the same sentence again and again before they understand the meaning.

ASSIGNMENT

Put up several small cards around your computer and other places with the word 'POINT!' written on them. Change them around every couple of days so they continue to catch your eye.

When you are hand pacing, you may speed up or slow down, depending on the material you are reading. However, while reading, remember to keep your hand moving! Do not stop. At first, you may miss some things. That's OK. Your brain is capable of processing at rates many times faster than you do now. It will also get lazy if you let it. Let your brain know that it must process what you read as you go. It is very capable of this, and will quickly learn how to remember what you have read. However, you must give it no alternative. If you miss something, let it go. You can pick it up later when you 'review' (see Chapter 11).

From this point forward, you will track underneath the line you are reading and remember the basic rule of hand pacing:

GO AS FAST AS YOU CAN WHILE MAINTAINING COMPREHENSION.

ASSIGNMENT
Read the following four paragraphs using your finger. Just trace underneath each line. Remember that you are in control of your speed. Match your speed to your comprehension.
Begin.

This will mean more to you than ever before. Do you remember when we talked about 'distracted reader syndrome' earlier? That's when you're reading along, thinking you're absorbing the material and then when you get to the end you realise (with horror) that you have almost no idea of what you read. Usually, the distraction is coming from within your head. You start daydreaming. Why? Well, let's face it; movies tend to be more fun than articles, reports or textbooks. That's what your brain was doing – running movies while it fooled you into thinking you were reading!

Remember when you learned how to read when you were at school? The teacher probably got you to read aloud to make sure you could do it. Once you demonstrated the ability to 'decode' the words, your teacher probably told you to keep reading silently to yourself. The problem with this was that you were only reading silently as far as the outside world could tell, but inside your head you were still pronouncing the words (sub-vocalising). That set up two barriers for you. One was that you could not read much faster than you could talk. That is called the sub-vocalisation barrier, which is to reading what the sound barrier is to flight. The other was that at some point your brain learned that if it pronounced the words, you believed you were reading. Eventually it had you saying the words but it stopped processing them – or at least not very deeply. At that point you experienced distracted reader syndrome.

In fact, if you've ever studied and learned to read a foreign language you will know this feeling. You can read that other language, sometimes quite well, without understanding a single thing you read! For instance, I'm a bit rusty in Spanish, but I can read it rather nicely. The only problem is I have almost no idea of what I'm saying.

For the first time in years you will know whether you are understanding what you are reading or not. Pointing at what you read gives that to you. It sets up a circuit between your brain and the material. If the circuit is broken you become aware of it immediately. Specifically, if what you're pointing at does not match up with what you're thinking about, the difference becomes obvious.

So how was that? Did reading along with your finger feel natural? Did it feel weird? Did it feel good? Did it get better as you went along? Are you still reading with your finger? Did you have a performance dip, or was it OK? Whatever your reaction now, in the big picture it does not matter too much. Soon you will read with accuracy and good comprehension. If it was a bit off then you will get better at it very soon.

Keep reading with your finger from now on. This is just about the most important technique in the book. Whatever you've heard about pointing at what you read, it is the single best tool for high comprehension, focus and concentration.

The flip turn

When you are reading along, using your finger to trace under the line, it's important to keep a good pace going. While you should not sacrifice comprehension for a steady pace, there is something to be said for keeping the brain active and focused. When it comes to efficiency with your time, the flip turn is important on multiple levels.

When I was researching reading techniques I went to libraries and parks to observe people reading, without their knowledge. If they had known they were being observed they would have behaved differently. I needed to know what people do naturally when they read, and how long it took them to do it.

I would sit or stand casually nearby, and when they turned a page I noted the time or started a stopwatch. I could usually tell when they flipped a page, and could almost always tell when they went from the left page to the right page by their head or eye movement. It usually took them between 90 seconds and 120 seconds per page. Sometimes I would walk by to see the titles of the books, and later I would go to a bookshop and look at the books to get an idea of how many words were on a page. Sometimes I would go up to people and ask them to show me the book as it looked interesting. When they showed me, I would quickly count the number of lines where they had been reading.

I began to notice, and this was something I was previously unaware of, how long it sometimes took people to turn the page when they were finished with the right-hand page. Usually they would turn the page fairly quickly in just a second or two. However, sometimes they could not quite grab it and would have to try several times to get traction. Often they would have to wet their finger to grip the page and turn it. This process could take anywhere from 3 seconds up to nearly 10 seconds if they were in no particular hurry. The average was about 4 seconds, which may not sound like much. Indeed, if you're taking upwards of 2 minutes (120 seconds) to read a page, then I will admit that 4 seconds is not much time. It's only 3 per cent of the time spent reading that page. But what if you are becoming a super reader? What if eventually you are reading a similar page in 20 to 25 seconds instead of 120 seconds? Now turning the page is taking upwards of 20 per cent of your reading time on that page, which is a lot of time for your finger to be flicking a page corner. This is not a productive use of your time.

The solution is simple. As your reading finger clears the first few lines of the right-hand page, move your other hand across and prepare the page for turning. It's poised to turn the page when you get to the bottom. The result? When your reading finger finishes the last word on the page, your other hand flips the page over and your reading finger comes down at the top left and picks up where you left off without missing a beat. It's a smooth, fluid motion; just like Olympic swimmers do when they get to the end of the pool. They flip over and push off the wall for power. You are doing the same thing with your reading!

When I watch people reading in my classes I have

often noticed that when people get to the bottom of a right-hand page, they hesitate and look back over the text a bit before turning the page. To me this means they do not believe they have absorbed the material. I want you to trust yourself. If you have previewed (chapter 7) and are pointing using hand pacing, you are getting loads of information. The time to find out is when you parrot (chapter 9). Furthermore, there is not usually anything that special at the bottom of the page. I do not observe people doing this on any other part of a page – only on the bottom right-hand side. This tells me quite clearly the readers are looking at this as their last chance to get it right on those two pages before turning. Since we have a review step built into our reading (chapter 10), we do not need to do that. We can continue with confidence that we are getting what we need, and if not we will check in at the proper time to assess our reading.

Remember that whatever information is on the last line of the right-hand page is only there by happenstance, depending on the size of the font and the amount of space between the lines. Therefore, dwelling on it is artificial. So I'm asking you to keep going when you get to the bottom, do the flip turn and keep reading on the next page.

READING IN BED

I'm often asked about whether it's OK to read in bed. I have some strong thoughts on this subject. The answer is: yes and no. I know there are few things in this world as nice as curling up under the cover with a great book. What you want to be careful about, however, is creating knock-on effects from that. Ivan Pavlov conducted one of the most famous experiments in history in the early 20th century, coming up with the concept of classical conditioning. He had a collection of dogs. He would ring a bell, and then bring them some meat. Ring the bell, bring the meat. It didn't take long for the dogs to associate the ringing bell with the meat. After a few times, ringing the bell would start the dogs salivating. They had become conditioned to respond to the bell. They would also generalise to other similar sounds.

My concern is that your body becomes conditioned to getting sleepy when you read. If the pattern is: read, feel drowsy, read, feel drowsy, read, feel drowsy then that can cause a problem. The worst case is when people like to read in order to fall asleep. If you must read in bed, put the book down at the very first sign of drowsiness. Do not carry on into nearly falling asleep. My students who have stopped reading in bed report that they no longer feel drowsy when they read during the day. My suggestion is to try it for 21 days in a row (or as often as you read in bed) and see the difference. The choice is yours. My job is to provide the tools and the means to test them.

ASSIGNMENT

Avoid reading in bed for either 21 days or 21 times (if you don't read to fall asleep every night). Do you notice the difference during the day when you read?

Reading from a computer screen

If you don't like reading from a computer screen and prefer to print documents out, try the following techniques for at least 21 days. Most people find that when they learn the skills of SuperReading™ they are able to read from a computer screen more successfully, especially if they have a positive attitude. If you make up your mind to have a good time with your improved skills, you will reap more benefit than if you look out for what might go wrong.

When you read from a computer screen, use the mouse cursor. It will not follow along as precisely as your finger on paper, but it will be close enough to keep your attention focused on where you wish to be. If you don't currently have a mouse with your computer, consider investing in a small USB mouse, which may be easier to use than running your finger along the words on the screen.

The position of your computer screen

The latest advice is to have the top of your computer screen just below eye level, especially if you tend to lean forwards. Try leaning forwards while keeping your eyes level. Notice how you tend to compress the vertebrae in your neck. That is not good for your health! For the latest research, look up 'computer ergonomics' (also known as human engineering) in a search engine for more information on best practice.

Positioning your computer screen for hand pacing

Most computers are not well positioned for reading using the hand pacing method. Here are the various options:

1 Use the mouse pointer to move along the line to keep you focused. It will not be a perfectly straight line, but it will do.
2 Get a desk that allows you to place the monitor within the desktop. Such desks have a hole cut into the top of the desk with a suspended, adjustable mount for your monitor. Use your finger on the screen. This should only be done for short periods of time, as it's difficult to properly support your arm and shoulder.

3 With LCD monitors you can really fly if they quickly dismount from their stand and sit right on your lap or the desk. It's like having an electronic book. You would have one finger on the screen and the other finger on the Page Down key or mouse wheel. It's the ideal option, though more expensive. You have to figure what your time is worth per hour and compare that to the cost of the monitor. The time to make such a decision is once you're competent with pattern reading (see chapter 11).

4 Tablets lie flat and can be used in either portrait or landscape mode. Their screens can rotate and flip over and around as well. They function like an electronic book and are excellent for fun and efficient reading. They are a bit more expensive but worth it if you plan on doing a lot of reading.

How to set up the text on your screen

Whatever kind of screen you are reading, find a way to narrow the columns of text. Make them as much like newspaper columns as possible. If the application has word wrap, simply grab the sides of the text and narrow it. The extra few seconds taken to arrange the page are well worth it for the speed and comprehension you gain. In MS Word, click View, then Web Layout to get word wrap. Now you can grab the side of the window and drag it to make the window narrower without losing any of the words. Make the line hold about eight to ten words across on average. This does not have to be precise, just approximate.

Remember that making the column narrower results in a document that has more pages. The amount of content is the same, but the document is now physically 'longer'. I bring this up because the apparent size of a document has a psychological effect on the reader. If someone hands you a two-page report, that feels different from being handed a 200-page report. Our reaction is totally different when the only difference is the length. You may experience something similar when you narrow the columns. Suddenly a three-page document is a ten-page document! Do not be fooled by that illusion. Just because you're hitting the Page Down key more often, you will be reading through it faster because the information is in bite-sized chunks!

Also be aware of the font size. The smaller the font the more likely it is that you will have to lean forward to see it clearly. That compresses the vertebrae in your neck and can cause health problems. The solution is either to change the font size or the percentage of magnification on the page. In an MS Word document, that drop down menu is located in View. You can either choose a predetermined value (100%, 150%, 200%) or left click the number and type in your own value.

Narrow column   **Wide column**

The ideal would be to get just the right number of words across your column as you can read in one or two glances. This will be looked at in more detail when you learn about Eye-Hop™ in chapter 8. As you progress in your Eye-Hop™ practice, you can use wider and wider columns.

The colour of the screen

Near-sightedness (or short-sightedness) is rising in the West. Some experts believe this may be due to squinting into brightly lit monitors and changing the shape of our eyeballs. At the least, looking at a bright monitor screen is going to be tiring on the eyes. In old films, the police would always shine a bright light at a suspect when questioning them. This was so uncomfortable that they would always confess. So why are we torturing ourselves when we read?

The answer is to either turn down the brightness or

change the background colour. You can do this in less than a minute. With Windows XP:

Click START
Control Panel /
Display /
Appearance /
Advanced /
Click on Window Text / Color 1 /

Then use the drop down menu to choose a light blue or light green (possibly very light pink).
Click OK

This will change the background colour in all of your applications, but the colour will not print out. It only affects your viewing panel. I have suggested a light colour because you still need contrast between the background and your text. If they are too close in value you will still be squinting to read and will have defeated your purpose!

ASSIGNMENT

Once you have set up your screen correctly and sorted out the appearance of your text, get a document up on your screen. Use the mouse cursor to read along. It does not matter whether you move the cursor under the line or on the line. Do it whichever way feels comfortable. Unlike your finger, the cursor is almost invisible and does not interfere with seeing the words. When I first started to teach this course in 1995, about one-third of the students were uncomfortable using the mouse to track along. As society has become more familiar with using computers, most people just adapt to it in a couple of days. If for some reason you take longer to adapt, remember the 21-day rule for adopting a new habit and look back to chapter 4 on reserving judgement.

SUMMARY

- Use your basic hand pacing technique from now on. A good attitude towards using your finger will make the transition from using only your eyes much easier. At some point, you will be completely used to this lifestyle change and it will be second nature for you.

- Sitting comfortably will make reading for long periods more tolerable. If a table or desk is not available and you are sitting in a chair, prop your forearms against your side. A pillow or two under the book will keep it at a comfortable distance from your eyes.

- Go as fast as you can while maintaining comprehension. Remember – comprehension is king!

- The flip turn will help your flow, and it is good psychologically. Knowing you are heading for it, and later practising it at speed, is proof that you've become a super reader.

- Reading in bed is not advised if it makes your eyes tired. You may be sacrificing good attention the next day.

- Reading from the computer screen is part of life, so make sure all that time spent is not at the expense of your physical well-being. Make sure you follow the latest hints and best practice for good ergonomics.

7.

Previewing

Once you have got to grips with hand pacing, and are comfortable with using your finger (or mouse cursor) to track your reading, you are ready to move on to previewing, one of the other top three techniques in this book. When taking the first reading test in chapter 5, you will probably have noticed how much easier it was to answer the questions after reading the text for the second time. This is because you were familiar with the information. You understood what it was about, who was involved and for what purpose. You may have remembered some facts and they made more sense the second time through. You could say that you 'previewed' the essay with your first read. However, you can do better than that. There are special strategies that can give you loads of good information without having to read all the text the first time. These strategies are called 'previewing'.

Previewing lets you know what's coming. It's a strategic way to get a peek ahead at what you will be reading. It serves some of the same functions as a movie preview. When you watch a preview, or trailer, it shows you enough of the movie to get you interested. One difference is that the movie preview doesn't give away too much. Previewing when you read can give you loads of valuable information.

There are three main ways to preview: key sentence previewing; name and number scan; and novel previewing. The first technique is usually people's favourite. It's the one that is used about 90 per cent of the time.

Key sentence previewing

Key sentence previewing is quite simple. Read the first sentence of each paragraph. Most authors load a lot of information into the first sentence. Try to only preview the first five to ten pages or so, if there are long chapters. It's hard to keep much more information in your head, especially when you're just starting off. The rule is to key sentence preview only as much as you can accurately recall.

ASSIGNMENT

Test your present abilities by reading five key sentences from a book and discovering how much you can recall from those. If you get them all, try to do more until you get a significant drop-off in your recall. It's like body building – each time you push yourself, you grow stronger. If right now you can recall four key sentences, work on that for a couple of days. Then work at mastering five. Then six, and so on.

After reading the key sentences, try forming mental pictures of each point as you go. It's OK to be outrageous. Mental pictures are a clever way to remember information. Pictures have far more power than most words and are usually far easier to remember. They trigger different parts of the brain, which use more imagination. When you make mental pictures, make them larger than life, with colour and sound if possible. The more ways you can hook into the concept you wish to remember, the more likely you will remember it. For instance, you can say the thing you want to remember several times while visualising (see more on this in chapter 12). This will conjure up your internal mental image, making the connection more complete.

As your mind strengthens, keep raising the bar. Between your brain stretching to keep up and the new techniques you will learn throughout the rest of this book, your abilities will grow. Once you have read the prescribed number of key sentences, be that ten or more, go back to where you started key sentence previewing and read all the words, including the key sentences, again. The double exposure will help your retention. Repetition is one of the five important keys to memory (there is more on this in chapter 13). Try the following fun test, which proves that repetition is a great way to learn.

Key sentence previewing

What is 6 x 6?

Did you get the answer right away?

Let's try another one.

What is 3 x 3?

Did you have to think hard? Did you have to put a hand to your head and close your eyes to concentrate and draw numbers in the air to figure it out? No? The answer just popped into your head, right?

OK, let's try something different. This time, when you look, try NOT to let the answer pop into your head. Ready?

What is 5 x 5?

The answer just popped into your head. That was easy.

You may have squeezed it out by thinking of something else, but it was right there for you, all ready and very accurate. No hard thinking – all it needed was mentioning. Don't you sometimes wish you could remember everything that easily? What made the answer come up so quickly? The answer is repetition. Years ago you learned the multiplication tables by sheer repetition, and still they pop up effortlessly. That's how powerful repetition is for learning. Fortunately, there are other methods for effective learning besides repetition. We will be exploring them in this book. For now, let's really drive the point home. Let's try one more case from the multiplication tables.

What is the answer to 17 x 17?

Hmmm. You don't get the same response from your brain now, do you? What happened? 17 x 17 was on the table, but you probably didn't spend as much time learning it. Therefore nothing sprang to mind when you looked at it. You saw the answer years ago, so you understand the concept and just after looking at it could have given the correct answer (which is 289, by the way). However, one look does not put the answer into your long-term memory, does it? That would take another one of the five keys to memory – namely emotion. If the last time you looked at 17 x 17 something highly emotional happened, you would probably remember it. Emotion seals in memories, but more on that when we get to it in chapter 13.

CASE STUDY

I once taught a group of teachers, one of whom was attending university at night. He was also working part-time somewhere else! After our second class, he went home and discovered that he had a test in two hours for which he hadn't even opened the book! Worse, it was in a required subject he had little interest in! The test covered the first hundred pages. He cracked open the binding (for the first time), and began doing key sentence preview. By the time he had to leave for the test, he had covered only sixty pages. He ended up getting 80 per cent in the exam! Would you say there's a lot of important information in those key sentences? He certainly did.

Alpha-omega – a special case of key sentence previewing

Alpha-omega means 'first and last' and refers to the beginning and ending paragraphs of an article or piece of writing. In a typical news story, for example, the first two paragraphs are supposed to tell you the 'who, what, when and where' of the article. Usually, the last paragraph is a summary of the article and is used to drive home the author's point, or 'why'. By reading the alpha-omega, you do at least two things: one, you have an excellent idea of what the story is all about, including the author's viewpoint; two, you can save a lot of time if this article does not interest you, based on what the main points are. You can parrot what you have read (see chapter 10).

Occasionally you come across an author whose writing style is a bit different. They put important information not only in the first sentence of each paragraph, but also in the last sentence of each paragraph. With these authors you may want to do alpha-omega on each paragraph as a means of previewing and/or reviewing (chapter 11).

You can also use alpha-omega with a whole book as a way of getting a quick overview of it. The alpha in this case is the front cover and front jacket flap, while the omega is the back cover and back jacket flap. Some people like to include the preface and table of contents as part of their alpha-omega. Either is fine. The idea is to preview the book so you know the basic plot, some of the characters and the author's point of view. Remember the old saying, 'You can't tell a book by its cover'? That is partially true. You can tell a few things about a book from its cover by using alpha-omega but remember to keep your mind open as there will be more to it than meets the eye. I have met people who refuse to read some books because they contain ideas with which the reader does not agree. You are developing powerful tools of comprehension, so I suggest that it is OK to read such books. Just because you read it does not mean you have to believe it. Aristotle said it best: 'It is the mark of an educated mind to be able to entertain a thought without accepting it.' They will probably reinforce what you already believe. Just let go of your fears and don't believe everything you read.

The bookmark preview

You can also use alpha-omega in a different way. You use a bookmark and go through an entire book looking for items of interest. Spending no more than five seconds per page, every time you come across an item you are interested in learning more about, you jot the page number down on the back of a bookmark. You go through the whole book in 15 minutes or less and have specific targets you know will be of interest to you. Keep the bookmark with that book, as it is now dedicated to the best hot spots of information. If the information in the book is of particular importance to you, because of your career, a vocation or education, you may want to take notes as you preview for later reference. You may well be able to bookmark around 30 to 40 places in the book that appear to be of high interest. Those that turn out to be real gems can be circled to make them stand out. You can even write a word next to them to remind you of the topic. Although the bookmark could become separated and lost from the book, this technique will particularly satisfy those people who feel it is horrible to mark a book directly or fold page corners to mark a place. Some people are not that attached to their books, some think marking their books makes them theirs, and others would not dream of 'damaging' a book.

Later in this book you will learn about a particularly useful note-taking method called Info-Mapping™, which will help you take notes for particularly easy reference and memory.

Name and number scan

Name and number scan

The second previewing technique is name and number scan. This is really suited to historical texts and research papers or any texts that are full of facts. Newspaper articles often have many facts in them. Scanning through them to pick up the who, what, when and where will give you the facts. Reading the full text will fill in the blanks. When you start to read, move your finger quickly down the page in a zigzag, looking for any names, such as those of people and places. Scan also for any numbers, such as dates, money, weights or how many of something there are. In either case, pause momentarily and make a mental note of the name or number. You can use the power of repetition and say the fact a few times. When you actually go back and read, you can fill in what the name or number was and why it was significant.

Becoming aware of all the facts in an essay or article can make you curious about how they all fit together. You may be wondering how 1887, the moon, Cambridge University and China all fit together. A curious mind works far better than a bored mind. Your brain holds on to all the puzzle pieces until they make sense. Holding on to them makes them remain in your memory longer.

ASSIGNMENT

Get a book that is likely to have a lot of names or dates or places. Scan down a few of the pages with your finger, looking for the name and number facts. Stop on each one for a couple of seconds. You can even say them aloud if you like. Then go back and read one of the pages. You will begin to notice how those facts jump back out at you. You will also notice how they tend to 'stick' a bit better in your memory. They will make more sense once you get the context of how they fit together.

Novel previewing

The third technique is particularly apt for reading novels, although it can be used with any material, particularly where the targeting of the writing is not easy or obvious. With key sentence previewing, it's fairly obvious where the key words are. Name and number scan works well when there are lots of facts sprinkled through the text. Novel previewing fills up the void the other two techniques leave behind when they are not ideal. In theory, you could use novel previewing all the time, except that the other two techniques are specialised for when the author has either placed their key information in the key sentences or distributed facts all through the text.

Some good news is that reading your novels more quickly, with the right tools, will greatly enhance your experience. They will happen more at the speed of real life. In a book it takes you 90 seconds to read about how beautiful a garden is. In real life you know it in a second or two. As a super reader you'll know in about 12 seconds. This will feel better because that's closer to how you really experience your life. Novel previewing is a great tool if you are taking a literature course. It will give you a really good feel for what is in the book, while adding to your understanding and recall.

Novels require a technique that is quite different from that needed for textbooks, magazines and many other forms of the written word. The reason is that novels often have something other books don't have. Read the sample below (don't forget to use your finger!):

> Dr Jones walked up to the old man. 'Have you seen James?'
> 'No, not since early this morning.'
> 'Was he here?'
> 'No. He was at the hotel.'
> 'The hotel where I'm staying?'
> 'Where are you staying?'
> 'I'm at the Fairmont.'
> 'No, he was at the Lawrence Towers.'
> 'Was his wife with him?'
> 'Yes. She looked younger than I remembered.'
> 'Yeah, surgery will do that.'
> 'Shall I tell James you were looking for him?'
> 'No. I have a little surprise for him.'

How is this different from other forms of writing? Novels have fewer paragraphs because they often have a lot of dialogue. As a result, key sentence previewing doesn't work as well for previewing novels. You need a different tool. You need novel previewing. It's quite simple and works remarkably well. In fact, you can use it for almost any text, though when there are paragraphs key sentence previewing is usually best.

Words words words words words words words words
words words words words words words words words
words words words words words words words words
words words words words words words words **Sir Richard
ordered the fleet to attack.** words words words words
words words words words words words words
Words words words words words words words words
words words words words words words words words
words words words words words words words words
words words words words words words words words
words words words words words words words words
words words words words words words words words
words words words words words words words words
words words words words words words words words
words words words words words words words words
words words words words words words words words
words words words words words words words words
words words words words words
words words words words words words words words
words words words **Their ship sank without a trace.**
Words words words words words words words words
words words words words words words words words
words words words words words words words words
words words words words words words words words
words words words words words words words words
words words words words words words words words
words words words words words words words words
words words words words words words words words
words words words words words

Novel previewing

Here's how novel previewing works. Simply drop down one-third of the page, read a line or two, drop another one-third, and read a line or two. Read just enough to get the idea of what's happening on that part of the page. You can also drop down by quarters, sampling three places on the page. This would be good to do when there is dense text with lots of words on the page. You will be amazed at how much of the story comes together for you.

ASSIGNMENT

Pick up a novel. Use novel previewing, dropping down a third, on a few pages. At first you can do three places per page. Just read enough to get the idea. Then write down what you remember. Now go back and read the pages. Compare how much was there with how much you picked up from the novel previewing. Usually the novel previewing technique gives you a fairly clear picture of what was happening on that page.

Students always worry whether novel previewing and therefore reading novels more quickly will spoil their enjoyment. The answer, of course, is no. First of all, you are free to read at any speed you like. You can speed up or slow down at your discretion, just like you've always done. The difference is that your range will be far wider. To me, the joy of a good book is that I get lost in it. I lose track of time and find myself immersed in this other world. When I stop, I have no idea of the time. One of the marks of having fun is losing track of time. Imagine laughing and laughing with your friends. Everyone's getting along and you feel great, and you have no idea how late it is. Were you all talking fast or slowly? Do you care? Does it matter? It's the same with reading. When you're fully into a book you have no idea whether you're reading quickly or not. You are probably reading faster than 'normal' because you know the subject, you like the characters and you can't wait to see what will happen next.

The question is, so what if you're reading even faster

than that? The book will end eventually. Maybe the author will write more! You may as well have some of your evening left after finishing it. Plus, there are plenty more great books out there.

NOTE: Some people respond negatively to novel previewing because they like the surprise of what's coming up and do not want to have a peep at what's coming up. At the other extreme there are people who read the last few pages, find out how it all ends and then begin reading their novel! If they like the ending, they will read the whole book. If the ending perturbs them, they will move on to another book.

The choice is yours. I do recommend previewing at least the first three chapters of a book to make sure you are very familiar with the main characters and situations. This is especially useful with novels where there are loads of people, organisations, technology and places to remember. Without a firm foundation you may be quite lost later on. Just be aware of this: whenever you read without previewing, your comprehension and recall will be lower than if you did Preview.

Previewing for readers of English as a second language

If your first language is not English, previewing may be even more important for you. There is really nothing that increases comprehension like previewing.

Vocabulary

If your second language is English, it may mean that you have a challenge with vocabulary. If you feel you run into a lot of words you don't know, I have some advice for you. Identify those words when you preview. Look at the words around them (the sentence they are in) and try to get the meaning from the context. In plain language, see if the words they are surrounded by give you the likely meaning. If you can't get the meaning, then you have a few choices:

1 You can hope that it will make more sense when you go back and read all of the text. This would give you more context.
2 You can look up the word right away and learn the meaning. This interruption is better during previewing than during reading. This is probably the safest choice, especially if you add the word to your vocabulary list.
3 Determine that the word is not that important; that you do not need to know its meaning. This is the most dangerous choice, as you may guess wrongly.

If English is not your first language (or whatever other language you are now reading in), this is of more importance. You may have more vocabulary words to learn than the average native English reader. Your understanding of a word is less likely to be the correct meaning.

There are also many slang usages that may not be obvious. Although it takes longer, looking up words you are unsure of will help your understanding of the text. If you think of it as a learning experience it will be easier to do. Being certain of meaning may save you from embarrassment later on. Keep a list of these words and review them periodically. Monthly would be very good. See the section on learning vocabulary on page 241.

Questions to ask that will help with previewing

Magnetic questions

Magnetic questions will really help with your previewing before reading as well as when using a technique called parroting (you will see more about this in chapter 9). These are basic questions that apply to most material, whether written or spoken. When you can answer these six questions you understand the material. The questions are:

> **Who?**
> **What?**
> **When?**
> **Where?**
> **Why?**
> **How?**

These simple questions cover the basic structure of information. These are the same questions asked by Rudyard Kipling in this extract from his poem *The Elephant's Child*:

> I keep six honest serving men
> (They taught me all I knew);
> Their names are What and Why and When
> And How and Where and Who.

Although we use them in a slightly different order, they are the same six questions and will serve us well too.

Who refers to people, organisations, characters, animals; whoever the subject of your reading material might be. For example, in an article about astronomy, the **Who** could be Galileo, Einstein, the Planetary Society or 'people who believe the earth is flat'.

What refers to the thing done (by a character) or a physical object in your reading material. Examples could be the first telescope, the Theory of Relativity, a black hole or the belief that the earth is at the centre of the universe.

When refers to time. Examples could be important dates, seasons, eras or simply an indication of before or after. For example, 'a long time ago', 'during the Bronze Age', '20 July 1969', or 'when he was a little boy'.

Where refers to location. These are physical places such as countries, cities, a room in a house, under her left eye, behind the door or page 277 in a book.

Why refers to the reasons for something happening (cause and effect). This magnetic question takes us deeper into the meaning of what we're reading. Examples might be 'because he felt driven to find the answer', or 'because it was important to know when crops should be planted', or 'because he knew how to ask the right questions'. **Why** questions are usually the hardest to answer because we must have a fairly deep understanding of the material. Discovering 'why' can give us a logical understanding of the world.

These first four questions are 'factual' in nature. They give us the bare facts. **Why** begs us to look beyond the facts into motivations or cause and effect. People who can answer **Why** questions show true understanding of what they have read. This is what *you* are aiming for. You want to go beyond simple factual recall into true understanding.

How refers to methods of getting things done, whether by humans, nature or whatever. For example, 'by working day and night for two weeks', or 'by fastening part A securely to part C', or 'by pure chance', or 'because she would not give up until the company agreed'. **How** questions are the nuts and bolts of the action in a story. They give us understanding of the methods used to achieve something or the mechanics of something happening. **How** can also quantify units of time, quantity and detail. **How** many people attended the meeting? **How** does this machine work better than the old model? **How** will you know when the project is finished?

To use the magnetic questions for previewing, write them on a card (used as a bookmark) near what you are reading. Glance at it before you start reading to remind your brain to be on the lookout for answers to these questions. While it's in your peripheral vision, your subconscious will be aware of it. Soon it will become second nature to be able to answer the magnetic questions after reading. For most of what you read, if you can answer those questions, you've got it! They are called 'magnetic' because they begin to draw the important information to you like a magnet! You can also use the magnetic questions for parroting (chapter 9) and reviewing (chapter 10).

ASSIGNMENT

For at least 21 days, carry a magnetic questions bookmark with you and leave it by the side of your reading. Glance at it for five seconds before you start reading. Notice how certain words are jumping out at you.

Title questions

Most people pay very little attention to the titles of what they are reading. In fact, they tend to just skip straight past them. I've got people to read an article and then asked them what the title was. In a sample of several thousand people, about a dozen knew the title. That's a pretty strong statistic for people attending a reading course. You might think they would really be on their toes and try their best. Well, at the beginning, maybe that is their best!

How to do title questions

Read the title of the book, chapter or story. Ask yourself magnetic questions about the title and mentally fill in your answers as you read.

For example, a book is entitled *The Four Entertainers*:

Who are these four entertainers?
What do they do as the four entertainers?
When did they become the four entertainers?
Where are the four entertainers working?
Why are there the four entertainers?
How did they become the four entertainers?

HINT: When asking title questions be sure to repeat as much of the title in your question as possible. It may seem tedious or repetitious, but that's part of the point. There are two advantages to this. One is that by repeating the words in the title you have a much better chance of remembering the title. By asking these rapid-fire questions you are generating the curiosity to find the answers. Your questions may or may not make sense. It doesn't matter one bit. You are generating interest in the story. When you have finished reading the book or article you should be able to either answer the question or know with confidence that the question did not apply.

Many people try to make the title questions technique more complicated than it is. It is a very simple procedure. It should not take longer than about fifteen seconds. Go fast, have fun and do not be concerned about making sense. Just asking a few quick questions is all it takes. Keep it simple.

SUMMARY

- Previewing allows your mind to prepare for the task ahead and greases the wheels for brilliant reading.

- With the possible exception of reading poetry, previewing is one of the most powerful ways to increase your ability to read at speed, understand and recall any text that you've read.

- Previewing is always in the top three of the tools that SuperReading™ graduates say made the most difference to their reading.

- If English is your second language, do a lot of previewing. It saves time and you have a better understanding of the material when you are finished. You are also likely to remember more.

- You are free to combine any and all of the previewing techniques. This can be especially helpful on 'bad days' when your cognitive abilities are not as efficient as usual.

8.

Eye-Hop™

My unique Eye-Hop™ exercises lie at the heart of learning how to become a super reader and they set SuperReading™ apart from any other type of speed reading. These exercises will lift you up to higher and higher reading speeds while maintaining your comprehension. When I am teaching I tell every class: 'Whoever does the most Eye-Hop™ sessions will see the highest percentage increase in their reading effectiveness (R.E.) score.' This almost always turns out to be true. Of course, you must also practise your reading each day!

We have already looked at the problems of reading one word at a time and pronouncing all the words in your head (see page 78). You are now at the point where you will begin to overcome that barrier to reading speed. Hopefully you have been reading along with your finger for a while now and it's beginning to feel more and more natural. I know this is a lifestyle change, but you will get used to it. Remember to reserve judgement (see the importance of this on page 44), but if you are already feeling good about hand pacing, that's great.

The next steps, which will take you anywhere from three to eight weeks to master, will work in tandem with your hand pacing skills and you will find that soon the two techniques will come together in a synergistic way.

The aim of the Eye-Hop™ exercises, examples of which are located at the end of this chapter on page 126, is to help you go from reading one word at a time to reading groups of words at a time, starting with groups of two words, moving on to three and four, to possibly five and six or more. You will learn, by repeating the exercises before going on to reading your own material, how to glance at a word group and understand its meaning at once. Once you start to do this you will save time but also you will reduce wear and tear on your eye muscles. The ocular muscles around the eye are among the weakest in the human body. When you read, the ocular muscles tend to refocus on every word. When you read four or five words at a time, they only need to focus a fraction as much. This will allow you to read longer with higher performance and less strain.

The concept of Eye-Hop™ has been around since about 1995. The first Eye-Hop™ was literally cut and pasted and then photocopied and a typical article took three to four hours to produce. I created the Eye-Hop™ stories like this for several years.

Several Silicon Valley programmers who had taken

my course offered to write programs for me that would do it automatically, but with no success. Then in 2000, a student called Reto Stamm approached me as I was putting away my materials. He also offered to write a program to make Eye-Hop™. It took him a couple of hours and a little tweaking, before the Eye-Hop™ program ran perfectly. Now anyone can make their own Eye-Hop™ in seconds, thanks to the genius of Reto Stamm.

How to Eye-Hop™

The progression of Eye-Hop™ is to start reading two words at a time. When you have mastered that, then you move up to three words at a time, then four words, then five. When you get fast at reading four words, you will notice that your brain is no longer pronouncing many of the words inside your head. You are getting the full meaning of the phrase without pronouncing it! This is known as 'the breakthrough'. If this doesn't happen for you with four words, it will certainly happen with the five-word Eye-Hop™. There is little chance of reading five words in half a second and pronouncing them all.

Before moving on to the basics of Eye-Hop™ you should turn to page 126, where you will find examples of the exercises. Take a very quick look at them now so that you understand what the two-word Eye-Hop™ looks like. Once you are ready to start work on the

Eye-Hop™ exercises, you will need to go to my website (www.superreading.com/eyehop) where you will find all the exercises you need, arranged in booklets. You will probably need to print out the four Eye-Hop™ booklets, as I know that working from printed copies works very well. You may be able to do Eye-Hop™ exercises on a laptop, but be very careful not to stress your arm and shoulder. Most people like to touch when they read and hop, so you need to decide whether you want to be touching your computer screen that often. Having said that, tablet PCs are brilliant for reading so perhaps consider one for your next computer purchase.

Each Eye-Hop™ booklet is a PDF file. The four booklets average about 50 single-sided pages each, totalling just over 200 printed pages. You may print them out as you need them, or all at once. Most people report they can print out the entire set of four booklets on one black ink cartridge with an inkjet printer. There are only graphics on the instruction page, which are not heavily ink intensive, and print well on your printer's text setting. The booklets print in 'landscape mode', though your printer will work that out for itself. Although the pages are numbered, I recommend stapling them. Either take them to a copy shop with a heavy duty stapler, or separate a booklet in half or thirds to at least keep part of it together. You do not want to have the pages loose, as it would be difficult to pick them all up if a booklet blew out of your hands on a windy day!

These are the basics of Eye-Hop™:

- Either lay the Eye-Hop™ exercises flat in front of you when you practise, or up at a slight angle if that suits you better.
- To Eye-Hop™ you pivot from your elbow and actually HOP with your index finger from word group to word group (some people do use other fingers such as the middle one, or all four fingers, but this is quite rare). When hopping, your hand actually **comes off the paper or the computer screen**. Your fingertip traces a little half-circle from group to group. When you land, aim for the middle of each word group. See the Eye-Hop™ diagram below or in your printed out Eye-Hop™ booklet. It summarises all you need to know.

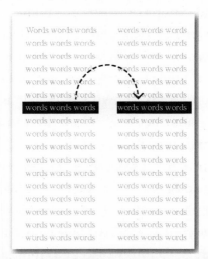

Use your finger to hop from column to column while doing the Eye-Hop™ **exercises**

- Slide the page up with your left hand as you go. (Left-handers reverse instructions as required.)
- Remember to go as fast as you can **while maintaining comprehension**.
- You need to do at least five minutes of Eye-Hop™ at a sitting (but not more than ten minutes, the first time – see below). It takes a few minutes to get into a rhythm. My suggestion is to read the Eye-Hop™ exercises at least three times per day for five to ten minutes per session. Try to manage at least 30 minutes of Eye-Hop™ per day. Forty minutes per day is ideal. Once you get used to it, there is no upper limit.
- Don't worry if you know the stories told in the exercises. It's actually OK to know these stories very well. The purpose of the exercises is to get you to understand groups of words at a glance. Even if they seem memorised, that's fine. In fact, you can preview these stories (as you learned in chapter 7), especially if English is not your native language. And if you make your own Eye-Hop™, which you will learn about below, you can do it in almost any language that uses Arabic letters.
- When your hand **consistently** moves from group to group so fast that it blurs, or it seems to slow you down compared to how fast you're picking up the words, move up to the next level (i.e. from two to three, or three to four words at a time). Once you move up a level, do not move back to the previous

level, even if you find you slow down in the new level, which does happen (especially moving from three-word to four-word Eye-Hop™).

* Finally, when you do the Eye-Hop™, stay relaxed. Keep your muscles loose. This is also true whenever you read. Staying relaxed is good advice for most activities.

WARNING! Reading for more than ten minutes with Eye-Hop™ is **not** recommended **the first time you try it.** There have been a handful of people over the years that got a headache from doing this. It's very rare, and it only happened to each of them once. I want to protect you.

NOTE: For now, the only time you hop is when you are actually doing the Eye-Hop™ exercises. You don't hop yet when reading text. Keep on using hand pacing for regular reading. Later you will merge your Eye-Hop™ skills with the hand pacing, but only when you are ready. I will explain more about that later. Once you're into the four-word Eye-Hop™ you can start to use it on regular text.

Making your own Eye-Hop™

One of the best pieces of news I have for you is that you can also produce your own personalised Eye-Hop™. You can do this quickly and easily by going online (www.superreading.com/hopify) and dropping any text in and clicking the 'Hopify' button. Here are the steps for creating your own Eye-Hop™:

- Locate the text you want to Hopify
- Highlight that text
- Click 'Control C'
- Open the website (www.superreading.com/hopify)
- Click once in the big box
- Click 'Control V'
- Choose the level of Eye-Hop™ you require
- Choose your spacing
- Click the Hopify button.

At this point you have two choices. You can print out from the screen, or you can export the hopified text to a program like MS Word. Then you can print it out from there.

Eventually your best choice will be to do the Eye-Hop™ directly on your computer screen using a tablet PC.

NOTE: When creating your own Eye-Hop™, start off with relatively simple material. This is especially true when doing the two-word and three-word Eye-Hop™. Really dense or technical material makes learning the skill more difficult. Once you have developed your competence, you can begin to use more difficult material. This is why the prepared materials you download begin with such simple stories as Aladdin. In the beginning it's more important to develop your skill than to try to absorb highly technical subjects. You can move on to those later on. In conclusion, keep your hopping materials simple and easy to absorb.

> **ASSIGNMENT**
>
> You can make your own Eye-Hop™ any time you like. Start off with the prepared two-word Eye-Hop™ booklet to make sure you have a good sample to begin with. Once you know how doing Eye-Hop™ feels then you may create your own. You will probably be able to do this within an hour of using the prepared Eye-Hop™.

Moving through successive levels

The beauty of Eye-Hop™ is that you expand your ability to absorb groups of words in easy to handle stages. On the following pages are examples of Eye-Hop™ stories and articles, which will give you the idea of how it works. Start by doing the two-word Eye-Hop™ at a pace that allows you to understand what you are reading. As always, go as fast as you can while maintaining comprehension. Once you have the feel for it after a couple of minutes, go at the same pace (or a bit faster) on the five-word Eye-Hop™. You will soon see that you cannot handle it if you do a hop about every second or so. It's simply too much information to grab all at once. The good news is that over the next few weeks you will be able to move up to that skill level and you will be able to handle it. If you try it now and cannot do it, you will better appreciate how far you will have come later. Some day you may read these words again and marvel at how you were able to increase your abilities.

Your next question might be, 'When do I move up from two-word to three-word Eye-Hop™?' Although this information was given a couple of paragraphs back, I know that your reading skills aren't 'super' yet, so I'm repeating it now! The simple answer is, when your finger is bouncing so fast from group to group that it becomes a blur, it's time to move up to the next higher word group. While you may find the two-word Eye-Hop™ less than challenging, I would like you to read through it completely at least once. Everyone is different. You may have to spend a week or more on the two-word. That's OK. Some people can actually start on the three-word Eye-Hop™ straight away, but I still get them to go through the two-word Eye-Hop™ at least once. There are important concepts to grasp in there.

It's very important not to move to the next level before you are ready. Make sure you are really blazing through before going on to the next higher word group. Likewise, don't stay too long on the two- or three-word Eye-Hop™. For example, it should not take you more than a week on the three-word Eye-Hop™, unless you found the two-word very challenging. It's probably better to err on the side of taking an extra hour or two before moving up.

Now, start reading at the beginning of the two-word Eye-Hop™ exercises. When you have read for between five and ten minutes, stop and begin again later from where you left off. Keep cycling through the stories until you are ready to move up to the next level. You may find yourself nearly memorising the stories. That's fine. The major purpose of Eye-Hop™ is to get your brain to recognise groups of words at a glance. The more you become convinced of your ability, the better you will do.

If you like you can preview a couple of lines per page to familiarise yourself the first time you go through a story. This may be particularly helpful if English is not your first language. And remember, the same rule applies in Eye-Hop™ as in hand pacing: hop as fast as you can while maintaining comprehension.

NOTE: If your first language is not English, previewing the Eye-Hop™ may help you a lot. This was not something I anticipated when I was developing Super-Reading™, but I noticed that students with English as a second language struggled a bit more with Eye-Hop™ than others. They hand paced more slowly, and their comprehension was lower. I found that previewing helped them to improve comprehension and see an increase in speed. If English is not your first language you will need to be a bit more patient with Eye-Hop™, particularly at four and five words, but you may find previewing will improve your ability.

Eye-Hop™ samples

Two-Word Eye-Hop™
Basic Astronomy

A few thousand years
ago, Man did not
even know whether the
Earth was round or
flat. A few hundred
years ago, he knew it
was round, but did
not know whether it
was the centre of
the universe, or just
one of the many
planets orbiting the Sun.
Today he is beginning
to wonder whether there
is life elsewhere in
the universe. And, if
there are intelligent beings,
how can we get
in touch with them.
For several thousand years
Man has wondered about
the nature and behaviour
of all things to be
seen in the sky.
He has learned a

great deal
the Sun,
planets, meteors,
the other
Our Sun
The bodies
are known
Those orbiting
known as moons.
the study of
heavenly bodies.
may think
that a
began several
ago cannot
the question:
life elsewhere.'
we consider
distances and
it's amazing
know as
we do.
that our
was born
five thousand

by watching
the Moon,
comets and
heavenly bodies.
is a star.
orbiting a star
as planets.
planets are
Astronomy is
all these
Some people
it strange
science that
thousand years
yet answer
'Is there
But when
the huge
time involved,
that we
much as
We know
Solar System
at least
million years ago.

Three-Word Eye-Hop™
Journey to the South Pole

The history of our involvement at the South Pole dates back to the early years of the 20th century. It is a story of great explorers, such as Scott, Amundsen, Shackleton and Byrd. It is a story which demonstrates the incredible advances in technology which have taken place during the last century. It all stems from our natural curiosity and our desire to know all we can about our world. Robert Falcon Scott of Great Britain led the first major expedition to Antarctica in 1901. He built a hut on Ross Island and from there did scientific and exploratory work. Scott, along with Dr Edward Wilson and Ernest Shackleton (later Sir Ernest) made the first journey to the interior of the frozen continent. They walked 200 miles south on the Ross Ice Shelf. It is doubtful whether they believed they had much chance of reaching the South Pole, but their march was the first in that direction. Their decision to turn back was

made in part
illness, which was
to scurvy (a
Following his return
became determined to
to lead his
1907 he returned
in charge of
greatest expeditions
His men became
climb Mt Erebus
on Ross Island.
the south magnetic
importantly they pioneered
the South Pole.
Jameson Adams
with four ponies,
the pole in
Dogsleds were
of 1901 to 1904
not work out
For this reason,
to rely on
The journey south
The ponies pulled
The explorers travelled
shelf, wondering if
the South Pole.
and they had
just 97 miles

because of Shackleton's
felt to be due
deficiency of vitamin C).
to England, Shackleton
return to Antarctica
own expedition. In
to Ross Island
one of the
in Antarctic history.
the first to
the 13,000-foot volcano
They also discovered
pole, but most
the route to
Shackleton, Frank Wild,
and Eric Marshall,
set out for
October 1908.
used in the expedition
and they did
well at all.
Shackleton had decided
ponies and manpower.
was remarkable.
very large loads.
over the ice
it would lead to
It did not,
to turn back
from the Pole.

Four-Word Eye-Hop™
The Optimist

There is a story	of identical twins.
One of them was	a hope-filled optimist.
'Everything is coming up	roses!' he would say.
The other was a	sad and hopeless pessimist.
He thought that Murphy,	as in Murphy's Law,
was an optimist.	The worried parents of
the boys brought them	to the local psychologist.
He suggested to the	parents a plan to
balance the twins' personalities.	'On their next birthday,
put them in separate rooms	to open their gifts.
Give the pessimist the	best toys you can afford,
and give the optimist	a box of manure.'
The parents followed these	instructions and carefully
observed the results.	When they peeked in
on the pessimist, they	heard him audibly complaining,
'I don't like the	colour of this computer...
I'll bet this	calculator will break...
I don't like this game...	I know someone
who's got a bigger	toy car than this...'
Tiptoeing across the corridor,	the parents peeked in
and saw their little optimist	gleefully throwing the manure
up in the air.	'You can't fool me!
Where there's this	much manure, there's
gotta be a pony!'	*Author unknown*

Five-Word Eye-Hop™
A humble Scottish farmer

This story begins with a poor Scottish farmer. One day while trying to make a living for his family, he heard a cry for help coming from a nearby bog. He dropped his tools and ran to the bog. There, mired to his waist in black muck, was a terrified boy, screaming and struggling to free himself. The farmer saved the lad from what could have been a slow and terrifying death. The next day, a fancy carriage pulled up to the Scotsman's sparse surroundings. An elegantly dressed nobleman stepped out and introduced himself as the father of the boy the farmer had saved. 'I want to repay you,' said the nobleman. 'You saved my son.' 'No, I can't accept payment for what I did,' the Scottish farmer said, waving off the offer. At that moment, the farmer's own son came to the door of the family hovel. 'Is that your son?' the nobleman asked. 'Yes,' the farmer replied proudly. 'I'll make you a deal. Let me take him and give him a good education. If the lad is anything like his father, he'll grow to be a man you can be proud of.' And that he did. In time, the farmer's son graduated from St Mary's Hospital Medical School in London, and went on to become known throughout the world as the noted Sir Alexander Fleming, the man who discovered penicillin. Years afterwards, the nobleman's son was stricken with pneumonia. What saved him? Penicillin. The name of the nobleman? Lord Randolph Churchill. His son's name? Sir Winston Churchill. Someone once said: What goes around comes around. It might be true.

Mastering Eye-Hop™

You will want to have fairly good comprehension while Eye-Hopping™. You can test your comprehension by parroting after a story (as you will learn in chapter 9). You should be able to remember at least 75 per cent of the content – not word for word, but the gist of the story with some interesting details such as names and places. The rule is to read as fast as you can while maintaining comprehension. This is especially true if you have previewed the Eye-Hop™ story (see chapter 7). If you have done poorly, then slow down a bit on the next story and parrot again. If your recall is still too low, and you are not overly stressed or distracted by things in your life, then preview the stories. If that does not help, then do not worry. Just keep going through the Eye-Hop™ exercises as best you can and eventually they will do their work for you. Then you will start pattern reading (to find out all about this, see page 162) when you are into either the four-word or five-word Eye-Hop™.

ASSIGNMENT

Do at least 40 minutes of Eye-Hop™ every day until you have mastered the five-word level.

SUMMARY

- The purpose of Eye-Hop™ is to move you from processing one word at a time to many words at a time. You progress through the levels, getting faster and faster on each level until your finger cannot physically keep up with your brain.

- At the two-word and three-word levels you will still hear all the words in your head as you process them. When picking up speed in the four-word level you will begin to experience some drop-off of the words pronounced while still understanding the meaning of those words.

- You should have fairly good comprehension when Eye-Hopping™.

- You can parrot (see chapter 9) to see what you recall. If your recall is very low, you probably need to slow down.

- Sometimes you slow down for a while when moving up to a next level (particularly when going from three-word to four-word).

- Your finger should come off the page when you hop, defining each word group as you land.

- You can create your own Eye-Hop™ by copying text and importing it into the Hopify website (www.superreading.com/hopify).

9.

Parroting

Parroting is an extremely useful technique for testing yourself on what you have read. It has a key role to play in boosting comprehension and recall. You can parrot at various points in your reading: certainly, while you are learning the techniques of SuperReading™, you should parrot at least once a day, after reading key sentences (see page 93). The idea is that you read a few key sentences, and then you find out how much you remember. For example, if you were to read eight key sentences you may be able to recall points from only five of them. Some people can only remember two or three points. Wherever you start is OK. It's where you end up that is important! Of course, when you are parroting, you will find that how much you can recall will depend on how you are feeling that day. We have already looked at some of the factors that can affect our reading abilities, but it is worth recalling them now:

- adequate sleep
- nutrition
- interest in the material
- stress
- your environment (noise, physical distractions).

In this chapter we will also look at some useful techniques for dealing with test stress in the exam room.

ASSIGNMENT

Pick up any book with paragraphs. Read eight key sentences (see page 93) and discover how many you can recall. With eyes open or closed, recall everything you can about what you just read. You don't do it verbatim; instead you are simply 'parro-phrasing'. This means that you are remembering the gist of the information.

Do this assignment at least three times to make up a good sample. Now the idea is to build up your ability over time, once you have taken on board the information in the rest of this chapter. This technique is called 'stair stepping' and is a very powerful way to build your skills. It allows you to know your level of skills when you begin, how fast you're making progress and where you end up.

How to parrot

There are three ways to parrot. Have a go at all of them and see which works best for you. Remember in chapter 3 you worked out what kind of learner you are?

If you are a visual or kinaesthetic type person you may find that the Info-Map™ technique (see pages 147–151) works particularly well for you. If you are more of an auditory person, you may find that verbal parroting works better. In either case you will want to practise both, as your skills will improve and your abilities will expand.

Parroting by writing

The first parroting method is to write down what you can remember. The best way to do this is by using the Info-Map™ technique for note taking. This is a great method for generating ideas, as you will see when you come to try it out. We will look at this technique again in much more detail in chapter 10, where it is used for reviewing what you have read, but to put it simply Info-Mapping™ is a technique to map out information instead of writing it down in serial order. One advantage of Info-Mapping™ is that you may record information in any order you choose, either by category or the order in which you remember it. Information is bullet pointed (using key words) to remind you of the various points you have read.

The idea is that when you have finished previewing and then reading your pages, write down the central theme within the circle or oval drawn in the middle of your Info-Map™. Send several lines (usually five to seven) out from the central hub and write down the main thoughts. From each one of these thoughts, extend a line or two. Write down other thoughts as you remember them. Try to group similar ideas together. Write as fast as you can without much regard to being neat.

When you are parroting by writing, you are either reading **or** writing. Do not look at the book, write, look at the book, and write. The best way is to read, put the book down, then create your Info-Map™ **from memory**.

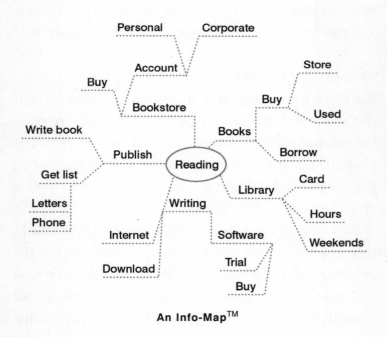

An Info-Map™

Parroting by telling

The second way to parrot is to tell what you remember to someone else. This makes absorbing the information multi-sensory. You see it, you say it and you hear it. In class students always stand up when parroting with someone else. That gets you to think on your feet (which may also come in handy for other situations).

It's been said that the best way to learn something is to teach it to someone else. In essence, this is what you are doing when you **tell** the other person what you've read. If you parrot with another person, you can hone your listening skills further by writing down what they have told you. In other words, parrot what they have parroted!

Parroting by pretending

The third way to parrot is to *pretend* someone is with you and tell them verbally about what you have read. Do **not** simply think about it in your own head as that tends to make you lazy and waste time. Thinking in your head takes a large amount of discipline to pull it off consistently and successfully.

Parroting aloud, however, forces you to face the truth. It proves that either you know it or you don't. Part of the art of SuperReading™ is never to be afraid to find out how you've done. If you do well, you are happy. If you do not do well, you simply see what you left out of the recipe and correct it for next time. You will not improve if you bury your head in the sand as denial has no place in any plan to improve your skills. There is a phrase used in NLP (neuro-linguistic programming) which is especially apt: 'There is no failure, only feedback.'

While you are telling your pretend companion about what you have read, use the magnetic questions (who, what, when, where, why, how – see page 108). They make a great starting point for quizzing yourself on the material you have read. Simply ask yourself 'Who was mentioned?', 'What did they do?', 'When did they do that?', 'Where did they do that?' and so on.

> **ASSIGNMENT**
> Parrot for at least one five-minute piece of reading every day. This time use the Info-Map™ technique (page 147).

Dealing with test stress

Some people get really stressed and flustered in testing situations such as exams. They feel like they know the information beforehand, but something awful happens when they walk through that doorway into the exam room. Their heart rate goes up, their palms get sweaty, their skin grows cold and sometimes their mouth goes dry. Their head may swim and their breathing goes shallow. These are all signs of panic. Are there solutions? Yes.

Using parroting techniques will get you testing yourself more thoroughly than your teacher, professor or anyone else. You will have much higher confidence, borne out of proving to yourself that you know the information. Memorising through pictures and imagination (see pages 192 and 230) will take the stress away from trying to get facts and concepts to simply stick in your head. Affirmations and visualisation will get you through the rough patches (see page 192).

You can also use a couple of physical methods to calm yourself down:

1 Make your breathing slow and deep for a couple of minutes. Only focus on your breathing – think of nothing other than the air entering and leaving your body. You can hold on to it for a few seconds when you fill your lungs.
2 The other technique is 'palming'. This will relax your eyes and your mind. Rub your hands together very fast with a good amount of pressure. When they heat up cup your eyes with them, letting the heel of your hand fit into your eye socket. Keep it there for five to ten seconds. This will relax the ocular muscles and give you a feeling of relaxation. It may take you a few seconds to get focused again! You will feel more calm and may even find yourself smiling.

You can also perform a minute of alphabet animals (see page 220).

Easy does it

Here's a specific strategy that works well for dealing with test stress. When you open your paper, preview the test (using the techniques in chapter 7), pick out all the easy items and do them first. This has three advantages. One is that you will definitely get credit for those questions. Another is that it will build your confidence. The third is that it will give you momentum to get going on the rest of the test.

SUMMARY

- Testing yourself is a great way to determine how much information you have gleaned from your reading.

- There are three ways to accomplish this: one is to write down what you remember; a second way is to tell someone else what you can recall; the third method is to pretend to tell someone else what you remember.

- Testing will ensure that you recall the information.

- If you only parrot in your head, you will tend to get lazy and not follow through. Saying the words out loud proves that you really do remember what you read.

- Use calming techniques in testing situations.

10.

Reviewing and embodying

Reviewing is a very useful technique that helps you to fill in the gaps and answer those questions that previewing and reading left behind. You use reviewing after you parrot what you've just read. As you review, you will need to keep the questions or gaps in your reading in mind and make mental notes when you discover the missing information. This is reading with a specific purpose and is known as targeted reading.

We will also look at Info-Mapping™ again in more detail in this chapter as it is a very valuable technique for aiding review and recall. Embodying is the act of putting information into long-term memory, or possibly medium-term memory. A difference is that repetition of the information over time (weeks to months) may be the factor that pushes medium-term memories into long-term ones. An embodied idea is one that requires very little thought to access and communicate. An example would be the answer to 6 x 6. It takes only a fraction of a second to say the answer, because that information has been embodied. It requires no great degree of intelligence or ability. The answer to 16 × 16 requires more thought and work. While the answer, 256, is something you know, it was probably not associated with the question of what is 16 × 16. You've heard tell of 256; you just didn't embody the fact that it is the product of 16 × 16. What you do have stored in long-term memory is the procedure for figuring it out, either on paper, in your head or with a calculator. In this chapter we will be looking at various methods for embodying information.

Simple reviewing techniques

Before going on to describe some helpful reviewing techniques I should tell you that if you have parroted (chapter 9) and you are already able to recall everything you need for that session, you may then skip reviewing. However, if you have previewed (chapter 7), read and parroted and realise you are missing something vital, then you need to go back and review the section containing the vital piece of information. Use the following simple techniques (which we have already covered in chapter 7 when you used them for previewing purposes) for better recall.

Key sentence

Read the key sentences (see page 93) of each paragraph again. They are most likely to be the first sentence of each paragraph, but may be the last sentence. Look at how the author organises the information and adapt to it.

Name and number scan

Scan the page for proper nouns and numbers to remind you of the facts in the text. Use your finger when you scan. Stop on each one for a second or two to let the information sink in. You can say the word(s) aloud for extra impact (see below for more on this).

Simple scanning

You can simply scan over material you just read to see if specific pieces of information, such as names, dates, places, etc. jump out at you. Remember to use your finger!

Further memory techniques for reviewing and recalling

There follows a range of techniques that you might find helpful when you are reviewing and recalling what you have read. Try all those that appeal to you and stick with the ones you like. While some techniques work better for some people than others, I would suggest trying each for at least 21 days or 21 times, and then judge which really works best for you.

- Use the Roman room memory technique (which you will find out more about on pages 233–239) to recall lists of items. Take each item to remember in turn and link it with the next object in the memory room.
- Use the short-term method of mental shouting, where you pretend you are in an expensive restaurant, standing on a table shouting out the thing you need to remember as loud as you can. (There is more on this too, on pages 230.)
- Emotion is another tool you can use to seal in information. Get excited about something and you're more likely to remember it. You can use joy or enthusiasm or countless other emotions. (Again, there is more on this, on page 229.)
- Strong imagery (see page 192) related to the topic will help a lot, as the right brain is activated by pictures.
- Acting the topic out in some way can be very powerful, as it gets the entire body into the performance. This can be very kinaesthetic, verbal and emotional all in one.
- Sheer repetition is another way. Simply go over and over the information until it sticks.

The most powerful method of repetition is 'spaced repetition'. This is where you do some repetitions and then wait to repeat them again. You can wait anywhere from minutes to days, depending on how much information you are trying to absorb. For example, if you wanted to remember that the capital of Belgium is Brussels or something more arcane, like the capital of Mongolia, which is Ulan Bator. If you were to look at that fact once a day for 21 days, you would probably remember it forever. So spend ten seconds on it one day and then another ten seconds the next day. Each time you do this you will experience the 'Oh yeah phenomenon'. When you ask yourself, 'What is the capital of Mongolia?' you may not remember at first. When you look at the answer, you'll get a rush of recall, and say, 'Oh yeah – it's Ulan Bator!' A couple of days later when you do it again, you may experience the same thing. Then you repeat this a week later and then a month later and so on each month. This will only have taken you five minutes, but spread out for 15 or 20 seconds at a time, it will have a huge effect on your remembering the answer. That little rush of recall really does something amazing in your brain and puts the information in your long-term memory almost effortlessly. All you have to do is choose the appropriate spacing to facilitate the remembering. The simpler and more familiar the information is the less spaced repetition you will need. For example, knowing that the Nile is the longest river in the world is relatively easy, because you've heard of the Nile, seen pictures of it, and can imagine it on a map. However, remembering that the Ob-Irtysh is the fifth longest river requires far more repetition because for most people they have either never heard of it and probably have no idea where it is (Russia). Remembering the Nile as the longest river could probably be embodied in five seconds once a day for a week. Remembering the Ob-Irtysh as the fifth longest river could take 15 seconds once a day for a week, then once a week for six weeks, and once a month for four months. There's no hard and fast rule, but I would say with the Ob-Irtysh example, if you had it well recalled after three months, I would do a couple of extra months just in case. The great thing about this method is that it takes so little time. Everyone can spare a few seconds in a day. You could even program the information to pop up on your computer or mobile phone on a regular basis until it is embodied.

Note taking by Info-Mapping™

As we have already seen in chapter 9, Info-Mapping™ is a form of laying out information in a graphic form instead of in a linear fashion like most people are taught in school. Instead of Roman numeral I, I (a), I (b), I (c), II, II (a), II (c), etc, the Info-Map™ spreads out in a radial fashion from the central hub. This style gives the note taker the freedom to place information wherever it seems to fit, and even if it does not fit well it doesn't matter that much. In practice, Info-Mapping™ is less stressful than a list because you do not have to remember information in the exact same order as the author. When trying to recall information (by parroting, see chapter 9), we sometimes feel that if there is a gap, we cannot proceed until we recall that fact. We feel stuck, frustrated and stupid. With Info-Mapping™ you can simply move on to another area and write down what you recall from there. As there is no sequence required, you are free to move in any direction.

You can use Info-Mapping™ to help you review and recall. When you have finished previewing and reading your material, write down the central theme in the circle or oval in the middle of your Info-Map™. Send several lines (usually five to seven) out from the central hub and write down the main thoughts at the ends of the lines. From **each one** of those thoughts extend as many lines as you need outwards from that thought or fact. Write down other thoughts as you remember them. Try to group similar ideas together. Write as fast as you can without much regard to being neat.

Only use one circle or oval, for the middle of your Info-Map™. This way, if you write something important, you can circle it later to draw attention to it. Six months later you will be able to look back at your Info-Map™ and instantly go to the most important points. Some Info-Mapping™ systems have you use colour to distinguish various categories of information from one another. Colours are great if you have the time and always have colours with you. If you don't, you've become dependent on a system that has a small drawback. If you want a way to distinguish categories, you can use shapes. You can use circles, squares, squiggly lines, zigzag lines, loopy lines, double lines, etc. As long as you have a pen or pencil you're in business.

Then:

- review the pages you have just read
- fill in the knowledge gaps in your Info-Mapped™ notes after you review
- review the material again to fill in any remaining gaps.

When you are reviewing using your Info-Map™, you are either reading or writing. Do not look at the book, write, look at the book, and write. The best way is to read, put the book down, then Info-Map™ from memory. (By the way, forget using a highlighter pen – this just trains your brain to be lazy.)

When you write, you can either write on the line or at the end of the line. The choice is yours. Below are two examples to show the difference. You could combine the two methods and save a bit of room. Topics can go on the line and notes can go after the line. Whatever you are comfortable with is what will work best for you. The idea is to end up with a map that resembles the way you put information together. That way, when you look back on it in the future it will still make sense to you. You have organised it in a similar fashion as to how your brain processes and stores information.

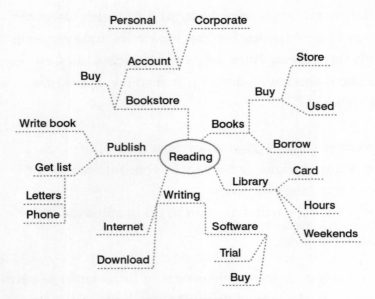

Information written on the line

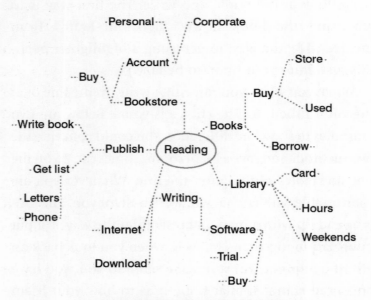

Information written after the line

In my classes I am always fascinated to see how, with the same instructions, everyone comes up with a totally different-looking map. Some are very neat and organised, some are helter-skelter, some are crowded and some look sparse. Each Info-Map™ reflects something of the personality of its creator. Whenever you create something it can't help but relate to who you are.

Advanced review techniques

Once your reading skills reach a certain level, you will be able to absorb and embody large amounts of information in a relatively short time. As you gently push yourself to do more and more each week, some amazing things will begin to happen. Eventually you will be able to read not only entire lines at a glance, but multiple lines. Some people, after a few months, are able to see and understand small paragraphs in a second or two. When this happens, it is important to just let the process take over. This is called relaxed focus, or directed relaxed focus.

You may feel like an observer watching the reading process as you read. This is a very right-brain activity. It must come with no analysing and no judgement (whether good or bad). The first way to experience this is by reviewing some information in a loop several times or more. This is not the same as when people don't understand something and have to go back over it several times for it to make sense. You already understand it. Now you are working to permanently retain it. When you have retained it, you can say that you have embodied it. To embody the information you read means to make it a part of you; almost on a physical level.

For example, if you were to pattern read (see chapter 11) this page over and over 10 or 20 times, going faster and faster, eventually the information would be going directly into your subconscious mind. You would find that you could bring up any part of it with ease and confidence. This method of combining repetition and pattern reading puts you in the zone far beyond what any standard reader could hope for.

Advanced Eye-Hop™

Simply hop down the page when you are reviewing, skipping several lines as you go. This works especially well when you're very fast at four-word Eye-Hop™, as your brain is picking up more content. A variation on this theme is the 'roving Xs'. Trace three big letter Xs down the page (see the diagram opposite) and then parrot. Use this pattern to review extra-wide columns because pattern reading is more difficult with really wide columns (see chapter 11 for a detailed explanation of pattern reading). You may have to do three hops to a line in some books and articles with very wide columns.

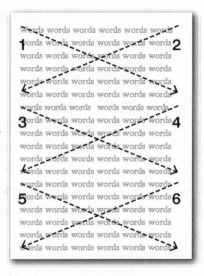

Roving Xs

Loop the loop

With this technique you simply make a looping pattern (see diagram overleaf) with your finger on the first page and repeat it on the facing page. Keep going for as many pages as you wish to review (you can also use this for previewing). Consciously you may not remember tremendous amounts. Subconsciously, your mind remembers everything. You may do one large loop on a page or two or three smaller loops. The diagram shows one large loop per page. You can experiment with other patterns as well. You could try a pattern like a lightning bolt, or a figure-of-eight. Sometimes being creative with a pattern gets you more interested in the text.

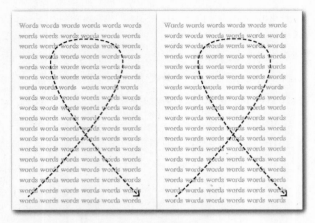

Loop the loop

Page scan

With this reviewing technique, you start at the bottom of a page and let your eyes move up the page like a scanning device. When you get to the top, let your eyes scan back down the same way. Again, this technique is most powerful when you've been going quite fast for a while with the four-word or five-word Eye-Hops™ (see chapter 8).

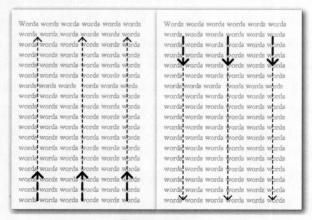

Page scan

Hop-drop

Hop-drop is a slightly different way of doing Eye-Hop™. Some people really like it. Others do not. Please try it while reserving judgement for at least 21 days. You lift your finger off the page and drop down a couple of lines, picking up the ones you go over as you proceed. You must be going quite fast on four-word Eye-Hop™ or fairly fast on the five-word for this technique to work. The narrower the column the better it works.

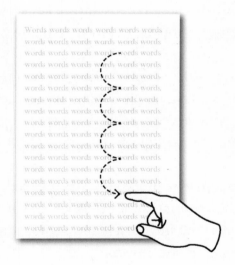

Hop-drop

NOTE: These are advanced techniques. You must be an advanced reader to take them on – in other words you should have progressed to the five-word Eye-Hop™ before you can benefit from them. Often they do not work well the first time you use them and this is another instance where reserving judgement is crucial.

Also be aware that on a particular day you may or may not be at your mental best. This is a good reason for reserve judgement for at least 21 days! That way you are sure to catch yourself on a good day and reap the benefits of a particular skill.

It seems that on different days different techniques work better. This may be due to various cycles in our day, month or season. The reason doesn't really matter. What's important is to recognise that we are sometimes different and we need to have a varied set of tools to deal with these differences. For instance, if key sentencing just isn't working for you today, switch to name and number scan.

If variety is the spice of life, then experimenting is the spice of reading. Switching things around may wake up your brain, forcing it to focus better. Avoid getting into mental ruts by changing your thinking and actions.

If you keep on seeing yourself as the reader you want to be, the appropriate tool will work for you. The key is to keep believing in yourself and seeing yourself using the information you absorb.

Hi-speed review

By reviewing significant chapters, or even entire books, the subconscious accepts the information in a subliminal fashion, because the speeds are so high that you are not consciously aware of every word. What you do is simply keep reading in your favourite pattern faster and faster and faster. Soon the concepts are coming together in pictures in your mind like a movie.

ASSIGNMENT

Take a particularly significant piece of information and read it at high speeds until it becomes imagery. This will take several times of reading through; the number of times varying from person to person and day to day. It may take five, ten or 20 loops. Eventually you will register the meaning pictorially wherever possible, seeing the information more than just understanding it. This effect depends a bit on the nature of the subject. Anything in the text you can picture will become more vivid with each repetition. You are looking to turn it more into an experience than just reading it. You are mentally running it over and over like an endless loop tape. Allow it to seep deeply into your subconscious. Like doing repetitions in weight-lifting, the information will build up in that part of your personality. The high-speed loop is a wonderfully simple concept which cannot be achieved as well by standard readers. Your ability to absorb multiple words at a glance enables you to benefit from high-speed review at a much more significant level.

Daily application

Always look out for ways to practise a concept on a daily basis. For instance, you might pick a self-improvement book like *How to Win Friends and Influence People* by Dale Carnegie. One of his concepts is 'You catch more flies with honey than with vinegar'. In sales, or any human relations, we see that being 'sweet' (nice) towards people takes you further than being a grouch or a critic. Focus on 'using honey' all day long. Opportunities will present themselves. You could even focus on one attribute for a week. Benjamin Franklin identified several areas in which he wished to improve himself. One was humility. He carried around a card with the word 'humility' written on it everywhere he went for a month. He claimed this helped him to be more humble. According to Franklin, 'Humility is the one thing that once you think you have it – you don't!'

Look for clever ways to remind yourself daily of how you might wish to change. Be creative. Whatever works for you is what's right. The same principle applies to reviewing information. If you review information daily until it is embodied, you will soon find it difficult to forget. The difference between 'review' and 'application' is that with application you are putting the information to use, which better seals it into memory. If information you wish to remember does not have a way to be applied, you can imagine teaching it to someone else. In that case, teaching is the application.

Keep a notebook

For permanent long-term recall, I recommend keeping a notebook (or file) that can hold the information you are interested in always having at your 'mental fingertips'. Keep key words and concepts in it and review it monthly. It will only take a few minutes and you will remember all these wonderful concepts. Some can be factual; some can be inspirational; and others can be instructional. A quick perusal will be all you need to remind you and further embody the concepts in your mind. Put a monthly reminder in your calendar to review this file. It is the essence of spaced repetition (see page 145) and the ultimate expression of reserving judgement.

SUMMARY

- Repetition is one of the most powerful ways to embody information. The more exposures spread over time (spaced repetition), the more likely you are to remember.

- Using techniques such as Hi-speed review, advanced patterns of Eye-Hop™, Loop the Loop, Roving Xs and Page Scan can work at a non-verbal level to help you retain information.

- Info-Mapping™ is not only multi-modal, it is a permanent record of what you wish to recall.

In this chapter we have looked at reviewing and embodying what you have read, and we have now come to the end of the section of this book that has introduced you to the basic techniques of SuperReading™. Now would be a good time to recap on what you should have learned so far. It is conveniently encapsulated in the acronym PREPARE:

Preview
REad
PArrot
Review
Embody

Put the underlined letters together and you have: P.RE.PA.R.E:

The first step is to **preview** the material so you know what's coming.

The second step is to **read** (using your finger, of course!).

Step three is a choice: **parroting** to see if you've gained enough information.

Step four is another choice based on what you learned in step three. If you are missing vital information, you then **review** to capture it.

Step five, **embodying**, is yet another choice: do I want to put effort into storing this information in medium- or long-term memory?

PART THREE:

Building on the Basics

11.

Pattern reading

By now you must have realised that there are many aspects of the art of reading and in this chapter we are going on to look at some more advanced techniques that will help you to build on the basics of SuperReading™, including perhaps the most important concept in this book – pattern reading.

REMINDER: To remind yourself of the basics you have already learned, use your hand pacing technique (see chapter 6) to read something you have just previewed. (In fact, are you reading these words using your finger right now?) When you read, read every word including the key sentences again (or you can use name and number scan or novel previewing – see chapter 7). This repetition will aid your recall later. And remember, always read as fast as you can while maintaining comprehension. Think about increasing your speed about 5 per cent or so per page. It's human nature to slow down but most of the time there is no real need to do this – it just tends to happen. If you concentrate you will find you can speed up 5 per cent with no loss to your comprehension. In fact, after a few weeks of prac-tise, speeding up will probably increase your comprehension and recall.

Gentle snap-back or carriage return

This is a simple technique that will help you to improve your hand pacing.

When you get to the end of a line that you are hand pacing, 'snap' your finger back to the left of the line of text (rather like the carriage return on an old manual typewriter). The snapping back is **not** a violent move. It is a firm, yet gentle snap. The intention of the action is to keep you moving and in flow with the text. It will help to challenge your brain to keep up.

When you get near the end of the line you may notice that you understand the whole line **before** your finger arrives at the last letter of the last word. As soon as you **know** the meaning of that line, snap down to the next line and do the same thing again.

Reading styles

You start reading after you have previewed a chapter, story or article that is greater than two paragraphs. For now, you will use **one** of the following techniques as you read. The first two, hand pacing and Eye-Hop™, are fundamental techniques, while the rest are more advanced. When you get to pattern reading on page 172 you will discover a technique that is the most important aspect of SuperReading™, and which will really help you to fulfil your potential.

Hand pacing

This is a brief reminder of the technique, which was explained in detail in chapter 6. Sitting in the proper reading position (see page 73), elbow on the table, you pivot your arm so your finger moves in a smooth, flowing motion across the page. The finger always remains in motion, although you may slow down or speed up, depending on the material.

Eye-Hop™

Again, this is a brief reminder of the technique that was described in detail in chapter 8. You can read with this method by making two or three hops with your eyes across a line, dropping down to the next line and continuing in the same manner. If you are reading a book with exceptionally long lines of small type, you may have to do more than three bounces in the beginning. As always, you are going as fast as possible, or taking in as much as possible while maintaining your comprehension.

Second word

After you've mastered the two-word Eye-Hop™, you can really begin to benefit from the hard work you've done. You are now able to process two to three words at a glance, especially if the words are relatively small. Now, to take further advantage of your growing skill, you can start your finger on the second word of a line instead of the first. Your brain will process both the first word and the second word (and possibly the third word). This will begin to save you even more time because you will get down the page a bit faster. This is because even though you are reading at the same speed, you are covering a slightly smaller area, so it will take you less time to cover each line.

ASSIGNMENT

Pick up a book and try reading a paragraph or two now, starting on the second word, and you'll experience this for yourself. After reading a couple of paragraphs, parrot (see chapter 9) to see how that worked for you. Your recall should be the same (or better) as when you start with your finger at the very beginning of a line. If it is not, it may be that you are thinking about the technique instead of what you are reading, thus taking up some of your attention and focus. Assuming you have been doing the Eye-Hop™ exercises in chapter 8, this technique **will** work for you.

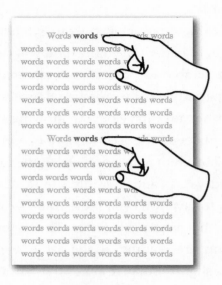

Second word

Short stroke

Once you have been reading fairly fast (about one line, or two hops per second or faster) in three-word Eye-Hop™ and are moving on to four-word Eye-Hop™ it's time for your next step – short stroke, which is an advanced form of hand pacing. Instead of starting with your finger at the first letter of each line and following through to the last letter of each line, you start in half an inch to an inch (1.5 to 2.5 cm) from the beginning and finish half an inch (1.5 cm) from the end. You will find that you can do this easily because you have been practising the Eye-Hop™ exercises. You are now taking in and comprehending at least three words at a time, probably four. If you start a line with your finger on the first letter, you are cutting off the two words that could be to the left of that point. So start further in to take advantage of your new ability.

The same holds true for the end of a sentence. Once you get near the end, you will find that you already know what it says.

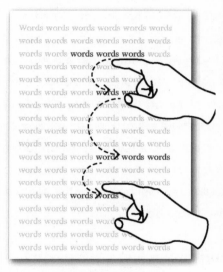

Word darts

Word darts

To prepare for short stroke, you first need to have a look at the concept of 'word darts', which is related to Eye-Hop™.

ASSIGNMENT

Find a book with reasonable-sized type (at least 11 or 12 pt or 16 character spaces (or less) per inch/2.5 cm).

Now, with the book open to pages with plenty of text, choose some random lines and place your finger near the middle of the line as if you were doing Eye-Hop™. Your finger will only remain there for a moment, just like when doing Eye-Hop™. However, instead of going left-right-left-right, move down the page to 'random' lines and just see what you get. In other words, you may hit the third line, the seventh line, the tenth, the fifteenth, the eighteenth and the twenty-fourth. Do at least a dozen of these word darts to get a good sample over a couple of pages. Afterwards, you should know approximately how many words you were picking up with each 'dart'. Most people will pick up three. Some may pick up three or four, and a few will pick up four or five. If English is not your first language, you may only pick up two. If you want to feel better, try the same exercise in your native language.

Starting short stroke

Once you have determined how many words you pick up using word darts, the concept of short stroke will make more sense to you. In fact, short stroke is very easy. Simply place your finger down about an inch (2.5 cm) or so into the text as you begin a new line and start reading from there. Likewise, as you approach the end of that line, you will notice that you understand all the meaning of that line before your finger reaches the end! Once you know what the line means, drop down to the next line and 'short stroke' that one about an inch. Keep going the same way to the bottom of the page as illustrated in the diagram.

Your brain has been getting used to picking up at least three words at a glance. This means that whenever you put your finger down on a page, your brain will pick up one to two words around it. Therefore, starting a line by putting your finger down on the first letter of the first word has your brain looking at the clear space to the left for information. You can now put your finger down on the second word in the line and still have picked up the first word!

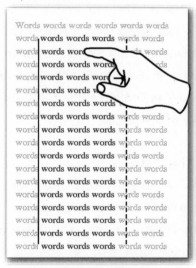

Short stroke

ASSIGNMENT

Begin with your finger near the solid line as shown in the diagram (about 2 cm in). When you get to about where the dashed line is you will already understand the remainder of the line. When that happens for you, drop down to the next line and begin again.

Short stroke will increase your comprehension after just a page or two of practice and will cut at least 20 per cent off your reading time. Later, when you are going fast (about ten lines, or 20 hops, in eight seconds) on the four-word Eye-Hop™, you can start even further in. Try different starting points until you find what's comfortable for you. Once you know that, you can stretch yourself each day to increase your abilities. For example, once you've mastered starting in at 2 cm, try 2.5 cm. The same goes for ending your reading on a line. Keep ending further and further from the end of the line. Once that is consistently comfortable try starting in at 3 cm. Eventually, your entire stroke on a line will only be about 2 to 3 cm, situated in the middle of the page.

Evolution of short stroke

As you are able to absorb more and more words, your finger stroke across the page will get smaller and smaller. By the time you are picking up three to four words at a glance, you will be able to shorten your stroke to size of the line marked 2. When you can pick up four or five words at a glance, your stroke will look like line 4. Eventually your stroke will be very short like lines 6 or 7. However, by that time you will probably be performing pattern reading (for more, see page 172 of this chapter). Sometimes you may still decide to use

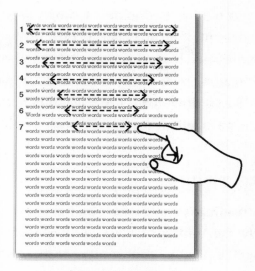

Shortening your short stroke

short stroke instead of pattern reading for various reasons, such as lack of sleep or stress.

Vertical drop

Try this useful technique once you are doing the five-word Eye-Hop™. When you are reading newspaper articles, you will know that you can simply drop your eyes down in steps once you have mastered the four-word Eye-Hop™ exercises (see page 130). Most newspaper columns are only five or six words across, so putting your finger down in the middle of the column gives you the whole line! After a little practice, you can simply flow down the column. When you do begin to flow, keep a bit of a sideways curve to your downward stroke. You will find that if you go straight down, you tend to be looking at single words again.

Some people find it easier to pick up two or three lines at a glance once they have become proficient at pattern reading, which we will look at next. Some people like to flow down the page; others like to hop down the page. Whatever works for you is the right way.

Pattern reading

Pattern reading is really what you have been aiming for since the beginning of your journey through Super-Reading™. In fact, pattern reading is the quintessential form of reading, which can help you reach your full reading potential. Many people have been amazed by its possibilities for both speed and comprehension.

Before trying the pattern reading technique (this includes the backwards S and Z, pages 177–183 below) you **must** be consistently going fairly fast in the four-word Eye-Hop™ (at least ten lines (20 hops) in eight seconds). If you are not yet consistent, please wait a few more days in order to have a good experience with this technique.

By the time you have reached this part of the book, you have probably been working your way through the SuperReading™ exercises for at least three or four weeks. You are reading these words with your finger using short stroke. Your comprehension is far better than it was before you bought this book and you've noticed far less drifting off (as described in chapter 2).

You've realised that previewing is extremely cool and useful (see chapter 7). You are getting through material faster and better than ever. Now, you're going to take it up to the next level. Pattern reading is different from what you've been doing up until now, although there are some people who start doing this naturally once they are going fast in the four-word Eye-Hop™. If you do turn out to be one of those people, there are a few pointers that will make pattern reading more powerful for you.

Over the past few weeks you have been preparing your brain to make this leap. Now is the time. You may or may not have noticed, but when you come back to the left column in Eye-Hop™, your finger sweeps towards it and you have actually read the words before you realised it consciously. To put it another way, by the time your finger lands on the word group, you already understand it! While this effect may not happen on every hop, it will begin to occur more often. Take a moment to think about this. Imagine doing your Eye-Hops™. See your finger coming back to the left column. If you understand the words either before your finger touches down or as it touches down, then you get my meaning. In other words, this skill is more advanced than your finger touching down, picking up the words and then moving on, as you were probably doing in the three-word Eye-Hop™.

This means that half the time you have been, in a manner of speaking, reading backwards! Yes, backwards!

Now it's time to take advantage of this skill to use a technique called backwards reading, which is a precursor to the full form of pattern reading.

Backwards reading

Backwards reading is a method that works really well for some people. It is **not** pattern reading but can be a useful additional skill. If you try the following assignment, you will find out whether or not you can benefit from this reading style. It is good to try backwards reading before going on to pattern reading because it will show you that you can read backwards, because of the right to left stroke on the Eye-Hop™.

Remember the 21-day rule for reserving judgement from chapter 4. A significant number of people have reported that at first backwards reading did nothing for them, but later on they tried it again very successfully. Part of this may be that many people simply don't believe that they could possibly read backwards. The fact is that when they try it again they have already done more impressive things than reading backwards, such as using the memory room (see chapter 13).

ASSIGNMENT

Follow these steps to ensure the highest degree of success in backwards reading:

1 Preview two pages, perhaps of this book or a newspaper.

2 Read those pages using your finger to trace under the lines from **right** to **left**. You can use short stroke (page 166) if you like.

Finger moving right to left

NOTE: Although your finger will be moving from right to left, your eyes will most likely be going from left to right. Somehow this can work quite well. You will find that it works best, the shorter the line. Wide lines make this process more difficult. So choose a book with relatively narrow columns. It would be even better to try backwards reading first in a newspaper or magazine. Once you have read the pages, parrot (see chapter 9) to see how much you remember. If your recall is acceptable, then this is a technique you can use from time to time.

I have found that backwards reading is very popular with engineers who use the technique to read their engineering journals. It may be that there's something about a logical mind which likes the anomaly of moving in one direction and reading in the other. One theory is that by going in the other direction you are forced to concentrate more on the material. Either way, I suggest starting off with familiar material to see if you get it at all. Most people are amazed that it works. In fact, by moving your finger in the opposite direction in which you are reading, your finger tends to become more of a background object. In some ways it's easier to ignore your finger in favour of seeing the words. I believe this is because you **know** you're not following your finger, so you are free not to let it guide your speed. However, you keep the benefit of letting it move you along because it 'forces' you to drop down to the next line and keep some momentum going.

The more you practise backwards reading the better you will get at it. Remember that what helps you get going at first is to have narrow columns with familiar text. It may be to your advantage to use backwards reading as a review tool (see chapter 10). Once you have seen that this can work, you can move up to pattern reading, which is really the beginning of the ultimate way to read.

Now that you've experienced backwards reading it's time to move on to combine the pattern of Eye-Hop™ (chapter 8) with the rhythm of hand pacing (chapter 6)

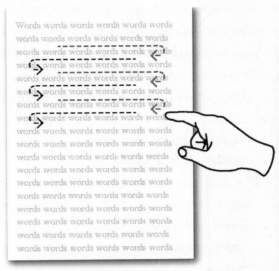

Backwards S

for the first form of pattern reading, known as the backwards S.

The backwards S

I suggest you practise this technique using a children's book to give yourself an easy time at first. See the assignment below for instructions.

ASSIGNMENT

Starting where you normally would on a page, that is the upper left, preview the material you want to read. Once you have previewed, go back to the beginning. You will be using the short stroke idea that you learned on page 166, but with a twist. When you get to the end of the first line of the first page, drop down to the next line and let your finger move from **right to left**. As you approach the left margin, drop down a line and move your finger **left to right**. Keep moving in this serpentine (snakelike) movement down the page. Go fairly fast. With this method you will observe two things:

1 Your comprehension will be better when you go **faster** (up to a point).
2 You have to trust yourself. This is because you will not be verbalising much in your head. You will understand without your internal voice giving you nearly as much feedback. You have to simply relax and **let it happen**.

Using this technique will help you to develop some really super speeds. Remember, once you've practised the backwards S technique for a few minutes, if you find your comprehension slipping, you may need to speed up instead of slow down. This method definitely involves faith and trust, because you will not know that you know the material until you parrot (chapter 9).

As you get used to this technique, bear in mind that everyone is different. While pattern reading using the backwards S technique, your eyes may follow your finger, or they may ignore your finger completely, or be somewhere in between. For many people, their finger becomes more of a 'pacing' tool than a 'pointing' tool. Your eyes may be going left to right (>>>) while your finger is going right to left (<<<)! It doesn't matter. Just find out which way works for you, and remember to reserve judgement, as always, for at least 21 days before deciding whether you like pattern reading or not. For most people it's a leap, so you need to keep your mind open and your finger moving!

If you have taken the rep test (in chapter 3), you will know by now the kind of learner you are. If you scored higher than 16 on 'digital audio' and tend to repeat things to yourself verbally (this is known as sub-vocalisation), pattern reading may possibly be more challenging for you. This is because your brain prefers hearing ideas in your own internal voice and does not willingly give that up. If you are patient and keep practising pattern reading, using visualisation techniques and affirmations to overcome your challenges, you will eventually realise that your sub-vocalisation reduces to an efficient level.

WARNING: You will be reading at some rather fast speeds. You will be previewing (chapter 7), so you will know a lot of information. However, there have probably been times in your life when you had to cram for an exam and decided you would read the material really quickly. Most people find that they absorbed very little information that way. Your brain has tracked those times and 'knows' you cannot read past a certain speed with any accuracy. You will probably exceed that speed with this method. It's quite possible that your mind will jump to the conclusion that it remembers almost nothing and tell you that when you've finished. Remember that this is impossible because you previewed! Your mind is playing an 'old tape', which you can now ignore. Confidently begin to parrot (chapter 9) and soon you will see that you remember impressive amounts of information. The case studies below illustrate this idea. If you give recalling a really good try, and you still cannot recall the material you've just read, then reread it. You may need to adjust your speed (while most people need to slow down, a large number of people actually need to speed up!).

CASE STUDIES

I had an engineer in class who was taking his last test in the final lesson. He did his 20-second preview and then proceeded to read. After reading the passage in about 25 seconds, he was shaking his head. I asked what the problem was. He told me he remembered nothing from the passage. I said, 'Just trust yourself. Take the test and remember to smile.' About halfway through the questions he had a look of near disbelief on his face. He called me over and said, 'This is incredible. I know all the answers. I guess I understood better than I thought!'

He did understand better than he 'thought'. This is because we're using a different thought process here. It's like watching playing cards flip by very fast. You know you know the cards, but there is no time to say them in your head. You recognise the king, the jack, the four of clubs.

If there were a card that did not belong there you would know that as well. You have been preparing for this for weeks. You are ready. Go for it and let it happen. Just let the story unfold for you. Remember, when you parrot and then review, you will be going even faster. Then reread and go even faster yet. Do it another time and go even faster. Each time you can go faster and understand more completely! Now you're doing it in seconds where before it took minutes!

There was a young woman in one of my classes who was on week five of the course. We were practising pattern reading. She had brought along a novel to read. There were 18 people in the class, which was a mixture of both students and professionals. As I walked around the room observing my students I noticed a nice smile on her face as she blazed through her novel. She was very absorbed by it. A few minutes later as I came back around I noticed the smile had been replaced by a frown and furrowed brow. I leaned over and asked her what the problem was. She looked up for a moment with a puzzled look on her face. 'I don't know what's happened. I was going along just fine, but now my comprehension has just dropped.'

I considered for a moment, and asked, 'How far did you preview?'

She flipped back a few pages and found the page she had previewed to. Now I knew what to say.

'You've gone past the pages that you previewed. Your comprehension dropped.'

She had a look of compete revelation. Her eyes were wide and her mouth was agape. She nodded with under- standing and said, 'Wow, that previewing really is powerful. Thanks.'

I walked off with a bit of a revelation myself. I now knew what to look for when people were pattern reading. I also have confirmation of just how powerful previewing is!

The Z

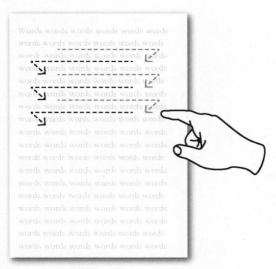

The Z

Another form of pattern reading that some people like is the Z. I would say that about 5 per cent of my students prefer this method. This works just like the backwards S we have just been looking at, only the movement is more sharply defined. Instead of a flowing motion that floats down the page, the Z is sharp and angular. Try both and see. You will probably like one and dislike the other. There is usually no middle ground.

The problem with the Z is that its sharp angles mean that even at its best, it is not as flexible a pattern as the backwards S, and is therefore not as fast. I would recommend the backwards S to most people, except perhaps those who operate with their 'left brain', such as engineers and lawyers, who might find it more diffi-cult to let go and enjoy the beauty of the flow of the S. However, such people may also find that using the backwards S may free up their thinking and expand their potential.

Pattern reading novels

As you will learn for yourself, reading with your finger flowing down the page while you absorb the informa-tion is a beautiful experience. Some readers have likened the feeling as being right up there with the best experiences of life. Pattern reading in a novel is particu-larly satisfying because you will experience the story closer to the 'speed of life' and at those speeds you become really 'engaged with the page' and filter out the rest of the world. The book not only comes alive, it becomes your universe for a while, so it becomes a true escape, which will transport you to other worlds and realities. After all, isn't that what reading should do for us?

ASSIGNMENT

Pick a simple book to start with. A novel is fine. If you have done your Eye-Hop™ exercises as prescribed, pattern reading should be easy for you. Easy or not, go for it. Relax and let it happen. Thinking about it as you read only gets in the way. Just know that you are doing it right. Your brain will do the rest.

Pattern reading and English as a second language

If English is not your first language, you need to be aware that the challenges of pattern reading will be greater than for those who learned to speak English first. Pattern reading involves massive processing of information as you go down the page. If you recall my warnings about starting with simple material, this goes double for those who did not grow up thinking in English. I recommend starting not only with simple material, but also with simple material in your native language. This all depends upon your level of English development. In my experience of teaching many students for whom English was not their first language, high-speed processing is held back when reading in a second language. It will take more time and more practice. You can do it; you just need to know that it may take anywhere from two to eight weeks longer to become proficient. I know that is quite a wide spread, but there is a huge difference in people's ability to learn languages. The average length I've observed in courses is from two to three weeks, but without knowing an individual it is impossible to be more precise.

My best advice for you if English is your second language is to keep practising and you will eventually get better and better with pattern reading. If you use visualisation techniques and affirmations, this will speed up your progress.

ASSIGNMENT

Try pattern reading in your most comfortable language with simple materials (even children's books). Prove to yourself that it's possible. Once you see that you can handle it, you will know that it's only a matter of time until you can master it in English.

The evolution of pattern reading

The following diagrams show how pattern reading evolves with practice. Over time you may progress through all the stages. The fourth stage is the ultimate reading experience. You are usually picking up multiple lines at a time and your eyes may even be going in other patterns down the page because of line breaks and other factors. It's one of the most difficult things to describe. Once you're really involved in it, especially with a novel, you can lose track of how you're actually progressing down the page. When someone is 'engaged with the page', the brain does whatever it needs to in order to follow the story. If you try to be conscious of how you're processing the words, the whole effect can stop. You need to simply 'let the book do half the work' and go along for the ride. You are guiding a half-conscious process, so play with it and see how far you can take yourself. What you are aiming for is a beautiful experience where the words flow into your mind, like water in a river. You develop a rhythm and a flow, which feels really good. Reading a novel should feel more like watching a movie.

1   The backwards S moves across, down and over the text in a flowing motion. It repeats on the next page where you do a flip turn.

Flowing backwards S

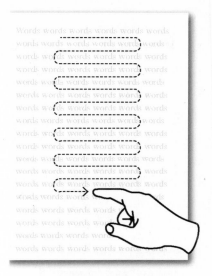

Short stroke backwards S

2 The backwards S then tightens up with short stroke. You go at the same speed but get down the page faster.

3 The pattern begins to stretch out into a stretched backward S as the brain picks up more and more information when you read multiple lines at once (see page 188).

4 The pattern stretches out further as the brain is able to process entire lines and even paragraphs.

Remember to always keep at least a slight curve to your motion to stop yourself from reading single words again.

Please reserve judgement on these techniques, as they often take time to develop. You may be fortunate to see immediate success with them, but even if that

Stretched backwards S

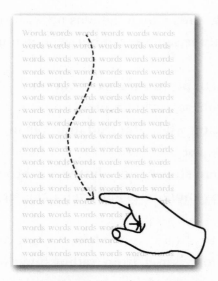

Further stretched backwards S

happens for you, there's still more development to come. That's why reserving judgement for at least 21 days or 21 times of practice is so valuable. The more open you are to possibilities the more likely it is that those possibilities will manifest.

The half-page speed-up

Once you are well into the four-word Eye-Hop™ you can begin to do something that will keep your reading skills fresh and growing. It's quite a simple technique. There are two reasons to do it and why I am introducing it now. One is to keep from backsliding into reading slowly or even one word at a time again. The other is to keep increasing speed until you reach an upper limit where you simply can't go any further on a particular level of material (such as novels, or a history textbook, or anything). It's like flying a plane up and up. At some point the air will no longer sustain the aircraft. You can't take a plane into outer space. At some point a given person simply cannot absorb information any faster. They have reached what I call their genetic limit. Nobody can read a million words per minute. On their best day, the limit will be somewhere between 100 and 1,000,000 w.p.m. That upper range is not negotiable beyond that point with that material. I've seen people read simple novels faster than 4,000 words per minute with impressive recall. With the enhanced focusing technique (see page 255) I've seen people absorbing information upwards of 5,000 to

10,000 w.p.m., though not with the kind of accuracy of pattern reading at 1,000 to 2,000 w.p.m.

Halfway down each page, speed up about 5 per cent or a little bit faster than you were going. When you learn about the speed visualisation technique in chapter 13 you will discover that you can speed up by 50 to 100 per cent and more and not lose any comprehension. In fact, you will often find that your comprehension increases.

To do the half-page speed-up you simply imagine there's a line across the page about halfway down. When you get to the imaginary line, boost your speed a bit. Even though I've suggested an increase of only 5 per cent, you may actually speed up 20 per cent or more. As long as you are maintaining comprehension you will be fine. Over time those little increases will add up. In the worst case, you won't be backsliding to lower speeds. In the best case, you will see highly significant increases over time with virtually no effort.

You can use this technique both for reading paper materials and on your computer screen. Let it become second nature and your skills will remain at their peak for years to come.

SUMMARY

- This chapter is about getting better and better. You are progressing from reading one word at a time to absorbing thousands of words per minute.

- Pattern reading uses a 'stair step method' of progressing – that is to say you take small steps beyond where you begin and make continual progress until you are pushing the limits of what you will ever be capable of doing.

- Everyone has a genetic limit, but between where you start and where you end up, the difference is remarkable and exciting.

12.

Visualisation and affirmation techniques

The visualisation and affirmation techniques you will find out about in this chapter are vital to improving your reading performance and will also help you to achieve other goals. Visualisation is especially helpful with novels, though it can relate to other reading as well. The ability to hold and manipulate imagery in your head is a powerful tool and will help you to see yourself performing better in many areas. The visualisation and affirmation techniques that are especially effective are picture visualisation, speed visualisation and positive affirmations.

Picture visualisation

It has long been known that the human brain is a goal-seeking mechanism that does especially well when the target is well defined. Visualisation is the best tool for this as it focuses your mind both consciously and subconsciously. The ability to create a mental image of what you want can be the essential ingredient in any project, and the more detailed and exciting you can make the image, the more precisely your mind will work to create it.

The following assignment will make you a master visualiser. You will need a magazine to practise with, preferably one with plenty of colourful advertisements and visually interesting pages. To get the full benefit repeat the assignment every day for 21 days.

ASSIGNMENT

STEP ONE:

Pick a page and turn it face down. (Ideally get someone else to pick the page for you.) With your eyes closed, hold the page up in front of you.

STEP TWO:

Open your eyes for about a quarter of a second. Close them again straight away. This is called a 'visual snap-shot'.

STEP THREE:

Recall what you saw, out loud. It should only be three or four of the main elements. If you remember much more than that, your eyes were open too long.

STEP FOUR:

Now view the page for five seconds. Recall everything you remember, including what you saw the first time.

STEP FIVE:

View the page for ten seconds. Recall everything you remember, including what you saw the first and second time.

STEP SIX:

Repeat step five twice more until you can remember most of what is on the page. You will find you are able to remember large amounts of detail very quickly.

NOTE:

- This is a great exercise to do with someone else. Warning to adults: children do very well with this one; you may be out-performed!

- Say what you are looking at when you when are viewing the page, like an announcer. Example: *There's a woman, white blouse, pearl necklace, dark hair, shoulder length, parted on my left, gold bracelet – left hand, looking to the right...*

- When working with a page, read only major titles. Do not read text, as this would take too much time. Be aware of text, such as how many sections of text are there, any colours and where they are on the page. Treat a block of text like a picture, for example: *'There's three blocks of text at the bottom. The text is white against a blue background.'*

When you have practised picture visualisation for a few days, you will notice your skill levels rising. When you feel this is happening, take one of these images and begin to change it in your mind. Make an element twice as big and move it around the page that you see in your mind's eye. Get it to interact with something else in the picture. Then, once you master this skill, use it to visualise **any** goal you set for yourself. Keep building the imagery until you see it as vividly as the magazine pages.

For example, each day, you could spend a couple of minutes seeing yourself reading faster than ever and recalling all that you read. With eyes closed, move your finger at speeds that take you down a page in two seconds. Then speed it up to one second and even faster. It's OK to go really fast in your imagination. You'll be surprised how at how soon your brain will begin to respond at similar speeds, especially once you have mastered the four-word Eye-Hop™ (see chapter 8).

Speed visualisation

Many top athletes use visualisation techniques to enhance their performance. Perhaps not surprisingly, speed visualisation can be applied to reading as well as sports. You will be ready to attempt this technique once you are going fast (about ten lines, or 20 hops, in eight seconds) in the four-word Eye-Hop™. The purpose of this technique is to get you reading faster to see that you can pick up more information at higher speeds. This technique will 'fool you' into reading faster than normal.

The idea is that you use your finger to read down an imaginary page at lightning speed while imagining that you understand what you read. To be clear, there is really no page in front of you – just a clear table or desk. This is not the time for weak spirits. This is the time to push yourself and break out of whatever thoughts are holding you back. You want to be pretending to pattern read, getting down each imaginary page in about one second or so.

You can see yourself picking up the information on the imaginary page any way you wish. The knowledge can be going directly into your brain, or it can travel up your arm, or it can play out like a movie in front of you. It does not matter. Just keep telling yourself that you are 'getting it'. At this point, confidence is more important than the thin veil of reality. When you believe that you are doing it your brain will comply and absorb more information at greater speeds.

It's helpful to think of things you like to do while going fast during this exercise. If you like skiing, or skating, or driving, or running fast, try keeping imagery and emotions from that type of activity in the background while you are doing this. The point is to get used to going faster while feeling good and confident. When you were practising the half-page speed-up (see page 189) where you increased your reading speed by 5 per cent halfway down the page, you will have felt a similar sense of exhilaration and concentration.

You can enhance this technique by playing fast, upbeat music as you are visualising yourself reading. Instrumental music is best as there are no words to interfere with your concentration. You could try

'Popcorn' by Hot Butter or 'Flight of the Bumble Bee' by
Rimsky-Korsakov.

ASSIGNMENT

Once you are going fast in the four-word Eye-Hop™, get
your music ready and perform this technique for about
90 to 120 seconds. Use a book that is of interest to you,
but not too highly technical, perhaps a novel or a self-
development or business book. Preview and read a
chapter to get into the flow of the book. Time yourself to
check your speed (words per minute). Then preview
another chapter. Halfway through the second chapter
(that you just previewed), start the music and do the
exercise. When the music ends, or two minutes have
passed, turn the music off or right down, pick up where
you left off and read as fast as you can while maintaining comprehension.

Most people find they naturally go faster because of
the speed they just experienced imagining they were
reading. Time yourself again, on the first half of the
latest chapter and then again on the second half after
the exercise. When you finish the chapter, parrot what
you remember from the latest chapter (see page 135).
You should find that you went much faster and your
comprehension was at least as good if not better. If it
was not better, do this exercise again in a day or two.
Keep doing it until you are going much faster (at least
25 per cent) and have equal or better comprehension.

Positive affirmations

Affirmations are statements we make about ourselves. Positive affirmations are usually statements about how we desire to be or how we want to act. They are employed to change the results we are getting in various parts of our lives, by expanding our comfort zones for that area. The most powerful affirmations begin with the words: 'I am...'

Make a claim for who and what you want to be **now**. Not in the future. The part of your brain you need to reach has little idea of the concept of 'future'. It only understands 'now'. Therefore, all positive affirmations need to be said in the present tense.

Try these affirmations to improve your reading:

I am a great reader!
I learn things quickly and easily.
I love to read and I'm great at it.

Many people know they are poor readers, and will tell you so. While it's good to have awareness of our weaknesses, it's another thing to promote them. Each time we do that, we convince our brain it's true and this will lower the electrical activity in the brain, matching results to expectations. After years of claiming a lack of skill, it will take some effort to reverse the situation. The way to do this is simple and effective. However, it will take some determination and persistence. You need to say an affirmation about 100 times a day. You can break this up into 5 sessions of 20 or 4 sessions of 25. Each session will only take a minute or so.

Say your affirmation with emotional feeling. Say it as if you really mean it. Your unconscious mind responds best to highly charged emotion and body movement. Embody these affirmations. Make them a part of you; especially those that stick in your throat or cause you dismay. Reading them silently is OK too, but saying them aloud adds more sense and feeling to the message.

Try looking at yourself in the mirror from time to time when you say your affirmations. Look right into your own eyes and say, 'I am a great reader' or whatever your affirmation is. This will drive it deeply into your mind. Think about it – you may well have said or thought you were a poor reader hundreds or thousands of times. It will take at least that many repetitions of your affirmation to reverse the programming. However, saying more than 100 a day will not yield much better results. Saying 3,000 in a row is not nearly as effective as saying 20 every couple of hours each day over a month. The value of continually reminding yourself over time cannot be underestimated.

The following positive affirmations are intended to address any underlying mental attitudes that would hold you back from either attaining or maintaining your SuperReading™ skills. (I've provided lots of affirmations and some are variations on a theme which might seem slightly repetitious but I've done this so you can find just the right ones to address your needs.) Read through the list to choose the ones that you want to focus on. If any seem hard to say, or silly or give you a strange reaction, they may have touched a nerve connected to a learning block. To overcome the block faster, say that particular affirmation over and over again.

Ideas and facts flow to me from the page.
I recall what I read easily and effortlessly.
I like reading. I flow along in a rhythmic motion, absorbing information as I go.
Understanding comes easily to me.
I do really well in tests, for I have tested myself more thoroughly than any teacher could.
When taking tests, I know that I know the material.
I deserve to be a great reader.
I relax and let the words flow into my mind.
As my finger sweeps across the page, I understand and remember what I read.
I am a great student.
I am a great learner.
My reading skills get better and better every day.
Each time I read, my comprehension gets better and better.
I like the feeling of having read well.
I allow myself to be the superb reader that I am.
There is so much good information around that I am thankful for having the gift of great reading.
Reading is fun for me and I get better at it every day.

I go easy on myself, for I know that some days are better than others when it comes to mental activities.
I appreciate the advantage of previewing and allow myself those rewards.
I enjoy reading stories. It's like watching a movie where I control the speed.
My mind works beautifully at giving me the knowledge I need.
I trust that I get all I need when I read.
When I read, my finger sweeps across the page, pulling the meaning into my mind.
It's OK for me to be a great reader.
I have a great brain and great skills. No wonder I'm such a great reader.
Reading for me is easy. I know what to do and I do it well.
All subjects are accessible to me, for I know how to learn.
When I read, it's OK not to get it all the first time around. I am aware there is more, and I'll pick it up next time.
I am an effective reader. I make good use of my time.
I know what great reading is, and I know I can do it.
I am a great reader.
I recall what I read with ease and accuracy.
I like reading rhythmically, absorbing facts as I go.
Understanding comes naturally to me now.
I am prepared to take tests, having thoroughly tested myself.

I am relaxed when taking tests, because I know
that I know the material.

I claim my right to be a great reader.

I feel relaxed as the words flow into my mind.

Using my finger to read helps me to understand
and recall information.

I enjoy previewing material.

I love learning.

My reading skills improve each day.

Each time I read, my comprehension improves.

I allow myself to be a great reader.

Reading boosts my confidence.

Reading has become my favourite activity.

I am kind to myself, because some days are better
than others.

I appreciate previewing and allow myself its rewards.

I enjoy reading stories. I can control the pace to
suit myself.

My mind works efficiently.

I trust that when I read I pick up all the key facts.

Reading is now such fun for me.

I get pleasure from doing such a great job at reading.

It's OK if I struggle at first to understand a book. I
am a super reader.

I am intelligent and a brilliant reader.

Reading for me is rewarding because I learn so much.

When I read, I understand most of the text the first
time. I pick up the rest when I review what I have
read.

My efficient reading saves me time.

I know what it takes to be a great reader, and I know I am one.

Nobody is perfect, including authors and editors. I forgive them for poor writing and organisation. I use my skills to understand their valuable ideas.

I use my reading skills to continually empower myself and others.

All I need to learn is accessible to me.

Written information is available to me faster and better every day.

With each passing day, I become a better and better reader.

I am thankful for my abilities, and I rejoice in using them.

It feels good to do things that enhance the quality of my life.

I take positive advantage of ideas and opportunities.

I have fun reading and learning about the important things in life.

I naturally attract the information and knowledge I need.

I see that reading well is a skill I can learn and use.

I apply my skills and grow stronger and better every day.

I accept my new skills and welcome them into my life.

I am relaxed and confident when I read.

I accept my reading skills, knowing there is always room for growth.

It's OK for me to practise and become a great reader.
I pick up good ideas when I read and incorporate
them into my life.
I practise my new skills and read better and better
every day.
I like myself regardless of practising my exercises.
I realise reading is a key to my future and I
consistently invest time in my skills.
I like myself when I read.
A calm, relaxed feeling comes over me when I read.
It's simple becoming a great reader and I become a
better reader all the time.
My ability to learn and remember grows and grows.
Reading and recalling becomes easier and easier
for me.
I like the feeling of smoothly reading across the
lines; the words flowing into my mind.
Parroting is fun for me. The more I parrot, the
better I get. Parroting gives me more confidence
every time.
I always know where I stand.
Whatever level I'm at is OK. I know great reading
is within my reach.
I continually move towards being a better reader
all the time.
No matter how I do on any given day, I see myself
as a great reader and learner.
Nobody does their personal best every day; I like the
direction in which my reading skills are moving.

ASSIGNMENT

Read the affirmations above out loud. Judge how each one makes you feel. Choose three of them – one that feels really good when you say it, one that makes you uncomfortable when you say it, and one that addresses a particular challenge you have. Do each one 100 times a day in five sets of 20, spread out during your day, like when you awake, after breakfast, before lunch, before dinner, before bedtime. Say them with feeling (win that acting award!). Embody them (through repetition and emotion).

Work on no more than three affirmations at a time. You can work on one, two or three affirmations at any one time. Do an affirmation for at least 21 days. Once you feel it's embodied and you have accepted it or the 'problem' associated with it is resolved, you may replace it with a new one.

NOTE: Affirmations may seem irrelevant or ridiculous to you. However, they can be very powerful. Remember that we do talk to ourselves subconsciously all day long, and that part of our subconscious brain does listen to what we say. So reserve judgement for at least 21 days and do yourself a favour.

Affirmations for speakers of English as a second language

If your first language is not English, you may want to consider saying affirmations in your first language. The patterns and thoughts you are overcoming are probably from the first eight years of your life. Whatever language you formed those ideas in may be the one to reverse them with. It depends on how well you think in English. If your immediate reaction to situations has you thinking in your first language, then that's probably the one to go with.

You can also do affirmations in both languages. Try both and see over time which has the most impact for you. Just be aware that saying affirmations in different languages may have different success rates.

ASSIGNMENT

Write out an affirmation that excites you and changes your thinking about yourself in a positive way. Be sure it is positive and refers to now and not the future. There should be no hint of the words: no, not, don't, won't, will, going to, will be, want. Do use the words 'I am' to begin your affirmation. For example, 'I am a great reader.'

SUMMARY

- The ability to see what you want to accomplish is paramount to achieving it.

- Using picture visualisation will bring your goal of being a super reader closer.

- Speed visualisation allows you to experience faster reading with high comprehension by building momentum.

- Affirmations are an excellent tool for helping you to address false or unhelpful beliefs which hold back your progress and growth.

PART FOUR

Further Techniques and Strategies

13.

Learning and memory

When we begin to turn on the real power of the brain, most of the challenges of learning limitations such as dyslexia fade away. In this chapter we will look at ways of learning and improving the memory that make reading more fun and accessible to all kinds of learners.

I had a 21-year-old student who had been labelled as dyslexic since primary school. In the third lesson of the course, he jumped up and yelled out, 'I understand this! This is amazing – I just read this and I understand it! This has never happened before. Wow! I can read. I can really read!'

'Education is not the filling of a pail – but the lighting of a fire.'

WILLIAM BUTLER YEATS

He was so excited that it took him a couple of minutes to calm down. He slapped his hand to his head and started talking about all the years of going to special schools and tutors and struggling so hard. Now it was so easy. At these schools they were trying to get him to think; SuperReading™ got him to read! The point is that most learning disabilities are disabling because the person is trying to do the task with only one part of their brain – the troubled part. Once you get more of the brain involved, the appropriate parts take over and do the job. Teamwork is the key. So do not label yourself. Just let your brain figure out a way as you go. You certainly will not do yourself any harm if you learn how to read fast!

A study of SuperReading™ was undertaken at London South Bank University in 2008. The findings showed that indeed dyslexic adults saw significant improvement in their reading abilities. Surprising to the experimenter, those students with the lowest scores to begin with saw the greatest percentage increase in their reading abilities. Most of them became better than non-dyslexic readers. While they were hopeful for some improvement, becoming a better reader than a non-dyslexic reader was more than most of them had hoped for. The results of the study are available online at www.alchemy.name/html/lsbu.html.

NOTE: A key to learning is focus. Staying in focus on your subject leads to learning so when you are studying, stick to one subject at a time. When you have been reading about algebra, for example, parrot that information (see chapter 10) and then take a break. Relax and recharge by meditating, working out, enjoying a conversation or whatever you wish. Now move on to history or whatever subject you wish to tackle next. This is such an important part of SuperReading™ that the next chapter (chapter 14) is devoted to looking at ways to focus your mind to help your reading efforts.

CASE STUDIES

Chris, aged 11, was one of the poorest readers I had ever come across. His mother told me that Chris had been seen by more than a dozen reading experts. When he took his first test, where most of the children in the class finished in less than three minutes, it took Chris nearly eight minutes. He could not answer a single question in the quiz. The next week he was still taking over six minutes to read, while the other children were mostly under the two-minute mark. Chris could now answer one question while the others were averaging seven or eight. Four weeks later there was not much improvement and I was concerned he would drop out. I gave my 'Hang in there' speech to the whole class, targeting Chris, who by this time was the only one who really needed it. I couldn't tell if I had reached him, as he had never made eye contact with me.

The next time we tested, something amazing happened. Chris's reading time dropped to just under three minutes. He correctly answered six out of ten questions. His reading effectiveness score (see chapter 3) skyrocketed. He looked me in the eye for the first time. Hesitantly, he asked, 'Mr Cole, is this really my reading score?' I came over and looked at his time, answers and graph. 'Yes. That's correct.' What happened next is something I will always remember. He looked up at me with what can only be described as an 'ear-to-ear grin'. I truly believe that was a turning point in his young life. From that moment on he was a different person. He began to fully participate in the class and interact with the other students.

At the end of the course Chris's mother approached me and thanked me profusely. She said that all his teachers reported a profound change in his attitude and performance. She felt that within another few weeks he would become the best reader in his class. And he did.

In that same course was a young woman of about 14. When she started, she presented herself as a bit of an airhead. She laughingly put herself down, revelling in her stupidity and 'ditziness', which I think she felt would somehow appeal to the boys in the class. This behaviour continued for about three or four weeks. Then something profound happened. As her test scores rose from about 50 to over 300, her attitude towards herself changed. Once she had tested twice at that level and saw it was real, she dropped the façade. Suddenly she looked quite studious and focused. She almost looked like a different person and she was certainly behaving differently. Her mother told me, 'I can't believe the change. Her marks are higher at school and she actually sits down to do her homework without a fuss. Last Saturday I found her lying on her bed reading a book.' I replied, 'That's great.' Her mother replied, 'You don't understand. This is a kid who never picked up a book in her life. She could have been out goofing around, but she decided to stay home and read. Whatever you're doing here, keep doing it. And thanks.'

I've told these stories here because I believe true learning should come from a love of learning. It's really asking a lot from people to love something they hate to do because it's painful. When we can read and have some fun with it, as I will show you later in this chapter, then learning comes about naturally.

Reading ability and intelligence

I've been asked if reading ability reflects intelligence. I believe it does to some degree but not as much as you might imagine. Of course you must have at least a few brain cells firing to understand what you read. If we were to measure intelligence by how much a person can recall from what they've read, then my graduates are geniuses! When you can go on and on about a book you read ages ago, people will believe that you are very intelligent too. I prefer to say that this course will make you look as intelligent as you really are, or more so!

There is a myth that we can only store a limited amount of information in our brains. Nothing could be further from the truth, **unless** you believe it. Then your brain will act accordingly. Remember: 'Whether you think you can, or whether you think you can't, you're probably right!' The human brain has about one hundred billion neurons, or brain cells. The possible number of neural connections in one human brain is far greater than the number of atoms in the known universe! So don't worry about running out of storage space. Your brain's true capacity is greater than you'll ever need. It's not about storage; it's about retrieval. This is where memory techniques come into play. Look back to chapter 10, where you learned some simple techniques for helping retrieval and recall, ranging from using emotion to spaced repetition.

Making learning fun and interactive

One of the best ways to learn is to make your learning fun. Make up games. Get physical and act out what's going on. Use all your senses to learn – or as many as are appropriate. Use your imagination to be silly and outrageous. Explain what you are learning to someone else; even if they are not actually there. You could even look in the mirror and explain it to yourself.

The saying goes, 'If you really want to understand something, teach it to someone else.' This is because teaching is the ultimate form of parroting (see chapter 9).

It's parroting with more feedback and questions! If you can't answer the questions, that tells you to go back and review (see chapter 10). And don't be shy. If there's something you don't know, or can't find again, revel in it. If you're blocked from understanding a piece of knowledge, there's probably a good reason for it. It usually indicates an unconscious cause for the blockage. There may be a hidden need your unconscious mind has for keeping you from understanding or even acknowledging it. Forcing yourself to gain that understanding can result in a breakthrough in your life. We all live in comfort zones. The mechanisms behind the comfort zones will use any means to hide information from us that is contrary to the hidden beliefs that support the non-resourceful belief. When a question in a textbook or a comment from an author brings it to our conscious attention, we have a small window of opportunity to look at it and realise a truth that has eluded us. An example would be reading an article that mentions follow-through. You have been told this is an area you need to work on. You don't recall reading the comment and go hunting for it. However, you just can't locate it. You scan a couple of times but it's just not jumping out at you. Most people would give up and let it go. The opportunity vanishes. They have missed out on a vital key to their success. Why? Because some destructive pattern needs them to be unaware of the trend they have not to follow-through. They remain at a low level of success. So when this kind of opportunity comes along, go for it!

Questions are an important part of learning. Use the magnetic questions you first encountered in chapter 7 (remember Who, What, When, Where, Why and How?). In particular, use Why and How a lot. These are the ones that really test your knowledge and understanding.

And importantly, do not judge yourself. Judging leads to bad feelings and lower performance. Whatever happens, just accept it and see yourself doing better in future. Remember: 'There is no failure, only feedback.' In fact, failure is fine. It is just another form of parroting. It tells you there are more things you have to do. And 'giving up' is not one of them!

ASSIGNMENT

Before you begin to learn something new, stop and ask yourself, 'What can I do to make this fun and interactive?' If you have no great answer to this question, think of one and do it, before you start to learn. If you need help in coming up with something, read on. Set a timer and see how much information you can absorb before the bell rings. If you learned six facts in two minutes, now try learning seven facts in two minutes. Or, imagine there are several people there with you and they are going to ask you questions. You learn as much as you can in a specific amount of time and pretend to answer their questions. Or imagine you are on a game show and you have to read an article and know at least five facts, and earn more money for all the facts you remember beyond five. The novelty of these activities will increase your attentiveness and recall. Use your imagination and come up with different scenarios.

Top tips for facilitating learning

Getting interested

When you are reading, your body language is important if you want to make the most of it. Have you ever seen somebody sitting at a table, with their head leaning against their hand at an odd angle? If you were selling something to this person, would you think that they were paying attention? Not a chance. If you sit to read in such a position of non-interest do you think that your brain can really be paying attention to what you are reading? It cannot. Pay attention to how you are sitting. Sit in the way that you would when you are keenly interested in something and your brain will follow along and absorb more information more quickly. Be truly interactive. Lean forward, keep your eyes wide open, have a happy or excited expression on your face and nod approvingly when you begin. You will find more on this in chapter 14 ('Artificial interest' on page 247).

Learning anomalies

Sometimes when we are learning a new skill or technique our abilities temporarily suffer. This is natural. Take any skill you are already familiar with, such as writing. What if you had to write with your other hand? Would that make a difference? Even signing your name would be very difficult and you could not copy your own signature unless you practised a lot. What about writing in the dark or blindfolded? Would that decrease your skill? Of course it would. With practice and determination, could you build up your skills again? The answer is yes, of course. Be aware of this when learning a new skill and your ability to overcome minor dips in performance will not upset you. You will know by now the importance of reserving judgement (chapter 4) and you should just keep forging ahead until your abilities catch up again.

Attitude

Another thing that facilitates learning is attitude. Being happy and feeling good opens centres of the brain that are important to effective learning. The easiest ways to get happier and therefore facilitate better learning are through smiling and imagery. Simply smiling, or laughing lightly, relaxes the body and the mind, and leads to pushing out negative mind chatter. The other thing that works well if your mind won't shut off is the use of vivid imagery, which was looked at in detail in chapter 12. Using imagery brings your right brain into play. Your right brain controls much of what you do, and is relatively non-judgemental. When the right brain is to the fore you can perform without the usual critical judgement that might get in your way.

My favourite way to clear the mind and adjust your attitude is called alphabet animals, a simple way to lift your mood and raise a smile, to put yourself in the right frame of mind for effective learning. This technique also works well to help you deal with negative feelings at any time.

ASSIGNMENT

Pick any letter of the alphabet. Think of an animal beginning with that letter. See that animal in your mind, either with your eyes open or closed. Get the animal to start moving. See it run or fly. See it go up a tree. Now see it dancing on a tree branch. Perhaps it's dancing a jig. Give it a top hat and tails – bright pink! And a green polka-dot tie. And now give it a cane. Set the scene to music in your mind – perhaps 'Puttin' on the Ritz'. Now get the animal to jump off the tree into a bucket of bright red paint. Its head pops up and the animal sticks its tongue out at you.

Now if you really managed to visualise that, you should be feeling pretty light-hearted by now and ready to do some effective learning.

Next time you try alphabet animals you can either go into a lot of detail with your animal or get it to interact with other things (for example you could see a 20-metre penguin in central London) or other animals. Once you've done a couple of these, they shouldn't take more than half a minute, you will find your mood will lift and a smile will come to your face. Sometimes just thinking about them can instantly lighten your mood.

The brain scan experiment

In the early 2000s I watched a TV documentary about a university experiment that got me jumping up and down with excitement. It seemed to prove convincingly that belief, which is closely tied to attitude, affects performance.

The TV screen was split into three parts. The middle and largest section showed a man sitting in a room at a table. On the table were a variety of puzzles that were numbered for clear identity. In the upper left corner of the TV screen was a shot of the room next door. In the room were two experimenters, separated from the man at the table by a one-way mirror (they could see him, but he could not see them).

The man was sitting under a portable MRI (magnetic resonance imaging) scanning machine. It was lowered down so it could take scans of his brain while still allowing him to see the table in front of him. In the upper right corner of the TV screen was the readout from the MRI. It showed a top-down view of his brain. Whenever electrical activity increased, the computer displayed the colour red in that location. The experimenters got him relaxed and then asked him questions to determine his 'at rest' electrical activity. They put three groups of people through this experiment. The first group was used to establish base levels of activity while at rest and when solving puzzles. They gathered data from a large group of people to see how much time it took to solve the various puzzles and to see which parts of the brain worked on the various kinds of problems. The first group, the control group, gave them all that basic information.

When one of the experimenters turned on the microphone, there was an audible 'CLICK' sound. The subject also heard the 'CLICK' sound when the microphone was turned off.

CLICK (on)
Experimenter: 'OK, Frank, do you see the puzzle near the number 1 on the table?'
Frank: 'Yes.'
Experimenter: 'Good. In a moment, when I say "Go", start solving that puzzle. When you are finished, raise your hand. We will be timing you. Do you understand?'
Frank: 'Yes.'
Experimenter: 'Very good. Ready . . . begin.'
CLICK (off)
Frank worked on the puzzle and when he finished, raised his hand.
CLICK (on)
Experimenter: 'OK. Now do the same with Puzzle 2. Raise your hand when you finish. Begin.'

CLICK (off)

Frank worked on Puzzle 2 and when he finished, raised his hand.

CLICK (on)

Experimenter: 'OK. Now do the same with Puzzle 3. Raise your hand when you finish. Begin.'

CLICK (off)

The experiment continued on through about ten different puzzles. This gave the experimenters a really good idea of how long it took to solve the puzzles and which parts of the brain were called into play. As the subjects went along, their electrical activity rose in response to the problem solving. We could see the rise displayed in red on the monitor from the scan.

Now the experimenters were ready to play with people's minds a bit ...

The second group they ran through their paces was the positive group. The experiment started off the same as the control group's. For the first four puzzles everything was the same. Then something different happened.

CLICK (on)

Experimenter: 'OK, Jeffrey. Now do the same with Puzzle 5. Raise your hand when you finish. Begin.'

But there was no CLICK OFF!

The subject, someone named Jeffrey, waited a couple of seconds and then began to work on Puzzle 5.

After a little while the two experimenters in the hidden booth had a conversation, which Jeffrey could hear clearly, that went something like this:

Experimenter 1: 'Wow, this guy is really smart!'
Experimenter 2: 'I know, he's very clever. He's solving these puzzles faster than anyone I've seen.'
Experimenter 1: 'I think we can get out of here early tonight.'
Experimenter 2: 'Great! Want to stop off for a coffee?'
Experimenter 1: 'Sure. Let's see if he keeps going like this.'

Jeffrey solves Puzzle 5 and raises his hand. There's a CLICK but he doesn't hear anything. There's a couple more CLICKS and he finally hears the experimenter's voice. The experimenter sounds a bit put off.

Experimenter: 'O – OK Jeffrey, good. Now do the same thing with Puzzle 6. Begin.'
CLICK (off)

Jeffrey now realises that he was not supposed to hear that conversation between the two experimenters. He thinks they accidentally left the microphone on. What Jeffrey does not know is that it was all part of the plan. They were actors who had a carefully written script to give the impression that they were really impressed with him.

When he first heard their conversation the electrical

activity in his brain increased. When Jeffrey started on Puzzle 7 he was feeling really confident. His electrical activity shot up and on the monitor we could see areas of his brain lighting up in red that had not shown any activity before. He outperformed the control group and got even better on Puzzle 8. His brain was lighting up like crazy! Jeffrey believed in himself because of the experimenters' conversation and his performance went through the roof.

It was at this point that I realised how important this experiment was. It showed in graphic form that our brain works harder and better when we believe in ourselves. Jeffrey was cleverer when he believed he was clever!

The experiment did not stop there. There was a third group – the negative group. It went something like this:

CLICK (on)
Experimenter 1: 'OK, Sam. Now do the same with Puzzle 5. Raise your hand when you finish. Begin.'
But there was no CLICK OFF!
The subject, someone named Sam, waited a couple of seconds and then began to work on Puzzle 5. After a little while the two experimenters in the hidden booth had a conversation that went something like this:
Experimenter 1: 'Jeez, where do they find these people?'
Experimenter 2: 'I know. This guy is like Forrest Gump or something.'

Experimenter 1: 'It's like watching paint dry.'
Experimenter 2: 'At this rate we'll be here all night. I'd better call my wife.'
Experimenter 1: [sigh] 'Yeah...'

The result was amazing. In real time you could actually see the red disappearing from the monitor. The scan revealed Sam's brain actually shutting down. The patterns went back to base level where he was sitting waiting to begin. The negative comments from the experimenters just sucked the life out of poor Sam. He took longer than the control group and couldn't even solve some of the puzzles. It was heart-breaking to watch. Fortunately, when the negative group finished, the whole scheme was revealed to them so they didn't go home thinking they were deficient. Their first few scores were shown to them and compared with the control group, so they could see they were 'normal'.

I share these results with you to demonstrate that how we view ourselves directly affects our ability to perform. By treating ourselves well we stand a better chance of increasing performance. This is related to another important subject: affirmations (see page 198).

Improving your memory

We now move on to the core section of this chapter – finding the keys to improving your memory. Memory is a fascinating subject. Your brain is holding on to millions and millions of pieces of information. It's all in there somewhere. The big question is: 'Where on earth is it?' Just imagine – you can have instant access to so many strange and bizarre facts. For example, think about … your refrigerator. What are you experiencing now? Are you seeing what's inside? Are you seeing the outside? Are you recalling the contents? A minute ago those facts were not in your consciousness. Now they are. In an hour they probably will not be in your consciousness again. We store so much information, but the key is not storage; it is retrieval and recall. The following elements of repetition, emotion, imagination, motion and association are known as the five keys to memory.

We have already touched on this subject in chapter 10 because memory techniques play a significant role in reviewing. Some of this information may already seem familiar, but that's OK, because the first key to memory is repetition!

Memory testing

Before we go on to discover the keys to memory, it would be interesting to test your memory skills as they are now. The best way to test your memory is with the help of another person. Get them to go to the list on the next page and read each word aloud after saying its number, starting with number 1. Ask them to count to five silently and continue with number 2, and so on.

When they get to number 20, wait five seconds and then take a minute to discuss between you something unrelated to the list, like your favourite movies, TV shows or books. After one minute, begin writing the words you remember by their number in a list, starting with the first word. If you cannot remember which number a word goes with, just write it down by any open number. Take no more than three minutes for writing your answers down.

After that, get the person to read the list back to you, saying both the number and the word. Circle the words that you got correct by their number. Those are worth 5 points. Words from the list that are by the wrong number are worth 1 point. Your answers may be plural or singular and spelling does not matter.

Memory test 1

Read aloud clearly and carefully. Say the number and the word; wait five seconds, go to the next word.

1 Mattress	11 Tree
2 Clarinet	12 Rainbow
3 Peanut	13 Ladder
4 Doughnut	14 Dairy
5 Car	15 Monitor
6 Pencil	16 Fork
7 Sellotape	17 Shirt
8 Eagle	18 Dream
9 Shoe	19 Brush
10. Cloud	20 Crayon

Allow five seconds after the last word, and then have a conversation for one minute. After that minute, it is time to write the answers down against the numbers, writing the first word first.

The five keys to memory

1   I have just said that the first key to memory is **repetition**. The more you repeat something, the more likely you are to remember it. Do you remember five times five? How about seven times seven? Of course you do. You cannot even keep the answers out of your head. Four times four? These facts are so deeply ingrained by repetition that you will always remember them. But how about 19 times 19? Probably nothing comes to mind. This is because there was not enough repetition in that case, since most people do not learn their times tables beyond 10 or 12. We see then that multiple exposures to information lead to permanent recall. The same thing is true when we read. The more times we see or experience the message, the more likely we are to recall it.

2   The next key to memory is **emotion**. We tend to remember that to which we have reacted with high levels of emotion. Take a minute to recall your most vivid memories. You will find that there is some emotional reaction when you recall them. The emotion served to seal in the memory. You can use this to your advantage by getting emotionally excited about specific things you wish to learn.

Even if you are acting, your brain cannot tell the difference. Your body will react as if the emotions are 'real'. Aristotle knew all about this. When he came to a critically important fact he wished a student to remember he would slap them across their face! Rest assured there are more reasonable methods of eliciting emotions and recalling information. One example is mental shouting where you see yourself standing on a table in an expensive restaurant, loudly shouting out the information you wish to recall. Shout it out several times in your mind.

3   The third key to memory is **imagination**. As Albert Einstein said, 'Imagination is more important than knowledge.' If you want to remember things really well, you have to engage your brain with your imagination. Words are simply sounds. These sounds only have meaning because we all agree to their meaning. The word 'boat' could just as easily mean 'fence' if we all agreed to change it. The things that transcend words are pictures and when we use pictures we use our imagination. No matter what you call a baby, we all know what one looks like and most of us react the same way upon seeing one. When we see a cute baby we react emotionally first, then the word comes to us. You can enhance memory using imagination by exaggerating something or by making it very silly. For example, if you need to recall a catfish, vividly see one swimming

around the room with you. Now make it 3 metres long. Now make it say 'meow' very loudly as it swims through the air. Physically grab its tail and hold on as it struggles to free itself. Act this out right now. Have it turn its head and hiss at you like a cat! Now you will remember 'catfish'. Reinforce it by saying out loud, 'Wow, this catfish can struggle!'

4   The fourth key to memory is **motion**. This has just been demonstrated with the catfish example above. Our eyes and brains are hardwired to respond to motion. We notice things that move, so make objects move in order to recall them better. More of your brain comes into play when you create action. Static objects tend to fade into the background and are forgettable. Imagine that you're visiting a zoo. You are looking at a herd of antelope simply standing there munching the plants. You're about to move on to the next pen. If you were recalling your day at the zoo, these antelope would not have been mentioned. Suddenly one of the antelope starts jumping up and down and running madly in circles. It jumps over several of the other antelope and starts spinning round. Now the antelope have become one of the highlights of the day and may even be the first thing you talk about. Why? Because of motion. Its movements made it special and helped you to remember them.

5   The fifth key is **association**. Associate the item you want to remember with something you already

know. What does it remind you of? Creatively link the item with something you know really well. For example, if you had to remember some information about a phone tree, you could link it with a real tree near your home or work.

One way to sum this up is to say that if you experience **movement**, **associate** with what you want to recall, **repeat** the process in some **imaginative** way with **emotion**, you will have no choice but to **remember** a piece of information! Now you have an acronym to remember: **M.A.R.I.E:**

MOVEMENT and
ASSOCIATION
REPEATED,
IMAGINED with
EMOTION

Memories are made permanent through repetition, but interestingly, the more emotions, movement and imagination you use, the less repetition you need! And of these, emotion is especially powerful. Emotion really seals in a memory. Look at your earliest life memories. They almost always have strong emotion attached to them. This is not coincidence. This is how your brain works. Use it. And, most of all, have fun when you use it.

ASSIGNMENT

The next time you need to learn something, consider M.A.R.I.E. and take steps to fulfil as much of it as possible. Remember to have a great attitude when you do it.

The Roman room

The Roman room memory technique dates back to the ancient days of the Roman Empire, when scholars used the objects in a room to remember items of importance. This technique will help you remember things in a particular order. It's a very easy system to learn, stands alone and does not interfere with other memory techniques you may use.

How to do the Roman room

The illustration below shows one of five elements of a kitchen including the dishwasher and the sink. For the first exercise you will use this area to help you remember a list of items. You will see the whole kitchen on the next page and will progress to remembering all 20 objects in the room.

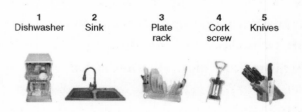

1	2	3	4	5
Dishwasher	Sink	Plate rack	Cork screw	Knives

A typical kitchen area

The procedure is to memorise the objects along each wall of our sample room (above) in the correct numerical order. You will always use them in this order. The first object to remember is the dishwasher. Imagine the dishwasher racks moving backwards and forwards and say to yourself 'dishwasher'. The next object is the sink. Say that it is a sink and see the swivelling tap, then do the plate rack, the corkscrew and finally the set of knives. The point of memorising these objects is to establish a permanent base of 20 'slots' where you will be associating other 'items' you wish to remember for work, school or anything else. In other words, this room (see full room below) is something you keep in your head just as it is, and from time to time you use it to remember lists of things that become attached to it. The room is a tool you use like file folders in a drawer to keep papers in a specific order so you can find them. Instead of folders, you have objects (dishwasher, sink, plate rack, corkscrew, knives).

Now, comes the practical bit: let's say you're going to the supermarket. You need five items. You have no paper. No problem!

The idea is to creatively merge an object in the kitchen with whatever it is you want to recall. You will do this by making the two things interact with one another using the following three steps:

Verbalise: say the first word you need to recall over and over again (repetition) out loud if possible.

Exaggerate: make the thing to remember bigger, brighter than it really is or imagine many of them. Make it unusual, such that if you saw one like this it would make a big impression on you.

Movement: we pay more attention to things that move than things that are still. This is why we use our finger (hand pacing, which we learned about in chapter 6) when we read. If there is action in your interaction you will recall the thing more easily.

In our example, the first item to remember on your shopping list is bread. See the bread (sliced or a loaf) thrown into the dishwasher. Perhaps the spray arm is spinning the bread around. Say to yourself: 'The dishwasher is spinning the bread.'

Next in the kitchen is the sink. Your next shopping item is facial tissue. See yourself pulling tissues out of the box and stuffing them into the sink. Or perhaps the sink is sneezing and you hand it a tissue. It blows its nose. Think of something totally outrageous. That way you will remember! Tell yourself that the tissues are helping the sink.

Next is the plate rack. You need some beach sandals and you have heard they are on special offer. How would you get the plate rack to interact with the beach sandals? Make it happen and tell yourself what you are creating.

Next is the corkscrew. Merge the corkscrew with peanut butter. Spread it on. Then carefully lick the corkscrew and feel the sticky peanut butter. Say to yourself that you are licking peanut butter off the corkscrew.

Last are the knives. You need to buy plastic cups. See yourself stabbing white plastic cups with the knives. Say what you are creating and seeing.

If you have more than five items to remember, keep going around the room. Your limit is 20 items. Experience shows that most lists you make will have fewer than 20 items.

ASSIGNMENT

The best strategy to memorise the room is to spend two minutes with a section of it about five times a day. Look at it, say it, close your eyes and repeat it verbally. Once you have it memorised, see if you can quiz yourself

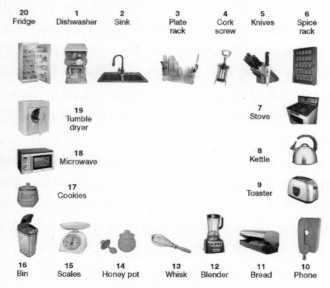

| 20 Fridge | 1 Dishwasher | 2 Sink | 3 Plate rack | 4 Cork screw | 5 Knives | 6 Spice rack |

| 19 Tumble dryer | | | | | 7 Stove |

| 18 Microwave | | | | | 8 Kettle |

| 17 Cookies | | | | | 9 Toaster |

| 16 Bin | 15 Scales | 14 Honey pot | 13 Whisk | 12 Blender | 11 Bread | 10 Phone |

The Roman room

going backwards around the section of the room. Eventually you need to memorise all 20 objects in the room, and know which object belongs on which wall. It is also very helpful to learn which numbers go with which objects.

Other rooms

You can also use your own room or rooms with this technique. I strongly suggest using five objects per space (wall or central area). The reason for always having five objects is for consistency. It makes remembering the number of each object easier and it is less confusing to have a consistent number of objects in each group as you go around. In that way, you are always sure when you get to a corner what number you are on. I also suggest four areas per room. In other words, the basic layout of rooms is fairly consistent; only the objects change from room to room.

If you are using a room from your life (bedroom, kitchen, den, office, the room you grew up in) and there are not enough objects in a given space, then simply add one in using your imagination. Just tell yourself that that object is now there. For example, along a wall in your bedroom is a lamp, chair, a window and a chest of drawers. That's only four objects. In your mind, you could imagine that next to the chest is a picture of a tree, or a cuckoo clock, or a trophy, or a plant.

HINT: Be sure not to duplicate objects, either in the

same room or in any of your rooms. For example, having a recliner in two of your rooms would potentially be confusing. Or having two stereo speakers in the same room could cause uncertainty as to which one was associated with which object to remember.

THOUGHT: Most people are literally amazed at how effective and easy this technique is for remembering things. You put a few seconds of creative work into each association and then let it go. When you come back to the beginning the thing you need to remember just pops out at you, as clear as can be.

HOPE: Memorising a room is really easy. All it takes is a bit of repetition. Just spend a minute or two here and there going over one section of five objects. It should not take more than about 40 minutes to memorise a room this way. Once you have it, you will always have it. Memorise the numerical position as well for instant access to any object in the room. For example, if someone asked me what the third longest river in the world is, I would think of the third object in the room, the plate rack. When thinking about rivers, I would access that particular information. In this case, it's 'yanking' a dish from the rack. Yanking reminds me of 'Yang', short for the Yangtze (*Yang see*). In about one to two seconds I would be saying the answer. No matter which river I might be asked, it would only take a second or two to know the answer, assuming I have memorised the numerical position of each object.

ASSIGNMENT
Use the Roman room technique to remember a shopping list (or similar) every time you get the chance.

Textbooks

While we are on the subject of learning, it would seem the right moment to talk about textbooks. In the past 20 years or so there has been a positive change in the quality of textbooks. For the most part, information is better organised, identified, illustrated and described. They also tend to be easier to understand. They often have good illustrations, questions at the beginning or end of chapters, summaries and glossaries. On the other hand, there's far more information to learn than ever before! The vast amount of information in some textbooks can be overwhelming. The following advice will help you get past the psychological barrier some people are faced with when looking at all this information.

We will now bring all your skills together and allow you to do very well with books you need to absorb in the future. Take a textbook you need to read and casually glance over it, looking through the table of contents, the front and back covers, preface, and leaf through using your imagination. Tell yourself how much fun it's going to be to understand all the great information contained within it. Example: 'I'm going to know all about string theory in a non-linear universe!' Take a look through the first chapter, noting unusual type, getting familiar with charts and graphs, and any pictures or diagrams. Look at these with a child-like sense of wonder, excited that soon you will master all this knowledge.

Then start breaking that first chapter into manageable chunks, telling yourself how soon you'll be understanding everything you see. The idea is to convince your brain that there is nothing scary here. There's nothing here you can't handle with time and tools. Take a small section of two or three pages and preview it as you learned in chapter 7. Then read it. Then review it. Parrot and determine if you need further review. Once you have a strong idea of the information, take on the next couple of pages or so. Stay in control of how much you are absorbing. It is essential to build a good solid foundation of knowledge when starting a new area of study.

There are two different schools of thought on unknown vocabulary words. One school says to look through the text, try to spot any words that you do not know and learn their meaning before reading. The other school says you should try to figure them out when you come to them from their context. If you cannot, then decide whether it is worth looking them up. The first way makes for a smoother reading experience when you get to the reading stage (after previewing – see chapter 7); while the second requires you to stop the reading process and consider what to do. I suggest trying both and deciding which works best for you (for more on this, see following section on learning vocabulary). You may want to look at the section with difficult vocabulary first. If your brain is all turned on, take advantage of that. Just make certain you are not simply avoiding Topic A by showing great interest in Topic B. Remember, first things first.

Think of learning as like eating a multi-course meal. You eat the meal one bite at a time. Cut, chew and swallow. Shoving all the food into your mouth at once isn't only uncouth, it's unproductive. The same is true for information. Your mind will reject too much knowledge at once, just as your stomach will do with too much food.

When you are reading your textbook, use the Info-Mapping™ method for taking notes; and use imagery and pictorial stories to remember facts (see page 192). Remember to avoid using highlighter pens – this just teaches your brain to be lazy.

The most important thing is to keep a positive attitude and smile as you look through your textbook. Those first impressions play a big part in determining how your brain will process and accept the information.

ASSIGNMENT

Take a new textbook that you need to read and use the bookmark technique (see chapter 7 on previewing) to preview it.

Remembering words: meanings and spellings

Vocabulary

Remembering vocabulary words does not have to be a difficult, painstaking process. There is a simple and effective technique, which does not require a great deal of thinking or stress. All it requires is a bit of time and diligence. Once you have made certain preparations, the rest of the process is as easy as listening to music.

Choose up to 18 words you do not know. Write them down with their meaning and a word or two that mean the same thing (synonyms) or put them in a sentence.

Record them on to a tape or on your computer. Use a strong, clear voice. Speak with authority. No mistakes or long pauses, so practise saying them first.

Lie down (don't fall asleep!) or sit quietly by yourself and listen to the recording 12 times in a row. Use headphones if you have them. Repeat every night for one week; then get someone to test you. They can ask you the meanings of the words in random order.

If you miss any of these meanings, include them in your list of words for next week. If you missed two words, then you can have a maximum of 16 **new** words in your next recording.

Keep doing this for as long as you want to learn new words. You can use the same procedure for spelling (see below). However, do **not** learn vocabulary and spelling in the same recording.

S-p-e-l-l-i-n-g-s

The steps to follow are the same as for vocabulary but to learn spellings, record yourself as you say the word in a clear, authoritative voice, then spell it out clearly, and say the word again. It is much easier to have the words and spellings written out in front of you as you record them.

Pause for a moment, and then do the next word. Again, the maximum number of words per recording is 18. If you are below the age of 10 or 11, your maximum number of words is 12. If you can handle more, then try bumping it up, but do **not** exceed 18 words at any age. The number of tape repetitions per evening, as with vocabulary, is 12.

REMEMBER: Do **not** mix spelling and vocabulary drills on the same tape recording. Leave some time between the two different drills.

SUMMARY

- Our attitude affects our beliefs and our abilities. Our brain works better when we believe we are good; and when we make learning fun!

- Use the Roman room technique to enhance your ability to recall lists.

- Remember the five keys to memory – movement, association, repetition, imagination and emotion (M.A.R.I.E.).

- Recorded repetition can effectively increase your vocabulary and improve your spelling ability.

14.

Focusing your mind

We have already seen how a key to learning is focus. This chapter looks at simple and effective ways to help you focus your mind and get completely absorbed in your reading, with outstanding results. It includes the exciting technique of enhanced focusing, which will offer you the chance to really let go!

As humans, we have an ability that takes us beyond any other living creature on the planet. We can **choose** to give our whole attention to one thing. Animals do this naturally. The lioness stalking the antelope is thinking of nothing else. One hundred per cent of her attention is devoted to that antelope. However, she cannot bring that intense focus to anything beyond her instincts as related to survival. There is no freedom of choice; only to focus on survival skills.

Have you ever heard about people who devote their whole lives to one thing, becoming totally involved with one idea? What happens to the efforts of these people? Don't they usually come up with something new and amazing? Well, maybe not every time. However, every time someone comes up with something amazing, it is because they got very involved with that subject. They got very focused and absorbed and before you knew it they discovered something wonderful.

You can do the same thing with your reading! You can get very focused and absorbed into your reading and achieve amazing things.

Getting focused

The first step is to **decide** that you are going to absorb the information. Then visualise a clear mental picture of you knowing the information (see chapter 12). The next step is to get focused on the material by employing your senses. Your senses are how you interface with the world. Every bit of information you get comes through one or more of your senses. In the following assignment you are going to combine your senses with your imagination. You will be using your vision, hearing, olfactory and kinaesthetic senses. The purpose of the assignment is to get focused by paying attention to what you are doing. This will help to shut out everything else so any distractions are minimised.

ASSIGNMENT

First, look at a piece of reading material, whether it's a book, journal or computer screen. You don't have to read it; just look at the shapes and colours on the page or screen. Now, visualise the words and pictures lifting off the page, going directly into your eyes and then up into your brain. Imagine a steady flow of information coming into you through your eyes.

Next, feel the book or paper. If it's a computer screen, simply turn your palms towards it. Imagine the words and pictures flowing from the page into your hands, moving up your arms and spreading all through your body. It's like dipping a paper towel into a colourful liquid. The liquid is absorbed into the material. Visualise all the words are being stored in your body and/or mind.

Now use your nose. Breathe in slowly and sense the words and pictures going right into your lungs. A few slow, deep breaths will do it. You can also feel the information spreading from your lungs to the rest of your body.

Finally, use your ears. As you begin to preview the material (see chapter 7), imagine the words coming into your ears like physical energy. Then speak the main words and thoughts from the text. Your mind will be more clear, relaxed and interested in the material. As you focus on the material to be absorbed, your attention is taken away from the distractions of your environment.

HINT: As is always the case, the clearer your reading area is, the easier it is to focus your mind. See page 251 for more on this.

Artificial interest

In chapter 13 I explained how getting interested is a matter of getting yourself into the right position to read. To take this further, you can generate artificial interest by getting into a position that suggests fascination. What you do is sit on the edge of your seat with your head forwards; feet flat on the floor. Think about it! This is how you sit when you are hearing something amazing. Open your eyes wide and look focused and intent. Say to yourself that this is fascinating stuff. If you tell yourself that it is, it will soon become more so. Pretend that you are interested and soon you will be. This is because every time you have been highly interested in something in reality, your body has reacted this way. When you put yourself into a physical state of interest, your brain responds the same way it did before: with interest.

Pretending to be interested can lead to **being** interested.

Also, as you read, watching for answers to the magnetic questions (chapter 7, Who, What, When, Where, Why, How?), the game is really afoot and you begin to get tuned in. If nothing else, you will become interested in the process of learning that is taking place.

ASSIGNMENT

Take a piece of reading you would normally be very reluctant to do. Pick it up (or bring it up if on-screen) and declare how wonderful it will be to read this material. Say to yourself how much you're looking forward to it and can't wait to get started. Declare how thankful you are to have this in your life. Sit in a posture of excited fascination and smile as you dig in. Every few minutes remind yourself how lucky you are to have this and keep smiling. When finished, note the differences between this and other times you have tried to read such material.

The enemies of concentration

How you are getting on with your reading can be a good barometer for how you are taking care of yourself in general. Several factors, all fairly controllable, can contribute to a lack of concentration and focus. Let's take them one at a time.

Lack of sleep

The amount of sleep needed is different from person to person. Some people seem able to function quite well with only four or five hours of sleep per night. Others would be useless with only that amount and require eight to ten hours to function well. Teenagers need more sleep but many are unlikely to get it, with school and other activities. Studies show that the ideal time for most teenagers to sleep would be from about midnight to 10 in the morning. They are really waking up fully about 10.30 a.m. The school system does not help with this requirement. The best we can do until society changes if you are a teenager is to get to bed 'early' and wake up in time to be ready for school.

On days when you have not had enough sleep, expect that your performance could be lower than usual. Taking this into account, you can compensate by doing extra previewing (see chapter 7). For example, you could combine key sentence previewing with name and number scan. If you are really tired but you must read, you may have to resort to reading aloud (while pointing).

ASSIGNMENT

Get to bed at a decent time tonight. Visualise yourself jumping out of bed in the morning energised and happy. Repeat for 21 days.

Poor nutrition

You are what you eat. Fresh fruit and vegetables provide the kind of nutrients that foster good mental performance. Be wary of 'heavy' foods (such as too many carbohydrates) that give you a bloated feeling. Your body must make neurotransmitters from what you feed it. The best transmitters are made from whole, healthy foods high in amino acids. Highly processed foods are not good for concentration. Caffeine seems to give a temporary boost, but some studies show it to be detrimental to memory.

Your brain works using neurotransmitters such as acetylcholine and not having enough reduces mental performance. Acetylcholine-rich foods include peanuts, egg yolks, meat, fish, milk, wheat germ, cheese and vegetables (especially cauliflower, broccoli and cabbage). You also need protein, which is found in meat, fish, nuts and dairy foods. You will also want to make sure you're getting enough omega-3, which is found in oily fish, or take a good quality supplement. Brain-boosting vitamins include the B complex, as well as A, C and E (so you can ACE your exams). The minerals manganese, magnesium, calcium and potassium are also beneficial to brain function.

ASSIGNMENT

Eat a balanced diet with fruit, vegetables and drink loads of water for one week. How do you feel? Repeat.

Stress

Have you ever tried to accomplish something important while your head was swimming with worry? Stress can affect focus, memory and patience (among other things). If you are worried about something, trying to do some reading will give you a good indication of just how much it's affecting you. It's very easy to judge because you will either remember something or you will not. Remember, when you are learning SuperReading™, you must not be afraid of the truth. If you don't remember something that's important you want to know about it, not pretend that you did remember it. If you have uncomfortable thoughts running in your head, then you are probably stressed.

Experts tell us there is good stress and bad stress. That is fine. For our purposes, any stress which lowers our reading ability is bad stress. What can you do? There are two kinds of fixes: short term and long term. Long-term fixes address the root cause of the stress. They can be time consuming. However, if something is bothering you that much, it may be your mind begging you to deal with it. Short-term fixes get you to forget about your problem for a while. Hopefully that's long enough to get on with the business at hand. An exercise like alphabet animals (page 220) can be quite helpful to lighten your mood and replace bothersome imagery and emotions.

> **ASSIGNMENT**
> Run through an alphabet animals exercise next time you are feeling stressed and need to learn something. Look through page 220, pick an animal and have fun with it.

Busy environment

A clear work area fosters good concentration. If work that needs your attention is within view, your subconscious mind is aware of it and your attention may be divided. Best practise is to have as many things as possible out of your vision. Remember the old adage, 'Out of sight, out of mind'.

A to-do list is also helpful, as writing it down lets your mind know it can release the thoughts surrounding those items. It is important to have a safe place to keep your list. Your mind must be certain that once something is on the list, it is safely filed away and cannot be forgotten.

ASSIGNMENT
Start making to-do lists. Keep them safely.

Noise pollution
Words can catch our attention. Odd sounds from the environment around you can do the same. Some people are even bothered by rhythmic sounds. Here are some techniques that will help you to avoid being distracted:

Visualisation (page 192) – see yourself absorbing information while surrounded by distractions. See a smile on your face.
Affirmation (page 198) – tell yourself how you are able to maintain focus in all conditions.

Finally, you can try **extreme focus** – consider that you might be distracted because your brain isn't challenged enough. You need to fill it with only one task; in this case, reading. Consider the following scenario. You just discovered a piece of paper that describes how to turn wood into gold. It's caught in a shredder and is slowly being pulled in. You only have about 20 seconds to read this piece of paper. Someone is asking if you would like to go to lunch later. There's an announcement on the public address system. Someone else just dropped some coins on the floor. Outside a dog is barking. Two people are arguing over who had the keys to the filing cabinet. Would you let any of that get in your way of reading that formula? No. You would be like a lion after its prey. You would completely ignore everyone and everything else. Isn't that right? You would be totally focused on that page.

The point is that if you are capable of concentrating in those conditions to discover how to turn wood into gold, you have the ability to focus under most conditions that are not threatening your immediate safety. So long as there's no fire you have the ability to concentrate and stay on task. What you need is the right motivation.

Quick focusing method

A development of the extreme focus technique described above is the quick focusing method, which will really help you to get your mind into a state of high concentration. In this method you read two (three, or four – it's up to you) books or pieces of writing at once, alternating between them every few seconds. You can experiment with how much time to spend on each book. After a minute or two (this varies), switch to the book you are more interested in. It can be one of the two or you can pick up a third book. Again, you can experiment to see what suits you best. As with all tools, what you prefer may vary from day to day.

Use as many different pieces for whatever length of time that you find solves your problem. For example, you could use four pieces for 15 seconds each. Or three pieces for 20 seconds each. Find the combination that works for you. You want to spend enough time to get the point but not so much time as you neglect the other material. It's all a matter of getting your mind into a state of high focus. Once you've achieved this state, reading the one text afterwards will seem easy. The concept is to overwhelm the brain with information, then allow it to focus on only one thing.

ASSIGNMENT

Imagine that you must read a piece of text or someone will be hurt. Put two other pieces of writing in front of you and read the three in turn for about ten seconds each. By trying to keep all that information in mind, you will crowd out the other bothersome thoughts. Do this for a minute or two until you are really focused. Then push one away. Continue for another minute. Take the second away so now you only have the one you're really interested in. Your level of focus should be sufficiently high to overcome whatever was distracting you before. This is fighting fire with fire. Your brain wanted to multitask and you have used the problem as a solution.

Enhanced focusing technique

And now for the ultimate in focusing! When you use the enhanced focusing technique you will be able to let it all go and really have some fun. If all goes well you may find that you are more challenged than at any time in your life. There is one caveat: you should have been practising pattern reading consistently well for at least a week (two weeks is better) before attempting the enhanced focusing technique.

The idea of this technique, which I use in the last class of my SuperReading™ courses, is to challenge your brain with a number of 'handicaps' in order to make it work harder. Under ordinary circumstances your brain 'feels' that it's capable of multitasking. It daydreams and runs various scenarios, conversations and theories, while you believe you are reading. It attends to sounds, noises and objects in your environment such as people, machinery, animals and anything else making a sound. The enhanced focusing technique can help you to overcome this 'problem' and increase your level of focus and concentration.

Experiments suggest that you can show a person a page of text for less than a second, and under deep hypnosis they can recall everything on the page. This technique will mimic this phenomenon to a certain extent, but without the deep hypnosis. And when you actually read the book afterwards, the information will seem familiar. You will catch on much more quickly than if you had not used this technique.

ASSIGNMENT

The first thing to do is find a book with large enough type that you do not have to squint to read, and preferably a title you have not read before, and which is not highly technical. Hardbacked books or large paperbacks are the best format. The type should not be too close to the gutter (the middle of the book when it is open). You will also need to have some music that you can play, preferably instrumental, although you may find that the extra challenge of words is OK. Some suggestions include:

Edgar Winter's 'Frankenstein'
Vivaldi's *Four Seasons*
Hot Butter's 'Popcorn'

Make a track list with one track playing after another. The order doesn't matter.

While the surprise and timing of what happens in a class may be difficult to reproduce, I am going to use some creative techniques here to mimic what happens. Remember that, as with other advanced techniques, it takes practise and repetition to master. The first time you do this exercise it could take 20 to 30 minutes. With practise it should take you about a minute or so to get deeply focused, but please do this at a time when you will not be interrupted, including answering the telephone. The advantage of being focused on one thing at a time is that you are not getting interference from other thoughts, topics or previous annoyances.

NOTE: This exercise requires you to undertake a bit of role play. If you can imagine that the scenario is real it will work better for you.
Let's do it!

- Follow all instructions.
- Sit down at a desk or table, and clear the area in front of you of everything except the book you have chosen to work with.
- I want you to think of a person, alive, not with you, who you care for very much. Close your eyes and let this person come to mind. When you have the person's name, turn the page.

NEWS FLASH!

Crazed space aliens from another dimension have invaded the Earth!

Among others, they have captured the person you were just thinking of.

They are demanding that you get all the information that you can out of the book in front of you…

In only 20 minutes!

If you don't, they will eject them into space – for an unpleasant death.

You must not only be a super reader, you must be a super hero!

Can you handle this challenge? Turn the page …

WHAT? I CAN'T *HEAR* YOU!

Can you handle this?

Along the way, there will be some challenges you have to face.

- Every half-minute or so, you must blink your eyes three times.
- Between blink times you must tap your feet on the floor three times.
- As you begin you can turn on the music – loud!
- If you can get someone else to quickly flick the lights on and off and make random noises from time to time, it's even better.
- You will need to flip pages really quickly, about one page per second!
- **Do not** use your finger to read – it will be busy flipping pages. If you accidentally flip more than one page at a time, just keep going.

You will get another instruction on the next page.

Start your music, turn the page and start flipping the pages for about five minutes while blinking and tapping.

REMEMBER, LIVES ARE AT STAKE!

Ready ... start the music and turn the page.

- Before you begin flipping, rotate your book so the text is upside down.
- When you get to the other end of the book, start again and keep on flipping for five minutes.
  Go!

180

Words words words words words words
words words words words words words
words words words words words words
words words words words words words
words words words words words words
words words words words words words
words words words words words words
words words words words words words
words words words words words words
words words words words words words
words words words words words words
words words words words words words
words words words words words words
words words words words words words
words words words words words words
words words words words words words
words words words words words words

After five minutes, please pause the music.

So, how did that go? Rate your performance so far on a scale of zero to 10, with 10 being terrific and zero being rubbish.

Say your number out load.

If your score was anything less than 10, I have a question for you.

How dare you?

How dare you judge yourself so harshly?

How do you know you're not the best person to ever try this?

After all, when was the last time you read a book upside down, with feet tapping, eyes blinking and flipping pages as fast as you can?

Never? Then how can you judge?

If you gave yourself a mark of 10, terrific. Well done.

If not, be certain that you are a 10 and carry on with the music and everything else.

Focus and go for it as if lives depend on you.

Start the music up again.

Go for another five minutes with the book upside down, tapping and blinking, then stop.

Good, now rotate the book so it's right side up again.

Continue scanning one page per second and tapping and blinking for five more minutes.

Great. Now scan the pages every two seconds.

Continue tapping and blinking for four minutes.

Go!

Well done! Super!

Now scan up the left-side page and down the left-side page, up the right-side page and down the right-side page, then flip the page.

Take two seconds to go up; two seconds to go down.

Go for four minutes!

Now scan up for four seconds and down for four seconds.

Cut back on the tapping and blinking.

Go for four minutes!

Good.

Now find your natural pace in order to absorb the information. You should still be reading quite quickly, covering a page in between three and six seconds. The music can be turned down a bit, but still pushing you along.

Keep going for five to ten minutes.

Fantastic!

The crazed space aliens have been appeased!

Your loved one has been returned and their memory of this incident has been wiped.

They will have no recollection of what happened to them.

You, on the other hand, have a fairly good idea of what your book is about.

This assignment should have demonstrated that you are now capable of absorbing information at really high speeds. Think of it as another previewing tool for a book (see chapter 7 for more on previewing). With some practice you may find that in about 20 minutes you can come away with more information than a person who has spent two to three weeks living with the same book.

What you have been doing here is fooling your brain into hyperactivity. By getting you to 'believe' it was a matter of life and death, you pooled resources not usually available. Next time you try this, simply imagine a similar situation, start with a book upside down for a minute or two and really get your brain up to speed. Once you're in high gear with the technique you can even switch materials after a minute or two and read something else. In other words, you do not have to turn the material you wish to read upside down. You can use other material to get yourself up to speed.

CAUTION: There is just one caution with this exercise: it does take up a bit of mental energy. Make sure you drink plenty of water afterwards and remember to eat nutritiously.

The power break

Research shows that every few hours your body uses up its best neurotransmitters, the chemicals that allow your nervous system to function. As the supply is used up, the body must replace them with a less effective version. When that supply gets used up, it must replace that one with an even less effective one, and so on all day long until we get what is known as our 'second wind'.

The problem is that these less effective transmitters cause wear and tear on our nervous system. By the end of the afternoon, our ability to concentrate and make good decisions declines. By the end of the work day we feel exhausted and spent. Even after a full night of sleep we still may not feel like we've caught up and that our cells have not got what they need to work at full capacity. In fact, what they need is a 'power break' or 'power nap' at some point during the day.

The solution is to take a 20-minute break to allow your body to manufacture more of the ideal neurotransmitters, which it cannot do when you are active. Only when you allow the body enough time to rest can it replenish the supply of these neurotransmitters. When it does, we feel refreshed, alert and calmly energised.

When is it the right time?

The body gives out clues as to when it needs a power break. They can be:

- feeling an itch
- yawning
- a leg 'falling asleep'
- feeling hungry before a mealtime
- loss of concentration
- eyes not focusing well
- feeling stressed before an important deadline.

If you are feeling some or any of these, it could be time to take your power break.

What should I do?

Find a quiet place, away from noise or distractions. Sit comfortably or lie down. Do nothing. Don't try to think or not think. Your task is simply to sit for 20 minutes. For the first few minutes you may have many thoughts racing through your head. They will go away. Just sit. Your body knows what to do.

You could try smelling some vanilla before you begin as its aroma is very relaxing. Just a few gentle sniffs will do it.

WARNING: It is most important that you do not break for more than 20 minutes.

After about 25 minutes or so, your body may start to go into its sleep stages (delta brain waves), which will cause grogginess instead of alertness. Use a timer set for 20 minutes to ensure you break for the proper amount.

One or two power breaks per day will make a big difference in your productivity. You will have more energy all day long and wake up more refreshed in the mornings!

NOTE: As you slip into right-brain mode as you relax, intuitive insights may come to you. Keep a pen and paper or recorder with you. Simply write or record any interesting thoughts, put down the device and close your eyes again.

ASSIGNMENT

When your body shows signs that it might need one, take a power break for between 17 and 20 minutes. Set an alarm and just sit there. Repeat once or twice a day for 21 days. How do you feel? Remember to keep a notepad or voice recorder with you for when great ideas spring up.

Getting focused

1 **Decide** to absorb the material.
2 **See** a clear picture of it done.
3 **Look** – imagine absorbing through your eyes.
4 **Feel** – imagine taking information in through your hands.
5 **Nose** – imagine breathing in all the words and pictures.
6 **Ears** – imagine the words flowing right into your ears.
7 **Speak** the main words and thoughts.

SUMMARY

- Decide what you want to achieve before you begin. As the famous writer Ralph Waldo Emerson said, 'Once you make a decision, the universe conspires to make it happen.'

- Artificial interest is often a life saver for people who have loads of dry, boring material to read.

While it is always helpful at any time, it is a real treasure for making the really dull stuff palatable.

- Defeating the enemies of concentration is so fundamental to good reading. While the basic techniques of this book go a long way, there is no reason to operate with strikes against you if it isn't necessary.

- Enhanced focusing is the ultimate focusing technique. Relax and enjoy it!

- The power break gets great reviews from people. What a simple way to save half your day. Try it for 21 days and look at the difference.

15.

Look to your future

Now you have come to the end of the main text of this book. What have you learned? In summary, loads!

In the first part of this book you discovered what SuperReading™ is all about and how it can help you (chapters 1 and 2). You have found out what kind of learner you are (chapter 3), how to test your reading effectiveness and monitor your progress (chapters 3 and 5). You know how important it is to reserve judgement with any new skill so you can embody that skill and fully benefit from it (chapter 4). You understand that you have to try it for at least 21 days or have 21 goes at it. You have discovered how to set reading goals and how to test yourself (chapters 4 and 5).

In the second part of this book, you learned the basic, essential techniques of SuperReading™. You discovered how to use hand pacing to point at what you are reading to keep your concentration (chapter 6). Then you learned how to P.RE.PA.R.E:

1 **Preview** the material so you know what's coming and improve recall (chapter 7)
2 **Read** (using your finger, of course!) (chapter 6)
3 **Parrot** to see if you've gained enough information (chapter 9)
4 If you are missing vital information, you then **review** to capture it (chapter 10)
5 **Embodying**: do I want to put effort into storing this information in medium- or long-term memory (chapter 10)?

Other very important aspects of basic SuperReading™ include the Eye-Hop™ and you learned how to progress from processing one word at a time to taking on four- and five-word Eye-Hops™ (chapter 8). You will also have discovered some very useful techniques for reviewing and recall, including Info-Mapping™ (see chapter 10 and 13).

In the third part of this book, you looked at some very useful techniques to help you build on the basics of SuperReading™, from pattern reading (chapter 11), visualisation and affirmation techniques (chapter 12), to methods for improving your memory, making learning fun and interactive (chapter 13), and focusing your mind (chapter 14).

You've now experienced SuperReading™. What's left to you now is knowledge. By investing some time each day in your personal development you can amass more useful information than you ever thought possible. The more you know, the more choices are available to you in your life.

From now on, schedule at least 30 minutes each day for personal reading to develop yourself. Choose a subject or topic that interests you and get a book on that subject. Using all your new skills, absorb the book and Info-Map™ it. This will take about eight hours. Get a second book on the same topic and do the same thing. This will take around six hours as much of the information will be similar. Add what you have learned to your Info-Map™. Get a third book on the topic. Look through the contents list and find out what's different. Read those sections and add the information to your Info-Map™. Get a fourth book ... Do the same again with any new information, which by now is only around 10 to 20 per cent of the content. This should take two hours at the most. Books five to ten should take you no more than an hour each to add to your Info-Map™. And so on. Then go to the internet for any up-to-the-minute information to add to your Info-Map™. After a few months you will end up being an expert on the subject. If it's for a hobby, you will have reached a new level. If it's for your career, the sky's the limit. If knowledge is power, you have indeed become powerful.

The more you read the more you will know.
The more you know the more you can do.
The more you can do the more useful you are.
The more useful you are the more you are worth.
The more you are worth the higher your self-esteem.
The higher your self-esteem the greater
can be your happiness.
The greater your happiness the more you may
attain peace.
Having achieved peace, you can truly begin
to help others.

Always read the best material you can, for it will
determine your future.

Your reading coach, Ron.

Appendices

APPENDIX A

It's about time

In chapter 1 you will have read of my quest, which I began in 1995, to find the solution to the problem of the apparent disappearance of time in a typical work day. I discovered that time disappeared into three areas: meetings, travel and reading. If you have been following the advice in this book you are probably well on the way to becoming a super reader, and the following strategies will save you even more time and help relieve or prevent stress.

'If you don't have enough money or time, you must prioritise.'

JOHN EDMUND HAGGAI

Christian motivational writer and speaker

On the telephone

Before you make a call, prioritise and **write down** the items you need to address. Tell the person when you call how many items you have to address, how long you believe it will take to go through them and confirm that they have the time to discuss them. Check the items off as you deal with them.

To finish: 'Thank you, that's all I have for now. Is there anything you need? I'll call you [soon, Friday, next week, etc ...]. Thank you. Goodbye!'

> **ASSIGNMENT**
>
> For the next 21 days, keep a pad by the phone and write down the points you're going to cover with them for at least three people per day. Time your calls to check you are sticking to your estimated time for the conversation.

'To-do' list

Make a written list of the things you need to do today. Have a separate list for things to do tomorrow. Prioritise the top five items and commit yourself to doing them. Before you go to sleep, close your eyes and visualise them all completed. You will often wake up with great ideas to get them done more efficiently. If you can delegate or bin any items, do!

There is another good reason for having a written

'to-do' list. It can help you focus when you read. How? Do you ever have thoughts spinning endlessly round your head? Do you sometimes keep rehashing the same thing over and over, like when you can't get a tune out of your head? If so, a 'to-do' list will help. I believe the swirling is the brain's attempt to not forget about it. The remedy is to convince your brain that it's OK to stop thinking about it by writing the item down and keeping it in a safe place, where your brain knows it cannot get away. Once that's done, your brain can relax in the confidence that the item will be handled and you will be able to focus on whatever you are doing, whether reading an article or anything else.

ASSIGNMENT

Try making 'to-do' lists for 21 days or 21 times and see what happens. Your mind will learn to let the items go and focus on whatever you want it to.

Filing

File items according to subject or date. Cross-reference your list using a program such as MS Excel. Only keep what you really need. When you file things keep in mind that you should be able to find it again in 30 seconds or less. That will force you to be more logical and thoughtful and to think about finding something easily six months from now. Consider this: if you were away and had to ask someone else to find that paper for you, how could you ensure that it would be really easy to tell them how to find it in 30 seconds or less?

Backing up your computer files on a regular basis can save days of work. I back mine up every Friday on to an external drive. Once per quarter I back up the external drive on to writeable DVDs. Those should be kept in an entirely different place from your computer, like a safe deposit box, or with a trusted friend or relative.

Scheduling

Make appointments for any activity that takes at least 30 minutes. This is called scheduling. Make appointments with yourself and keep them. In the context of this book, make and keep appointments to do your reading practice every day (and to do the Eye-Hop™ exercises in chapter 8).

Only keep one calendar (a computer back-up is OK). If you have two or more calendars you are inviting mayhem into your life. Eventually you will schedule an appointment that conflicts with one on the other calendar. Remember, 'A man with a watch knows what time it is. A man with two watches is never sure.'

Waiting

Always take something with you to do when you know you will have some waiting to do. Reading a book is a great idea. Or you can Info-Map™ projects (see chapter 10). Write a note to a friend. Plan out your next day. Do your Eye-Hop™ exercises (see chapter 8). Review your goals. Write down some goals. Always turn waiting time into productive time.

> **ASSIGNMENT**
>
> Choose a book that you wish to absorb and put it in your briefcase, handbag, rucksack, car or anywhere that makes sense to you. Do it now. Then pull it out and read it whenever you're in a queue or waiting for something. Pretend that you are being paid by the minute to read that book.

Ideas

Keep a small notebook or voice recorder with you at all times. Whenever an idea comes to you record it. Later you can transfer your ideas into a more permanent file on your computer. Every couple of months glance through your ideas file. From time to time the moment will be right for one of your ideas. By having them fresh in your mind you will be ready when opportunity knocks.

They say 'Opportunity only knocks once'. I think there's more to it than that. I believe opportunity has a sense of humour. Not only does it only knock once, but sometimes it knocks very softly just to see if you're listening.

ASSIGNMENT

Keep an ideas file. Review them from time to time, such as monthly or quarterly. You will be surprised at what you've come up with. From time to time the timing will be right and you'll be able to capitalise on them.

SUMMARY

- Preparing for phone calls saves time while adding clarity.

- A to-do list not only keeps you more organised, it allows you to read with better focus.

- Good filing saves time and reduces stress.

- Proper scheduling saves time and reduces your stress levels.

- Turning waiting time into productive time makes your life easier.

- Recording our ideas leads to creative solutions and better focus.

APPENDIX B

Reading tests and answers

The tests

These are the remaining reading tests following on from Test 1 in chapter 5. For much more information on testing look back at chapter 5 to remind yourself. Have a timer (stopwatch) and a pen ready. Start your stopwatch; then begin to read. No note taking! Make sure you have a piece of paper to hand to cover up the questions so that you don't see them as you are reading.

Test 2: Antony van Leeuwenhoek

Antony van Leeuwenhoek was an unlikely scientist. A Dutch tradesman from a family of tradesmen, he was not wealthy and earned no university degrees. He only spoke Dutch.

Yet with skill, diligence and curiosity, free of the scientific dogma of the day, Leeuwenhoek made some of the most basic and important discoveries in biology. He discovered bacteria, parasitic microscopic organisms, sperm cells, blood cells, and microscopic nematodes and rotifers. His research opened up a new entire world of microscopic life to scientists.

Leeuwenhoek was born in 1632. His father was a basket-maker and his mother's family were brewers. He started in business as a fabric merchant. He also worked as a surveyor and a wine assayer. Sometime during the 1660s, Antony van Leeuwenhoek learned to grind lenses. He made simple microscopes and began observing with them. He was inspired by Robert Hooke's illustrated book *Micrographia*, which showed Hooke's own observations with the microscope.

Leeuwenhoek is known to have made over five hundred 'microscopes', of which fewer than ten have survived. In basic design, probably all of Leeuwenhoek's instruments were simply powerful magnifying glasses, not compound microscopes of the type used today. Those were invented almost forty years before Leeuwenhoek was born. Sometimes he is referred to as 'the inventor of the microscope'. That would have been impossible.

Early compound microscopes were not practical for magnifying objects more than about twenty or thirty times. Leeuwenhoek's skill at grinding lenses allowed him to build microscopes that magnified over two hundred times, with clearer and brighter images than any of his colleagues could achieve. What helped was his curiosity to observe almost anything that could be placed under his lenses, and his care in describing what he saw. He hired an illustrator to make drawings of the things he saw, to accompany his written descriptions. Most of his descriptions of micro-organisms are instantly recognisable.

In 1673, Leeuwenhoek began writing letters to the new Royal Society of London, describing what he had seen with his microscopes. His first letter had observations on the stings of bees. For the next fifty years he corresponded with the Royal Society. His letters, written in Dutch, were translated into Latin or English and printed in the Philosophical Transactions of the Royal Society. In 1680 he was elected a full member of the Royal Society.

His descriptions of tooth plaque are among the first observations of living bacteria ever recorded.

Note down your reading time; then answer the questions on the next page.

Time: _____

QUESTIONS FOR: Antony van Leeuwenhoek

1. In what year was Antony van Leeuwenhoek born?
2. What did van Leeuwenhoek's father do for a living?
3. Who wrote the book *Micrographia*?
4. What was invented almost forty years before van Leeuwenhoek was born?
5. What magnification did van Leeuwenhoek's microscopes achieve?
6. Whom did van Leeuwenhoek began writing letters to in 1673?
7. In what material did van Leeuwenhoek observe living bacteria?
8. How many microscopes did van Leeuwenhoek make?
9. In what two languages were van Leeuwenhoek's letters published?
10. Name one of the other careers van Leeuwenhoek had.

Now go back to the previous page and read the article again.

Time yourself!

When you have finished answering go to page 301 and get the answers. Grade yourself.

Test 3: Conway Twitty

Conway Twitty was born Harold Lloyd Jenkins on 1 September 1933 in Friars Point, Mississippi. Jenkins was named by his great-uncle after his favourite silent movie actor, Harold Lloyd. The family moved to Arkansas when Jenkins was ten years old, and it was there that Jenkins formed his first singing group, the Phillips County Ramblers.

Two years later, he had his own local radio show every Saturday morning. Jenkins also practised his second passion, baseball. He received an offer to play with the Philadelphia Phillies after high school, but he was drafted into the army, which effectively ended that dream.

Discharged from the army, Jenkins again pursued a music career. Upon hearing Elvis sing 'Mystery Train', he began writing rock'n'roll songs. He worked with Sam Phillips, the owner and founder of Sun Studios in Memphis, to 'get the right sound'. None of those tracks were released.

Jenkins felt that his real name wasn't marketable, and he changed to his show-business name in 1957. Looking at a road map, he spotted Conway, Arkansas, and Twitty, Texas. He changed his professional name to 'Conway Twitty'.

Twitty's fortunes changed in 1958, while he was with MGM Records. His first Top 40 hit was 'It's Only Make Believe'. It was actually the B side of the single 'I'll Try'. Though it only made it to number two, it sold eight million copies. The record took nearly one year in all to reach and stay at the top spot of the charts in America and the UK. With his deep, resonant voice, some people thought it was Elvis recording under a different name. Twitty racked up nine Top 40 hits in his career.

Conway Twitty always wanted to record country music and in 1965 he switched genres. At first some country DJs refused to play his songs because he was well known as a rock'n'roll singer. His first top five country hit, 'The Image of Me' came in July 1968, followed by his first number one country song, 'Next in Line', that November.

In 1970, Conway recorded and released his biggest hit ever, 'Hello Darlin'', which spent four weeks at the top of the country chart. His music has appeared on other media, including TV's *Family Guy* and the video game *Grand Theft Auto: San Andreas*. With two Grammys, Conway Twitty was inducted into the Country Music Hall of Fame in 1999.

Note down your reading time; then answer the questions on the opposite page.

Time: _____

QUESTIONS FOR: Conway Twitty

1. What was Conway Twitty's real name?
2. What was the name of his first singing group?
3. Twitty wanted to play baseball. What city offered him a contract?
4. What Elvis song inspired Twitty to begin writing rock'n'roll songs?
5. Twitty's first Top 40 song was 'It's Only Make Believe'. What song was the A side of the record?
6. How many copies did 'It's Only Make Believe' sell?
7. What was the title of Twitty's first number one country song?
8. In what year was Twitty inducted into the Country Music Hall of Fame?
9. Who founded Sun Studios in Memphis?
10. What was Twitty's biggest country hit, which spent four weeks at number one?

Now go back to the previous page and read the article again.

Time yourself!

When you have finished answering go to page 302 and get the answers. Grade yourself.

Test 4: David Livingstone

David Livingstone was a Scottish missionary and explorer of the Victorian era, now best remembered because of his meeting with Henry Morton Stanley, which gave rise to the popular quotation, 'Dr Livingstone, I presume?'

Livingstone was born in the village of Blantyre, South Lanarkshire, Scotland. He studied medicine and theology at the University of Glasgow. While working in London, Livingstone joined the London Missionary Society, becoming a minister.

From 1840 he worked in what is now Botswana, but was unable to make inroads into South Africa because of Boer opposition. He married fellow Scotsman Robert Moffat's daughter Mary in 1844, and she travelled with him for a brief time, despite being pregnant. She later returned to England with their children.

From 1852 to 1856, he explored the African interior, and was the first European to see Victoria Falls, which he named after Queen Victoria. Livingstone was one of the first Westerners to make a journey across Africa. The purpose of his journey was to open trade routes, while accumulating information about the African continent. Livingstone was a proponent of trade and missions to be established in central Africa. His motto, inscribed in the base of his statue at Victoria Falls, reads 'Christianity, Commerce and Civilisation'.

He believed the key to achieving these goals was the navigation of the Zambezi River. He returned to Britain to raise funds, and to publish a book on his travels. He resigned from the missionary society. Livingstone returned to Africa as head of the government-funded 'Zambezi Expedition', which was to examine the natural resources of south-eastern Africa. The Zambezi River turned out to be completely unnavigable.

The expedition lasted six years. Livingstone was an inexperienced leader and had trouble managing a large-scale project. His wife Mary died on 29 April 1863 of dysentery, but Livingstone continued to explore, eventually returning home in 1864 after the government ordered the expedition recalled.

In March 1866, Livingstone returned to Africa to seek the source of the Nile. Livingstone was taken ill and completely lost contact with the outside world for six years. Henry Morton Stanley, sent by the *New York Herald* newspaper in 1869, found Livingstone on the shores of Lake Tanganyika in 1871. Stanley joined Livingstone, and together they continued exploring the north end of the Tanganyika.

Despite Stanley's urgings, Livingstone was determined not to leave Africa until he completed his mission. He died from malaria in 1873.

Note down your reading time; then answer the questions on the next page.

Time: _____

QUESTIONS FOR: David Livingstone

1. In what Scottish village was Livingstone born?
2. What subjects did Livingstone study at university?
3. Livingstone first worked in what part of Africa?
4. What was Mary Livingstone's maiden name?
5. Livingstone was the first European to see what African landmark?
6. The inscription on Livingstone's statue reads, 'Christianity, Commerce and _____'?
7. Which river did Livingstone believe was paramount to his goals for Africa?
8. How long did the government-funded expedition last before being recalled?
9. What did David Livingstone die from?
10. What newspaper sent Stanley to find Livingstone?

Now go back to the previous page and read the article again.

Time yourself!

When you have finished answering go to page 302 and get the answers. Grade yourself.

Test 5: William Morris

William Morris was one of the principal founders of the British Arts and Crafts Movement and is best known as a designer of wallpaper and patterned fabrics. He was a writer of poetry and fiction, and an early founder of the socialist movement in Britain.

The tragic conflict in Morris's life was his unfulfilled desire to create affordable – or even free – beautiful things for common people. The real-life result was always the creation of extremely expensive objects for the discerning few. In his utopian novel *News from Nowhere,* everybody works for pleasure only, and beautifully handcrafted things are given away for free to those who appreciate them.

Morris was born in Walthamstow near London. His family was wealthy, and he went to Exeter College, Oxford, where he was influenced by John Ruskin. He met his wife, Jane Burden, a working-class woman whose pale skin and coppery hair were considered by Morris the epitome of beauty.

The artistic movement Morris and his friends made famous was the Pre-Raphaelite Brotherhood. They disfavoured the rough industrial manufacture of decorative arts and architecture, and favoured a return to hand-craftsmanship, raising craftsmen to the status of artists.

Morris left Oxford to join an architectural firm, but found himself drawn to the decorative arts. In 1861, he founded the firm of Morris, Marshall, Faulkner &

Company. Throughout his life he continued to work in his own firm, although it changed names. Its most famous incarnation was as Morris and Company. His designs are still sold today under licences given to Sanderson & Sons and Liberty of London. In 1877 he founded the Society for the Protection of Ancient Buildings. His preservation work resulted indirectly in the founding of the National Trust.

Morris and his daughter May were among Britain's first socialists, working with Eleanor Marx and Engels to begin the socialist movement. In1884 he organised the Socialist League.

Morris's book, *The Wood Between the Worlds*, is said to have influenced C. S. Lewis's Narnia series, while J. R. R. Tolkien was inspired by Morris's books *The House of the Wolfkings* and *The Roots of the Mountains*.

After the death of Tennyson in 1892, Morris was offered the Poet Laureateship, but declined. William Morris died in 1896 and was buried in the churchyard at Kelmscott village in Oxfordshire.

Note down your reading time; then answer the questions on the next page.

Time: _____

QUESTIONS FOR: William Morris

1. William Morris is best known as a designer of wall-paper and _____?
2. Morris's utopian novel was entitled _____?
3. Where did Morris go to college?
4. His wife's maiden name was _____?
5. The artistic movement he helped made famous was the Pre-Raphaelite _____?
6. In 1877 he founded the Society for the Protection of _____?
7. Name one person Morris worked with to begin the socialist movement in Britain.
8. What was Morris's daughter's name?
9. *The House of the Wolfkings* influenced what author?
10. Which Poet Laureate died in 1892?

Now go back to the previous page and read the article again.

Time yourself!

When you have finished answering go to page 303 and get the answers. Grade yourself.

Test 6: Ezra Pound

Ezra Weston Loomis Pound was a poet, critic and intellectual. He was a major figure of the modernist movement in the first half of the twentieth century. He is generally considered the poet most responsible for defining and promoting a modernist aesthetic in poetry. In the early twentieth century, he opened a seminal exchange of work and ideas between British and American writers, and was famous for the generosity with which he advanced the work of such major contemporaries as Robert Frost, Marianne Moore, Ernest Hemingway and, especially, T. S. Eliot. Pound also had a profound influence on Irish writers William Butler Yeats and James Joyce.

His own significant contributions to poetry begin with his promotion of Imagism, a movement in poetry, which derived its technique from classical Chinese and Japanese poetry, stressing clarity, precision, and economy of language, and forgoing traditional rhyme and meter in order to, in Pound's words, 'compose in the sequence of the musical phrase, not in the sequence of the metronome'. His later work, for nearly fifty years, focused on the epic poem he entitled *The Cantos*.

Pound was born in America, where he attended several universities. In 1908 he moved to Europe, settling in London after spending a brief stint working as a tour guide in Gibraltar, and several months in Venice.

In the years before the First World War, Pound was

responsible for the appearance of Imagism and Vorticism. These two movements helped bring to notice the work of poets and artists such as James Joyce and Robert Frost.

Pound believed William Butler Yeats was the greatest living poet, and befriended him in England. Pound eventually became Yeats's secretary, and soon became interested in his occult beliefs. During the First World War, Pound and Yeats lived together at Stone Cottage in Sussex, England, studying Japanese, especially Noh plays. In 1914, Pound married artist Dorothy Shakespear.

In 1920, Pound moved to Paris, where he worked among a circle of artists, musicians and writers who were revolutionising the whole world of modern art. He was friends with Ernest Hemingway, whom Pound asked to teach him to box.

In 1924, Pound left Paris permanently and moved to Italy. During the Second World War, Pound created propaganda for the Axis, and later faced charges of treason in America. He spent twelve years in St Elizabeth's mental hospital in Washington, DC. Upon release, he moved to Venice, where he is buried today.

Note down your reading time; then answer the questions on the next page.

Time: _____

QUESTIONS FOR: Ezra Pound

1. Which movement in poetry is derived from Chinese poetry?
2. Name two major contemporary poets whose work was advanced by Pound.
3. Pound worked for fifty years on what poem?
4. In what year did Pound move to Europe?
5. What was the name of Ezra Pound's wife?
6. What was the name of the place where Pound lived with Yeats?
7. Imagism stresses three qualities. Please name one.
8. Imagism and Vorticism helped to bring notice to two poets. Please name one.
9. In what Washington, DC, hospital did Pound spend twelve years?
10. Where did Pound work as a tour guide?

Now go back to the previous page and read the article again.

Time yourself!

When you have finished answering go to page 303 and get the answers. Grade yourself.

Test 7: Ansel Adams

Ansel Easton Adams was an American photographer, known for his black and white photographs of California's Yosemite Valley.

Adams was the author of numerous books about photography, including his trilogy of technical instruction manuals: *The Camera*, *The Negative* and *The Print*.

He invented the zone system, a technique allowing photographers to translate the light they see into specific densities, giving them better control over finished photographs. Adams pioneered the idea of visualisation of the finished print based upon the measured light values in the scene being photographed.

Adams was born in San Francisco, California. When he was four, he broke his nose on a garden wall in an aftershock from the 1906 San Francisco earthquake. His nose appeared crooked for the rest of his life.

He became interested in photography when his Aunt Mary gave him a copy of *In the Heart of the Sierras* while he was sick as a child. The photographs piqued his interest enough to persuade his parents to holiday in Yosemite National Park in 1916, where he was given a camera as a gift.

Adams disliked the uniformity of the education system and left school in 1915 to educate himself. He trained himself as a pianist, and alternated between a career as a photographer and a concert pianist. Photography won out, as did Yosemite, where he met his future wife, Virginia Best.

At the age of 17 Adams joined the Sierra Club, a group dedicated to preserving the natural world's wonders and resources. He remained a member throughout his lifetime and served as a director. Adams was an avid mountaineer and participated in the club's annual 'high trips'. It was at Half Dome in 1927 that he first found that he could make photographs that were, in his own words, '. . . an austere and blazing poetry of the real'. Adams became an environmentalist, and his photographs are a record of what many of these national parks were like before human intervention. His work promoted many of the goals of the Sierra Club and brought environmental issues to light.

Adams was the recipient of three Guggenheim fellowships during his career. He was elected in 1966 a Fellow of the American Academy of Arts and Sciences. In 1980 Jimmy Carter awarded him the Presidential Medal of Freedom, the nation's highest civilian honour. The Minarets Wilderness in the Inyo National Forest was renamed the Ansel Adams Wilderness in 1984 in his honour.

Note down your reading time; then answer the questions on the next page.

Time: _____

QUESTIONS FOR: Ansel Adams

1. Name two of Adams's three instruction manuals.
2. What was the name of the technique Adams invented to help photographers translate light into densities?
3. On what did Adams break his nose when he was four years old?
4. In which National Park did Adams's family holiday in 1916?
5. What was Adams's wife's name?
6. What group did Adams join at the age of 17?
7. Who awarded Adams the Presidential Medal of Freedom?
8. The Minarets Wilderness was in which National Park?
9. In 1927, Adams photographed what natural feature?
10. How many Guggenheim Awards did Adams receive?

Now go back to the previous page and read the article again.

Time yourself!

When you have finished answering go to page 304 and get the answers. Grade yourself.

The Answers and Scoring

Remember that you do not score your tests until you have completed both the test and the re-test.

Here's how to score your tests:

1 When you get an answer totally correct both in the test and the re-test, give yourself a score of 10.

2 Give yourself a zero when you get an answer wrong or leave it blank. Numerical answers must be totally correct or you score zero.

3 Score 5 for a partially correct answer. For example, if the correct answer is 'Alexander Fleming', you get 5 points for 'Fleming' and 10 points for 'Alexander Fleming'.

4 Add up your numbers – this gives you your comprehension score. For example, 70 points represents 70 per cent comprehension.

5 Turn to Appendix C to calculate your Reading Effectiveness (R.E. score).

The first set of answers goes with Test 1 in chapter 5 on page 65.

Test 1: George Stephenson

1 Wylam
2 Ten years
3 Blucher
4 Flanged
5 Gravity
6 Edward Pease
7 Locomotion
8 Experiment
9 Cuts or embankments or (stone) viaducts [need one only]
10 Rocket

Test 2: Antony van Leeuwenhoek

1 1632
2 Basket-maker
3 Robert Hooke
4 Compound microscopes
5 Over 200 times
6 The Royal Society of London
7 Tooth plaque
8 Over 500
9 Latin and English
10 Fabric merchant or surveyor or wine assayer

Test 3: Conway Twitty

1   Harold Lloyd Jenkins
2   The Phillips County Ramblers
3   Philadelphia
4   'Mystery Train'
5   'I'll Try'
6   Eight million
7   'Next In Line'
8   1999
9   Sam Phillips
10 'Hello Darlin''

Test 4: David Livingstone

1   Blantyre
2   Medicine and theology
3   Botswana
4   Moffat
5   Victoria Falls
6   Civilisation
7   The Zambezi
8   Six years
9   Malaria
10 *New York Herald*

Test 5: William Morris

1   Patterned fabrics
2   *News from Nowhere*
3   Exeter College, Oxford
4   Burden
5   Brotherhood
6   Ancient Buildings
7   Eleanor Marx or Freidrich Engels (surname OK)
8   May
9   Tolkien
10 Tennyson

Test 6: Ezra Pound

1   Imagism
2   Robert Frost, Marianne Moore, Ernest Hemingway
    or T. S. Eliot
3   *The Cantos*
4   1908
5   Dorothy Shakespear
6   Stone Cottage
7   Clarity, or precision, or economy of language
8   James Joyce or Robert Frost
9   St Elizabeth's
10 Gibraltar

Test 7: Ansel Adams

1   *The Camera, The Negative* and *The Print*
2   The zone system
3   A garden wall
4   Yosemite
5   Virginia Best
6   The Sierra Club
7   Jimmy Carter
8   Inyo
9   Half Dome
10 Three

APPENDIX C

Calculating Your Reading Speed

To calculate your reading speed, count the number of words on several full lines of your book to get an average. Multiply by the number of lines on a page. Depending on the type of book you are reading, the number of words per page is likely to fall somewhere between 150 and 400. Time yourself reading a page (or two) and see where the time and words per page meet on the following chart. This is your reading speed. For example, if you take 20 seconds to read a page with 300 words, your word per minute reading speed will be 900.

00.01 to 00.30 SECONDS

Time	150	175	200	225	250	275	300	325	350	375	400
00:01	9000	10500	12000	13500	15000	16500	18000	19200	21000	22500	24000
00:02	4500	5250	6000	6750	7500	8250	9000	9600	10500	11250	12000
00:03	3000	3500	4000	4500	5000	5500	6000	6400	7000	7500	8000
00:04	2250	2625	3000	3375	3750	4125	4500	4800	5250	5625	6000
00:05	1800	2100	2400	2700	3000	3300	3600	3840	4200	4500	4800
00:06	1500	1750	2000	2250	2500	2750	3000	3200	3500	3750	4000
00:07	1286	1500	1714	1929	2143	2357	2571	2743	3000	3214	3429
00:08	1125	1313	1500	1688	1875	2063	2250	2400	2625	2813	3000
00:09	1000	1167	1333	1500	1667	1833	2000	2133	2333	2500	2667
00:10	900	1050	1200	1350	1500	1650	1800	1920	2100	2250	2400
00:11	818	955	1091	1227	1364	1500	1636	1745	1909	2045	2182
00:12	750	875	1000	1125	1250	1375	1500	1600	1750	1875	2000
00:13	692	808	923	1038	1154	1269	1385	1477	1615	1731	1846
00:14	643	750	857	964	1071	1179	1286	1371	1500	1607	1714
00:15	600	700	800	900	1000	1100	1200	1280	1400	1500	1600
00:16	563	656	750	844	938	1031	1125	1200	1313	1406	1500
00:17	529	618	706	794	882	971	1059	1129	1235	1324	1412
00:18	500	583	667	750	833	917	1000	1067	1167	1250	1333
00:19	474	553	632	711	789	868	947	1011	1105	1184	1263
00:20	450	525	600	675	750	825	900	960	1050	1125	1200
00:21	429	500	571	643	714	786	857	914	1000	1071	1143
00:22	409	477	545	614	682	750	818	873	955	1023	1091
00:23	391	457	522	587	652	717	783	835	913	978	1043
00:24	375	438	500	563	625	688	750	800	875	938	1000
00:25	360	420	480	540	600	660	720	768	840	900	960
00:26	346	404	462	519	577	635	692	738	808	865	923
00:27	333	389	444	500	556	611	667	711	778	833	889
00:28	321	375	429	482	536	589	643	686	750	804	857
00:29	310	362	414	466	517	569	621	662	724	776	828
00:30	300	350	400	450	500	550	600	640	700	750	800

00.31 SECONDS to 1 MINUTE

Time	150	175	200	225	250	275	300	325	350	375	400
00:31	290	339	387	435	484	532	581	619	677	726	774
00:32	281	328	375	422	469	516	563	600	656	703	750
00:33	273	318	364	409	455	500	545	582	636	682	727
00:34	265	309	353	397	441	485	529	565	618	662	706
00:35	257	300	343	386	429	471	514	549	600	643	686
00:36	250	292	333	375	417	458	500	533	583	625	667
00:37	243	284	324	365	405	446	486	519	568	608	649
00:38	237	276	316	355	395	434	474	505	553	592	632
00:39	231	269	308	346	385	423	462	492	538	577	615
00:40	225	263	300	338	375	413	450	480	525	563	600
00:41	220	256	293	329	366	402	439	468	512	549	585
00:42	214	250	286	321	357	393	429	457	500	536	571
00:43	209	244	279	314	349	384	419	447	488	523	558
00:44	205	239	273	307	341	375	409	436	477	511	545
00:45	200	233	267	300	333	367	400	427	467	500	533
00:46	196	228	261	293	326	359	391	417	457	489	522
00:47	191	223	255	287	319	351	383	409	447	479	511
00:48	188	219	250	281	313	344	375	400	438	469	500
00:49	184	214	245	276	306	337	367	392	429	459	490
00:50	180	210	240	270	300	330	360	384	420	450	480
00:51	176	206	235	265	294	324	353	376	412	441	471
00:52	173	202	231	260	288	317	346	369	404	433	462
00:53	170	198	226	255	283	311	340	362	396	425	453
00:54	167	194	222	250	278	306	333	356	389	417	444
00:55	164	191	218	245	273	300	327	349	382	409	436
00:56	161	188	214	241	268	295	321	343	375	402	429
00:57	158	184	211	237	263	289	316	337	368	395	421
00:58	155	181	207	233	259	284	310	331	362	388	414
00:59	153	178	203	229	254	280	305	325	356	381	407
01:00	150	175	200	225	250	275	300	320	350	375	400

APPENDIX D

Reading Effectiveness (R. E.) Scores

Once you have completed a test, look up your time in the left-hand column of the following tables (do this for both the test and then for the re-test). The number immediately to the right of your reading time is your words per minute (w.p.m.) score. Make a note of this.

The numbers across the top of the chart refer to your comprehension score. If, for example, you got five answers correct (5 x a score of 10), follow down the 50 column until it meets the row your time is on. The number where the column and row meet is your reading effectiveness (R.E.) score. The following charts are broken down into one-minute chunks to make it easier to quickly find your scores.

0:01 to 0:30 seconds

COMPREHENSION SCORE

Time	w.p.m.	10	20	30	40	50	60	70	80	90	100
00:01	24000	2400	4800	7200	9600	12000	14400	16800	19200	21600	24000
00:02	12000	1200	2400	3600	4800	6000	7200	8400	9600	10800	12000
00:03	8000	800	1600	2400	3200	4000	4800	5600	6400	7200	8000
00:04	6000	600	1200	1800	2400	3000	3600	4200	4800	5400	6000
00:05	4800	480	960	1440	1920	2400	2880	3360	3840	4320	4800
00:06	4000	400	800	1200	1600	2000	2400	2800	3200	3600	4000
00:07	3429	343	686	1029	1371	1714	2057	2400	2743	3086	3429
00:08	3000	300	600	900	1200	1500	1800	2100	2400	2700	3000
00:09	2667	267	533	800	1067	1333	1600	1867	2133	2400	2667
00:10	2400	240	480	720	960	1200	1440	1680	1920	2160	2400
00:11	2182	218	436	655	873	1091	1309	1527	1745	1964	2182
00:12	2000	200	400	600	800	1000	1200	1400	1600	1800	2000
00:13	1846	185	369	554	738	923	1108	1292	1477	1662	1846
00:14	1714	171	343	514	686	857	1029	1200	1371	1543	1714
00:15	1600	160	320	480	640	800	960	1120	1280	1440	1600
00:16	1500	150	300	450	600	750	900	1050	1200	1350	1500
00:17	1412	141	282	424	565	706	847	988	1129	1271	1412
00:18	1333	133	267	400	533	667	800	933	1067	1200	1333
00:19	1263	126	253	379	505	632	758	884	1011	1137	1263
00:20	1200	120	240	360	480	600	720	840	960	1080	1200
00:21	1143	114	229	343	457	571	686	800	914	1029	1143
00:22	1091	109	218	327	436	545	655	764	873	982	1091
00:23	1043	104	209	313	417	522	626	730	835	939	1043
00:24	1000	100	200	300	400	500	600	700	800	900	1000
00:25	960	96	192	288	384	480	576	672	768	864	960
00:26	923	92	185	277	369	462	554	646	738	831	923
00:27	889	89	178	267	356	444	533	622	711	800	889
00:28	857	86	171	257	343	429	514	600	686	771	857
00:29	828	83	166	248	331	414	497	579	662	745	828
00:30	800	80	160	240	320	400	480	560	640	720	800

0:31 to 1:00 minute

COMPREHENSION SCORE

Time	w.p.m.	10	20	30	40	50	60	70	80	90	100
00:31	774	77	155	232	310	387	465	542	619	697	774
00:32	750	75	150	225	300	375	450	525	600	675	750
00:33	727	73	145	218	291	364	436	509	582	654	727
00:34	706	71	141	212	282	353	424	494	565	635	706
00:35	686	69	137	206	274	343	411	480	549	617	686
00:36	667	67	133	200	267	333	400	467	533	600	667
00:37	649	65	130	195	259	324	389	454	519	584	649
00:38	632	63	126	189	253	316	379	442	505	568	632
00:39	615	62	123	185	246	308	369	431	492	554	615
00:40	600	60	120	180	240	300	360	420	480	540	600
00:41	585	59	117	176	234	293	351	410	468	527	585
00:42	571	57	114	171	229	286	343	400	457	514	571
00:43	558	56	112	167	223	279	335	391	447	502	558
00:44	545	55	109	164	218	273	327	382	436	491	545
00:45	533	53	107	160	213	267	320	373	427	480	533
00:46	522	52	104	157	209	261	313	365	417	470	522
00:47	511	51	102	153	204	255	306	357	409	460	511
00:48	500	50	100	150	200	250	300	350	400	450	500
00:49	490	49	98	147	196	245	294	343	392	441	490
00:50	480	48	96	144	192	240	288	336	384	432	480
00:51	471	47	94	141	188	235	282	329	376	424	471
00:52	462	46	92	138	185	231	277	323	369	415	462
00:53	453	45	91	136	181	226	272	317	362	408	453
00:54	444	44	89	133	178	222	267	311	356	400	444
00:55	436	44	87	131	175	218	262	305	349	393	436
00:56	429	43	86	129	171	214	257	300	343	386	429
00:57	421	42	84	126	168	211	253	295	337	379	421
00:58	414	41	83	124	166	207	248	290	331	372	414
00:59	407	41	81	122	163	203	244	285	325	366	407
01:00	400	40	80	120	160	200	240	280	320	360	400

1:01 to 1:30 minutes

COMPREHENSION SCORE

Time	w.p.m.	10	20	30	40	50	60	70	80	90	100
01:01	393	39	79	118	157	197	236	275	315	354	393
01:02	387	39	77	116	155	194	232	271	310	348	387
01:03	381	38	76	114	152	190	229	267	305	343	381
01:04	375	38	75	113	150	188	225	263	300	338	375
01:05	369	37	74	111	148	185	222	258	295	332	369
01:06	364	36	73	109	145	182	218	255	291	327	364
01:07	358	36	72	107	143	179	215	251	287	322	358
01:08	353	35	71	106	141	176	212	247	282	318	353
01:09	348	35	70	104	139	174	209	243	278	313	348
01:10	343	34	69	103	137	171	206	240	274	309	343
01:11	338	34	68	101	135	169	203	237	270	304	338
01:12	333	33	67	100	133	167	200	233	267	300	333
01:13	329	33	66	99	132	164	197	230	263	296	329
01:14	324	32	65	97	130	162	195	227	259	292	324
01:15	320	32	64	96	128	160	192	224	256	288	320
01:16	316	32	63	95	126	158	189	221	253	284	316
01:17	312	31	62	94	125	156	187	218	249	281	312
01:18	308	31	62	92	123	154	185	215	246	277	308
01:19	304	30	61	91	122	152	182	213	243	273	304
01:20	300	30	60	90	120	150	180	210	240	270	300
01:21	296	30	59	89	119	148	178	207	237	267	296
01:22	293	29	59	88	117	146	176	205	234	263	293
01:23	289	29	58	87	116	145	173	202	231	260	289
01:24	286	29	57	86	114	143	171	200	229	257	286
01:25	282	28	56	85	113	141	169	198	226	254	282
01:26	279	28	56	84	112	140	167	195	223	251	279
01:27	276	28	55	83	110	138	166	193	221	248	276
01:28	273	27	55	82	109	136	164	191	218	245	273
01:29	270	27	54	81	108	135	162	189	216	243	270
01:30	267	27	53	80	107	133	160	187	213	240	267

1:31 to 2:00 minutes

COMPREHENSION SCORE

Time	w.p.m.	10	20	30	40	50	60	70	80	90	100
01:31	264	26	53	79	106	132	158	185	211	238	264
01:32	261	26	52	78	104	130	157	183	209	235	261
01:33	258	26	52	77	103	129	155	181	206	232	258
01:34	255	26	51	77	102	128	153	179	204	230	255
01:35	253	25	51	76	101	126	152	177	202	227	253
01:36	250	25	50	75	100	125	150	175	200	225	250
01:37	247	25	49	74	99	124	148	173	198	222	247
01:38	245	24	49	74	98	122	147	171	196	220	245
01:39	242	24	48	73	97	121	145	170	194	218	242
01:40	240	24	48	72	96	120	144	168	192	216	240
01:41	238	24	48	71	95	119	143	166	190	214	238
01:42	235	24	47	71	94	118	141	165	188	212	235
01:43	233	23	47	70	93	117	140	163	186	210	233
01:44	231	23	46	69	92	115	138	162	185	208	231
01:45	229	23	46	69	91	114	137	160	183	206	229
01:46	226	23	45	68	91	113	136	158	181	204	226
01:47	224	22	45	67	90	112	134	157	179	202	224
01:48	222	22	44	67	89	111	133	156	178	200	222
01:49	220	22	44	66	88	110	132	154	176	198	220
01:50	218	22	44	65	87	109	131	153	175	196	218
01:51	216	22	43	65	86	108	130	151	173	195	216
01:52	214	21	43	64	86	107	129	150	171	193	214
01:53	212	21	42	64	85	106	127	149	170	191	212
01:54	211	21	42	63	84	105	126	147	168	189	211
01:55	209	21	42	63	83	104	125	146	167	188	209
01:56	207	21	41	62	83	103	124	145	166	186	207
01:57	205	21	41	62	82	103	123	144	164	185	205
01:58	203	20	41	61	81	102	122	142	162	183	203
01:59	202	20	40	61	81	101	121	141	161	182	202
02:00	200	20	40	60	80	100	120	140	160	180	200

2:01 to 2:30 minutes

COMPREHENSION SCORE

Time	w.p.m.	10	20	30	40	50	60	70	80	90	100
02:01	198	20	40	60	79	99	119	139	159	179	198
02:02	197	20	39	59	79	98	118	138	157	177	197
02:03	195	20	39	59	78	98	117	137	156	176	195
02:04	194	19	39	58	77	97	116	135	155	174	194
02:05	192	19	38	58	77	96	115	134	154	173	192
02:06	190	19	38	57	76	95	114	133	152	171	190
02:07	189	19	38	57	76	94	113	132	151	170	189
02:08	188	19	38	56	75	94	113	131	150	169	188
02:09	186	19	37	56	74	93	112	130	149	167	186
02:10	185	19	37	55	74	92	111	129	148	166	185
02:11	183	18	37	55	73	92	110	128	147	165	183
02:12	182	18	36	55	73	91	109	127	145	164	182
02:13	180	18	36	54	72	90	108	126	144	162	180
02:14	179	18	36	54	72	90	107	125	143	161	179
02:15	178	18	36	53	71	89	107	124	142	160	178
02:16	176	18	35	53	71	88	106	124	141	159	176
02:17	175	18	35	53	70	88	105	123	140	158	175
02:18	174	17	35	52	70	87	104	122	139	157	174
02:19	173	17	35	52	69	86	104	121	138	156	173
02:20	171	17	34	51	69	86	103	120	137	154	171
02:21	170	17	34	51	68	85	102	119	136	153	170
02:22	169	17	34	51	68	85	101	118	135	152	169
02:23	168	17	34	50	67	84	101	117	134	151	168
02:24	167	17	33	50	67	83	100	117	133	150	167
02:25	166	17	33	50	66	83	99	116	132	149	166
02:26	164	16	33	49	66	82	99	115	132	148	164
02:27	163	16	33	49	65	82	98	114	131	147	163
02:28	162	16	32	49	65	81	97	113	130	146	162
02:29	161	16	32	48	64	81	97	113	129	145	161
02:30	160	16	32	48	64	80	96	112	128	144	160

2:31 to 3:00 minutes

COMPREHENSION SCORE

Time	w.p.m.	10	20	30	40	50	60	70	80	90	100
02:31	159	16	32	48	64	79	95	111	127	143	159
02:32	158	16	32	47	63	79	95	111	126	142	158
02:33	157	16	31	47	63	78	94	110	125	141	157
02:34	156	16	31	47	62	78	94	109	125	140	156
02:35	155	16	31	46	62	77	93	108	124	139	155
02:36	154	15	31	46	62	77	92	108	123	138	154
02:37	153	15	31	46	61	76	92	107	122	138	153
02:38	152	15	30	46	61	76	91	106	122	137	152
02:39	151	15	30	45	60	75	91	106	121	136	151
02:40	150	15	30	45	60	75	90	105	120	135	150
02:41	149	15	30	45	60	75	89	104	119	134	149
02:42	148	15	30	44	59	74	89	104	118	133	148
02:43	147	15	29	44	59	74	88	103	118	133	147
02:44	146	15	29	44	59	73	88	102	117	132	146
02:45	145	15	29	44	58	73	87	102	116	131	145
02:46	145	14	29	43	58	72	87	101	116	130	145
02:47	144	14	29	43	57	72	86	101	115	129	144
02:48	143	14	29	43	57	71	86	100	114	129	143
02:49	142	14	28	43	57	71	85	99	114	128	142
02:50	141	14	28	42	56	71	85	99	113	127	141
02:51	140	14	28	42	56	70	84	98	112	126	140
02:52	140	14	28	42	56	70	84	98	112	126	140
02:53	139	14	28	42	55	69	83	97	111	125	139
02:54	138	14	28	41	55	69	83	97	110	124	138
02:55	137	14	27	41	55	69	82	96	110	123	137
02:56	136	14	27	41	55	68	82	95	109	123	136
02:57	136	14	27	41	54	68	81	95	108	122	136
02:58	135	14	27	40	54	67	81	94	108	121	135
02:59	134	13	27	40	54	67	80	94	107	121	134
03:00	133	13	27	40	53	67	80	93	107	120	133

3:01 to 3:30 minutes

COMPREHENSION SCORE

Time	w.p.m.	10	20	30	40	50	60	70	80	90	100
03:01	133	13	27	40	53	66	80	93	106	119	133
03:02	132	13	26	40	53	66	79	92	105	119	132
03:03	131	13	26	39	52	66	79	92	105	118	131
03:04	130	13	26	39	52	65	78	91	104	117	130
03:05	130	13	26	39	52	65	78	91	104	117	130
03:06	129	13	26	39	52	65	77	90	103	116	129
03:07	128	13	26	38	51	64	77	90	103	116	128
03:08	128	13	26	38	51	64	77	89	102	115	128
03:09	127	13	25	38	51	63	76	89	102	114	127
03:10	126	13	25	38	51	63	76	88	101	114	126
03:11	126	13	25	38	50	63	75	88	101	113	126
03:12	125	13	25	38	50	63	75	88	100	113	125
03:13	124	12	25	37	50	62	75	87	99	112	124
03:14	124	12	25	37	49	62	74	87	99	111	124
03:15	123	12	25	37	49	62	74	86	98	111	123
03:16	122	12	24	37	49	61	73	86	98	110	122
03:17	122	12	24	37	49	61	73	85	97	110	122
03:18	121	12	24	36	48	61	73	85	97	109	121
03:19	121	12	24	36	48	60	72	84	96	109	121
03:20	120	12	24	36	48	60	72	84	96	108	120
03:21	119	12	24	36	48	60	72	84	96	107	119
03:22	119	12	24	36	48	59	71	83	95	107	119
03:23	118	12	24	35	47	59	71	83	95	106	118
03:24	118	12	24	35	47	59	71	82	94	106	118
03:25	117	12	23	35	47	59	70	82	94	105	117
03:26	117	12	23	35	47	58	70	82	93	105	117
03:27	116	12	23	35	46	58	70	81	93	104	116
03:28	115	12	23	35	46	58	69	81	92	104	115
03:29	115	12	23	34	46	57	69	80	92	103	115
03:30	114	11	23	34	46	57	69	80	91	102	114

3:31 to 4:00 minutes

COMPREHENSION SCORE

Time w.p.m.	10	20	30	40	50	60	70	80	90	100
3:31 114	11	23	34	45	57	68	80	91	102	114
3:32 113	11	23	34	45	57	68	79	91	102	113
3:33 113	11	23	34	45	56	68	79	90	102	113
3:34 112	11	22	34	45	56	67	79	90	101	112
3:35 112	11	22	33	45	56	67	78	89	100	112
3:36 111	11	22	33	44	56	67	78	89	100	111
3:37 111	11	22	33	44	55	66	77	88	100	111
3:38 110	11	22	33	44	55	66	77	88	99	110
3:39 110	11	22	33	44	55	66	77	88	99	110
3:40 109	11	22	33	44	55	65	76	87	98	109
3:41 109	11	22	33	43	54	65	76	87	98	109
3:42 108	11	22	32	43	54	65	76	86	97	108
3:43 108	11	22	32	43	54	65	75	86	97	108
3:44 107	11	21	32	43	54	64	75	86	96	107
3:45 107	11	21	32	43	53	64	75	86	96	107
3:46 106	11	21	32	42	53	64	74	85	95	106
3:47 106	11	21	32	42	53	63	74	85	95	106
3:48 105	11	21	32	42	53	63	74	84	95	105
3:49 105	10	21	31	42	52	63	73	84	94	105
3:50 104	10	21	31	42	52	62	73	83	94	104
3:51 104	10	21	31	42	52	62	73	83	94	104
3:52 103	10	21	31	41	52	62	72	83	93	103
3:53 103	10	21	31	41	52	62	72	82	93	103
3:54 103	10	21	31	41	51	62	72	82	93	103
3:55 102	10	20	31	41	51	61	71	82	92	102
3:56 102	10	20	31	41	51	61	71	81	92	102
3:57 101	10	20	30	41	51	61	71	81	91	101
3:58 101	10	20	30	40	50	61	71	81	91	101
3:59 100	10	20	30	40	50	60	70	80	90	100
04:00 100	10	20	30	40	50	60	70	80	90	100

4:01 to 4:30 minutes

COMPREHENSION SCORE

Time	w.p.m.	10	20	30	40	50	60	70	80	90	100
04:01	100	10	20	30	40	50	60	70	80	90	100
04:02	99	10	20	30	40	50	60	69	79	89	99
04:03	99	10	20	30	40	49	59	69	79	89	99
04:04	98	10	20	30	39	49	59	69	79	89	98
04:05	98	10	20	29	39	49	59	69	78	88	98
04:06	98	10	20	29	39	49	59	68	78	88	98
04:07	97	10	19	29	39	49	58	68	78	87	97
04:08	97	10	19	29	39	48	58	68	77	87	97
04:09	96	10	19	29	39	48	58	67	77	87	96
04:10	96	10	19	29	38	48	58	67	77	86	96
04:11	96	10	19	29	38	48	57	67	76	86	96
04:12	95	10	19	29	38	48	57	67	76	86	95
04:13	95	9	19	28	38	47	57	66	76	85	95
04:14	94	9	19	28	38	47	57	66	76	85	94
04:15	94	9	19	28	38	47	56	66	75	85	94
04:16	94	9	19	28	38	47	56	66	75	84	94
04:17	93	9	19	28	37	47	56	65	75	84	93
04:18	93	9	19	28	37	47	56	65	74	84	93
04:19	93	9	19	28	37	46	56	65	74	83	93
04:20	92	9	18	28	37	46	55	65	74	83	92
04:21	92	9	18	28	37	46	55	64	74	83	92
04:22	92	9	18	27	37	46	55	64	73	82	92
04:23	91	9	18	27	37	46	55	64	73	82	91
04:24	91	9	18	27	36	45	55	64	73	82	91
04:25	91	9	18	27	36	45	54	63	72	82	91
04:26	90	9	18	27	36	45	54	63	72	81	90
04:27	90	9	18	27	36	45	54	63	72	81	90
04:28	90	9	18	27	36	45	54	63	72	81	90
04:29	89	9	18	27	36	45	54	62	71	80	89
04:30	89	9	18	27	36	44	53	62	71	80	89

4:31 to 5:00 minutes

COMPREHENSION SCORE

Time	w.p.m.	10	20	30	40	50	60	70	80	90	100
04:31	89	9	18	27	35	44	53	62	71	80	89
04:32	88	9	18	26	35	44	53	62	71	79	88
04:33	88	9	18	26	35	44	53	62	70	79	88
04:34	88	9	18	26	35	44	53	61	70	79	88
04:35	87	9	17	26	35	44	52	61	70	78	87
04:36	87	9	17	26	35	43	52	61	70	78	87
04:37	87	9	17	26	35	43	52	61	69	78	87
04:38	86	9	17	26	35	43	52	60	69	78	86
04:39	86	9	17	26	34	43	52	60	69	77	86
04:40	86	9	17	26	34	43	51	60	69	77	86
04:41	85	9	17	26	34	43	51	60	68	77	85
04:42	85	9	17	26	34	43	51	60	68	77	85
04:43	85	8	17	25	34	42	51	59	68	76	85
04:44	85	8	17	25	34	42	51	59	68	76	85
04:45	84	8	17	25	34	42	51	59	67	76	84
04:46	84	8	17	25	34	42	50	59	67	76	84
04:47	84	8	17	25	33	42	50	59	67	76	84
04:48	83	8	17	25	33	42	50	58	67	75	83
04:49	83	8	17	25	33	42	50	58	66	75	83
04:50	83	8	17	25	33	41	50	58	66	74	83
04:51	82	8	16	25	33	41	49	58	66	74	82
04:52	82	8	16	25	33	41	49	58	66	74	82
04:53	82	8	16	25	33	41	49	57	66	74	82
04:54	82	8	16	24	33	41	49	57	65	73	82
04:55	81	8	16	24	33	41	49	57	65	73	81
04:56	81	8	16	24	32	41	49	57	65	73	81
04:57	81	8	16	24	32	40	48	57	65	73	81
04:58	81	8	16	24	32	40	48	56	64	72	81
04:59	80	8	16	24	32	40	48	56	64	72	80
05:00	80	8	16	24	32	40	48	56	64	72	80

5:05 to 7:30 minutes

COMPREHENSION SCORE

Time	w.p.m.	10	20	30	40	50	60	70	80	90	100
05:05	79	8	16	24	31	39	47	55	63	71	79
05:10	77	8	15	23	31	39	46	54	62	70	77
05:15	76	8	15	23	30	38	46	53	61	69	76
05:20	75	8	15	23	30	38	45	53	60	68	75
05:25	74	7	15	22	30	37	44	52	59	66	74
05:30	73	7	15	22	29	36	44	51	58	65	73
05:35	72	7	14	21	29	36	43	50	57	64	72
05:40	71	7	14	21	28	35	42	49	56	64	71
05:45	70	7	14	21	28	35	42	49	56	63	70
05:50	69	7	14	21	27	34	41	48	55	62	69
05:55	68	7	14	20	27	34	41	47	54	61	68
06:00	67	7	13	20	27	34	40	47	53	60	67
06:05	66	6	13	20	26	32	39	45	53	58	66
06:10	65	6	13	19	26	32	39	45	52	58	65
06:15	64	6	13	19	26	32	38	45	51	58	64
06:20	63	6	13	19	25	32	38	44	51	57	63
06:25	62	6	12	19	25	31	37	44	50	56	62
06:30	62	6	12	19	25	31	37	43	49	55	62
06:35	61	6	12	18	24	30	36	43	49	55	61
06:40	60	6	12	18	24	30	36	42	48	54	60
06:45	59	6	12	18	24	30	36	41	47	53	59
06:50	59	6	12	18	23	29	35	41	47	53	59
06:55	58	6	12	17	23	29	35	40	46	52	58
07:00	57	6	11	17	23	29	34	40	46	51	57
07:05	56	6	11	17	23	28	34	40	45	51	56
07:10	56	6	11	17	22	28	33	39	45	50	56
07:15	55	6	11	17	22	28	33	39	44	50	55
07:20	55	5	11	16	22	27	33	38	44	49	55
07:25	54	5	11	16	22	27	32	38	43	49	54
07:30	53	5	11	16	21	27	32	37	43	48	53

7:35 to 8:00 minutes

COMPREHENSION SCORE

Time w.p.m.	10	20	30	40	50	60	70	80	90	100
07:35 53	5	11	16	21	26	32	37	42	47	53
07:40 52	5	10	16	21	26	31	37	42	47	52
07:45 52	5	10	15	21	26	31	36	41	46	52
07:50 51	5	10	15	20	26	31	36	41	46	51
07:55 51	5	10	15	20	25	30	35	40	45	51
08:00 50	5	10	15	20	25	30	35	40	45	50

Reading Effectiveness Progress Graph

Example: Test 1 scores of 75 and 200

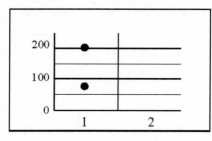

Fill in the following graph to keep track of your progress. Plot both your test R. E. score and your re-test R.E. score, one above the other. They should go above the Test Number. In other words, both your first scores from Test 1 should go above the 1.

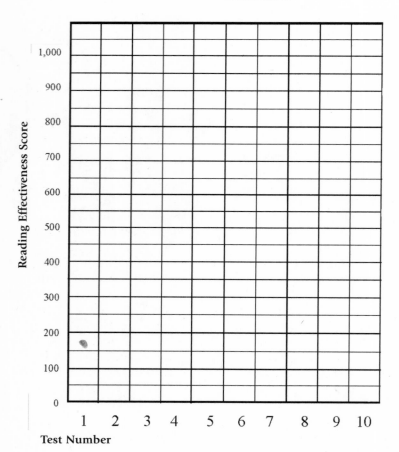

Reading Effectiveness Score

Test Number

Index

Entries in **bold** indicate charts and illustrations.

acetylcholine 250
acting out 145
Adams, Ansel 297–9, 304
ADHD *see* attention deficit
    hyperactivity disorder
affirmations 192, 198–207
  assignments 205, 206
  and distractions 252
  examples 200–5
  for speakers of English as a
      foreign language 205
alphabet animals technique
    220–1, 251
analogue audio 36, 40, 42
application 158
Aristotle 98, 230
artificial interest 218, 247–8,
    266–7
assignments
  achieving excellence 23
  affirmations 205, 206
  backwards reading 174–5,
    175
  Eye-Hop™ 123, 132
  focus 246, 248–52, 254,
    256–7, 266
  goal setting 50
  hand pacing 76, 77

ideation 51
key sentence previewing
    93–4
learning skills 217–18,
    220, 233, 236–7, 239,
    241
magnetic questions 111
memory skills 236–7, 239
name and number scan
    101
novel previewing 105
parroting 135, 139
pattern reading 177–8,
    184, 185
reading in bed 84
reading effectiveness
    testing 68
reading from a computer
    screen 89–90
reserving judgement 47
reviewing 157
second word 165, **166**
time-management skills
    275, 276, 278, 279
visual, audio and
    kinaesthetic learning
    42
visualisation 193–4, 197

word darts 167–8, 169–70
association, and memory
227, 231–2
attention deficit
hyperactivity disorder
(ADHD) 5
attitude 215
and learning 34–6,
219–21
poor 31–2
positive 11, 72
audio
analogue 36, 40, 42
digital 36, 40, 43
see also visual, audio and
kinaesthetic (VAK)
learning

backwards reading 173–83,
175
backwards S 177–82, **177**,
183, 186–7, **186**, **188**
basic reading technique
71–160
embodying 142–3, 147,
158, 160
Eye-Hop™ 115–33
flip turn 79–82, 91
hand pacing 72–91
parroting 134–41, 160
P.R.E.P.A.R.E. acronym
160, 268–9
previewing 92–114, 160
reviewing 142, 143–60
sitting posture 73–4, **74**,
90
bed, reading in 83–4, 91
beliefs 14, 72
Best, Virginia 304
Bly, David 10
brain 215, 250

see also left brain; right
brain
brain scan experiment 221–6
brain waves, delta 265
brainstorming *see* ideation
breaks 211–12
power breaks 263–6, 267
breathing techniques 140

caffeine 249
calendars 277
Carnegie, Dale 158
carriage return 163
Carter, Jimmy 298
case studies 7–8, 12
key sentence previewing
97
learning and memory
212–14
pattern reading 180–2
slow readers 21–2
cause and effect 110
challenges, overcoming
19–33
chunking 240
classical conditioning 83
comfort zones 52, 216
comprehension 4–5
average 17
and Eye-Hop™ 120, 132,
133
and hand pacing 73, 77,
78–80, 90
and novel previewing 106
and pattern reading
162–3, 172, 180–2
poor in fast readers 24
and previewing 106
and reading effectiveness
55, 56, 60–1
scores 313, 314–25

and speed visualisation
198
computer screens 84–90, 91
  colour 88–9
  and computer ergonomics
    85
  and font size 87
  and hand pacing 85–6
  using mouse pointers 84–5
  position of 85
  screen text 86–8
concentration *see* focus
conditioning, classical 83
confidence 225–7
Cooper, Ross 25
cynicism 35–6

delta waves 265
dialogue 103
digital audio 36, 40, 43
distraction
  agents of 248–53, 267
  'distracted reader
    syndrome' 23, 77–8
drifting off 23
dyslexia 24–5, 210–11

Einstein, Albert 29, 230
embodying 142–3, 147, 158,
  160, 269
Emerson, Ralph Waldo 266
emotion, and memory 96–7,
  145, 227, 229–30, 232
Engels, Friedrich 292
engineers 176, 180, 183
English as a second language
  and affirmations 206
  and Eye-Hop™ 125
  and pattern reading 184–5
  and previewing 106–8
  and reading effectiveness

testing 58–9
  and vocabulary 107–8
enhanced focusing technique
  189–90, 255–63, **260**,
  267
environment, and focus
  251–3
exaggeration 235
excellence 22–3
experience 45–6
eye dominance 20
eye muscles, damage to 19,
  116
Eye-Hop™ 5–6, 10, 88,
  115–33, 269
  advanced 152, **153**
  assignments 123, 132
  booklets 118–20, **119**
  and comprehension 120,
    132, 133
  and English as a second
    language 125
  and hand pacing 116
  and hop-drop 155
  making your own 121–3
  mastering 132
  and page scan 154
  and pattern reading 164,
    173
  and previewing 125
  progress in 123–5
  and reading effectiveness
    score 115
  safety tips 121
  samples 126–31
  second word 165
  skill levels 123–5, 126–31
  technique 117–21
eyesight 245–6
  ocular dominance 20
  poor 20–1, 88

see also ocular muscles

failure 217
fatigue 263–4
filing 276–7
flip turn 79–82, 91
focus 211–12, 244–67
    and artificial interest
        247–8, 266–7
    assignments 246, 248–52,
        254, 256–7, 266
    and choice 244, 245, 266
    enemies of 23, 248–53,
        267
    enhanced focusing
        technique 189–90,
        255–63, **260**, 267
    extreme 252–3
    and power breaks 263–6,
        267
    quick focus method 253–4
    relaxed 151–2
    and the senses 245–7, 266
font size 87
Ford, Henry 14
Franklin, Benjamin 18, 158
Frost, Robert 294, 295

gentle snap-back 163
Glasgow, Arnold H. 32
goal setting 47–50

Haggai, John Edmund 274
half-page speed up 189–90
Hamilton, Scott 32
hand pacing 72–91
    assignments 76, 77
    and comprehension 73,
        77, 78–80, 90
    and computer screens
        85–6

and Eye-Hop™ 116
and the gentle
        snap-back/carriage
        return 163
    and pattern reading 163–4
    see also short stroke
happiness 219, 271
hatred of reading 11
headaches 121
hearing/audition 245–6
    see also visual, audio and
        kinaesthetic (VAK)
        learning
Hemingway, Ernest 294, 295
Hooke, Robert 282
hop-drop 155–6, **155**
humility 158
hypnosis 255

ideas 278–9
ideation (brainstorming)
        50–1
illiteracy 16
imagery 145, 157, 195, 219
imagination
    and memory 227, 230–1,
        232, 235–6, 238
    see also enhanced focus
        technique
importance of super reading
        skills 15–17
Info-Mapping™ 100, 142,
        147–51, **150**, 269–70
    creating from memory 137
    and parroting 136, **137**
    and reading goals 49
    textbooks 241
information superhighway
        26
'inner voice' 36
intelligence 214–15

interest, artificial 218,
247–8, 266–7

Joyce, James 294, 295
judgement, reserving 44–7,
219
about yourself 217
contract for 46–7
on pattern reading 179,
187–9
on reviewing 155–6

key sentence previewing
Alpha-Omega 97–9
bookmark preview
99–100
and reviewing 143–4
kinaesthetic sense 245–6
see also visual, audio and
kinaesthetic (VAK)
learning
Kipling, Rudyard 109

learning 210–43
anomalies 218–19
assignments 217–18, 220,
233, 236–7, 239, 241
and attitude 34–6, 219–21
blocks to 216
brain scan experiment
221–6
case studies 212–14
facilitation 218–21
and focus 211–12
fun and interactive 215–18
new skills 45–6, 51–2
psychology of 34–6
from textbooks 239–41
see also visual, audio and
kinaesthetic (VAK)
learning

learning
challenges/disabilities
24–5, 210–11
left brain 29, 183
Leonardo da Vinci 29
Lewis, C. S. 294
Livingstone, David 288–90,
302
Livingstone, Mary 288, 289
Lloyd, Harold 285
logic 29
London South Bank
University 25, 211
loop the loop 153, **154**, 159
love of reading 11

magnetic questions 108–11,
217
magnetic resonance imaging
(MRI) 221–6
Maltz, Maxwell 52
M.A.R.I.E. acronym 232–3
Marx, Eleanor 292
memory
assignments 236–7, 239
and association 227,
231–2
embodying 142–3
and emotion 96, 145, 227,
229–30, 232
and imagination 227,
230–1, 232, 235–6,
238
long term 142–3, 146
M.A.R.I.E. acronym 232–3
medium term 142–3
and motion 227, 231, 232,
235
and notebooks 159
and the parroting
technique 134–41

and repetition 227, 229,
232, 234, 238
reviewing 142, 143–58
Roman room memory
technique 233–9, **233**,
236
storage capacity 215
testing 227–9
for words 242–3
see also recall; retrieval
mental shouting 145
Michelangelo 29
minerals 250
Moawad, Bob 11
Moffat, Robert 288
monitors *see* computer
screens
mood lifts 219–21
Morris, Jane 291
Morris, May 292
Morris, William 291–3, 303
motion, and memory 227,
231, 232, 235
mouse pointers 84–5
music 196–7

neurotransmitters 250, 263
new skills, learning 45–6,
51–2
nice, being 158
Nietzsche, Friedrich 26
Noble, Charles C. 49
noise pollution 252
note-taking *see*
Info-Mapping™
notebooks 159
novels
pattern reading 183–4
previewing 93, 102–6, **104**
nutrition 249–50

ocular dominance 20
ocular muscles, damage to
19, 116
olfaction 245–6
opportunities, readiness for
278
organisation
poor 30–1
see also time-management
skills

page scan 154, **154**
page turning 79–82
'palming' technique 140
'parro-phrasing' 135
parroting 108, 133, 134–41,
159–60, 268–9
by pretending 138–9
by telling 137–8
by writing 136–7
failure as 217
and pattern reading 180–1
teaching as 215–16
technique 135–9
and test stress 139–41
patience 32
pattern reading 152, 162–91
backwards reading
173–83, **175**
backwards S 177–82, **177**,
183, 186–7, **186**, **187**,
188
case studies 180–2
and comprehension
162–3, 172, 180–2
definition 172–4
and English as a second
language 184–5
evolution 185–9
and Eye-Hop™ 164, 173
gentle snap-back/carriage

return 163
half-page speed up 189–90
and hand pacing 163–4
novels 183–4
and parroting 180–1
and previewing 179–82
progress measurement 191
reading styles 163–4
second word 165, **166**
short stroke 166–7,
    168–71, **169**, **171**, 187,
    187
speed of 172, 178, 179–81,
    189–90
as ultimate goal of reading
    172
vertical drop 171–2
word darts 167–8, **167**
the Z 182–3, **182**
Pauling, Linus 50
Pavlov, Ivan 83
PDF files 118
perfectionism 22–3
Philips, Sam 285
phobias, about tests 56–7
picture visualisation 41,
    192–5, 207
posture, seated 73–4, **74**, 90,
    218
Pound, Dorothy 298
Pound, Ezra 295–6, 303
power breaks 263–6, 267
P.R.E.P.A.R.E. acronym 160,
    268–9
Presley, Elvis 286
pretence 138–9
    see also enhanced focus
        technique
previewing 92–114, 160,
    268–9
and the enhanced focus

technique 262
and the Eye-Hop™ 125
key sentence previewing
    93–9, **95**
magnetic questions 108–11
name and number scan
    93, 100–1, 144
novel previewing 93,
    102–6, **104**
and pattern reading
    179–82
for readers of English as a
    second language
    106–8
title questions 112–13
prioritising 274–5
progress measurement
    12–14, 32
for reading effectiveness
    326, **326**, 68
stair step method of 191

questions
magnetic 108–11, 217
title 112–13
quick focus method 253–4

reading effectiveness (RE)
    level 54–69
assignments 68
and comprehension 55,
    56, 60–1
and English as a second
    language 58–9
erratic scores 57–8, 69
and Eye-Hop™ 115
progress graph 322, **322**
scoring 9, 59–61, 69, 115,
    212–13, 313
test phobias 56–7
testing yourself 54–69

reading tests 13–14,
281–309
Ansel Adams 297–9, 304
Antony van Leeuwenhoek
281–4, 301
Conway Twitty 285–7, 302
David Livingstone 288–90,
302
Ezra Pound 294–6, 303
George Stephenson 61–7,
301
phobias about 56–7
scoring 301–4, 309–22,
322
William Morris 291–3, 303
recall 227, 230–2
average 17
and emotion 96
and key sentence
previewing 93–4
and notebooks 159
and novel previewing 106
and parroting 134
and pattern reading 162–3
poor, of fast readers 24
and repetition 94–6
and reviewing 142,
143–57
and visualisation 193–4
regression
conscious 26–7
unconscious 26–7, **27**
relaxed focus 151–2
repetition 94–6, 112–13,
145–7, 152
and memory 227, 229,
232, 234, 238
and pattern reading 162
spaced 145–7
representational system
preference test (Rep Test)

37–41
results, time to achieve
positive 9–10
retrieval 215, 227
reviewing 142, 143–60, 269
advanced 151–7
assignments 157
hi-speed 156–7
and Info-Mapping™
147–51
right brain 29
and imagery 219
inspirational/creative
nature of 29
and power breaks 265
and reviewing 151–2
Roman room memory
technique 145
roving Xs 152, **153**
Ruskin, John 291

scanning, simple 144
scepticism 35–6, 51–2
scheduling 277
second wind 263
second word 165, **166**
self-belief 14
senses, and focus 245–7, 266
short stroke 166–7, 168–71,
169, **171**, 187, **187**
short-/near-sightedness 88
sitting posture 73–4, **74**, 90,
218
skimming 24
sleep deprivation 248–9
smell, sense of 245–6
'speed reading' 4–5
speed of reading 16–17
calculation 305–7
fast 24
fluctuations in 72

pattern reading 172, 178, 179–81, 189–90
scores 309, 310–21, **310–21**
slow 21–2, 23
speed visualisation 190, 195–7, 207
spellings 243
stair step method 135, 191
Stamm, Reto 117
standard reading, overcoming the problems of 26–32
Stanley, Henry Morton 288, 289
Stephenson, George 61–7, 306
stress 139–41, 250–1
sub-vocalisation 28–9, 78
   barrier 78
subconscious mind 152, 156–7, 205
   see also unconscious mind
success 10, 14–15
Sun Microsystems 4

tablets (computers) 86, 118
targeted reading 142
Taylor, Jim 8
teaching 215–16
teenagers 248–9
telephone skills 275
tests
   representational system preference test (Rep Test) 37–41
   stress over 139–41
   see also reading tests
textbooks 239–41
time-management skills 274–9

assignments 275, 276, 278, 279
filing 276–7
ideas 278–9
prioritising 274–5
scheduling 277
telephone skills 275
'to-do' lists 275–6
waiting 277–8
title questions 112–13
'to-do' lists 252, 275–6
Toffler, Alvin 16
Tolkien, J. R. R. 292
touch 36
Twitty, Conway 285–8, 302

unconscious mind 199, 216
   see also subconscious mind

van Leeuwenhoek, Antony 281–4, 301
verbalisation 234
vertical drop 171–2
Victoria, Queen 288
vision 20–1, 88, 245–6
   see also ocular muscles
visual, audio and kinaesthetic (VAK) learning 34–43, 179
   analogue audio 36, 40, 42
   assignments 42
   digital audio 36, 40, 43
   and parroting 135–6
visual snapshots 193
visualisation 192–7, 207, 219–21, 246
   assignments 193–4, 197
   and distraction 252
   and goals 195
   picture visualisation 41, 192–5, 207

speed visualisation 190, 195–7, 207
vitamins 250
vocabulary 30, 107–8, 240–3

Wacker, Watts 8
waiting 277–8
Windows XP 89
Word (software) 86–8
word by word reading 28
word darts 167–8, **167**

word wrap function 86–7
words, memory for 242–3
words per minute score (w.p.m.) 60, 309, 310–22

Yamada, Kobi 17
Yeats, William Butler 210, 294, 295

Z, the 182–3, **182**

About the author

Ron Cole has been a trainer and personal coach since 1993. He learned his trade while living in Silicon Valley, California. He had been running a small advertising company for over five years when he signed up for a goal-setting course. What he learned there changed his life. Not only did his profitability nearly triple in six months, new ways of thinking and working infused themselves into his daily work.

After a few months Ron was asked to assist in teaching one of the courses. The thrill of helping people improve their lives was too much to resist. Over an 18-month period Ron dissolved his advertising agency and went into coaching full time. After another two years he started his own small company, offering coaching services.

Eventually his clients asked for help in managing their time better. This led to three areas of interest: travel, meetings and reading. For travel, Ron recommended books and audiotapes for continual learning. He taught best practice techniques for running smooth, productive meetings. Ron had experienced a speed reading course, but felt something more was needed for the kind of highly technical reading many of his clients were faced with. Over six months he experimented and came up with the basics for dealing effectively with large volumes of dense information.

After a year he got his first corporate client, Hewlett-Packard. He went from teaching a maximum of 8 people to 25! HP ordered three more courses and a new career began. Feedback from those professionals helped hone the course into a tight package which eventually included memory skills, visualisation and motivational tools.

As the course spread to more companies, many of the delegates wanted their children to benefit from these skills. Some companies held family classes where adults and children took classes together. This was quite an experience for both groups. The adults were hard-pressed to keep up with the children, and the children benefited from seeing that adults were still interested in education. Eventually some schools brought the course in and the improvements were impressive. In one school the benefits were so profound that the students finished the entire curriculum in almost half the time!

At the writing of this book it's been 14 years, having taught thousands of people, from lawyers to teachers, engineers to bank managers and sales professionals to fourth-year students. They all now have one thing in common: reading is more fun, fast and productive.

Ron also teaches writing courses, NLP, goal achievement, negotiation, networking, visualisation, remembering names, organisation and presentation skills. His personal coaching skills include sales coaching and productivity.

If you would like more information about Ron's courses and coaching services, visit:

www.alchemy.name or
www.ofcourseihaveawebsite.com